Heinrich Schenker
Selected Correspondence

CONTRIBUTORS
TO THIS VOLUME

Ian Bent
David Bretherton
Marko Deisinger
William Drabkin
Martin Eybl
Christoph Hust
Kevin C. Karnes
John Koslovsky
Lee Rothfarb
John Rothgeb
Hedi Siegel
Arnold Whittall

Heinrich Schenker
Selected Correspondence

Edited by
Ian Bent, David Bretherton,
and William Drabkin

THE BOYDELL PRESS

© Contributors 2014

All Rights Reserved. Except as permitted under current legislation no part of this work may be photocopied, stored in a retrieval system, published, performed in public, adapted, broadcast, transmitted, recorded or reproduced in any form or by any means, without the prior permission of the copyright owner

First published 2014
The Boydell Press, Woodbridge

ISBN 978 1 84383 964 4

The Boydell Press is an imprint of Boydell & Brewer Ltd
PO Box 9, Woodbridge, Suffolk IP12 3DF, UK
and of Boydell & Brewer Inc.
668 Mount Hope Ave, Rochester, NY 14620–2731, USA
website: www.boydellandbrewer.com

A catalogue record for this book is
available from the British Library

The publisher has no responsibility for the continued existence or accuracy of URLs for external or third-party internet websites referred to in this book, and does not guarantee that any content on such websites is, or will remain, accurate or appropriate.

Designed and typeset in Adobe Jenson Pro
by David Roberts, Pershore, Worcestershire

Heinrich Schenker

Selected Correspondence

Edited by
Ian Bent, David Bretherton,
and William Drabkin

THE BOYDELL PRESS

© Contributors 2014

All Rights Reserved. Except as permitted under current legislation no part of this work may be photocopied, stored in a retrieval system, published, performed in public, adapted, broadcast, transmitted, recorded or reproduced in any form or by any means, without the prior permission of the copyright owner

First published 2014
The Boydell Press, Woodbridge

ISBN 978 1 84383 964 4

The Boydell Press is an imprint of Boydell & Brewer Ltd
PO Box 9, Woodbridge, Suffolk IP12 3DF, UK
and of Boydell & Brewer Inc.
668 Mount Hope Ave, Rochester, NY 14620–2731, USA
website: www.boydellandbrewer.com

A catalogue record for this book is
available from the British Library

The publisher has no responsibility for the continued existence or accuracy of URLs for external or third-party internet websites referred to in this book, and does not guarantee that any content on such websites is, or will remain, accurate or appropriate.

Designed and typeset in Adobe Jenson Pro
by David Roberts, Pershore, Worcestershire

Contents

List of Illustrations   vii
Notes on Contributors   ix
Preface and Acknowledgments   xi
Editorial Method   xvii
Abbreviations   xx
Biographical Notes on Correspondents and Others   xxi
General Introduction   xxix

I THE EARLY CAREER

1 Schenker as Composer   2
2 Schoenberg and Schenker's *Syrian Dances*   30
3 Johannes Messchaert and Performance   44
4 The Society for Creative Musicians and Schoenberg's Music   53
5 Julius Röntgen: Editing and Ornamentation   59

II SCHENKER AND HIS PUBLISHERS

6 Cotta and the New Musical Theories and Fantasies   74
7 Otto Erich Deutsch and the "Moonlight" Sonata Facsimile   93
8 Universal Edition and the *Tonwille* Dispute   106
9 Drei Masken Verlag and *The Masterwork in Music*   130

III SCHENKER AND THE INSTITUTIONS

10 The Sofie Deutsch Bequest and the Vienna Academy   152
11 Invitations to Serve: Guido Adler   179
12 The Photogram Archive   187
13 Professorial Sorties: Ludwig Karpath and Wilhelm Furtwängler   208

IV BEETHOVEN'S NINTH SYMPHONY

14 Genesis of *Beethoven's Ninth Symphony*   226
15 Paul von Klenau and Beethoven   237
16 Georg Dohrn and the Ninth Symphony   251

V CONTRARY OPINIONS

17 Expedient Mutuality: Schenker and August Halm 256
18 Expectations Unfulfilled: Schenker and Furtwängler 294
19 Open Disagreement: Schenker and Paul Hindemith 318

VI ADVANCING THE CAUSE

20 Fighting the Propaganda War: Walter Dahms 326
21 Hamburg and Moriz Violin 350
22 Further Inroads into Germany: Felix-Eberhard von Cube 387
23 Collecting Sources: Anthony van Hoboken 418
24 Edinburgh Outpost: John Petrie Dunn 441
25 The Seminar Years: Felix Salzer 454
26 Letters from America: Hans Weisse 465

Select Bibliography 491
Transcription and Translation Credits 498
Index 503

Illustrations

(Plates 1–11 appear between pp. 52 and 53)

1. Letter: Schenker to Max Kalbeck, May 19, 1897 (© From the Holdings of Special Collections & Archives, UCR Libraries, University of California, Riverside)
2. Letter: Schenker to Moriz Violin, March 7, 1929 (© Special Collections & University Archives, University of California, Riverside)
3. Letter: Schenker to the Vienna Academy, December 13, 1927 (© Special Collections & University Archives, University of California, Riverside)
4. Draft letter: Schenker to Hindemith, November 10, 1926 (© Special Collections & University Archives, University of California, Riverside)
5. Letter: Felix-Eberhard von Cube to Schenker, October 20, 1931 (© Special Collections & University Archives, University of California, Riverside)
6. Letter: Hans Weisse to Schenker, October 15, 1931 (© Special Collections & University Archives, University of California, Riverside)
7. Postcard: Moriz Violin to Schenker, December 5, 1925 (© Special Collections & University Archives, University of California, Riverside)
8. Postcard: Otto Erich Deutsch to Schenker, August 5, 1920 (© Special Collections & University Archives, University of California, Riverside)
9. Schenker, *Syrian Dances* (1898), cover (© Special Collections & University Archives, University of California, Riverside)
10. Cube and Schenker: cartoon (1924) (Felix-Eberhard von Cube © Cube family)
11. Schenker's study-bedroom (© Special Collections & University Archives, University of California, Riverside)

(Plates 12–43 appear between pp. 180 and 181)

12. Heinrich Schenker (1927) (Felix-Eberhard von Cube; © Special Collections & University Archives, University of California, Riverside)
13. Heinrich Schenker (undated) (© Special Collections & University Archives, University of California, Riverside)
14. Schenker's gravestone, Central Cemetery, Vienna (© Iby-Jolande Varga, 2003)
15. Heinrich and Jeanette Schenker (1919) (Ludwig Bednař; © Special Collections & University Archives, University of California, Riverside)
16. Jeanette Schenker (c. 1912) (Atelier Kosel, Vienna; © Special Collections & University Archives, University of California, Riverside)
17. Jeanette Schenker (1925) (Atelier d'Ora; © Special Collections & University Archives, University of California, Riverside)
18. Jeanette Schenker (1927) (Felix-Eberhard von Cube; © Special Collections & University Archives, University of California, Riverside)
19. Eugen d'Albert (W. Höffert, Berlin; © Special Collections & University Archives, University of California, Riverside)

20 Ignaz Brüll (Fritz Luckhardt; © Austrian National Library, Picture Archive)
21 Max Kalbeck (W. C. Hans; © Austrian National Library, Picture Archive)
22 Ferruccio Busoni (Willinger; © Austrian National Library, Picture Archive)
23 Josef Weinberger (Lillian Fayer-Barylli; © Austrian National Library, Picture Archive)
24 Johannes Messchaert (1896) (Wegner & Mottu, Amsterdam; © Special Collections & University Archives, University of California, Riverside)
25 Julius Röntgen (1896) (Deutmann & Zonen, Amsterdam; © Special Collections & University Archives, University of California, Riverside)
26 Otto Erich Deutsch (1927) (Atelier Pietzner-Fayer; © photos: Studio Fayer, Vienna)
27 Emil Hertzka (Tom Richard von Dreger; © Universal Edition, Vienna)
28 Alfred Einstein (1927) (Atelier Pietzner-Fayer; © photos: Studio Fayer, Vienna)
29 Otto Vrieslander and Herman Roth (1917) (© Special Collections & University Archives, University of California, Riverside)
30 August Halm (1916) (© German Literature Archive, Marbach)
31 Joseph Marx (c. 1932) (Max Fenichel; © Austrian National Library, Picture Archive)
32 Guido Adler (1935) (© Austrian National Library, Picture Archive)
33 Robert Haas (1927) (Atelier Pietzner-Fayer; © photos: Studio Fayer, Vienna)
34 Anthony van Hoboken (1927) (Atelier Pietzner-Fayer; © photos: Studio Fayer, Vienna)
35 Wilhelm Furtwängler (© Austrian National Library, Picture Archive)
36 Ludwig Karpath (© Austrian National Library, Picture Archive)
37 Paul von Klenau (Trude Fleischmann; © Trude Fleischmann)
38 Walter Dahms with Margarete Ohmann (c. 1925) (© Special Collections & University Archives, University of California, Riverside)
39 Aline and John Petrie Dunn (1930) (© Special Collections & University Archives, University of California, Riverside)
40 Moriz Violin (c. 1901) (Schwertführer, Berlin; © Special Collections & University Archives, University of California, Riverside)
41 Moriz Violin, cartoon (1931) (Felix-Eberhard von Cube; © Special Collections & University Archives, University of California, Riverside)
42 Felix Salzer (© Constance Old)
43 Hans Weisse (c. 1913) (Franz Hofer, Bad Ischl; © Special Collections & University Archives, University of California, Riverside)

The editors, contributors and publishers are grateful to all the institutions and persons listed for permission to reproduce the materials in which they hold copyright. Every effort has been made to trace the copyright holders; apologies are offered for any omission, and the publishers will be pleased to add any necessary acknowledgement in subsequent editions.

Notes on Contributors

Ian Bent is Emeritus Professor of Music at Columbia University, New York. He has worked widely in the history of music theory and analysis. His books include *Analysis* (1987, with William Drabkin), and *Music Analysis in the Nineteenth Century* (1994). He has published articles in the field of Schenker studies, and was initiator of *Schenker Documents Online*.

David Bretherton is Lecturer in Music at the University of Southampton, having previously served as a postdoctoral research assistant for *Schenker Documents Online*. He has published articles and delivered conference papers on Schubert's songs, Schenker, and digital musicology. His doctoral thesis, on "The Poetics of Schubert's Song-Forms" (Oxford 2008), was supervised by Suzannah Clark.

Marko Deisinger teaches at the Department of Analysis, Theory and History of Music, at the University for Music and Performing Arts, Vienna. His doctoral dissertation was on the Viennese court Kapellmeister Giuseppe Tricarico, and he has since conducted research on music-historical relationships between Italy and the Habsburg court in Vienna in the seventeenth century. He transcribed Schenker's diaries 1918–30 for *Schenker Documents Online*.

William Drabkin, Emeritus Professor of Music at the University of Southampton, is Editor of *Music Analysis*, and also of the translations of *Der Tonwille* and *The Masterwork in Music*. He has written biographical studies of Schenker and his circle based on material in the Schenker archives, and has translated much of Schenker's diary and correspondence for *Schenker Documents Online*. He has also published an edition of Beethoven's principal sketchbook from 1821 (Artaria 197).

Martin Eybl is Professor of Music History at the University for Music and Performing Arts, Vienna. His research is focused on aesthetics and music theory in the early twentieth century, editions of early music, and Austrian music of the eighteenth century. From 1994 to 2006 he was director of the Schenkerian analysis program at the University.

Christoph Hust is Professor of Musicology at the University for Music and Theater in Leipzig. His books deal with seventeenth-, eighteenth-, and twentieth-century music and music theory, and he has produced editions of eighteenth-century texts about music (Nichelmann, Koch, Burney). His interests lie in methodological approaches to music theory and analysis.

Kevin C. Karnes is Professor of Music at Emory University, Atlanta, Georgia, USA. His books include *Jewish Folk Songs from the Baltics: Selections from the Melngailis Collection* (2014), *A Kingdom Not of This World: Wagner, the Arts, and Utopian Visions in Fin-de-Siècle Vienna* (2013), and, with Walter Frisch, the revised edition of *Brahms and His World* (2009).

John Koslovsky teaches music theory at the Amsterdam Conservatory and is an affiliate researcher in the humanities at Utrecht University. His research in music analysis and in the history of music theory has appeared in the *Journal of Schenkerian Studies, Theory and Practice, Intégral*, the *Dutch Journal of Music Theory*, the *Rivista di analisi e teoria musicale*, and *Music Analysis*.

Lee Rothfarb has taught at the University of Michigan, and at Tulane and Harvard Universities, and is Professor of Music at the University of California, Santa Barbara. He has published three books, *Ernst Kurth as Theorist and Analyst* (1988), which won the Society for Music Theory's 1989 Outstanding Publication Award, *Ernst Kurth: Selected Writings* (1991), and *August Halm: A Critical and Creative Life in Music* (2010).

John Rothgeb is Associate Professor of Music Emeritus at the State University of New York at Binghamton. A leading Schenkerian analyst and theorist, he has written articles on many aspects of music. He has also translated Oswald Jonas's *Introduction to the Theory of Heinrich Schenker* and several of Schenker's writings, including *Counterpoint* (with Jürgen Thym), *Beethoven's Ninth Symphony*, and the four elucidatory editions of Beethoven's late piano sonatas.

Hedi Siegel is on the Techniques of Music faculty of Mannes College of Music in New York. She has translated several of Schenker's writings, including *A Contribution to the Study of Ornamentation* (1976), *J. S. Bach's Chromatic Fantasy and Fugue* (1984), and essays in *The Masterwork in Music*. She edited *Schenker Studies* and, with Carl Schachter, *Schenker Studies 2*.

Arnold Whittall is Emeritus Professor of Music Theory and Analysis at King's College London. His books include *The Music of Britten and Tippett* (1982), *Musical Composition in the Twentieth Century* (1999), *Exploring Twentieth-Century Music* (2003), and *Introduction to Serialism* (2008). He is currently preparing a collection of essays, *British Music after Britten*, and continues to edit the Cambridge University Press series *Music since 1900*.

Preface and Acknowledgments

THE framework for all Schenkerian historical and biographical studies—and of a great deal else besides—is provided by Heinrich Schenker's own filing system, i.e. the folders in which he stored his ever-increasing mass of working papers, correspondence, diaries, and other materials at his apartment. This system was evidently a joint creation: the product of Schenker's own legalistic mind, but also significantly of Jeanette's organizational powers. How far back the two were acquainted is unknown, but she may have done secretarial work for him during the summer vacations that her family spent together with him between 1903 and 1909.[1] It was in 1910 that Jeanette left her first husband, Emil Kornfeld, and their sons Erich and Felix in Aussig (Ústí nad Labem) to share her life with Schenker in Vienna.[2]

In 1911 Jeanette started taking down the contents of Schenker's diaries from dictation using her stenographic skills and copying them in her neat hand. At some point she organized the disparate-sized sheets and scraps of paper that constituted his early diaries and paginated them; and in 1912 she compiled an index of all the diaries from 1896 to September 1912 in a small, alphabetically tabbed book—an invaluable, but little-known, biographical resource.[3] In later years, after the couple's marriage in 1919, there are records of their purchasing folders, labeling them, and filing papers away.[4] There are also records of their purchasing two boxes of index cards for the cataloguing of papers.[5] Additionally, Jeanette took down Schenker's lesson notes and copied them into "lessonbooks," starting with January 15, 1912. She copied extracts from documents for his use and took down many important items of correspondence in shorthand, writing

---

[1] Communication from Heribert Esser, May 1, 2007. The first mention of Jeanette in Schenker's diary is: "July 6 [1909]: to Steinach / 19th: arrival of J[eanette] K[ornfeld] / 20th: departure for Switzerland with Floriz and Felix Pollak."

[2] September 20, 1910, never to see them again, with the exception of Felix, whom she encountered in Theresienstadt concentration camp (communication from Heribert Esser, July 22, 2007).

[3] This index is held with the diaries in the Oswald Jonas Memorial Collection, Box 4, folder 9, and is glued to p. 1045, in the middle of 1915.

[4] E.g.: "Large-format folders and labels purchased for *Free Composition* [...] The first ordering of the folders for *Free Composition* with the marked-up labels completed; three full containers yet to be put in order" (diary, December 18–19, 1930); "A folder created for Urlinien" (September 25, 1927); "The letters taken from the folder and placed in a box" (December 7, 1927); "The thick folder of letters emptied; letters 27–29 examined, ordered, and filed away" (November 1, 1929).

[5] E.g.: "Cards for the card file (*Kartothek*) purchased" (March 16, 1927); "Lie-Liechen puts the card file in order" (December 3, 1927); "The second card catalog (*Zettelkatalog*) purchased at Schwanhäuser (20.40 shillings)" (February 21, 1928); "Card-file and cards for the Urlinie graphs purchased" (December 7, 1928).

first drafts for Schenker to amend and copy out; on other occasions she made file copies of letters of which he needed a permanent record (there are examples of both situations in the present volume). She also helped draft his theoretical and analytical texts and thoughts. Schenker once declared that in addition to being an excellent cook Jeanette "stands fully equipped at my side intellectually"; and in a codicil to his will he stated: "Without her practical help down to the very last detail, it [*Free Composition*] would not be complete."[6]

After Schenker's death, Jeanette re-assembled his papers into 84 folders.[7] She entrusted the extensive correspondence that Schenker received from Universal Edition and Drei Masken Verlag, and sundry other correspondence (together with his scrapbook, lessonbooks, unpublished theoretical works, draft materials for *Free Composition*, analyses and sketches for works by Bach, Beethoven, Chopin, and Brahms, and items of his library) to Ernst Oster at the time of his emigration to the United States in 1938. Oster bequeathed these materials to the New York Public Library, and they were catalogued by Robert Kosovsky in 1989–90 as "The Oster Collection: Papers of Heinrich Schenker" (OC). A finding list was published in 1990 and a complete set of microfilms was issued.

Immediately prior to her deportation to Theresienstadt in 1942, Jeanette entrusted a second large batch of folders, including all the diaries, and correspondence to and from over 400 correspondents (together with her husband's compositions, scores, and biographical materials) to Erwin Ratz, who had twice prevented her deportation but was unable to protect her on the third occasion. Ratz kept the materials safe in Vienna throughout the war, selling them in the mid-1950s to Oswald Jonas, who in 1965 took up a professorial position at the University of California, Riverside. After Jonas's death in 1978, the collection was transferred to the University by his family, along with his own papers and those of Moriz Violin, who had died in San Francisco in 1956, the whole collection being named "The Oswald Jonas Memorial Collection" (OJ).[8] One result of this merging of three sets of papers was the re-integration of the massive two-way correspondence between Schenker and Violin, amounting to some 1,026 items— far and away the largest single personal correspondence. This Collection was catalogued by Robert Lang and JoAn Kunselman and a checklist made available in 1982, with the help of Irene Schreier Scott, Heribert Esser, Hellmut Federhofer, and Genoveva Violin Windsor; a printed version of this checklist was published in 1994.

Before both of those transactions, in April 1936, Jeanette had sold six folders (containing Schenker's studies of thoroughbass in J. S. Bach and C. P. E. Bach and analyses of compositions by J. S. Bach, Haydn, Mozart, and others) to Felix Salzer, who fled to the United States in 1939. To these were added Salzer's own

---

[6] "[…] my wife prepares such wonderful meals, the same wife who, like me, eats potatoes and moreover also stands fully equipped at my side intellectually" (letter to August Halm, November 2, 1922); codicil dated May 20, 1934.

[7] Counting folders 11 and 11a–i as separate folders.

[8] An overview of the Oswald Jonas Memorial Collection, with introduction and itemized inventory of contents can be found online at http://www.oac.cdlib.org/findaid/ark:/13030/tf4j49n9zc/.

papers after his death in 1986, and the entirety was bequeathed to the New York Public Library in 2001, where it was catalogued by John Koslovsky in 2007 and named "The Felix Salzer Papers" (FS).[9] Salzer's own papers included his surviving correspondence, among which were the letters and postcards that Schenker had written to him (thus providing the counterpart to those that Schenker received from Salzer), and a small amount of correspondence from Hans Weisse to Schenker.[10]

The Oswald Jonas Memorial Collection opened to the public (initially with some restrictions) in 1979. Charlotte E. Erwin and Bryan R. Simms were among the first to explore its contents, producing a dual-language edition of the letters from Arnold Schoenberg to Schenker in 1981.[11] But the lion's share of early research into this archive was undertaken by Hellmut Federhofer, who spent five months working at Riverside between October 1980 and February 1981 excerpting entries from the diaries and transcribing letters to and from Schenker. Much of the resulting material is incorporated into his *Heinrich Schenker nach Tagebüchern und Briefen in der Oswald Jonas Memorial Collection* (1985), in which he sought to establish an accurate biographical framework, and to open up areas of Schenker's life and work that had for various reasons hitherto been out of public view. Notable among these were Schenker's relations with artists, scholars, and writers on music in Vienna; his opinions of composers and contemporary performers; and his "world outlook" on the issues of genius, journalism, commerce, trade, politics, wealth, religion, and Jewry. Every student of the development of Schenker's life and thought is indebted to this ground-breaking book and to the articles that Federhofer wrote in the 1980s, as well as to his 1990 edition of Schenker's early music criticism.[12]

Federhofer did not, however, have access to the Oster Collection. Since the late 1980s this Collection has provided a rich source of materials for investigations across the entire field of Schenker studies. The numerous collections of analytical sketches and drafts have proven especially rewarding in examining the development of Schenker's graphic techniques, and also for studying Schenker's approaches to individual pieces of music. The Collection has enabled scholars to chart the slow coming to fruition of *Free Composition* and to study, and in some cases retrieve for publication, theoretical works that Schenker left incomplete. Increasingly scholars have been drawn to the files of correspondence, to the lessonbooks, and to Schenker's scrapbook as sources for biographical information, intellectual development, and publication and reception history.

---

[9] An overview and detailed description of the Felix Salzer Papers can be found online at http://archives.nypl.org/mus/20415.

[10] A detailed typescript description by Robert Kosovsky of Jeanette's distribution of Schenker's papers and copies of Jeanette's list of the contents of the 84 folders are included on reel 1 of the set of forty-seven microfilm reels of the entire Oster Collection issued by the New York Public Library.

[11] Charlotte E. Erwin and Bryan R. Simms, "Schoenberg's Correspondence with Heinrich Schenker," *Journal of the Arnold Schoenberg Institute* 5 (1981): 23–43.

[12] For these works by Federhofer see Bibliography.

The web-based *Schenker Documents Online*, which aims to provide a complete, open-access, annotated dual-language edition of all of Schenker's correspondence in both directions, together with his diaries and lessonbooks, began in 2004.[13] It has had access not only to the three collections discussed above but also to correspondence in many other libraries, archives, and private collections in Austria, Germany, the Netherlands, and the USA.

The largest of these is the cache of 444 items, overwhelmingly letters written by Schenker to Universal Edition, housed at the Vienna Library in the City Hall (Wienbibliothek im Rathaus, formerly the Wiener Stadt- und Landesbibliothek (WSLB)), but on loan from Universal Edition's archive. The transatlantic "marriage" of this cache with materials in the United States enables scholars to bring together the two sides of this major correspondence, consolidating over 1,400 items—the largest Schenker correspondence of any type. Several other caches have similarly provided the counterparts to items in the three main collections.[14] More documents continue to come to light, often as a result of *Schenker Documents Online*'s inquiries, adding to the existing corpus, sometimes supplying the reciprocal side of an existing one-sided correspondence, occasionally bringing a new correspondent into the fold.

Most recently, in 2012 twelve items from Schenker to the Photogram Archive were tracked down in the Austrian National Library (PhA/Ar), complementing those already known from the Archive to the Schenkers; and, during the preparation of this volume, thirteen letters to and from the Vienna Academy were unearthed in the archive of the Academy (now UfMdK), providing crucial new evidence to complement the known correspondence.[15] Items from all these matched collections are included in this volume.

The present volume is in part a product of *Schenker Documents Online*, and its contributors are all contributing scholars to that website. Here the roughly 450 selected documents have been assembled under six general, broadly chronologically arranged themes, the contents of which are themselves presented in roughly chronological order in such a way as to cause communications from and to different correspondents to intersect with and play off against one another.

---

[13] Its url is: http://www.schenkerdocumentsonline.org/index.html. Currently some of the material is still located at http://mt.ccnmtl.columbia.edu/schenker/; this is due to be moved to the main site within the next two years.

[14] The collection of 209 items of correspondence between Schenker and J. G. Cotta in the Cotta Archive (CA), German Literary Archive, Marbach, when collated with materials in OJ, brings the total two-sided Cotta correspondence to 325 items. The collection of 51 items from Schenker to Felix-Eberhard von Cube located by William Drabkin in an apartment in Hamburg and photocopied by him in the 1980s, when collated with 52 items in OJ and OC, yield a total of 103 items of correspondence between Cube, his father Gustav, and Schenker (and whereas the Hamburg originals seem now to be lost, the photocopies have been deposited in OJ). Until 2007 only letters from Anthony van Hoboken were thought to survive; but in that year letters and postcards from Schenker to Hoboken came to light in the hands of an antiquarian dealer, and these have since been acquired by OJ.

[15] These documents were hunted down by Marko Deisinger and Martin Eybl with the kind assistance of the staff of those institutions.

These documents are accompanied by interpretive commentary in the General Introduction and the twenty-six chapter introductions.

THE editors wish to express their thanks to the following institutions for their invaluable help in placing documents and photographic materials at our disposal for this book and for providing information: Special Collections and University Archives at the University of California, Riverside (Dr. Melissa Conway, Head; Sarah M. Allison, Eric Milenkiewicz); the Music Division of the New York Public Library (Dr. Robert Kosovsky, Curator of Rare Books and Manuscripts); the Vienna Library in the City Hall (Dr. Karl Ulz); the Music Collection of the Austrian National Library, Vienna (Dr. Thomas Leibnitz, Director); the archive of the University for Music and Performing Arts, Vienna (Dr. Lynne Heller, Archivist; Erwin Strouhal); the German Literature Archive, Marbach (Dr. Eva Osswald and Dr. Birgit Slenzka of the Cotta Archive); the Hargrett Rare Book & Manuscript Library, University of Georgia, Athens, GA (Charles Barber, Assistant Director); the Johannes Messchaert Collection, Westfries Archive, Hoorn, Netherlands (Jan de Bruin); the Röntgen Archive of the Netherlands Music Institute (Dr. Frits W. Zwart, Director; Rik Hendriks); Universal Edition, Vienna (Astrid Koblanck, Director; Aygün Lausch, Heinz Stolba; Katja Kaiser, Archivist, and former archivists Martin Sima, Angelika Glatz, and Ronald Kornfeil); Mannes College the New School for Music (Dr. Joel Lester; Ed Scarcelle, Librarian); the Alban Berg Complete Edition (Dr. Regina Busch); the archive of Terezín (Theresienstadt) Memorial (Alice Beranková); Ursula Kralupper of Studio Fayer, Vienna; V. A. Heck Antiquariat, Vienna (Uta Schweger); the Orpheus Trust (Dr. Primavera Gruber); the State Library, Berlin (Dr. Helmut Hell, Jean Christophe Prümm); and the University of the Arts, Berlin (Antje Kalcher).

The editors are grateful to the following individuals for information and assistance directly or indirectly in the preparation of this book: Paul Banks, Antony Beaumont, Caroline Bent, David Carson Berry, Elizabeth Brinsden, Heribert Esser, Hellmut Federhofer, Niels Krabbe, Rosemary Moravec, Alexander Odefey, William Pastille, Kathryn Puffett, Andrea Reiter, Irene Schreier Scott, Nigel Simeone, Nakoma Two Wolves (Diana Windsor). They also wish to thank their fellow contributors to this volume for help and advice given over and above the providing of their contributions. They wish finally to express gratitude to the volume's copyeditor, Kathryn Puffett, and typesetter, David Roberts, for their skill and professionalism, and also to the editorial team at Boydell & Brewer for their help and encouragement throughout.

A grant from the Arts and Humanities Research Council of Great Britain has assisted the production of this volume.

The editors are pleased to acknowledge the following copyright holders: Horst Boehm of the Alban Berg Foundation; Vivian Rehmann of Breitkopf & Härtel; Mario Busoni (Ferruccio Busoni); the German Literary Archive, Marbach (J. G. Cotta); Claus-Eberhard von Cube (Felix-Eberhard von Cube); Cristina Teixeira Coelho (Walter Dahms); Elisabeth Schiemann (Otto Erich Deutsch); Elisabeth Furtwängler (Wilhelm Furtwängler); Eberhard Halm (August Halm); Susanne Schael-Gotthardt of the Hindemith Institute in Frankfurt (Paul Hindemith);

Anthony van Hoboken Jr. (Anthony van Hoboken); Corinna Boskovsky (Paul von Klenau); Thomas Leibnitz of the Austrian National Library (Photogram Archive, Robert Haas, Julius von Kromer); the Executors of the Estate of Hedwig Salzer (Felix Salzer); Lawrence Schoenberg (Arnold Schoenberg); Aygün Lausch and Astrid Koblanck of Universal Edition, Vienna (Universal Edition, Emil Hertzka, Alfred Kalmus, Ernst Roth, Barbara Rothe); Genoveva Violin Windsor and Nakoma Two Wolves (Moriz and Valerie Violin); Andrew Parker and Bronwyn Cooper (Hans Weisse); the Netherlands Music Institute (Julius Röntgen); Dr. Lynne Heller of the University for Music and Performing Arts Vienna (Academy/Hochschule for Music, Vienna, Wilhelm Bopp, Joseph Marx, Franz Schmidt, Alexander Wunderer); and Dr. Melissa Conway of Special Collections and University Archives at the University of California, Riverside. In addition, the editors have written assurances that there are no claims under intellectual copyright on correspondence by Drei Masken Verlag and its representatives (C. Alberti, Albert Böhme, August Demblin, Alfred Einstein), Johannes or Johanna Messchaert, or Julius Röntgen.

After extensive inquiries, correspondence from the following are deemed to be in the public domain: the Ansorge Society Vienna; Theodor Baumgarten; Sofie Deutsch; John Petrie and Aline Dunn; Ernst Lamberg; Fritz Mendl; Heinrich and Jeanette Schenker (who had no children together; nor are any progeny from Jeanette's first marriage known to survive); Simrock; Georg Tomay; Siegfried Türkel; the Society of Viennese Music Critics; Josef Weinberger; and Hermann Wunsch.

Every reasonable effort to trace copyright owners has been made. We would be pleased to hear from those whom we have been unable to locate or have inadvertently omitted, to whom we extend our apologies.

Editorial Method

The Texts of Correspondence

ALL correspondence items presented in this volume were originally written in German. They have been transcribed and edited, then translated into English. (See Transcription and Translation Credits, at the back of this volume.) For every document, the full text has been given: no ellipses have been introduced. As a result, longer letters may cover a wider range of topics than is encompassed by the theme of the chapter in which they occur. The editors see this as an advantage, since it enables the reader to get a fuller sense of the interchange between correspondents and a better feel for the psychology of the writer (and the recipient).

In translating these texts (though matters vary from translator to translator) we have aimed at an idiomatic English rather than a literal rendering of the German. We want all texts to read as naturally and as clearly as possible. As part of this policy, we have occasionally allowed ourselves to enlarge slightly upon the text; but when doing this we have been careful not to stray beyond the stated or implied content of the German. Anything added to that content is supplied in square brackets. Editorial annotations are in italic type within square brackets. (Occasional square brackets in an original text have been converted to parentheses.) We have adopted American rather than British usage; this governs spellings, construction, punctuation, occasionally the choice of a word or phrase, and the format of dates. At the same time we have avoided the use of obscure or outdated idioms. In the music examples slight imprecisions in such matters as alignment in the original have been regularized, but care has been taken not to alter the musical or theoretical sense. Editorial accidentals and key signatures have been added only when absolutely necessary. Examples bearing corrections are represented by their final version.

Titles of works present a special case. For Schenker's own writings, these are rendered in English, either adopting the title of a published English translation or devising our own where none exists. The same policy has generally been adopted for publications by Schenker's pupils and associates. Works by other authors are given in the original language except where a widely accepted English translation exists. Institutions, on the other hand, are rendered in English. There are two exceptions to these rules: the title of Schenker's *Der Tonwille* has been left untranslated, as has the institutional term *Hochschule*, which does not have a clear equivalent in English ("college," "academy," and "conservatory" are approximate) and whose translation as "high school" would be misleading.

In cases where the final copy of a letter is not known to survive but a draft of that letter exists among Schenker's papers, we have presented the draft. Drafts in Jeanette's hand have often been heavily edited by Schenker, confronting the editor with more than one option. Wherever possible, we have presented what we believe to be the final version of the draft text. When, as is often the case, Schenker's annotations are indecipherable, we have presented either the last decipherable version or the base text of the draft, with the situation described in a footnote.

We have used footnotes for a variety of purposes: to explain an ambiguity or uncertainty in the German or the meaning of a technical musical term; to describe a paleographic feature of the original document; to provide background information, especially political, cultural, or social; to describe the circumstances of the writing of a given item; to elucidate an allusion, or to identify the source of a quotation; to cite a publication or a musical composition referred to; to supply brief biographical particulars (though when a name occurs in more than one chapter of the volume, the biography for it is supplied in Biographical Notes on Correspondents and Others at the front of the volume); or to cross-refer from one item to another, or from one part of the volume to another.

The Use of Diary Entries

In many cases, whereas Schenker preserved the letters and cards received from a given correspondent, his own side of the exchange is not known to have survived. (We should remember that some of his correspondents were deported to concentration camps, others disappeared, others fled the country.) Since Schenker summarized in his diaries the content of all important incoming and outgoing correspondence, our primary purpose in introducing diary entries is to supply something missing from one side of the exchange or the other.

Schenker also used his diary to record face-to-face meetings, at home, in a coffeehouse, or at a place of business. Where such discussions form an essential part of the thread of a correspondence, we have included Schenker's record. Such summaries are often less constrained than the language of letters, affording a more candid and vivid sense of the people involved and their interactions.

Format

Each document is preceded by a heading; this gives the author(s) and addressee(s), with the firm that they represent where applicable, the type of document, and the date or dates of writing. Below this is given the shelfmark of the document (see "Library and Collection sigla" under Abbreviations below).

While the content of the body of a letter and any postscript(s) has been presented in full, along with salutation, valediction, and signature(s), other elements of a document may have been suppressed or supplied elsewhere. In particular, datelines (at the head or foot of a letter) have been suppressed and subsumed within the document heading (though if a letter was written over several days, the subsequent datelines have been retained and the date range given in the heading). Letterheads (printed, typed, stamped, or handwritten) giving the name and address of the author have in general been suppressed, as have addresses given at the foot of letters, and recipient addresses in either position, except where the geographical location of the author or recipient is itself significant. In many cases the letterhead or address is included on the first occasion and suppressed thereafter until any change of address occurs. This particularly affects writers such as Wilhelm Furtwängler and Anthony van Hoboken, who traveled frequently and wrote from many different places. Where printed letterheads have been included, they have often been simplified by omission of telephone numbers, telegram addresses, addresses in cities other than the primary one, bank codes, and graphic elements. In the case of postcards and lettercards, sender and recipient addresses have been treated in the same way as in letters; other matter, such as postmarks, stamps, adverts, and pictures and their captions, have been suppressed, unless the information contained in them is relevant to the content of the item, in which case it has been footnoted.

Indentation of paragraphs has been regularized. The spacing of the valediction line(s) and signature(s) in the original has been approximated; where these have been squashed at the bottom of a page or turned up a margin, they have here been regularized as normal, stepped indentation. Marginal additions have where possible been incorporated into the text at the relevant point.

Abbreviations

Library and Collection sigla

CA	Cotta Archive, Schiller National Museum / German Literature Archive, Marbach, Germany
DLA	German Literature Archive, Marbach, Germany
FS	The Felix Salzer Papers, Music Division, New York Public Library, New York, USA
JM/Ar	Johannes Messchaert Collection, Westfries Archive, Hoorn, Netherlands
NMI	Netherlands Music Institute, The Hague
OC	Oster Collection, New York Public Library, USA (File 1B = copies or drafts of outgoing letters; 12 = miscellaneous materials; 18 = recent miscellaneous correspondence; 24 = correspondence relating to *Der Tonwille*; 30 = correspondence on Schenker's desk at his death; 52 = Universal Edition correspondence; 54 = Drei Masken Verlag correspondence; 82 = materials relating to Beethoven)
OJ	Oswald Jonas Memorial Collection, University of California at Riverside, Riverside, CA, USA (Boxes 5–8, 70, and 89 = outgoing correspondence; 9–15 = incoming correspondence; 35 = biographical materials; 72 = photographic materials)
ÖNB	Austrian National Library, Vienna, Austria
PhA/Ar	Photogram Archive, Music Collection, Austrian National Library, Vienna, Austria
Rothg	Personal library of John Rothgeb
Sbb	State Library in Berlin, Music Division, Berlin, Germany
UG	Hargrett Rare Book & Manuscript Library, University of Georgia, Athens, GA, USA
UfMdK	University for Music and Performing Arts, Vienna
WSLB	Vienna Library in the City Hall (Wienbibliothek im Rathhaus), Vienna, Austria (formerly Wiener Stadt- und Landesbibliothek)

Other abbreviations

DMV	Drei Masken Verlag
UE	Universal Edition
comp.	compiled by
ed.	edited by
edn.	edition
repr.	reprinted
rev.	revision; revised (by)
transc.	transcription; transcribed by
transl.	translation; translated by
vol.	volume

Biographical Notes on Correspondents and Others

Included below are those correspondents (marked *) and others who are represented in this volume in more than one selection. Biographical information about any person who appears in one selection only is usually given either in the introduction to that selection or in a footnote at the first appearance of his or her name.

*Guido Adler (1855–1941)   Austrian music scholar. As the first Professor of musicology at the University of Vienna (1898–1927) he established musicology as an academic discipline in Austria. He edited the *Denkmäler der Tonkunst in Österreich* from its inception in 1893 until 1938 and organized many conferences and festivals, notably that for Beethoven in 1927. Like Schenker, Adler gained a doctorate of law from Vienna University and studied with Bruckner at the Conservatory; his numerous doctoral students included Anton Webern, and, from Schenker's circle, Hans Weisse and Felix Salzer. (Plate 32)

*Eugen d'Albert (1864–1932)   German pianist and composer, notably of operas and musical comedies. Schenker was acquainted with him from at least 1894, receiving support from him for his early published work. (Plate 19)

Wilhelm Altmann (1862–1951)   German librarian and musicologist. He joined the staff of the Royal Library (Prussian State Library) in Berlin in 1900, becoming director of the Music Collection (1915–27). Schenker was in contact with him between 1919 and 1934 about sources and photographic materials.

Carl Bamberger (1902–87)   Viennese conductor and writer on music. A pupil of Schenker's from 1920 to 1924, he pursued a career in conducting. He and his wife Lotte later taught at the David Mannes Music School (from 1938 or 1939).

Paul Bekker (1882–1937)   German writer on music. As chief music critic for the *Frankfurter Zeitung* 1911–23 he was an influential figure. An advocate of Wagner, Liszt, and Franz Schreker, he was ideologically opposed to Schenker, who denigrated his Beethoven monograph (1911) in the elucidatory editions of the late piano sonatas.

Aristide Briand (1862–1932)   French politician, advocate of trade unions, leader of the French Socialist Party. He was eleven times Prime Minister of France between 1909 and 1929, and the winner (with Gustav Stresemann) of the Nobel Peace Prize in 1926 for the Locarno Treaties. In 1929–30 he put forward a plan for a European union, which Schenker denounced in *Masterwork 3*.

*Ignaz Brüll (1846–1907)   Austrian composer and pianist. A member of Brahms's circle and the first editor for UE of Mozart's keyboard music, he was acquainted with Schenker between 1897 and 1906 and performed some of Schenker's compositions. (Plate 20)

*Ferruccio Busoni (1866–1924)   German-Italian pianist and composer. He edited and made piano transcriptions of works by Bach and others; his artistic manifesto *Sketch of a New Aesthetic of Music* dates from 1907. He supported the publication of Schenker's music at Breitkopf & Härtel, and in 1903 conducted Schenker's *Syrian Dances* in an orchestration by Schoenberg. (Plate 22)

Friedrich Buxbaum (1869–1948)   Austrian cellist. He was a member of the Vienna Philharmonic (1893–1900) and the Rosé Quartet (1900–21), and professor at the Vienna Conservatory/Academy (1902–38). He founded the Buxbaum Quartet in 1921, and performed chamber music with Moriz Violin in the 1920s.

*Felix-Eberhard von Cube (1903–88)   German theorist and composer. After studying with Schenker (1924–26), he taught at the Rhineland Music Seminar, Duisburg (1927–31), and subsequently with Moriz Violin at the Schenker Institute in Hamburg until it closed in 1934. After war service, he reopened the school in 1947 as the Heinrich Schenker Academy; his *Lehrbuch der musikalischen Kunstgesetze*, designed for the Academy, was published in an abridged English translation in 1987. (Plate 10)

*Walter Dahms (1887–1973)   German writer on music, composer, violinist, and conductor. He became a strong supporter of Schenker around 1913, corresponding with him for nearly two decades, but was prevented by war service from studying with him. He shared many of Schenker's views on music and politics and was awarded a Sofie Deutsch stipend in 1920. (Plate 38)

*Otto Erich Deutsch (1883–1967)   Austrian music biographer, bibliographer, and cataloger. In 1919 he briefly took over the book dealership Seidel & Son, Vienna, then became Hoboken's personal librarian (1926–35); his first collaboration with Schenker was as series editor of UE's facsimile editions, beginning with the "Moonlight" Sonata (1921). He acted as an intermediary in Schenker's negotiations with DMV (1926–30), and the two collaborated on a revised edition of Schubert's "Unfinished" Symphony (1927–28). A leading documentary biographer of the 20th century, he was an enthusiastic supporter of the Photogram Archive. (Plate 26)

*John Petrie Dunn (1878–1931)   Scottish music theorist and pianist. He studied piano at the Stuttgart Conservatory before joining the faculty in 1902, then moved to Kiel Conservatory, becoming its deputy director, and later returned to Edinburgh as concert pianist and theory teacher at the University of Edinburgh (1920). He was the author of books on piano playing and orchestration, and the translator of an abridged *Counterpoint 2*. (Plate 39)

*Alfred Einstein (1880–1952)   German musicologist. He was the author of biographies of Schütz and Mozart and books on the Italian madrigal and the Romantic period. He prepared the editions of *Riemanns Musiklexikon* in which Schenker first gained an entry, and, as head of music publications at DMV in the mid-1920s, oversaw the initial phases of the *Masterwork* yearbooks. Editor of the *Zeitschrift für Musikwissenschaft* for fifteen years, Einstein was dismissed from that post because of his Jewishness. (Plate 28)

Robert Haas (1886–1960)   Austrian musicologist, specializing in the music of the Baroque and Classical periods and in performance practice. As head of the Music Collection of the Austrian National Library 1920–45 he oversaw the establishment and growth of the Photogram Archive. (Plate 33)

*August Halm** (1869–1929)   German writer on music, composer, conductor, and teacher. He taught at the Freie Schulgemeinde in Wickersdorf 1906–10 and 1920–29. He was also music critic of the *Süddeutsche Zeitung*. Halm corresponded extensively with Schenker from 1916 to 1927; the two men were in agreement on the state of European music, but disagreed on other matters, including the relative merits of Brahms and Bruckner. (Plate 30)

*Viktor [Victor] Hammer** (1882–1967)   Austrian painter, sculptor, printer, and typeface designer. From 1922 he ran a printing press in Florence, while maintaining a studio in Vienna until 1939, when he moved to the USA. First in touch in 1913, he became a close friend of Schenker's in the 1920s, making a mezzotint portrait of the theorist in 1925.

Friederike Hauser   A friend of Moriz and Valerie Violin, Hans Weisse, and the conductor Wilhelm Furtwängler, who often stayed at her home in Vienna (IX, Universitätsstrasse 2) when giving concerts in the city.

*Emil Hertzka** (1869–1932)   Austrian music publisher. Associated with UE from 1903, he was its director from 1907 until his death. He was responsible for modernizing the company and changing its direction by signing contracts with progressive composers such as Mahler, Richard Strauss, Schoenberg, and Schreker, making agreements with or buying out other publishers, launching in-house journals to promote its catalog, and forging links in other countries. Hertzka handled Schenker personally, seeing through his publications from the *Instrumentation Table* (1908) to *Der Tonwille* (1921–24), and taking over the New Musical Theories and Fantasies from Cotta; their relationship went through alternate periods of crisis and calm, culminating in a break in 1925, but resumed in 1928. (Plate 27)

Robert Hirschfeld (1857–1914)   Austrian writer on music, teacher of music aesthetics at the Vienna Conservatory/Academy 1881–1914. He was a music critic for the *Neues Wiener Tagblatt*, the *Wiener Abendpost*, the *Österreichische Rundschau*, and other journals and co-founded the Vienna Concert Society. He was sympathetic to Wagner but hostile to Mahler, and was a member of Schenker's circle in the 1900s.

*Anthony van Hoboken** (1887–1983)   Dutch musicologist and collector. He amassed an enormous library of books and music, mainly first and early editions of works by Baroque and Classical composers. He was a pupil of Schenker's in piano, theory, and composition, and was one of the most important patrons of his last decade. In 1927, at Schenker's instigation, he launched the Photogram Archive and chaired its Board of Trustees. (Plate 34)

Bronisław Huberman (1882–1947)   Polish violinist. One of the leading soloists of the first half of the twentieth century, he also taught at the Vienna Academy from 1934 to 1936.

*****Max Kalbeck** (1850–1921)   German music critic. He moved to Vienna, becoming the highly influential music critic of the *Neue freie Presse* from 1883, and was the author of a four-volume biography of Brahms (1904–14). (Plate 21)

*****Alfred Kalmus** (1889–1972)   Austrian music publisher. He was for a long time Emil Hertzka's assistant at UE, later becoming the head of the New York office of the publishing house. In his capacity as editor of the Philharmonia series of miniature scores, Kalmus oversaw Schenker's and Deutsch's revised edition of Schubert's "Unfinished" Symphony and (in New York) the *Five Analyses in Sketchform* (1932).

Leo Kestenberg (1882–1962)   Hungarian pianist and educator. He was the music adviser to the Prussian Ministry of Science, Culture, and Education from 1918 and Director of the Central Institute for Education and Teaching (Berlin) from 1922. He wrote books on music education and was involved, with Georg Schünemann, in reforming all levels of music education in Prussia in the 1930s. He invited Hans Weisse to deliver a lecture on Schenker in Berlin in December 1930. He was removed from his post in 1932 on account of his Jewishness; in 1938 he emigrated to Palestine.

Paul Khuner (1884–1932)   Viennese industrialist, manufacturer of Kunerol (an early form of margarine). His wife was a pupil of Weisse's, and in 1931 he gave Schenker a subvention of 5,000 shillings to help with the printing costs of *Free Composition*.

Albert Kopfermann (1846–1914)   German musicologist. He worked at the Royal Library (Prussian State Library) in Berlin from 1878 to 1914, becoming director of the Music Division in 1908. Schenker corresponded with him over the photographic copies of Beethoven sources for the elucidatory editions that he was then preparing.

Alfred Lorenz (1868–1939)   German musicologist, best known for his four-volume study *Das Geheimnis der Form bei Richard Wagner* (1924–33) and an article on development in the "Eroica" Symphony first movement (1924). He taught music theory and history at the University of Munich from 1922, becoming Professor there in 1926.

Ferdinand Löwe (1865–1925)   Austrian conductor. He taught at the Vienna Conservatory/Academy 1884–1922, serving as its director 1919–22, and was a founding director of the Vienna Concert Society and conductor of its orchestra. Schenker may have known Löwe since the 1880s; they were close friends in the first decade of the twentieth century.

*****Joseph Marx** (1882–1964)   Austrian composer and educationalist. He taught composition, harmony, and counterpoint at the Vienna Academy 1914–52, serving also as its director (1922–24), and was the first rector of the Music Hochschule in Vienna (1925–27). A conservative but influential music critic for the *Neues Wiener*

Journal 1931–38, he supported the proposed introduction of a textbook based on Schenker's *Theory of Harmony* at the Academy. (Plate 31)

Siegfried Ochs (1858–1929)   German choral conductor, founder in 1882 of the Berlin Philharmonic Chorus, also editor of J. S. Bach cantatas and the *St. Matthew Passion*.

*Reinhard Oppel (1878–1941)   German composer, music historian, and theorist. He taught theory at Kiel Conservatory 1911–24, then lectured in theory and history at the University of Kiel until 1931, with a post also at the Leipzig Conservatory 1927–40. He carried on a voluminous correspondence with Schenker between 1913 and 1935 and had occasional lessons. He assisted Schenker with the preparation of *Brahms: Octaves and Fifths*, and remained in touch with Jeanette Schenker until 1939.

Richard von Perger (1854–1911)   Austrian conductor and educator. He was concert director of the Vienna Society of the Friends of Music (1895–1907) and concurrently the director of its Conservatory (1899–1907).

Ferdinand Pfohl (1862–1949)   German writer on music. He was music critic for the *Hamburger Nachrichten* from 1892 to 1932, and also taught music theory and history as co-director of the Vogt Conservatory 1913–34. He was an influential figure in Hamburg's musical life and wrote several books on Wagner, including a major study of his life and works (1911).

Oskar Posa (1873–1951)   Austrian conductor and composer. He worked at the Graz Opera House from 1911 to 1913 and, as a member of Schoenberg's circle, co-founded the Society for Creative Musicians in Vienna.

*Julius Röntgen [Roentgen] (1855–1932)   German composer, conductor, and pianist. He lived in Amsterdam for most of his professional life, where he was director of the Conservatory 1912–24. He was a regular accompanist for Julius Stockhausen, Johannes Messchaert, and Pablo Casals. He also edited the keyboard music of J. S. Bach for UE, and other Baroque chamber works. (Plate 25)

Herman Roth (1882–1938)   German writer on music. He was a music critic in Leipzig and Munich, and later taught in Stuttgart and Berlin; he edited works by Bach, Handel, and other composers. His textbook *Elemente der Stimmführung* (1926) was influenced by Schenker's *Counterpoint*.

Alphons von Rothschild (1878–1942)   Art collector and philanthropist. A member of the Vienna branch of the Rothschild family, he was a major collector of artworks, furniture, manuscripts, and stamps. A piano pupil of Schenker's prior to 1899, he was also Schenker's first important patron, financing the publication of *Theory of Harmony* and *Counterpoint 1*.

*Felix Salzer (1904–86)   Austrian (later American) music theorist and teacher, pupil of Hans Weisse in the 1920s, then of Schenker as part of the latter's seminar (1931–34); he also earned his doctorate under Guido Adler at the University of Vienna. After Schenker's death he taught at the New Vienna Conservatory, and he succeeded Weisse at the David Mannes Music School, New York, in 1940, becoming its director 1948–55. His first book, *Sinn und Wesen der abendländischen Mehrstimmigkeit* (1935), was written with Schenker's encouragement. His compendious *Structural Hearing: Tonal Coherence in Music* (1952) was for many years the leading textbook in Schenkerian analysis. (Plate 42)

Jeanette Schenker [Lie-Liechen, Lie-Lie] (1874–1945)   Wife of Heinrich Schenker. She was born Jeaneth Schiff; with her first husband, Emil Kornfeld, she had two sons, then she left him in 1910 to be with Schenker in Vienna; the couple married in 1919. From 1911 she worked as Schenker's shorthand secretary and amanuensis, writing up his diaries and correspondence, and drafts of his writings. After his death she oversaw the publication of *Free Composition*, sold the greater part of her husband's library, organized his papers, and entrusted these to safekeeping. She was deported to the Theresienstadt concentration camp, where she died a few months before the end of World War II. (Plates 15–18)

Julia Schenker (1826–1917)   Mother to at least six children, of which Heinrich was the fifth. Schenker was much attached to her, and she represented a close link with his Jewish background. In her last years she lived with his older brother Wilhelm and his wife in Kautzen; Schenker was much involved in arranging the rituals for her death.

Moriz [Mozio] Schenker (1874–1936)   Schenker's younger brother, a banker with the Austrian Provincial Bank, later the Treuga Bank; he oversaw Schenker's financial affairs, and on his behalf negotiated a settlement with UE in 1925; but in 1929 Schenker wrestled with him to regain his savings, in part to finance the publication of the "Eroica" Symphony analysis (*Masterwork* 3) and *Free Composition*.

Franz Schmidt (1874–1939)   Austrian composer, pianist, and cellist. He studied at the Vienna Conservatory, returning there to teach cello (from 1901), piano (from 1914) and counterpoint and composition (from 1922); he was director of the Academy (as the Conservatory became) 1925–27 and subsequently served as rector of the recently formed Music Hochschule (1927–31). Before World War I Schmidt was for many years also a cellist in the Vienna Philharmonic Orchestra and at the Court Opera.

Fritz Stein (1879–1961)   German organist and conductor. He was director of music at the University of Jena and the city's organist from 1906. He taught at the University of Kiel from 1920, becoming professor in 1928; from 1933 to 1945 he was director of the Music Hochschule in Berlin.

Jane Stirling (1804–59)   Amateur Scottish pianist. She was a pupil and later a close friend of Chopin, to whom she gave assistance on his final concert tour of Great Britain in 1848–49. Her collection of printed copies of works by Chopin, annotated by the composer, was the principal source of Édouard Ganche's influential "Oxford" edition of Chopin (1928–32).

*Karl Straube (1873–1950)   German organist, teacher, and choral conductor. He was organist and Kantor at the Thomaskirche, Leipzig, and in 1919 he founded the Church Music Institute at the Leipzig Conservatory. He was a friend of Wilhelm

Furtwängler; both musicians sought to interest the major Leipzig publishing houses, C. F. Peters and Breitkopf & Härtel, in Schenker's analysis of the "Eroica" Symphony.

Charles Sanford Terry (1864–1936)   English music historian. He taught at the University of Aberdeen from 1898 and was Professor of music there from 1903 to 1930, specializing in the music of J. S. and J. C. Bach.

Fritz Ungar (1898–1988)   Austrian publisher. He founded the Phaidon Verlag in 1922 and the Saturn Verlag in 1926. Ungar was a cousin of Oswald Jonas and with Saturn published a pair of early books on Schenkerian theory by Jonas (1934) and Salzer (1935).

***Moriz Violin [Floriz]** (1897–1956)   Austrian pianist and teacher. He was the music director of Wolzogen's Buntes Theater in Berlin (1901–02), then returned to Vienna to teach the advanced piano class at the Conservatory/Academy (1908–12). In 1921 he moved to Hamburg, where he taught at the Vogt Conservatory before founding a Schenker Institute in that city (1931), only to return to Vienna after the National Socialists came to power. From 1935 to 1938 he taught in the Schenker Institute within the New Vienna Conservatory, moving to the USA (with Schoenberg's assistance) after the annexation of Austria (1938) and finding employment in San Francisco. Violin was Schenker's closest friend and confidant, with whom he shared the familiar "Du"; more than 1,000 items of correspondence between Violin and his wife Valerie ("Wally") and the Schenkers survive from a period of three decades. (Plates 40, 41)

***Otto Vrieslander** (1880–1950)   German composer and musicologist. He lived for much of his life in the Munich area, moving to Switzerland in 1929. Although a pupil of Schenker's only briefly (1911–12), he remained a member of Schenker's closest circle, and their correspondence (1910–35) may amount to well over 800 items. Vrieslander assisted with the drawing of music examples and graphs for *Masterwork 2* and prepared a revision of the *Theory of Harmony*, which was intended as a textbook at the Vienna Academy. He also made an "elucidatory edition" of pieces by C. P. E. Bach for UE (1914) and wrote a monograph on the composer (1923). (Plate 29)

George Wedge (1890–1964)   American organist and educator. He studied at the Institute of Musical Art in New York (returning there later as its dean), then taught at New York University 1920–27 and the Curtis Institute of Music, Philadelphia, 1924–26. He is reported to have introduced Schenker's ideas into his teaching as early as 1925 and was thus probably the earliest proponent of Schenkerian theory in the USA.

***Josef Weinberger** (1855–1928)   Austrian music publisher. The music publishing house of Weinberger, founded in Vienna in 1885, brought out editions of light opera and popular instrumental music; it published the original edition of Schenker's *Syrian Dances* (1898). With Bernhard Herzmansky and Adolf Robitschek, Weinberger co-founded UE in 1901 with the aim of providing standard Austrian editions of Classical repertory and school music. (Plate 23)

***Hans Weisse** (1892–1940)   Austrian (later American) composer, theorist, and teacher. He was formally a pupil of Schenker's from 1908 to 1921, and for part of that time a piano pupil of Moriz Violin's; he also completed a doctorate in musicology under Guido Adler at the University of Vienna. Weisse taught privately in Vienna throughout the 1920s, his pupils including Oswald Jonas and Felix Salzer and several American musicians, among them Gerald F. Warburg and Victor Vaughn Lytle. He emigrated to the USA in 1931, teaching at the David Mannes Music School and Columbia University and creating a base upon which Schenkerian theory would flourish in American academia. (Plate 43)

General Introduction

THE present volume brings together some 450 pieces of correspondence to and from the Austrian music theorist Heinrich Schenker. These have been arranged in six sections, each concerned with an aspect of Schenker's long and wide-ranging career in music. Each section contains several individual chapters that cover the correspondence relating to a specific topic or episode: the publication of a single work, the negotiations with a publisher over a series of publications; an exchange with a particular correspondent at a particular time, a musical work that became a focal point in Schenker's life, and so on. Broadly speaking, the chapters are arranged in chronological order, as are the larger sections themselves.

The title of this volume avoids the word "letters" so common on the title pages of editions of correspondence. While letters may be in the majority in the Schenker correspondence, many other formats are found therein too, including postcards, picture postcards, telegrams, calling cards, printed announcements and invitations, bank documents, and so on. Nor is this the only sense in which our volume is more inclusive than some other editions of composers' correspondence. The editors treat the "Schenker correspondence" as not just those items emanating from Schenker's pen but rather as the whole, two-sided exchange of communications. There are several reasons for making this decision.

The first is a practical one: despite what has been said in the Preface, there are still many instances of correspondence for which only the "other" side is available—those of Dahms, Dunn (with the exception of one item), and Weisse (with five exceptions), for example. It should be said immediately that the Schenker correspondence is in general *not* a trivial one; on the contrary, it is a substantive body of material, long on discussion of deep and important issues, short on appointment-making and small talk. And that holds true for both sides of the exchange of letters; thus where Schenker's side is absent, there is value still in presenting the incoming communications, from which in any case some of what Schenker has previously said can be retrieved. Moreover, those incoming letters often report: "I hear from Vrieslander that …," "Weisse tells me …," "I gather that Hoboken is …," and so on. Indeed, there is a sense in which Schenker's correspondence is but one facet—to be sure, the major one—of a larger entity: the Schenker *community*. Among Schenker's circle there was constant intercommunication. Alliances, animosities, collaborations—some temporary, some long-lasting and deep-rooted—existed among its members. Schenker shows himself keenly aware of these crosscurrents, sometimes holding himself aloof, often bringing diplomacy to bear, occasionally adding fuel to the flames. Those counted as pupils, colleagues, and friends make up a moderate-sized group, whereas the greater network of communications is extensive and diverse, including publishers, performers, educators, journalists, academics, and those who consulted Schenker from far and wide for advice, information, or news of his publications, or who sought instruction from him. Amidst all of these, Schenker emerges as a controlling force, seeking advantage for his cause, ever striving for the betterment (as he saw it) of German culture and society, and indirectly of humanity.

There is a second, related reason: What started as the enterprise of a lone figure with a powerful sense of his own mission grew, from the 1910s onward, into a discipleship of men, and indeed women,[1] proclaiming not just a theory but an entirely new way of listening to and experiencing music. In this way, Schenker's voice had by 1930 become the voices of many in a geographically expanding domain.

Then there are Schenker's diaries. Numbering more than 4,000 meticulously inscribed pages written over a period of forty years, these extraordinary documents on the one hand chart the momentous events of Europe—war, treaties, the fall of monarchies, hyperinflation, poverty and hunger, and the rise of democracy, Marxism, and fascism—and on the other hand they detail the practicalities of domestic life and his relationship with the beloved Jeanette. Crucially, these diaries also record the daily inflow and outflow of correspondence, the main points of each item being summarized, sometimes supplemented with Schenker's reactions. It is these summaries that furnish the third reason for including both sides of Schenker's correspondence, for where his side is not known to survive the editors have been able to use his summaries of his own outgoing letters and postcards as proxies for the items themselves. Or, put conversely, they are able to use the letters of others as a scaffolding for the reconstruction of Schenker's part in the discourse even when that is not available.

We must not forget that diaries are as fallible as any other human document; this is particularly so in Schenker's case, for we know his diaries were written up not daily but typically weekly and sometimes even months later, often during the ensuing summer (he records precisely when that process took place). Just how he preserved the information in the meantime is something about which we can only speculate: he may have made notes, or kept rough drafts of diary entries until he had dictated them to Jeanette. Evidently some accuracy was lost in the process: the surviving correspondence is occasionally misdated in the diaries, and sometimes important items are left unrecorded altogether.

However judiciously selected, the items of correspondence chosen for this volume cannot adequately represent the 7,000 or more that are known to survive. The editors have striven to provide a cross-section of the types of document, topics, and styles of writing encompassed by the totality. But they encountered several obstacles, the first being that more than half of the correspondence has yet to be studied. Many whole sets of correspondence have, to the best of our knowledge, never been broached: for instance, the eighty-nine items of correspondence with the musicologist and editor Herman Roth, the forty-two pieces with the art critic and painter Adalbert Franz Seligmann, and the thirty-two items from Hilda

---

[1] Most notably his long-standing and loyal pupils Angi Elias and Marianne Kahn (both of whom had their own pupils, to whom they no doubt disseminated Schenker's ideas) and Evelina Pairamall, and to a lesser extent also Greta Kraus and Trude Kral from his seminar of 1931–34, and above all Jeanette. Nor should we forget the role that his female patrons Irene Mayerhofer (Graedener), Jenny Eissler, and Sofie Deutsch, as well as Angi Elias, played in Schenker's advancement.

Rothberger, wife of businessman and medal engraver Alfred Rothberger. Only a tiny fraction of the correspondence with Schenker's brothers Wilhelm and Moriz (159 items) has yet been examined, as is the case also for that with Jeanette's brothers and sisters and their spouses, Paul and Anna Schiff, Victor Schiff, and Arnold and Rosa Weill (forty-seven items). Then again, while frequent exchanges between Schenker and his sister Schifre and her family are recorded in the diaries, a mere seven items survive, and no letters are preserved at all between Schenker and his mother Julia. As a result, Schenker's family and that of his wife are entirely unrepresented in this volume, regrettable though that is.

Timing ultimately worked against two chapters originally planned for inclusion in this volume: that presenting correspondence with Reinhard Oppel, who taught theory at Kiel Conservatory from 1911, Kiel University from 1924, and Leipzig Conservatory from 1927; and that with the artist Viktor Hammer, whose mezzotint portrait of Schenker (1926) is the most celebrated visual image we have of the theorist.[2] A somewhat different obstacle arose with respect to the correspondence with Otto Vrieslander, who was Schenker's pupil and active supporter in many roles from 1912 to the theorist's death. Jeanette eventually returned Vrieslander's letters to him, and the resulting dual-sided collection, which apparently numbers in excess of 800 items—making it the second largest of all the personal correspondence sets—is now in private possession.[3] Its inaccessibility creates the single greatest lacuna in the entire Schenker correspondence, and one can only hope that it will become available to scholars sooner rather than later—not least because of the far-reaching correspondence Vrieslander conducted with Jeanette between her husband's death and her deportation to Theresienstadt.

Other exclusions were self-imposed because of the inevitable limits of space; of these, Schenker's communications with journal and newspaper editors while serving as music critic in Vienna between 1891 and 1901 would have deserved a place in Section I; and his correspondence with Universal Edition over the elucidatory editions of the late Beethoven piano sonatas and over his final three publications, *Five Analyses in Sketchform*, Brahms's study of parallel octaves and fifths in the musical canon, and *Free Composition*, had a rightful claim to a place in Section II.

The editors have elected instead to offer more material on a limited number of issues, so as to achieve depth in preference to sheer coverage. In so doing, they have arranged the selections in such a way as to show off Schenker's correspondence in many different lights: artistic, intellectual, business, professional, polemical, and private, and encompassing his work in composition, performance, editing, source studies, theory, pedagogy, and analysis.

---

[2] For Oppel see Timothy L. Jackson, "Heinrich Schenker as Composition Teacher: The Schenker–Oppel Exchange," *Music Analysis* 20, no. 1 (March 2001): 1–115; For Hammer see Hedi Siegel, "Looking at the Urlinie," in *Structure and Meaning in Tonal Music: Festschrift in Honor of Carl Schachter*, ed. L. Poundie Burstein and David Gagné (Hillsdale, NY: Pendragon, 2006), pp. 79–99.

[3] See Federhofer (1985), pp. 213–16 and *passim*; *Schenker-Traditionen*, pp. 246–47, 196–99; and *New Grove Dictionary of Music* (2001) and *Grove Music Online*.

xxxii *General Introduction*

What follows is an overview of the six main sections of the volume. Here the editors offer some interpretation of and broader reflection upon the material contained in each of those sections with the occasional speculation that goes beyond the scope of the individual chapter introductions and the footnoting of the correspondence items.

SECTION 1, **The Early Career**, presents several facets of Schenker's artistic and professional life prior to the publication of his *Theory of Harmony*. Schenker's earliest years in Vienna were devoted to law studies at the University and music at the Conservatory. He spent a little over two years at the Vienna Conservatory, little of it in the study of composition *per se* (he was in Bruckner's harmony and counterpoint lectures); but in the 1890s he devoted considerable time to composition and by the turn of the century had assembled a portfolio of some fifty works or works-in-progress, of which eight had appeared in print. Schenker had the good fortune to win the support of two eminent pianist-composers of the day, Eugen d'Albert and Ferruccio Busoni. Both spoke on his behalf with leading German music publishers, and both performed his solo piano works to win support for them among the concert-going public. The *Fantasy* for piano Op. 2 was especially close to Busoni's heart: he succeeded in getting Schenker to revise it so that its three sections were run together as an uninterrupted work; and he went so far as to suggest new titles for these sections, giving the work as a whole a more programmatic orientation.

"These pieces have a touch of genius about them" (*Diese Stücke sind genial*), wrote Busoni of Schenker's *Syrian Dances* in 1900. The German word *genial* is far stronger than the conventional usage of its mild English cognate: it means "imbued with genius," and that sentiment boosted Schenker's self-image as a composer, for in response he wrote that Busoni's kindness "gives me constant encouragement, and emboldens me to strive further." It is instructive, therefore, to follow the trajectory of this one work from before its publication in 1899 in a first, piano four-hands version, through Busoni's warm-hearted reaction, to its modest success in concert, and heart-rending to see Busoni's engagement of Schoenberg to orchestrate the accompaniments and the Berlin performance of this second version in 1903, in which Schenker must have invested his highest hopes, only for the work's catastrophic reception by the press to shatter his self-confidence as a composer.

By contrast, Schenker's collaboration with another leading performer of the day—the Dutch baritone Johannes Messchaert—brought lasting happy memories from his early Viennese years. It is Schenker's only known stint as a touring artist, and one he undertook primarily as a singer's accompanist.[4] Although the tour lasted only a number of weeks, Schenker recorded the impact that Messchaert's artistry had on him in letters to other correspondents (see the letter to Cube of April 29, 1928) and in his writings on music long after the event;[5] it is even mentioned in the tiny entry on Schenker in *Riemanns Musiklexikon* of

---

[4] He also accompanied the bass singer Eduard Gärtner in the 1890s and early 1900s in major Viennese concert venues; see Federhofer (1985), p. 19, fn. 37.

[5] See *Tonwille* 6, vol. 2, pp. 35–36 (Ger. orig., 41).

1929, three decades later. For Schenker, Messchaert's art represented the antidote to intoxication with opera, which is why he placed it higher than that of the leading Italian tenor of the time, Enrico Caruso. How much of Schenker's own artistic sensibility, conversely, rubbed off on the singer is an interesting point of speculation: Messchaert's approach to diction and declamation, which so impressed the young Schenker, is in part recorded in an essay that was brought out posthumously in 1927.[6] Schenker acquired a copy of this and noted that its content agreed precisely with his own recollections.

As Schoenberg wrote to Schenker in 1904, "You [...] oblige me to pay you the compliment of giving the real reason why we regard your involvement as essential. Is it necessary to emphasize that we are delighted to find one intellect among musicians?" One wonders what these words—assuming they were genuinely meant—were based on: most likely on Schenker's ten years of writings as a critic, perhaps also on private conversations while the two men were in collaboration over the *Syrian Dances*. Or perhaps Schoenberg was merely using flattery to recruit another member to his planned Society for Creative Musicians. Schenker's side of the correspondence is lost, and the diary does nothing to help us; but his responses were clearly evasive, for he seems not to have attended any of the meetings.

With hindsight, the spectacle of Schenker acting as agent for a publisher is a strange one indeed. But on March 15, 1901, he wrote to Julius Röntgen to recruit him to the fledgling Universal Edition's new series of Austrian practical editions of classical works. Schenker had been aware of Röntgen since at least 1896[7] and admired him as a "deep-thinking, deep-feeling" pianist, not in the virtuoso mold. Josef Weinberger had published Schenker's *Syrian Dances* in his own publishing house in 1899, and early in 1901 as one of the three founders of Universal Edition[8] had offered Schenker his own part in the new editorial venture. Both Röntgen and Schenker opted for eighteenth-century keyboard music: Röntgen for works by J. S. Bach,[9] Schenker for sonatas by C. P. E. Bach, the manuscript of which he handed over in the final week of 1901.

Perhaps his choice of Carl Philipp Emanuel led Schenker to a close engagement with the *Essay on the True Art of Playing Keyboard Instruments*, which in turn led to his writing of *Ornamentation* and so to a life-long interaction with Bach's "master text." What is clear is that it inducted him also into the world of editing and arranging: next to arrangements of organ concertos by Handel (1905), and

---

[6] Johannes Messchaert, *Eine Gesangstunde*, ed. Franziska Martienssen (Mainz: Schott, [1927]), a copy of which was in Schenker's library at his death.

[7] Schenker heard Röntgen at a concert by Johannes Messchaert on February 5, 1896, describing him in his review of the concert as: "A pure artist, a pure human being, a charming artist, a charming human being." Federhofer (1990), pp. 318–19; see also ibid, pp. 325–28.

[8] The others were Bernhard Herzmansky of Doblinger and Adolf Robitschek.

[9] His contributions included the Inventions, the French and English Suites and Partitas, the Italian Concerto, the Chromatic Fantasy and Fugue in D minor, and the *Well-tempered Clavier*.

keyboard concertos by C. P. E. Bach (1907–08, unpublished[10]), then to scholarly critical editions of J. S. Bach's Chromatic Fantasy and Fugue in D minor (1910: ironically to replace that of Röntgen) and Beethoven's piano sonatas. Moreover, the publication of the edition of C. P. E. Bach sonatas and the *Ornamentation* study within six months of one another in 1903[11] was the exemplar for all his later, elucidatory editions. As the correspondence with Röntgen shows, Schenker still had his own interests as a composer very much at heart. Notable, though, is that his remark about the delayed tonic in Brahms's G minor Rhapsody, Op. 79, No. 2, in his letter of April 13, 1901, foreshadows the commentary on this passage in his *Theory of Harmony*.[12] This in turn might remind us that the precursor to the harmony manual, Schenker's unpublished essay in treatise form, "The Tone System,"[13] probably dates from around 1903. Perhaps, then, the years 1901 to 1903, when his aspirations as composer and performer still lingered, might be seen in a new light, as the period during which editing and theorizing began to converge as the parallel, inter-related activities that were to dominate his work as a mature music scholar.

SECTION II, **Schenker and his Publishers**, presents some of the exchanges between Schenker and the firms that published his principal works as editor and theorist—J. G. Cotta in Stuttgart, Universal Edition in Vienna, and Drei Masken Verlag in Munich. It is hardly surprising that the letters to these three publishers should be among the most voluminous collections in the surviving papers and also among the most completely preserved. For although he repeatedly professed that he was not a businessman, and that he was forever placing himself and his work at the mercy of the publishing industry, Schenker kept careful records of his dealings with publishers lest they cause him financial damage by breaching the terms of their contracts with him. His training in the law was invaluable, and he became increasingly embroiled with the firms that he approached to bring out his editions of music, his major theoretical texts, and his analytical monographs, yearbooks and pamphlets.

With Cotta, a firm with whom he had no prior connection when he offered them his *Theory of Harmony* in 1905, Schenker conducted an entirely cordial correspondence, accepting all of their recommendations, even though they did not always accord with his artistic principles. This may in part be explained by Schenker's relatively obscure status as a scholar in the early years of the century: he had published (with Universal Edition) only his volume of keyboard music by

---

[10] See Schenker's diary, pp. 10, 29–33; Federhofer (1985), p. 2, fn. 7, p. 19, fn. 37.

[11] Sonatas edition submitted December 28, 1901, released February 10, 1903; *Ornamentation* submitted October 4[?], 1902, released July 24, 1903 (information from correspondence and the publication registers in the archive of Universal Edition, Vienna).

[12] *Harmony*, pp. 35–36, Ex. 28 (Ger., pp. 49–51, Fig. 32).

[13] Given the name "Das Tonsystem" by Jeanette, this survives as a manuscript and typescript (OC 31/360–87 and 388–417). See Robert W. Wason, "From *Harmonielehre* to *Harmony*: Schenker's Theory of Harmony and Its Americanization," in *Fourth International Schenker Symposium*, vol. 1, pp. 213–58.

C. P. E. Bach and its associated study of ornamentation. Indeed, he made little headway with Cotta at first; and it was only with the intervention of one of his composer-pianist supporters, Eugen d'Albert, that the publishers changed their mind and agreed to bring out the *Theory of Harmony* as a single, large volume, on a commission basis; this was the first of what were to become three volumes of New Musical Theories and Fantasies. Cotta repeatedly warned Schenker not to overextend himself, either by splitting *Theory of Harmony* into two half-volumes, or by including an Afterword that was not central to the topic. Holding out the hope that this additional text would at some point appear on its own, Schenker continued to work on the next main part of his Theories and Fantasies, provisionally entitled "Psychology of Counterpoint" as a way of distinguishing it from popular textbooks on the subject. While he was working on it between 1906 and 1908, the *Counterpoint* project became so large that publication as a single volume would have been unthinkable; Cotta duly brought out the first half-volume, which Schenker had submitted in 1908, but the remaining volumes of the Theories and Fantasies were much longer in the making and were entrusted to Universal Edition in 1921.

The principal casualty of the change of publisher was the Afterword to the *Theory of Harmony*, which had grown to a 125-page essay by the time the latter had appeared. Described for a time as the "capstone" of the entire Theories and Fantasies project, it would have been Schenker's only writing on music history (a subject in which he professed little interest), one that would have shown music to be in constant decline during the 19th and early 20th centuries. When one considers how quickly the text became dated—for the Schenker of 1906, the "moderns" were Bruckner, Wolf, and Richard Strauss—it is surprising that he continued to hold out the hope of publishing it as late as 1923, by which time a new generation of composers with yet more radical agendas constituted the dominant figures in discourse on contemporary music.

Cotta's attitude to Schenker was never more than lukewarm; Universal Edition were far more willing to support his agenda for the reform of the classics and the pedagogical tradition. This may be in part the result of their relatively recent arrival on the scene, in part a desire to support the work of Vienna-based authors, and perhaps above all a shared view of a what constituted a well edited text of a musical classic. It is not surprising that most of Schenker's work for Universal Edition in the first two decades of their association was in the realm of music editing and performance practice; in these more musicological products, which reached a climax in the elucidatory editions of the late Beethoven piano sonatas, there is a clear separation of musical text and verbal commentary, and Schenker's deepest sense of respect for the German "masters" is perhaps most tangible. One of the happier collaborations during the Universal Edition years was that with Otto Erich Deutsch, who was commissioning editor of a series of facsimile editions of Viennese composers. Together they produced a facsimile edition of Beethoven's "Moonlight" Sonata, at a time when Schenker's mind must have been preoccupied by incipient thoughts about the Urlinie and a theory of structural voice-leading levels. (Years later, Deutsch and Schenker were to collaborate—without receiving any credit for it—on a revised edition of Schubert's "Unfinished" Symphony for the Wiener Philharmonischer Verlag, a UE imprint.)

The publication of *Der Tonwille* got off to a shaky start. Secure in his understanding of a paragraph in his contract with Universal Edition that guaranteed him sole responsibility for the content of these pamphlets, Schenker set out his hardening political views in the leading article, "The Mission of German Genius." The company's director Emil Hertzka, who was normally well-disposed to Schenker's speaking his own mind, turned against the increasingly polemical tone of what Schenker wrote under the rubric "Miscellanea," the final part of each pamphlet, devoted to a discussion of musical topics—and even non-musical topics—in a cultural and political context. Schenker's outspoken francophobia, together with what Hertzka saw as gratuitous attacks upon the Frankfurt music critic Paul Bekker and other respected writers, eventually led to a complete breakdown in the once cordial relationship between publisher and author. Embittered by Hertzka's lack of support for his work, Schenker accused his publisher of withholding royalties from the sale of his works, of delaying the appearance of the pamphlets and so stifling the dissemination of his creative work, and of exploiting the success of the Beethoven editions (which, in the meantime, had expanded to include text-critical editions of all thirty-two sonatas). Schenker fought a campaign to save *Der Tonwille*, exerting pressure on friends and pupils to purchase additional copies as proof that the work was still in demand. Hertzka went so far as to guarantee regular publication by converting it from a set of free-standing pamphlets into a quarterly periodical; but the loss of trust between the two was too great; and when Schenker discovered a publishing house, Drei Masken Verlag, willing not only to take it over but also to more than double its scope—making it a yearbook of over 200 pages—he arranged a settlement with Universal Edition that put an end to *Der Tonwille*.

In spite of an auspicious beginning with Drei Masken Verlag and a friendly correspondence with their head of music, Alfred Einstein, Schenker's relationship to his new publishing house began to unravel in little over a year. The publisher had underestimated the difficulties in interpreting Schenker's terminology and the graphic symbols attached to it (special dies had to be ordered from the print foundry), and Schenker had underestimated the time needed to produce a coherent text comprising many analyses, each with its own set of music examples and graphic illustrations. Although he sent the manuscript for *Masterwork 1* to Munich by the June 1925 deadline, he made many changes to the text at proof stage, and this incurred both severe delays to publication and substantially higher production costs. Things came to a head in June of the following year when the manuscript for the second yearbook was dispatched within days of the first appearing in print: lacking any means to judge the commercial success of *Masterwork 1*, Drei Masken Verlag was determined to postpone production of the second yearbook until the fall. Schenker's initial fury at this suggestion— he accused the firm of breach of contract, noting further that the concept of a yearbook would be meaningless without continuity in the form of a series of volumes—gradually subsided in recognition that his work would ultimately be better served by a delay in its appearance than by a new legal battle. By agreeing to a revised timetable, he also gained the sympathy and support of three close members of his circle: Otto Erich Deutsch, whose personal acquaintance with Einstein helped restore relations between author and publisher and who himself spent much time proofreading the second yearbook; Otto Vrieslander who, being based in Munich and understanding the latest developments in Schenker's graphing technique, worked directly with the engravers on the music examples; and Anthony van Hoboken, who helped finance the production costs of the yearbook.

With the publication of *Masterwork* 2, Schenker's relationship with Drei Masken Verlag reached an amicable conclusion. But he was to return to the Munich firm once more, in the spring of 1930, after learning that neither of the two main Leipzig houses (C. F. Peters and Breitkopf & Härtel) was interested in his latest work, a monograph on Beethoven's Third Symphony. Once again the ever-diplomatic Deutsch came to the rescue and arranged for Schenker's "Eroica" to be published on a commission basis as a third *Masterwork* yearbook. Publication followed more quickly, partly on account of the narrower focus of the volume, partly thanks to the enthusiasm and professionalism of the Viennese calligrapher Georg Tomay, who understood exactly Schenker's needs in the four dozen analytical examples and thirty-five pages of foreground graphs that dominate the volume; copies arrived in Berlin in December 1930, to coincide with a public lecture on Schenkerian theory given there by Hans Weisse.

SECTION III, **Schenker and the Institutions**, shows an individual grappling with an uncongenial world of officialdom and professional affiliation. For Schenker throughout his career, authority was something to be resisted, to wrestle with, to challenge. Indeed, from this section of the volume he might seem to emerge as anti-authoritarian and anti-establishment. Over the Sofie Deutsch bequest, he was in conflict indirectly with a charitable institution and the Ministry of Education, and directly with the Vienna Academy. In his dealings with Guido Adler it was the academic musicological community with which he declined to engage. The request that he serve on a panel of jurors for the Rothschild Artists' Foundation must have created a tension for him between on the one hand his loyalty to both Alphons von Rothschild (as former pupil and patron) and the Jewish Religious Community (to which he paid taxes), and on the other hand his instinct to distance himself from the person who had by 1916 come to embody musicological orthodoxy. That tension showed also (especially in the diary entries) over the invitation in 1926 to serve on the Beethoven Centenary Committee: he accepted, but then did not involve himself and turned down the opportunity to lecture.

Even with the Photogram Archive, an institution of his own invention set up to support his work and on the board of which he sat, he refused to involve himself in several of its public initiatives including, extraordinarily, the Archive's official opening: "I shall firmly keep my distance from these things. I shall stay at home." The long-running quest for a professorial position again exposed the dilemma for him, and his 1910 letter to Cotta (given in this volume in a footnote) bespeaks that dilemma, balancing "the attendant advantages in honor and remuneration" of such a position against the "sacrificing of my freedom."

Schenker's anti-establishment attitude and the high value he set on personal liberty seem to contradict the pro-aristocratic and anti-democratic views that he so fiercely and so ubiquitously espoused. However, for him aristocracy did not equate with worldly authority, nor democracy with individual freedom. Monarchy and aristocracy were of a higher order, were passed down through families, and were ultimately God-given. The authorities that Schenker resisted were man-made creations: governments, ministries, professional bodies, commercial companies. He admired Rothschild because he saw him as coming from a long, aristocratic line (the Vienna Rothschild family's ennoblement in fact dates back to 1822), whereas he secretly despised Mrs. Deutsch as being a product of commercial success, and therefore middle-class and "new money." Both were his patrons, deserving of his gratitude; but in his mind they fell into different categories. He felt contempt for the numerous people upon whom "profession-specific honorary titles"[14] were bestowed, especially during the Weimar Republic as part of the system of "Orders of Merit for Service to the Republic," whom he perhaps saw as time-servers and sycophants.

While not actually claiming that he himself was imbued with genius—certainly not putting himself on a par with Beethoven and Brahms[15]—he nonetheless saw his theoretical vision as unique and coming from a higher source. This goes some way toward explaining why he refused to collaborate with anybody outside his own circle: there would have been an incompatibility of minds that would have made such cooperation futile.

SECTION IV, **Beethoven's Ninth Symphony**, takes a single, major work with which Schenker had a career-long involvement. The correspondence concerning Beethoven's Ninth Symphony is testimony to Schenker's belief that analysis, performance, and textual criticism were inseparable aspects of music study. A book on the Ninth—probably of modest dimensions—was mooted as the first of a series of independent "handbooks" emanating from the Afterword to the *Theory of Harmony* and demonstrating the preeminence of the masters. Cotta declined to issue this handbook before the Afterword—now conceived as an independent essay—had appeared; but they also showed little interest in bringing the latter out as the third volume of the New Musical Theories and Fantasies.

Schenker found more sympathy for a study of the Ninth in his home town. In 1910 he received an invitation from the Association of Viennese Music Critics to give a series of lectures on the work, which Universal Edition would then issue in print form. The lectures did not materialize, but Universal Edition offered Schenker a contract for a book-length study of the Ninth Symphony, which he duly completed in the middle of the following year, and which was published in 1912. Schenker had hoped that this would be complemented by a critical edition of

---

[14] *Berufsspezifische Ehrenzeichen*: these included, for example, Court Counselor, Chamber Counselor, Government Counselor, Medical Counselor, Veterinary Counselor, Commercial Counselor, Economic Counselor, and Education Counselor. There were also counselorships for people who worked in the mountains, forests, and in the building industry.

[15] "That I am no Sebastian Bach, no Handel, no Beethoven, Haydn, or Mozart, no Schubert, Mendelssohn, Schumann, or Brahms—this I know better than all of you. Before them I am dust, not worthy of the wind that bears it aloft"; *Tonwille* 5, vol. 1, p. 222 (Ger. orig., 54).

the score, but the estimated costs of this were prohibitive. Nonetheless, the Ninth Symphony "monograph" ushered in a period of relatively stable relations with Universal Edition, which saw the first three volumes of the elucidatory edition of the late Beethoven sonatas published, and the laying of the groundwork for a series of handbooks that evolved into the *Tonwille* pamphlet series.

The symphonic work of Beethoven is the subject of a rich exchange of letters, and personal encounters, with the Danish conductor and composer Paul von Klenau. Klenau saw no contradiction in his support for Schoenberg's school of composers and his adulation of Schenker's writings on the classics, and wrote to Schenker repeatedly for advice on the performance of the "Eroica," the *Missa solemnis*, and the Ninth. Schenker's replies and his notes on their meetings (summaries of which were written up by Jeanette) reveal his advocacy for performing these works at tempi significantly faster than were customary at the time He was compelled to defend the metronome markings that Beethoven provided for his symphonies, assuring Klenau that the works would not seem rushed so long as he kept the goals of Beethoven's linear progressions in mind and understood the composer's articulation marks.

Schenker also used his conversations with Klenau to stress the importance of consulting autograph scores, which give much more insight into Beethoven's intentions. (In this regard, he mentioned his revisions to the text of the Fifth Symphony, recorded in the *Tonwille* serialization of his essay on the work.) The same applies to an exchange of letters a few years later with the conductor Georg Dohrn, director of the Breslau Orchestral Society, concerning his forthcoming performance of the Ninth: Schenker cited certain features of the autograph score of the Ninth and also commended to Dohrn his textual notes on the Fifth.

SECTION V, **Contrary Opinions**, identifies certain respects in which some of Schenker's associates diverged from his views and the ways in which they chose to express their differences. On the whole, Schenker's correspondents were friendly, if not deferential. It was not merely that they were fearful of confrontation and so avoided making remarks that might, upon being misunderstood, provoke a hostile response framed in legalistic language. Many were genuinely indebted to him for having enriched their lives in almost unimagined ways through the wisdom he imparted about musical structure and meaning: to Hans Weisse he became a "spiritual father," and other pupils and musicians with whom he came into contact undoubtedly thought of Schenker in similar terms.

There were times when, for these admirers, Schenker's overbearing political sentiments or partisan musical stances became too much to suffer in silence. But expressions of disagreement were confined to specific cases, for instance Walter Dahms's condemnation of the German command during World War I, and Weisse's refusal to accept—perhaps even to believe—Schenker's adulation of the songs of Otto Vrieslander.

Writers and composers with whom Schenker clashed either took no notice of him (Ernst Kurth) or rebutted his claims in their own work (Paul Bekker, Arnold Schoenberg). It is, therefore, all the more endearing to find a composer of some renown—Paul Hindemith—pleading with Schenker to consider his work in greater detail, confident that the closer scrutiny of the music would lead to a change of judgment on the theorist's part. (What few musicians outside his closest circle did not realize was that, while Schenker's theories underwent considerable development, his likes and dislikes hardly changed over the span of his life.)

The most fruitful exchange of artistic views is found in the lengthy correspondence with August Halm, a near-contemporary who, like Schenker, wrote prolifically about music from an independent vantage point, i.e. without holding an important position at a major institute of higher learning. Their correspondence is on the whole cordial, perhaps because both held out the (forlorn) hope of an endorsement of what they treasured most in life: for Schenker, the wider dissemination of his theories; for Halm, recognition as a composer. Without bringing himself to accept Halm's music, or his opinions on the music of others (notably Brahms and Bruckner), Schenker was clearly touched by Halm's untainted idealism and devotion to music: in the brief "Literature" section in the "Eroica" Symphony essay (*Masterwork* 3, pp. 67–68; Ger., pp. 100-01), Schenker paid eloquent tribute to Halm's masterful thematic analysis, and his dedication to music analysis in general.

By contrast, Schenker's turbulent friendship with the eminent conductor Wilhelm Furtwängler, the most successful of all the musicians with whom he came into contact, shows little evidence of intellectual reciprocation. For one thing, Furtwängler was too open-minded about, or fond of, the music that Schenker deprecated (Stravinsky, Bruckner, Wagner), and had neither the music-theoretical foundations nor the literary skills with which to express himself adequately to Schenker. Not only did he lack any understanding of sonata form, as Schenker deduces (with some astonishment) from a conversation dating from April 1925, but he also seemed utterly unconcerned with textual matters, regarding a musical score as something to be committed to and ultimately conducted from memory, rather than an object to be set alongside a composer's sketch or autograph manuscript.[16]

SECTION VI, **Advancing the Cause**, in contrast to Section V, brings to the fore the measure of agreement and common cause that existed between Schenker and certain of his associates. From about 1920 Schenker was convinced that he had advanced music theory sufficiently beyond the points taken by Fux in counterpoint and C. P. E. Bach in thoroughbass that his work would be remembered long after his death; by the end of the decade he had won over a sufficient number of converts to his cause to reassure himself that his place in the music history books, and that of his writings in music theory seminars, was as good as secure. All his converts, in turn, were beginning to find their places in the Schenkerian world of the future. Outposts of Schenker studies were established in Germany: Felix-Eberhard von Cube promoted his teaching in

---

[16] The point arises in the diary entry for December 8, 1927: Furtwängler met Schenker at Hoboken's house and was unimpressed by Hoboken's collection of first editions. "I've got everything up here," he remarked, pointing to his head. Schenker, who had recently completed his extensive textual study of Schubert's "Unfinished" Symphony, was evidently disappointed at not finding in Furtwängler a willing conversation partner with whom to discuss his latest finding.

the industrial Rhineland; Moriz Violin brought Schenker's performing world to Hamburg, only to discover a nascent Schenkerism in that city too. Schenkerian thought was also beginning to thrive outside German-speaking lands, despite the absence of English translations of his writings (the English foreword to the "Moonlight" facsimile excepted): at the University of Edinburgh, a pianist by the name of John Petrie Dunn was teaching counterpoint and orchestration according to Schenkerian principles, and in America there was an increasing clamor for Schenkerian pedagogy in conservatories.

Although circumstances prevented Walter Dahms from studying music with Schenker formally, he was among the earliest to see in Schenker's writings the basis of a reform of music teaching. Dahms and Schenker fell out over Germany's conduct of the war; and yet while Schenker dropped the occasional disparaging remark about Nietzsche, Dahms's support of Schenker's German-centered cultural stance never wavered. And if, like August Halm, Dahms held a more liberal view of what constituted great music and chose to write about a greater range of musical genius, he was nothing but adulatory about the theorist's latest writings, the "Miscellanea" pages not excepted. The correspondence nonetheless retains a formal air, with each writer replying frankly to the other without in any way compromising his own stance.

In Moriz Violin, by contrast, Schenker had a correspondent to whom he could unburden himself freely. Their correspondence is the only one in this volume in which the familiar form of address ("Du") is used: the origins of this uncharacteristically close friendship have yet to be investigated, but the correspondence shows that it embraced an element of shared Jewish identity. Violin, widely recognized as a pianist of unquestionable musical sensitivity, had a performer's intuitive approach to music and musical issues; and his perceptive portrayal of cultural life in Hamburg—to which he moved in the early 1920s, partly to escape Vienna's stifling cultural atmosphere—captures the different environments in which he and his friend worked.

Violin seems to have been keen on fostering Schenkerian sensibilities in his teaching, and he eventually came into contact with musicians who knew about Schenker and knew something of his work. One of them was the Altona city organist, Carl Friedrich Wilhelm Hannemann; the other was a pupil of Violin's named Harry Hahn, who taught Schenkerian theory on his own initiative at the local composers' co-operative, using large-format sketches for illustrating voice-leading techniques, and whose essays and graphic work made an impression on Schenker himself. But the most important step that Violin undertook was to transform the conservatory at which he worked into nothing less than a "Schenker Institute" at which his friend's aesthetic outlook would flourish in both the studio and the classroom. Unable to persuade Hans Weisse to be the theory teacher at his new school, Violin (with Schenker's approval) offered the job to Felix-Eberhard von Cube, who resigned his post in Duisburg to take up this opportunity to promote his teacher's cause in his teacher's name.

The rise of National Socialism put an end to Violin's idealistic plans, and he returned to Vienna in 1933, after which the almost monthly exchange of long letters between Violin and Schenker is reduced to a trickle of relatively short communications.

Long before his relocation to Hamburg, Cube was determined to be a "foot soldier" in Schenker's army, fighting the cause wherever he went. Schenker, for his part, recognized a gifted musician in the young man who arrived in Vienna in late 1923 to study with him, one whose talents he was unable to nurture fully because Cube's father stopped supporting his education after barely two years' study. Cube's unswerving dedication to the cause took him to other cities in northern Germany—Düsseldorf and Cologne—where he presented seminars on Schenkerian analysis. Cube willingly accepted Schenker's quasi-paternal guidance, and was always eager to show his appreciation of his teacher's help, long after formal tuition had stopped. At no time was this more evident than in the summer of 1928, when Schenker turned sixty: Cube sought the cooperation of bookshops in Duisburg and Essen to mount an exhibition of Schenker's writings and editions, and he wrote an impassioned, poetic (and slightly misleading) account of Schenker's rise to prominence on the Viennese pedagogical scene, which was printed in two north-German newspapers.[17]

In later years, as part of the preparation of teaching materials for Duisburg and, above all, for the Schenker Institute in Hamburg, Cube sent draft voice-leading analyses to his teacher for approval; these included an analysis of the first prelude from Bach's *Well-tempered Clavier*, Book I, and the first-movement theme from Beethoven's Piano Sonata in A♭ major, Op. 26, both of which feature in Schenker's late published work. His teacher did not comment on Cube's more scientific explorations of the tonal system, but Cube persevered with these in his later, unpublished writings.

In Anthony van Hoboken Schenker found a pupil who was ideal in almost every respect. He was a gifted musician who was not only attracted to Schenker's latest theory but also understood the scope—and limitations—of its application to performance; he persevered with work on analysis, devoting considerable time to Brahms's Intermezzi Op. 117.[18] As an enthusiastic collector of first and early editions of music, he had amassed an enormous library of musical sources, and his dedication to textual matters complemented Schenker's more ideological approach to primary materials and Otto Erich Deutsch's "purely philological" interests, as Schenker characterized them.

Hoboken's immense wealth was to prove a blessing to Schenker throughout the last ten years of his life, when the Dutchman was a regular pupil of his. The realization of the Photogram Archive, a project born in the spirit of the elucidatory editions, would have been unthinkable without Hoboken's financial support. And he went so far as to guarantee the printing costs of *Free Composition* and so enabled Schenker, in spite of declining health, to work steadily on it during the last five years of his life; for this financial security Schenker apostrophized Hoboken, in

---

[17] "Ein Meister der Musiktheorie," *Rhein- und Ruhr-Zeitung*, July 24, 1928, and, in modified form, *Duisburger General-Anzeiger*, June 28, 1928.

[18] A twenty-eight-page typescript copy of his unpublished study of Op. 117, No. 1, is preserved as OC 14/2, and an earlier typewritten draft with numerous handwritten emendations by Schenker as OC 14/3. Hoboken's studies of Op. 117 are recorded in Schenker's lessonbooks between March 15, 1928, and April 8, 1929.

the foreword to *Free Composition*, as a man "whose name is indissolubly connected with this work" and for that reason alone has gained immortality.

Inevitably, a man of Hoboken's wealth created enmity within Schenker's circle, and one sometimes gets the impression that the success or failure of one Schenkerian initiative or another was dependent more upon Hoboken's purse than upon Schenker's intellectual authority. Schenker, who resented wealth for its own sake, often spoke unflatteringly about his patron behind his back. Thus, for example, he did not conceal from Cube his displeasure that Hoboken would not contribute a modest sum to establish a pilot program in Schenkerian analysis at the Hochschule in Cologne in the late 1920s. He compared Hoboken unfavorably with Felix Salzer, who, though far less affluent, subsidized the first performances of Weisse's Octet and the post-concert receptions. And he privately blamed Hoboken, at least in part, for the collapse of other initiatives that arose during the last decade, including the proposed "communications" or "yearbook" attached to the Photogram Archive, and a collected edition of the works of C. P. E. Bach projected in twenty volumes.

The Edinburgh-based John Petrie Dunn had studied piano and composition in Germany, but it was only from reading Schenker's New Musical Theories and Fantasies that he claimed to have gained insight into the innermost workings of music. One may therefore read his first letter to Schenker (April 18, 1926) almost as an act of desperation: Was *Free Composition* already out of print, as his local bookseller had feared, and was Dunn therefore to be deprived of the last chapter of this most important of contributions to music theory? Having successfully made contact with his guiding spirit, Dunn soon embarked on an English translation of parts of *Counterpoint* 2 adapted for his university students and had plans to expand this project to other sections of the book. A lengthy extract from the Ninth Symphony monograph in Dunn's *A Student's Guide to Orchestration* (London: Novello, 1928) marks the first appearance of a quotation from Schenker's work in an English publication.

As the only native English-speaking musician with whom Schenker corresponded regularly, Dunn steered well clear of politics, and took special care not to bring up any matter on which the two might disagree, e.g. Wagner's orchestration. Culturally the two shared almost the same ideals: Dunn's disparaging remarks about jazz are, if anything, even more uncompromising than Schenker's pronouncements in the "Miscellanea." Being hampered in his university teaching by Professor Donald Francis Tovey on one side and an "old pedant" on the other, Dunn was never destined to make a major contribution to the dissemination of Schenkerian theory: his mimeographed translations from *Counterpoint* reached only a handful of students over a period of a few years. Nonetheless his death in a road accident at the age of 52 came as a shock to Schenker, who had already put Edinburgh on the map of places his theories had conquered.

By contrast with Dunn, Felix Salzer's musical interests were more wide-ranging than Schenker's. A pupil of Weisse's until the latter's departure for the United States in the fall of 1931, Salzer did not come into direct contact with Schenker until Weisse's little seminar (which also included Trude Kral, Greta Kraus, and Manfred Willfort) reconvened in Schenker's apartment on the Keilgasse, and he became Schenker's private pupil only after the latter lacked the strength to teach them as a group. Salzer's admiration for the music of the Middle Ages and Renaissance did not prove a hindrance to the new teacher–pupil relationship; on the contrary, Schenker seems to have shared some of his private passions, e.g. for folk music, and in particular for the musicianship of Béla Bartók, thus belying sentiments he had expressed elsewhere that Brahms was the one true purveyor of the Hungarian idiom in art music.

In the 1930s Salzer's greatest achievements—the universalizing of Schenkerian theory, and its establishment at the forefront of the American music theory scene—lay well in the future. At this time, Schenker's hopes for the wider dissemination of his work were pinned on Hans Weisse, who had been his student from as early as 1908 and who remained in close contact with Schenker right until his departure for New York (via Hamburg and its Schenker Institute) in mid-September 1931. As with so many others of whom he had high expectations, Schenker blew hot and cold about Weisse publicly and privately. He envied Weisse his ease in establishing good relationships with influential people, and his natural ability to communicate; but he was also fearful that Weisse might commit an analytical gaffe, e.g. through the presentation of a faulty voice-leading analysis at a public lecture, and so put his entire project at risk. Weisse's boundless self-confidence, however, proved more beneficial to the Schenkerian cause than his teacher could have imagined, and Schenker was not a little startled by the success of Weisse's enterprise at the David Mannes Music School and (a year later, in 1932) at Columbia University.

Weisse began to free himself from Schenker's force-field as he became settled in New York and won adherents to his teacher's understanding of musical structure. True until the end in recognizing Schenker as his "spiritual father," he came to recognize that Schenkerism could take root in the United States only if it cast away the political and cultural ideology that had underpinned it in Austria and Germany. He welcomed the appearance of text-free—and thus demagoguery-free—publications like the *Five Analyses in Sketchform*, and went so far as to propose that the analytical examples and foreground graphs for Schenker's "Eroica" analysis be published separately as teaching materials for a Mannes seminar on the symphony. He was later to ruffle feathers by suggesting, similarly, that the volume of music examples for *Free Composition* could likewise be published on its own, without text. In a quasi-valedictory letter to Violin, which closes this volume, Weisse defends his view of that long-awaited, posthumous publication as "the weakest, from a literary point of view" of all of the Master's writings. This is characteristic of his view of Schenkerian theory as a musical phenomenon that will triumph in the end because of what it is, and as something that belongs more to the future than to the past.

I
The Early Career

I
Schenker as Composer

UPON applying in September 1887 to study at the Vienna Conservatory, Schenker was pronounced "qualified to be placed on probation in the first year of the advanced class (*Ausbildungsklasse*) in composition," and would "at his own wish be assigned to the class of Franz Krenn." Alongside this he was to study piano with Ernst Ludwig. But Schenker evidently changed his mind about composition, opting instead in the first year for harmony and in the second year for counterpoint, both with Anton Bruckner. Not until the third year, 1889/90, did he enroll in a composition class, this time with Johann Nepomuk (Hans) Fuchs.[1] However, he withdrew from the Conservatory altogether on November 20, 1889, having completed his studies for the doctorate of law at the University of Vienna.

No doubt the death of his father at the end of 1887, followed by the arrival in Vienna from Galicia of family members in need of support, had a bearing on his abandonment of musical studies. When precisely Schenker embarked on composition with serious artistic intent is unclear: certainly by 1890, perhaps earlier—as Schenker's encomium upon Ludwig's death might suggest: "He had the leisure and will to take me under his wing when I entered the Conservatory on an imperial scholarship. It was he who paid attention to my compositions."[2] By 1903, when his editorial and theoretical interests were beginning to blossom, composition faded, as the final diary entry in this selection, from 1931, ultimately records.

Just under fifty compositions are known, ten of them bearing opus numbers.[3] Most are preserved in the Oswald Jonas Memorial Collection (boxes 22–23). The majority are songs for solo voice with piano, or pieces for solo piano or piano four-hands. In addition, there are three sets of pieces for chorus, some movements for piano trio, others for string quartet, a serenade for horn and piano, and incidental music to *Hamlet*. Of these works, eight appeared in print; the

---

[1] Federhofer (1985), 5. The relevant matriculation document is reproduced in *Rebell und Visionär: Heinrich Schenker in Wien*, ed. Evelyn Fink (Vienna: Lafite, 2003), 48–49.

[2] Diary March 14, 1915; Federhofer (1985), 7.

[3] Robert Lang and JoAn Kunselman, eds., *Heinrich Schenker, Oswald Jonas, Moriz Violin: A Checklist of Manuscripts and Other Papers in the Oswald Jonas Memorial Collection* (Berkeley: University of California Press, 1994), 67–75; Benjamin McKay Ayotte, ed., *Heinrich Schenker: A Guide to Research. Routledge Music Bibliographies* (New York: Routledge, 2004), 5–39. Identified compositions in the Oster Collection Finding List, 25 (OC 10/17v), 29 (OC 10/75), 174 (OC 50/2), 369 (OC Schenker/1–4); possible unidentified compositions: 24 (10/1 and 8), 27, (10/50), 85 (32/2), 86 (32/25), 94 (32/125). Graphs of some of the compositions are preserved in the Oster Collection: Op. 2, No. 1 (15/15–17), Op. 4, No. 1 (15/18–22).

remainder are in manuscript at differing stages of completion. Those referred to in the correspondence given here, together with known performances, are:

Op. 1   Two Pieces for Piano (Vienna: Doblinger, [1892]): 1. Etude, 2. Capriccio / "To Julius Epstein"

[no opus number]   Serenade for Horn and Piano / "To his dear friend, Louis Savart"
performances: November 5, 1893, March 5, 1894, Vienna, Savart [OJ 35/5, [2, 5]]

Op. 2   *Fantasy* for Piano (Leipzig: Breitkopf & Härtel, 1898) / "To F. Busoni"
performance: second section, January 8, 1899, Klagenfurt, Schenker [OJ 35/5, [6]]

Op. 3   Six Songs for Solo Voice with Piano Accompaniment (Leipzig: Breitkopf & Härtel, 1898, 1901):
1. Versteckte Jasminen, 2. Wiegenlied, 3. Vogel im Busch, 4. Ausklang, 5. Allein, 6. Einkleidung
performances: No. 2 December 1, 1900, Vienna, Gärtner, Zemlinsky [OJ 12/40, [3] = OJ 14/23a, [1]]; No. 4 March 19, 1902, Vienna, Gärtner, Schenker [OJ 35/5, [20, 23]]

Op. 4   Five Pieces for Piano (Leipzig: Breitkopf & Härtel, 1898) / "Dedicated to Eugen d'Albert"
performances: two pieces, January 24, 1898, Vienna, d'Albert; No. 2 January 8, 1899, Klagenfurt, Schenker [OJ 35/5, [6]]

Op. 5   Two-voice Inventions (Leipzig: Breitkopf & Härtel, 1898) / "Dedicated to Mrs. Irene Mayerhofer"

Op. 6   Three Songs for Low Voice with Piano Accompaniment: 1. Heimat, 2. Nachtgruss, 3. Wandrers Nachtlied, 3a. Meeresstille
performances: No. 3a (with unpublished song "Blumengruss") January 19, 1895, Vienna, Gärtner, Schenker(?) [OJ 35/5, [4]]; Nos. 1 and 2 January 26, 1905, Vienna, Gärtner, Willy Klasen [OJ 35/5, [29, 31]]

Op. 7   [Three songs for mixed chorus], 1. Was ich liebe? (MS), 2. Die Nachtigall (MS), 3. Vorüber (published in a collection of 51 choruses by the Vienna Singakademie [copy preserved as OC 50/2], to which the piece is dedicated)
performance: No. 3 December 18, 1903, Vienna, Singakademie [OJ 35/5, [25, 28]]

Op. 10   *Ländler* for Piano (Berlin: N. Simrock, 1899) / "To Mr. Wilhelm Kux."

Of these, the letters concerning the *Fantasy* Op. 2, are of particular interest: in them we can trace the transformation under Busoni's guidance of three separate short pieces into a single, larger structure.

The correspondence that affords glimpses of Schenker's composing activities encompasses two publishers (Breitkopf & Härtel and Simrock), one organization (the Vienna Singakademie), and five individuals (Eugen d'Albert, Ignaz Brüll, Ferruccio Busoni, Max Kalbeck, and Detlev von Liliencron). The more than 300 letters and postcards between Schenker and Moriz Violin dating from 1896 to 1905 may yield further evidence of Schenker's brief career as a composer. Pertinent diary entries are few and far between; surviving concert programs furnish valuable information, and have been presented in abbreviated form below.

IAN BENT

❧ Breitkopf & Härtel to Schenker (letter), October 16, 1895
OJ 9/20, [5]

BREITKOPF & HÄRTEL
Leipzig
Nürnberger Strasse 36

Dear Sir,

It was very kind of you to send us your Five Pieces for Piano, Op. 2 [*recte* Op. 4], with which we have now become acquainted. Without doubt they will attract many admirers. It is of course not easy to gain acceptance for new piano compositions. For us there is an additional consideration: we have a large number of works that we have already accepted and still have to produce and publish. Accordingly, we have felt obliged for the time being to refrain from taking on anything that is not incontrovertibly necessary. We deeply regret that under such circumstances we are compelled to return your manuscript to you, but nevertheless thank you for the trust you place in us.

With kind regards,
Yours most truly,
Breitkopf & Härtel

❧ D'Albert to Schenker (letter), April 5, 1896
OJ 9/6, [12]

Hotel & Pension du Lac
ON LAKE GARDA   Riva. Hotel du Lac

Dear, revered friend,

I have long been intending to write to you, and must earnestly ask your forgiveness for not having gotten round to it before now. I am enchanted by your Pieces for Piano. If I have not played any of them so far, this is due solely to the fact that I have given almost no concerts this year other than the Brahms evening in

Berlin, but have instead devoted myself entirely to the orchestration of my opera *Gernot*.[1] We have been here since the end of January and have greatly enjoyed the peace and quiet. Now the idyll is over; tomorrow we travel slowly back to Dresden and on to Coswig, only to travel to London at the end of the month, where I have to give seven concerts—the first under Mottl's direction. I am now starting to play the piano again, and your opus shall be the first new piece on my agenda. It will be a great pleasure for me to study it, of that I am sure.

As concerns the young Szalit,[2] it is a real pity that she has not come here rather than going to Abbazia to recuperate. The effect would have been just the same, and I would have been able to teach her for another two months.

I did not suggest this, because Mr. Szalit expressly told me in Vienna some time back that there was no possibility of breaking away from Fischhof[3] before the end of April. I am naturally very happy that the young lady is not studying with this piano fop, and wholeheartedly concur with the idea that she should study with you for the time being, for you are a serious musician and will point the young lady in the right direction. If you see Mr. Szalit, please give him my best thanks for his kind letter. I should very much like to know as soon as possible whether the young lady is definitely coming to me, and if so when. As to her health, I do not think that Lake Starnberg could have a detrimental effect—quite the contrary. I should also like to know how to divide up my teaching; for this year I could be at her disposal only from the end of June to the end of September—i.e. three months—in Leoni[?] on Lake Starnberg. Not until next year would I be in one place for a longer period of time: March to November. So would you take over the continuation of the young lady's study on my behalf in the intervening period? Please let me know your feelings about this.

Enclosed at long last is the vocal score of *Ghismonda*.[4] The opera was a great success, but the rotten Dresden press maligned it from top to bottom so that the remaining performances were played to an empty house. The dear Dresden public just lets its views be dictated by their criticism and has no judgment of its own. When one sees with what resources the successful opera scribblers of today contend, one might as well give up any attempt to persevere with a serious work.

As soon as I play something of yours, I will send you the program. Where do things stand over a publisher? Breitkopf & Härtel are somewhat sluggish—it is not worth thinking of them. Please avail yourself of my services: whatever lies within my meager power I will do.

With cordial greetings from me and best regards from my wife, I remain, in anticipation of an early reply.[5]

    Your ever true
    Eugen d'Albert
Address until April 16: <u>Coswig</u> nr. Dresden
  April 17–26: <u>Baden-Baden</u> Hotel
    Badischer Hof

---

[1] *Gernot*: opera on libretto by G. Kastropp, first performed Mannheim, April 11, 1897. Schenker received an invitation to the première (OJ 9/6, [17]), but evidently did not attend.

² Paula Szalit (1886 or 1887–1920): Polish pianist and composer who came to public notice early as a child prodigy and was taught by Robert Fischof, then studied temporarily with Schenker before moving to Eugen d'Albert. In 1896 Schenker described her in a review as "a nine-year-old child, a wondrous talent" and spoke of her "superb rhythm, elegantly developed dexterity, [...] wholly subtle pedal technique such as the most mature of all virtuosos possess" (Federhofer (1990), 321), and praised her improvisations.

³ Robert Fischhof (1856–1918): Viennese pianist, pupil of Anton Door, Anton Bruckner, Franz Krenn, later Leschetizky and Liszt; from 1884 to 1918 Professor of piano at the Vienna Conservatory (Academy).

⁴ *Ghismonda*: opera on libretto by d'Albert after K. L. Immermann, first performed Dresden, November 28, 1895.

⁵ No reply is known to survive.

D'Albert to Schenker (letter), January 2, 1897
OJ 9/6, [14]

> Frankfurt a.M.–Sachsenhausen
> Letzter Hasenpfad 91

Dear friend,

Most cordial thanks for your printed Pieces for Piano [Op. 1]! I am even more pleased with them in print than in manuscript—if that were possible. I have begun negotiations with another publisher to have your remaining compositions published by him. Let us hope I will succeed. When the right moment arrives to send him something, I will alert you.

I sent you the libretto of *Die Abreise*.¹ There are still a few errors: p. 7, line 11 from the bottom must be "Jugend" not "Fugend"; p. 18 line 14 from the top "Im" instead of "Dem"; line 15 "erfreuet mich" instead of "gehört für mich"; also, on p. 24 line 10 it should read "Der Versuch" instead of "den Versuch." I hope to be able to send you the score soon.

On January 24 I am due to play in Vienna. Since I am giving a Beethoven evening (at special request of Mr. Gutmann), I cannot play your Pieces for Piano this time; but perhaps another opportunity will present itself at which I can be useful to you by performing the pieces. I am entirely at your disposal—needless to say, where time permits.

With cordial greetings and retrospective New Year's good wishes, and also from my wife,

> Your devoted
> Eugen d'Albert

¹ *Die Abreise*: opera on a libretto by F. von Sporck after A. von Steigentesch, first performance Frankfurt, October 20, 1898.

🎵 Brüll to Schenker (letter), January 23, 1897

OJ 9/23, [1]

Dear Dr. [Schenker],

I am delighted that Mr. Violin would like to play something from your composition[s], and I am happy to put at your disposal for this purpose the evening in March (I believe it will be March 19) that I am arranging.

Since Mr. Violin's address is unknown to me, may I ask you please to tell him <u>provisionally</u> on my behalf that I will be delighted for him to participate in compositions of yours—what's more, perhaps with one of his own works as well?

I do not insist on your giving me some of your work to look through, but it would be of great interest to me. If you wish to give me the honor of a visit, then please let me know in advance the time you will be coming, and please exclude the days 28, 29, 30, and 31 of this month, and on the other days avoid 1–3 o'clock.

   With kind regards,
    Yours most truly,
     Ignaz Brüll

Vienna IX
Liechtensteinstrasse 4, 1st floor

🎵 Diary entry, February 7, 1897

Visits to Goldmark and Brüll. Favorable, it seemed to me even genuinely favorable judgment of my compositions.

D'Albert plays the variations from my *Fantasy* at sight (Hotel Bristol). The artist himself has an unfullfilled personality: he lacks what the great artist has, what the great human being has . . . subdued appearance.

🎵 D'Albert to Schenker (letter), May 8, 1897

OJ 9/6, [18]

               Heidelberg

Dear friend,

If only I knew everything as definitely as that I am going to play your compositions! I would have done it long ago, but could not find five minutes to study them thoroughly. After I left Vienna I was in Russia, then I had unbroken rehearsals for *Gernot*—I hope that the pandemonium will soon stop so that I can take it easy. The first thing then shall be to learn your pieces by heart. In the forthcoming winter I will play them, for sure—not for your pleasure, but for mine.[1]

I am hugely pleased that I shall be able to see you at the meeting of the Society of Composers, and that you will be able to hear my *Gernot*. I am absolutely counting on seeing you in Mannheim on the 26th—we can go into detail about everything then.² I sent the piano-vocal score to your old address, so I hope you have received it. On the 10th I travel to England for ten days to do concerts, and do not get back here until the 21st. My wife and I thank you cordially for your kind good wishes, and send you both our warm greetings.

> So rest assured of the promise
> of your faithful
> Eugen d'Albert

In great haste!

So you will see the young Paula on the 26th: she is doing excellently.³

---

¹ In a letter of June 11, 1897, d'Albert was to write: "Are you in agreement with Busoni's proposal: *Fantasy in Three Parts*? I have mastered the difficult pieces." (OJ 9/6 [19]).

² Schenker's diary for May 31, 1897, records: "Back from Germany—from the trip to Mannheim (Tonkünstler festival), Frankfurt, Heidelberg, etc. Did not form any encouraging impressions: no signs of new sources of art springing up anywhere." (OJ 1/1, 2b).

³ In what is perhaps the first glimpse of him as teacher, Schenker records in his diary sometime between February and September 1897: "Paula Szalit prepared for concerts: among other things, J. S. Bach's fugues in C♯ minor (five voices) and E♭ minor." (OJ 1/1, 3).

❧ Schenker to Kalbeck (letter), May 10, 1897
OJ 5/19, [3]

Dear Sir,

I do not flatter myself by presuming that you have taken notice of my literary efforts in Harden's *Die Zukunft*, in the *Wiener Neue Revue* or in *Die Zeit*. Closer to my heart would be if you would do me the honor of listening to some of my compositions, upon which Brahms, not to mention Goldmark, d'Albert, and Busoni, have pronounced with much—perhaps overmuch—appreciation.¹ Please do not for a moment think I am covertly asking you to publicize me in your writing. All I have in mind is to introduce myself in the very best circles here as a composer before d'Albert plays something of mine. May I hold out any hope?²

> With great respect,
> Dr. Heinrich Schenker

---

¹ Both of the opening sentences are terminated with question marks, which cannot be rendered in translation.

² On May 17, Kalbeck invited Schenker to visit him and bring his music (OJ 12/7, 1).

🎔 Busoni to Schenker (letter), [May 17, 1897]
OJ 9/27, [1]

Greatly revered Dr. [Schenker],
After all that Maestro Goldmark[1] has told me about you, it will be a great pleasure for me to become acquainted with you personally. —May I ask you kindly to call on me the day after tomorrow (Wednesday) in the morning?[2]

Through a mistake on the part of the doorman, a first letter from me that was prepared for you was not delivered. Please forgive me for the double inconvenience by

    yours truly,
    With kind regards,
    Ferruccio B. Busoni

---

[1] Karl Goldmark (1830–1915): Hungarian Jewish composer, especially of opera, who lived much of his life in Vienna.

[2] The letter that follows indicates that Schenker came to him a day earlier than proposed, on Tuesday May 18.

🎔 Schenker to Busoni (letter), dated May 18, 1897
Sbb B II 4413

Highly revered Sir,
As I left you, delighted by your kind reception and happy about your spoken and written praise for the items of mine, I took myself off to see Maestro Goldmark. I gave him your letter and told him you were in favor of Peters. The good old master promptly wrote me a glowing, a really glowing recommendation to Peters, with whose publishing house he was certainly well acquainted. On the strength of that, I wrote Peters a letter in which I informed him, so to speak in private, of your flattering praise for my Scherzi and, in particular, Variations. Just imagine, a letter came straight way from him, from which I gathered that he prefers not to take on such serious stuff. He never once asked to see the Variations, but he did the Legend, Scherzi, and the five piano pieces that pleased you so much. I also noticed that he asked to see these items only out of courtesy toward Goldmark, without taking the latter's recommendation particularly to heart. After a couple of days my recruitment by the publisher was at an end: Peters regrets .... For myself, the only thing that is painful is the fact that the old master's recommendation had to come to nought for me. I told Goldmark none of this. For the rest, I believe that Peters would not really concern itself with such serious items.

In the midst of my dejection, there came by chance a heart-warming, truly heart-warming letter from d'Albert, who informed me from Heidelberg that during the forthcoming winter he would definitely play something of mine. He invited me to Mannheim where we could discuss many things. Perhaps I will appear there with my friend Rosé,[1] who plays quartets (needless to say, with three others). Will I meet you there, too? How that would please me! You did me a power of good, not because you praised my works, but by the manner in which you praised them.

Now, as you can see, I am in a position to send the manuscripts of mine that you would most like to have. It would be better if I could send you the items printed! But what am I to do? Do you know a publisher? Would you care to recommend me to him? Perhaps Kistner, or Rieter-Biedermann, Aibl, or Simrock? What do you think of that? Or should I perhaps, armed with a recommendation from you, set off and hawk myself around some publishers? Goldmark was very pleased to hear that you had firmly promised to help me, and to play something of mine. If you do this, it will surely be a big help! Please forgive this long epistle, but since I no longer felt able to turn to Goldmark it was necessary for me to say all of this to you—you who were so cordial toward me.

Have you by any remote chance read my article about Brahms in Harden's *Die Zukunft* No. 32?[2] On the matter of tempo in the Brahms concerto, I took the liberty of taking Mr. Weingarten to task in the Vienna *Neue Revue*.[3]

Is it fair, do you think? With best wishes to you, and I kiss the hand of your esteemed wife,

I remain
Dr. Heinrich Schenker

---

[1] Arnold Rosé (1863–1946): Austrian violinist of Rumanian birth. Rosé was concertmaster of the Vienna Philharmonic Orchestra and at the Court (State) Opera from 1881 to 1938. He taught at the Vienna Conservatory/Academy from 1893 to 1901 and 1908 to 1918. In 1882 he founded the Rosé Quartet, which became one of the leading chamber ensembles of Europe. The friendship between Rosé and Schenker was to wane after the Quartet gave the premières of Schoenberg works in 1907 and 1908, despite Rosé's commitment to the German-Austrian Classical repertory.

[2] "Johannes Brahms," *Die Zukunft* 19 (May 8, 1897): 261–65; Federhofer (1990), 230–35.

[3] "Die Berliner 'Philharmoniker'," *Neue Revue* 8, no. 16 (April 16, 1897): 495–97; Federhofer (1990), 222–24, referring to Brahms's Piano Concerto No. 1 in D minor.

❧ Schenker to Kalbeck (letter), May 19, 1897

OJ 5/19, [4] (Plate 1)

Dear Sir,

Once again, warmest thanks for your patience of yesterday. I wonder whether I shall increase it by sending you a few articles by myself? What will interest you most is the fact that I received per article from *Die Zeit* 18 Florins and from the *Neue Revue* 10 Florins.

Everything[1] was written amidst the bitterest of troubles, and bears the scars to no ordinary degree. How thankful I should be if the great event of my life were to emanate from your circle, i.e. a publisher!

With most devoted greetings,
> Yours,
>> Heinrich Schenker

[1] At this point Schenker is presumably speaking of his compositions, or both his compositions and his journalistic work, and of the period after his father's death in 1887.

❦ Busoni to Schenker (letter), [c. May 20, 1897]
OJ 9/27, [2]

Dear Dr. [Schenker],

Your second epistle sounded more consolatory than your first; more consolatory for me, too, who take an active interest in your fortunes.

I should be delighted if something were to materialize with Lienau,[1] for which I should of course like to do anything that I can, and will do as soon as the opportunity arises.

In the meantime, the package containing music has also arrived, the content of which confirmed my excellent impression throughout.

How would it be (a subjective idea and nothing more!) if you were to combine your ~~Ballade~~ Legend and Variations into a single work, perhaps entitled *Fantasy*? The C major Scherzo would make a good middle movement, which, by the way, I would much rather have without Trio, "as a single outpouring."

So, for example: *Fantasy*,

1. In modo d'una leggenda
2. Intermezzo umoristico
3. Finale, alla variazione.

I believe that in this form your work would not be inferior to Schumann's Op. 17.[2]

Sadly, I shall not be able to come to Mannheim, but please, if you have a chance, convey my greetings to d'Albert. Congratulate him on his success with *Gernot*, as for my part I most heartily do.

I have not read your article on Brahms,[3] but am eager to catch up with it.

Warm thanks for the music that you kindly sent. The Ballade made a fine, serious impression on me. —

If nothing comes of Schlesinger, then we will go on trying.

> With cordial greetings,
>> Respectfully,
>>> Yours
>>>> F. B. Busoni

[1] Robert Lienau: Berlin music publisher. The elder Lienau had bought the Berlin firm of Schlesinger in 1863, adding his name to it. Schenker had met the younger Robert Lienau on May 18 or 19, played some of his music to him, and been invited to play

before the elder Lienau. Schenker reported this to Busoni in a letter of May 19 (Sbb B II 4414).

[2] Schumann, *Phantasie*, Op. 17, for piano, similarly in three sections: 1. Durchaus fantastisch und leidenschaftlich vorzutragen; Im Legenden-Ton, 2. Mäßig. Durchaus energisch, 3. Langsam getragen. Durchweg leise zu halten.

[3] "Johannes Brahms," *Die Zukunft* 19 (May 8, 1897): 261–65.

Busoni to Schenker (letter), June 2, 1897
OJ 9/27, [3]

Most revered Dr. [Schenker],

I can answer you today only in haste and briefly, first to thank you for your friendly epistle, and secondly to assure you of the sincerity of my praise. Nevertheless, even though your things please me especially, you must prepare yourself for the fact that your compositions, thanks to the intense subjectivity with which they are imbued, will not become popular overnight.

That is, however, the fate of any worthwhile artistic product—on the other hand, I am no prophet, and could be mistaken in my conjecture.

I shall willingly try out your Legend, Scherzo (without Trio) and the Variations (perhaps with one or two modifications) on the public some day. But my authority is by no means so assured that the very fact of my playing your work will constitute a wholesale and incontrovertible recommendation for it. This truth really came home to me recently when I tried to introduce Nováček's concerto.[1] I regard the dedication as an honor that I cannot refuse.

   With friendly greetings, I remain
    Yours very truly,
     Ferruccio Busoni

I should still like, when the opportunity arises, to discuss the small changes to the *Fantasy*.

[1] Ottokar Nováček (1866–1900): Hungarian violinist, violist, and composer, who studied in Vienna and Leipzig, won the Mendelssohn Prize in 1885, and later emigrated to the USA. Busoni premièred his piano concerto in 1894.

Schenker to Busoni (letter), August 31, 1897
Sbb B II 4415

Highly regarded Sir,

You are the only person who has at his fingertips the solution to the question, so I must, willy nilly, trouble you. A friend of mine, albeit not rich, but all the more willing to make the sacrifice, has offered to have some of my things printed at his expense.[1] This would relieve me of worries about publishers who print the worst music (recommendations from Schütt, Leschetizky work wonders here!), and who would treat my pieces as if they were even worse than what they usually print. Now, leaving aside an opus that was published five or six years ago in Vienna,[2] I should like to start afresh with the *Fantasy*, then perhaps the five shorter pieces, followed by a string quartet or trio. With the chamber music, I will allow myself time to wait for success with Rosé, our best chamber musician—i.e. in his concerts.

Since you were so very kind as to promise me some artistic advice regarding the *Fantasy*, I must ask you whether you will be coming to Vienna this season and will give me the opportunity to act on your advice. I will gladly wait the next couple of months, high time though it is to go before the public.

Thanking you most cordially in advance for your efforts,

    I remain in sincere admiration
      Yours most truly,
        H. Schenker

---

[1] Those of Schenker's patrons at this time known to us were Alphons von Rothschild, Irene Mayerhofer, and the Eissler family (none of whom could be described as "not rich"): the most likely person is Moriz Violin.

[2] Two Pieces for Piano, Op. 1 (1892).

Busoni to Schenker (letter), August 31, 1897
OJ 9/27, [5]

Highly revered Dr. [Schenker],
I am absolutely delighted at the favorable turn of events on the publishing front, and with all my heart wish you an initial success from which countless others may yet follow.

Had you waived the honorarium, I now venture to say, the procurement of the house of Breitkopf & Härtel for undertaking the publication and also the printing costs of one of your works would perhaps have been not quite so difficult.

Certainly under the "smoother" circumstances that now prevail it would be not inadvisable to place the name of this world-class firm at the foot of your compositions. Breitkopf & Härtel have sometimes been prepared to do this in the case of good works in return for payment of expenses.

I am to play in Vienna on December 16, and am likely to stay there for several days.

My suggestions regarding pianistic matters are not compositional in nature: an artist of your caliber has no need of the latter.

What I had in mind was principally to propose a few technical pianistic changes to facilitate a more supple performance. To effect the transformation of the three pieces organically into a single *Fantasy*—my general idea—is a matter for you alone, and a task that might perhaps afford you some artistic satisfaction.

If you think you can wait until December, then we can have an interesting little discussion in person. If not, then I would have a crack at tackling the less clear and persuasive ways of notating some passages. In the meantime, accept the most cordial greetings of

>Your sincere and most friendly
>F. Busoni

❧ Schenker to Busoni (letter), September 4, 1897
Sbb B II 4416

Most revered and best Sir,

Thank you, thank you for your heart-warming words! I shall gladly wait, since to do something in person is always more accurate than doing it in writing.

As regards Breitkopf & Härtel, I must admit I have still not made the attempt. At the same time, however, I am fearful lest even waiving any honorarium would not elicit an obliging response. How happy I would be to spare my friend the money, if I had any prospect! Peters returned my materials despite my having waived the honorarium, and despite Goldmark's recommendation. I would even go to Kistner or Aibl so as to save money without demanding anything for myself, but where do I get the recommendations from?

One more thing before I end: Would you be interested in writing a short piece about something close to your heart for Harden's *Die Zukunft*? Not that I conduct business for Harden, but it would give me, and surely thousands of others, pleasure to read something interesting about art or the state of art today by you, since you write so excellently and in so natural a way. Believe me, it would please me as much as Harden, just for its intrinsic interest. If it took your fancy, I would then write asking Harden to invite you as suits you best, and things could proceed from there.

What do you think about that? I myself am writing fewer and fewer essays, and correspondingly more short notices.

>With most cordial, sincere and friendly greetings,
>Yours,
>H Schenker

❧ Busoni to Schenker (letter), September 11, 1897
OJ 9/27, [6]

Dear Dr. [Schenker],

Warm thanks for your friendly, ever-welcome words!

I will be very happy to act as an intermediary between you and the house of Breitkopf, and am—while unable to make any promises—not at all without hope.

Will you now forge the *Fantasy* together, in order to present it to the latter publisher as a fully valid test of your talent? And for these purposes, shall I return the manuscript to you?

The Breitkopf people do not go all out for instant success as do other publishers, who have shown themselves so noncommittal toward you. That is, however, why they don't shower largesse in the form of honoraria. Also, where they recognize something of quality they are more steadfast and persistent than the sensation-mongers.

The prospect that you kindly hold out to me of being able to have a spot available in Harden's *Die Zukunft* is very attractive to me. Although I do not have the time right now to put something literary together, I do have something in mind for a later occasion to articulate something for which entrée to a few columns in a periodical such as Harden's would be extremely welcome.

So thank you for that, and let me have your answer soon.

  With respectful greetings,
   Yours truly,
    Ferruccio Busoni

Schenker to Busoni (letter), [mid-September 1897?]
Sbb B II 4418

Most highly revered, best Sir,

Your kindness is extraordinary. I still have a manuscript of the prospective *Fantasy* and am getting down to the work. One thing I absolutely must achieve, either with your help or with my friend's money: to conquer the house of Breitkopf & Härtel! I am very curious to see whether d'Albert will today (and where?) make good the promise that he recently so kindly reiterated. I hear clearly from your sympathetic, kind letters that you will one day play something of mine. I only wish that the time were now at hand.

In conclusion, I will take the liberty of showing you the finished *Fantasy*, so that justice may run its course.

  With best, most heartfelt greetings,
   Yours,
    H. Schenker

Schenker to Busoni (letter), September 25, 1897
Sbb B II 4417

Most highly revered, best Sir,

There! I am done with my *Fantasy*! I hope that as a unity it will please you every bit as much as, perhaps even better than, in its separate parts. Now I am waiting with impatience for December 16. When I take a look at the new works arriving from the various publishing houses, then for a thousand reasons it really pains me not yet to have been able to get into print! Nevertheless, I hope soon, very soon to attain my right.

  With best wishes and thanks for your encouragement,

> I remain
> Yours most truly,
> H. Schenker

🎼 Breitkopf & Härtel to Schenker (letter), November 9, 1897
OJ 9/20, [8]

Dear Sir,

We have, with thanks, received your Five Pieces for Piano [Op. 4], which, if we are not mistaken, we have already seen on a previous occasion.

Under current circumstances, given the volume of works still to be put into production, it is not easy for us to contemplate new undertakings. However, since you have so kindly expressed yourself ready to assume the initial production costs we will not deny you your wish, especially since Mr. d'Albert has so kindly interceded on behalf of your work.

We normally have 250 copies of such works printed as the first edition. This would amount to about 173 marks.

We take the liberty of drawing together the conditions relating to the account in a contract[1] that we submit to you in two copies with the request that, if you find it satisfactory, you return one copy to us signed. We would then proceed immediately, ensuring in so doing that No. 2 can also be published as a separate item.

> With kind regards,
> Yours truly,
> Breitkopf & Härtel

---

[1] The contract for the Five Pieces for Piano, Op. 4, dated October 30, 1897, is preserved as OJ 9/20, [7].

🎼 Breitkopf & Härtel to Schenker (letter), December 22, 1897
OJ 9/20, [9]

Dear Sir,

To our especial pleasure, we have been able to complete your Five Pieces for Piano, Op. 4, before the beginning of the holidays. We have the honor of dispatching ten copies to you in accordance with our agreement, with the comment that we will embark on the general distribution to music retailers on January 2, 1898. We hope, in the interests of both parties, that great success will be achieved with them.

According to the enclosed statement of account, the balance of our costs amounts to 85.75 marks, for the kind remittance of which we should be most grateful.

With kind regards,
Yours most truly,
Breitkopf & Härtel

❧ D'Albert to Schenker (letter), January 17, 1898
OJ 9/6, [28]

Der Reichshof
Berlin W.

Dear Dr. [Schenker],
You will soon now have occasion to set aside your displeasure with me at the rare appearance of your Pieces for Piano on my programs, so please make every effort to do so. The best opportunity for us to get together is after my concert on Thursday evening.[1]

Goodbye for now, dear Dr. [Schenker],
With cordial greetings,
Yours most truly,
Eugen d'Albert

---

[1] D'Albert's recital in the Bösendorfer-Saal on January 24, 1898 included two of Schenker's Five Pieces for Piano, Op. 4 (advertised as "Two Pieces for Piano, Op. 4") alongside works by Beethoven, Chopin, Liszt, d'Albert and others (*Neue freie Presse*, No. 12003 (January 23, 1898): 14). In February or March 1898 d'Albert wrote: "What I have done for your Pieces for Piano is really nothing: later on, however, you will be happy with me: one should never play fewer than five of them." (OJ 9/6, [31]), and October 6, 1898, "When do your new pieces appear? I shall be playing the Five Pieces for Piano more often this winter—and <u>better</u> than in the past." (OJ 9/6, [30]).

❧ Schenker to Kalbeck (letter draft), [c. January 20, 1898?]
OJ 5/19, [6]

Dear Sir,
I have accidentally mislaid my copy of the *Berliner Tageblatt*, but I hope to be able to come up with another one tomorrow or the day after.—
E. d'Albert astonishes me with the announcement of four pieces from my Op. 4 for Monday evening. Consequently, the very thing you recommended to me—a première of my works—seems to be coming to pass of its own accord. The progress is late in starting, but it should become gratifying. Certainly not on Monday to begin with, since the pieces are not suited to public taste, but in the next year, I hope, when Busoni intends to play a large *Fantasy*, Op. 2, a work about which he is proclaiming the most complimentary things in writing and by word of mouth to Goldmark and others, and which he even praises, in an uncharacteristic torrent of fervor—*sit venia verbis*[1]—as a work that is not inferior to Schumann's

Fantasy. Though all this is excessive—for example, the claim that the variations contained in that work are the best since the Brahms "Handel" Variations(!)—still I may at least hope that Busoni will work on my piece with real enthusiasm. Compared to this, success is but a trifle. A real appreciation, even in the smallest measure, that comes from a real man, will please me more than all the compliments of the ignorant masses.

If Rosé will also perform my string quartet[2] as intended, then I think that I can consider myself established, and able to fish out the various pieces of music I have lying on my desk.

Perhaps adverse fate finally will become good to me and, after some dreadful, truly appalling years, lead me toward a better future. Then the one thing I would congratulate myself for is that I have only myself (not even my friends or a patron) to thank for everything, everything, food, music, performers, every piano and theory lesson, every chance to make money. As difficult as it is, is there a more satisfying feeling?

I don't know why, but my heart gives me leave to tell you—and you alone—all these emotional matters. I have a feeling that only you could pass a just and humane judgment on a fate such as mine. I trust, therefore, that you will grant pardon for this unburdening to

      Yours very respectfully
      H. Schenker

[1] *sit venia verbis*: "forgive me for saying so myself."
[2] Four items (one fragmentary) for string quartet—Aria, Scherzo 3, Largo, and further sketches—are preserved as OJ 23/25–28. None were ever published.

❧ Schenker to Busoni (letter), February 15, 1898
Sbb B II 4419

Until we meet on March 8![1]

Most revered, most dear friend,

I believe I have at long last finished doing all that you asked for, and send you my *Fantasy*. Let me thank you once again for your invaluable encouragement to create this work on a larger scale. If only its performance were at the level of your encouragement!

I already told you that d'Albert, for some reason still incomprehensible to me, suddenly announced my [Five] Pieces. Because the program was overlength, he played only two of them instead of all four [*recte* five] (i.e. Nos. 1 and 2). I told him straight out at the time that I was not in agreement with the performance, and he confessed to me candidly that it was precisely because he did not feel he had fully mastered the pieces that he opted to play fewer of them on the first occasion, rather than exposing me and himself to the danger of an inadequate performance. As it happens, no damage was done. On the contrary, Kalbeck reviewed even so slender an event very favorably, etc.

Meanwhile, I realized how right you were when you advised me to go public on the first occasion with the *Fantasy*, i.e. with a larger-scale work. Only one thing consoled me: I told myself there was no defense against the unpredictable, and the unpredictable is what d'Albert's concert was for my cause.

Heuberger and the *Neue freie Presse* did not review d'Albert's concert at all, because there was a guest appearance[2] at the same time in the Opera House by Mrs. Lili Lehmann. In any case, you can well imagine what I think of the newspaper scribblings for the great public. Thus in mentioning Kalbeck and Heuberger by name, I mean only to refer to the unavoidable consequences of a step into the public arena, nothing more.

And now that you have the *Fantasy* in your possession, let me ask you where things stand with the approach to Breitkopf & Härtel or any other publisher. Do you <u>want</u>, are you <u>able</u> to intercede, either in person or in writing, with me on hand or in some other form? I asked d'Albert, who sent me a very warm—a really very warm—recommendation for Breitkopf & Härtel, whether he was willing to update his recommendation (which was general and valid for all my works). It was important not to hurt him, though he knows that you are looking after all aspects of the *Fantasy*. He was even wise and obliging enough to tell me that he would always, under all circumstances, be at my disposal.

So what I must do now depends on you. I don't think you need d'Albert's assistance. It will be enough if I can prove to the publisher, with your promise in writing (will that be OK?), that you intend to play the piece, today or tomorrow, or in two or five years' time. If you can spare a little time in the course of the season, please be so kind as to advise me! I am even happy to come to Berlin (only for a couple of days, for reasons of that thing called money) if you think that necessary or worthwhile for my own purposes or those of the publisher. In short, I remain ever your devoted companion and friend, receptive to your wishes and suggestions.

   H. Schenker

Most cordial, most devoted greetings to your wife.

---

[1] Busoni was to be in Vienna and he and Schenker had arranged to meet; however, according to Sbb B II 4420, March 15, they missed one another.
[2] Bellini's *Norma* was performed at the Court Opera on January 24, 1898. Norma was one of Lehmann's noted roles.

❧ Breitkopf & Härtel to Schenker (letter with enclosure), February 16, 1898
OJ 9/20, [10]

Dear Sir,

Thank you for sending us the *Neues Wiener Tagblatt* for February 12, 1898. We are delighted to see from this that two of your Pieces for Piano, issued by our publishing house, were performed with great success by Eugen d'Albert.

We came across the following review in the *Hamburger freie Presse* of January 23, 1898, which may possibly not yet have come to your attention.

    With kind regards,
     Yours most truly,
      Breitkopf & Härtel

[*enclosed handwritten copy from the* Hamburger freie Presse:]

> In his Op. 4 Schenker brings us five new pieces for piano. The very fact that Eugen d'Albert has accepted the dedication of these five pieces for piano is evidence enough of their intrinsic worth. They are, so far as one can judge at first sight, not too difficult; they nevertheless present a few challenges to the pianist's technique, as is true most particularly of the first and third pieces.
>
> But the professional performer as well as the advanced amateur will be able to draw much that is beautiful out of these pieces and find many stimulating ideas in them. Individual sections, such as the Allegretto in the first piece and the Andante, are truly superb.

❦ Busoni to Schenker (letter), February 19, 1898
OJ 9/27, [7]

Revered friend,

I am in possession of your letter and the manuscript, and previously I also received a postcard and the Five Pieces published by Breitkopf.

For all of these my warmest thanks and heartfelt appreciation.

Your *Fantasy* deserves its name, for it is full of fantasy, significant as a whole, interesting throughout with a broad sweep to it, and finely crafted development. It gives me wholehearted joy to be able to pay tribute to these distinguished features (which are no small matter). I do so unreservedly.

I think I should comment that in the construction of this piece the linking passages to the three sections (in themselves exhilarating and rich in content) are however perhaps unduly drawn out, such that instead of three sections there are in truth five that can be discerned.

On the other hand, I can only admire the way in which you have connected the three parts organically and fashioned out of them a <u>single whole</u>.

I cannot refrain from saying that from time to time your subjectivity makes its case in a highly subjective way. It is as if you were making music within your own four walls and only for yourself. Only a public that knows and <u>loves</u> you <u>personally</u> will be able to understand and enjoy such passages—but such a <u>public</u> does not exist. Let me cite, as a good example of this, variations 6 and 7, which I really would advise cutting out altogether.

I have reiterated again and again that I will speak up in support of the work with my limited powers and still more limited influence, and I abide by that. And it is not by my promise that I will be guided, but by my conviction.

I am so busy that I must stop, much though I should like to carry on writing. I will have the pleasure of continuing our discussion in person in Vienna on March 8.

>With cordial greetings,
>Yours very truly,
>F. Busoni

My wife sends friendly greetings.

Brüll to Schenker (letter), April 12, [1898?]
OJ 9/23, [9]

Highly revered Dr. [Schenker],

I wanted to call on you to render my heartfelt thanks in person for the things you sent me. However, an accumulation of work has prevented me, and the possibility that I might not find you in, or might disturb you.

I have enjoyed playing through your Inventions [Op. 5] and Songs [Op. 3]. Everything that you create is extraordinary, and bears the stamp of a deep spirit and significant talent. "Ausklang" is truly moving, and no less so "Allein" [Op. 3, Nos. 4 and 5]. Most heartfelt thanks!

>In friendship,
>Yours truly,
>Ignaz Brüll

Breitkopf & Härtel to Schenker (letter), May 3, 1898
OJ 9/20, [11]

Dear Sir,

We have given thorough consideration to your *Fantasy*, Op. 2, which you most kindly sent us. It is a serious work which, in our opinion, demands pianists and listeners of equally high caliber. In the absence of these, there is bound to be some contradiction. We think highly of your work, to which Mr. Busoni has so kindly given his support, and, despite many practical difficulties for its production at our expense, we should like to ask if we might assume that the honorarium may be made dependent on the degree of success.

The two letters from Mr. Busoni will be returned, having been duly noted.

In looking forward to your esteemed answer, we remain

>With kind regards,
>Yours most truly,
>Breitkopf & Härtel

❦ Schenker to Busoni (letter), May 5, 1898
Sbb B II 4422

Dear friend,

Breitkopf & Härtel have finally taken on my *Fantasy*. How grateful I am to you for that!

At last I consider myself saved—at least from immediate need. Now it is a matter of getting the work thoroughly into circulation among musicians, and letting it become well known. I owe it all to you—you whom I value so greatly!

One question:

When once I expressed my desire to dedicate the *Fantasy* to you, you couched your answer in such a way as to leave me unclear whether I might dedicate my opus to you. Are you, perhaps, an "enemy" of dedications? If that were so, I would be the last person to repay your friendship to my opus with a hostile act. But if that isn't the case, then please don't begrudge me the satisfaction of placing your name above the *Fantasy*.

I hope to make it to your historical concerts in Berlin. Scarlatti appears not to have written any concertos with orchestra. What a pity!

But until then, please tell me candidly how you feel about the dedication.

With thanks to you once again and cordial best wishes to you and your wife,

> I remain
> Your devoted
> H. Schenker

❦ Busoni to Schenker (letter), May 6, 1898
OJ 9/27, [8]

Dear Dr. [Schenker],

I am delighted and honored over the dedication, which I accept with sincere thanks. I congratulate you on the publication of your *Fantasy* and from the bottom of my heart wish you an era of good fortune.

> Your cordially devoted
> F. Busoni

Excellent if you come in the autumn!

❦ Breitkopf & Härtel to Schenker (letter), July 20, 1898
OJ 9/20, [13]

Dear Sir,

We are indebted to you for affording us the opportunity to become acquainted with your Songs for Mixed Chorus [Op. 7] and your *Ländler* for piano [Op. 10]. We certainly find these works interesting.

Although we feel able to assume that these compositions will meet with attention among real musicians, we are not at all able to gauge how successful we will be in introducing them to a wider market.

In view of our many other large-scale undertakings, we have accordingly decided to return the manuscripts to you herewith, with many thanks.

> With customary kind regards,
> Yours most truly,
> Breitkopf & Härtel

❦ Simrock to Schenker (letter), August 29, 1898
OJ 14/24, [2]

N. Simrock
Music Publisher
Friedrich-Strasse 171
BERLIN W. 8

Dear Sir,

Our proprietor was in Berlin for a few days passing through,[1] and on this occasion took a look at the manuscript that you had submitted. Provided that you make no further demands, but would be content with six free copies, Mr. Simrock is not disinclined to undertake the publication of your Op. 10. We are in the meantime returning the manuscript to you because there are a couple of passages on pages 7 and 8 that are not completely intelligible. Please in any case go through the manuscript once again very carefully and ensure that it is entirely free of ambiguities. Subsequent corrections, made after the piece has been engraved, incur exceptional costs and delays, and must therefore be avoided if at all possible.

> In looking forward to your esteemed reply,
> With kind regards,
> N. Simrock

---

[1] Simrock had written to Schenker on July 29, 1898, thanking him for the material submitted and telling him that their proprietor was away and would not return until the fall.

❦ Schenker to Busoni (letter), [September/October 1898]
Sbb B II 4426

Dear, good friend,

In a few days I hope at last to be able to send you my *Fantasy*, printed. Breitkopf & Härtel sent me two proofs, which I have already sent back corrected. It is my wish that the work may still make the same favorable impression on you today as it did all that time ago!

Now I am once again in a position to announce a welcome success. Believe it or not, N. Simrock has, without any recommendation, accepted some harmless *Ländler* [Op. 10] of mine (honorarium: six free copies!), so these will soon be out. I sent the cheery opus off at random and—lo and behold!—Mr. Simrock has really taken it. Where honoraria are concerned, I have stopped pestering publishers—in the end they would merely send my music back to me.

Since fortune is smiling on me so, I venture to ask something of you. Could you send a few lines of recommendation about the enclosed small *a capella* choruses [Op. 7] for me to Mr. Siegfried Ochs, your fellow Berliner? Here in Vienna, I will not again try to offer the small choruses to Mr. [Richard von] Perger. My reason is the extraordinary indolence on the part of that conductor. I am sending you the choruses so that you can see whether you feel able in good conscience to recommend them. If yes, I should be very grateful for the approach, for, as you can well imagine, if I write larger-scale choral works, [it will be advantageous for me[1]] that you are on friendlier terms with Mr. Ochs than I can claim to be. If you were willing in that case—in order to save yourself the trouble of writing, packing and mailing things off—to send[2] the score with a few words to Mr. Ochs, I would be if possible even more grateful, and reassured that in your dealings with me you are taking care of everything in the way most convenient for you. Of course, this is only if my choruses please you! If not, then back to Vienna with them!

    Until we meet again!
    Best greetings, and I kiss the hand of your esteemed wife,
      Your devoted
      H. Schenker

---

[1] The top of the page is torn, taking away the first line, so this reconstruction is speculative.

[2] *schicken*: The sentence makes little sense as it stands. Perhaps Schenker is asking Busoni to "take" the score to Ochs and offer his recommendation in person.

❧ Breitkopf & Härtel to Schenker (letter), October 22, 1898
OJ 9/20, [14]

Dear Sir,

Our music engraving shop has been so overburdened recently that it has unfortunately taken until today for us to be in a position to dispatch to you the free copies of your *Fantasy*.

Hoping for a favorable reception for this work among music lovers, we remain

    With kind regards,
      Yours most truly,
        Breitkopf & Härtel

❧ Schenker to Busoni (letter), October 24, 1898
Sbb B II 4423

Dear, good friend,

Please find enclosed "your" *Fantasy*, which I should like to commend anew to your well disposed judgment. May it meet with your approval also in this format, as it did on the first occasion when still the work of a copyist.

How sorry I am that I cannot hear your concerts in Berlin! But you yourself have made it impossible for me by giving them not within one week but over several. How was I, poor devil, to hold out for that many weeks in Berlin? I shall be patient until Vienna, where I shall be seeing you soon. Most cordial greetings to you and your highly esteemed wife,

   From your
   H. Schenker

❧ Schenker to Kalbeck (letter), October 28, 1898
OJ 5/19, [7]

Dear Sir,

In grateful recollection of your very real cooperation during the past year, I take the liberty of sending you, enclosed, the work of mine that is so highly prized by Busoni. Busoni recommended it to the publisher. Perhaps you may be interested if I at the same time tell you that Mr. Simrock in Berlin has acquired a harmless little work in spite of my having approached him <u>without any recommendation</u>! Now I have courage.

   In genuine admiration,
    Yours truly,
     Heinrich Schenker

❧ Brüll to Schenker (letter), November 6, [1898]
[OJ 9/23, [10]]

Dear Dr. [Schenker],

I am indebted to you for what you so kindly sent me. Your *Fantasy* is aptly named: it is imbued with fantasy. Fantasy, <u>big</u> ideas, an organization that occasionally evokes late Beethoven, as if you were wanting to connect to him in order to build on to him—also it has an element of Sturm und Drang. I was also pleased to renew my acquaintance with the shorter pieces that you gave my brother.[1] I am quite besotted with the G major piece.[2]

   Most cordial greetings, revered Dr. [Schenker],
    from your most devoted
     Ignaz Brüll

[1] Eugen Brüll (1856–1927): a banker.
[2] Schenker forwarded this letter to Breitkopf & Härtel who, in returning it, informed him that distribution would start January 2, 1899 (OJ 9/20, [15]). They sent him six free copies on December 7, 1898 (OJ 14/24, [3]).

ᛞ Breitkopf & Härtel to Schenker (letter), February 10, 1899
OJ 9/20, [18]

Dear Sir,

We were delighted to see from your letter of February 9 that during the concert tour of the major cities of Austria-Hungary that you undertook with Mr. J. Messchaert, January 7 to February 4,[1] you performed two of your own compositions (Legend from Op. 2 and No. 2 from Op. 4), published by us, with great success.

With kind regards,
Breitkopf & Härtel

[1] (See chapter 3.)

ᛞ Simrock to Schenker (memo), May 30, 1899
OJ 14/24, [5]

Dear Sir,

Please excuse the belated reply.[1] Our proprietor was away. We regret that we are not in a position to take on the publication of the manuscripts you sent to us. The *Ländler* that we published have up to now elicited no inquiries whatsoever.

With kindest regards,
pp. N. Simrock

Manuscripts:
Dances of the Chassidim,[2] two volumes in manuscript
Item 3: Four Choruses for Mixed Chorus

[1] Simrock had written to Schenker on May 3, 1899 that their proprietor was away until late May, and they would not be able to give him a decision on the work submitted before then.
[2] Early title of what were later published as *Syrian Dances* (see chapter 2.)

🎼 Simrock to Schenker (memo), November 29, 1900
OJ 14/24, [6]

Dear Sir,
    In returning to you herewith the items that you kindly submitted to us, we have with regret to inform you that we are unable to take further the items you kindly offered us.[1] We are unusually heavily committed and are accordingly not in a position at the moment to undertake new obligations.

    With kind regards
        pp. N. Simrock
        [illegible signature]
For simplicity's sake, we take the liberty of returning to you straightaway the packet that you recently sent us.

[1] Which items Schenker had submitted is unclear. The postscript appears to refer to a second packet returned without its contents being considered.

🎼 Detlev von Liliencron to Schenker (letter), April 19, 1901
OJ 12/40, [2]

My new address:
Alt-Rahlstadt nr. Hamburg

Highly revered Master Schenker,
    I have received your interesting letter and your magnificent compositions [Op. 3],[1] forwarded to here, while we were in the throes of moving house. I immediately sat down at the piano and played and "sang" them—and, you will be pleased to hear, found "Wiegenlied" <u>absolutely enchanting</u>, though I was downright livid at the bellowing of little Wulff in the next room. Nothing on earth is more frightful than the howling of a baby. The little rascal, as I yelled at him afterwards, didn't deserve to have been the source of inspiration for a composition so wonderful, so exquisite. Then "Vogel im Busch" also pleased me especially. Infinitely graceful. A thousand thanks!
    I am addressing this to Breitkopf & Härtel, because you had not given me your <u>exact</u> address in Vienna.
    With heartfelt thanks for so much that is beautiful, and dear, and interesting from you,
        I am your
            Baron Detlev Liliencron

[1] Detlev von Liliencron (1844–1909): German lyric poet and writer of ballads and novellas, whose poetry, notably *Rides of the Adjutant and Other Poems* (1883), influenced that of Rainer Maria Rilke and Hugo von Hofmannsthal; c. 1900/01 he worked as "senior literary director" of Wolzogen's Überbrettl cabaret. Schenker

set three of his poems: "Versteckte Jasminen," "Wiegenlied," and "Vogel im Busch" as his Op. 3, Nos. 1–3. This letter and a postcard from him to Schenker survive. Liliencron was also set by Brahms ("Auf dem Kirchhofe,"—which intrigued Schenker from 1907 to the graph in *Free Composition*, a full graphing being planned for a never-published second volume of *Five Analyses in Sketchform*), Reger, and Richard Strauss.

Breitkopf & Härtel to Schenker (letter), June 30, 1901
OJ 9/20, [26]

Dear Sir,

On the occasion of this year's statement of account for sales of your composition:

Five Pieces for Piano, Op. 4

not a single sale was, unfortunately, made, which in the interests of both parties we regret.[1] In compliance with the contract, we do not fail to inform you of this fact, and we hope that we will be able to bring you more favorable information on this in the future.

With kind regards,
Breitkopf & Härtel

[1] Schenker had received statements of account in 1899 and 1900, with payments of 40.50 marks for forty-five copies and 27 marks for thirty copies respectively sold, and would receive in 1902 37.50 marks for fifty-six copies. Again in 1903 no sales would be recorded "of your works."

Breitkopf & Härtel to Schenker (letter), October 28, 1902
OJ 9/20, [30]

Dear Sir,

Thank you for turning to us again in good faith with regard to the publication of your Three Songs, Op. 6. Much as we would like to maintain long-established associations, we must nevertheless regretfully inform you that strictest limitations are now imposed on us where new publications are concerned. We still have in train such a variety of material, in part left over from last year, that even summoning all our resources we will scarcely be able to complete the quickest jobs in the next few months. We have accordingly resolved to cease taking on any new tasks for the time being, even when no risk for us would be attached to the work. We cannot expect you to hold out indefinitely, and will not think ill of you if you avail yourself of more favorable prospects for publication elsewhere.

In returning your manuscript to you with thanks, we remain,
>With kind regards,
>>Yours most truly,
>>>Breitkopf & Härtel

❧ Vienna Singakademie to Schenker (letter), December 1, 1903
OJ 35/5, [1]

Your Excellency,

The undersigned Board of Directors has decided to arrange for your chorus "Vorüber" [Op. 7, No. 3], which you so graciously dedicated to the Singakademie, to be performed at the second concert of the Vienna Singakademie (December 18), and takes the liberty most devotedly of inviting Your Excellency herewith to conduct the said work yourself.

In respectfully requesting an affirmative reply to the address of the President, Mr. Friedrich Ehrbar, Vienna IV, Mühlgasse 28 by December 2, we remain

>With kind regards,
>Board of Directors of the
>VIENNA SINGAKADEMIE
>>Jost Kramer[?]
>>Secretary

❧ Diary entries, October 3–4, 1931

[October 3:] Bringing order to my compositions!

[October 4:] The work of bringing order to my compositions continued. […] 5–6:15 p.m.: I show Lie-Liechen my compositions, veritable "treasures," in the world of today as unequaled as my theories! Those around me, and the public, valued and admired my works highly, deservedly so—but I was clear in my own mind that I was never going to attain the status of a master, let alone surpass it—on the contrary, I felt an obligation to place before the world only that which I alone knew.[1] However, I am prouder than ever today of what I was able to offer by way of composition!

---

[1] Schenker's decision to abandon composition may have been influenced by the disastrous reviews that the 1903 performance of the *Syrian Dances* in Berlin prompted (see chapter 2).

2
Schoenberg and Schenker's *Syrian Dances*

IN 1903 the twenty-nine-year-old Arnold Schoenberg found his first publisher, Dreililien Verlag, and was taken on as a teacher of harmony and counterpoint at the Schwarzwald School in Vienna. Additional income came from work as an arranger for Universal Edition. Since 1900 Schoenberg had regularly made piano reductions (including one of selections from *The Barber of Seville* for piano four-hands) and also orchestrated "some 6,000 pages of operettas by Zepler and others,"[1] so it was presumably his reputation as a safe pair of hands that led to his engagement—at Busoni's suggestion—to orchestrate Schenker's *Syrian Dances*, which Busoni would première in Berlin in November 1903. Dealing entirely with the work in hand, and the possible ways of paying for it, the 1903 letters from Schoenberg to Schenker—supplemented here by letters to and from Busoni, Weinberger, Breitkopf & Härtel, Ignaz Brüll, and Max Kalbeck—do not make it clear when the two actually met, although the brief note probably written on September 21 indicates that Schoenberg hoped to call on Schenker the following day. No replies are extant.

Schoenberg's *Verklärte Nacht* had received its first performance in Vienna on March 18, 1902, and on February 28, 1903, he had completed his first major orchestral work, *Pelleas und Melisande*, which would not be performed until January 1905. It is therefore unlikely that in 1903 Schenker knew anything of his compositions. Similarly, there is no way of telling what Schoenberg knew of Schenker's life and work, three years before the publication of Schenker's *Theory of Harmony*. In his own *Theory of Harmony*, first published in 1911, Schoenberg commented that he had read "some of" Schenker's "four years ago."[2] He also stated that, while there might well be some common ground between the two on such matters as the nature of "strong," ascending harmonic progressions, Schenker was already being led astray by "unbecomingly vigorous polemics against modern artists."[3] As for composition, no comments from Schoenberg about the *Syrian Dances* have survived.

By 1923, as the twelve-tone method was finally becoming a workable compositional technique, Schoenberg had turned more bitter, and more barbed, writing that "the main thing impressing the decline or downfall of our art and culture on all these Spenglers, Schenkers, and so forth, has been an awareness of themselves as totally lacking in creative talent."[4] Schenker in turn was no

---

[1] O. W. Neighbour, "Schoenberg, Arnold," *New Grove Dictionary of Music and Musicians*, 2nd edn. (London: Macmillan, 2001), ed. Stanley Sadie with John Tyrrell, vol. 22, 599.

[2] Arnold Schoenberg, *Theory of Harmony*, trans. Roy E. Carter (London: Faber & Faber/Faber Music, 1978), 119.

[3] Ibid., 318.

[4] Arnold Schoenberg, "Those who complain about the decline" (1923), in *Style and Idea*, ed. Leonard Stein, transl. Leo Black (London: Faber & Faber, 1975), 204.

less scathing in 1926, referring in detail to Schoenberg's *Theory of Harmony*, and characterising its author as wanting "above all, to be the godfather to new chords." Schenker then exclaimed sarcastically—"Ah, how convenient he makes things for his students, and also for the composers of modern music."[5]

The abiding differences between the two have been debated by Carl Dahlhaus: "musical coherence, in Schenker's theory, unlike Schoenberg's, is not an embodiment of the consequences extracted from unrepeatable material, but an unalterable *nomos* which governs the varying formations of the foreground. Schenker, for whom the nature of a matter is contained in its origins, seeks the law concealed behind the manifestation. Schoenberg on the other hand, aspiring more to ends than to origins, follows the consequences that emerge from a musical idea. His traditionalism consists less in the discovery of the past in the present than in the discovery of the future in the past."[6]

ARNOLD WHITTALL

[5] "Further considerations of the Urlinie: 2," *Masterwork* 2, 15–16 (Ger., 35).

[6] Carl Dahlhaus, "Schoenberg and Schenker," in *Schoenberg and the New Music*, transl. Derrick Puffett and Alfred Clayton (Cambridge: Cambridge University Press, 1987), 140. The *Syrian Dances* were published, in their original four-hands version, in October 1898 (*Hofmeisters Monatsbericht*, 462) by Josef Weinberger.

♪ Breitkopf & Härtel to Schenker (letter), June 28, 1899
OJ 9/20, [19]

Breitkopf & Härtel
Leipzig
Nürnberger Strasse 36

Dear Sir,

Thank you for kindly sending us your *Hebrew Dances*.[1] We are glad to have considered this work, the value of which we acknowledge.

However, after mature consideration we must regretfully tell you that we are unable at this time to offer to publish it. We currently have our hands full with all manner of major undertakings, including the collected edition of Berlioz's works and the *Lieder und Gesänge* of Loewe. We hardly need emphasize how extensive these works are, and that we are accordingly obliged to harness all the resources at our command in order to complete these jobs by the planned deadlines.

We see from your esteemed letter that two renowned Viennese publishers have been competing for your work. Since you are therefore in a position to arrange for prompt publication, you will no doubt not think ill of us if under the prevailing circumstances we return your composition to you.

With greatest respect,
Breitkopf & Härtel

¹ *Hebräische Tänze*: Schenker's early name for the *Syrian Dances*; he also considered *Tänze der Chassidim*.

❧ Schenker to Kalbeck (letter), September 6, 1899
OJ 5/19, [8]

Dear Sir,

If you wanted to further the interest that you have kindly shown in me, it would be good of you to let me come with my new pieces (Simrock, Weinberger). I should very much like, with a young friend—a pianist from the Brahms circle whom you surely know[1]—to show off to you a new piece for piano four-hands for which I at last received my first honorarium, and with which I achieved the greatest success last season in private circles.

It is my hope that Busoni will play my Op. 2 this year.

In sincere admiration,
Yours truly,
Dr. H. Schenker

[1] Almost certainly Moriz Violin.

❧ Schenker to Busoni (letter), November 6, 1899
Sbb B II 4429

Dear, good friend,

I have edged forward once again by a paltry amount with a first measly honorarium! But that is all a prelude! Sadly, the stipend has not, I am sure of that, been dealt with, as a result of which I was prevented from coming to Berlin to confer with you about some frightfully tricky things for the forthcoming edition.[1]

The picture on the title page is horrific. Instead of a regular orthodox Jew they have used a dancing girl. Thus is one misunderstood by the publisher.[2]

When are you coming to Vienna?

Your faithful and deeply appreciative
H. Schenker

I kiss the hand of your wife.

[1] Presumably the C. P. E. Bach edition that Schenker was preparing for Busoni.
[2] Reference is to the cover of *Syrian Dances* (see Plate 9).

🎵 Busoni to Schenker (letter), [c. November 7, 1899?]
OJ 9/27, [9]

Revered friend,[1]

In great haste, between one trip and another, thank you for sending me the terrific, original, atmospheric, Secessionist[2] *Syrian(?) Dances*, which afford me <u>real</u> pleasure.

It is wrong of you—forgive me a bit of well-intended pedantry—to construe much of what you do as a <u>prelude</u> to something still to come, since everything that happens in the present is <u>of principal concern</u>, and since the correct <u>use of the present</u> is made only by the application of this principle. This is what my experiences have taught me. At the beginning of our career we await special occurrences, in the expectation that these will announce themselves by special attributes. Later only that which has occurred appears as an occurrence.

   More in writing or in person in Berlin!!
   Cordial greetings,
    Yours,
     F. Busoni

---

[1] Federhofer (1985), 81, dates this letter to 1898; but as Busoni is replying to Schenker's remark about a "prelude" to future work, the letter must surely have been a direct response to Schenker's of November 6, 1899.

[2] The Vienna Secessionist movement (*Sezession*) had been founded by Gustav Klimt, Josef Hoffmann, and other artists in 1897.

🎵 Brüll to Schenker (letter), November 7, 1899
OJ 9/23, [4]

Dear Dr. [Schenker],

I received your nice letter of the 1st in Abbazia and was delighted with its contents.

And today you delight me with your *Syrian Dances* and the note that accompanied them. I believe that, through their distinctive melodic beauty and the skillful—and original—manner of their development, the *Dances* will cause a sensation. My most heartfelt thanks.

Does the dedication[1] call for an explanation? Even if—as is not the case—the dedication were not of recent date, anyone who is acquainted with you knows that your intention can only be to give pleasure to your very dear, erstwhile pupil.

   With cordial greetings,
    Your most devoted
     Ignaz Brüll

---

[1] "Alphons frh. v. Rothschild zugeeignet" ("dedicated to Baron Alphons von Rothschild").

🎵 Josef Weinberger to Schenker (letter), January 5, 1900
OJ 15/12, [5]

Josef Weinberger
Vienna I
Kohlmarkt No. 8
(Entrance Wallnerstrasse 1)

Dear Professor,
    I should be greatly indebted to you if you would be so kind as to arrange for a note to appear against the *Syrian Dances* on the programs of the Gärtner concerts that these have just been published by my publishing house.
    With most grateful thanks in anticipation,

        Yours with kind regards,
        Josef Weinberger

🎵 Concert Program, Bösendorfer-Saal, Vienna, January 26, 1900
OJ 35/5, [14–19]

Artists: Eduard Gärtner (baritone); Heinrich Schenker, Moriz Violin (piano)

Mendelssohn, "Schilflied," "Pagenlied," "Schlafloser Augen Leuchte," "And'res Maienlied"

[Oskar C.] Posa, "In einer grossen Stadt," "Irmelin Rose"

Brüll, "Der Abschied" (première), "Trinklied" (manuscript)

Wolf, "Nun lass' uns Frieden schliessen," "Nachtzauber," "Das Ständchen," "Elfenlied"

Schenker, *Syrian Dances*, for piano four-hands (première)

[Eduard] Schütt, "Öffnet' ich die Herzensthür," "Am Birnbaum," "Ewig mein bleibt, was ich liebe!"

[Vítězslav] Novák, *Gypsy Songs* [Op. 14,] Nos. 3 and 4 (première)

[Robert] Franz, "Vergessen," "Ständchen," "Auf dem Meere," "Wenn der Frühling auf die Berge steigt"

❧ Busoni to Schenker (letter), February 11, 1900
OJ 9/27, [11]

Dearest friend,

I was highly delighted at your friendly communication—and equally delighted by your *Syrian* (why the disguise?) *Dances*, which I have played through frequently and successfully with good musicians and pianists.

These pieces have a touch of genius about them.

The major tasks that I have confronted lately (they can be seen from the programs), the birth of a child, and the loss of my best friend Nováček to death, have all rained down—indeed, thundered down—on me virtually simultaneously, and have thrown me into utter confusion. Hence the delay in writing.

My warmest thanks to you and most cordial greetings.

In highest esteem,
Yours,
F. Busoni

❧ Busoni to Schenker (letter), August 25, 1903
OJ 9/27, [12]

Dear and revered friend,

I owe you so much—the answer to your letter, thanks for your lovely, unusual edition of C. P. E. Bach's work, which I admire. Yet, conscious of all my debts, I have the audacity to ask something more of you!

Hear me out, please. The concerts initiated last year, which bear the name "Orchestral Evenings: New and Rarely Performed Works," are to be continued and moreover to become a regular occurrence. Two more will take place, on October 19 and November 5.

I would very, very much like to have you on the program, and thought that an <u>orchestrated selection</u> from your *Syrian Dances* would present you to good advantage. Do you have the pieces scored for orchestra? They "cry out" for such treatment. Please help me make my wish come true, and write back to me by return with your thoughts.[1]

With most cordial greetings,
Yours most truly,
Ferruccio Busoni

---

[1] Schenker reported this in a letter of August 27 to Moriz Violin: "An hour ago I received a letter from F. Busoni of an amiability and practical value for me that would be unthinkable in Vienna. He wants to perform my *Syrian Dances* in Berlin."

Schenker to Busoni (letter), August 30, 1903
Sbb B II 3550

[Upper Austria] Gmunden[, Esplanade 13]

Dear and greatly revered friend,

My thoughts on the matter are quite different. I should prefer to make the score myself, regardless of whether or not Schoenberg has already done it (which I may know in a few days' time). I shall then be in a position, if only success is granted me, to sell the score and with it to earn some money, which I need so badly.

Are you in agreement with this?

A speedy answer is requested by

Your faithfully devoted
H Schenker

The *Neue freie Presse* published something very nice about my edition. I hope you, too, will be pleased to hear this.

Schenker to Busoni (letter), [c. September 1, 1903?]
Sbb B II 3549

Dear and greatly revered friend,

Your kind letter has gone a long way round before reaching me, which is why the return reply that you asked for has been so long delayed. How happy I am at your letter, happy above all that a man of your status is prepared to promote me! I must now tell you how matters stand.

Some three years ago I played the *Syrian Dances* with a friend in the Bösendorfer-Saal. On that occasion, they appealed to a musician named Arnold Schoenberg (who has since moved to Berlin, and who, on the recommendation of Richard Strauss,[1] received the Liszt Stipend for three years), so much so that he asked me if he might orchestrate the pieces. He is in fact a virtuoso orchestrator (also has some interesting scores, so people tell me), and earns his living by necessity from orchestration, just as I had to make my living a few years ago in part by journalistic writing. I had no option but to respond with pleasure to Schoenberg's spontaneous request, but referred him to my publisher, to whom I had regrettably sold the pieces too cheaply (considering that they sell well), including all arrangements, etc. And now I believe that the pieces would be available <u>ready orchestrated</u> from the publisher, except that either the publisher did not ask anyone, or no one took it on.

I myself had thought about orchestrating them at the outset,[2] but it seemed to me more tactful, more artistic, to give them first in piano four-hands form, even though I had the sound of the orchestra clearly in my head. — Now let me ask you, dear, good friend, whether you wish to have the pieces in <u>my own orchestration</u>, or whether you <u>can</u> perform them as orchestrated by Arnold Schoenberg. In the former case, I would have to throw myself wholeheartedly into doing them as fast as possible, having them copied, etc. I wrote to the publisher to establish whether Schoenberg had tackled the piece for him at that time. I definitely would like to seize this golden opportunity that you are offering me, and I should very much like it to be you to whom I owe my first success (for that is what I firmly believe it will be). So please kindly answer me whether Schoenberg's orchestration will suffice for you. In the meantime, let us hope that my publisher will reply and the situation will be cleared up.

You will be pleased to hear that the concerts of the Society of the Friends of Music and the Singakademie are wanting to perform something of mine. Ah! If only all of this would materialize! For I am desperately in need. The fight that I have been waging with little support since the thirteenth year of my life[3] has all but worn me down completely. My thanks, my sincere thanks, for the keen interest that you have taken in me!

> Your ever-faithful devotee
> sends most cordial greetings to you and your wife,
> Heinrich Schenker

---

[1] In a note from 1944, Schoenberg recalled: "Strauss, in 1902, having glanced through the (then unfinished) scores of my *Pelleas* and *Gurrelieder*, procured for me the 'Liszt Stiftung' for two years at 1,000 marks yearly": *A Schoenberg Reader: Documents of a Life*, ed. Joseph Auner (New Haven: Yale University Press, 2003), 302.

[2] Schenker produced a *Table of Instrumentation* in 1906, which was published two years later by Universal Edition.

[3] i.e. 1880/81: Schenker's oldest sibling, Marcus, died in 1880 (Federhofer (1985), 4), and it may be that Schenker—the youngest child but one—dated his sense of family responsibility not just to the death of his father Johann in 1887, after which he bore the main burden, but back to this time, when he perhaps had to hold his large family together: see diary entries for September 3–5, 1927. (Thanks to Lee Rothfarb for his work on Schenker's education, and for this interpretation.)

Busoni to Schenker (letter), September 3, 1903

OJ 9/27, [13]

Dear Dr. [Schenker],

I leave to <u>you</u> the choice of instrumentation for your *Dances*. May I take the liberty of just pointing out the following to you?

1) Should you approve of Schoenberg's own orchestration as a composer, then you will have your delightful pieces ready-clad in fitting tone colors, and will spare yourself a job.

2) We create an opportunity for Schoenberg to have <u>his</u> name on the program as well.

3) If the success that we expect is achieved, then he can arrange your other works, and from <u>this</u> you can profit financially.

I leave in your hands not only the decision, but also any arrangements with Schoenberg. I only ask you to let me know the former as soon as possible, and for delivery of all the necessary materials for the concert on October 19.

One further suggestion: Won't you call the child by its right name, and entitle your series of dances simply *Jewish Dance Melodies?* The impact would be all the greater. — Whether or not we perform them complete remains still to be determined.

I thank you for your willingness and your confidence in me, and I send you friendly greetings.

    Yours truly,
    Ferruccio Busoni

UE to Schenker (letter), September 4, 1903
OC 52/11

Universal Edition & Co.
Maximilianstrasse 11
Vienna [I]

Highly revered Sir,

Imperial Counselor Weinberger instructs me to inform you, in provisional response to your esteemed letter,[1] that it is impossible for him to deal with the matter of your *Syrian Dances* from a distance, and asks you kindly to wait for his return, which should be in a few days.

The letter from Busoni will be returned by registered post.

With most respectful greetings,

    Yours truly,
    Leder[?]

1 letter returned

---

[1] Schenker's letter is not known to survive; it evidently enclosed a letter from Busoni.

Schoenberg to Schenker (letter), September 12, 1903
OJ 14/15, [1]

    Payerbach 126

Dear Dr. [Schenker],

I have indeed made a start on the orchestration of your "Syrians," and that is just as well, since it could be that I will need longer than I first hoped. I finished the first dance today. I still do not know when they will all be completed, but I doubt if it will be before the end of next week. More likely considerably later—perhaps towards the end of the week after next.

And now, in order to avoid any possible misunderstanding later on, a word about the fee.

If it turns out that you have to pay for the orchestration yourself, I would charge you 100 Gulden for it. However, if Weinberger is paying, I would not do it for less than (please note: less than!) 150 Gulden. But if possible (see above) considerably more!

I raise this matter now because this fee is—understandably—somewhat higher than I have received for operettas. But I have already realized from the first piece (nineteen pages of score, which I could normally complete with ease on the first day) that this work will require much more effort on my part. I have therefore spent thirteen full working days on the first piece. That should sufficiently clarify the level of the fee.

I hope that, if Weinberger is paying, you can obtain more than this minimum. I have fixed it only because I want to do the work and in order not to delay mentioning any possible difficulties in that respect.

I shall send you the completed piece at once. Please write fully if you have any requests. But I think it will be quite good. It is just a pity that there is a little too much *ff* (*fortissimo*) in all the pieces. As one can imagine, this means many fewer orchestral tone colors. But this will hardly be a serious drawback.

One more thing: I have approached Busoni about my symphonic poem.[1] Nothing involving you, of course! I did this since I found out by other means that he was continuing with his concerts.

In conclusion: we had forgotten to agree on a "selection." I think it would be better to leave Busoni to choose after the first rehearsal, so that the "chosen" pieces can be those that work best. It should make little difference to the fee, especially for you, if we were to leave one out, so you should have no objection. I look forward to your response and am

  With best wishes,
   Yours,
    Arnold Schoenberg

---

[1] *Pelleas und Melisande*, composed between February 1902 and July 1903. Busoni asked Schoenberg to send him the score, and wrote to the composer (October 15, 1903) praising his orchestration, but he never conducted the work. It was first performed in Vienna, conducted by the composer, on January 26, 1905.

Schoenberg to Schenker (letter), [September 15, 1903?]
OJ 14/15, [2]

Dear Dr. [Schenker],

Many thanks for your letter. I accept your kind offer.[1] It came so unexpectedly that—taking your kindness literally—I must respond with something equally unexpected: I can confirm what you have been saying all along about Reichenau.[2] I am coming to Vienna tomorrow afternoon. Will I find you at home during the afternoon (around 3 to 3.30) the day after tomorrow (Wednesday), or will you be elsewhere? In any case, best wishes for the present.

    Cordial greetings,
     from your
    Arnold Schoenberg

Vienna IX, Porzellangasse 56 c/o Kramer

[1] The communication to which this responds is not known to survive.

[2] "ich werde Ihnen Wasser auf Ihre Reichenauer-Mühle erzählen": evidently an allusion to something said previously. There are two towns in Austria with the name Reichenau (one of which is occasionally mentioned in Schenker's diaries), and one in Switzerland; equally, it could refer to someone of that name.

Schoenberg to Schenker (letter), [September 21, 1903?]
OJ 14/15, [3]

Dear Dr. [Schenker],
 Without any news from you or Violin, I will take the liberty of seeking you out tomorrow morning, about 11 o'clock. Will you be at home?

    Cordial greetings,
    Arnold Schoenberg

Schoenberg to Schenker (letter), [September 29, 1903?]
OJ 14/15, [4]

Dear Dr. [Schenker],
 I have left No. 3 for you at the coffeehouse—with luck No. 4 around 6 p.m. tomorrow.

    Cordial greetings,
    Arnold Schoenberg

Schoenberg to Schenker (letter), [c. September 30, 1903]
OJ 14/15, [5]

Dear Dr. [Schenker],
 You will receive piece No. 4 tomorrow. I have had very bad toothache and have not been able to work. My only activity: the swelling of my face!

    Cordial greetings
    [unsigned]

❦ Weinberger and Hertzka (UE) to Schenker, October 6, 1903
OJ 15/12, [7]

Dear Professor,
    Enclosed is Dance No. 3 with the exception of the first violins, which will follow in an hour's time.
    Please return this Dance corrected, as quickly as possible, after which Nos. 1, 2, and 3 will be dispatched to Busoni immediately.
    No. 4 is due to arrive this afternoon and will be sent to Busoni, probably uncorrected.

        Respectfully yours,
        Josef Weinberger   Hertzka[1]

[1] The appearance of Emil Hertzka's distinctive signature on this letter is surprising, since he did not join UE until 1907.

❦ Weinberger and Hertzka (UE) to Schenker (letter), October 6, 1903
OJ 15/12, [8]

Esteemed Sir,
    Owing to unforeseen eventualities, viz. that two copyists have fallen ill and a third is behind-hand with other work, the completion of the copying has been set back by one or two days. This should be of no consequence, however, since you expressly told me that the parts must be sent off to Busoni at the latest on the 8th of the month, and this deadline will be met despite the disagreeable circumstances.
    Nos. 1, 2, and 3 with a complete set of duplicate copies will be ready this evening or at the latest early tomorrow morning; No. 4 in the course of tomorrow.[1]

        Respectfully yours,
        Josef Weinberger   Hertzka

[1] Schenker records in his diary for October 7–9, 1903: "Orchestral parts for the *Syrian Dances* for Busoni's Evening in Berlin corrected."

❦ Schoenberg to Schenker (letter), [October 13, 1903?]
OJ 14/15, [6]

Dear Dr. [Schenker],
    I have already looked for you several times at the coffeehouse as well as at your home, to find out how things stand. Have you already sent the material to Busoni? How has he responded? When are you usually in the coffeehouse? Or at home?

Best greetings,
Arnold Schoenberg
Vienna IX, Liechtensteinstrasse 68/70, II/22

❧ Diary entry, November 4, 1903

To Berlin with Floriz, at Brodes' place. Tempi too fast in Busoni's performance. Bad "reviews." Influenza ...

❧ Concert Program, Beethoven-Saal, Berlin, November 5, 1903
OJ 35/5, [38–47]

Orchestral Evenings (New and Rarely Performed Works), with the Philharmonic Orchestra, promoted by Ferruccio Busoni

First Evening, November 5 at 7.30 p.m., Beethoven-Saal, with José Vianna da Motta

[PROGRAM:]

D'Indy, "Symphonic Introduction" to *The Stranger*, Act 2

Debussy, *Prelude to the Afternoon of a Faun* (eclogue by Stéphane Mallarmé)

Berlioz, "Trojan March" from *The Capture of Troy* [Part 1 of *The Trojans*]

Franck, *The Djinns*, symphonic poem for piano and orchestra (after Victor Hugo), pianist José Vianna da Motta

Nielsen, *The Four Temperaments*, Op. 16, conducted by the composer

Schenker, *Syrian Dances*, orchestrated by Arnold Schoenberg[1]

---

[1] The reviews of this performance were largely disastrous. Two typical examples are: "Finally came *Syrian Dances* by Heinrich Schenker (Vienna), orchestrated by Albert [sic] Schoenberg [...] The *Syrian Dances* came over as banal in the highest degree. [...] The *Dances* conjured up drunken dervishes or belly dancers." (*Tägliche Rundschau*, Berlin, November 9, 1903); "Schenker's *Syrian Dances* are manifestly conceived for piano, and may perhaps in the latter mode of performance make a far better impression as unpretentious conversation music than they do in their garishly decked-out orchestral garb, whose gaudy display of magnificence is tiresomely incongruous with the threadbare shabbiness of their content. Mr. Busoni, who as conductor otherwise brought laudable circumspection to the evening, could here have done more skillfully to damp down the shrill tonal effects." (*Deutsche Warte*, Berlin, November 13, 1903). Only the *Neue freie Presse* of Vienna (November 19, 1903) reviewed it favorably: "In the concert that Ferruccio Busoni put on with the Philharmonic Orchestra, among other works the *Syrian Dances* by the Viennese

composer Heinrich Schenker was played. This original and melodic work, which is familiar to the Vienna public, achieved great and well deserved success in Berlin."

❧ Schoenberg to Schenker (letter), undated [November 10, 1903?]
OJ 14/15, [7]

Dear Dr. [Schenker],

I need to speak to you urgently and will therefore call at your apartment tomorrow at about 2 pm. Should you be busy around midday and write to me accordingly, please set a morning time, since I am not free in the afternoons.

    Cordial greetings,
      Yours,
    Arnold Schoenberg

❧ Weinberger (UE) to Schenker (letter), November 17, 1903
OJ 15/12, [6]

Dear Professor,

Now that the performance of your *Syrian Dances* by Busoni has taken place, I should like to ask you very kindly to report to me on how it went and in due course to let me have newspaper reviews.

Since I shall be attempting to set up a further performance of the *Dances*, and Mr. Busoni now no longer needs the orchestral material for this work, I should be greatly obliged if you could get the parts back from him and have them sent to me at the earliest opportunity.

Since all correspondence on this matter was effected through you, it seems right and proper that it should be you who reclaims the material from Mr. Busoni.

Looking forward with interest to your esteemed reply, I remain,

    Respectfully yours,
      Josef Weinberger

❧ Diary entry by Schenker, November 18, 1903

Prague, too, books the *Syrian Dances*.

3
Johannes Messchaert and Performance

ONE of the most celebrated vocalists of his day, the Dutch baritone Johannes Martinus Messchaert (1857–1922) enjoyed an illustrious career as a soloist, pedagogue, and choral conductor. (See Plate 24.) It was not as an opera singer that Messchaert made his name but as a singer of lieder and oratorio; above all, his performances of Schubert lieder and his role as Christ in Bach's *St. Matthew Passion* earned him accolades in the German and Dutch press. Having studied with the Frankfurt-based vocal pedagogue Julius Stockhausen, Messchaert went on to collaborate with the pianist Julius Röntgen, with whom he established his solo career and helped co-found the Amsterdam Conservatory of Music in the 1880s. While Messchaert and Röntgen concertized throughout the Dutch- and German-speaking lands, no city received them as openly as Vienna, where Messchaert won the admiration of Brahms, Richard Strauss, and Mahler, among others.[1]

Messchaert was by all accounts, then, a master of vocal technique and of song, and it is no wonder that Schenker too would laud him as one of the greatest singers of his age. While still in the early stages of his career as a music critic, Schenker reviewed at least two performances by Messchaert and Röntgen favorably in February of 1896 ("A deep feeling for the text and its tones makes [Messchaert's art] true to both poetry and music, and with artistic truth beauty is achieved.").[2] In that year Schenker had also become personally aquainted with the baritone, and in 1899 Schenker and Messchaert put together their own small concert tour of the Austro-Hungarian Empire (from January 8 to February 3), with Schenker as Messchaert's accompanist. Although Schenker seems to have tired somewhat of the tour, the musical collaboration with Messchaert undoubtedly had left a lasting impression. Some twenty-nine years after their collaboration, Schenker wrote to Felix-Eberhard von Cube:

> The concert tour with Messchaert furnished me with insight into the utterly and uniquely subtle workshop of this singer, whom I readily acknowledge to be the greatest singer of all times and places. He towers above the proudest

---

[1] See Federhofer (1985), 178–80, and Oswald Jonas, "Heinrich Schenker and Great Performers," *Theory and Practice* 28 (2003): 123–35, also the entry in *Biografisch Woordenboek van Nederland*. Messchaert's pupil Franziska Martienssen dedicated two books to Messchaert's vocal style, including performance analyses of selected Schubert lieder. See F. Martienssen, *Johannes Messchaert: ein Beitrag zum Verständnis echter Gesangskunst* (Berlin: B. Behr, 1914; repr. as *Die echte Gesangkunst, dargestellt an Johannes Messchaert*, ibid., 1920); F. Martienssen, ed., *Eine Gesangstunde: allgemeine Ratschlaege nebst gesangstechnischen Analysen von einigen Schubert-Liedern / von Johannes Messchaert* (Mainz: Schott, 1927). Of the last item, Schenker commented (diary, December 20, 1927): "In earlier years, I often used to talk about individual features of his great artistry; they have been reproduced in the most faithful way in this little book."

[2] For these reviews, see Federhofer (1990), 318–19, 323–25.

Italian examples of all centuries, including Caruso; unfortunately the world knows nothing of his rank, nor could they understand anything, since Messchaert never sang in the opera house, which is the only artistic trough from which the masses feed.[3]

The tour with Messchaert, in other words, was quite possibly the highest artistic collaboration of Schenker's career as a pianist. The entire known extant correspondence of Messchaert and Schenker is presented below, along with the 1899 tour schedule and recital program.

JOHN KOSLOVSKY

[3] Letter from Schenker to von Cube, April 29, 1928. Schenker spoke favorably about Messchaert in *Tonwille* 6, vol. 2, 35–36 (Ger. orig., 41) and *10*, vol. 2, 148 (Ger. orig., 27).

Messchaert to Schenker (postcard), October 8, 1896
OJ 12/54, [1]

Dear Sir,

Many thanks for your songs with which I was delighted to acquaint myself. I would have loved to put them on our program, but then I would first have to put songs on the program that have already been sent to me by other composers. I think I could very well put together an evening featuring Viennese composers. Warm greetings; I look forward to seeing you again.

    Your devoted,
       Joh. Messchaert

Tour Schedule and Program, January 8 to February 3, 1899
OJ 35/5, items 52, 53

Date	Venue	Accompanist
January 8	Klagenfurt	Schenker
January 11	Graz	Schenker
January 13	Trieste	Schenker
January 15	Brünn (Brno)	Schenker
January 17	Lemberg (L'viv)	Schenker
January 19	Vienna, Musikverein small hall[1]	Röntgen
January 21	Budapest	d'Albert[1]
January 24	Linz	Schenker
January 26	Vienna, Musikverein small hall	Röntgen

| January 30 | Aussig | Schenker |
| February 3 | Budapest | d'Albert |

[1] Reviews of these recitals show that Schenker was not the only accompanist on this tour. Röntgen seems to have been soloist and accompanist at the two Vienna recitals; it is unclear whether in Budapest d'Albert performed both roles, or whether he played only the solo items while Schenker (who was present in Budapest) accompanied the songs.

ʂ Recital Program for Tour
OJ 35/5, item 54

[Programs varied slightly from venue to venue; the list of alternatives is given below.]

Loewe	"Der Nöck," "Kleiner Haushalt"
Bach	Fugue
Schubert	"Meeresstille"[1], "Liebesbotschaft," "Nacht und Träume"[2]
(or) Brahms	"Feldeinsamkeit"
Grieg	"Wiegenlied," "Mit einer Wasserlilie"
Four old Netherlandish Folksongs	
(or) Schenker	"Legend"[3], from *Pieces for Piano*[4]
Chopin	"Polonaise"
(or) Wolf	"Zur Ruh'," "Weylas Gesang," "Der Tambour," "Elfenlied"
Schumann	"Die beiden Grenadiere"

[1] Of this song Schenker wrote in *Tonwille* 6, vol. 2, 35–36 (Ger. orig., 41): "Permit me, in this connection, to remember, alongside that great poet [Goethe] and great composer, the great singer Johannes Messchaert, recently deceased, who in his interpretation of 'Meeresstille' achieved the corresponding effect by elongating the notes in so utterly peaceful a way that they sounded like messages emerging from the silence rather than notes issuing from the human breast. Only at the word 'ungeheurn' did any tone creep into the voice, swelling almost imperceptibly, as far as 'ungeheure Weite,' but pulling back immediately. The effect was to render the silence at the end all the more fearful and believable."

[2] Of this song Schenker wrote in *Tonwille* 10, vol. 2, 148 (Ger. orig., 27): "we find an extremely expressive use of a similar *sospiro* across measures 22–23; one has to have heard it sung by the incomparable J. Messchaert, in order to comprehend the gripping effect of what is basically a naturalistic compositional trait."

[3] The opening section of Schenker's *Fantasy*, Op. 2 (1898), is marked: Movimento solenne, non troppo lento, A modo di Leggenda.

[4] Op. 4, No. 2 (Allegretto grazioso), as confirmed in a letter from Breitkopf & Härtel to Schenker of February 18, 1899.

✥ Johanna Messchaert to Schenker (letter), January 9, 1899
OJ 12/54, [2]

Dear Dr. Schenker,

I write to you with a rather large request, and I beseech you to keep this letter a secret from my husband.

You can't imagine how much fear and worry I have when my husband goes on so long a journey, and for this reason I ask you ever so kindly and insofar as it is possible to take care of my husband, for instance to ensure that he does not sing too much, that he does not push himself with encores, that he is well nourished, and that he takes a break on the train; and in case he falls ill (heaven forbid!) that you send me a telegraph immediately. Until January 25th the address is Plantage Parklaan 14, and after the 25th it is Vondelstraat 51. You will certainly laugh at me, but you are also married and so you will understand very well my concern.

   Warm greetings, yours respectfully,
    Joh[a] Messchaert
     Alma

Apologies for my bad German!

✥ Johanna Messchaert to Schenker (letter), January 18, 1899
OJ 12/54, [3]

Dear Dr. Schenker,

Cordial thanks for your warm letter. I am now much more at peace, since I know that my dear husband has not only a thoroughly musical accompanist but also a considerate travel companion. I will never forgive you for having told my husband about my secret [letter], but I am not angry about it.

With much joy I read about your mutual success. With warm greetings,

  Yours respectfully,
   Joh[a] Messchaert
    Alma

✥ Messchaert to Schenker (letter), February 10, 1899
OJ 12/54, [4]

Dear Dr. [Schenker],

Though I find myself here in the chaos of moving, I can no longer put off writing a few words to you. It will not be much and not so beautiful, not correct, and lacking clear German, but it comes from a warm heart.

I must express my most cordial thanks for your friendship, your affection, your patience with me and your seriouness and devotion at our rehearsals and concerts. Although I would like it very much, I dare not express the hope that we will be able to make music together more often, because I believe I have to conclude from some of your remarks that for your part it was not as pleasant as you had thought it would be and I sometimes felt as if I were responsible for your boredom and your loss of time.[1]

I hope that you will nonetheless still retain just a bit of our friendship!

Our new house is most charming! And if some of the rooms are not as big as those in our previous dwellings, it makes up for it with a certain coziness. It may surprise you to be receiving a message from me in Amsterdam because I should still be in Basel, but the Arlberg train line from Vienna to Basel has given me a cold. At night it was 23–24 degrees![2] And the railway gives bonuses to every stoker or train conductor who uses the least amount of coal!!!!!! Because of this, God help me, I had to cancel many concerts! Now, dear Dr. [Schenker], in all "dignity" I must take my leave, because at every moment I am being disturbed by carpenters, wallpaper hangers, painters, smiths, gardeners, etc. etc. etc.

Please accept (also on behalf of my wife, who naturally has had a dreadfully wearisome time) a thousand warm greetings and a thousand thanks for everything, I hope to see you again very soon.

  Your cordially devoted
  Joh. Messchaert

[1] On February 4, from Budapest, Schenker wrote to Moriz Violin "My last port of call! Thanks be to Jehova! Tomorrow in Vienna." (quoted Federhofer (1985), 19).

[2] Messchaert must be referring to temperatures in Fahrenheit.

Messchaert to Schenker (postcard), February 16, 1899
OJ 12/54, [5]

Dear Dr. [Schenker],

Many thanks for your message and your letter. I am once again standing with one foot in the train,[1] for this reason my short card. I have heard neither from [Arnold] Rosé, nor from Grünfeld,[2] nor from Tendler,[3] nor from Mery.[4] My wife is momentarily not at home, otherwise she would certainly leave you her greetings.

  In haste,
  Your
  J. Messchaert

[1] Messchaert's metaphor, which is derived from the expression "to stand with one foot in the grave" and suggests the boarding of a train that is about to depart, implies that he is in a hurry, or constantly on the move.

[2] Ludwig Grünfeld (1852–1924): theater and concert agency in Vienna.

[3] Carl Tendler: sheet music dealer, Graz.

[4] Béla Mery: sheet music dealer, Budapest.

❧ Messchaert to Schenker (letter), March 2, 1899

OJ 12/54, [6]

FERD. HEGER'S
QUEEN ELISABETH HOTEL
Vienna

Dear Dr. [Schenker],

I have to abandon my intention to visit you directly upon my arrival. With my well-known respect for the Viennese climate I hope you will be able to understand. Yesterday one felt the bad weather even in one's room. Today it seems to be better. At least I see the sun! How are you? Perhaps I shall see you tonight at *The Creation*![1] That would be wonderful!

If the weather improves I will come for a visit.

>   In the meantime warm greetings.
>   Your
>   Joh. Messchaert

[1] The performance took place that evening in the great hall of the Musikverein with a Miss Hiller, Mr. Raval, and Messchaert as soloists.

❧ Messchaert to Schenker (letter), undated [March 3, 1899?]

OJ 12/54, [A]

My dear Dr. [Schenker],

Too bad that you didn't come in for a moment. I would very much have liked to shake your hand!

I hope I will still be able to see you.

I am doing much better, thank God, and I hope that tomorrow evening I will be able to sing well.[1]

>   With warm greetings,
>   Your
>   Joh. Messchaert

[1] Messchaert was giving a recital of Hugo Wolf songs with Sophie Sedlmair in the Bösendorfer-Saal on March 4.

❦ Messchaert to Schenker (postcard), postmarked June 26, 1899
OJ 12/54, [7]

Dear Dr. [Schenker],

Many thanks for your card. [Oskar] Posa is splendid! This is music, poetry, sonorous beauty, formal mastery, everything of the highest order! I am extremely thankful that you made yourself known to me. I still often think of our tour together, with its joys and sufferings! I am in correspondence with Rosé, Grünfeld, Bösendorfer[1] etc. etc. etc. I think Bösendorfer does not wish to give his hall to Rosé, and I wish only to sing there. Goodbye to us.

A thousand greetings, also from my wife.

> Your warmly devoted
> Messchaert

[1] Ludwig Bösendorfer (1835–1919): Austrian piano manufacturer. The reference in the next sentence is to the Bösendorfer-Saal, the most popular concert hall in Vienna between 1872 and 1913.

❦ Messchaert to Schenker (postcard), August 25, 1899
OJ 12/54, [8]

Kallwang, Upper Styria

Dear Dr. [Schenker],

My warmest thanks to you and the Mayerhofer[1] family for your friendly postcard, which came precisely on my birthday! A thousand thanks!

> With warmest greetings
> Your devoted friend,
> Joh. Messchaert

[1] Irene Mayerhofer (1854–1923): close acquaintance and patron of Schenker, wife of Hermann Graedener.

❦ Schenker to Messchaert (letter), undated, [January/February 1900?]
JM/Ar, [1]

Dear, revered Professor,

I must write to you from the heart in what follows. So out with it! Posa told me that you are not satisfied with the monetary terms of your tour in Austria this year. I can certainly understand that. As you were explaining the issue of Grünfeld last night, I had a sudden idea which, because I was in the presence of others, I immediately suppressed. I would like to share with you the ideas that came to me last night, still warm from their first impulse. They are open, honest, without side agenda, and come merely out of a personal affection for you and for your distinctiveness as an artist. Well then!

I have said it to you before, and I will say it again: the province simply cannot pay for your honorarium, at least <u>not on a yearly basis</u>. I am younger than I look, but I am also more clever than the impresarios when it comes to knowing people. Anyone who has suffered as much as I will know people. If you and [someone as big as] a Rubinstein were to suggest about 100 florins, that would be nice for the province. In these rural regions people value only money and know <u>absolutely nothing</u> about art. Of what use is it that you provide a master like Röntgen and then charge only 400 florins: the province will not take the offer. Therefore I make the following friendly offer: I could make myself available to you for a possible tour of the province, without <u>honorarium and anonymously</u>—in this way you <u>can charge less</u> and still <u>make a gain</u> on your trip. You would not have to pay me <u>anything</u> (this would be <u>between us</u>, because Grünfeld would not go for it); I will gladly pay for food and lodging myself, and I would only ask that the train tickets (which I can't eat), and which however cost up to 140 florins, be reimbursed to me. I also have rich friends to whom I could turn if it were not possible for me to do you this favor. You would not need to use my name for the impresario or for the music societies: you are bringing your accompanist with you, and that is enough! Isn't it? With respect to soloists, <u>the societies</u> should choose their soloists if they wish to. But if you absolutely <u>must</u> have one of your accompanists, because perhaps it can't be any other way for one reason or another, you would have to write to me <u>a few months</u> beforehand, because I assure you, I would do it as well—Beethoven, Chopin, Schumann, Brahms (not Schenker)—as any one else. Of course you do not have to mention my name, because then the province itself would refuse me as a pianist altogether. You see that I do not want the slightest gain in reputation or money for myself. I simply wish to serve you. It would also be better this time around, since I understand you much better and your manner of singing, which was so <u>new</u> to me! I also think I understand our circumstances, our country and our people better than you do, and I can prepare the way so that the people are sympathetic to you.

I would like to do all I can for you: I merely ask you to leave this friendly offer unanswered. I would not be offended if you did not want to make use of it. All I want is for you to <u>do something</u> that <u>works best for you</u>; but I also want the province to hear something of your art: that is precisely my duty and mission. Who knows if some future Mozart, Beethoven, or Brahms were to hear you? If you need me—and that is the punch line of this overly long letter—please write to me, because I would travel with you, even if you want to travel to Germany or Bavaria etc., under the same conditions, without honorarium and anonymously.

I send my warmest greetings to and to your dear wife, and I remain

    Your devoted
    Dr. Heinrich Schenker

Send my warmest and best greetings to Professor Röntgen!

ᛞ Messchaert to Schenker (postcard), postmarked February 17, 1900
OJ 12/54, [9]

Dear Dr. [Schenker],

As you wrote to me, you did not want <u>any</u> direct answer to your wonderful letter. I would have loved to answer it immediately but I am constantly "en route." And this will last a while longer. In the meantime many thanks for your tremendous kindness and warmth. Perhaps another time. Until then, a thousand greetings.

   Your devoted,
    Joh. Messchaert

ᛞ Messchaert to Schenker (postcard), April 28, 1901
OJ 12/54, [10]

Victoria Hotel Amsterdam

Dear Dr. [Schenker],

For now I have still not arrived home and I ask for forgiveness if I must leave you waiting for a long time for a message from me.

   Many greetings
   Your
    Joh. Messchaert

1 Letter, Schenker to Max Kalbeck, May 19, 1897

2 Letter, Schenker to Moriz Violin, March 7, 1929, p. 1

3 Letter, Schenker to the Vienna Academy, in Jeanette Schenker's hand, December 13, 1927, p. 1

4 Draft letter, Schenker to Paul Hindemith, p. 4, in Jeanette Schenker's hand with emendations by Schenker, November 10, 1926

5 Letter, Felix-Eberhard von Cube to Schenker, October 20, 1931 (p. 1, top only)

6 Letter, Hans Weisse to Schenker, October 15, 1931 (p. 1, top only)

7 Postcard, Moriz Violin to Schenker, December 5, 1925

Wien, am 5. August 20

Sehr geehrter Herr Doktor!

Ich teile Ihnen mit, dass mir Herr SPEYER in London die Aufnahme seiner Skizzenblätter für die nächste Zeit in Aussicht gestellt hat, und dass, wie ich aus einem Aufsatz von FRIMMEL in der "Österreichischen Rundschau" eben ersehe, MANDYCZEWSKI vor einiger Zeit ein anderes Skizzenblatt zur Mondschein-Sonate aus dem Besitze des Herrn Dr. Wilhelm Kux in Wien veröffentlicht oder besprochen hat. Bevor ich mich auch um die Reproduktion dieses Blattes bemühe, bitte ich Sie, mir zu sagen ob Sie es kennen, und aufgenommen wissen wollen.

Mit besten Grüssen Ihr ergebener Deutsch

8 Postcard, Otto Erich Deutsch to Schenker, August 5, 1920

9 Schenker, *Syrian Dances* (1898), cover

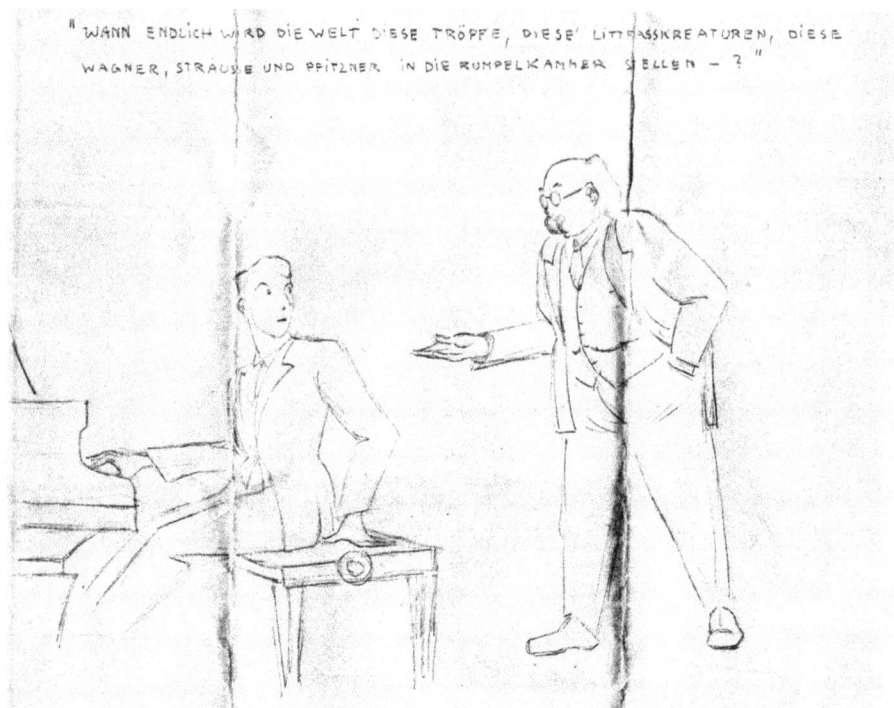

10 Lesson with Schenker: cartoon by Cube in letter to his father, January 20, 1924: "When, at last, will the world consign these nincompoops, these poster boys, these Wagners, Strausses, and Pfitzners, to the junk room?"

11 Schenker's study-bedroom, 8 Keilgasse, Vienna III, at the time of his death

4
The Society for Creative Musicians and Schoenberg's Music

THE invitation to Schenker to attend a meeting "to consider possible ways of setting up a society to sponsor the performance of 'modern music'," of which Schoenberg was a co-signatory, and the dispatch of an invitation to the event of the Ansorge Society on February 7, 1904, leave open the question as to how much of Schenker's thinking about such music was known to those inviting him. The Society for Creative Musicians[1] was duly established on April 23, 1904, but despite having Mahler as its honorary president—he also conducted Strauss's *Sinfonia domestica* at one of the concerts—it lasted only until March 1905.

The subsequent letters from Schoenberg would appear to indicate that Schenker had not completely rejected all such overtures. But by February 5, 1907, and a concert at which Schenker heard the première of Schoenberg's String Quartet, Op. 7, the scene was set for a definitive parting of the ways. Despite commenting in his diary that he found the quartet "a single long-drawn-out atrocity!", Schenker returned three days later for the First Chamber Symphony, confiding to his diary only that it was "an embarrassing fiasco."

That Schoenberg (or someone on his behalf) was still sending invitations to Schenker in November of 1907 evidently does not mean that Schenker had expressed any enthusiasm for continuing to receive them; and even before the 1911 publication of Schoenberg's *Theory of Harmony* Schenker's dislike of what the composer stood for was vividly apparent in his reaction to Universal Edition's decision to publish Schoenberg's Second String Quartet, Op. 10, and Three Pieces for Piano, Op. 11. Schenker wrote to Emil Hertzka on February 7, 1910, sarcastically noting the latter's willingness to promote "anti-musical music."

ARNOLD WHITTALL

---

[1] *Vereinigung schaffender Tonkünstler*: a difficult title to translate. By "schaffend," the organizers probably intended to designate musicians who were composers (for which *Komponist* was also available), as distinct from performers; but another distinction was perhaps also in their minds, that between "creative" (i.e. original, innovative) and uncreative (i.e. unoriginal, imitative) composers. For further discussion of the Society, see Mark D. Moskovitz, *Alexander Zemlinsky: A Lyric Symphony* (Woodbridge: The Boydell Press, 2010), 90–93.

Zemlinsky, Gutheil, and Schoenberg to Schenker (letter), January, 1904
OJ 14/15, [8]

Dear Sir,[1]

The undersigned take the liberty of inviting you to a meeting at 8 pm on January 21 at Hopfner's Restaurant, [Vienna] I, Kärntnerstrasse (private room). The aim of the meeting is as follows:

Anyone who compares the musical situation in Vienna with that in even smaller cities in Germany will be forced to recognize that for a long time the "city of music" has sadly lagged behind in the minimal progress that can be demanded these days even from those cultural centres that rest on the laurels of earlier times. Those who suffer most from this are the new and youngest creative artists, the rising generations of composers not only in Vienna but also throughout the Empire. Whereas in Germany public and press do not simply take a snobbish interest in serious younger artists, but even respond with warmth and esteem, here their efforts are invariably greeted with total silence.[2]

The notable success of the newly established Ansorge Society[3] leads us to conclude that in Vienna a change for the better is possible, and that a public for modern music can in fact be identified and educated in Vienna, if serious, committed people make a vigorous attempt to do so.

At the above-mentioned meeting, to which for now only a small number of seriously interested people have been invited, we aim to consider possible ways of setting up a society to achieve this goal, through the sponsorship of performances (orchestral, chamber music, lieder, etc.).[4]

The undersigned express the hope that such a burning issue will not leave you indifferent, and that you will agree that only collective action can further our objectives: we therefore urge you, if you aim to attend the meeting, to reply to Mr. Alexander von Zemlinsky, Vienna III, Obere Weißgärberstrasse 16.

    Respectfully yours,
    Alexander von Zemlinsky[5]
    Court Music Director Gustav Gutheil[6]
    Arnold Schoenberg

---

[1] This form letter is written in Suetterlinschrift by an amanuensis, and signed by the three signatories.

[2] This adverse comparison of Vienna and Austria-Hungary to Germany might already have met with Schenker's approval in 1904: it certainly agreed with his feelings later in his career.

[3] Society—named after composer and pianist Conrad Ansorge (1862–1930)—formed in 1903 to promote great art, old and new, by performances and lectures. Zemlinsky was a co-founder. It eventually merged with the Academic Union for Art and Literature in 1911.

[4] The outcome of this meeting was the foundation of the Society for Creative Musicians.

[5] Alexander Zemlinsky (1871–1942): Austrian composer of operas, choral, orchestral, and chamber works and lieder, conductor; music director of the Carl Theater in Vienna from 1899, the Folk Opera 1906–10, the German Regional Theater in Prague 1911–27, and the Kroll Opera, Berlin 1927–30, emigrated to USA in 1938.

[6] Gustav Gutheil (1868–1914): music director of the Weimar Court Theater, husband of the soprano Gutheil-Schoder from 1899.

Ansorge Society to Schenker (invitation/ticket), February 11, 1904
OJ 14/15, [9]

VIENNA ANSORGE SOCIETY
VIENNA VIII-2, FLORIANIGASSE 58

Guest ticket[1] for Dr. Schenker for the Ansorge–Grube–Schoenberg evening, to take place at 7 p.m. on February 11, 1904, in the General-Vereins-Saal, Vienna I, Eschenbachgasse 11.

Price: _ kronen _ Heller

[1] The document is printed in Art Deco typography, with the Ansorge emblem and handwritten entries.

Schoenberg to Schenker (letter), [February 12, 1904?]
OJ 14/15, [13]

Dear Dr. [Schenker],
  Too bad!!! I would have liked to know your thoughts.
  The subcommittee session is at my place: 5 o'clock.
        Cordial greetings,
        Arnold Schoenberg

Schoenberg to Schenker (letter), [February 16, 1904?]
OJ 14/15, [10]

ARNOLD SCHOENBERG,
VIENNA IX,
LIECHTENSTEINSTRASSE 68/70

Dear Dr. Schenker,
  You underestimate the importance of attending our discussions—rather too much, in fact—and thereby oblige me to pay you the compliment of giving the real reasons why we regard your involvement as essential. Is it necessary to emphasize

that we are delighted to find <u>one</u> intellect among musicians? That counts for more than factional divisions, at least in my experience. We are meeting from 5 o'clock onwards. – – – so if you leave at 7 o'clock, all will be settled. You'll come then!!

    Cordial greetings,
    Arnold Schoenberg

❧ Schoenberg to Schenker (letter), February 25, 1904
OJ 14/15, [11]

Dear Dr. [Schenker],

I don't believe that anything important can happen at the Friday session:[1] on the contrary, I see this session as completely superfluous, since one person alone could do everything that remains to be done. Nevertheless, despite this you will still find us together at 7 o'clock, since we begin only at 6. Whatever happens, however, I should be happy if you could come to my place on Friday evening and perhaps you would like to stay for supper? In any event, we could chat about a number of matters. I would therefore be delighted if you would give me this pleasure. It is too expensive for me to go to a restaurant—and also out of consideration for my wife, who would otherwise have to remain unhappily alone the entire evening. I therefore hope to see you here and look forward to your confirmation of this.

    With cordial greetings,
    Yours,
    Arnold Schoenberg

[1] Friday February 26 or March 4.

❧ Schoenberg to Schenker (letter), [1904?]
OJ 14/15, [12]

Dear Dr. [Schenker],

I get the feeling you're angry with me! Was I too hasty yesterday?

In any case, you have completely misunderstood me. I didn't want to know your attitude as a critic but as a creative artist. And in my case it has much less to do with you than with Grund[?] and Braun. Because, from you, in advance, I expected a wide mental horizon.

My aim: because of this clear difference of opinion, to settle on an open contract.

Thus, I sought to unite, not separate. You must concede that!

Please come here tomorrow, Thursday, at 5 o'clock for a subcommittee meeting.

    Most cordial greetings,
    Arnold Schoenberg

🎵 Schoenberg to Schenker (letter), [c. February 1, 1907]
OJ 14/15, [14]

Dear Dr. [Schenker],

I am very sorry that you did not attend:[1] I would have liked you to be there, for I am sure you would have received a different impression. However, perhaps you can still come to Rosé's concert (February 5) when my string quartet will be performed!!!

Perhaps I can give you a printed score. — the Chamber Symphony is on the 8th.

        Cordial greetings,
        Schoenberg

---

[1] Presumably the "Modern Lieder Evening" presented on January 26, 1907, comprising exclusively Schoenberg's Two Songs, Op. 1; Four Songs, Op. 2; Six Songs, Op. 3; and Eight Songs, Op. 6, on texts by Richard Dehmel, Gottfried Keller, Nietzsche and others.

🎵 Diary entry, February 5 and 8, 1907

[February 5:] D minor Quartet of Schoenberg, by [the] Rosé [Quartet]. A single, long-drawn-out atrocity! If there were such a thing as criminals in the realm of art, one would have to count this composer among their ranks, as one born such, or perhaps merely turned, criminal. Without feeling for key, motive, measure, on its own terms just utterly threadbare, without a trace of technique, and nevertheless at the same time constantly the hugest non-existent, total sham.

[February 8:] Concert by the Wind Music Society: d'Indy, *Song [and Dances]*, Op. 50 [for wind sextet], very well written. Wolf-Ferrari [Chamber Symphony in B♭ major, Op. 8] devoid of talent, indolent, brought down by lack of technique right through to the sonorities of the "Female Choruses." Schoenberg [Chamber Symphony, Op. 9]—an embarrassing fiasco on the part of the composer and his friends!

🎵 Schoenberg to Schenker (printed invitation), [c. November 1, 1907]
OJ 14/15, [15]

Dr. Heinrich Schenker

Arnold Schoenberg invites you to a performance of compositions by his students on November 7, 1907 at 7.30 p.m. in the Gremium Hall of the Viennese Merchants' Guild, Vienna I, Schwarzenbergplatz 16.

This invitation, whose return is requested if unable to attend, serves as a ticket.

To be performed:

1. Erwin Stein (student of counterpoint): four-part choral fugue, arranged for piano four-hands.
2. Alban Berg (student of counterpoint): double fugue for string quintet, with piano accompaniment (in the manner of a written-out continuo part).
3. Rudolf Weyrich: Adagio for string quartet.
4. O. de Ivanow: String Quartet, movements 2 and 3 (Adagio and Scherzo).
5. Dr. Anton von Webern: Piano Quintet, movement 1.
6. Rudolf Weyrich: Rondo for piano.
7. Alban Berg: songs.
8. Heinrich Jalowetz: songs.
9. Wilma von Webenau: pieces for piano.
10. Dr. Karl Horwitz: String Quartet, movements 1 and 2 (Allegro and Adagio).

Performers:

Frl. Etta Tomasz, piano

Frl. Elsa Pazeller, singer

Dr. Oscar Adler string quartet

Dr. Georg Helm

Heinrich Jalowetz

Heinrich Geiger

Josef Loyda, violin

5
Julius Röntgen:
Editing and Ornamentation

WHILE Schenker first witnessed Julius Röntgen perform five years before he wrote his first extant letter to him, we do not know when the two men first met or communicated with each other.[1] In his letter of March 15, 1901 to the Leipzig-born composer, pianist, and accompanist, Schenker invited Röntgen to join him in preparing practical editions of keyboard works from the classical canon, a commission from Josef Weinberger, co-founder of the publishing firm of Universal Edition. Röntgen accepted and completed no fewer than eight volumes of music by J. S. Bach the following year. Schenker's correspondence with Röntgen ranged far beyond matters related to the commission, however. With his letter of April 13, 1901, Schenker sent Röntgen copies of two of his recently published scores: Six Songs, Op. 3, and Two-voice Inventions, Op. 5. Röntgen replied on April 22, expressing thanks and sharing his candidly ambivalent impressions of Schenker's compositions.

Outwardly, their friendship was unaffected by this exchange. When their correspondence resumed in 1908, their mutual respect seemed as genuine as ever. Schenker offered advice about publishing in Vienna, Röntgen expressed regret about not seeing Schenker on a trip to Austria, and the two traded thoughts about performance practice, inspired by Schenker's gift of a copy of the second edition of *A Contribution to the Study of Ornamentation* (1908). But in a diary entry of January 13, 1907, Schenker recorded impressions of Röntgen's musicianship that belied—or at least complicated—the respect conveyed in his letters. Speaking of Röntgen in the same breath as the composer and keyboardist Max Reger, Schenker described Röntgen's playing as warm and passionate, but "without artistic understanding or any creative breath whatsoever." Röntgen's last surviving note to Schenker, a lettercard of February 10, 1915, looks back fondly and with evident nostalgia at their earliest encounters, sometime prior to 1900.

KEVIN C. KARNES

---

[1] Federhofer (1990), 318–19 (February 5, 1896); Federhofer (1985), 189.

Schenker to Röntgen (letter), March 15, 1901
NMI C 176-02 (= OJ 5/18, [A])

Revered, dear Professor,

Do not be frightened by a matter of business alone!

Austria has recently been preparing to emancipate itself from Germany—specifically, from the two largest discount houses,[1] Breitkopf & Härtel and Peters. A committee is making preparations for a new edition, to include <u>all</u> works in the musical literature!! The project, in spite of the enormous number of collaborators, is naturally projected to take <u>several years</u>, and I personally know from an authoritative financier that the undertaking rests soundly upon a foundation of millions. The edition should delight not only the eastern hinterlands (the Balkan provinces, etc.), but will also touch upon Germany, England, France—in short, it will radiate outward in all directions. And successes have already been scored, prompting both the financier and the committee to dream of fat years to come!

To ensure that the project is stamped with an international character, the committee has turned to the most distinguished foreign artists (from Germany, France, etc.) as collaborators. The first round of work, addressing a number of urgent tasks, is already in full swing.

The publisher Weinberger with whom I spoke briefly, expressed to me his misfortune at not having seen you again in Berlin. He wanted to ask, in person, whether you wish to participate, what you would like to edit, etc. Unfortunately, Prof. Messchaert has declined for lack of time. In his place, <u>Stockhausen</u>, <u>Iffert</u>,[2] etc. are contributing.

After determining that the work would come with a <u>very good</u> honorarium, I have taken it upon myself, <u>having been called by Weinberger to help</u>, to invite your participation, and to ask you to take on whatever seems most appealing to you. By no means take me to be an agent. As an artist, I naturally have the most ardent wish to play an edition (annotations, fingerings) prepared by you, whom I esteem so highly, in sharp contrast to those mere-virtuosos. I think that Weinberger, the most influential member of the committee, is eager to hear what might be expected from you in terms of important works by Beethoven, Scarlatti, or Schumann. The accursed Prof. Barth[3] has greedily seized Scarlatti (eighteen pieces) for himself!

In short, I ask that you tell me whether you are ready to contribute your exceptional talents. Give me your "yes" in words, and I'll send your letter directly to Weinberger. Everything else will then be settled contractually between you and Weinberger (or the committee).

Please, say "yes"!

(My new publications[4] will be finished soon, and I will send them as promised.)

   With best wishes,
    Yours truly,
     Dr. H. Schenker

---

[1] "discount houses": probably intended as a derogatory characterization.

[2] Julius Stockhausen (1826–1906): German baritone in opera and oratorio, one of the greatest interpreters of German song of his day. Despite Schenker's statement,

Stockhausen does not appear to have completed any editorial work for UE. August Iffert (1859–1930): German baritone, who taught at the Dresden Conservatory.

[3] Karl Heinrich Barth (1847–1922): German pianist, teacher at the Stern Conservatory in Berlin, later at the Berlin Music Hochschule. Barth's edition of *Domenico Scarlatti: Klavierwerke* was published by UE.

[4] Simultaneously with his letter of April 13, 1901, Schenker sent Röntgen a packet of materials, the contents of which can be deduced from that and the following letters as his own compositions.

❧ Röntgen to Schenker (letter), March 18, 1901
OJ 13/27, [1]

Amsterdam

Most revered Dr. [Schenker],

First of all, many thanks for your letter and for so kindly sharing your views, which I value so highly!

It will be a pleasure to contribute something to the great undertaking about which you write. In principle, I happily say "yes," but my final decision must depend upon what kind of edition is desired. I already see from your remarks that a mere critical reproduction of the original text is not intended. Will the edition follow a set of general principles, or will each of the individual editors be left to follow his own path?

Is it a matter, e.g., of merely marking fingerings, phrasings, etc., or must this be an <u>instructive</u> edition in the manner of Cotta's?[1]

I would not like to undertake a work in the latter sense. Another question: Is this to be a complete edition, i.e., covering all the works of a composer? Or could one limit oneself to a selection? E.g., some of Mozart's piano works (apart from the sonatas), the Fantasies, A minor Rondo, B minor Adagio, and also some of the smaller, lesser-known pieces? That would seem more practical to me than bringing out the entire mass, in which there is much that is of only historical interest. A selection of Mozart's piano works would be an enticing project for me! Then I thought about Bach's six sonatas for piano and violin, which have appeared only in quite useless popular editions. The older version of the sixth sonata—including the two wonderful adagios—has still not appeared, except in the big Bach Collected Edition.

I would therefore be very grateful if you would tell me a bit more about the operative artistic foundation of the entire undertaking!

For fun, I am sending you a joke that I played years ago with Bülow.[2] It is an "arrangement" of one of my piano pieces for a Bülow-enthusiast female student, who was very good at "hitting the wrong notes."

Here you will see what you have to fear from me as an "arranger"!

Send the thing back to me sometime, preferably quite soon, along with the Inventions, which I am eagerly awaiting!

I am sorry that I was in such a bad state during my last visit to Vienna, and that I therefore made so little use of our time together. Unfortunately, Messchaert was "influenza-ed"[3] by me and had, until just recently, been dealing with that. But he is now fit as a fiddle at the Bach Festival in Berlin, and we have concerts here on the 26th.

I've been thoroughly enjoying [Oskar] Posa's violin sonata and new songs—those have been occupying me most intensely!

Enough for today; I write in great haste.

Would you be kind enough to pass my provisional acceptance along to Mr. Weinberger?

I hope to hear more of the details soon, and then, hopefully, to be able to say something more certain.

With cordial greetings,
In admiration,
Yours truly,
Julius Röntgen

Your discretion please regarding "Über-Bülow"[4] (see above)!

---

[1] A reference to Cotta's "Instruktive Ausgabe klassischer Klavierwerke."

[2] Hans von Bülow was one of the collaborating editors of Cotta's "Instruktive Ausgabe klassischer Klavierwerke"; in particular, vols. 4 and 5 of *Beethoven's Sonaten und andere Werke* in that series were edited by him. His editions were a frequent target of Schenker's polemical attacks. Schenker is referring here to Bülow's edition of C. P. E. Bach keyboard sonatas (Leipzig: Peters, 1862).

[3] A pun: Röntgen apparently "influenced" (*influenzirt*) Messchaert by giving him influenza.

[4] "Über-Bülow": presumably the joke-piece described earlier.

❧ Schenker to Röntgen (letter), April 13, 1901
NMI C 176-01

Revered and dear Professor,

Many thanks for your agreement to contribute! I hope you have also reached an agreement with Weinberger & Co. I have not seen Weinberger for some time and I know virtually nothing about how it turned out. If you assert that what you have to offer is your intellectual property (in a higher sense than the typical services of all too many editors), you may indeed insist on a higher honorarium than usual. And Weinberger will approve it. At least that is what I will do with regard to the edition of C. P. E. Bach that I've promised to undertake. In truth, I do not know if I should be more fearful of the colossal task ahead or overjoyed at so much beauty. Do you know the Sonata in F major, the second in Breitkopf & Härtel's Urtext volume? It is so endlessly fine and, in stark contrast to the modern first-and-second-subject merchants, presented so freely and lavishly, in such a multifarious manner! Who today writes with such genius as we see on the last eighth-note of measure 4 in the first movement? How exquisitely it moves back and forth, coming and going, like a slight muscular movement, like the merest twitch! Nothing is thick, nothing coarse, in no way dolled up. Will and execution, both working delicately, marvelously!

The fact that Bülow could leave this sonata aside would be incomprehensible to me if I had not earlier been inclined to judge him somewhat more lowly than highly. And if I have understood your teasing lampoon of Bülow, you too feel that he is a figure less worthy of beatification, less worthy of being taken seriously, than the great starstruck masses believe. I might take this opportunity to say that even Brahms too did not overestimate him; it was indeed Brahms who threw a wet towel on the *furor teutonicus* when the Germans were clamoring for a national monument after Bülow's death. I went to Brahms then, at the behest of Harden in Berlin, and he said, "What's this? I have pledged money and support, but only for a cemetery monument in Hamburg. Bülow deserves no more; he was only a music director! Does Wagner have a monument? etc." How lovely that Brahms, despite all his feelings of thankfulness, had the courage to say it. This is my view too regarding the question of a monument.

And now a few more words about what I have sent you as promised. I hope that Invention No. 2, of which I am very proud, may arouse your interest.[1] It is indeed rather quick—passionate, I think, deliberate, very expressive! It is here, primarily, where I've breached modernism. It would make me very happy if this Invention pleased you.

In contrast, I am absolutely certain that you must—that you simply must—find one of the songs pleasing (so firmly am I convinced of this, and I say so nevertheless with all the modesty that you and I both deserve): "Der Ausklang."[2] There is, incidentally, a strange, uncanny reason for this. Consider this: Prof. Gärtner,[3] who just this year hosted a Lieder evening of the "young," which included works by R. Strauss (around fourteen to sixteen songs by eight or ten composers were performed), wanted to sing two of my songs—"Wiegenliedchen,"[4] of course, because he found the *pp* and so forth so agreeable (and moreover because it provided a pleasant counterbalance to the other novelties, which, as is common practice today, obliterate the German song style completely, tear the vocal cords to shreds, and regard key and tonality as vanquished), and also the above-mentioned "Ausklang." Now, it happened that he needed to sing more songs by his accompanist, Mr. Zemlinsky, because the following week, in his capacity as music director of the Carl Theater, the latter was to conduct Gärtner's operetta ("one hand washes the other"). And so he could only sing "Wiegenliedchen," with which, by the way, he scored perhaps the greatest success of the evening . . .

But now consider this (and here comes the tragedy): On the same evening as the concert, almost the same hour, even the same minute in which Gärtner performed [my work], the uncommonly congenial author of the poem "Leuchtende Tage"—the author of "Ausklang"—died in Berlin, before the end of his thirty-second year!! If Gärtner had sung "Ausklang" at that moment, how strange the coincidence would have been!

Oh! Read Jacobowski's book of poetry!—What a pure, loving man! A touching disposition.

From everything I've sent, it will be obvious to you that I take no pleasure in getting wrapped up in enharmonicism and chromaticism, as people are so fond of doing today in the most childish of ways. The reason for all the present carrying on is the following view of mine: No one has such a brilliant sense of tonality that he is able to write with such brilliant, multifaceted inventiveness (and, in turn, in such multifaceted forms) as, e.g., Schumann, in the Intermezzo, Op. 4, No. 5, where the actual tonic, D minor, makes its first appearance in mm. 20–21, after a long, utterly beautiful, tarrying in F major—and indeed undergirded by a <u>different</u> motive! And at first, <u>*pp*</u>! Only in measure 29 is it *ff*, D minor, the eighth-note motive *ff*, and above it, however, a <u>new</u> ballad <u>from out of this D minor</u>. — Or Brahms's G minor Rhapsody, which you play so well: The tonic G (major) first appears in measure 9 (and how it is hidden!), and the actual tonic, G minor, finally in measure 11! How it all unfolds! How it moves toward the tonic! And then without much ado, the tonality makes its way toward D minor!

And a most brilliant example of enharmonicism in the E minor Sonata of Beethoven, in the first movement around measure 37 and after. This B♭, this B♭ major!!!

And so I say: Most people today, because their lack of talent in art cannot unfortunately transform itself into talent, and restlessly sensing that <u>something</u> must be changed in their art if dreaded boredom is to be avoided, feel that they must transform and alter—most rashly—even the tones themselves. The more monotonous they are themselves in terms of invention and talent, the more the notes must be altered, and ever more rashly, so that the monotony of the composer is not betrayed.

I firmly believe that one must not hand a child key, tonality, modulation, chromaticism, or enharmonicism any more readily than one hands a child fire. It is indeed no joke. And above all, synthesis!—which must have spirit in every nook and cranny, and the less conspicuous it is, the more beautiful; if obtrusive, then all the more contrived.

In conclusion, revered, dear Professor, one more thing: Should Professor Messchaert, at some point, feel like singing "Ausklang" (<u>only out of the most sincere</u> convictions, of course!), I hope that Mr. Gutmann[5] will not make trouble. Because when Mr. Eugen d'Albert played some of my piano pieces here a couple years ago, Mr. Gutmann paid the 15-florin royalty (novelty royalty) out of his own pocket, without saying a word to d'Albert or to me. I learned about it two years later in the presence of Prof. Becker and Dr. Rottenberg[6] from Frankfurt; Gutmann, however, could not be persuaded to let the money be returned by d'Albert or myself. I hope this will be resolved.

If this is getting overly long, then perhaps it has succeeded in making you more acquainted with me.

A thousand greetings,
Yours, in great admiration.
H. Schenker

---

[1] Schenker, Two-voice Inventions, Op. 5 (Leipzig: Breitkopf & Härtel, 1901).

[2] Schenker, Six Songs for Solo Voice with Piano Accompaniment, Op. 3 (Leipzig: Breitkopf & Härtel, 1898, 1901), No. 4, "Ausklang" (text by Ludwig Jacobowski).

[3] Eduard Gärtner: bass singer who performed chamber music and songs with Schenker, Moriz Violin, Paul de Conne, and others. Schenker sometimes

accompanied him in song recitals in the 1900s, and Gärtner gave performances of songs by Schenker and also by Schoenberg (Federhofer (1985), 19, 49–50).
4 Schenker, Six Songs, Op. 3, No. 2, "Wiegenlied" (text by Detlev von Liliencron).
5 Albert J. Gutmann: agent and concert promoter. It seems as though a concert by d'Albert, arranged by Gutmann, at which one of Schenker's works was performed, was not financially successful. Rather than acknowledging this fact to either d'Albert or Schenker, Gutmann apparently absorbed the loss himself, and paid Schenker's royalty "out of his own pocket." Schenker's concern regarding Messchaert's possible interest in performing some of his songs might be explained by the fact that Messchaert, like d'Albert, was also represented by Gutmann.
6 Hugo Becker (1864–1941): German virtuoso solo cellist and chamber music player, who taught at the Hoch Conservatory in Frankfurt, Berlin, and the Royal Swedish Academy before being appointed to the faculty of the Berlin Music Hochschule in 1909. Ludwig Rottenberg (1864–1932): Austrian conductor and composer, music director at the Frankfurt Opera 1893–1926.

❧ Röntgen to Schenker (letter), April 22, 1901
OJ 13/27, [2]

Most revered Dr. [Schenker],

At last a word of thanks for your letter, which was so rich in content! Don't mistake the delay for indifference! To the contrary: your Songs and, above all, Inventions have occupied me intensely; but I did not want to write until I had developed a somewhat more intimate relationship with the material at hand, and that did not come immediately to me.

In the Inventions you tread upon fairly twisted paths, and it is not always easy to follow you. In particular, the purely musical essence is not always readily apparent, even though the technical aspect is immediately interesting and impressive. In this respect, I am drawn most strongly to the piece in F♯ minor—but more, thus far, through reading it than through playing it. There is much that sounds quite daring to me, even though everything is entirely logical. On it, you can safely write, as Bach did on his inventions: "a clear way at the same time to acquire a strong foretaste of composition." In contrast, "refreshing of the spirit" seems to take somewhat of a back seat.[1]

Considering how well I have become acquainted with the Inventions thus far, it is possible that my opinion will change. In any case, I will return to the works frequently, and I look forward to discussing them with you further in the future!

I have not yet spent a great deal of time with the Songs, since I've had many other things to do in recent weeks. The Bach edition I took on[2] has occupied me during every free hour (for the latter purpose, your Inventions are very well suited!), and everything else had therefore to be pushed back.

To me, "Ausklang" stands out among the songs. The marvelous text has found immediate expression in the music, and the song must make a profound impression. The other songs seem a bit less natural to me (with the exception of the delightful "Wiegenlied"!). But the texts are of a wittier sort, and you have illustrated everything interestingly! The last song is least to my liking—it seems, to me, to be too heavy for the clever text in places (the G♯ minor episode). As I said, however, I must probe them further and ask that you consider these few words as merely provisional.

Messchaert is coming to Amsterdam in a day or so. I'm looking forward to playing through the songs with him, especially "Ausklang."

And now you must make do, for today, with this overly brief reply to your highly stimulating letter, and once again many thanks for everything,

  Yours, in great admiration,
  Julius Röntgen

[1] Röntgen quotes, apparently to signal his approval of Schenker's adherence to expectations associated with the genre, and without syntactic coherence, from Bach's inscription on the title page of the fair copy of his Inventions and Sinfonias, BWV 772–801 (1723). "Gemüths-Ergötzung": This term appears on the title pages of the first editions of Bach's four volumes of Clavier-Übungen (1731–42). The spelling used by Röntgen, however, is found only in Bach's second volume, containing the Italian Concerto (BWV 971 [1735]) that Röntgen was then editing for UE. My thanks to Stephen Crist for his help in identifying the source of these quotation.

[2] The identity of the edition to which Röntgen refers is unclear. During this period, Röntgen's editorial work for UE was extensive. His editions of Bach's Little Preludes and Fugues, Two- and Three-Part Inventions, French Suites, English Suites, Partitas, Italian Concerto, D minor Concerto, and *Chromatic Fantasy and Fugue* all appeared in 1902.

❧ Röntgen to Schenker (lettercard), October 14, 1901
OJ 13/27, [4]

Dear, honored Dr. [Schenker],

Your "indiscretion against the will"[1] has made me extraordinarily happy, and it would be lovely if we had it to thank for the fact that the firm of Messchaert-Röntgen did not go bankrupt[2] in Vienna!

Gutmann's tactic is not lovely, however. Two years ago, when he came with the high offer, we agreed on the condition that it would also hold for the following year, assuming continuing success. He responded agreeably to this. I recently wrote to him plainly about this, of course without a trace of hope that it would be of any use. He began his letter of reply with this lovely line: "I stand in the front line of enthusiastic friends of art." And then he complained about the "bad times" he is always compelled to face. Now, Rosé's offer[3] has personally made me very happy. Whether it will be realized this year is still uncertain. In any case, Messchaert is tied to Gutmann, with whom he has made an exclusive commitment to three concerts in January.

On the 18th I have a concert here [Amsterdam] with Messchaert, and I will find out then how the affair has played out. I will discuss your letter with him then, and he can respond for himself to your suspicions concerning his view of your relationship with Rosé. I have not heard a single word from Messchaert, which makes me think that your view is correct!

And what have you been doing lately? You spoke in your last letter of a larger piece of work!

Have you finished your work on C. P. E. Bach? I worked the whole summer to fulfill my Bach obligations! It surprises me now that the printing proceeds so slowly. I was given October 1 as the latest possible date for publication, and I stayed up until around 6 o'clock every morning for that reason.

My own most recent work was a four-hand arrangement of old Dutch dances from 1550, probably the oldest monument of Dutch instrumental music.[4] It would be fun to play them with you sometime! If nothing comes of Messchaert-Röntgen, I will come with Eldering, our extraordinary violinist,[5] and perform the three Brahms sonatas for the Viennese.

Thus I say farewell and offer the most heartfelt greetings in the meantime!

    Yours truly,
       in friendship,
          Julius Röntgen

[1] "Ihre 'Indiscretion wider Willen'": inexplicable on present documentation; perhaps there had been personal contact during the Messchaert-Röntgen visit to Vienna, or perhaps a letter from Schenker is missing. Only one item of correspondence intervenes between this and the previous letter: a humorous lettercard jointly from Röntgen and Oscar Posa, not included here.

[2] "Banquerot": French *banqueroute* (bankruptcy).

[3] This may refer to an invitation from the violinist Arnold Rosé to collaborate in one of his Concerts Soirées. A similar case arose five years earlier with Eugen d'Albert, who, like Messchaert, was represented by Gutmann, and did not wish to imperil his relationship with Gutmann by working with another agent or promoter (letter to Schenker, April 24, 1896). Alternatively it may refer to Alexander Rosé, who ran a concert agency and a music retail and rental business on the Kärntner Ring.

[4] Röntgen's *Oud hollandsche boerenliedjes en contradansen* was published in five volumes between 1897 and 1916 (Amsterdam: De Algemeene muziekhandel, and Leipzig: Breitkopf & Härtel).

[5] Bram Eldering (1865–1943): Dutch violinist. He taught at the Amsterdam Conservatory of Music from 1899, then moved to the Cologne Conservatory in 1903, where he taught until his death.

❧ Röntgen to Schenker (letter), August 8, 1908
OJ 13/27, [6]

Fuglsang, via Nykøbing
Falster
Denmark

Honored Dr. [Schenker],

It made me very happy to hear from you once again! Your letter was forwarded to me here and found upon my return from Norway.

I will gladly connect with Mr. Steiner,[1] whom you have recommended so warmly, but I would like to get to know him somewhat better before I give my promise for a concert tour with him. I would not want people to speak of a "decrescendo" if I made a return appearance in Vienna without Messchaert. You will certainly understand that! Could not a meeting with Mr. Steiner be arranged? E.g., in Berlin? If need be, I could get there from here toward the end of August for a day, or possibly in September from Amsterdam, albeit with greater difficulty.

In any case, we can surely correspond about it.

I am very eager to see your new work, and will be able to have a look as soon as I am once again in Amsterdam.

Have you heard that a piano quintet by myself was recently awarded a prize by the Concert Society?[2] I had hoped that the Society would publish the work, but that seems not to be the case.

Could you perhaps give me the name of a local publisher who might be inclined to publish it?

With best greetings,
Yours truly,
in friendship,
Julius Röntgen

---

[1] Presumably Franz Steiner, who corresponded with Schenker in 1908 and 1913.

[2] The Wiener Konzertverein was founded in 1900 principally to support an orchestra whose programming—often popular and sometimes explicitly pedagogical—would be directed at audiences not traditionally inclined to attend Philharmonic programs. The Society's orchestra persists today as the Wiener Symphoniker.

❧ Röntgen to Schenker, September 23, 1908
OJ 13/27, [7]

Highly revered Dr. [Schenker],

I have long owed you a response and thanks for your letter[1] and for your *Contribution to the Study of Ornamentation*, which I have read with the greatest interest and will study still further.

Most of its contents took the words right out of my mouth, especially the more general remarks about the latest advertising article by Riemann, "The Mannheim

School,"² and about Bülow's extravagances.³ I am now really looking forward to becoming acquainted with your C. P. E. Bach edition, and am eagerly awaiting it. After I read your essay I had to confess, with a feeling of shame, that I actually know Philipp Emanuel much too poorly.

I have, of course, been occupied with the subject of ornamentation myself, since many questions confronted me when editing the elder Bach. I have my own views about this difficult subject, which I would like very much to discuss with you some time in person.

I think that not everything can be handled by the inflexible rule, "every ornament is subtracted from the following note"—especially not in the case of composers after Bach. Good taste must also be permitted to play a role. To me, Bülow goes much too far in this respect. Already with Mozart I find it more tasteful in many cases to take appoggiaturas of more than two notes before the main note.⁴ How much more delicate does this sound:

than

(see the Lebert and Stark Cotta edition),⁵ especially when the pupil plays the ornament with an accent on D♯ and with the necessary stiffness (encouraged by the type of the notation).

Why not regard such ornaments as little connecting notes, and why must they always be hung like a weight on the note that follows?

In any case, I cannot swear by Bülow's dogma, which allows for no exceptions to the rule whatsoever.

But enough about this, until we speak some day.

Just a couple more words about Mr. Steiner, whose acquaintance I recently made here.

In spite of the congenial impression that his personality and his vocal abilities have made upon me, I could not grant him his wish to perform in concert together. He will inform you of my reasons.

I cannot make a good appearance with someone making his debut, and I have always refused to do so.

But Mr. Steiner did not make the trip in vain. I recommended a brilliant young man to him, whom he has engaged for his concert. He is coming soon to Vienna in order to prepare the program with Steiner, and I hope that you will get to know him. His name is Willem Andriessen,⁶ and he recently received, in an outstanding way, our Conservatory's Prix d'Excellence.

Allow yourself to hear him improvise a fugue sometime, and you will be amazed!

He did that here before the assembled public, on a highly cunning theme given to him by Arthur de Greef.[7]

Perhaps we will see each other in Vienna again this winter. I want to give a couple of concerts with my son, who is presently solo cellist in Zürich,[8] and I have written directly to Gutmann about it.

Concerning my Quintet, I would be very thankful if you could give me the name of a publisher with whom I could get in touch. Since the work was awarded a prize in Vienna, I would like very much for it to be published there as well.

Enough for today, and thanks once again for the Bach [sic]. I hope to get to know your new work right soon.

      With best greetings,
        Yours most truly,
          Julius Röntgen

[1] The letter is not known to survive, nor did Schenker record its writing in his diary.

[2] Hugo Riemann, ed., *Sinfonien der Pfalzbayerischen Schule (Mannheimer Schule)*, Denkmäler Deutscher Tonkunst, ser. 2: Denkmäler der Tonkunst in Bayern 3/1, 7/2, 8/2 (Leipzig: Breitkopf & Härtel, 1902–07). Schenker dedicates much of the Foreword of the second edition of *Ornamentation* to a critique of Riemann's statements on behalf of the Mannheim symphonist Johann Stamitz, whose contributions were, in Schenker's view, far less significant than those of C. P. E. Bach. Schenker does not name Riemann as his target, but he makes his identity clear (Eng. transl. (1976), 12–13; Ger., 2).

[3] In his Introduction to *Ornamentation*, Schenker criticizes Bülow's editorial practice as evinced in the latter's edition of C. P. E. Bach's piano sonatas (*Sechs Klavier-Sonaten*, ed. Hans von Bülow [Leipzig: C. F. Peters, 1862]). In this volume, as quoted in Schenker's book, Bülow likened his undertaking to preparing an "arrangement" of Bach's scores for a modern audience (Eng. transl., 16–19; Ger., 4–5).

[4] There may be some confusion regarding terminology here. In *Ornamentation* Schenker uses Röntgen's term—*Vorschlag*—narrowly, to denote the appoggiatura. The ornament shown in Röntgen's example, however, is what Schenker would call an "ascending turn" (*Doppelschlag von unten*) or "slide" (*Schleifer*) (Eng. transl., 107–08; Ger., 54–55). Schenker corrects Röntgen on this point, albeit obliquely, in his letter of October 3, 1908.

[5] Sigmund Lebert's edition of Mozart's A minor Rondo, K. 511 (Stuttgart and Berlin: J. G. Cotta, 1892); he quotes from m. 1. With Ludwig Stark, Lebert authored the widely distributed and influential *Grosse theoretisch-praktische Klavierschule*, published by Cotta with four-part appendix (1858, 23rd edn 1904 by Max Pauer).

[6] Willem Andriessen (1887–1964): Dutch pianist and composer, student of Röntgen, Daniel de Lange and others at the Amsterdam Conservatory, who went on to cultivate a significant career as a solo pianist and staunch advocate of new music in the Netherlands. He was appointed to the piano faculty of the Conservatory in The Hague in 1910. He was a member of a musical family: his brother Hendrik was also a composer, as were Hendrik's two sons, Jurriaan and Louis, the latter being a significant figure in the avant-garde of the later twentieth century.

[7] Arthur de Greef (1862–1940): Belgian pianist and composer, professor of piano at the Brussels Conservatory from 1887.

⁸ Engelbert Röntgen (1886–1958): Dutch cellist, principal cellist of the Philharmonic Orchestras of Rostock and later Zürich, and from 1912 of the Vienna Court/State Opera.

☙ Schenker to Röntgen (letter), October 3, 1908
NMI C 176-03

Highly revered Professor,
 First, the subject of greatest interest to you. I inquired whether the Concert Society plans to publish your prize-winning composition, and I learned from a friend who is on the board of directors—[Ferdinand] Löwe is in Munich at the moment—that the work is entirely and exclusively your property. So then I went to the only publisher in question here in Vienna, Mr. Herzmansky (Dohnányi's publisher), and told him about the situation. First he said that chamber music published in Vienna does not make its way over to Germany—sad enough, but a fact nonetheless. But he asked nevertheless about your requirements regarding the honorarium, and when I was able to tell him reassuring things about the matter he said that it would then be best if he could somehow hear the work in public, in order to form his own opinion (?sic!). To this I replied: I believe that the Concert Society will certainly bring the work to performance itself. Otherwise, the invitation, jury, prize, etc. would have made no sense. All the better, replied Mr. Herzmansky, I will listen to it and give you the news. That was the extent of our dialogue.
 Now I think that it would not be so difficult for me, perhaps, to persuade Löwe to give the earliest possible performance of your work. But I would encourage you to think about the truth that slipped out a bit to the publisher, about the extent to which publishing chamber music in Vienna is generally worthwhile. Our publishers live with operetta—they live off it and for it—and have no standing in Germany. While anything and everything finds its way to us from abroad, works edited here can penetrate abroad under only the most favorable of circumstances. No money! No advertising! Schnitzler, Bahr, Hofmannsthal,—they are all published abroad. Brahms, Dvořák, Goldmark also come to us from abroad. Think about this difficulty, and make up your mind about it. You need not doubt that I will work gladly, incessantly, and with all of my strength to assure that your path here is a smooth one.
 Now a small correction. My edition is already a few years old, and was accompanied at its birth by *A Contribution to the Study of Ornamentation*, the second edition of which is now in your hands. There you will find it emphasized repeatedly that the subtraction for the appoggiatura only is made from the following note, thus in contrast the ∾ and all other ornaments go beforehand, just as you also obviously feel. I have provided the psychological and historical basis for this feeling. It is thus theoretically correct, just as your feeling requires (cf., e.g., p. 59, §2; p. 60, §3ff.; p. 63, §6; p. 66, §9 etc.; p. 71, §1!), and it makes me happy that we are in agreement on this question.

Mr. Andriessen seems to be a completely splendid young man. Unfortunately I have not been able to hear him yet, but I hope to soon. Prof. Violin and Mr. Steiner have certainly spoken most appreciatively to me about his abilities.[1]

>So much in haste!
>With best greetings,
>Yours very truly,
>H. Schenker

---

[1] Thanks are due to the late Maximilian Aue and Peter Höyng for their help with a particularly difficult passage in this letter.

Röntgen to Schenker (lettercard), February 10, 1915
NMI C 176-03

Most revered Dr. [Schenker],

Your postcard was a great joy for me, for which I thank you most heartily. It was like a greeting from the good old Vienna days, when you and Brahms sat on the stage in the Bösendorfer-Saal and listened to us, when we drank good wine together in the Klosterneuburger Keller. Your loving lines stirred up all of these memories anew. So until we see each other again sometime—with the Röntgen Trio,[1] I hope, whose leader sends you the most friendly greeting!

>[unsigned]

---

[1] Röntgen Trio: Julius Röntgen (piano) and his two sons, Julius (violin) and Engelbert (cello).

II
Schenker and his Publishers

6
Cotta and the New Musical Theories and Fantasies

THE grand German publishing house of J. G. Cotta goes back to 1659, when Johann Georg Cotta acquired the management of the bookshop of Tübingen University through marriage. At about the same time he established his own publishing business, and the name "J. G. Cotta" soon became attached to both the retail store and the publishing firm. In the 1790s Cotta became associated with Schiller, and soon after with Goethe, of whose collected works it published the third edition in 1806–10. In the latter year, the firm moved from Tübingen to Stuttgart (where it remains today under the name Klett-Cotta). Subsequently it published the collected works of Herder, Schelling, and Pestalozzi, and works by Hölderlin, Hebel, Kleist, Rückert, and other important German literary figures. The firm remained in family control until 1889, when it was sold to Adolf and Paul Kröner. In 1905, when Schenker proposed his New Musical Theories and Fantasies, Adolf Kröner was its sole proprietor.[1]

Schenker's association with the name of Cotta lasted fifteen years. That he was conscious of the prestige that this brought him is clear from the deferential tone that he adopted in his letters, and the readiness with which he accepted Cotta's advice. The contrast between this and the manner he adopted toward Universal Edition and Drei Masken Verlag is striking.[2]

The Schenker–Cotta correspondence comprises 325 items. The selection below covers the twelve months from initial contact in 1905 to publication of *Theory of Harmony* in 1906,[3] and concludes with some of the final communications of 1920 and 1921. It therefore passes over the correspondence concerning *Counterpoint*.

To summarize the latter briefly, on September 23, 1908, Schenker submitted the manuscript for that volume, with some material, including the Introduction, still to come. Only two weeks later he proposed publishing what he had submitted plus his Introduction as "the first half-volume" so as to catch the Christmas trade, leaving the smaller second half-volume to be delivered the following Easter. He

---

[1] *Lexikon des gesamten Buchwesens* (Stuttgart: Anton Hiersemann, 2nd edn. 1987–), vols. 2, 187–88; 4, 237.

[2] On the contrast with his dealings with UE, see Ian Bent, "'Niemals also ist der Verleger ein "Mäzen" des Künstlers': Schenker and the Music-Publishing World," in *Essays from the Fourth International Schenker Symposium*, vol. 2, ed. L. Poundie Burstein, Lynne Rogers, and Karen M. Bottge (Hildesheim: Georg Olms, 2013), 121–33.

[3] Robert Wason traces the early history of the *Theory of Harmony* in "From *Harmonielehre* to *Harmony*: Schenker's Theory of Harmony and its Americanization," in *Essays from the Fourth International Schenker Symposium*, vol. 1, ed. Allen Cadwallader with John Patrick Connolly (Hildesheim: Georg Olms, 2008), 231–58, especially 215–24, 248–51.

had made a similar proposal for *Theory of Harmony*, against which Cotta had advised. They balked again this time, but eventually acquiesced. The second half-volume had crystallized in Schenker's mind by May 1909 as covering three- and four-voice counterpoint, "Bridges to Free Composition," "Free Composition," and an Epilog. Volume 3 was then to be *The Decline of the Art of Composition*, which he described as "the capstone of the whole work." The latter was an outgrowth from the *Theory of Harmony* that he planned to complete in fall 1909.[4]

Counterpoint 1 was published on October 4, 1910, by which time Schenker was already offering Cotta his planned *Little Library*, a series of analytical booklets on individual works (which would eventually coalesce as *Der Tonwille*), singling out in particular Beethoven's Ninth Symphony, to illustrate the theoretical principles set forth in his New Musical Theories and Fantasies. In 1920, Schenker again offered Cotta the *Little Library*, and also a complete edition of Beethoven's piano sonatas, both of which Cotta declined. Ultimately, as the final items in the selection show, Universal Edition took over publication of *Counterpoint 2*, and thirteen years later *Free Composition*, volume 3 of the series, and the republication of the earlier volumes. The *Decline* remained unpublished.

IAN BENT

[4] For more on the history of the *Decline* and its place in the New Musical Theories and Fantasies, see William Drabkin, "Schenker's 'Decline': An Introduction," *Music Analysis* 24, nos. 1–2 (March–July 2005): 3–33.

❧ Schenker to Cotta (letter), November 8, 1905
CA 1–2

Dear Sir,

Dr. Wilhelm Goldbaum[1] has agreed to provide any information regarding me personally or my work as an artist. In referring you to him, I take the liberty of putting the following proposal to you:

I have written a book entitled "New Musical Theories and Fantasies by an Artist,"[2] and should be greatly honored if you would do me the favor of accepting this in your highly esteemed publishing house on commision.[3]

First let me explain my anonymity.[4] A critical edition of C. P. E. Bach, published by order of Universal Edition here, to which I have written a supplementary book, *A Contribution to the Study of Ornamentation*, has had such success with the press and public that, in accordance with a long-standing human foible, hostile opinions have suddenly been expressed about my work as a composer, despite its successes in performance, and despite the fact that firms such as Simrock, Breitkopf & Härtel, Weinberger, etc. have published my works. So as not to jeopardize my future work, I elected to assume anonymity for the time being.

Moreover, as a harmony textbook with a continuously reasoned scholarly text subdivided into short paragraphs, my book includes some commentary sections containing quite robust criticisms of modern dilettantism, for example of the alleged "mastery" of Bruckner, Strauss, Reger, etc.[5] These criticisms, however, far from being merely asserted in journalistic fashion, are bolstered by arguments theoretical in nature. Now, it was important to me to let the dust from these attacks settle, in order not to be disturbed while writing volume 2, a *Psychology and Critique of Counterpoint, Based on New Principles*.

At the same time, precisely in view of these attacks, it seemed advisable to select a neutral publishing house that had not printed Bruckner, Strauss, etc. It is for this reason that I was advised here—where the book, despite all the secrecy, is awaited with great excitement by specialists, disciples, and pupils, as Dr. Goldbaum can certainly attest—that I should turn to you with a request for inclusion in your commission-publishing house.[6]

This I do herewith, asking you at the same time in the first place to let me have an answer in principle.

I should be greatly indebted if you would be so kind as to bear in mind that I am anxious to see the book in print as soon as possible.

      With kind regards,
        I remain,
          Dr. Heinrich Schenker

---

[1] Dr. Wilhelm Goldbaum: perhaps editor at the *Neue freie Presse* (*Lehmann's allgemeiner Wohnungs-Anzeiger* 1906), he helped Schenker with aspects of the volume (see below).

[2] The formulation "New Musical Theories and Fantasies" was, if the correspondence and contract are to be believed, intended as a volume title at this stage. The title of volume 1 emerged as *Theory of Harmony*, and thereafter "New Musical Theories and Fantasies" was adopted as the series title.

[3] "on commission": This phrase refers to a business arrangement—properly called "commission publishing house" (*Kommissionsverlag*)—whereby a work was undertaken by the publisher and full accounts were rendered to the author, and upon receiving bills the author would advance the necessary sums, or—as in the case of Schenker—call on his patron to do so.

[4] For the first edition authorship was given on the title page as "by an Artist." In December 1907 Karl Grunsky inquired of Cotta as to the identity of the author and whether in his forthcoming review for the *Schwäbische Merkur* he might divulge it. Schenker instructed Cotta not to disclose his name. On June 5, 1908, Schenker decided that his name should be placed on the title page of *Counterpoint 1*, and in due course anonymity was finally lifted for the second edition of *Theory of Harmony* (1910).

[5] Only two of the five passages alluded to here are included in the abridged English translation: *Harmony*, 174 (Reger omitted), 208 (Bruckner omitted), 285–87 (Bruckner), 220 fn. 3 (Strauss), 226 (Strauss omitted) (Ger.: 220–23 fn. 1 (Reger), 273–77, 376–78 (Bruckner), 291–93 fn. 1, 299–304 (Strauss)).

[6] Schenker had approached Universal Edition, who rejected the proposed work on April 13, 1905, and again in the autumn, when he met with a temporizing response on October 21. Between the two approaches he turned to Breitkopf & Härtel on June 23, and they rejected the book on September 6.

Cotta to Schenker (letter), November 9, 1905
OJ 9/31, [1] (= CA 3)

HEIRS OF J. G. COTTA'S BOOK DEALERSHIP
STUTTGART AND BERLIN

November 9, 1905

Dear Sir,

Thank you very much for the kind proposal of your book New Musical Theories and Fantasies, by an Artist, contained in your letter. We must however, with regret, inform you that we are not in a position to contend for the publication of the work because we are already overextended with numerous other undertakings.

Respectfully yours,
Heirs of J. G. Cotta's Bookdealership

Cotta to Eugen d'Albert (letter), November 14, 1905
OJ 9/31, [2]

Mr Eugène d'Albert, Dresden on the Elbe,
         Hospice Hotel, Zinzendorfstrasse

Highly revered Sir,

In receipt of your kind letter of yesterday, we are happy to tell you we are much inclined, given the circumstances of which you tell us, to issue Dr. Heinrich Schenker's new book in our publishing house. The fact that you, highly revered Sir, have undertaken to intercede is for us a mark of its literary and artistic worth, and prompts us to ask Dr. Schenker to send us the manuscript, since we had responded to his letter of proposal of the 8th of this month that we had regretfully to decline on account of our being overburdened with work on hand. Unless you advise us to the contrary, we will now write to him saying <u>that, your having drawn his qualities to our attention once again, we should now like him to submit his material</u>.

Before reaching a definitive decision, which could occur quickly, we must however certainly familiarize ourselves with its content, because Dr. Schenker himself wrote to us that its text "contains quite robust criticisms of the alleged mastery of various composers." We are most unlikely to have any objection to these, but we would still like to look through the manuscript in any case, before we reach a contractual agreement.

We remain, with the greatest respect

Yours truly,
Heirs of J. G. Cotta's Book Dealership

❧ Cotta to Schenker (letter), November 15, 1905
OJ 9/31, [3] (= CA 4)

Dear Sir,

Mr. Eugen d'Albert, with whom we enjoy good business relations, has drawn our attention favorably to your work "New Musical Theories and Fantasies, by an Artist" after we had been obliged to answer your recent direct inquiries in the negative on account of the heavy demands of other undertakings. In view of this change of circumstances, we are, however, now disposed to take your kind proposal further, and accordingly ask you to send your manuscript to us for inspection.

With kind regards,
Heirs of J. G. Cotta's Book Dealership

❧ Schenker to Cotta (letter), November 22, 1905
CA 5–6

Dear Sir,

I am delighted at the latest welcome turn of events, and take the liberty of submitting to you herewith my manuscript for your inspection.

The only thing I have held back is the Afterword, so that I can give it a second reworking. It is about one gathering long, and deals with the cyclic technique[1]—regrettably now lost—of our great masters.

If I may at this point express one wish, it is that you not let too many specialists examine my manuscript. The issue is really one of the priority of my idea, which I should like to be sure is safeguarded as completely as possible through the commission. In particular, I fear lest Professor Riemann or any "Riemannian" might get his hands on it. It is precisely against "musical mathematics" as represented by Riemann that my book is expressly directed. No one in the world is more eager than Professor Riemann to appropriate every new idea to himself alone, to present it as coming from himself alone. He currently commands the market place, and no longer allows anyone even a small patch.

Please do not keep me waiting too long for your decision.

I am also enclosing the table of contents of the book in a typewritten copy, so as to facilitate control of the paragraphs and marginal rubrics (and how they are to be printed).

With kind regards,
Yours,
H. Schenker

---

[1] "Cyclic form" was Schenker's term at this period for first-movement sonata form having three parts (exposition, development, recapitulation), the first and third parts themselves comprising three thematic groups, hence tripartite at two levels. The form, or technique, is fully described in "Decline of the Art of Composition" (the unpublished later iteration of the Afterword), where the non-schematic nature of

this organization of material is stressed, in contrast to Riemann's alleged schematic view of the form.

❧ Cotta to Schenker (letter), December 5, 1905
OJ 9/31, [4] (= CA 7–8)

Dear Sir,
   Since the arrival of your manuscript "New Musical Theories and Fantasies, by an Artist," for the dispatching of which our grateful thanks, we have investigated the matter thoroughly, and can now inform you that we are happily prepared to take on the commissioning publication. We have set down the conditions that we propose to you in the enclosed draft of a publishing contract.[1]
   In addition to this, we note that the payment incumbent on you according to clause 3 ought to amount to about 3,100 marks. This figure is however based only on an entirely approximate estimate, since your manuscript presents considerable difficulties for precise calculation. The printers estimate the extent as twenty-five gatherings, with an Afterword of one gathering still to come,[2] according to your kind letter of the 22nd of this month. Your takings upon sale of the edition would—at any rate, on the basis of a provisional estimate—amount to around 5,252 marks. With all of these figures we must, as said before, add the proviso that the final yield will vary above or below the estimate.
   In awaiting with interest your esteemed response to our proposals above, we remain
                    with kind regards,
              Heirs of J. G. Cotta's Bookdealership
   A copy of the contract with our signature will be sent to you as soon as we have received the enclosed copy back from you completed.

[1] CA [205], not given here, is an excerpted copy of the full contract.
[2] 26 gatherings: the eventual volume comprises 30 [x + 1–29] gatherings of 16 pages each = XVI + 464 = 480 pages.

❧ Schenker to Cotta (letter), February 5, 1906
CA 12–13

Dear Sir,
   I confirm with thanks receipt of the proofs and of your letter of the 27th of last month.[1] I will send on the examples that you require as soon as I possibly can.
   As concerns the setting of the music examples,[2] while I can well appreciate your plan to enhance the outward appearance of the many examples by placing them separately from the text, I have nevertheless, after careful consideration, come to the conclusion that it would be preferable to locate them where they are actually

discussed, in order to avoid the doubly undesirable situation of their occurring too early (to my mind disturbingly so), and on the other hand of the reader then being obliged to leaf back to them. However, in order to come some way toward the right idea conveyed by your manner of setting, I am considering—for reasons of necessity and feasibility, if nothing else—separating the examples by interspersing short explanations.

The best place to identify the composer of any given example is obviously, in my view, <u>directly above the example</u>, in the right-hand corner.

The explanations of the examples could then be set in different, <u>smaller</u> type.[3]

In the four gatherings of proofs that have so far reached me, I have myself carried out the change outlined above in red ink, so as to alert the typesetter.

Where the title is given on each gathering, <u>my name must be removed</u>, for reasons of anonymity.

To get back to your esteemed letter: it will clearly be more practicable if you will very kindly make the manuscript of the relevant passages available to me for a short time so as to prevent any errors from creeping in as regards the <u>extent</u> of the missing examples.

Enclosed are the first two gatherings of proofs, for which more corrections were needed than had perhaps been expected on account of the change in layout—and also on account of the large size of the notation and the small format. It is precisely this situation that inclines me toward caution and prompts me to ask if you would very kindly first send me galley-proofs rather than gatherings in page make-up.

For the rest, gatherings 3 and 4, which will follow shortly, show that as the volume proceeds the corrections should not be so extremely numerous as they are in the first two gatherings.

With kind regards,
    Yours truly,
        H. Schenker

---

[1] That letter contained a list of missing music examples.

[2] "setting": Cotta used single-impression typesetting for music (i.e. small pieces of metal type combining note-heads, stems, and stavelines: a system developed by Breitkopf in the 1750s), rather than engraving (as used for most of Schenker's later publications).

[3] The book as published drops into a smaller type in the main text (as apart from footnotes) in two situations: (a) brief linking explanatory text between music examples, (b) longer sections labeled "Note" (*Anmerkung*) which deal with specific issues, e.g. the nature of horizontal line, scale-step, polyphony, and monody.

❦ Diary entry, between May 1 and 22, 1906

Alphons von Rothschild[1] guarantees his financial support of the work.

---

[1] Rothschild eventually paid 4,300.30 marks for the publishing costs of *Theory of Harmony*.

Schenker to Cotta (letter), May 29, 1906
CA 25

Dear Sir,

Herewith I send you the corrected proofs for the final gatherings of Part I, and I seize this opportunity to broach with you the idea as to whether it might not be appropriate to produce Part I on its own as the first volume (1). You see, the Afterword is likely, in the enlarged scope of the work, to amount to five to seven gatherings[1] and might perhaps therefore very suitably make up a second volume if put together with Part II. However, I leave the settlement of this proposal entirely to your professional judgment.

At all events, I ask you please to send me further galley-proofs. It would be very convenient if I could have finished correcting Part II by the end of June.[2] I should be greatly indebted to you for this.

    With kind regards,
    Yours truly,
    H. Schenker

---

[1] The Afterword, eventually entitled "The Decline of the Art of Composition—a Technical-Critical Study," was never published, but survives in a typescript draft with Schenker's corrections. For an edition with translation by William Drabkin, see *Music Analysis* 24, nos. 1–2 (March–July 2005): 33–232.

[2] Schenker, who normally spent the summer months in the Tyrol, departed on July 10, 1906, for Ötz.

Cotta to Schenker (letter), May 31, 1906
OJ 9/31, [8] (= CA 26)

Dear Sir,

We confirm receipt of your esteemed letter of the 29th of this month with grateful thanks, as too of corrected proofs for the end of Part I of your book Musical Theories and Improvisations [sic]. We should like, for technical and commercial reasons relating to the book trade, to advise against your suggestion of dividing the book into two. We gather from your esteemed communication that the Afterword originally estimated at one gathering will now occupy five to seven gatherings. Not only will the sum named by us provisionally for production costs at the initial costing be considerably exceeded by the far-reaching increase in extent now envisioned, but also the high shop price brought about through this will have a deleterious effect on the sales of the work. Even if the question of costs touches only you directly, we would emphatically not like to conceal our misgivings from you, and recommend you to restrict the extent of the Afterword if at all possible.

In accordance with your wishes, we will speed up as far as possible the sending of further galley-proofs.

                    With kind regards,
            Heirs of J. G. Cotta's Bookdealership

❧ Schenker to Cotta (letter), June 4, 1906
CA 27

Dear Sir,

I am most grateful for your kind cautionary letter of May 31. One volume let it be, then. But I have now decided to publish the Afterword separately under some such title as "Beethoven or Wagner?: An Afterword to the New Musical Theories and Fantasies." Don't you think that is the best way forward, seeing how great a store I set by the Afterword, and how impracticable—indeed even undesirable, considering the views it expresses—a reduction is at this stage? A statement at the end of the main work will also alert the reader to the Afterword, to be published separately but simultaneously, and vice versa.[1] Please let me know whether this plan is acceptable to you.

But let me yet again ask you to give me the opportunity to finish at least the <u>music examples to Part II</u>. I should much prefer to go through these once again correcting them on the originals themselves; and since I should like to get out of Vienna at the end of June, weary as I shall be from the term's teaching and my work, it would be convenient to be able to use my own library. In the country it would be virtually impossible to carry out the corrections of the music examples, since I by no means have in my head which works are quoted in Part II, and therefore these would perhaps have to be taken with me. Might it perhaps be possible for you very kindly to keep this in mind?

            With grateful thanks once again, I remain
                With kind regards,
                    H. Schenker

---

[1] The announcement in the *Theory of Harmony* appears in the Foreword, on p. vii: "For the same reason, I will not neglect, before the publication of my *Psychology of Counterpoint* and to reinforce and put into practice the present *Theory of Harmony*, to publish a supplementary text entitled 'The Decline of the Art of Composition—a Technical-Critical Study.'"

❧ Cotta to Schenker (letter), June 5, 1906
OJ 9/31, [9] (=CA 28)

Dear Sir,

We are grateful for your esteemed letter of the 4th of this month, from which we gather that you have in mind separating the Afterword from the main work, Musical Theories and Fantasies, and publishing it under separate title, along the lines of "Beethoven or Wagner." Since you lay great stress on the Afterword, considering the views it expresses, we agree with your opinion. However, we would strenuously advise you against releasing the Afterword and the main work simultaneously, since we are convinced that this is less than advantageous to the sales of the main work. Conversely, there would be nothing against publication of the Afterword perhaps six months or a longer period of time after the appearance of the main work. The separate appearance of the individual parts is very common, especially in scholarly works, and by this means the part appearing later as a rule helps promote the sales of the earlier part by renewing attention in it.

We will gladly comply as far as possible with your wish to receive the music examples of Part II for correction no later than the end of June. The printers have promised to supply text that includes music examples within it by the end of this month; music examples that appear without text (as appendix), on the other hand, will not finish being set until the beginning of July. In any case, we will do everything in our power to speed up completion.[1]

 With kind regards,
 Heirs of J. G. Cotta's Bookdealership

---

[1] Proof corrections continued until the beginning of November. On September 24 Cotta wrote that in view of the increased extent of the volume and "the extraordinarily numerous and extensive corrections that in places [...] are tantamount to their having to be reset from scratch," the costs that Schenker would have to bear would be considerably greater than estimated.

❧ Diary entry, September 21, 1906

In the evening some clever advice received from Dr. Goldbaum concerning the title page and the final chapter.

❧ Schenker to Cotta (letter), October 1, 1906
CA 41–42

Dear Sir,

In receipt of your esteemed letter of September 24, 1906, let me make it plain that I would of course be prepared to honor the additional work that has been created.

What I am particularly concerned to do, however, is to make clear to you that I must, not least for practical, commercial reasons, incorporate the material that has been reserved for the Afterword in some form into the work. In view of the fact that this part (which, moreover, I will present not as an Afterword but as an organically integrated third and last section of the "Practical Part"[1]) includes virtually no music examples, and hence its printing could be done very quickly, I take the liberty of asking you to be patient with me and my book just a little longer. I am convinced that, despite this, it will still be possible for the book to appear on the right side of Christmas, since all the conceptual work is done.

What is lacking in writings of all kinds about music (manuals, guides, historical works, and the like) in Germany and everywhere else is a mode of criticism for works of art that is based on compositional factors. What one usually reads and hears is a journalism ignorant of artistic matters; or—as in the case of artists and theorists—a way of thinking that is theoretically pretentious, but (because based on false theories) wholly erroneous, sometimes pedantic, sometimes obsequious. The clamor among the German public for guidance in the created values appears to me, precisely now when the dilettantism of those who compose attracts huge crowds, to be at its most intense, though I have no desire to inquire whether that clamor betokens merely the usual curiosity or a higher engagement with art. The proof of this lies in the keen demand for books of all kinds on music—something that is undeniable. However, the fact that this demand has not hitherto resulted in any extraordinary commercial success on the part of any published book is not to be attributed to the public, but rather to the works themselves, which, as I have already said above, are utterly inartistic and naïve. The abstractions from the nature and practice of our greatest masters, and the redeployment of these, have proved so inadequate that masters such as Brahms and Beethoven are dragged down to the level of Mahler, Reger, etc., without realization that the latter are dilettantes, and far, far from being artists, let alone "masters."

In the course of Parts I and II of my book, while constantly seeking the way toward art, I have frequently had occasion to devise specific arguments against modern dilettantism. That is, I have forged the weapons with my own hands in order to be able to commence battle, so it is only natural that I should burn to make use of those weapons. I have frequently been invited, in Vienna, Berlin, and elsewhere, to account for my disapproval of modern musical goings-on in lectures and essays. I have turned down all such requests because the public, its hearing and reading in so parlous a state, could never have followed me. Now at last I have an opportunity to offer what has been quite widely awaited from me in an organic form for the use of the public, artists, and critics. Should I let this unique opportunity go? How could I possibly do that?! I take it as my moral duty to say what I know, and not to be deterred by costs and other such considerations. And who knows whether it will not be just the final section that will be the principal attraction for most of my readers?

For this reason, I ask you to be patient with me just a little longer. Within a day or two I will present you with about a third of the final section, together with the title page of the book and the preliminary announcement for which you ask.

    With kind regards,
      Yours truly,
        H. Schenker

---

[1] The book as published is divided into two large sections entitled "I. Theoretical Part" and "II. Practical Part." The latter is subdivided into five sections, none of which corresponds to the material designated at this time as the Afterword. By September 1907 Schenker had decided to publish the latter material as volume 3 of New Musical Theories and Fantasies, after volume 2, *Counterpoint* (which was still envisioned as a single volume), had been published, under the title *The Decline of the Art of Composition*.

⁋ Cotta to Schenker (letter), October 2, 1906
OJ 9/31, [13] (=CA 43)

Dear Sir,

From your esteemed letter of the 1st of the month we understand that you wish your Afterword to be published directly in conjunction with the main work, Theories and Fantasies, and in one volume with the latter. Permit us to take this opportunity of repeating our request of May 31: to restrict the extent of the Afterword as far as possible, not only so as not to jeopardize sales by necessitating an insupportable price, but also in the interests of completion well before Christmas. The latter reason in particular has in the meantime become still more urgent! If we wish to spare the book from being submerged in the flood of literary Christmas gift items, then it must be sent in the first week of November. That way, it will reach the retail booksellers in mid-November and can be made available to interested readers just before the onslaught of the Christmas trade. Any new scholarly items that appear at the end of November or even as late as December languish unnoticed in the majority of the retail stores until after Christmas. And since shortly after Christmas we begin the run-up to the impending Easter book fair accounting, they may be returned to the publisher at the next fair.

Rest assured that our urgings are made solely with a view to serving the interests of your book to the full extent in our powers. In accordance with your esteemed letter, we hope to receive with all haste the manuscript still lacking, and remain

        With kind regards,
          Yours truly,
       Heirs to J. G. Cotta's Bookdealership

⁋ Diary entry, October 9, 1906

Finalizing of the title page with the help of Dr. W. Goldbaum and Seligmann.[1]

---

[1] Adalbert Franz Seligmann (1862–1945): Austrian art critic, writer, and painter, who was at this time writing for several newspapers, including the *Neue freie Presse*, and who corresponded extensively with Schenker between 1902 and Schenker's death.

⁋ Cotta to Schenker (letter with invoice), November 10, 1906
CA 54–55

Dear Sir,

We have the honor today of informing you that your book Musical Theories and Fantasies is finished and is ready to be shipped out to the book trade. Of the contractually agreed twelve free copies, we are dispatching ten paperbound to you by the same post. Two bound copies will follow at the beginning of next week.

In accordance with the agreements made between us, we enclose herewith our account of the production costs as well as of the advertising, marketing, and commercial costs, to a total of 4,300.30 marks.

We venture to express our hope that the finished product may meet with your approval, and the book moreover with great success.

With kind regards,
Heirs of J. G. Cotta's Bookdealership

Dr. Heinrich Schenker, <u>Vienna III</u>
<u>Musical Theories and Fantasies, volume I</u>
Print-run 1,100, extent 39¾ gatherings

Typesetting	M.	1,631.15
Proof corrections	M.	847.55
Printing	M.	379.–
Dust jacket	M.	23.40
Paper	M.	456.30
Stitching and binding	M.	202.–
Advertisements	M.	300.–
Marketing and Commercial outlays	M.	560.90
[Total:]	M.	4,300.30

❧ Diary entries, November 20 and 22, 1906

[November 20:] Telegram to Rothschild: price. Utter despair and tension!

[November 22:] 4,300 marks received from Rothschild, together with letter in his own hand about sending the sum of money.

❧ Rothschild to Cotta (telegram), November 22[?], 1906

CA 57

j g cotta bookdealership stuttgart

am sending you by today's post for the account of dr heinrich schenker a check for four thousand three hundred marks 30 pfennigs = rothschild =

Cotta to Schenker (letter), November 26, 1906
OJ 12/27, [1]

Dear Sir,
We herewith acknowledge with thanks the arrival of the amount of 4,300.30 marks via the banking house of Freiherr von Rothschild, Vienna, with which we have fully discharged our notification of the 10th of this month. We dispatched the review copies indicated by you on the 23rd of the month.[1]

>With kind regards,
>pp. Heirs of J. G. Cotta's Bookdealership
>H. Kurz

[1] Schenker requested review copies to be sent to Robert Hirschfeld, Julius Korngold, Max Kalbeck, Hans Liebstöckl, Ludwig Karpath, Richard Robert, and Max Graf, and complimentary copies to Eugen d'Albert and Karl Goldmark.

Diary entry, December 2, 1906

At Baron Alphons's place. Thanks for his support. Non-committal response regarding volume 2.[1]

[1] Rothschild did in due course pay the costs of *Counterpoint 1*, though five months late, in March 1911. Schenker began submitting manuscript for *Counterpoint* on September 23, 1908. Proofs circulated between October 1908 and summer of 1910, and Schenker received his free copies of *Counterpoint 1* on October 4. The first batch of manuscript for *Counterpoint 2* was delivered to Cotta on October 4, 1920.

Cotta to Schenker (letter), October 5, 1920
OJ 9/31, [45] (= CA 181–182)

Dear Dr. [Schenker],
We have the honor of informing you that Mr. Otto Vrieslander delivered the manuscript of Section 3 (continuation of the New Musical Theories and Fantasies, volume 2, first [sic] half-volume) to us yesterday. The manuscript comprises 320 written sides, and does not yet, according to Mr. Vrieslander, represent the conclusion in its entirety. Instead, the latter should follow in a short while, but Mr. Vrieslander was unable to give us a more precise idea of the date on which this might occur.
For us to make a start on printing the present manuscript is for several different reasons out of the question at this time. First and foremost, confirmation would be required that the conditions of publication as set out in our publishing contract of December 1905 can apply also for the continuation of your work. We can

determine the production costs, which would have to be calculated on the basis of these conditions, only once the manuscript in its complete, definitive form is in our hands. We should just like to point out that these production costs will be incomparably higher under current difficult conditions than was the case for volumes 1 and 2/1 of your work, and, moreover, that for the same reasons the shop price of 35 pfennigs per printed gathering set in §2 of our publishing contract is no longer remotely adequate. To subdivide the conclusion of your work yet again by publishing the section that Mr. Vrieslander has brought us now, then later to publish the conclusion as an appendage to this (and to the pagination, also) when the latter comes to hand, we do not, in view of uncertainty, consider opportune. The long gap between the appearance of volumes 1 and 2/1, and the even longer time that has elapsed since the appearance of 2/1, have undoubtedly had an adverse effect on the sales of your work. This effect would be exacerbated if we were now to publish what is admittedly a continuation but only an incomplete continuation and still not the completion of the work.

We should like therefore to recommend that you send us as soon as possible the manuscript of the conclusion, which is still lacking. Only then can we get down to the necessary calculations on the basis of which you will be in a position to make your further decisions.

We will meanwhile hold the manuscript that Mr. Vrieslander brought us in our safe-keeping.

       With kind regards,
        Yours truly,
        Heirs of the J. G. Cotta's Bookdealership

Schenker to Cotta (letter), November 6, 1920
CA 183–184

Dear Sir,

A regrettable misunderstanding has arisen. What I have submitted to you through Mr. Otto Vrieslander is the <u>conclusion</u> of my *Counterpoint*, volume 2.

My theory of counterpoint is, in this form, completely self-sufficient, quite as much as in all passable manuals of counterpoint, such as, for example, Bellermann, Cherubini, Riemann, etc., etc. In fact, I exceed the customary scope by several sections.

I could be struck dead at this culminating moment and you would not find anyone who could speak of my counterpoint theory as a torso. Nobody has even the faintest idea that beyond my *Counterpoint* something, the most important thing of all, remains still to be said, and yet that it is no longer counterpoint as such.

There is thus nothing to prevent you from printing the manuscript that was delivered to you; on the contrary, now that it is complete at last, my *Counterpoint* will undoubtedly acquire as many friends as the other textbooks.

In the light of this, I now invite new proposals from you, since no doubt the old purchase price is out of date.

In view of the fact that sales to date have remained low, it would be advisable to print only 500 copies. While having the advantage of lower costs for me, this would keep open the possibility of my eventually combining what I shall send you later with this section, and this would emphasize the main idea extraordinarily well. But, as I have already said, since nobody knows a thing about what I shall be sending you, sales of the completed *Counterpoint* will remain unaffected by it. In view of this future possibility, the section submitted for printing should appear only stitched.

I told Mr. Vrieslander himself all of this, but unfortunately he appears not to have made it sufficiently clear to you.

I should be obliged to you, my dear sir, if you would put your new proposals to me, including letting me know the approximate number of gatherings and the costs.

  With kind regards,
   Yours truly,
    Dr. Heinrich Schenker

Cotta to Schenker (letter), November 16, 1920
CA 185–187

Dear Dr. [Schenker],

We return today to the esteemed letter with which you replied to our letter of October 5.

We take it from your letter that the manuscript delivered to us by Mr. Vrieslander in fact represents the conclusion of volume 2 of your Musical Theories and Fantasies, i.e. of your *Counterpoint*. Nevertheless, you wish to reserve the right to append an Afterword to this, the second half-volume of volume 2, at a later stage. For this reason, you wish volume 2/2 to be issued in an edition of 500 copies, only stitched.

On the strength of this, we have now carried out a calculation on the basis of the manuscript in our hands. In the typographical arrangement used hitherto, this yields a generous 20 printed gatherings.[1] Whereas volume 1, produced in 1906, with a scope of 30 printed gatherings and an edition of 1,100 copies, generated total costs in the amount of 4,300.30 marks, and volume 2/1, printed in 1910, with roughly the same extent and likewise an edition of 1,100 copies cost 3,859.15 marks, the production and marketing costs as well as the out-of-pocket expenses for volume 2/2, with an extent of only c. 20 gatherings and an edition of 500 are estimated in the region of 24,000 marks! In this connection, we should point out that this total is reckoned on the basis of current prices, that these prices are however subject to fluctuation (which, with conditions as they are, are bound in the future only to rise), and that we must on that account reserve the right expressly to change this calculation. We should furthermore emphasize that a paper is available to us that we could still procure at a markedly low price, and that we have entered our business expenses into the calculation at a rate considerably below what has for some time now been necessary and customary for us.

The high level of production costs would—as is easy to see—inevitably result in an altogether uncommonly high shop price, so long as one has in mind getting a profit margin, however modest, out of it. The shop price in this case could not be set lower than 80 marks per stitched copy!

Then again, this is a price that, with regard to the extent of 20 gatherings, must be viewed as excessively high, one that would, precisely on account of this circumstance, bring discredit upon the publishing house of Cotta. We are unable therefore to agree to publish the book under these conditions.

The highest price that we consider viable and on which we could proceed with our firm would be 45 marks. At this level, however, the takings from sales fall short of the total production costs and expenses, which, as stated above, are predicted to be around 24,000 marks; instead, there would be an uncovered over-run of some 10,000 marks.

In order to alleviate this loss for you, we are prepared, for our part, to go some way to accommodate you by forgoing any share in the takings from the book, but rather to surrender these exclusively and at their full value to you. As an exception in this case, we will content ourselves with the approximate recovery of our expenses, which have however already been calculated into the previously cited total of production costs of c. 24,000 marks.

On the other hand, you will understand if, faced with radically changed working conditions that require us each time to make prompt fulfillment of our obligations to our suppliers, we propose to you an alteration to §3 of our publishing contract to the effect that half of the total production costs, 12,000 marks, is payable to us in cash before printing, the other half fourteen days after completion of the book.

We leave it entirely to your discretion whether you wish us to produce volume 2/2 under these terms and look forward with interest to your valued response.

   With kind regards,
   Heirs of the J. G. Cotta's Bookdealership

---

[1] *Counterpoint 2* as eventually published comprised one unsigned gathering of 26 unnumbered pages + 16 (1–16) of 16 pages + one (17) of 8 pages = 290 pages.

❧ Schenker to Cotta (letter), January 23, 1921
CA 188

Dear Sir,

Your esteemed letter of mid-November 1920 was for me uncommon evidence of a high-minded readiness to accommodate for which I was all the more grateful in that it concerned not me as a person but the cause espoused through me. In my joyous first reaction, I overestimated the financial possibilities available to me. That is to say, I myself, as an artist wholly without means, did not originally come into the equation; but sadly I had to tell myself that there can be no thought of help from foreign sources, especially given the precariousness of exchange rates nowadays. Even in those days, Baron Dr. Rothschild, although a pupil of mine for several years, was unable to resist remarking that the 3,000–4,000 marks (which was surely an infinitesimal sum for him) was "a lot of money." My pride would not permit me to go back to him, especially since I could point to having had some little "success," as he understands it. Since no other ways forward had emerged, I saw the urgent completion of my work jeopardized.

In this difficult position, I opened my heart to my Viennese publisher, Director E. Hertzka. And lo!, he surprised me with an immediate offer to cover the costs not only of the second half-volume but also all further volumes (of the serial work, to which my *Theory of Form*, my *Decline of the Art of Composition*, etc. are still to be added) himself. His only condition is that he also be able to take over the volumes of this work that have already appeared. Since he already has published so many works of mine, e.g. the monograph on Beethoven's Ninth Symphony, works on C. P. E. Bach, the *Last Five Sonatas of Beethoven in an Elucidatory Edition*, etc., and also recently the series *Little Library*, not to mention collected editions of the sonatas of Beethoven as well as of Mozart and Haydn,[1] he anticipates such great success from the publicity for all these works that he dares take on the great risk (he puts a figure of 1½ million kronen on it, at today's values) attached to this comprehensive theoretical work.

You can see, my dear Sir, that with this offer a prospect opens up that relieves me of the principal worry of my life. For even if I never have in mind drawing financial profit from the work, it is a matter of the deepest concern to me that what I alone can say today be sayable on the broadest possible front, and that it must be said in the interests of the art of music.

The evidence already evinced of your great readiness to accommodate encourages me to come to you with an entreaty to dispense altogether not only with a renewal of our contract but also with the original commission-publishing house. So continually evolving a work may indeed in any case have been only a burden to you, uncompensated by any kind of advantages. I therefore hope that you will have no further difficulties in granting my request. It is part of my nature—which is expressed also in my works, hence needs no emphasizing—that I shall remain always duly grateful to you for all the kindnesses you have shown me in the past.

In the event of your agreeing to this, it would be up to the publishing house to settle the business side. The long delay, which has in any case hampered (as a result of wartime conditions, as also of the economic conditions today) the appearance of the latest volume, makes it my duty to implore you not to delay making your decision.

      With kind regards,
      Yours truly,
         Dr. H. Schenker

---

[1] Planned editions of the Haydn and Mozart piano sonatas did not materialize.

Cotta to Schenker (letter), February 5, 1921
OJ 9/31, [46] (= CA 189–190)

Dear Dr. [Schenker],

We refer to your esteemed letter of the 23rd of last month, bringing us the news that you have found a patron in the person of your Viennese publisher, Director E. Hertzka, who will take entirely upon himself the risk associated with the continuation of your work *New Musical Theories and Fantasies*. We congratulate you unreservedly upon this solution to your difficulties, highly propitious as it is for you.

Sorry though we are to sever our link with your work, which we have been handling in our publishing house for fifteen years now and value highly, we must of course unquestionably step aside in the face of the rare, propitious offer that has been made to you from the other quarter. Therefore, in accordance with your wish, we declare ourselves willing to cancel our commission-publishing-house contract of 1905 and our related agreements of 1908–09, and to return to you the stocks in hand of your two volumes. We ask you to let us know to whom to send these stocks (freight costs to be charged).[1] We will then have a final account sent to you.

We will arrange forthwith for the manuscript of Section III that Mr. Otto Vrieslander delivered to us last October to be returned to you as a registered packet insured for 3,000 marks.

With kind regards,
Heirs of J. G. Cotta's Bookdealership

---

[1] Stocks of volumes 1 and 2/2 were transferred two weeks later. Volume 2/2 was printed, and delivered to the publisher on November 30, 1922, Universal Edition's reeditions of volumes 1 and 2/1 had been printed already by February 21, 1921 (eleven copies of 2/1 and 431 of 2/2 were seized by the Gestapo on March 26, 1940; presumably stocks of *Theory of Harmony* had been exhausted; UE Archive, publication print book).

7
Otto Erich Deutsch
and the "Moonlight" Sonata Facsimile

SCHENKER'S correspondence with Otto Erich Deutsch is among his largest. The earliest known letter from Deutsch dates from June 25, 1913;[1] but prior to this, in late 1912, both were apparently speakers at a public lecture series at the Society of the Friends of Music,[2] and in addition Schenker's diary entry for February 24, 1913, reports an evening spent with Deutsch following a lecture by Schenker's pupil Sofie Deutsch.[3] The correspondence reached its peak in the late 1920s and early 1930s and mostly concerns Schenker's publications; it also includes numerous social invitations, which attest to an increasingly close relationship between the Schenkers and the Deutsches. After Heinrich's death, the Deutsches remained close to Jeanette, and Otto Erich's last known letter to Jeanette, in which he mentions his plans to visit London and New York, is dated May 3, 1939. In the event, Deutsch's Jewish ancestry compelled him to flee Austria, and he lived in England from 1939 to 1951 (initially interned as an "enemy alien"[4]) before returning to Vienna.

The selection of correspondence presented here dates from the early 1920s— happier times for both couples. The Schenkers had finally been able to marry in November, 1919, and Otto Erich and Hanna were to have their son Franz Peter in the following July. These years also saw the first significant scholarly collaboration between Schenker and Deutsch: the publication in 1921 of a manuscript facsimile of Beethoven's "Moonlight" Sonata as the first volume in the series *Musical Rarities: Viennese Connoisseur Prints*,[5] of which Deutsch was general editor.

By this time Schenker had already published his elucidatory editions of Beethoven's Opp. 109, 110, and 111, and that of Op. 101 and the complete edition of Beethoven's piano sonatas were to appear over the next few years. These editions were rooted in Schenker's study of original manuscripts and first editions, and the elucidatory editions in particular included transcriptions of manuscript sketches and descriptions of autographs, so Schenker was clearly convinced that there was both a need and a demand for this kind of publication. The facsimile edition of the

---

[1] In this letter, Detusch reports on the location of the manuscript collector Carl Meinert.

[2] A press announcement for the lecture series, dated September 15, 1912, is preserved in the Oswald Jonas Memorial Collection in Box 11, folder 22.

[3] See chapter 10. Sofie was unrelated to Otto Erich.

[4] On the internment of Deutsch and others in wartime Britain, see Suzanne Snizek, "The Abyss and the Berries," in *The Impact of Nazism on Twentieth-century Music*, ed. Erik Levi (Vienna: Böhlau, 2014), 197–222.

[5] *Musikalische Seltenheiten: Wiener Liebhaberdrucke*. The series also included facsimiles of works by Haydn, Mozart, Schubert, and Brahms.

"Moonlight" Sonata can be seen as a continuation of his interest in demonstrating the value of composers' autograph manuscripts for the interpretation of their works, as well as being part of an emerging fashion for facsimile editions of composer autographs.[6]

Deutsch, a keen bibliophile and collector of Schubert first editions, was likewise committed to the importance of composers' manuscripts, as well as of historical documents in general; indeed his scholarly reputation today rests on his documentary biographies of Schubert, Handel, and Mozart, and his thematic catalogue of Schubert's works. In Deutsch, then, Schenker had found a natural ally, one who not only offered moral and intellectual support but also had the practical and diplomatic skills that would see Schenker's aim realized.[7] The Deutsch-Schenker partnership—and friendship—grew and lasted because their endeavours and areas of expertise were complementary, and because of Deutsch's respect for and deference to Schenker. In the selection below, we see Detusch actively tracking down and obtaining reproductions of several "Moonlight" sketch leaves, almost as if he were Schenker's research assistant rather than the series editor.

DAVID BRETHERTON

---

[6] For Beethoven alone there were facsimiles from DMV (Munich) of the piano sonatas Opp. III (1922) and 78 (1923), from Kistner & Siegel (Leipzig) of the Ninth Symphony (1924), and from Henri Piazza (Paris) of the "Appassionata" Sonata (1927).

[7] In this regard, consider Deutsch's early role in the founding of the Photogram Archive, recorded in his letter of January 8, 1927 (see chapter 12).

❧ Deutsch to Schenker (letter), January 8, 1920
OJ 10/3, [5]

Dear Professor,

Following consultation with Director Hertzka, I can tell you that he wants to include only facsimiles of Beethoven sonatas in our series of connoisseur prints, and not textually cleaned editions of these works. He asks you and me initially to take on a facsimile of the "Moonlight" Sonata, with accompanying elucidations. For these luxury editions, only 8 percent of the retail price can be offered to the editors (as a maximum); this will still earn us some 1,600 kronen if we assume a print-run of 200 copies at 100 kronen. This is a conservative estimate. If you insist on a fixed fee, I could pay you 1,000 kronen from my own account upon publication of the book. Your work will consist of: the provision of the source material, the wording of the title, the manuscript of your brief commentary (about four landscape pages in large print), and supervision of the proofreading. [You will receive] three complimentary copies of the work.

If, because of the (materially insignificant) competition from the Copenhagen publisher who is also printing a connoisseur edition of the "Moonlight" Sonata,[1] or for more fundamental reasons, you would prefer to produce a facsimile of a different Beethoven sonata, then please send me your new proposal. Likewise, please let me know whether you would also recommend a new edition of the sonata edited by Prieger.[2] Then be so kind as to remind me what you recommended by Mozart.

With respect to Beethoven, you ought to be free to make your own plans for the *Little Library*.[3]

Your *Theory of Harmony* was in fact not in stock in Vienna. Universal Edition gave me inaccurate information about this.

I would note that a royalty of 8 percent of the retail price for a luxury edition, for which the publisher has high costs and the sale price is higher as a result, seems appropriate to me, and that I get much less as an editor. Your collaboration would be an honor for me, not a commercial venture.

        Please give my regards to your dear wife.
        Yours very truly,
        Otto Erich Deutsch

PS I would need the photographs immediately, your manuscript if possible by February 1. Another Schubert volume of mine, a Mozart volume, and a Haydn volume will appear in the first instance.[4]

---

[1] Probably Wilhelm Hansen, the leading Danish music publisher in the twentieth century. No facsimile edition by Hansen of the "Moonlight" Sonata, however, is known to exist.

[2] Erich Prieger had previously published a manuscript facsimile of Beethoven's Piano Sonata in A♭ major, Op. 26 (Bonn: Friedrich Cohen, 1895).

[3] *Kleine Bibliothek*, the working title from 1910 to 1921 for what was to become *Der Tonwille* in 1921.

[4] These volumes in Deutsch's "Viennese Connoisseur Prints" series comprised the autograph scores, respectively, of five early Schubert songs, two rondos by Mozart (K. 485 and K. 511), and twelve Scottish folksong arrangements by Haydn.

Hertzka (UE) to Schenker (letter), January 14, 1920
OC 52/446

Dear Professor,

In receipt of your valued letter of the 9th of this month, I take the liberty of informing you that I am still in Vienna because I have not yet been able to get away on account of the current highly uncertain conditions for travel and the Bavarian rail stoppage. Should the conditions improve to some degree, I have in mind to travel to Frankfurt.[1]

The idea of publishing bibliophile editions of all the Beethoven sonatas is still not achievable at the present time. However, we want in any case to do the "Moonlight" Sonata, and Mr. Otto Erich Deutsch is the general editor of these bibliophile editions. He has also undertaken to reach agreement with you regarding the edition, so you will no doubt be hearing more from him. I have already mentioned that I should very much like to publish afresh the collected Beethoven sonatas in an edition by you,[2] provided that a complete new engraving will not be necessary, since this is altogether out of the question at a time like the present. If we could do this in conjunction with the Little Library, that would of course be highly congenial, and I accept your apportionment, namely 20% of the retail price. To fix the honorarium for the Beethoven edition <u>per page without footnotes</u>, is entirely agreeable to me; I should just like to ask you what supplementary honorarium you want to bring into the equation. — As concerns the prices under consideration for the Little Library, your calculation is illusory these days. The basic costs fluctuate from day to day. In terms of today's prices, one would have in any halfway respectable presentation to reckon on a retail price of 5–8 kronen per sixteen-page gathering.

I am sending you at the same time the contract for Op. 101 and ask you to return the same furnished with your signature, upon which you will receive the first tranche of the stipulated honorarium of 7,500 kronen.

With most cordial greetings,
Yours truly,
Hertzka

---

[1] Hertzka had agreed to pick up photographs from the collector Louis Koch in Frankfurt.

[2] *L. van Beethoven: Klaviersonaten nach den Autographen und Erstdrucken rekonstruiert von Heinrich Schenker*, 4 vols. (Vienna: UE, 1921–23).

❧ Deutsch to Schenker (letter), January 16, 1920

OJ 10/3, [7]

Dear Professor,

I acknowledge with many thanks your postcard of the 14th and your calling card of the 15th of the month, the attachment to which I return herewith. Today I spoke with Director Hertzka, who has already replied to you, and I am writing concurrently to the Board of the Beethoven House in Bonn. Hertzka plans to have more than 200, in fact 500 copies of the Beethoven volume printed, so that your royalty would increase by one-and-a-half times. We are also planning to bring out the volume with French and English texts alongside the German, something which I trust you will endorse. If we have no luck with Bonn we would like to use your other source material, whose publication we also plan, with your consent and cooperation. The Berlin Library and Mr. Koch[1] (in whose possession, I assume, are the manuscripts of Opp. 28, 110, and 111) will probably cause no trouble; nor will Mrs. Wittgenstein[2] (Op. 109). I wrote to my former colleague, the Ukrainian Legation Counselor Dr. Vladimir Zaloziecki, concerning Op. 106, also to Peters in Leipzig concerning Mozart's A minor Rondo, which Dr. Hans Gál is supposed to bring out.

Could we print the measures missing from the beginning and end of the "Moonlight" Sonata autograph on separate pages, as they appear in the first edition, in front of and at the end of the manuscript facsimile? The variants[3] would also have to be reproduced. You are very welcome to say what you want about this correction and the value of the manuscript to all editions. I ask you merely to refrain from polemics in this salon-like situation; your sober observations will be evident to the experts without them, while the foolishness of former editors will be easy to discern.

The cost of new photographs will be borne by Universal Edition.

The Prieger edition,[4] like that of Mozart's *Requiem* (Schnerich),[5] may be reprinted only with the permission of the former editors.

You should not sell yourself too cheaply to Universal Edition or to me, even if you reuse the commentary in the *Little Library*.

I edit the bibliographical and musicological publications for Universal Edition, and I pay the editors myself. In addition to three complimentary copies, you will receive 8 per cent of the retail price of each copy sold. A formal contract will follow.

Allow me to draw your attention to Kinsky's catalogue of autograph manuscripts of the Heyer Museum in Bonn (the Society of the Friends of Music and I each have a copy of it).[6]

Yours very truly,
Otto Erich Deutsch

---

[1] Louis Koch (1862–1932): Frankfurt collector of music autographs and manuscript dealer, who owned (among other manuscripts) the autograph score of Beethoven's Sonata in A major, Op. 101. The Prussian State Library in Berlin owned the autograph scores of Opp. 110 and 111; the score of Op. 28 was in the collection of the Beethoven House, Bonn, in 1904.

[2] Leopoldine Wittgenstein (1850–1926): mother of the pianist Paul Wittgenstein and the philosopher Ludwig Wittgenstein. The autograph of Op. 109 was auctioned in the 1940s and acquired by the Library of Congress, Washington.

[3] By *Varianten*, Deutsch probably means Beethoven's sketches for the sonata, three leaves of which were reproduced in the edition and discussed in Schenker's commentary.

[4] *As dur-Sonate op. 26 von Ludwig van Beethoven: Facsimile*, ed. Erich Prieger (Bonn: Friedrich Cohen, 1895).

[5] *Mozarts Requiem: Nachbildung der Originalhandschrift Cod. 17561 der K. K. Hofbibliothek in Wien in Lichtdruck*, ed. Alfred Schnerich (Vienna: Gesellschaft für Graphische Industrie, 1913).

[6] Georg Kinsky, *Musikhistorisches Museum von Wilhelm Heyer in Cöln: Katalog, IV: Musik-Autographen* (Cologne: Wilhelm Heyer, and Leipzig: Breitkopf & Härtel, 1916).

❦ Deutsch to Schenker (postcard), February 12, 1920
OJ 10/3, [8]

Vienna, II, Valeriestrasse

Dear Dr. [Schenker],

Today I received notification from the Board of the Beethoven House that we may have reproduction rights for the manuscript only in return for a financial share. With the agreement of Director Hertzka, I offered the Society 5% of the retail price. More news to follow.

    Yours truly,
    O. E. Deutsch

❦ Deutsch to Schenker (postcard), June 15, 1920
OJ 10/3, [10]

Dear Professor,

On returning from my trip, I found the Beethoven House's authorization for the reproduction of the C♯ minor Sonata. They also give the name of a Bonn photographer. I would, however, like to spare us having new photographs made, if possible, and therefore ask you to send your white-on-black prints to me or Universal Edition, so that we can determine whether they are satisfactory for reproduction. With best wishes to you and your wife,

    Yours very truly,
    Deutsch

❦ Deutsch to Schenker (postcard), August 5, 1920
OJ 10/3, [13] (Plate 8)

Dear Dr. [Schenker],

I can inform you that Mr. Speyer of London[1] has promised me the photographs of his sketchleaves in the near future. Additionally, I have just seen, in an article by Frimmel in the *Österreichische Rundschau*, that some time ago Mandyczewski published or spoke about another "Moonlight" Sonata sketchleaf, in the possession of Dr. Wilhelm Kux in Vienna.[2] Before I try to get a reproduction of this page too, I ask whether you know of it and would like to have it included.

    With best wishes,
    Yours truly,
    Deutsch

---

[1] Edward Speyer (1834–1929): London-based collector of music autograph manuscripts. (A description of his collection was published in *The Musical Times* of June 1906.)

[2] Wilhelm Kux (1864–1965): Austrian banker and philanthropist, collector of musical autograph manuscripts and instruments.

❧ Deutsch to Schenker (letter), August 16, 1920
OJ 10/3, [14]

Dear Professor,
I thank you for your letter of the 8th of the month and your kind wishes. I wrote to Director Kux and await news from him. Things are moving ahead slowly with Universal Edition, but my lack of time is also to blame. In any case, the Beethoven volume will be published first.[1] Today I received a letter from Speyer in London, in which he writes that he is currently in the countryside, and that this makes it difficult for him to have the sketches photographed. He did however send me a printed facsimile of another page with sketches for the "Moonlight" Sonata, in the Fitzwilliam Museum, Cambridge, which was reproduced in a *Musical Times* Special Supplement on May 1, 1903,[2] with the following comment: "The passage above sketched by Beethoven is in the last movement of his pianoforte sonata … [Op. 27, No. 2], beginning at bar 23." I assume that you do not know this sketchleaf, and I will ask for a photograph from the museum, if you wish. The reproduction, which Mr. Speyer has only lent me, can probably be found in Vienna.
With best wishes to you and your dear wife, I remain,

   Yours truly,
    O. E. Deutsch

[1] That is, Schenker's "Moonlight" will be the first to appear in Deutsch's series of facsimile editions.
[2] The supplement appeared in the March, not the May, 1903, issue of *The Musical Times*.

❧ Deutsch to Schenker (letter), September 13, 1920
OJ 10/3 [15]

Dear Professor,
I thank you most sincerely for your card of the 19th of last month, and ask you to let me know whether, in the manuscript of the "Moonlight" Sonata, thirteen measures are missing from the beginning, as well as the final measures. It seems that the lost cover contained not only the title and final bars, but also the first page of the autograph.
Universal Edition is hoping, if possible, to reproduce two pages of the manuscript on each folio page, one underneath the other, and to have opposite them a page of printed music edited by you. I ask you to comment on whether or not you agree with this proposal.

At the same time, I am writing to Director Kux, who returns your greetings, for permission to have his sketchleaf photographed, as he has already agreed.

Please do not neglect to examine the sketchleaf in *The Musical Times*, so that we can decide whether to make a reproduction of it, too.

With best regards to you and your dear wife,

>Yours truly,
>Deutsch

Deutsch to Schenker (letter), October 1, 1920
OJ 10/3, [16]

Dear Professor,

I take the liberty of enclosing the images of Kux's manuscript; I ask you to study the sketchleaf, then forward it at the earliest opportunity to Universal Edition for reproduction (with an appropriate label).

I am writing to the Cambridge museum today about the sketchleaf there.

>With best wishes,
>Yours truly,
>Deutsch

1 encl. (three photographs)
by registered mail

Deutsch to Schenker (letter), November 6, 1920
OJ 10/3, [17]

Dear Professor,

I take the liberty of enclosing two photographic prints of the "Moonlight" Sonata sketchleaf in the Cambridge Museum, which was reproduced in part in *The Musical Times*.[1] Mr. Speyer of London sent me these photographs and also told me that his own Beethoven sketches, which he has not had photographed, begin with the second part (the development) of the finale, after the double bar, and also treat the second theme in a somewhat varied form.

When you have worked on the enclosed sketchleaf, as well as that of Mr. Kux, please return them to me for reproduction. The production of the entire manuscript is in progress.

>With best wishes,
>Yours truly,
>Deutsch

2 encl.

---

[1] In his diary, Schenker records having received the "Cambridge sketches for the Moonlight Sonata" on November 5, 1920; it is likely that Deutsch's diary record was misdated by a day or two.

♣ Deutsch to Schenker (letter), November 26, 1920
OJ 10/3, [20]

Dear Professor,
    Unfortunately I am only now able to reply to your postcard of the 20th of the month.
    Our connoisseur edition will be reproduced by photolithography. The so-called "Cambridge sketches" are in the Fitzwilliam Museum in Cambridge, and half of them (one page) were reproduced in *The Musical Times* as a special supplement on March 1, 1903, as I have already written on August 16 this year.
    Yesterday I received the news from Mr. Speyer that he has finally had his sketchleaf photographed in London for us, and I should receive the photograph in a few days. I therefore ask you to put your Preface on hold until I have forwarded this photograph to you.
    With best wishes,
        Yours truly,
        Deutsch

PS Mr. Speyer also wrote that he has no [other] sketches of piano sonatas by Beethoven; however, he does have a letter from Beethoven to Schlesinger in Paris, which deals with corrections to the C minor Sonata (Op. 111);[1] see Thayer's biography, 2nd edition, 1908, vol. 5, p. 584.

Universal Edition urgently requires a prospectus for the Beethoven day from me. For this purpose, I would like to have a look at your Preface: could I possibly see it in the next few days? Please at least lend it to me in its present state for twenty-four hours.

---

[1] Probably letter 1190 in *The Letters of Beethoven*, ed. Emily Anderson (London: Macmillan, 1961); it is currently owned by the Beethoven House, Bonn.

♣ Deutsch to Schenker (letter), December 11, 1920
OJ 10/3, [21]

Dear Professor,
    Yesterday I received the enclosed photographs of the Speyer sketches, with a photographer's receipt for £1.16.–. I hope this leaf meets your expectations. I ask you to make the necessary changes in the manuscript of your accompanying Preface, and return the Preface with the photographs to me soon.
    The photographs of the Bonn manuscript have been severely delayed by a shortage of chemicals and glass at the factory in Cologne responsible for them, but they should still be ready in December. The prospectus for the entire series will be issued on Sunday. Your corrections were used.[1]

>   With best wishes,
>   Yours truly,
>   Deutsch

2 enclosures

[1] Schenker placed a question mark in the margin. What Deutsch probably means is that he has made use of Schenker's draft commentary (see letter of November 26) in preparing the prospectus for his series of facsimile editions.

❧ Diary entry, December 21, 1920

Connoisseur edition finished, and letter to Deutsch with request for contract.

❧ Deutsch to Schenker (letter), December 23, 1920

OJ 10/3, [22]

Dear Professor,

I confirm with thanks the receipt of your Preface to the Beethoven volume, including the five photographs, and shall send you a formal contract in the next few days.

>   With best wishes,
>   Yours truly,
>   O. E. Deutsch

❧ Deutsch to Schenker (letter), January 30, 1921

OJ 10/3, [23]

Dear Professor,

Before the latest increase in postage costs comes into effect, I want to fulfill my long overdue obligations to you regarding the contract, which have been hitherto held up by an incredible amount of overwork. I hope that you are happy with the wording, which is quite similar to that used for Kalbeck[1] and Mandyczewski.[2]

The Bonn photographs are finally now ready, and will be sent to me once Universal Edition has paid. The size of the sketch reproductions must then be agreed.

I am sorry that you did not send your commentary to me first. I must see it before the translator does, and I will retrieve it from Universal Edition. You will receive an edited version, perhaps even with the English translation.[3]

You can return the Frimmel books to me when it is convenient.

The printers' misunderstandings are bad; they are even internally inconsistent.

Thank you for the Schubert stamp.

Best wishes to you and your wife!
>Yours truly,
>>Deutsch

2 encl.[4]

---

[1] *Johannes Brahms, Drei Lieder,* "Mainacht", "Sapphische Ode", "Nachtwandler", ed. Max Kalbeck (Vienna: UE, 1921); vol. 3 in Deutsch's series of connoisseur prints.

[2] *Joseph Haydn, Zwölf Schottische Volkslieder, für eine Singstimme mit Klavier, Violine und Violoncello,* ed. Eusebius Mandyczewski (Vienna: UE, 1921); vol. 2 in Deutsch's series of connoisseur prints.

[3] See Deutsch's letter of January 16, 1920, in which a single, trilingual edition is mooted. In the end, UE brought out separate editions, in German (UE 7000) and in English translation (UE 7000a). According to the publisher's publications book altogether 560 copies were received from the printer on September 19, 1921; a small number of these were bound in half-leather and individually numbered as a "special issue."

[4] Presumably two copies of the contract, as Schenker would have signed and returned one copy to Deutsch. A translation of this document, dated December 16, 1920, is given below.

❧ Deutsch and Schenker (contract), dated December 16, 1920
OC 52/485

C O N T R A C T

between Dr. Heinrich Schenker, Vienna III, Reisnerstrasse 38, and Mr. Otto Erich Deutsch, Vienna II, Valeriestrasse 26.

1. Dr. Schenker will undertake the edition of the "Moonlight" Sonata by Beethoven in a facsimile of the manuscript and of three related sketchleaves for the collection "Connoisseur Prints for Music Lovers," which Mr. Deutsch is editing for the publishing house Universal Edition & Co., Vienna.

2. Dr. Schenker will write a Preface for this volume, which will be translated into English if necessary, at the publisher's expense.

3. Dr. Schenker will receive from Mr. Deutsch as honorarium 8% (eight percent) of the normal price for each copy sold, with one-time settlement after the Easter Book Fair each year; but upon publication of the volume, the honorarium of half the edition as first installment in advance. Furthermore, three complimentary copies after publication of the volume.

4. This letter of agreement is binding for legal successors.

Vienna, December 16, 1920[1]
>Otto Erich Deutsch

[1] Deutsch has back-dated the contract to coincide with the 150th anniversary of Beethoven's birth; this explains, in part, the six-week discrepancy between the date on the contract and that on the covering letter: January 30, 1921. (See also Schenker's diary entry of December 21, 1920, above.)

❦ Deutsch to Schenker (postcard), June 28, 1921
OC 24/22

Dear Professor,
Thank you for your kind postcard of the 26th of the month. I was very surprised to hear that you have moved,[1] and wish you luck for the new home and your summer trip. I cordially return the greetings from you and your dear wife. Let us hope that the prints of our connoisseur edition will appear soon and be as successful as your *Tonwille*, the first issue of which I have read with great interest.

> With best regards,
> Yours very truly,
> Deutsch

[1] The Schenkers moved into Keilgasse 8, apartment 12, in May 1921.

❦ Deutsch to Schenker (letter), September 24, 1921
OJ 10/3, [24]

Dear Dr. [Schenker],
The Beethoven volume is in fact now almost ready: only the English translation of the Preface still requires a thorough revision, on account of the awkward, severely Germanized wording of certain phrases.

Furthermore, since the numbers representing keys and individual tones have been transcribed very hastily and imprecisely, and have not been improved in the revision, I have asked Dr. Kalmus to show you the latest revision of the English Preface one more time. Your photographic prints of the manuscript are with Dr. Kalmus, and I ask you still to be patient a little while longer until the completed facsimile pages have been so arranged, in a sample print-out, that we may safely give the authorization to publish.

This can perhaps be done as early as next week, and Dr. Kalmus will then allow the images to be sent to you immediately. The sonata will appear this fall, and you can be assured that its publication will not have been delayed one day by me. The fee (a percentage, as I recall, calculated in kronen or in marks) will in fact have increased substantially as a result of the delay.

I would be very delighted to welcome you and your wife at my (our) place soon.

With the best regards,
> Yours truly,
>> Deutsch

⁂ Deutsch to Schenker (letter), November 15, 1921
OJ 10/3, [25]

Dear Professor,

I thank you for your card of the 12th of the month, and have flagged the two advance payments for the luxury edition of the "Moonlight" Sonata on the list of Seidel's Book Dealership.[1] Both copies are therefore to go to Mr. Vrieslander, including the one designated for Mr. Hoboken. However, not by cash on delivery, because this is now hardly possible abroad.

With best regards to you and your wife, I sign as
> Yours truly,
>> Otto Erich Deutsch

[1] L. W. Seidel & Son, Vienna I, Graben 13, which Deutsch had taken over in November 1919.

⁂ Deutsch to Schenker (postcard), dated December 28, 1921
OJ 10/3, [26]

On behalf and for the account of our Mr. Otto Erich Deutsch, we have today, through the Austrian Credit Institute for Public Enterprises and Works, paid into your account at Deutsche Bank in Berlin

> marks 1,200.--/twelve hundred marks/

>> Respectfully,
>> SEIDEL'S RETAIL BOOK DEALERSHIP
>>> D.

Letter will follow.
> Yours,
>> Deutsch

8
Universal Edition and the *Tonwille* Dispute

SCHENKER'S correspondence with Universal Edition spanned thirty years, from 1901 to his death in 1935, and involved all UE's principals—Josef Weinberger, Josef Wöss, Barbara Rothe, Alfred Kalmus, Hans Heinsheimer, Hugo Winter, and Ernst Roth. But it was with one person that Schenker primarily dealt: Emil Hertzka. Soon after his arrival as UE's director in 1907, Hertzka gave Schenker his personal attention: of the approximately one thousand surviving items of correspondence between Schenker and UE, no fewer than six hundred are with Hertzka. Schenker's periodical *Der Tonwille*, a decade in the planning and full of promise, ultimately proved an impediment: it soured the relationship, and brought about the move to another publisher.

The crisis over *Der Tonwille* was not the first in that relationship: there had been periods of dissension and temporary breakdown before. But that which began in 1922 and raged until its tumultuous end in 1925 was of a different order. It laid bare Schenker's distaste for commerce, his suspicion of the business world's perceived deceitfuness and sharp bookkeeping practices; it brought out Schenker's fiercely guarded intellectual autonomy, his resistance to editorial encroachment, and his paranoia at what he saw as UE's reluctance to publicize his work and ultimately its active concealment of that work from the public. At a personal level, it exposed the conflict between Schenker's brand of Jewishness—assimilationist, German-nationalist, politically and socially conservative—and the cosmopolitan, internationally minded, democratically inclined Jewishness that Hertzka represented. On the other hand, it reveals the respect, one could even say affection, that Hertzka had for Schenker, and the apparent decency with which he struggled to communicate with him.

The sixteen letters and two telegrams offered here, selected from over four hundred surviving items of correspondence from 1922 to 1925, trace the deteriorating relations between Schenker and Hertzka to the point at which communications were broken off and dealings were placed in the hands of lawyers.

The seeds of the crisis go back to the fall of 1920. By September Schenker had already submitted a certain amount of copy for *Der Tonwille*, and from this UE produced samples of typography and music engraving. On November 10 Schenker handed in the text of the highly polemical lead article "The Mission of German Genius," proofs of which he was correcting by December 17, while on December 20 he handed in the copy for the first movement of his Beethoven Fifth Symphony study. It was not until after Christmas that the "Mission" proofs arrived on Hertzka's desk.

IAN BENT

☙ Hertzka (UE) to Schenker (letter), December 30, 1920
OC 52/561

Universal Edition & Co.
Vienna I
Karlsplatz 6
(Musikverein Building)

Dear Professor,
    Unfortunately, it was not possible for me to answer your esteemed letter of the 22nd of the month prior to the holidays. But before I write to Cotta,[1] we really ought first to have a discussion of the matter between ourselves, so please give me the earliest opportunity for doing so. Such a discussion is all the more necessary because I have only just now read the proofs of your article "The Mission of German Genius" and urgently need to speak with you in this regard. Should it not be easy for you to find the time, I should of course be glad to call on you, and I can make myself available to you even during the two days of forthcoming holiday.
        With most cordial greetings,
            Yours truly, in admiration,
                Emil Hertzka

[1] Hertzka was in discussion with Cotta at this time over the transfer to UE of *Counterpoint 2* and future volumes of the Musical Theories and Fantasies (See chapter 6).

☙ Diary entries, January 4 and 5, 1921

[January 4:] From Hertzka (express): expects me tomorrow between 3 and 5 o'clock. — [January 5:] At Hertzka's [office]: Preface[1] is "holy," "magnificent," but, given his business associations in New York,[2] he would not dare to present it to foreign readers; he suggests printing it separately, and for a while I consider having the essay printed in *Counterpoint 2*, which he has nothing against; finally he hits upon the idea of setting up a fictitious publishing house:[3] ". . and now you can write whatever you want." Moved by this, Lie-Liechen leaps up to shake his hand warmly, remarking how good it is when two people, each versed in his own profession, come to an agreement; whereupon he says: "You must know that I cherish your husband." [...] — To Floriz (express): things went well with Hertzka.

[1] That is, "The Mission of German Genius."
[2] *protokollirt in New-York*: a difficult phrase. Since little is known of Hertzka's business relations with American publishers at this time it suggests that he had an agreement or understanding with a company or companies in New York.
[3] The "Tonwille-Flugblätterverlag" (Tonwille Pamphlet Publishing House), under which imprint *Der Tonwille* alone was published for its first six ("occasional") issues, changing to a quarterly publication in 1924, at which point the imprint changed

to "Tonwille-Verlag" (Tonwille Publishing House). Only the final issue, IV/4 = 10 (October 1924), released in January 1925, appeared over the imprint "Universal Edition Wien." The fictitious publishing house was attached to the sheet-music house Albert J. Gutmann, which was by this time owned by Universal Edition.

Kalmus (UE) to Schenker (letter), February 21, 1922
OC 52/512

Dear Professor,

We acknowledge with thanks receipt of the Urlinie engravings for the Beethoven and Mozart sonatas,[1] as also of the proof of the engraved examples numbered according to their sequence and the galley proof belonging to it, and moreover the proof copy of *Op. 109*.[2]

As concerns the last-named work, we can implement the corrections in the music section without more ado. But unfortunately it is another matter where the corrections to the text section are concerned, since the type is no longer standing and only matrices[3] of it are to hand, and for printing purposes these can be used only unaltered. Every change would entail the complete resetting of the whole page, and needless to say nowadays that would incur huge costs. Accordingly, however much we welcome a revision of the work, it is regrettably impossible to undertake a resetting of the elucidation, and we hope that you will understand this is at the present time an insurmountable obstacle. The correcting of the music section will still mean an essential revision by comparison with the old edition.

Now as concerns *Der Tonwille* issue 2, because its extent has already grown too great,[4] we are going to have to hold the conclusion of your treatment of "Beethoven's Fifth Symphony" to the next issue. But now the printers need precisely the small type[5] in which no fewer than nine full columns of this article are set; and among the "Miscellanea" we have a further large quantity of small type to set. In view of this, and at the same time the fact that the type, of which our stocks are unfortunately only small, is also needed for a different, urgent job, we have no alternative but to break up this article, with its examples already engraved, to prepare matrices, and to print the next issue from the plates poured from the matrices, so that the type can in the meantime be reused. We are therefore delivering the complete conclusion of the "Beethoven Fifth Symphony" with a request that you look through the same once again, before the type is broken up. We will then begin this conclusion with a new page, and must then see to it in the next issue that the other articles are so arranged that there is no blank space. Please kindly send the proof-pulls back by return post, so that we can have the work carried out as fast as possible.

Director Hertzka is delighted that you approve his idea of the "Urlinie Edition,"[6] and we look forward to hearing particulars from you.

With kind regards,
p.p. Kalmus

N.B. A complaint has been sent urgently to the printers in Graz.

[*added by hand:*] We have just received the answer that further columns are underway.

---

¹ *Tonwille* 2, "Beethoven's Sonata in F minor, Op. 2, No. 1" and "Mozart: Sonata in A minor," vol. 2, 72–95, 55–71 (Ger. orig., 7–24, 25–48, with two double-sided Urlinie leaves appended).

² The elucidatory edition of *Op. 109*, published in 1913, of which a second edition was in progress and would be published in January 1923.

³ matrix: a mold (often made of papier maché) in which the face of the type is cast. This process enables the typesetter to break up (distribute) the type and return its components to the compartments of the type case for reuse.

⁴ *Tonwille* 2 as ultimately published comprised forty-eight pages—already sixteen pages over the contractual limit (issue 1 had run to fifty-six pages). The continuation of "Beethoven's Fifth Symphony" was deferred to issue 5 and ran to forty-two pages, and its conclusion to issue 6, which ran to thirty-seven pages, both plus their appended Urlinie leaves.

⁵ *Tonwille* uses two type sizes, of which the smaller, "Petit-Schrift," was used for the Secondary Literature sections of analytical articles, and in two-column layout for the "Miscellanea" (with the exception of *Tonwille* 1, which was set in the larger type and single column throughout).

⁶ This refers to Schenker's complete edition of the Beethoven piano sonatas. In a letter of February 11, 1922, Hertzka proposed that Schenker produce an Urlinie graph for each sonata, and that this be included with the corresponding sonata and the result marketed separately as Schenker's "Urlinie Edition." A contract was produced, but the project was never realized.

❧ Hertzka (UE) to Schenker (letter), May 2, 1922
OC 52/564–565

Highly revered Professor,

The printed proof of the second part of *Der Tonwille*, "Miscellanea," by you has just been put before me, and its contents have come to my attention for the first time.

It is acutely embarrassing for me to have to inform you that, after mature consideration, I am not in a position to publish this anthology, highly interesting as it certainly is, in its entirety. The primary reason for this is that by virtue of this appendix the cost of the second issue would be increased dramatically, and would compel me to place a retail price on it that would render the issue unsalable. Permit me to point out that we envisioned the issues of *Der Tonwille* as comprising two gatherings, i.e. thirty-two pages.¹ Since it now turns out that the section without the "Miscellanea" already takes up forty-eight pages, that reaches the maximum that we may run to. Apart from that, our contract says expressly that the *Little Library*, i.e. *Der Tonwille*, examines various topics in the field of music. In the fourteen pages of "Miscellanea," no topics whatsoever in the field of music are examined, but only topics in the field of politics and demagoguery. I consider it my duty to say to you that I would never have decided to publish *Der Tonwille* had I been aware that it would deal with a very wide range of things that have nothing whatsoever to do with music. Our contract contains the clause that we respect your right to free expression of opinions without any limitations, but it is self-evident that this clause referred to the treatment of topics in the realm of music.

Unpleasant though I have always found aggressive *ad hominem* polemic, I have acquiesced patiently to it in *Der Tonwille* as in the elucidatory editions so long as it related to musical matters because I hold you yourself and your judgment in the highest esteem, and acknowledge unreservedly your authority in all matters to do with music. But when it goes beyond that, I cannot possibly let it go uncriticized, and I would be very pleased if on the occasion of our next meeting an understanding could be reached between us on the handling of the matters in question.

As concerns the specific case of the fourteen pages, what would be most welcome to me would be if in view of the three-gathering make-up of the second issue this item could be dispensed with altogether. We could, by mutual agreement, extract some material from the "Miscellanea" and incorporate it into the third issue. Should you on the other hand be firmly of the opinion that even the second issue ought to contain some miscellaneous material, I might possibly be prepared to admit something of the order of four pages' worth (in the first issue there were five and a half pages).[2] The second issue would then have fifty-two pages (the first had fifty-five pages), and would thus be far and away larger than we envisioned in the contract.

My preference would be if you would give me the pleasure of a visit very soon so that we could talk the matter through in person, and if you would reply to this letter not in writing but face-to-face.[3]

      Ever in warm admiration,
      Yours very truly,
      Emil Hertzka

---

[1] Clause 1 of the contract, July 10, 1920, reads: "I relinquish to you the exclusive and sole publishing right as well as translation right of the work authored by me 'Little Library' which is envisioned as a succession of two-gathering issues appearing from time to time, of which a maximum of twelve are to appear per year."

[2] Part of the "Miscellanea" was a diatribe against the Beethoven biographer Paul Bekker, a personal friend of Hertzka and chief music critic of the *Frankfurter Zeitung*, which Hertzka had already rejected from the elucidatory edition of *Op. 101* and which Schenker had sought to include in *Tonwille 2* under the subtitle "Music Criticism." Defending his position in a letter written the very next day, Hertzka remarked: "Admittedly, I find Paul Bekker's spiteful jostlings shameful, but I can quite well understand from the human point of view that someone whose ears you have boxed many a time will one day want to take his revenge. Unfortunately, *Der Tonwille* will be read by fewer people than the *Frankfurter Zeitung*." The item remained unpublished, but can be read in the English translation of *Der Tonwille*, vol. 2, 161–65).

[3] No meeting is recorded in Schenker's diary.

Diary entry, May 4, 1922

From Hertzka (letter): raises objection to "Miscellanea"! Great upset; I immediately draft a letter.

Diary entry, May 18, 1922

To Hertzka (letter): I protest against presumption of political activities, inciting strife between nations, etc.

Hertzka (UE) to Schenker (letter), May 19, 1922
OC 52/312–313

Dear Professor,
    Only in the last few days have I gotten around to reading your article on music criticism. I do not know Bekker's original article.[1] The majority of future readers of *Der Tonwille* will also not be acquainted with him. Thus there is no one who knows the relationship between the quoted passages and the whole article; nor does anyone know whether and to what extent the quotations are the central point or only side issues. This said, I already believe that you have given Mr. Bekker a hard time, and that no one can ever in his whole life have insulted him in such a manner.
    However, there is one thing that I would very much like to have seen in the article, and I can only infer that you have deliberately left it unsaid, because I would otherwise really have been baffled by it. You have given poor old Bekker a thorough thrashing, but have not refuted him. I cannot believe you did this just to spare him, and I would very much like to have seen you prove to Mr. Bekker that criticism is something for which absolutely no aptitude is necessary, that in this sphere there is no aptitude whatsoever,[2] and that he who has the greatest knowledge of his subject is under all circumstances the best critic. It surely ought to have been possible to prove beyond doubt that knowledge of one's subject offers security. Why do you not prove that to him? Why do you say instead that all our accumulated knowledge of the subject offers no security? If today's knowledge of the subject offers no security, what on earth *does* offer security? Do you not think it is dangerous to concede that to Mr. Bekker? Could one not surely decide for oneself whether or not knowledge of one's subject offers security? You write, at any rate, that there must be a knowledge of one's subject that offers security. Who then has this knowledge of his subject? Naturally, Mr. Bekker doesn't have it. By your own assertion, you yourself appear not to think that you possess this knowledge of your subject already. In that case, who on earth *could* possess it? What Bekker writes about Beethoven's Ninth, Bekker says on his own behalf. He writes expressly "I can." If he had wanted to allude to you, he would surely not have used the "I" form. Why do you assume that Bekker would have shrunk from naming you if he had meant to refer to you, after not having been at all shy about

speaking of you so disrespectfully most recently in the *Frankfurter Zeitung*.[3] What Bekker says about emotional involvement in artistic judgment seems to me to be absolutely right, and I believe that, in saying that, he is giving expression to the opinion of very many people who are neither dishonorable nor stupid nor both. I also believe that on important questions one can be of different opinions, and that insults do not denote stupidity or dishonorableness or both, particularly not a refutation. I certainly do not agree with Mr. Bekker in all respects, and I should be very happy if you were thoroughly to refute him. But do you really think it constitutes a thorough refutation when you time and again use a democratic view of life as a target for insult and ridicule, and taunt him for not going down a mine despite all his support for the position of the workers?

I do not entirely understand your wish to remain stationary for millenia with a "well-understood Beethoven" and to express the opinion that then human mediocrity would instead make progress. If composition had stopped at the death of Beethoven, then we would have no works by Chopin, Brahms, Schumann, Mendelssohn, etc., who are surely also people who always figure in your list of geniuses as well, and I believe that in a further hundred years a new Schenker will be able to extend the Gotha[4] of genius-aristocracy with further names.

I do not consider myself able or qualified to polemicize on social problems. But I find it impossible to believe that a genius-aristocracy would flourish better in the context of imperialism and militarism than in the context of democracy. The Greek people lived long before the Germans, and I do not believe that you would have completely to deny genius and genius-aristocracy to this no less imperialistic and militaristic people.[5]

With the above I have made clear my misgivings openly. Please take them only in that spirit: as the opinions of a lay reader of *Der Tonwille* expressed with the aim of drawing attention to what seem to be weak points in your argument. However dazzling your article on German genius seemed to me, I was not in agreement with much of it; the dispute with Bekker seems to me no more successful this time.

Thus, before I pass this article on for printing, I should like to recommend you to look it through one more time. Quite apart from all that I have already said, it seems to me also to be too long.

If, despite all of this, you wish it to be printed unaltered, then, in view of the great veneration that I have for you, I will send the whole article for printing without flinching and have it published in *Der Tonwille*. I myself am off to Germany tomorrow morning for eight or ten days. Dr. Kalmus has authority from me to get to work on the printing in accordance with your wishes.

In hoping that you will not take offense at my candid expression of opinion, and that our relationship, which is of paramount value to me, will not be impaired in any way on account of the "Miscellanea," I remain

   In highest regard and admiration,
   Yours very truly
   Hertzka

---

[1] Paul Bekker, "Kritik und Persönlichkeit," *Frankfurter Zeitung*, November 7, 1919.

[2] In Schenker's view, "aptitude" (*Begabung*) was a superficial attribute, whereas "knowledge" (*Wissenschaft*) was profound. Bekker had written "criticism is not a matter of understanding, or of knowledge […]. It is a gift from heaven […] an aptitude which one either has or has not […]." Schenker's response was "since when is ignorance reckoned as a 'gift from heaven' […]?" (For Schenker's essay, see *Masterwork 2*, 161–65.)

[3] Paul Bekker, "Musiker-Faksimiles," *Frankfurter Zeitung*, March 25, 1922.

[4] Gotha: *Almanach der Gotha*, directory of the European nobility and monarchies, first published in 1763 by C. W. Ettinger in the town of Gotha and published annually from 1785 to 1944.

[5] Hertzka seems to have lost the thread of the argument here. What he presumably meant to say is that genius-aristocracy flourished in ancient Greece, even though it was the cradle of democracy.

❧ Diary entry, May 22, 1922

To Kalmus (letter): I give the order to print article, even against Hertzka's censure.

❧ Hertzka and Kalmus (UE) to Schenker (letter), June 3, 1922
OC 52/568

Dear Professor,
  Now that I have returned from my travels in Germany, I should like imperatively and as quickly as possible to speak with you in person about the matter that is unresolved between us. Since I take it that your time is not encumbered by lessons during the Pentecost holidays, please would you convey to the bearer of this letter when and where I can speak with you on Sunday or Monday?

>With kind regards,
>Yours very truly,
>for Director Hertzka
>Dr. Kalmus

❧ Diary entry, June 4, 1922

For half an hour, Hertzka indulges in pacifist international, cosmopolitan, democratic avowals. He gushes about compromises and says he was always able to solve difficulties. He labels me an idealist. Then I speak up and position the meaning of "Miscellanea" as apolitical and directed only against a democracy hostile to art. We part on good terms because Hertzka promises to make non-binding comments only in the margins and to send "Miscellanea" by Tuesday.

❧ Hertzka (UE) to Schenker (letter), June 10, 1922
OC 52/569

Dear Professor,

In accordance with our face-to-face talk of a few days ago, I have at last, after very detailed perusal, reached the point at which I can send you the "Miscellanea" for your opinion. This would have happened on Thursday but for some important foreign trips and meetings, and I wanted to collect it today and send it to you by messenger so that I could pass the material to the printers on Monday.[1] Imagine my consternation when Mr. Kalmus handed me the second issue of *Der Tonwille* this morning, already published! He cited the agreement reached with you by which neither the "Miscellanea" nor the "Anti-Bekker" was to be included in this issue. I was unable to apprise him of our conversation as we were both enormously overburdened in the past few days, and I thought there was no question of the issue's being printed for the time being. Sadly, there is now nothing that can be done, and I believe the second issue is extremely handsomely presented and will have well-deserved success.[2]

As regards the possible use of the "Miscellanea," please let me know what you now would like. We can hold part of it for issue 3 and discard the remaining part; or else, as you originally envisioned, release the essay to you so that you can have it separately printed at your discretion.

Since you have already done a great deal of work for issue 3, it will not be difficult to bring the issue out in the late fall, and I look forward with keen interest to what you have to say in this regard.

With most cordial greetings, and in warm admiration and esteem,

    Yours truly,
    Emil Hertzka

At all events, I am delighted that *Tonwille* 2 is out, and that with it a new building block in your unique "monument of genius" has been laid.

---

[1] The chronology here is confused. Hertzka intended to get the material to Schenker on Thursday, June 8, then planned either to collect it from him on Saturday, June 10, so as to pass it to the printers on Monday, June 12, or to collect it from Schenker on June 10, and return it to him by messenger with revisions in time to get it to the printers on June 12.

[2] In communications to pupils and friends over the next month, Schenker reports Hertzka's "deceptions," or "infringements."

❧ Diary entry, November 19, 1922

8:00 Furtwängler, 8:30 Weisse and his wife; ample meal! Furtwängler praises my unconditionality, contrasting it with his conditionality stemming from his profession! […] He also expresses the opinion that Hertzka is "sabotaging" me[1] and voluntarily expresses his willingness to inquire in Leipzig with Peters and Breitkopf & Härtel.

[1] In a letter of August 30, 1922, Kalmus had informed Schenker of Hertzka's wish to drop a section of the "Miscellanea" concerning Felix Weingartner from *Tonwille 3* to save space, continuing: "May I ask you to comply with Director Hertzka's wishes, and not to construe this as 'censorship terrorism'," which implies that Schenker had already described Hertzka's editorial activities in these terms.

Diary entry, November 21, 1922

At Hertzka's: [...] I say openly that I am being sabotaged and cite the opinion of others—Hertzka feigns feeling hurt! I accuse him of protecting Bekker against Vrieslander, but not me against Bekker; and when I also make several slanderous comments about his actions several times, he comments, in contradiction to a statement made a year ago: I support everything that is honest!! He promises to publish the third and fourth issues quickly.

Diary entry, February 18, 1923

To Hertzka (letter): I do not do anything behind Vrieslander's back and wish that nothing be done;[1] I propose a word substitution or a footnote from the publisher in which the editorial staff reserves the right to its judgment; I give the advice not to proceed with a biased, terroristic approach, burdening me only with the work, the *force majeure*, insults, while affording others friendship and protection. Thank you for presents.

[1] Otto Vrieslander had submitted an article to one of UE's house journals, *Musikblätter des Anbruch*, which included polemics against Paul Bekker and Hermann Kretzschmar. Hertzka wrote to Schenker on February 16 asking if he would support him in striking out the two passages.

Hertzka (UE) to Schenker (letter), February 20, 1923
OC 52/574

Dear Professor,
The course of action that you suggest for the Vrieslander article is the one to which I shall adhere. The shortening of an article in periodicals is often necessary, even without the consent of the author. We have however found a way out: we will publish the first half right away without alteration (the issue should still appear this week), the second half in the March issue after successful negotiation with Vrieslander.[1]
You do me an injustice when you consider that I was "unjust, biased, and totally terroristic." If only you were able to observe me closely at work, you would quickly be obliged to recognize that the opposite is the case. If Bekker were to try to insult or defame you in the *Musikblätter des Anbruch* or in any other periodical with

which I am associated, or in a book that I was to publish, then I would probably put a stop to that far more energetically than was the case, conversely, with Schenker against Bekker. I have a horror of *ad hominem* polemics, and regret it even when people of high standing bring personal matters to the fore over matters of substance. Your advice to hold myself aloof from bloodless battle is no doubt well-intentioned, but you really must not forget one thing: that this battle is actually going to have to be settled to a small extent behind my back.

It is precisely because I am not biased, and would prefer to practise benign neutrality toward all sides, that I take no pleasure whatsoever in seeing personalities whom I value in a periodical that is close to my heart at loggerheads with one another. Just imagine: if it were to occur to Mr. Bekker to attack you in the *Musikblätter des Anbruch* and, if, citing the hospitality granted to the insults from the other side, he were for his part to answer back with insults, then I would naturally be obliged vigorously to reject his impertinence in publishing something of that sort, and you can well imagine the consequences.

I ask you please to believe me when I say that I place the highest value on the work that you do and on your publications—and not just since recognition for the importance of your books and writings has won through, but from the very outset, standing up for you wholeheartedly. That I cannot go along with your German-nationalist views is perhaps shortsightedness on my part, for which I must beg you to excuse me. Since my youth, which I spent partly in Italy, France, etc., and through my unbroken, intimate contact with high-standing non-German people, I am supranationally oriented.

Nevertheless, stay well-disposed to
Yours truly in admiration,
Emil Hertzka

[1] Otto Vrieslander, "Henrich Schenker und sein Werk," *Musikblätter des Anbruch*, 5th year, no. 2 (February 1923): 41–44; no. 3 (March 1923): 72–79. Footnote on p. 77 reads: "Note by the editorial staff: Responsibility for these words and other polemics in this article rests solely with the author."

🎼 Schenker to Hertzka (UE) (letter copy), July 9, 1923
OC 52/577–579

Letter to Hertzka from Galtür, July 9, 1920[1]

Numerous people have approached me by various means (mail, music retailers, etc.) in connection with the Bach article that appeared in the June issue of *Die Musik*,[2] asking after the Tonwille Pamphlets Press and where they can obtain issues 1 and 2 that are cited there. I am not in a position to answer them all, and accordingly ask you to insert an ad about *Der Tonwille* in *Die Musik*, by which means you could avoid damage being done to the publishing house as well as to me, and do a service for the future. I do not know whether such an ad has ever previously appeared in *Die Musik*; all I know is that ads from UE are to be found in the June issue and also in the July issue, which has just arrived, but none concerning me. I would also especially ask you to set the tone of the ad as you did at the beginning. You cannot do enough by merely wanting to do justice by me, i.e. the highest tone available to you is at one and the same time good enough and yet too little, so secular[3] is my achievement.

I know from several conversations with you how your mind works over a publicity drive when it is a matter of Schenker. You suddenly become skeptical—you who travel from city to city mixing with the great and the good and are extolled as a master of the publicity drive. It is no accident that, following the article by Vrieslander, the sales of my publications promptly shot up. And if you were to recommend my publications, most particularly *Der Tonwille*, to the retailers—as in the past you wanted to send them the *Anbruch*, so that they could display them in their windows or in other ways—the success would instantly be more compelling. But something holds you back!

The publicity for the [New Musical] Theories and Fantasies has long been incommensurate with its value, and it is clear to see that you are discriminating against it—for example, by contrast with the shoddy work of Schoenberg, which belongs to the eleventh century or to Kagran.[4] My *Theory of Harmony* was epoch-making; the very fact alone that my book came out earlier than, and was a prerequisite for Schoenberg's *Theory of Harmony*, proves that. Certainly if you wanted to appeal to a better judgment, I would know no reason why the tone of the ad should be so muted. Does not my work have a complete *Counterpoint*, as well—something that Schoenberg lacks? It is the only *Counterpoint* that your firm has published, and even that seems to leave you cold. You ought, dear Director, to come back at me that you are constantly advertising the Beethoven edition. But that edition is a glorious gift to UE and not for me. The New Musical Theories and Fantasies and *Der Tonwille* are Schenker, and only a publicity drive for these works would be one for Schenker.[5]

Right now, while I am free of teaching commitments, I am in a position to draft issues 5, 6, 7, and 8 of *Der Tonwille*, but the form that the issues take depends upon the speed of the printing. In the fifth issue at long last—the issue is short by a mere eleven pages—the Fifth Symphony essay would be polished off; but dare I start on the Third Symphony of Brahms in a later issue when the continuation will follow in six months or even later, judging by the rate of printing, which has managed just the four issues since 1921?[6] And even if I could secure a net profit by winning over a loyal following of purchasers, what good would that do me and *Der Tonwille* if you (and sadly your printing house as well) are against it?

It is no use, dear Director, you must put your cards on the table as to whether or not you are my adversary, as many of the best musicians in Germany believe, or whether you can at least muster enough of a publisher's objectivity to allow even my work to flourish under your protection. I think it high time that UE took over *Der Tonwille* itself (nobody can track down the fictitious publishing house, and with good reason) and promote it more briskly, so that [*remainder missing*]

---

[1] The final page (or possibly more) is missing. The copy is in Jeanette's hand, with no corrections in Schenker's hand. His diary confirms that the letter was written, and this copy made.

² Heinrich Schenker, "Joh. Seb. Bach: Wohltemperiertes Klavier, Band I, Präludium c-moll," *Die Musik* 15, no. 9 (June 1923): 641–51.

³ *säkular*: Schenker presumably means "secular" in the sense of valid for all times, hence of eternal significance (cf. *in saecula saeculorum*, "for ever and ever")—in his phrase, that his work is "of ultimate truth."

⁴ A derogatory view of Schoenberg's *Theory of Harmony* (Vienna: Univeral Edition, 1911, 3rd edn. 1922): "to belong to the eleventh century" means to be valid for one age, a past one, therefore of no relevance to the modern world. Kagran is part of Donaustadt, the 22nd district of Vienna; "nach Kagran gehören" was probably a Viennese colloquial term of abuse.

⁵ The German of these two sentences is strangely formulated; Jeanette herself seemed to doubt the latter by placing question-marks over two words.

⁶ *Tonwille* 4 had just been released, on June 20, 1923; *Tonwille* 5 would not be published for another eight months, on February 23, 1924, so Schenker's suspicions were well justified. Schenker never published a study of Brahms's Symphony No. 3, Op. 90, though several sketches for graphs are preserved in the Oster Collection.

Diary entry, October 10, 1923

From 4:30 to 6:00 at Hertzka's office [...] We finally switch to the main topic, to *Der Tonwille*! I roll out the question of a double issue¹ and in response he surprises me with the offer, to send out two issues in close succession now, and immediately thereafter to start releasing a "quarterly publication," also reflecting this in the title. Now I am free of the tight constraints and I am happy to steer toward the world of sonatas. Volume 4 thereby also takes on the tighter construction in which only it can be realized!²

¹ Schenker is proposing that *Tonwille* 5 and 6 be released as a double-issue in order that the entire remainder of his article on Beethoven's Fifth Symphony can be published together.

² Schenker presumably means that volume 4, i.e. *Free Composition*, will no longer have to deal with lengthy analyses. His intention was that the *Tonwille* pamphlets, and later the *Masterwork* yearbooks, by providing a pool of extended examples, would allow *Free Composition* to be more theoretically oriented. He notes in his diary (June 20, 1926): "I explain to him [John Petrie Dunn] that *Der Tonwille*, like the yearbooks, was intended to include examples in order to take the strain off *Free Composition*."

Schenker to UE (letter), April 2, 1924
WSLB 322 (=OC 52/588)

To Universal Edition

I am today returning *Der Tonwille* issue 6 to Mr. Detoni,¹ without imprimatur, and must on this occasion comment:

In September 1923 I handed over the material; in October, to satisfy a proposition by Director Hertzka, I took on a new task for issues 5 and 6, and delivered it on time.[2] What he said was: "in two weeks' time issue 6 will follow on the heels of issue 5," and today I must yet again go to work on issue 6! A music example to which I had given my imprimatur has gone missing, a <u>new one has been presented to me in an impossible state</u>; <u>other music examples are still lacking</u>—in short, when we should already be bringing out issue 8 (issue 7 is already in your hands), we are still tinkering with issue 6!!

The martyrdom that I have suffered since 1921 on account of a handful of short *Tonwille* issues, the never-ending hold-ups, the blaming of printers, having to do issues twice over, the injury done to the enterprise—the Fifth Symphony essay began in 1921 and its "second continuation" <u>will</u> appear <u>in 1924</u>!—the damaging effect on earnings, etc., etc.: the sacrifice that I have to bear is far too great, all on one side, and in breach of contract. From now on, sadder and wiser, I shall learn my lesson and take care not to submit material that is going to be subject to such huge delays.

I ask you therefore to expedite issue 6 as much as possible. I am also waiting for the galley proofs of the "Appassionata" essay for issue 7! Here we are now in 1924, the year in which, according to Director Hertzka's own declaration, and to the published announcement, we are due to release four issues! Or is the "quarterly publication" itself to be just as much of a fiction as that the "pamphlets" were real "pamphlets"?

With kind regards,
H. Schenker

---

[1] Josef Anton Detoni: technical writer, later publisher, employed by Universal Edition from c. 1920, who acted as intermediary between Schenker and the printers and engravers between 1920 and 1924.

[2] Referring to the meeting of October 10, 1923 (above).

Diary entry, May 26, 1924

In the meeting[1] I repudiate the bookkeeper. Hereupon we go into detail on individual matters. [...] I give him the *Tonwille* contract to read. Suddenly he starts fantasizing about twelve issues, à la Reclam,[2] etc.!—repeats, though, his assurance of a quarterly publication. As usual for a publisher, he expresses his regret at the poor sales of *Der Tonwille*, as if this had to do only with me and not also with his business methods; when I cited the number of copies of the first issue sold, he said: "Ah, I am pleasantly surprised by that." He still declares that he is not in a position to include *Der Tonwille* in UE. I, and also Lie-Liechen, come out in favor of the way of thinking up to now, preferring the anonymous publisher.

---

[1] The meeting involved Hertzka, Schenker, Jeanette, and Schenker's brother Moriz.

² Schenker is referring to pamphlets produced cheaply and in quick succession, by analogy with *Reclams Universal-Bibliothek*, a series of modestly priced paperback issues of classical texts—beginning in 1867 with the two parts of Goethe's *Faust*—issued by the publishing house of Philipp Reclam Jr.

⁊ Schenker to UE (telegram), July 17, 1924
WSLB 333

ischgl tel galtuer[1]

await express title page Tonwille quarterly publication issue 1 january march universal edition that I have already corrected otherwise will take action and institute legal proceedings the incessant malicious fooling around has got to stop = schenker

[1] The telegraph clerk in the Tyrolean village evidently took the message down by dictation, mangling it in several places, including typing "Tonwille" as "don wille." An expansion of the message might be: "I await by express mail [a proof of] the title page [reading:] 'Der Tonwille / Quarterly Publication / Issue 1 (January/ March) / [imprint:] Universal Edition,' which I have already corrected [once before]. Otherwise I will take action and institute legal proceedings. The incessant, malicious fooling around has got to stop. — Schenker." That is, Schenker claims to have seen and corrected a proof of the title page that carried the publisher's imprint "Universal Edition," and has since received another with "Tonwille-[Flugblätter?] verlag" substituted.

⁊ UE to Schenker (telegram), July 18, 1924
OC 52/520

Are sending new proof-sheet title page inside title page already sent on 14th. [/] Music[*sic*] Edition[1]

[1] The proof sent out on July 18, annotated "second proof, 2.30 July 18," does indeed bear the imprint "Universal-Edition A.-G. I., Karlsplatz 6." Nevertheless, the title page as published would read "Tonwille-Verlag."

Schenker to UE (letter), September 13, 1924
WSLB 344

To Universal Edition

1). On August 18 you wrote me under point 4: "We have arranged for our advertising department to make available to this firm a number of prospectuses, and <u>we hope that this firm</u> will do its utmost to promote sales of *Der Tonwille*."[1] Today I hear that UE <u>has sent neither prospectuses nor issue 7</u> to André in Frankfurt am Main. It is the duty of the <u>publishing house</u> <u>itself</u> to nurture sales, and certainly not to put up resistance just when friends of the author are about to take on the work of the publisher.[2] Those friends could do a lot, but they see themselves being prevented by breach of contract on the part of the publisher himself. It would be better if you had ceased your "We hope" and instead made what you have written and what I have passed on to my friends a reality.

2). On August 2 you wrote me: "On the <u>5th of the month</u> we will then arrange for <u>all the remaining letterpress</u> for issue 8 to follow," etc. We are in the midst of issue 9 and I have seen nothing of the remainder of issue 8. All of this is injurious to my work and to me.

3). The July statement of account for New Musical Theories and Fantasies has still not arrived. Today I suffer damage through such improper dilatoriness, where 15% is offered on three-month notice, where, precisely because of that, authors receive quarterly statements of account.

4). At Haslinger's, people still know nothing of issue 7, at Doblinger's nothing of issue 6, at …[3] nothing whatsoever of my Beethoven edition. I ask the publishing house to cease these injurious actions and to honor everything that is owed me in my contract. I say this in all seriousness, for my patience is at an end.

      With kind regards,
      Dr. Heinrich Schenker

---

[1] In a letter of August 2 Schenker had raised, among other issues, difficulties that André of Frankfurt was experiencing in obtaining information about *Der Tonwille*.

[2] The Hamburg industrialist Max Temming, a patron of the arts, had been approached by Moriz Violin in 1923 with a view to his supporting the sales of *Der Tonwille*, and in December 1924 paid for a copy of the first seven issues of the journal to be sent to ten leading German music-historical institutes. Schenker had also begun to use his pupils to bolster sales of the journal. (See chapter 21.)

[3] Schenker writes three dots and does not enter a name.

❧ Diary entry September 6, 1924

In the Gutmann music store; the manager complains more than a little about difficulties caused by Universal Edition, he also praises the Peters edition for their paper and printing; he excuses himself repeatedly for not being able to do anything for *Der Tonwille* if the publisher does not provide any publicity, saying Gutmann is only a retail outlet, not a publishing house now—so now we understand why subscribers do not know what is going on.

❧ Hertzka (UE) to Schenker (letter), September 16, 1924
OC 52/657

Dear Professor,

I have just been told that you maligned us in a wholly unjustified manner to one of the employees of the Gutmann music store. May I ask you to give your own account of this story? I am unable to give this report any credence, though it comes from someone accustomed to speaking the truth.[1]

In awaiting your most <u>immediate</u> and <u>precise</u> account, I remain

  With kind regards,
  Universal Edition & Co.
  Hertzka

[1] Schenker's reaction in his diary was: "The coward right away twists it into a joint issue with the other men, whom I did not intend to target at all."

❧ Schenker to UE (letter), September 18, 1924
WSLB 345

To Universal Edition

I have today received your letter of the 16th of the month. I freely admit that, in keeping with my character, with which you are familiar, a few days ago I expressed my justified disapproval of the observed action taken against me, and that I expressed it forcefully.[1]

  With kind regards,
  Dr. Heinrich Schenker

[1] The second sentence had been drafted by Schenker's attorney for this case, Theodor Baumgarten, to whom he had been recommended by his brother Moriz two days earlier.

❧ Schenker to UE (letter), September 24, 1924
WSLB 348 (=OC 52/658–659 (draft))

To Universal Edition

To your letter of September 20, which has just reached me, albeit unsigned, I have the following to say:

The release of the three issues of the quarterly publication for 1924 still to appear is not, in my opinion, at your whim; on the contrary, you are <u>obligated</u> to have these three issues appear within the space of this year.

Your splitting up of issue 2 of the quarterly publication I reject as contrary to our contract.

It is not my doing that the first issue did not appear until the end of August. Rather, this, as you know only too well, is to be attributed to your constant contraventions of the contract. What is more, I cannot permit the consequences of this injustice to continue subsequently to work against my contractual rights.

Your view of the limitation to which an issue of the quarterly publication is to be subject contradicts the express agreement of October 10, 1923, with Director Hertzka, as stated in his words: "The issues of the quarterly publication can be somewhat larger." Those words displayed a correct apprehension of the character of a quarterly publication. The sudden directive about the two-gathering limit is in any case already untenable, because the first issue [IV/1 = 7] is 44 pages long. (I might incidentally say that the second issue ought not substantially to exceed this size.)

The content of every issue is carefully considered by me, complete in itself yet at the same time contributing a specific component to the larger overall plan. I must have said this a thousand times. For that reason, I will permit no encroachment upon my proper authorial rights, and I will tolerate no alteration to the way my material is apportioned, particularly now that correction of proofs is complete. I therefore insist that the second issue appear in the form in which I prepared it, as shown by the galley proofs that I sent back for page make-up. It is no less in the interests of the publishing house than in mine that the periodical appear as I create it, to the best of my abilities as artist and writer. The subscribers have a right to read me just as they know me and as they expect of me.

It looks to me as if you want to make the previously internal rift caused by you into an outward break. I will therefore meet your wishes halfway, and propose that we dissolve our relationship as regards *Der Tonwille* after the appearance of the second issue [IV/2 = 8]. You made plain through your actions just how uncomfortable it was and is for you, most recently by unilaterally altering the title page of the first issue to which I had given my imprimatur and in place of "Universal Edition" (which, by the way, is cited as the publisher in the abbreviations list,[1] correctly so on the basis of the title page submitted to me), suddenly set "Tonwille-Verlag."

With kind regards,
Dr. Heinrich Schenker

[1] The list of abbreviations on the reverse title page of issue IV/1 (= 7) (January/March 1924) does indeed include the line: "Tw. = Heinrich Schenkers 'Der Tonwille' (UE)." This remained unchanged in issues IV/2–3 (= 8–9) and IV/4 (= 10).

❧ Barbara Rothe (UE) to Schenker (letter), September 26, 1924
OC 52/601

Professor Heinrich Schenker,[1]

In response to your letter of the 24th of the month, we would entreat you above all to refrain from any kind of polemic aimed at us, and to deal with the questions and differences of opinion before us as briefly and to the point as possible. If you feel yourself not in a position to do this, then we ask you to nominate a representative for these purposes with whom a calm and objective exchange is possible.

The situation is in brief that we still intend, as we notified you in our previous letter, to release three issues of *Der Tonwille* this year. It is neither technically nor materially possible for us to produce a total of more than six gatherings, hence ninety-six pages, within the coming three months. There exists no contractual obligation to make the issues larger than two gatherings. Some expedient must be found so that we can achieve what is possible, in order that the publication of the volumes not be impeded or altogether prevented by insistence on impossible demands. One always possible way ahead—though by no means welcome to us—would be for us to publish the second and third volumes as a double issue comprising four gatherings, thus sixty-four pages such that the fourth and final volume of the year would have the regular extent of thirty-two pages.[2]

We believe that you will see from what we have laid out above that we wish to resolve the question of the appearance of the next few volumes by agreement, and we look forward to your reply to this by return. Although in principle we deplore reacting with raileries and recriminations, we should nevertheless make clear that in raising the question of altering the publisher, namely from Tonwille-Verlag to UE, you have forgotten the conversation that we had before the summer vacation.[3] When we insisted on tying the change-over of "Tonwille" to the published work of UE, along with full artistic freedom for you as editor, to a certain right of censorship when it comes to personal and national-political attacks, you made very clear that under these conditions you would prefer "Tonwille-Verlag" to continue to appear as the publisher. Of this we took note at the time, and accordingly retained it as the publisher's imprint. So there can be no question of absolute autonomy in this, and equally untenable are all the other conclusions that you draw from adhering to the publishing firm.

As to your suggestion that we dissolve our relationship as regards *Der Tonwille*, we reserve our reply until the questions of the three issues still to appear have been completely settled.

   With kind regards,
   Universal Edition & Co.
    pp Rothe

[1] The absence of salutation marks a new stage in the deteriorating relations between the two men, and a partial withdrawal on Hertzka's part. Barbara Rothe was UE's office manager (Bureau-Chefin) between 1908 and at least 1929.

[2] IV/2–3 were ultimately produced as a double issue comprising fifty-six pages and accommodating the entire essay on Brahms's "Handel" Variations, Op. 24; IV/4 comprised forty-two pages.

[3] i.e. May 26, 1924: this remark indicates that the true author of the letter is Hertzka, albeit signed by Barbara Rothe.

❧ Hertzka (UE) to Schenker (letter), November 10, 1924
OC 52/605

Doctor Heinrich Schenker

We acknowledge receipt of your letter of the 5th of the month and would prefer it if you would comment upon the following questions in the matter of the dissolution of the letter of agreement over *Der Tonwille*:

1) Do you have in mind to continue the editing of this little library *Der Tonwille* with any other publisher, or are you thinking of not publishing any further articles of this kind?

2) Would you, in the event that a settlement of the disputed question were possible, continue *Der Tonwille* such that you would produce a two-gathering issue each quarter-year in return for a once-and-for-all-fixed payment, in addition to which a lump-sum payment for the previous ten volumes would be forthcoming, whereupon no further statements of account to you would have to be issued. Once sales figures for ten issues are available, the publishable value of the *Der Tonwille* issues can then be approximately assessed.

As regards point 2), we should like to comment as follows: The continuation of the series appears to us desirable in the interests of music education. If the series were to be continued by another publisher, that could happen under the title *Der Tonwille* only if the publisher were to take over the publishing rights, stocks, engraved plates, etc. in their entirety. We doubt if a publisher could now be found who would declare himself ready to do that.[1] For the good of the enterprise, we would set aside all personal elements and make an attempt to continue the work, so long as by modifying the contract any possibility of vexation, dispute, or ill-temper were precluded. Perhaps with impartial mediation by a neutral third party it might be possible to formulate such a letter of agreement.

The discontinuance of *Der Tonwille* altogether would surely be to the great detriment of the ten already existing volumes, of which large stocks are in hand. This discontinuance would moreover not make a favorable impression of yourself as editor.

Despite the currently less than satisfactory state of relationships, we can, for the good of the enterprise, and leaving all personal factors aside, put forward a substantive agreement, provided that from your side there is good will to do that.

In anticipating your response we remain
Sincerely yours
Universal Edition & Co.
Hertzka

[1] In fact, negotiations for the takeover of *Der Tonwille* were already going on with Drei Masken Verlag by November 1924. A contract would be issued in February 1925 for a yearbook with the title "*Das Meisterwerk in der Musik*," Schenker would begin submitting material for it in June 1925, and UE would release the material assets of the periodical in December 1925. (See chapter 9.)

❦ Schenker to UE (letter), December 4, 1924
WSLB 362 (= OC 52/682–683 = OC 52/609)

To Universal Edition,[1]

The accident, about which mention has been made,[2] has unfortunately delayed the reply that I promised you to your letter of November 10. I now take the liberty of acquainting you with the following as regards the enterprise:

It is clear in view of the success of my *Tonwille* that my resolve to continue this periodical is for me unshakeable. In your letter you yourself have described its continuation as desirable for several reasons, or more correctly: you decry the discontinuation of the periodical.

You must surely appreciate what it is that prompts me to break my ties with you and to entrust the enterprise to another publishing house. It is not the sort of accounting that has been practised, but your downright sabotaging attitude toward my work and the dissemination of the periodical. It goes without saying, therefore, that even the fixed payment that you kindly offer affords me no provision, above all no guarantee, that the periodical will be managed by you in a way that is not injurious to it or to me.

I have every reason to believe that I will place *Der Tonwille* with another publishing house.

In order to bring about a smooth solution satisfactory to both parties, I will suggest to the publisher in question the acquisition of the ten issues. To this end, I ask you please, in keeping with your letter of November 10, for information on the following points:

1) What was the print-run of the issues?

2) How many copies of them are still available, and what price are you asking for the stocks?

3) What are you asking for the material assets (engraved blocks, plates, etc)?

You refer on the financial side to the great detriment that the cessation of *Der Tonwille* would be to the issues that have already appeared. But please do not forget that in the four years of its existence *Der Tonwille*—as I have again and again remonstrated with you—has suffered such enormous damage at your hands in financial and moral respects that I have a rightful claim upon compensation. I would, however, so as to avoid the unpleasantness of needing to demonstrate the damage I have suffered, rest my claim if, considering your repeated and so emphatic affirmation of the quality of the enterprise, you were to facilitate in every possible way the takeover of the ten issues.

   Looking forward to a speedy response from you,
    I remain, with kind regards,
     H. Schenker

---

[1] This letter underwent extensive drafting, and benefited from Baumgarten's advice.
[2] Schenker swallowed a large fish bone, which lodged painfully in the colon and had to be removed on November 18.

Hertzka to Schenker (letter), December 5, 1924
OC 52/610

Dear Dr. [Schenker],[1]

In receipt of your letter of the 4th of the month, I must inform you that we have no intention of giving away the publication of the ten issues of *Der Tonwille*. Hence there is no need for us to answer the three questions you have put to us.

   With kind regards,
    Universal Edition & Co.
    Hertzka

---

[1] This is the last letter that Hertzka wrote to Schenker before the dissolution. It thus marks the final breakdown of trust toward Schenker. Although correspondence flowed continually between Schenker and UE over proofs and complimentary copies, and the dispute with the bookkeeping department over accounts and subscription raged through most of 1925, the two men did not communicate directly. In May 1925 UE engaged its attorney, Gustav Scheu, and from then on communication on all the vexed issues was channeled between two parties' lawyers, each receiving instructions from his client, and threatening or trying to avert legal proceedings.

  Matters came to a head in early November 1925 when Baumgarten and Schenker drafted a formal complaint against UE covering the publisher's imprint of *Der Tonwille*, breach of contract, failure to provide adequate publicity, accounting errors, mishandling of subscriptions, and secrecy and obstructiveness on the part of UE's officials. Whether this was ever presented to the "press police" is unclear. Meetings earlier in the year had failed to produce agreement; now a top-level conference was proposed, bringing Schenker and Hertzka face to face for the first time in eighteen months. Hertzka had resisted having the two attorneys present at this, but ultimately agreed to the format of a dialog between himself and Schenker with the two attorneys in attendance, plus Hugo Winter to deal with bookkeeping issues, and Jeanette Schenker.

🎼 Diary Entries, December 9 and 10, 1925

[December 9:] Meeting from 10 to 12:30: it runs a very animated course; Hertzka cannot contain himself and unburdens his offended heart with statements that we vigorously deny. He turns down the settlement, in spite of it saying in the letter "… it is just the sums of money … ." He attempts to make a settlement with regard to *Der Tonwille*, but I fend this off because I am worried about the fate of the [Beethoven] sonatas, and offer a package deal. Several times we are on the point of breaking off the meeting, but it is Hertzka who gives way and initiates further discussion. He makes a suggestion with regard to *Der Tonwille*, including the monographs. Finally, at the last minute, we agree to meet again tomorrow.

[December 10:] Up at 6.30! While getting dressed, Lie-Liechen has a good idea: to suggest a middle course between the two points of view! Hertzka does not want to make a settlement—I do not want any royalties; so an annual payment should be made that corresponds roughly with the royalties. I gladly seize this suggestion, we come up with the sum: something like 3,000 or 2,500 shillings! Thus at the very beginning of the meeting I surprise even Baumgarten,[1] and Hertzka himself holds back for a while; then he asks me to name the sum, without basically appearing to be happy with this suggestion. I name it—more silence follows—Winter breaks it with the observation that this sum does not correspond to the facts and is prohibitively expensive.

Now the matter is approached head-on, but I succeed in arguing that the sonatas should be taken care of first. After a lot of to-ing and fro-ing we consent to agree to take one half [of the named sum]—but Hertzka does not even like the taste of this. Dr. Baumgarten has the idea of reducing the number of years [of payment] after my death to ten (instead of thirty); he communicates this to Hertzka, who accepts the suggestion primarily, it must be conceded, on account of his having misunderstood Baumgarten's suggestion because of his hearing difficulties and taken the ten years to be the absolute limit of his obligation. The goodwill of this moment seemed great, and from his heart there stormed forth: "And how much are you demanding for the theory books [New Musical Theories and Fantasies]?" (!) By chance, however, the question went from Baumgarten to Winter, and the misunderstanding was cleared up—Hertzka could not retreat any further and was tied to paying 12½ million kronen for the sonatas! Only now do we declare ourselves in agreement with the settlement on *Der Tonwille*, even with payment in installments. Hertzka also accepts my suggestion regarding the "Moonlight" Sonata: 500 shillings. — Writing up of the agreement, and conclusion![2]

---

[1] Theodor Baumgarten, attorney employed by Moriz Schenker and seconded to represent Schenker in his battle with UE in 1924–25.

[2] It was not until November 27, 1928, that Schenker wrote again direct to Hertzka, receiving a reply on December 21. Only twenty-three letters between the two survive from after the 1925 breakup. Hertzka died on May 9, 1932, so was not involved with Schenker's final publications: *Five Analyses in Sketchform* (1932), "Johannes Brahms: Octaves and Fifths" (1933), and *Free Composition* (1935, posthumous).

❦ Baumgarten to Schenker (letter), December 18, 1925
OC 52/538

Vienna I, December 18, 1925
KÖLLNERHOFGASSE I

Dear and highly revered Dr. Schenker,

Today I received the following letter from UE:

"In response to your esteemed letter of December 14 of this year we are having delivered to you by messenger:

<u>196 engraved blocks [of music examples] for *Der Tonwille* issues 1–10</u>

<u>13 gatherings of proofs of engraved music examples</u>

8 matrix tables[1] (= 16 pages) of small type for Beethoven's Fifth Symphony (from *Tonwille* issue 1).

After communications with the printers Otto Maas & Sons, all the remaining type for the *Tonwille* issues has already been distributed, and matrices were not made."

I have not yet opened the packet.

Please take note of the above communication. I remain with best greetings to you both

Yours truly,
Baumgarten

---

[1] *Materntafeln*: meaning unclear. There is no small type in the Fifth Symphony article in *Tonwille* 1; presumably reference is to the small-type section, pp. 15–42 of *Tonwille* 5.

9
Drei Masken Verlag
and *The Masterwork in Music*

Even before severing his ties formally with Emil Hertzka and Universal Edition in 1925 (see chapter 8) Schenker was already in negotiations with a publisher to continue the *Tonwille* series of short analytical and theoretical essays. The Munich firms of R. Piper and Drei Masken Verlag (DMV), both of which had considerable experience in fine book production, were initially considered. With the help of Otto Vrieslander a cordial relationship was begun in late 1924 with DMV, for whose music catalog Alfred Einstein was responsible. Much of the correspondence with Schenker was undertaken by a Mr. Demblin—probably the historian August Demblin, whose *Czernin und die Sixtus-affaire* was published by the firm in 1920.

What DMV offered Schenker represented a considerable improvement on the *Tonwille* format. Instead of a quarterly publication of small pamphlet-sized volumes, they proposed a yearbook comprising fifteen gatherings (of sixteen pages each) modeled on their *Mozart Jahrbuch* (of which only three volumes appeared between 1923 and 1929); the publishers also insisted on a new title, and *Das Meisterwerk in der Musik: ein Jahrbuch von Heinrich Schenker* was agreed upon. The manuscript was to be delivered by July 1, so that the yearbook could be in print in time for the Christmas sales.

Although Schenker spared no effort to meet the first deadline—the manuscript for the first yearbook was duly sent off before he and Jeanette left Vienna for their summer vacation—the publishers were somewhat caught off guard by the novelty of the voice-leading graphs and other musical illustrations. Moreover, Schenker made numerous corrections to the text after it was set in galley proofs, with the result that both the cost of and the time needed for production far exceeded DMV's initial estimate: by the time the first yearbook appeared in print, Jeanette had already finished copying the manuscript of the second and was about to send it to the publishers.

Initially DMV refused to publish the second volume, preferring to wait until they had a clearer idea of sales of the first volume. Schenker threatened legal action, but was dissuaded from taking the firm to court on the grounds that this would only further delay the appearance of his work. In the autumn of 1926 they agreed to proceed with *Masterwork* 2 on condition that Schenker assume some of the production costs and minimize late corrections. To achieve those ends, Vrieslander assisted with the music examples, Otto Erich Deutsch helped with proof corrections, and Anthony van Hoboken contributed to the production costs.

Schenker spent much of the late 1920s completing and revising a lengthy analysis of Beethoven's "Eroica" Symphony, one for which the graphs were yet more complex. He tried unsuccessfully (in spite of some help from Wilhelm Furtwängler) to interest one of the two great Leipzig music publishing houses, C. F. Peters and Breitkopf & Härtel, in taking it. With Deutsch's mediation once again, DMV agreed to publish it—as a third yearbook, despite the lapse of two years since the appearance of *Masterwork 2*—on the condition that Schenker assume all the production costs.

Masterwork 3 was published in early December 1930, just in time to be displayed at a lecture on Schenker's theories delivered by Hans Weisse at the Central Institute for Music Pedagogy in Berlin. Six months later—again through Weisse's agency—Furtwängler made a gift of 3,000 marks to Schenker, which covered more than half the production costs.

Concerned as they were with the inordinately high production costs of the yearbooks, DMV changed printing houses with each volume. Waldheim-Eberle (Vienna) printed the first yearbook, Mandruck (Munich) the second, C. G. Röder (Leipzig) the third. For the reproduction of the music illustrations for the "Eroica," Schenker—on Deutsch's advice—enlisted the help of Georg Tomay, a Viennese music calligrapher and autographer. (Tomay proved so skillful in preparing Schenker's graphs that he was subsequently entrusted with the preparation of the *Five Analyses in Sketchform*.)

The twenty-six items included in this selection represent about a tenth of the surviving correspondence concerning the *Masterwork* yearbooks. The only letters from Schenker to DMV that have been traced are drafts, in Jeanette's hand; all bear extensive corrections in Schenker's hand.

WILLIAM DRABKIN

❧ August Demblin and Alfred Einstein (DMV) to Schenker (letter), November 27, 1924
OC 54/2

DREI MASKEN VERLAG & CO.
MUNICH, KAROLINENPLATZ 3

Dear Dr. [Schenker],

Concerning the matter in which Mr. Vrieslander has hitherto taken over the negotiations between us, permit us now to approach you yourself, and to clarify our position.

We need not emphasize how much we look forward to coming in contact with you. But you will find it understandable that we pass on to you full responsibility for making arrangements with Director Hertzka; we wish to deal with you alone, and not have anything to do with Universal Edition. Moreover, we openly admit our purely business interest in the undertaking. Thus we must ask you to attempt to provide information about the production costs, the size of the print-run, and the frequency of appearance of the issues of *Der Tonwille* that have so far appeared. What seems to be required, in effect, is the acquisition of the whole of *Der Tonwille*, in spite of the very unsatisfactory layout of the issues; if this is unsuccessful and if one were obliged to leave the previous stock in Hertzka's hands, then we could only imagine a new series with a new title.

You will of course keep us informed about the further progress of your dealings with H; of our greatest interest and our goodwill, you may be assured!

    With best regards,
        Drei Masken Verlag & Co.
        p.p. Demblin, on behalf of the publishers
                                                A. Einstein

❦ Schenker to DMV (draft letter), December 9, 1924
OC 54/5–7

Sent by registered mail on December 9

To my letter of December 4 to Universal Edition, enclosed here, I received by return of post the letter of December 5 which is also enclosed.[1]

It is possible that Director Hertzka will accept the takeover of the ten issues [of *Der Tonwille*] as a principal requirement of the new publisher, or wishes to thwart our relationship by [your] refusal [to agree to this]. But it is also possible that he is reluctant to disclose numbers [of copies in stock] to me and to you; perhaps vengeance is also playing a part and that he intends to sabotage the ten issues outright. For he will stop at nothing that is humanly possible.

I now believe that there is nothing left for us to do than to begin a new series with a new title. What would you say to the title "Die Urlinie"?[2]

Could the earlier subtitle be retained? If not, then I would suggest "Quarterly Publication" etc.

The Fraktur typeface should be kept, likewise the format; otherwise a second music example on one page would allow no space for any further text.

In terms of content, I would start by gradually presenting all of Chopin's Etudes, and Brahms's four symphonies, rounded off by Mozart's three great symphonies, which would make it possible to create monographs [from them]; also to include the remaining symphonies of Beethoven, the greatest of Haydn, Schubert,[3] and so on, along with essays of various sizes, and the Miscellanea.

Please be so kind as to acquaint me with your draft contract, your view about the title and the form of the whole, so that I shall soon be able to decide on the appropriate content of the issues and work on them.

---

[1] Schenker's letter of December 4 survives as a final copy and two drafts. Hertzka's letter of December 5 can be found in chapter 8 above.

[2] [Schenker's note:] Further titles will be suggested in the letter.

[3] Of these works, Schenker published analyses of Mozart's Symphony in G minor K. 550, Beethoven's "Eroica" Symphony, and two Chopin etudes, Op. 10, Nos. 5–6, in the three *Masterwork* yearbooks. Analyses of two further etudes from Op. 10 (Nos. 8 and 12) appear in the *Five Analyses in Sketchform*.

August Demblin and Alfred Einstein (DMV) to Schenker (letter), January 20, 1925
OC 54/12

Dear Dr. [Schenker],

We apologize profusely for returning to the matter of *Der Tonwille* only today; it was not so easy for us to obtain the necessary information.

That was somewhat devastating. The main point is that *Der Tonwille* appears in a print-run of only 800 copies. Accordingly, we must concede to Director Hertzka that he is making a sort of complimentary gift, which he is able to make as the publisher of your large theoretical writings and your editions of Bach and Beethoven.[1]

For us the task is much greater. We must retain the previous subscribers to your issues and gain a large number of new ones. We believe that this will be possible only on an entirely new basis. Not merely the title would have to be changed, to spare us any confrontation with Universal Edition, but also the format; and we should like to suggest to you a yearbook for which you would make available to us a manuscript with the overall size equal to the four monthly issues, thus comprising about fifteen gatherings, on July 1 of every year, so that we could publish it in good time before Christmas. For a title, of the ones you suggested we thought "The Masterwork in Music: a Yearbook by Heinrich Schenker" to be the best. For you, the new format would admittedly have the disadvantage that you would be obliged to prepare a large amount of material at once; however, we believe that the effect of such a yearbook would be much greater, and deeper, than that of the smaller issues.

For a royalty, we would like to suggest to you 15 percent of the store price of a paperback copy; upon delivery of the manuscript, you will receive a corresponding advance. We will send you a draft contract that goes into greater detail as soon as we have been informed of your agreement, in principle, with our suggestions.

We enclose the letter of December 5, 1924, from Universal Edition.

      With best regards,
      Drei Masken Verlag & Co.
         p.p. Demblin, on behalf of the publisher
                                      Einstein

1 enclosure

---

[1] Annotation in Schenker's hand in the bottom margin: "Thus the figures given by the printers [Otto] Maas on February 14, 1925, are confirmed. The first issues [of *Der Tonwille*], 800–1,000 [copies]. Then fewer. No. 10, 700."

◊ Schenker to DMV (draft letter), January 28, 1925
OC 54/16–18

I agree to your suggestion of a yearbook with sincere conviction. However difficult it may be to complete the work in the narrow time-frame, I will summon all my strength so that I can deliver the first book to you by July 1. I shall soon send you a small part of my manuscript, with the request that you have it set, so that I can gain an idea of the overall size of the manuscript.

Having reached an agreement with you in principle, I now request a draft contract.

You may probably already know from statements made by Vrieslander that I am by no means a businessman; otherwise I would have long ago got the better of my Viennese patriotism and abandoned the Model Institute for Personal Un-businesslike Lack of Integrity, which is what Director Hertzka is. Nonetheless the demands of the day bid me to be concerned to understand what you mean by 15 percent of the [store price of a] paperback volume, i.e. how much that would roughly be, translated into figures. I cannot work that out, since I do not have any idea of the planned print-run or the price of an individual copy—what I know is simply the genuinely great and strenuous work that I must accomplish.

May I add that I leave it to you, in good faith, whether at your discretion you might perhaps offer me a fixed fee instead of a percentage royalty, as for example UE did with the Ninth Symphony and the elucidatory editions of the last sonatas of Beethoven.

I am pleased to see that you have the humor to see through Director Hertzka's "complimentary gift" to me (with payments that have been shown to have been withheld from me—which I contested!). For fully eight years, from one meeting to the next, he urged me into the "Little Library," which had already been announced in my monograph on the Ninth Symphony; but when he actually received the first issue, he could not think of anything else than to make it a "complimentary gift" in such a manner.

[unsigned]

◊ C. Alberti (DMV) to Schenker (letter), September 1, 1925
OC 54/33

Dear Dr. [Schenker],

Forgive us for leaving your letter of the 23rd of the previous month unanswered until today. We had hoped to give you a positive decision. On account of there being so many holidays taken at this time, we have not been able to progress with your work as far as we ourselves had hoped. We have obtained calculations from various printing houses; however, on account of great differences in cost, we cannot yet reach a decision. We must therefore, regrettably, inform you that we shall not be able to count on the start of proofs in the next two weeks. We assure you, however, that we shall choose a printing house in such a way that quick typesetting and printing can be achieved.

It would in any event be most advantageous if we were to receive the manuscript for the 1926 yearbook sooner, as such difficult work must be undertaken with a great deal of special care if one is not to experience undesirable surprises afterwards.

We therefore ask you to continue to be patient and remain,

With kind regards,
Drei Masken Verlag & Co.
p.p. C. Alberti

Schenker to DMV (draft letter), October 16, 1925
OC 54/37

As you can imagine, your last communication, from October 13, surprised and distressed me. Permit me to comment on this.

In this past year, merely to keep my word at all times for the sake of our agreement, I have already "rushed" in a superhuman way; so it would really not matter to me if I were to risk rushing still further, since the most important thing is to publish by the end of 1925—objectively, morally, and financially—which has already brought about so much work for me. For this reason I declare myself prepared to dispatch the proofs as quickly as possible—I shall make almost no corrections, unless the setters and printers are especially inept!—so that you need not fear any holdup on my part. We would still have a very good chance of meeting the Christmas deadline, at the very least. If, however, it is impossible for you to get hold of the proofs by the middle of November, or the beginning of December, then there would be no problem per se in our back-dating the first yearbook. In the meantime, I am continuing the work for 1926 (the second yearbook), which was begun a long time ago, and promise to send it to you absolutely on time. By then the printer will have long been found, and nothing would stand in the way of publishing the second yearbook (1926) by the deadline to which we have agreed.

With this in mind, I ask you to enable us still to publish in, say, December!

With kind regards,
Yours truly,
H. Schenker

Alfred Böhme (DMV Vienna) to Schenker (letter), January 14, 1926
OC 54/56

DREI MASKEN VERLAG & CO.
VIENNA I, WALLNERSTRASSE 4

Dear Dr. [Schenker],

Forgive us for not answering your letter of January 6 until today. Our entire staff were completely engaged in the end-of-year inventory and winding-up.

It is correct, at any rate, that a reproduction of the [autograph] score of Mozart's *Don Giovanni*, in Paris, will appear in our series of facsimile prints. Of Beethoven's Piano Sonata, Op. 57, nothing is known here.[1] Also we do not know when the Mozart score will appear, and we have written to our Munich house so that they may get in touch with you regarding the date of publication.

We have also communicated to our Munich house your expressed wish to have the Urlinie graphs in the 1926 yearbook twice as wide as they are now, with the reasons given. The remaining work will now be taken care of, step by step.

  We remain,
    With kindest regards,
    DREI MASKEN VERLAG & Co.
    Böhme

---

[1] A facsimile of Beethoven's "Appassionata" Sonata, Op. 57, was to be issued in Paris in 1927, by the printing firm of Henri Piazza.

❧ Alfred Böhme (DMV Vienna) to Schenker (letter), June 5, 1926
OC 54/79

Highly revered Professor,

  In response to your postcard concerning the appearance of the yearbook for 1925, we can tell you the following:

The bookbinder is hard at work on the production of the covers of the work and is likely to need a few more days for it. After the work had already been printed and while it was being bound, there was, unfortunately, a last-minute delay, for which the firm of Waldheim is fully and solely responsible and which we were powerless to do anything about. The firm of Waldheim had made an offer, with an estimate of the cost for the binding work; and after they had printed, they suddenly declared that they could no longer hold to this price. It would have been about 50% higher, something which, when multiplied, would have been applied to the financial calculations and would have had an effect on the determination of the price of the book in the shops. We were therefore compelled to transfer the bindery work to a different Viennese bookbinder. In addition, a small delay has arisen as a result of the two holidays outside the normal range of events (Whit Monday and Corpus Christi), through which two full working days were lost. Finally, the Munich house has additionally asked that the title for the binding should not be set with letters that are already available, as was the case with the trial cover sent to you; instead, a design of a very simple, tasteful typeface was prepared, and that had to be engraved.

As already mentioned above, all the difficulties have now been resolved, and the book bindery has been working since Tuesday on the binding. The binding will thus be finished next week; yet we recommend, in your interest as well as in ours, not to press us to bring out the edition early, for the sake of the two days, but to let the volumes dry thoroughly at the book bindery. Otherwise the danger arises that, if the book is sent out early, the covers will warp. We remain,

 With kind regards,
 DREI MASKEN VERLAG & Co.
 Böhme

August Demblin (DMV) to Schenker (letter), June 21, 1926
OC 54/88

Dear Professor,

As we recently informed you, the manuscript of your second yearbook has arrived. Concerning the printing of this, we cannot reach a decision with absolute certainty in this regard since we must first await the commercial results of the first volume before we decide to take it on.[1] We are somewhat concerned about these results, since the price of the book had to be set very high as a result of the high production costs; in particular, the correction costs were a quite significant factor, and indeed because the changes you made after the work was typeset were very considerable. We thus find ourselves compelled, in accordance with the agreement in our contract, to deduct the sum of 347.74 marks (these are the correction costs that exceed 10% of the printing costs) from your account, which we shall take into account only when calculating the percentage royalty.

The remainder of your advance of 250 (two hundred and fifty) marks will be paid to you through our Vienna house.

 With the expression of our kind regards,
 Drei Masken Verlag & Co.
 p.p. Demblin

---

[1] An annotation in Schenker's hand in the to margin of this letter indicates his displeasure at its contents: "See the contract, §8, [and] letter of September 1, 1925."

Schenker to DMV (draft letter), June 24, 1926
OC 54/91–92

On the basis of §8 of our contract concerning the yearbook *The Masterwork in Music*, I was just at the point of starting work on the manuscript for the third yearbook, 1927, when your letter of June 21 surprised me today. From it I infer that the third yearbook, 1927, is in all circumstances no longer welcome, and as you are informing me of this promptly I now consider myself free of contractual obligation with respect to a third yearbook.[1]

However, I shall certainly not allow a retroactive arrangement applicable to the second yearbook, according to your statement of June 21; and I insist upon your obligation to prepare the manuscript of the second yearbook, which I sent you in accordance with the contract, <u>for printing</u> and <u>to bring it out by the "deadline" of November 1926</u>. I delivered the manuscript for the first yearbook in the middle of June 1925, and it would have been your responsibility to have told me by July 1 [of that year] at the latest that you would not take a second yearbook or that you, making use of §8, recommended a change in the contract. Notwithstanding this, you let me work for a year and only now, when you have the manuscript in your hands, do you wish, on account of various other circumstances to which the contract does not apply, to put to one side the matter of whether you will "decide to accept the manuscript": I now declare all in breach of contract.

I leave all feelings aside, and deal with you from the standpoint of "business" with respect to your letter [of June 21], and request an answer within a week, whether you are adhering to your standpoint, whether you do so by not replying, or indeed … [*illegible text*], then I would see myself compelled immediately to seek the help of the judiciary to protect an agreed and contractually fulfilled achievement of mine.

All other questions in your letter I shall, for the time being, set aside.

       With kind regards,
       H. Schenker

---

[1] Many words in this hastily written and heavily corrected draft are illegible; the following translation is, in places, approximate.

August Demblin (DMV) to Schenker (letter), July 9, 1926
OC 54/95

Dear Professor,

Owing to the absence of one of our directors, we were unable until today to reply to your letter of the 24th of last month, in which you object to our being unable to proceed at this very moment with the production of the new volume of your yearbook. Even if we take a different position in the interpretation of §8 of our contract, and do not believe that our previous request that you might wish to send us the manuscript of volume 2 at your earliest convenience prevents us from having recourse to §8, we should most certainly wish to accommodate you as far as possible, and to produce the new volume as soon as the conditions in the book market somehow permit it. This is, however, in no way the case at present; and as we would have to keep the price of the volume at the same level as the first, and in view of the shortage of money among potential purchasers of this book, we would probably be able to sell only a small portion of the print-run; this is something that can be neither in your interests nor in ours.

We should like, therefore, to suggest to you that the matter be postponed until the early fall, the end of September or the beginning of October, as we hope that by then we shall be able to see somewhat more clearly into the near future.

Please let us know whether you are agreed to this suggestion.

With the expression of our kind regards,
   Drei Masken Verlag & Co.
   p.p. Demblin

Schenker to DMV (draft letter), July 14, 1926
OC 54/96–99

While preserving my point of view, I shall gladly agree to your suggestion of delaying the matter until the beginning of October.

I remain adamant about the publication of the manuscript you have in your possession as the 1926 yearbook, but am prepared, in order to accommodate you, to agree to a delay of its appearance, as has been the case with the 1925 yearbook, even though I shall suffer significant financial damage as a result. If you do not want to burden your budget for this year with two yearbooks, then I shall accept that; but the manuscript should still go into production in the course of 1926, so that it can still appear as the 1926 yearbook in the first half of 1927.

I would certainly never have written *The Masterwork in Music* as a one-off book, and most certainly not in the way it was written as a yearbook for 1925. There is a difference between a book and a yearbook; you know this as well as I.

The "yearbook" necessitates a periodicity; the title was the result of your suggestion and wish, and you too regarded the yearbook as the continuation of *Der Tonwille*, which however did not appear as a single issue.

Thus it happens that, even in the 1926 yearbook, I have been able to broach topics of the broadest contemporary interest, which I was not yet able to air in the 1925 yearbook, which was the first yearbook. Just as each yearbook of mine will take on a specific form, so the yearbooks will hang together with each other. As you yourself suggested 250 pages, and were aware of the content as well as the form of *Der Tonwille*, you would surely have known the approximate production costs as a result of your experience (I am thinking in particular of your Mozart yearbooks); for this reason I am astonished that you give, retrospectively, the matter of cost as the reason for non-fulfillment.

My works have most certainly created no financial losses for Universal Edition. Most of them have (in spite of sabotage) reached several print-runs; and their value for the publishing house is something that I can best judge from the large sum of money that Director Hertzka conferred upon me as royalty during our last negotiation, as well as also from the fact that he has pledged to complete one of my works, etc.

I would rather, I believe, ask your patience—even for business reasons—than have you threaten to destroy my work even before the first reviews have appeared!

   [*unsigned*]

❧ Alfred Einstein (DMV) to Schenker (letter), December 11, 1926
OC 54/109

Dear Dr. [Schenker],

I am concerned that your letter of November 18[1] still lies here unanswered; and I would like to take this opportunity to give you an explanation of the situation entirely from my personal point of view.

The publishing house is of the opinion that it is not bound to bring out the second volume of *The Masterwork in Music*; and it has turned to its legal adviser, from whom it has been strengthened in its belief that a battle over the publication will, in the greatest likelihood, go in its favor. I personally would very much wish to avoid a trial occurring between you and Drei Masken Verlag, and I fancy that perhaps a cheaper arrangement can take place whereby the publisher can compensate you appropriately for the trouble that you have taken over the second volume. Please write to me, to say whether you might possibly be agreeable to this (in any event, the sum will not be exorbitant), and then I shall make this suggestion here at the publishing house. — In any event, I am leaving tomorrow for a few weeks' holiday, but would request that you address your reply to me personally.

        With most cordial greetings and best wishes,
        Yours very truly,
        Alfred Einstein

[1] Schenker's letter complained that DMV had not yet, as promised, declared whether or not it would publish *Masterwork 2*, nor had it advertised *Masterwork 1*.

❧ Schenker to DMV (draft of two letters), January 8 and 10, 1927
OC 54/116

Vienna, January 10, 1927[1]

1) Since you have declined, on financial grounds, to publish the second volume of my yearbook *The Masterwork in Music*, I request that you hand over the manuscript of this volume to my representative, Mr. Otto Erich Deutsch.

I must reserve the right to claim compensation for the damages which arise from your breach of our contract.

    With kind regards,

2) A group of pupils would like to make your contract with me with regard to *The Masterwork in Music* financially easier.

Mr. Otto Erich Deutsch, who is the authorized representative of this group, also has my authority to reach an agreement with you, which in this sense represents an addendum to our contract.

    With kind regards,
    [*unsigned*]

[1] Because these letters are typewritten, they were not composed by Schenker himself. His diary entry for January 7 records a meeting with Anthony van Hoboken and Otto Erich Deutsch, who "suggest to me two courses of action, depending on the attitude of the publishers." It may be that Hoboken and Deutsch brought these drafts with them—forward-dated, to allow time for Schenker to reflect on the matter before replying to the publishers. At the bottom of the page is written, probably in Schenker's hand, "January 8, 1927." —From the content of the publishers' next letter (January 17), it is clear that Schenker had agreed to the second course of action, and that Deutsch had then made immediate contact with the publishers.

August Demblin (DMV) to Schenker (letter), January 17, 1927
OC 54/119

Dear Dr. Schenker,
As you will have at any rate already learned from Mr. Otto Erich Deutsch, we are, on the basis of the proposal made to us by Mr. Deutsch (i.e. by the group of pupils he represents) with your agreement, prepared to typeset the second volume of your yearbook *The Masterwork in Music*. We even hope that it can be published before the end of March.

At the same time we assure you that we are also prepared to publish a leaflet, which you may wish to write in reply to attacks or reviews that the second volume of the yearbook may encounter.

Our bookkeeping department is at the same time receiving the instruction to remit the portion of the honorarium, 250 marks, which is contractually due to you.

In so far as we may give expression to our delight that, under these conditions, it is still possible for the second volume of your yearbook to be published by our house, we send greetings,

with the expression of our kindest regards,
Drei Masken Verlag & Co.
p.p. Demblin

Otto Vrieslander to Schenker (letter), February 10, 1927
OC 54/129

Most revered, dear Dr. Schenker,
I enclose the Symphony in G minor, with which you will, I hope, be tolerably pleased. In executing this work, I have not let the most subtle subtlety go unused. The slurs, dotted slurs, strokes, etc. etc. have been drawn as finely and as close to the staff lines as necessary, clarity permitting, so that the *picture* remains clear—which is of course your principal concern. You will therefore note that, in spite of the increased number of your signs, a desirable clarity has been secured in this way. I could of course have lined the paper myself; but I see that even if I make the space between the staves even wider, there is no gain in clarity. Mistakes will hardly be found, as I have undertaken the revision myself in the most precise

possible way, unless a misunderstanding has crept in. Moreover, I was thoroughly informed about the changes as a result of your detailed commentary. In the course of being reproduced, the pages will probably be cut up into pieces; for this reason I have always written on *one* side of the paper. This would be better as a model for the engraver's copy, in case you were to proceed in this direction. I have not yet received Haydn's "Chaos," though Einstein informed me a few weeks ago about graphs that are to be copied; so I am expecting new work. I will, at some point, inquire about this.

Accept, both of you, my most sincere greetings. And return the master copy to me at your earliest convenience, so that I can give it to the Drei Masken Verlag.

   Yours truly,
   Otto Vrieslander
Munich 38, Walhallastrasse 9

❦ Otto Vrieslander to Schenker (letter), February 15, 1927
OC 54/132

Most revered, dear Dr. Schenker,

After looking at my master copy, Dr. Einstein said immediately, only without thinking further about it: This must be engraved, since from a copy *of such quality* the engraver could produce everything in the most faultless way. I informed him of the fact that you, in effect working only for pocket money, would no longer be in the mood to pay an inordinate sum of money for additional corrections and that you would have been most displeased to find that you had eventually been charged far more than 300 marks. Stern silence on Dr. Einstein's part and a rather foolish facial expression. Yet even that no longer applies in the event that I rewrite the manuscripts. I also told him that, so long as I were to remain here [in Munich], I would read the corrections until, say, the last set, which would of course have to go to you.

We indeed decided on engraving, the clarity of which is more readily guaranteed, but above all because we can expand the width of the [pages in the] supplement[1] (since, indeed, an empty page makes this widening possible alongside the text, as we already explained in the presence of Messrs. Deutsch and Hoboken), such as would not be possible by means of photolithographic reproduction. In accordance with this decision I immediately entered the slurs encompassing the interval of a third in the sections of the G minor Symphony, which I would otherwise have had to omit; in addition, I have immediately changed the ⸻ fourth-progression ⸻ since this is now of course possible once again. I also alerted him, especially in the fugue, to the double division of the Urlinie figures $\frac{5}{1}$ with the <u>two</u> line-heights and the difference in their level. And so on and so forth.

Since I will also be reading the corrections, you can put your faith in me entirely. Regarding the slurs, of which mine are much too similar to strokes (i.e. straight lines) and which you would rather have rounder, more vaulted, so as not to be confused with actual straight lines, I shall also arrange what is required.

Regarding my question about "Chaos" and further parts of the Symphony, he said that <u>Mandruck had not said a word about particular difficulties</u>. With this, however, I was not satisfied, so instead I asked Dr. Einstein if I could speak personally with the corrector so that, in case he thinks there are problems, I can first complete a manuscript so that you will not have additional expenses for additional corrections chalked up against you, for that is the very thing that we want to avoid as far as possible. That was also Hoboken's view at the time. In the meantime I am *intentionally* writing up these points once again in a letter to Dr. Einstein, so that he cannot later wriggle out of things with some lame excuse about—who knows?—imprecise or even false instructions, etc. He will have this letter tomorrow, and I shall make a carbon copy, which I shall send on to you, so that you are in the picture.

When I now receive further manuscripts I shall of course, in spite of the engraving process, send my master copies to you in Vienna as before, so that you are in the picture and can undertake any additional <u>improvements</u> that may still be necessary.

Deutsch wrote to me, I would like [you to know], since he had earmarked me—and told Haas about it—to give a lecture about bibliography as concerns Beethoven; whereupon I replied to him that I would give a lecture only if I could speak about Schenker's Beethoven editions, and this quite expressly only if he were not to cut the time alloted to a most ludicrous limit. To speak about Beethoven bibliography *per se* is something that others could do just as well as if not better than I, even if I would not like to deny that I know several important things about this matter. But to ramble on, just for the sake of rambling on, for that I have no desire; if however it comes to blathering, then [I shall do so] only in relation to you and your editions, so that the blathering can at least be put together a bit fruitfully; otherwise it is really no different from an intellectual giving a lecture to other intellectuals over a snack in a coffeehouse about the solution to the world's problem[s]. By which everyone is thinking: Hey, I knew that, and more, all along. —About *my* subject, one could of course not make this claim. For this, however, I will probably receive a clear rebuff; of this I am in no doubt.

Enough for today. As soon as I have an answer from Dr. Einstein, you will hear further. I shall also make the matter most urgent.

Most cordial greetings to the two of you. That I am curious about Dunn is something you can well imagine. I should like to make the man's acquaintence, since I would have quite a lot of stimulating things [to talk about] with him; for England is a fruitful place for such things. I personally do not have any expectations of England (apart from the sympathy in which I have always held this country), since the English have nourished themselves on our Handel, Haydn, Weber, Beethoven and, lastly, Chopin, whereas their own nation[s] had only pretty words, phrases and—a nice burial for their great musicians. The touching story of Miss [Jane] Stirling, who gave Chopin 25,000 francs as he faced starvation, is something I shall always find wonderful. Likewise the £50 sterling for Beethoven shortly before his death, which touched him so deeply. The Parisians in the first case, the Viennese in the second, had only "a nice pompous funeral!" for their great ones. Therefore the English Schenker also delights me.

Yours truly,
OV

[1] The extra pages of graphs and Urlinie-Tafeln, held together by a paper band at the back of each yearbook.

❧ Otto Erich Deutsch to Schenker (letter), March 16, 1927
OC 54/137

Dear Dr. [Schenker],

Thank you for your postcard. I am enclosing the proof sheets 61–70, which were not finished yesterday, and a copy of the Haydn sketch for "Chaos." Mandyczewski wrote about this in 1889 in Kratochwill's magazine. From Poszony, the manuscript made its roundabout way to America. The photograph is not available or has been mislaid. The copy, made from a line etching, ought to suffice; it is certainly better than the print in Schmidt's *Haydn*.[1] Both are probably derived from the reproduction in Mandyczewski's article, which is not present in the Society of the Friends of Music. It is certainly available in the National Library, for example.

The inscription "Collection Poszonyi" must be omitted.

Please return the page to me. I have borrowed it.

All issues of *Der Tonwille* may be found in the Reading Room of the Society of the Friends of Music (Library).

Most truly,
Yours,
O. Deutsch

2 enclosures

[1] Leopold Schmidt, *Joseph Haydn*. In the second edition of this work (Berlin: Harmonie-Verlag, 1906) the sketch is reproduced on p. 105.

❧ List of review copies of *The Masterwork in Music*, volume 1
OC 54/193

	Review Copies	
	Schenker Yearbook	
[Recipients]	[City]	[Dispatch date, intended journal]
1. Otto Vrieslander	Munich	29.6.26
2. August Halm	Wickersdorf	"
3. M. Violin	Hamburg	"
4. Herman Roth	Stuttgart	"
5. Prof. Dr. Altmann	Berlin-Fr.[1]	"

6.	Preuss. Staatsbibliothek	Berlin	"	
7.	Frau Elsa Bienenfeld	Vienna	"	*Neues Wiener Journal*
8.	Frau Hedwig Kauner	"	"	*Wiener Morgenzeitung*
9.	Dr. Ernst Decsey	"	"	*Neues Wiener Tagblatt*
10.	Dr. D. J. Bach	"	"	*Arbeiter-Zeitung*
11.	Dr. Hans Liebstöckl	"	"	*Die Stunde*
12.	*Basler Nachrichten*	Basel	26.7.26	
13.	*Der Bund*	Bern	"	
14.	*Neue Zürcher Zeitung*	Zurich	"	
15.	*Berliner Börsen-Courier*	Berlin	"	
16.	*Berliner Lokalanzeiger*	"	"	
17.	*Deutsche Tageszeitung*	"	"	
18.	*Vossische Zeitung*	"	"	
19.	*Berliner Tageblatt*	"	"	
20.	*Deutsche Allgemeine Zeitung*	"	"	
21.	*Berliner Börsen-Zeitung*	"	"	
22.	*Münchner Neueste Nachrichten*	Munich	"	
23.	*Allgemeine Musikzeitung*	Berlin	"	
24.	*Die Musik*	Stuttgart	"	
25.	*Zeitschrift für Musik*	Leipzig	"	
26.	*Neue Musikzeitung*	Stuttgart	"	
27.	*Die Musikwelt*	Hamburg	"	
28.	Prof. Dr. A. Herget	Komotau[2]	29.7.26	
29.	Fratelli Bocca	Turin	"	
30.	Prof. Dr. Karl Schmidt	Friedberg	18.8.26	
31.	Alexander Berrsche	Munich	7.9.26	
32.	Prof. Dr. R. Oppel	Kiel	9.9.26	
33.	*Il pianoforte*	Turin	14.9.26	
34.	Ludwig Unterholzner	Augsburg	"	
35.	Dr. Frotscher	Danzig	"	
36.	Dr. Paul Mies	Cologne-Sülz	18.9.26	
37.	*Deutsche Akademiker[?]-Zeitung*	Vienna	18.10.26	
38.	*Symphonia*	Nijmegen	"	
39.	*De Musick*	Amsterdam	11.11.26	
40.	*Das Orchester*	Berlin-St.[3]	25.11.26	
41.	*Magdeburgische Zeitung*	Magdeburg	5.1.27	

---

[1] Probably Friedrichshain, a district of Berlin.

[2] A town in the Sudetenland lying close to the border of Saxony (Germany). Its German population was expelled after World War II, and the town is now known by its Czech name Chomutov.

[3] Probably Steglitz, a district of Berlin.

🎵 Karl Straube to Schenker (letter), May 14–16, 1930
OC 54/218

Leipzig, May 14, 1930
Grassistrasse 30^{III}

Highly revered Dr. [Schenker],

Forgive me for writing to you late, but I was in Holland and was unable to speak with Breitkopf & Härtel until after my return.

The fears that I harbored, that my efforts would be in vain, have unfortunately materialized. Counselor Dr. Volkmann[1] told me that the turnover in the music book publishing house has been catastrophic; since the onset of the financial collapse, works devoted to musical issues are hardly sold, and for this reason it is impossible to consider accepting a new arrangement with the publishing house.

May 16, 1930

In the last two days I have once more negotiated with C. F. Peters about taking over the publication of your work. Only today did I receive—unfortunately—another negative decision.

I am eternally sorry to have to report to you about these futile efforts.

    With loyalty and devotion
    Yours as ever,
    Karl Straube

[1] Ludwig Volkmann (1870–1947): a partner in the family firm of Breitkopf & Härtel.

🎵 August Demblin (DMV) to Otto Erich Deutsch (letter), May 22, 1930
OC 54/224

Dear Professor,

We received your kind letter of May 17 and inform you that we are gladly prepared to take on also the third volume of Dr. Schenker's yearbook in our publishing house. Please let us know above all what sort of print-run is envisioned; we imagine that this time, too, 1,100 copies (i.e. 1,000 copies plus an additional 10%) should be printed. As soon as you have informed us, we shall have a calculation made immediately which, of course, could only be made in the first instance with approximate figures and will thus not be binding.

    With the expression of our kind regards,
    Drei Masken Verlag & Co.
    p.p. Demblin

[*Note to Schenker, in Deutsch's hand:*]
My reply: Please calculate for [both] 500 and 1,000 (550–1,100) copies.
May 23, 1930   Deutsch

NB: I recommend that you begin in the Fichtegasse 1a: Georg Tomay, mornings from 8 to 12. You have been announced. He recommends (as I do) calligraphy (ink), which can then be stereotyped photographically (print). That will be clearer than autography, from which only exact copies can be made. The stereotypist can then prepare any size (including the same size).

Wilhelm Furtwängler to Schenker (letter), May 30, 1930
OC 54/298

BERLIN W.
HOHENZOLLERNSTRASSE 9

Most revered Mr. Schenker,

I have just heard from Professor Straube how the matter of your contract has turned out. I am incensed about this, and for my part I have written once again to the proprietors of Breitkopf & Härtel. I shall myself be coming to Leipzig in the middle of the month, and will also take the opportunity of speaking in person with the gentlemen.

I would very much like to know from you how long you can hold out before submitting your work to Hertzka. I would possibly then try once more to interest Max Hesse's publishing house, which is known to publish Kurth's books. I find the whole thing a cultural scandal, I will not let the matter rest as it is, so long as is in my power to do something about it.

You have probably heard that I have stepped down from my position in Vienna.[1] For this reason I shall, unfortunately, be unable to have the pleasure of seeing you for some time. Nonetheless I would be grateful if you would let me know when you are going into the mountains, and where. Perhaps we shall be able to meet some time this summer.

For today, in great haste, with kindest greetings,

    Yours,
        Wilhelm Furtwängler

P.S. Have you listened to Toscanini?
Best greetings to your wife!

---

[1] Furtwängler resigned his post from the Vienna Philharmonic in April 1930, after a period of three years as principal conductor. He had been unwell during the 1929–30 season, and he evidently found the task of directing the Berlin and Vienna Philharmonic orchestras exhausting. He did, however, return regularly to Vienna to conduct there.

Georg Tomay to Schenker (letter), July 9, 1930
OC 54/199–200

Special Office for Musical Works
Georg Tomay
Vienna I, Fichtegasse 1a

Dear Professor,

I am sending you imprints of the music examples and [original] manuscripts. All things that are indicated in green are things missing, which I have found when comparing with the manuscripts. With the things indicated in purple pencil, I ask you whether this should be printed. In the meantime, a change of plan has been introduced: the music appendix[1] will be printed not in Vienna, but by Röder in Leipzig. Of the imprints that are being sent to you today, a single copy will be made in Vienna and in fact on transparent paper; they will be newly printed in Leipzig using the blueprint process. Apparently, Roeder reckons that the entire printing of the music appendix will cost 200 marks, and Piller had suggested 1,400 shillings just for the five large sheets that are being sent to you today. I find it quite unbelievable that Leipzig can consider the entire work, which is a good two and a half times as extensive, as already finished; and all this should come to a quarter of the costs in Vienna. The Urlinie graphs, which I am marking up for the blueprint process, must of course be done again, as they have already been worked on for the lithographic process.

Now I ask you, dear Professor, to take your time and look through the large sheets carefully; you can make any further corrections that you wish. Please be so kind as to indicate all changes, mistakes, etc., with any colored pencil, except for green and purple, and to sign the sheets. I shall take full responsibility for any shortcomings, and likewise the printing house[2] will not have any grounds for reckoning on mistakes since the matrices will reach the hands of the printers free of mistakes—at any rate, however, the printing house will, before printing, also have to send an imprint, so that this can be compared with the corrected large sheets.

As soon as I send you Urlinie matrices for your inspection, I shall, dear Professor, also send you instructions for marking the corrections. These matrices are not so awkward, and you, Professor, can mark up everything, however only with a normal pencil: no ink, no colored pencils, and also no indelible pencils—but, Professor, you are after all in Galtür to rest, and not to work; I shall also leave you now, dear Professor, in peace and send you something for inspection only about two weeks from now.

The sheets that I sent you today also do not have to be studied immediately, since I shall be doing the retouchings myself and Piller has finished with his work.

Most respectfully, with cordial greetings to your gracious wife,

    Yours most faithfully,
    Georg Tomay

PS: Please return just the imprints. I no longer need the original manuscripts; these would increase your postage costs!

[1] The graphs and Urlinie-Tafeln—called *Bilder* in the publication—which were printed separately and secured by a paper wrapper at the back of the yearbook.
[2] The firm of C. G. Röder in Leipzig, which printed the *Masterwork 3*.

❦ Georg Tomay to Schenker (letter), July 24, 1930
OC 54/203

Dear Professor,

I am sending you the first, second, and third movements; there are twenty-two leaves of blueprint matrices for your kind consideration. For the fourth movement, twelve and a half leaves have been prepared (note stems, slurs, beams, and annotations) and should reach you, dear Professor, in a week at the latest. On the large printed sheets, the corrections have already been carried out; I must only go back over and compare all the music examples.

On the matrices that are going out to you today you need not exercise any special care; and you can, dear Professor, indicate any corrections with the usual pencil. I ask you only: <u>Do Not Use Ink</u>. To make it easier to read the graphs, I recommend that you place a piece of white paper underneath. In the first movement, I have marked a few questions. The second and third movements have been prepared by my young female assistant, and here I ask you kindly to take greater care in the reading of the proofs. All three of us have worked on the fourth movement together. When you return the matrices, I believe that, once again, you need not send your manuscripts; it will suffice to enter the corrections.

I shall have control copies made here, on account of the printing house, so that no mistakes on the part of the printing house can be passed on.

Allow me to present a request, a payment of 200 (two hundred) shillings as of August 1; I have wages to pay, and must also turn down much work since I do not wish to delay your work.

Thanking you in advance, I remain

With kind regards, yours most truly,
Georg Tomay

❦ August Demblin (DMV) to Schenker (letter), July 24, 1930
OC 54/230

Dear Dr. [Schenker],

By now you have surely been informed by telegram of the arrival of your manuscript. We promptly forwarded the manuscript to Röder and asked for an immediate confirmation of receipt. You will, then, soon receive the galley proofs of the text (in duplicate copy, with your manuscript); and we request that you forward the copy that you work through to us as soon as possible to <u>our</u> address, likewise to direct to us any questions that may arise in the course of production. Professor Deutsch will also receive a set of proofs, for control; we assume, however, that we shall receive the corrected proofs only from you. Should you wish anything further in this regard, please let us know—possibly through Professor Deutsch.

    With kind regards,
    Drei Masken Verlag & Co.
    p.p. Demblin

℘ Bank receipt for a payment from Wilhelm Furtwängler, June 1, 1931
OC 54/278

DEUTSCHE BANK UND DISCONTO-GESELLSCHAFT
BRANCH OFFICE: Mannheim, Heidelbergerstrasse

                       Mannheim, June 1, 1931

To: Dr. Hans Weisse,
Vienna XIII,
Wattmanngasse 5

  3,000.– three 1,000-mark banknotes on behalf of Dr. Furtwängler

III
Schenker and the Institutions

10

The Sofie Deutsch Bequest and the Vienna Academy

ONE of the less familiar corners of Schenker's world, this correspondence affords a glimpse into Viennese philanthropy and institutional politics. It centers around a bequest, made in a will of 1915, for two stipends a year to be awarded to "impecunious skilled composers"—stipends that were placed in the lifetime gift of Schenker. No sooner had the bequest been made than attorneys contested it. Matters were complicated by the fact that the annual yield for these stipends was part of the interest on a large bequest to the Association for the Feeding and Clothing of Hungry Schoolchildren in Vienna:[1]

> Fifty percent shall, yearly upon my death date, be distributed in two equal parts to two impecunious skilled composers or similarly qualified composition pupils. Dr. Heinrich Schenker, [Vienna] III, Reisnerstrasse 38, is to adjudicate on these stipends for his lifetime. The stipends can also be awarded to the same applicants in more than one year.[2]

When in 1924 the Association was wound up, the stipendiary part of the bequest was in an anomalous position, and a court ruling was required. This ruling only made matters worse for Schenker, for it placed the stipends in the hands of the Vienna Academy for Music and Performing Arts—the former Vienna Conservatory, and long-term focus of Schenker's professional and personal animosity. Schenker was himself a Doctor of Law of Vienna University, so was equipped to fight his corner; he appealed the terms of the ruling, and in 1927 a verdict in his favor was handed down.

Thus the correspondence is a tale of legalistic infighting, which we view largely from Schenker's vantage point. It also offers some insight into Schenker's complex psychology: a man who never held an official position, who accepted no public honor, an outsider with a distrust of the Viennese professional world and many personal enmities, but who was suddenly given (in addition to a pension) the power of exclusive patronage. His reactions to being placed in this position are fascinating to trace through the exchange of letters and diary entries.

In a sense, Mrs. Deutsch set Schenker an impossible task, for from as early as 1907 he had been speaking of the decline of art music and referring to Brahms as "the last master of German music"; indeed within a month of hearing of the

---

[1] Verein zur Speisung hungernder Schulkinder in Wien, founded by Betty Kolm in 1912, active during the War under the presidency of Anka Bienerth; part of an overarching women's charitable organization, the Bund österreichischer Frauenvereine, it was later apparently absorbed into the Schwarz-Gelbes Kreuz (Black-and-Yellow Cross), founded by Anka Bienerth in 1914.

[2] The will was made on February 2 and 10, 1915, and is quoted in a letter of May 21, 1924, from the Association to the Vienna Academy.

bequest he wrote "I intend to decline the right to award Mrs. Deutsch's stipends merely because I do not expect to be able to find two worthy candidates every year."[3] Potential candidates for the stipends were thus, by his own definition, scarce or nonexistent. Already in 1917 he quietly changed the word "composer" to "musician" (of course in those days many a performer and writer on music was also a composer), and "impecunious" became "of rank." It should therefore not come as a shock that after winning his argument in 1927 he threw in the towel.

Sofie Deutsch (1858–1917) was a wealthy Viennese Jewish socialite (unrelated to Otto Erich Deutsch) who invited members of her large circle of acquaintance to her apartment for elevated conversation and chamber music evenings and did charitable work. Her brother Fritz Mendl was a leading Austrian industrialist who bore the honorific title of Chamber Counselor; he and her second brother Heinrich together headed the large bakery and pastry company Ankerbrot (Anchor Bread), which by 1920 had one hundred branches. Sofie was a piano pupil of Schenker's from about 1902 onward, and a patron and supporter of his work. In all probability Schenker continued to teach her less for her talent than as a source of income. He considered her a flawed character and exclaimed frequently in his diaries at her "miserliness," "egotism," "greed," concern with material possessions, and moral weakness. He spoke of her once in 1908 as "an eternally restless person, sinking into the dirt over and over again, a genuine Hedda Gabler character." He was, however, perhaps fond of her, accepted the presents she showered on him, and appreciated the fact that she accepted Jeanette in the years leading up to the Schenker marriage in 1919 when so many others ostracized her.

The correspondence falls into four broad areas: that with Sofie Deutsch herself and Fritz Mendl; that with the attorneys Siegfried Türkel (pro-Schenker), Hugo Friedmann (contra), and Ernst Lamberg; that with the administration of the Academy for Music and Performing Arts; and that with the recipients of the awards. Several of the attorneys' letters are fragmentary, Schenker having torn them up and used the blank versos for other purposes.

IAN BENT

---

[3] Diary entry, January 28, 1917, recording a letter to Alfred Stern of the Rothschild Artists' Foundation. In 1921 he wrote "the present generation is destined to be a tragic clown among generations" of composers, lacking the capacity to reclaim German genius: *Tonwille* 1 (1921), Eng. transl., vol. 1, 19 (Ger. orig., 20).

❧ Sophie Deutsch to Schenker (letter), January 26, 1916
OJ 10/4, [1]

It is with great joy that I inform you of my decision to place at your disposal, for the purpose of publishing your future works, the sum of 10,000 marks in annual withdrawals of up to circa 3,000 marks, which will be remitted in installments upon presentation of publishers' accounts to the officials of my banking house, the Vienna Bank Association, Vienna X, Keplerplatz. Of this total sum, an amount of up to 1,500 marks is meanwhile also freely at your disposal without presentation of supporting documentation. My banking house is receiving instructions from me to this effect at the same time.

I thank you, highly revered master, for giving me the opportunity to furnish some small proof of my undying gratitude, and I wish you well-earned, unalloyed success with your selfless work in the interests of your sacred art.

  In heartfelt friendship, your grateful pupil,
   Sofie Deutsch
   [Vienna] I, Albrechtgasse

❧ Diary entry, January 6, 1917

At about 11 a.m. we go to the Sanatorium Auersperg to inquire in person after the condition of Mrs. Deutsch and learn, to our utter consternation, that she has died during the previous night around 11:30 p.m. The receptionist gave bone caries as the cause of death. In this manner, so many symptoms became explicable after the event that neither she herself, nor we, nor even the doctors were able to explain. There was no question whatsoever of its having been mere fish poisoning, and all treatment of the stomach was nothing but incorrect treatment. We were taken so unawares by the event that for a long time neither of us could take the idea in. For myself, who surely had the most to gain from the deceased's recovery and recuperation, nothing remains but to regret the irrevocable fact that she has not lived for a few more years in order to be convinced even more fully at first hand of the triumph of my ideas and proposals. I feel bound to surmise that after conquering her illness she would have resolved even more willingly than before to turn her life away from empty externals and more toward the inner world. And even if she already appeared exalted by the little that she wrested from her character on the basis of my advice, how very much more elevated would she have felt if she had fully complied with that advice, to which approaching old age would have given even greater impetus. Now all of that is over and done with, and she departed this life before reaching her full bloom, about which she secretly thought perhaps as much as I did, and incidentally every bit as isolatedly as she has lived her entire widowhood. Who knows whether, in the hour of her death, even her servant girl was in her room?

❧ Fritz Mendl to Schenker (letter), January 12, 1917
OJ 12/52, [1]

FOODSTUFFS HEADQUARTERS[1]
THE PRESIDENT

Dear Dr. Schenker,

 In the execution of the will of my sister Sofie Deutsch, deceased the 5th of this month, I have the honor of notifying you that my sister in this her will has designated and ordered stipends for impecunious skilled composers and similarly qualified composition pupils, and that the annual determination as to these stipends on each occasion should be in your gift.

In this matter I deem it advisable in the interests of a smooth and consistent implementation of the wishes of the deceased to hold a discussion, and I request you to do me the honor of calling on me on Monday the 15th of this month at 12 noon in the Foodstuffs Headquarters, Vienna I, Trattnerhof 1, 4th floor.

Since it unfortunately often happens that I am called away suddenly, I ask you in any case to ascertain by telephone at 11 a.m.—No. 16546, 12166, 17375—that I am on the premises in the Foodstuffs Headquarters.

I take this opportunity also to notify you that my sister decreed in her will that 2,000 kronen are to be paid to you each year in two installments of 1,000 kronen on January 1 and July 1 of each year, and has in addition left you a legacy of 5,000 kronen.

With cordial best wishes to you and your dear wife,

    Yours truly,
    Mendl

---

[1] This was possibly a wartime organization designed to feed the citizens of Vienna.

Diary entry, January 15, 1917

At 12 noon at Fritz Mendl's place: he repeats what he has already communicated in writing, but also confesses to having been in on the instruction that Mrs. Deutsch gave to the Bank Association. He suggested that I approach Dr. Türkel, and that it would still be possible to treat the issue as a matter of interpretation. I purposefully mentioned the difficulty of getting back from the Wallmodengasse,[1] but it still did not occur to Mendl to place his automobile at our disposal for the return journey—all the better for us.[2] Also rather mean-minded was that he did not deal with the instruction immediately,[3] for which he submitted the paperwork; we were no less surprised by the fact that he did not himself immediately pay out the money due to us. He told us how the previous day—Sunday—he had given himself over to the pleasure of hunting, which was a lesson specifically to me that the death should therefore not be the cause of greater upset to us than it was to the brother of the deceased lady. — To Floriz (by pneumatic postcard): I inform him of the outcome: a six[?]-year pension and a stipend.[4]

---

[1] Fritz Mendl lived at Vienna XIX/1, Wallmodengasse 11, hence they met not at the Foodstuffs Headquarters but at his home.
[2] "our," "us": evidently Jeanette and Heinrich went together.
[3] Presumably the instruction that Mrs. Deutsch gave the Bank Association.
[4] What prompted Schenker to write "6" (which is written over something illegible) is not clear.

❧ Siegfried Türkel, attorney, to Schenker (fragmentary letter), March 10, 1917
OC 16/29r, 28v, 27v

Dear Professor,

I am definitely in favor of your putting forward a claim for your honorarium. As I have already taken the liberty of informing you, I have been so to speak dispossessed and have almost no say in the estate. You see, the executor of the estate has only to insure compliance with the terms of the deceased's will, while having no influence at all over the carrying out of that compliance.

I certainly cannot deny the danger that the pension will not be granted to you until June 1917. The question has not yet come up for discussion and ought not to come up for discussion so long as the inventory has not been completed, since the Association has not yet submitted an inheritance claim, let alone committed itself to a period of deliberation for submitting the same. Chamber Counselor Mendl has nothing whatsoever personally to do with the estate. I take charge for him of the office of the executor of the will and it falls into neither my competence nor that of Chamber Counselor Mendl actually to make payments of legacies.

Your esteemed letter, dear Professor, [*part of document missing*] matter to the Anchor Bakery, the cashier of which also takes care of the private financial affairs of Chamber Counselor Fritz Mendl, and that always gives rise to a time-delay. The Chamber Counselor, as the Professor will certainly know, is dreadfully in demand as the President of the Foodstuffs Headquarters.

I know from personal experience how very highly the Chamber Counselor values you, and far be it from the Chamber Counselor to make any kind of difficulties for you. In the matter of the Bank Association and the honorarium, I would however firmly advise you, if things do not happen immediately, to undertake certain steps, for in legal affairs, sadly, good fortune does not happen of its own accord.

    With cordial greetings,
    Yours very truly,
      Türkel

❧ Schenker to Hugo Friedmann, attorney (letter draft/copy), March 12, 1917
OC 1B/19–20

Dear Dr. [Friedmann],

From the most recent letter of the Bank Association, Keplerlatz 11, to me, I gather that you in your capacity as Curator of the estate of Mrs. Sofie <u>Deutsch</u> are probably aware of the fact that I, besides a small legacy and a pension, also had a letter of credit in the amount originally of 10,000 marks.

Without in any way wishing to influence a decision with what I am about to write, I feel compelled at this moment to acquaint you with just the <u>spirit</u> of this document, since for reasons that are public in nature I am acutely concerned that my name be clear of any misunderstanding in connection with money. The deceased was a pupil of mine for well over fifteen years and was readily convinced of the imminent successes of my theoretical works in Germany and further afield, even though I did not show her absolutely everything. Now, it irked her greatly that I sold off at simply rock-bottom prices works the value of which is already so well recognized, and contented myself with a mediocre honorarium from my publisher. True enough, this honorarium certainly represents a tidy sum by Austrian standards, especially when measured in terms of the difficult sales of such thoroughly highbrow works as my own; nevertheless Mrs. Deutsch was right in what she felt. Thus it was that, one New Year's Day in a restaurant where she used to eat with me after lessons, she surprised me with a proposal to place my future major works on an independent financial footing for me in order to emancipate me from the publisher, for which purpose she wished to provide the requisite sum of money.

It did not come easily to me to forgo the publisher's annually stipulated honorarium,[1] with which I was at least secure against all worries about sales. All the less since by the time the next large volume was to come out—perhaps in 1920 or 1921—five or six years would have gone by that would already have directly netted me almost the same figure as that which Mrs. Deutsch had settled on me. Add to that the risk that through illness or death the next volume might never be completed, so that by that time I would have had to bear just the loss of the publisher's honorarium. Nonetheless, on purely ethical grounds alone, I accepted the deceased's proposal with gratitude, and on the basis of her wish relinquished my claim upon the publisher—a wish that she expressed <u>repeatedly</u>, even <u>in front of witnesses</u>.

The form that the deceased chose may primarily be due to the fact that I <u>declined</u> any <u>personal advantage</u>, even the benefit of interest on the sum, and intended the latter simply, without interest and even perhaps only for the work.

That Mrs. Deutsch was fully aware of my own great material sacrifice is evident from the very wording of her letter to me, in which she herself asserts this expressly. I have handed the letter over in the original to Dr. S. Türkel.

If I have accepted Mrs. Deutsch's proposal at all, I have done so, what is more, consciously in order thereby to give her the opportunity to reciprocate the very many troubles that I took on her behalf over so many years outside the lessons and above and beyond my teaching. Out of the same consciousness, I shall accept the small legacy as well as the pension, for it is my way of accepting what is offered me only after I have already given of myself many times over.

I gladly seize this opportunity also, dear Dr. Friedmann, to indicate to you where I stand <u>on the matter of the stipends</u>. The latter has taken even me by surprise, even though the impetus for it may have come from a first suggestion from me made very fleetingly in conversation, which probably goes back all of ten years. Still, now I know neither the amount nor the precise form of the stipends. Nevertheless I must reiterate to you also what I have already said on the subject to Chamber Counselor Mendl and Dr. Türkel: I fear that I will scarcely be able to fulfill the wishes of the deceased, greatly though it does me honor, for the specific reason of the shortage of suitably qualified candidate material. I recently declined for the same reasons the most flattering summons to serve on the jury of the Rothschild Artists' Foundation[2] (with Prof. Guido Adler and Prof. Alfred Grünfeld). Once again, these are reasons that lie in my public field of operation, and which prohibit me from awarding prizes to works that do not meet the demands that I myself set up. Already, now, in connection with several instances, I take the greatest imaginable trouble to keep a lookout for worthy candidates, but I doubt if I will come up with more than three or four people.[3] This is not, however, my last word on the subject. I hear that in the event of the stipend not being awarded it is to revert to the Association for the Feeding—and rightly so, for better to feed hungry children than gratuitously to nurture unskilled musicians.

Just one final word: I await the decision as to whether the pension for January–July 1917 will be paid out, naturally <u>after</u> all the transactions have been completed. Should this not be the case, then I would be obliged, admittedly belatedly, to submit my claim for the <u>honorarium</u> also for January to end of June, since I receive a <u>season's</u> honorarium from my pupils and have received this for all of the many years from Mrs. Deutsch.

With kind regards,
[*unsigned*]

---

[1] It is unclear which publisher and which honorarium are referred to here—Cotta did not pay him honoraria; UE did, but not annual ones—or whether Schenker did in fact forgo any honorarium from either publisher.

[2] The Rothschild Artists' Foundation, from which Schenker had received an award in 1899.

[3] Schenker certainly took up the search for a suitable candidate promptly, for on January 13 he wrote to Hertzka: "Is not Mr. Franz Mittler, who wrote me so nicely from the front line today via UE about my Beethoven edition, a young composer, a product of your publishing house?"; and on February 16: "I take the liberty of asking you in confidence whether he is in any sense impecunious." Hertzka replied that to the best of his knowledge Mittler's family was comfortably off.

❧ Diary entry, March 12, 1917

To Dahms (letter): I mention the stipend as a possible contribution to his stay in Vienna or even in Berlin.[1]

---

[1] Walter Dahms had been wanting to come to Vienna from Berlin to study with Schenker since 1914, but had been prevented in part by military service. This would have been a clear breach of the terms of the stipend. (See chapter 20.)

Türkel to Schenker (letter), March 13, 1917
OC 16/30v, 31v, 33v

DR SIEGFRIED TÜRKEL
COURT AND IMPERIAL ADVOCATE
CHANCELLERY: VIENNA VII, MARIAHILFERSTRASSE 26

Dear Professor,
    A thousand apologies for the error that I committed. For I really was unaware that you were, so to speak, a colleague, and I was always under the impression that you were a Doctor of Philosophy.[1]
    So very kind a man have I found you to be, dear Professor, that I hope you will think no further ill of me for this error. You will in the meanwhile, dear Professor, have received my communication that the 5,000 kronen has already come into my hands. As mentioned before, there was not the slightest reluctance to oblige on the part of the Chamber Counselor, but I had to address myself to the Chamber Counselor.
    The Chamber Counselor was happy to communicate this information to me, and I shall be delighted to be of service to you.

> I am, Sir,
> with kind regards,
> yours very truly,
> Türkel

[1] Clearly Schenker had informed Türkel in his last letter that he was a D. Jur., not a D. Phil.

Schenker to Türkel (letter draft/copy), March 17, 1917
OC 1B/23; OJ 14/40b

Dear Dr. Türkel,
    Enclosed is a letter received today from Dr. Friedmann.[1] On the basis of this Talmudic explanation (I myself am a Jew), one is led to the conclusion that I should be able to grant the stipend only after my death! What a turn the matter has taken since the Chamber Counselor's letter to me, which showed not a trace of this hair-splitting! And now that I have once more been thrust into this affair, I will go further and offer you, purely for your own private use, the following drastic explanation in appreciation of our common musical interests. I esteem the Chamber Counselor up to the present moment as a man to whom I would, among the many industrialists, bank directors, etc. that I have encountered in the course of my life, soonest accord the attribute of "having a touch of genius." I concede this opinion not solely on the basis of the man himself: one day, some two to three years ago, he asked me through Mrs. Deutsch whether I could place a girl in a band?! Me and a women's band! — *sapiente sat*. This is the root of the matter. So the Chamber Counselor sees a man to whom is evidently granted higher status

in Germany than Hugo Riemann or Hermann Kretzschmar, than [Hans von] Bülow, etc., to whom the majority of the German new generation pays homage and whom it emulates, but of whom people in Austria itself know very little, all because I once divulged to Mr. [Moriz] Benedikt that [Julius] Korngold etc., etc. Mr. Alfred Rothberger,[2] Stephansplatz 9, once told me that, when in London as guest of a major cloth merchant he asked his host where the grave of Walter Scott was, the counter-question came back: "Is that Scott the dealer in cheviot wool?" However, his hostess said in a sugary voice: "Oh no, that is surely the fairytale teller." For ten to fifteen years I frequented Vienna I, Ehendorferstrasse 2, the house of a great—of the greatest—timber merchant, as a friend of the family. I quickly made a mental note to myself that Mr. Eissler[3] ran a big timber business, but conversely in all those years the remarkable gentleman asked me, over a cup of coffee, which newspaper I wrote for. In the end, I gave up visiting the house. A certain level of consideration has to exist.

In your capacity as an attorney, you must be as well acquainted as I am with the nature of rich people. Now, happily I am constituted such that I do not under any circumstances give them precedence, least of all when they insistently make claims on money. (Mrs. Deutsch knew a thing or two about that.) I tell rich people to their faces that the true beggars and spongers of the world are the rich people, and when millionaires give themselves airs, I just say: I am a *Milliardeur e basta*! In actual fact, rich people squirmed before me when it was a matter of a couple of measly pennies, like the most wretched garbage collectors, whereas it was easy for me to forgo his money and everything else when this is what he emphasized.[4] I beg you, dear Dr. Türkel, to explain my complete indifference *in puncto* all sums of money along these lines. I follow your advice, but go no further. Moreover, in the case of Mrs. Deutsch I really do have a right to a great deal. Please do not forget that I published my New Musical Theories and Fantasies with Cotta of Stuttgart in 1906 and 1910 without any letter of credit or guarantee, etc. It sufficed, it will suffice, because it has to suffice. I shall appear in your chancellery as you request at the end of March, and remain until then with best wishes yours truly

[unsigned]

PS At the same time I am writing a couple of lines direct to the Chamber Counselor to thank him for his kindness.

Disclaimer[5]

I have received a sum of 10,000 (ten thousand) kronen from Chamber Counselor Mendl, and cede to him under liability for advisability and profitability up to the sum of 10,000 kronen my legacy, pension or other emoluments from the estate, or demands and claims against the estate, of Mrs. Sofie Deutsch, deceased January 5, 1917.

Should this disclaimer not be recognised by this estate, or by the court, or should these emoluments of 10,000 kronen not in part or whole be disbursed by the estate to Chamber Counselor Fritz Mendl within two years through the hands of Dr. Siegfried Türkel, then I have of course to reimburse Chamber Counselor Fritz Mendl for these sums through the hands of Dr. Siegfried Türkel out of my own resources. Any interest accruing to me from the transactions of the estate for these sums is due to Chamber Counselor Fritz Mendl, while I on the other hand, in the event that I receive no interest from the estate for these 10,000 kronen for the period of two years, shall have no interest to pay to Chamber Counselor Fritz Mendl for this.

   [*unsigned*]

The disclaimer is to be stamped with 100 kronen and the stamp overwritten upon the first lines.

---

[1] Not known to survive.

[2] Alfred Rothberger (1873–1932): joint head of the Rothberger Houses of Business, garment manufacturer, located centrally at Stephansplatz 1, 9–11, and a friend of the Schenkers. He was also a designer and engraver of medals, and designed a medallion of Schenker in 1925.

[3] Moritz B. Eissler: head of Eissler Bros., timber merchants. Schenker frequented their house from either 1894 or 1899 to 1909, when relations were broken off. Moritz's wife, Jenny Eissler, was one of Schenker's patrons.

[4] "his … he": Schenker unconsciously shifts from plural to singular here. He frequently spoke of "the rich man" (*der Reiche*), referring to the class of rich people. Here he has been speaking in the plural, but then has reverted to his more usual practice. It is thus probably best to read these as "their … they."

[5] *Cession*, lit. cession, assignment, transfer.

❧ Diary entry, dated April 12, 1917

To Dahms, Vrieslander, Roth (postcards): I inform them that things remain according to my original plan.[1] — To Dr. Türkel (letter): I inform him that on Mrs. Deutsch's death date in <u>each</u> of three succeeding years, or even otherwise, I shall have <u>1,600 kronen</u> available for distribution, in spite of all the representative officials and Dr. Friedmann. I recount the simple course of events, that I had, on the basis of the Court Counselor's letter, still in Dr. Friedmann-less times, hit on the idea of taking advantage of the endowment productively, and to this end have commissioned one work each from two Munich composers, with a promise of a modest financial contibution from the resources of the endowment; in a third case it is a matter of a Berlin composer to whom I have undertaken to give instruction.[2] The moment Dr. Friedmann thwarted my plans, I sought and received the solution to this conflict from a third person. So now I can patiently await the representative's decision. If it is favorable, I would be available; if not, then enough reverence will at any rate now have been shown.

---

[1] According to Schenker's diary of April 11, 1917, his pupil Angi Elias gave him 10,000 kronen in cash, and Schenker proposed to her that she "substitute for Mrs. Deutsch" so that he could give money to Walter Dahms, Otto Vrieslander, and Herman Roth, to which she agreed (OJ 2/7, 647–648). It may be that the disclaimer of March 17 was not activated, and that Schenker was here assuring the three recipients that money was still available (albeit now via Elias).

[2] Munich: Herman Roth and Otto Vrieslander; Berlin: Walter Dahms.

ꙮ Schenker to Türkel (draft letter), February 24, 1918
OC 1B/34r

Dear Dr. Türkel,[1]

In thanking you most warmly for having eased my access to you, which had without that been impossible for me recently, I hasten by return post herewith to <u>abide by</u> the disclaimer already surrendered by me on June 1, 1917. Apart from the fact that I may by no means stand in the way of Mrs. Figdor[2] (all the less so as in accordance with your communication the latter lady raised no objections at the time on her own part against the letter of credit), I will <u>avoid</u> any legal proceeding that would have required my putting forward evidence by summoning witnesses to show that I have in fact already given the amount of the letter of credit in advance with my accomplishments, and have in addition also suffered the most considerable damage—what's more, in the midst of the war—through the denial of the document.

I would, dear Dr. [Türkel], surely otherwise have repeated the disclaimer, even if you had not been in a position to convey to me (at any rate without obligation) the favorable position on the legacy question. In the light of all the experiences I have had, I am today merely being practical as regards this kind granting of access. I gave my disclaimer purely for the reasons then stated; but I must freely reserve to myself the right to go back on it, possibly even publicly, in the event that I were to have to suffer still further damage with respect to the rumors that may deprive me in part or whole of the inheritance due to me in accordance with the deceased's wishes, and to which she through her high valuation of my accomplishments may wholly unintentionally have given rise. How once before I had to suffer damage for a long, long time as a result of the fact that a pension was conjured up for me purely on the basis that I gave lessons to the young Baron [Alphons] Rothschild, a pension of which I neither then nor to this day have ever seen a penny.

I also take this opportunity to inform you that, on January 5, i.e. the death date of Mrs. Deutsch, I disbursed out of the resources of the subsidiary legacy kindly paid out to me at that time by Chamber Counselor Mendl the <u>first</u> sum through the <u>Vienna Bank Association</u> to Mr. <u>Otto Vrieslander</u>, composer, of Ebersberg, nr. Munich. In so doing, I at long last lift the veil of secrecy from why I at the time insisted on precisely this legacy more than on my own honorarium: for it is I myself who am the "third person" of whom I wrote to you at the time *sub rosa*. To a certain degree I had in mind a defense of honor, not only my own but also that of Mrs. Deutsch as well as of the Chamber Counselor. You will recall that I had no desire to take on the matter of the stipends, and that only through endless persuasion on the part of the Chamber Counselor, as too from yourself, did I let myself be talked into it. Faced with the Chamber Counselor's letter to me, and then also faced with its being held up to me in conversation, I surely at least had cause to doubt altogether that the stipends would ever be viable. But once committed to the matter, I dispensed the stipend money in the manner in which Mrs. Deutsch had reason to expect me, and indeed did expect me, to do; instead of awarding it to questionable products, I <u>bestowed</u> it by preference upon two reputable composers whose works appeared to me important,[3] and promised a third composer, whose name you may quite frequently have encountered in [Julius] Korngold's feuilletons along with quotations from his authoritative opinions, and to whom Mrs. Deutsch herself had contemplated giving over her own lesson-hours for the duration of her journey to Japan (and who is the critic for one of the most highly respected daily papers in Berlin[4]), quite specifically that I would facilitate his stay in Vienna by means of money from the foundation, in which case I myself then fully intended to give him instruction free of charge.

Now, I divulged to these gentlemen by name the source of the award—I had to do that because I did not want to get a bad name for myself by appearing to be a benefactor of money when I am in any case overburdened as a benefactor of instruction. As the doubts arose, it was too late, at least in the cases of these three gentlemen, to deviate or to go back on the commitment. It was a different matter in cases where after the initial approach to individual potential candidates I nevertheless did not commit myself to any one composer or any one work.

The sum amounted to 1,020 marks, i.e. one third of that legacy. On January 5 next, the second musician should have his turn, and finally as the third the Berlin composer.

Unfortunately, I could not have done otherwise, as you yourself will admit.

With best wishes, Yours truly,
[unsigned]

PS I should be greatly obliged to you, dear Dr. [Türkel], if in your letter to Dr. Friedmann you would date my disclaimer to the day June 1, 1917, on which I wrote to him for the first time—so long as this does not conflict in any way with your interests. For me a very great deal would hang on this determination, now as well as later.

---

[1] This draft is heavily edited by Schenker; only the final reading, insofar as it can be determined, is given here, but the finished letter is not known to survive.

[2] The Figdor family was evidently fighting on the side of the Association for the Feeding and Clothing of Hungry Schoolchildren in Vienna. The family was related to Sofie Deutsch (a Karl Figdor (1846–1910) was related by marriage to Heinrich Deutsch (1850–99), Sofie Deutsch's husband). One of its members, Richard Figdor, was a pupil of Schenker's from early 1919 to sometime in the 1920/21 season.

[3] August Halm and Otto Vrieslander.

[4] Walter Dahms.

❧ Schenker to August Halm (letter), December 9, 1918
DLA 69.930/4

Dear Professor,

Two years ago a female student of mine died, an older woman who had had the benefit of my instruction for sixteen years. She left a will in which she designated an association as primary beneficiary, as well as establishing two stipends for artists, the disposition of which she assigned exclusively to me. If the present circumstances in music were not so hopeless, what happiness it would have to bring for someone, supported by the trust of the deceased, to jump to aid wherever obstacles (publishers!) foil this or that plan! However, I had little desire to take on the pleasant duty, just as in another case I declined to share jury duty with our music historian, Professor Guido Adler.[1] But the brother of the deceased and the executor of the will succeeded at least in coaxing me into a trial. I had some artists in mind and awaited the first distribution of money from the bequest in order to take action. However, all manner of complications (external to me) came up in the handling of the bequest, such that it still occupies the court up to this moment, and such that the endowment of the stipends has fallen through altogether. Even though the brother of the deceased woman is one of Austria's richest industrialists, it nevertheless did not occur to him to take advantage of his high rank in society. Fortunately, another wealthy female student,[2] who has been coming to me for over eighteen years, has put me in the position of keeping my word in those cases that I had in mind.

On January 5, as the death date of the deceased, the amount is to be paid out. I therefore ask you whether it would be agreeable if around that time I were to transfer the sum of 1,600 kronen to you for your purposes? Last year, that still amounted to over 1,000 marks. With the low exchange rate of the kroner, I do not know whether this year the same amount in marks would result.

In asking for your friendly consent, I also request information as to in what manner I could convey the sum to you. Do you perhaps have a representative here in Vienna? If not, I would make an attempt to secure <u>permission</u> from the regulatory agency (such is of course necessary <u>in all circumstances</u>).

As you see, assuming your consent, I am inquiring today in order to undertake the matter as soon as possible. To be safe, I ask that you send your reply to me by <u>registered mail</u>.

Are the circumstances of your activities very constrained, or are you getting the upper hand on the untold woeful confusion in political matters, which in my opinion is to be traced solely to Karl Marx, just as the musical confusion is to be traced to Richard Wagner?

With best greetings,
Yours very truly,
H. Schenker

---

[1] i.e. on the judging committee of the Rothschild Artists' Foundation. Schenker gave two divergent reasons for refusing this approach, depending on convenience: that there were insufficient qualified composers to merit awards, and that he did not wish to serve alongside Adler, who had already been approached.

[2] Angi Elias.

ꙮ Türkel to Schenker (letter), December 27, 1918
OJ 14/40a

Dear Professor,

In receipt of your letter of December 25, 1918,[1] I take the liberty of observing that I do not rightly understand for what reasons you, Professor, give me this information. If, Professor, you make donations and distribute awards out of your own or collective resources, then that is a purely private matter for yourself, which really ought to be of no interest to me as your representative. I therefore do not understand what, Professor, you mean by saying that this year as well as last year you have fulfilled the duty which you feel it your right to carry out on the basis of communications made to you. Needless to say, you ought not to count on restitution of such amounts as have been overspent by you without any authorization. I took the liberty of drawing this to your attention in person, Professor, at the time. I made clear to you that no obligation is placed on you, and accordingly that you also have no entitlement to make payments of any sort in another's name and accordingly also have no right to restitution of any kind.

But under these circumstances I also do not understand why you notify me, as your representative, of these private actions, which have nothing to do with the Deutsch matter and with my representation of your person.

I take the liberty of addressing this letter to you so that, with a grasp of your letter on my part that is free of contradiction, the error may not be incurred on your part that you are obligated or entitled today to payments of any sort whatsoever. It goes without saying that anything you do by way of restitution in your own name or capacity is your affair and has nothing to do with me.

   With greetings,
    and kind regards,
     Yours very truly,
      Türkel

[*handwritten in pencil:*]

Dear Professor,
I beg you not to construe this letter as an unfriendly act. I should, however, like to avoid any misunderstanding.

   With greetings,
    Yours,
     Türkel

---

[1] Not known to survive, but Schenker's diary records: "Letters to Türkel and Friedmann about the final decision to award Halm a stipend."

Türkel to Schenker (letter), November 3, 1919
OC 16/37v–36v

Dear Professor,
I have received a letter from Dr. Friedmann, the contents of which are as follows:
"I refer, in regard to your inquiry as to the situation concerning the matter of the legacy, to the communication already conveyed to you that, in view of the circumstance that the testatrix was not an Austrian citizen, her total personal assets were not approved by the fiscal authority for control designation; and I am proceeding, after assembling all the evidence from the State Office of Finance, to effect approval with evidence that the beneficiaries are Austrian citizens.

To this end, I require proof that Dr. Schenker is an Austrian citizen, and I ask you to procure this for me if at all possible."

> I remain,
> With kind regards,
> Türkel

Please attend to this as soon as possible.

Diary entry, May 5, 1920

I go to Dr. Friedmann: he greets me in a friendly manner as a musician "philologist" venerated by his son, as he says. He gives surprising information about the lack of piety of the Mendl family vis-à-vis their deceased sister, regarding a lack of concern in the matter of a gravestone, unwillingness to aid the estate even with the smallest of advances, about scandalous events surrounding the acceptance of keepsakes, etc. The attorney does not shy away from calling the family vulgar and agrees with me for turning down Chamber Counselor's wife as a student. And even with Mrs. Deutsch, this was a case of her only wanting to "grate" against me! However, it is very strange that, according to what he said, Mrs. Deutsch once borrowed money from her brothers at a low interest rate in order to lend it out at higher rates! Dr. Friedmann also regretted that Dr. Türkel is apparently much too servile to admonish his clients for taking such a stance. He promises to take care of the matter soon and advises for this reason against the disclaimer.

Diary entry, November 21, 1923

To court at 12:00: Dr. Lamberg and the Privy Counselor lay out the case; the Supreme Court suspends the valorization duty, accordingly it would not contradict the law if I were to be set at 2,000 kronen per year. The lawyer offers me 2 million in compensation from supposedly 150 million for the sale of the house. The Association and the Figdor family split nearly 140 million evenly. I have no difficulty forgoing the 2 million to benefit needy German composers, which is also noted in the file. In return, the court recognizes the stipend in the amount of 1½ million per year. — In that respect things go differently from what the wise people had predicted. I express my willingness to distribute it, especially after the kind Court Counselor advised me to do so and confirmed from his own experience how even such a small additional payment should not be underestimated in these current times of dire need.

ᘛ Ernst Lamberg to Schenker (letter), December 7, 1923
OJ 12/31, [1]

>Attorney in Law
>Dr. Ernst Lamberg
>VIENNA I,
>MAHLERSTRASSE 14

Dear Professor,

As per our agreement legally entered upon re the estate of the late Mrs. Sofie Deutsch, I take the liberty of informing you that I shall be in a position on the 10th of this month to remit the sum of 2,000,000 kronen to an address to be provided by you. I shall then convey to you the documentation concerning the correct remittance. With greatest respect, I ask you please to notify me of this address.

I take this opportunity also to inform you that I shall likewise transfer to you punctually the sum of 1,500,000 kronen as stipend for musicians, which is to be ready for disbursement for the first time on January 5, 1924. Please then be so kind as to inform me what determination you have made as regards this sum.

In conclusion, I take the liberty of bringing to your attention the fact that the Association for Feeding and Clothing Hungry School Children also had to take precautions against the event that the Association might be dissolved. Against this event, the decision was reached, with the permission of the court, to transfer upon the dissolution of the Association a quarter of the capital assigned to the Association from out of the estate of the late Mrs. Sofie Deutsch, i.e. circa 74,000,000 kronen, however, rounded up to a sum of 20,000,000 kronen, to the Academy for Music and Performing Art, with the request that the yields of this capital be used in the spirit of Mrs. Sofie Deutsch's will as stipend[s] for musicians, and to leave to you, dear Professor, for your lifetime, to dispose to whom these stipends are to be awarded. This latter stipulation is however valid, as mentioned, solely in the event of the Association's being dissolved. Until that time, 1,500,000 kronen will be placed at your disposal each year, which is to be disbursed on the death date of Mrs. Sofie Deutsch, thus on January 6 [recte 5], as stipends for musicians.

In closing, I most respectfully ask you to inform me whether you wish to collect the sum of 1,500,000 kronen from my chancellery, or where I should dispatch this sum to.

I should mention in this connection that I shall place this sum at your disposal on January 2, 1924.

I remain, with kind regards,
Yours truly,
Dr. Lamberg

⚓ Diary entry, December 18, 23, 24, 1923

[December 18:] From Dr. Lamberg (letter delivered late, sent via Reisnerstrasse dated December 10: 2 million are available. Where should they be sent?; the 1½ million are also ready. — We hurry to the German embassy, speak with the secretary, who gives us a postal payment form, fills it out himself, names me as sender. I send this selfsame postal payment form to Dr. Lamberg in a letter: I ask for the stipend amount to be sent to Mozio [Moriz Schenker] who will receive instructions from me. I want to preserve the confidentiality of the recipient. [...] To Mozio (letter): I ask him to transfer the sum to Dahms, if necessary from my money.

[December 23] To Dahms (letter): I explain the origin of the 1½ million, ask him to excuse me for sending without asking.

[December 24:] From Mozio (letter): he has remitted 487 lire to Dahms—the matter is "resolved," since the money from Dr. Lamberg has been deposited in the meantime.

⚓ Hermann Wunsch to Schenker (letter), January 31, 1924
OJ 15/31, [1]

Berlin W 30
Aschaffenburgerstrasse 8

Revered Professor,[1]

From the "German Assistance," I received your donation in the amount of 2,000,000 Austrian kronen. Permit me to express my sincere thanks to you for your magnanimous benefaction! I hope very soon to have the pleasure of being able to justify myself to you in artistic terms for having accepted the donation.

I have intentionally hesitated to publicize my musical compositions, so even you may in all likelihood barely be acquainted with my name. The performance of my Second Symphony in Munich (Hausegger) was really the first attempt; that it bore fruit so richly, as it now appears, delights me and justifies to some degree my reticence. The symphony will now receive its second performance as early as February 11 in Breslau; further performances are planned.

I will take the liberty of letting you have further news of myself from time to time, if you will not think ill of me for doing so.

At the moment, I am working on my Third Symphony, and I hope that it will be possible for me to have a performance some time in Vienna at which I might be present and would surely not neglect to pay you my respects to you.

Once more, my gratitude to you!

I remain,
> With kindest regards,
> Yours,
> Hermann Wunsch

[1] Hermann Wunsch (1884–1954): German composer and conductor, a Rhinelander, teacher of composition at the Berlin Music Hochschule from 1937, head of the advanced classes in theory and composition and director of the department for new music from 1945 to his death. Schenker probably knew about him from a fulsome article featuring him in the *Rheinische Musik- und Theater-Zeitung* of February 23, 1924, which described him as a composer of symphonic works, tone poems, solo and orchestral songs and spoke of his gift coming "from our great German masters."

Lamberg to Schenker (letter), July 1, 1924
OJ 12/31, [2]

Dear Professor,

I have the honor of informing you that the Association for Feeding and Clothing Hungry Schoolchildren in Vienna at its last General Meeting on May 19 of last year took the decision to dissolve itself.

Against this event, on the basis of a court order, a quarter of the capital assigned to the Association from out of the estate is to be given over to the Academy for Music and Performing Arts with the request that the yields of this capital be used in the spirit of Mrs. Sophie Deutsch's will and the decision over the stipends be left to you for your lifetime.

The Asssociation is assigned a sum of 74,000,000 kronen out of the estate.

The Association has now decided at its General Meeting of May 19 to bestow the sum of 20,000,000 kronen on the Academy for Music and Performing Arts.

I have notified the Academy of this bestowal and have received from the same the following letter:

> The Directorate of the Academy for Music and Performing Arts has the honor, on the basis of the esteemed letter of the Association for Feeding and Clothing Hungry Schoolchildren in Vienna, of announcing that the Academy is willing to take over the sum of 20,000,000 kronen assigned to it under the testimentary provision of Mrs. Sophie Deutsch as endowment, to administer this endowment under the name "Sophie Deutsch Stipendium for Musicians" and to divide the monetary yields annually into two equal parts for two impecunious skilled composers and similarly qualified composition pupils as well as for the lifetime of Dr. Heinrich Schenker to leave the decision over the awarding of the stipends to him on the basis of slates of three candidates per stipend supplied to him by the Music Academy.[1] The Director: Joseph Marx m.p.

With greatest respect, I therefore request you kindly to come to agreement with the Academy for Music and Performing Arts as concerns the decision assigned to you punctually before the next anniversary of the death of Mrs. Sofie Deutsch (January 5).

> I remain with specially kind regards,
> Yours very truly,
> Dr. Lamberg

[1] The requirement of a slate of candidates does not appear in the letter from the Association to the Academy of May 21, 1924, but was slipped in by the Academy Director, Joseph Marx, in a letter to Dr. Lamberg of June 27, 1924, and is reiterated here.

Schenker to Lamberg (letter draft/copy), July 8, 1924
OJ 5/24, [1]

Your esteemed letter of July 1 has reached me in Galtür, where the postal service is less fluid than in Vienna.

I adopt a different standpoint on this question. Not once since the days in which it was first discussed, hence not since the time of Fritz Mendl, Dr. Türkel, and Dr. Friedmann, nor even of you yourself or the Court Counselor, have I ever heard the idea of limiting the discharge of the duty that I was to undertake. What the deceased enunciated in her will alone captures her intention, but long before then she had also been accustomed to expressing it again and again by word of mouth. In bequeathing a <u>considerable stipend</u>—never did she dream that something so utterly different might arise, otherwise she would have drafted her will differently—she was not for a moment thinking of a so-to-speak local stipend linked to an academy or school of some sort but of artists anywhere in the world, to whom assistance was to be brought for any reason whatsoever, even if they were already known and regarded. (For example, the 2,000,000 kronen that I offered as a present were handed over by the Berlin Central Bank to the symphonic composer H. Wunsch in Berlin for whom Hausegger strove so very hard. In many ways I am reminded of old Arnold Mendelssohn, etc. Mrs. Deutsch had in mind similar cases in placing reliance on the considerable sum of money and my impartiality and sense of responsibility.)

So far from her mind was the customary type of stipend that she expressly explained in her will that the stipend money was <u>to revert to the Association</u> after my death.

Even though, to be sure, things have now taken a different path, even though the Association has gone into dissolution, I really still cannot see why the last vestiges of the deceased's piety need be denied by the Association, by you, by the Academy, or by me. What I mean is: The Academy ought to welcome the opportunity to exhibit a little patience in absorbing the piety offered; it is coming into the stipend in no way directly at the wish of the deceased, but only by accident, and it ought to honor this with gratitude. Even if it is the case that my work—just between ourselves—will outlive all the academies in the world, nonetheless physically the

Academy will outlive me, so it really still has time, ample time, to take control of the stipend at its own discretion. However, so long as I live, the Academy should make it a matter of honor to fulfill the wishes of the deceased, all the more so since it has in mind to adorn the stipend with her name. Accordingly, I beg you to impart all this to Dr. Marx (whom I do not know personally) and get over to him the wishes of the deceased, which surely cannot strike him as severe. I have absolutely nothing against Dr. Marx, nor against the Academy either. But for the time being the situation is another matter altogether. The Academy has time on its side.

In the same spirit, I ask you also to instruct the Academy to place the interest at my disposal in good time, so that I can distribute the money discreetly to where merit already gained has in some way been severely incapacitated.

    With kind regards,
    [unsigned]

Lamberg to Schenker (letter), July 11, 1924
OJ 12/31, [3]

Dear Professor,

I am in receipt of your letter of the 8th of the month. I take the liberty of observing that the legal position is that the Association for Feeding and Clothing Hungry Schoolchildren alone was obligated to leave the decision regarding the stipends in your hands.

In the event of the Association's dissolution, the deceased has made no provision of any sort, thus a solution needs to be sought that approximates as closely as possibly the wishes of the deceased.

This solution is contained in the court decision conveyed by me to you whereby the 20,000,000 kronen are to be bestowed upon the Academy with the request that it disburse the stipends and leave the choice in your hands for your lifetime.

This has happened, and the Academy's decision has been communicated to you.

Accordingly, nothing lies in my power, and it is also absolutely not my job to induce the Academy to change its position. If you are of the opinion that the Academy ought not to reserve its [right to produce a] slate of threes, and [if you] place such great value on the [right to] exclusive decision, then I must ask you to come to terms directly with the Academy over this matter. I do not doubt that in personal discussion with Professor Marx you will settle the matter in a manner agreeable to both parties, for which there is surely enough time after your return from vacation, since the next stipend disbursement has not to be made until January 5, 1925.

    I remain with kind regards,
      Yours truly,
        Dr. Lamberg

Schenker to Joseph Marx (letter), December 3, 1924
UfMdK Z 641/1924, [1]

Highly revered Court Counselor,[1]

Attorney Dr. Ernst Lamberg notified me in his letter of July 1 of this year that the Artists' Stipend of Mrs. Sophie Deutsch, who was for twenty years a pupil of mine, has been placed in the hands of the Academy, and that the latter has decided to put forward its own slates of candidates just during my lifetime. In turning now directly to you, I seek to win your support for a slight change in this solution which, while not being detrimental to the newly acquired rights of the Academy, temporarily at the same time complies with the differently construed, true intention of the testatrix.

I will not dig far back into the past and detain you needlessly, but only acquaint you with what is necessary.

Not only from the many conversations that I had with my pupil, but also from the provision set out clearly in her will, I know that she was thinking of awards made to artists, who, irrespective of whether young or old, whether residing in Austria or Germany or somewhere else, irrespective also of whether they are affiliated to a school or are already a well established name, should obtain the (still in her day considerable) sum of money for the alleviation of need, or as assistance (e.g. for the publication of a planned work), from me. So exclusively was this her wish that in her will she expressly earmarked the capital allocated for the stipend to pass entire at my death to the Association for Feeding Impoverished Schoolchildren! In order to protect thoroughly the artists receiving the stipend, my pupil wished me to conduct the award process in strictest secrecy so that no third party might get to hear anything whatsoever of the making of the award. Moreover, the brother of the testatrix (the well-known proprietor of the "Anchor Bread" factory), the attorney handling the estate, and ultimately in early 1924 the legal counselor were wholly in accord with this testimentarily expressed wish when they asked me to take on the distribution. In the first three years after the death of the testatrix, even before the matter was clarified, I in fact dispensed the stipend entirely secretly to three artists of rank, and then however I stopped awarding it, since it appeared that the stipend would never get off the ground.

Now, I do not need to expatiate further to you, dear Court Counselor, wherein the current solution contradicts the wishes of the testatrix. I do not know from which quarter and for what reason disrespect has in the above sense been shown toward her. Nor do I know why the Association failed even to consult me when passing its final resolution. After I expressed my misgivings to Dr. Lamberg in writing, he recommended in his letter of July 11 of this year that I take the matter up directly with you.

Thus, I ask you now whether you are willing to join me in honoring the wishes of the deceased, which were so clearly expressed, and to relinquish to me trustingly for the remaining years of my life the disposal of the interest so that I am once again in a position to carry out the honorary office in secrecy. In the event that you, dear Court Counselor, find no cause to share in these considerations of respect, I would, I have to say, be bound to forgo any cooperation, certainly not out of animosity toward the Academy—that is far from my mind—but in the consciousness that I would be contravening the wishes of my deceased pupil.

I hope to find you well disposed toward my request, and remain

with great respect
Yours very truly,
H. Schenker

[*in lower margin of page 1 in another hand:*] 20,000,000 kronen dispensed from the Central Savings Bank, Municipality of Vienna N34513, under "Sofie Deutsch Music Stipend."

---

[1] There is a draft of this letter, dictated December 2, in Jeanette's hand with extensive alterations by Schenker. In addition to the underlinings shown here, there are in the finished letter many other, fainter underlinings that may or may not be by Schenker, which have been disregarded here.

Marx (Vienna Academy) to Schenker (letter), December 13, 1924
OJ 12/51, [1]

ACADEMY FOR MUSIC AND
PERFORMING ARTS

I have the honor of informing you *pro tem* in response to your esteemed communication of December 3, 1924, that I have with pleasure forwarded your wishes in regard to the form of awarding of the

Sophie Deutsch Stipend for Musicians

to the Federal Ministry for Education as the decision-making authority and once the decision has been reached I shall notify you of it.

The Director:
Marx

Franz Schmidt (Vienna Academy) to Schenker (letter), October 21, 1925
OJ 9/4, [1]

Highly revered Court Counselor,[1]

Further to the letter of December 13, 1924 addressed to you by my predecessor in the Academy administration, I take the liberty of informing you that the Federal Ministry of Education has requested the Academy's administration in collaboration with the professorial college and in accord with the Finance Procurator in Vienna to prepare a founding letter and to present it to the Federal Ministry of Education for approval. The Federal Ministry of Education has expressly decreed that any limitation of the right of award, which was conferred upon you for your lifetime, in the form of a slate of three candidates is to be avoided as being contrary to the originator's wishes.² And that we are to be in contact with you as to how in your opinion the awarding of the stipends after your death—and it is my sincere hope that that will lie in the far distant future—could be conducted in fullest compliance with the wishes of the testatrix, and the procedure deemed appropriate for this should be adhered to in the foundation letter.

I respectfully request you, highly revered Court Counselor, in the spirit of this ministerial directive to set out for me as precisely as possible all your wishes in this regard so that I can take these into account when drafting the foundation letter. I will of course also submit the completed draft to you for your comment.

> In expressing my kind regards,
> I am yours most truly,
> Franz Schmidt

---

1. Schenker, of course, was not a Court Counselor; Schmidt was either mistaken or deliberately attributing to Schenker a higher social status than he possessed.
2. This verdict was conveyed in a letter from the Ministry to the Academy dated February 23, 1925, thus the Academy had waited eight months before informing Schenker.

❧ Schenker to the Vienna Academy (fragmentary draft letter), October 30, 1925
UfMdK Z 641 D/1925, [1]

Highly revered Court Counselor,
In thanking you for your kind letter of October 21, 1925, I hasten to reply to your question:

I request the Academy after my death to take the Sofie Deutsch Stipend under its auspices and to administer it without restriction of any sort.

With this declaration not only do I satisfy the inclinations of my heart and of my convictions, but also the foundress would today think and act in no other way. If she—as do I today—had had the choice between different academies or other institutions she would undoubtedly have accorded the Vienna Academy the precedence that genuinely is due to it. My only regret is that the stipend, which could originally be reckoned among the most valuable of its type—for example the Mendelssohn or Meyerbeer Stipend in Berlin—has been whittled away so severely through the years-long administering of the inheritance, through the unexpected lawsuits against the estate, and the general devaluation of currency. Unfortunately, nothing more can be done about that, and it is incumbent upon us only to fulfill our duty as well as possible.

The conferment has to take place on the death date of the testatrix, January 6 [*recte* 5].

Once again, in thanking you for your cooperation and troubles, I remain
>Yours very truly,
>Dr. Heinrich Schenker

🙛 Schenker to Vienna Academy (letter copy), December 17, 1926
UfMdK Z 767 D/1926, [1]

To the Administration of the Academy for Music and Performing Arts,

In the spirit of the letters exchanged by us on October 21, 1925, and October 30, 1925, I take the liberty of inquiring whether I shall be in a position on January 6 [*recte* 5], 1927, the anniversary of the death of the foundress, Mrs. Sofie Deutsch, to be able to distribute the interest on the invested capital for this year and the years that have gone by. Thanking you cordially in advance for your kind attention, I sign with expression of high regards,
>Yours most truly,
>[*unsigned*]

🙛 Wunderer (Vienna Academy) to Schenker (letter), December 21, 1926
UfMdK Z 767 D/1926, [1]

Dear Court Counselor,

I take the liberty, in response to your esteemed letter of the 17th of this month, of drawing to your attention the fact that, in the spirit of the express decree issued by the Federal Ministry of Education, any limitation of the right of award conferred upon you for your lifetime with respect to the "Sophie Deutsch Musician Stipend" is to be refrained from as being contrary to the originator's wishes. You are of course within your rights to dispense the accumulated interest on the capital after January 1, 1927 in accordance with your discretion.
>In expressing my kind regards,
>I am yours most truly,
>Wunderer[1]

---

[1] Alexander Wunderer (1877–1955): Viennese oboist, member of Vienna Philharmonic 1900–37, oboe teacher at the Vienna Academy 1919–39, professor from 1924; chosen as Director of the Academy in 1927 but not confirmed by the Ministry of Education; decorated in 1927 for services to the Austrian Republic; taught also at the New Vienna Conservatory and later at the Salzburg Mozarteum.

🎼 Schenker to the Vienna Academy, December 31, 1926
UfMdK Z 767/D/1926, [4]

In thanking you cordially for your letter of December 21, 1926, I should like to express my joy that at long last the wishes of the foundress can reach fulfillment. It only remains for you to be so kind as to acquaint me with the amount of the accumulated interest on which a recipient may be fortunate to expect, and at the same time to let me know where and by what means I can withdraw the sum of money and forward it on the anniversary of the foundress's death, which falls in the coming week.

   With kind regards,
    Yours very truly,
     H. Schenker

🎼 Marx and Wunderer (Vienna Academy) to Schenker, January 11, 1927
UfMdK Z 767/D/1927, [2]

Dear Court Counselor,

 In reply to your valued letter of December 31 of last year, which unfortunately and through no fault of my own has found its way belatedly back to my desk, I take the liberty of informing you that the interest amounts to about <u>430 shillings</u> and can be collected at any time at the Academy cash desk against acknowledgment of receipt.

   With expression of kind regards,
    Joseph Marx

🎼 Vienna Academy to Schenker (letter), February 3, 1927
OJ 9/4, [3]

Highly revered Court Counselor,

 The Rectorate of the Hochschule and the administration of the Academy for Music and Performing Arts, in accordance with an advisory issued by the Federal Ministry of Education in accord with the Finance Procurator in Vienna, has to draw up a founding letter for the

     Sophie Deutsch Musician Stipend

whereby, as already repeatedly emphasized, any limitation of the right of award conferred upon you for your lifetime is to be desisted from as being contrary to the originator's wishes, you are respectfully requested in pursuance of an advisory from the Federal Ministry of Education to make known how in your opinion the awarding of the stipends after your death could be conducted in fullest compliance with the wishes of the testatrix, since the procedure deemed appropriate is to be adhered to in the foundation letter.

      The Rector: For the Academy Director:
      Marx   A. Wunderer

❧ Schenker to the Vienna Academy (fragmentary draft letter), February 7, 1927
OJ 5/4, [3]

It would perhaps be sufficient to refer to my letter of October 30, 1925, in which I answered your question once before; but I gladly repeat the content of that letter here:

I request the Music [Academy] in Vienna <u>to take over</u> the Sofie Deutsch Musician Stipend <u>with unrestricted administration</u> after my death.

This I believe accords in the most worthy fashion with the wishes of the testatrix.[1]

    [unsigned]

---

[1] This draft in Schenker's hand contains numerous revisions. The reading given here aims to represent only his latest thoughts, since the finished letter is not known to survive.

❧ Schenker to Vienna Academy (letter copy), dated December 13, 1927
OJ 5/4, [4] (Plate 3)

Dear Court Counselor,[1]

On January 6, 1928, I would have been due once again to award the Sofie Deutsch stipend. However, my experience of last year has taught me that the testatrix's wishes can no longer be fulfilled, since in the meantime the amount of the stipend has been still further whittled away by the fall in the rate of interest, such that I no longer dare offer it to the musicians of distinction that the testatrix had in mind above all.[2] The possibility would still be open to me, of course, of allowing the interest to accumulate over several years; but then I would by virtue of my advanced age have few occasions left in which to fulfil the honorary duty with regard to the testatrix.

I have accordingly decided to withdraw at this point, and ask you to make the dispensation of the stipend from as early as 1928 a responsibility of the Academy. The Directorate will doubtless always identify from among the pupils of the institution a young man who can be helped out of some current need even with such an amount.

And now I should like to thank you once again, revered Court Counselor, for having been willing in times past on the basis of my declaration to install me in the honorary office. I bow to the pressure of time in placing the office once again in your hands.

[unsigned]

[1] This draft or copy, dictated and taken down by Jeanette Schenker with annotation by Schenker, incorporates his modifications.

[2] Schenker is stretching the truth here, for Mrs. Deutsch's will spoke of the stipends as intended for "impecunious skilled composers and similarly qualified composition pupils."

II
Invitations to Serve: Guido Adler

For a half century prior to the German annexation of Austria Guido Adler was the principal shaper of musicological discourse in the organized academic community of the Habsburg Empire. After completing a doctorate under Hanslick, Adler began his professorship at the German University in Prague. There he worked to lay foundations for an ambitious reimagining of music-historical study, grounded in the empirical examinations and inductive, text-critical analyses that characterized the "Vienna School" of art-historical research under Rudolf Eitelberger, Alois Riegl, and Moriz Thausing.[1] Adler's move to the University of Vienna in 1898 introduced his vision of musicology to a new generation of scholars. The publication of *Der Stil in der Musik* (1911) projected that vision beyond the boundaries of empire and across the span of the twentieth century.[2]

Schenker's first recorded contact with Adler occurred on October 25, 1901, when Adler invited Schenker to give a lecture to the International Musicological Society. Schenker accepted and was invited again. Yet Schenker's relationship with Adler soon devolved in a manner that highlights his lifelong difficulties accommodating and relating to members and institutions of official academic society. By the time Schenker's pupil Hans Weisse began his doctoral studies with Adler in 1914 (Schenker had recommended Weisse to Adler), Schenker's distrust of Adler's motives and methods was well established. Diary entries show Schenker repeatedly engaging Weisse in conversation about Adler's lectures, only to disparage what Weisse reported.[3] In his diaries, Schenker twice recounted Weisse's claim that Schenker's books were excluded from Adler's seminars— possibly revealing Schenker's anxieties about being unaccepted.[4] Indeed, Schenker also recorded those moments when Adler seemed to offer qualified praise of his work. For his part, Weisse appears to have vigorously defended Schenker and his teachings in Adler's company.

The ambivalence that marked Schenker's relations with Adler and the ministerial culture he represented is vividly revealed in a series of documents from 1926–27. On February 10, 1926, Adler approached Schenker about joining a conference committee to help plan Vienna's Beethoven centennial celebration, and Schenker apparently agreed. The following January 28 Adler asked Schenker to lecture at the conference. Schenker declined, feeling incapable or disinclined

---

[1] Kevin C. Karnes, *Music, Criticism, and the Challenge of History* (New York: Oxford University Press, 2008), 38–47.

[2] Guido Adler, *Der Stil in der Musik* (Leipzig: Breitkopf & Härtel, 1911).

[3] Federhofer (1985), 49–52.

[4] Diary entries of May 29 (see below) and October 24, 1914, in Federhofer (1985), 50–51; also see Nicholas Cook, *The Schenker Project* (New York: Oxford University Press, 2007), 272–73.

to adapt his work to anticipated limitations of time and audience, or (as his diary entry of February 11, 1927, suggests) because of his distaste for professional musicology. Yet that entry also reveals Schenker's persistent sense of being shunned by Adler and the Viennese establishment. After the centennial, on April 4, Adler asked Schenker to sit for a portrait for inclusion in a commemorative album. Evidently Schenker did not respond. His diary entry of May 11 suggests that his silence was deliberate.

KEVIN C. KARNES

❧ Adler to Schenker (letter), October 25, 1901
OJ 9/3, [1]

INTERNATIONAL MUSIC SOCIETY
Regional chapter: VIENNA IX, Türkenstraße 3

Dr. Heinrich Schenker, Esq.[1]

On behalf of the committee of the Vienna chapter of the IMS, we write to inquire politely whether you would be inclined to give a lecture. We would like to hear your suggestion about topic and date. Awaiting a quick reply and your obliging acceptance, we have the honor of signing,

for the committee,
Guido Adler

Koner, Secretary

---

[1] The first three letters from Adler to Schenker are handwritten by an amanuensis under a printed letterhead and signed by Adler. The remainder are typewritten.

❧ Adler to Schenker (letter), July 2, 1902
OJ 9/3, [2]

Dear Sir,

Recalling the willingness you expressed last autumn to give a lecture for the IMS, we write to inquire politely whether you are willing to deliver the lecture in question this coming season. Should you decide to give it in the fall, we request a brief description.

For the head of the IMG,
Guido Adler

Koner, Secretary

12 Heinrich Schenker, portrait, Galtür, August 1927 (Felix-Eberhard von Cube)
13 Heinrich Schenker, portrait, undated
14 Heinrich Schenker, gravestone, inscription "*po nikbar* [Here lies] Here lies the body of one who perceived the soul of music and communicated its laws, as the great musicians understood them, and as no one before him had done [–] Heinrich Schenker 1868–1935"
15 Heinrich and Jeanette Schenker, portrait, November 30, 1919 (Ludwig Bednař)

16 Jeanette Schenker, portrait, c. 1912 (Atelier Kosel, Vienna)
17 Jeanette Schenker, portrait, October 1925 (Atelier d'Ora)
18 Jeanette Schenker, portrait, Galtür, August 1927 (Felix-Eberhard von Cube)
19 Eugen d'Albert, portrait (W. Höffert, Berlin), inscribed "To my true friend, Dr. Heinrich Schenker, as a memento, Eugen d'Albert Frankfurt am Main, October 6, 1898"

20 Ignaz Brüll, portrait (Fritz Luckhardt)
21 Max Kalbeck, portrait (W. C. Hans)
22 Ferruccio Busoni, portrait (Willinger)
23 Josef Weinberger, portrait (Lillian Fayer-Barylli)

24 Johannes Messchaert, portrait, April 1896 (Wegner & Mottu, Amsterdam)
25 Julius Röntgen, portrait, April 1896 (Deutmann & Zonen, Amsterdam)
26 Otto Erich Deutsch, portrait, May 1927 (Atelier Pietzner-Fayer)
27 Emil Hertzka, painted portrait (Tom Richard von Dreger)

28 Alfred Einstein, portrait, May 1927 (Atelier Pietzner-Fayer)
29 Otto Vrieslander and Herman Roth, photograph, February 1917
30 August Halm, photograph, Esslingen, 1916
31 Joseph Marx, portrait, c. 1932 (Max Fenichel)

32 Guido Adler, drawn portrait, 1935
33 Robert Haas, portrait, May 1927 (Atelier Pietzner-Fayer)
34 Anthony van Hoboken, portrait, May 1927 (Atelier Pietzner-Fayer)
35 Wilhelm Furtwängler, portrait

36 Ludwig Karpath, portrait
37 Paul von Klenau, portrait (Trude Fleischmann)
38 Walter Dahms with Margarete Ohmann, photograph, Monte Rosso, c. 1925
39 Aline and John Petrie Dunn, photograph, Marienbad, August 1930

40 Moriz Violin, portrait, c. 1901 (Schwertführer, Berlin), inscribed "As I arrived in Berlin full of hope. Floriz"
41 Moriz Violin, 1931, cartoon (Felix-Eberhard von Cube)
42 Felix Salzer, photograph, Sils Maria, Switzerland
43 Hans Weisse, portrait, with framed portrait of Brahms, c. 1913 (Franz Hofer, Bad Ischl)

꧁ Adler to Schenker (letter), October 5, 1902
OJ 9/3, [3]

Dear Sir,
    We write to inquire whether you would be inclined to give another lecture for the IMS this year. If so, we would request that you kindly tell us the topic (presumably the promised lecture on ornamentation[1]), and date—the lecture schedule is open from January onwards.
        Yours truly,
        Guido Adler
Koner, Secretary

[1] Schenker had completed his *A Contribution to the Study of Ornamentation* (Vienna: UE, [1903]) at about this time.

꧁ Rothschild Board of Directors to Schenker (letter), December 3, 1916
OJ 12/26, [2]

Highly esteemed Sir,
    In the name of the Board of Trustees of the "Baron von Rothschild Artists' Foundation" I have the honor of respectfully informing you, highly esteemed Sir, that at the meeting of this Board on November 13 of this year it was resolved to inquire of you whether you would be willing to accept the honorary office of a juror in conjunction with the expert adviser Professor Guido Adler and his co-adviser Professor Alfred Grünfeld.
    The Board of Trustees looks forward in pleasurable anticipation [to hearing] that you are well-disposed to comply with the invitation extended to you, in the interests of this Foundation, which serves artistic causes.
        With kindest regards,
          The President,
            Dr. Alfred Stern[1]

[1] Alfred Stern (1831–1918): Viennese attorney, from 1881 member of the Board of Directors of the Jewish Religious Community for thirty-one years, and its President for fifteen years, and a strongly anti-zionist voice.

꧁ Diary entries, December 5, 8, 13, 1916

[December 5:] Letter from the committee of the [Jewish] Religious Community: wishes me to take on the honorary post of juror with Adler as expert adviser and Grünfeld as co-adviser.

[December 6:] To Floriz (postcard): I ask him to meet me, if possible on Friday, to give me some tips on how to say "No" to the Religious Community.

[December 8:] After lunch, to Floriz in order to hear his ideas on the matter of Adler and the Religious Community.

[December 13:] Letter dictated to the Board of Trustees, written out by Lie-Liechen.

❧ Jewish Religious Community to Schenker (letter), December 17, 1916
OJ 11/58, [1]

Dear Dr. [Schenker],
　　Concerning your letter of the 10th of the month,[1] I cannot help expressing my regret that you have declined to undertake the duty of juror on the "Rothschild Artists' Foundation."
　　Precisely the fact that you represent a trend in art that does not correspond with today's admittedly not common but nonetheless quite widely held views would have made your participation on the panel of jurors seem to me particularly desirable.
　　I am convinced that on this panel total objectivity will pertain in the judging of the works before it, that there can be no question of a bias in one direction or another, and that the verdict that the jurors will deliver will limit itself solely to whether the proposed works demonstrate evidence of genuine talent, promising for the future. It has always been thus in the many years of existence of the "Rothschild Artists' Foundation," and thus it surely will remain in the future. Hence I can only express my keenest regret at your refusal, which I shall nonetheless lay before the Board of Trustees.[2]

　　　　　　With kindest regards,
　　　　　　Dr. Alfred Stern

---

[1] This date is perhaps in error: Schenker's diary has no record of his writing to the Community on the 10th.

[2] In a letter of December 9, 1918, to August Halm, Schenker remarked that he had "declined to share jury duty with our music historian, Professor Guido Adler." His mind was undoubtedly swayed by unfavorable reports of Adler from his student Hans Weisse, including that of May 29, 1914, recorded in Schenker's diary: "Weisse recounts that my writings are missing from the Seminar Library. It is transparently clear from this that Professor Adler would prefer to keep them from his students. That he does not succeed in this, however, is plain from reports by Weisse, who attests that most of the young people have read or are reading my *Theory of Harmony*, etc., and in many cases accept them."

Adler to Schenker (letter), February 10, 1926
OJ 9/3, [4]

BEETHOVEN CENTENNIAL CELEBRATION
UNDER THE HONORARY DIRECTION OF
PRESIDENT DR. MICHAEL HAINISCH
MARCH 26–30, 1927

ADDRESS: FEDERAL MINISTRY OF EDUCATION
(BEETHOVEN CENTENNIAL CELEBRATION)
VIENNA I, MINORITENPLATZ 5

March 26, 1927, will be the hundredth anniversary of Beethoven's death in Vienna. To commemorate this day, a celebration consisting of artistic, academic, and social events will be held in Vienna from March 26 through 30, 1927. All institutions and individuals who wish to pay tribute to this hero of music are invited. We respectfully invite

... YOUR ESTEEMED SELF ...

to serve on the Conference Committee of the Beethoven Centennial Celebration

[remainder of page 1 cut off]
        For the Executive Committee:
           Guido Adler

under whose authority is issued an invitation to the meeting of the Conference Committee on Thursday, February 18, at 5:45 (quarter to 6) in the Institute for Music History at the University (the right-hand door off the ramp, in the right parterre).[1]

---

[1] There is no record in his diary of Schenker's having attended this meeting.

Diary entry, February 17, 1926

To the Ministry (letter): I confirm my membership of the Committee.

Adler to Schenker (letter), January 28, 1927
OJ 9/3, [5]

Highly revered Dr. [Schenker],
    Permit me to inquire whether you would like to give a lecture in the Beethoven section of the conference, and to invite you to do so if you so wish. I would not want to see your name and person missing from the list of lecturers. Enclosed is the program and announcement.

With kind regards,
Guido Adler

❧ Schenker to Adler (incomplete draft letter), February 7, 1927
OJ 5/3, [1]

Highly revered Court Counselor!
 For your honorable invitation my warmest thanks. To achieve your aim, however, will be—as I expressly regret—impossible for me, since I feel compelled to express myself on the theme of Beethoven only in the ways evinced in my works hitherto; since this requires, for technical reasons, more time and exposition than is possible within the framework of such a conference. [*Text partly indecipherable*]

❧ Diary entry, February 9, 1927

After teatime, at the moment at which we want to step outside, Mr. [Otto Erich] Deutsch arrives; he asks me not to turn Adler down. With all haste, I go over the reasons that have compelled me to say no.

❧ Diary entry, February 11, 1927

I give Hoboken my grounds for turning Adler down; I had drawn up a list of arguments for this purpose! They culminate in the point that I do not want to make the mistake made by the Jew in Galsworthy's *Loyalties*, by entering into the circle of musicologists and making fun of them, as I have been doing for thirty-five years. The Musicological Congress is, moreover, a sort of sideshow of the Beethoven Festival; it is not organically connected to it; our dear Court Counselor Adler is merely using this occasion to put on airs and allow his horde of dandies to parade their historical wisdom. This is fine for someone who has an appetite for such atrocities: he could also wolf down stones! Last of all, the most important argument: even if I were to bring my offering, I would surely not be mentioned in the *Neue freie Presse* or, at most, in a roundabout way in a hastily assembled official article by Adler on what was on offer, wherein my name and the title of my lecture would be mentioned with a few kind words.

❧ Adler to Schenker (form letter), April 4, 1927
OJ 9/3, [6]

The program for the Centennial Celebration includes the dedication of an album to the National Library and the Museum of the City of Vienna, with portraits of the illustrious guests who contributed to the brilliance of the festival in such generous ways.

For this reason the Executive Committee most kindly asks that you contact the studio of Pietzner Fayer, Vienna I, Opernring 1 (across from the Opera; tel. 6426), to which the artistic production of the album has been entrusted, to have your photograph taken free of charge.

With heartfelt thanks for your friendly collaboration on our memorable project,

> with kind regards,
> on behalf of the Executive Committee
> of the Beethoven Centennial Celebration,
> Guido Adler

❧ Atelier Pietzner-Fayer to Schenker (letter), May 10, 1927
OJ 11/1, [1]

VIENNA I, OPERNRING 1

We take the liberty of referring to the invitation to all contributors to the Beethoven commemorative album for the National Library and the Museum of the City of Vienna, which was sent to you by the Music-Historical Institute.

May 5 was set as the final deadline for the photographs for the album, and all those involved have in fact kindly responded to the summons.

We are now on the point of assembling the album[1] and note with regret that your portrait is still lacking. It would be a matter of great regret if you alone were missing from the album, and since we are of course committed to the wholesale success of this valuable work we stand ready to do all that we can to facilitate your involvement, too. We are accordingly for you extending the final deadline originally set for May 5 until May 20, and sincerely hope that it will prove possible for you to call on us before then—since the photography will really require no more than a few minutes—with a view to our taking your photograph at no cost to yourself.

We should be most grateful for a communication by telephone (6426), since we are holding open the space for your portrait

> With expression of our
> highest regards
> PIETZNER – FAYER
> Fayer

---

[1] For items in this album, see Plates 26, 28, 33, 34.

❧ Diary entry, May 11, 1927

To Pietzner (postcard): I do not belong in the album, as I have not been brought into the position—either from my own efforts or those of others—of taking part in the Festival.

❧ Schenker to Adler (letter), May 31, 1933
UG 32/5, [2]

Greatly revered Court Counsellor,
    Please accept my most sincere thanks for the kind gift of your Brahms article.[1] It seems to me that the very fact that so many reservations are still expressed about Brahms assures him an immortal place among men. There will be no end to puzzling over him—and how could there be an end to it when our general understanding of purely musical craftsmanship still stands so far behind the craftsmanship displayed by Brahms!

        With sincere esteem,
        Yours very truly,
        H. Schenker

---

[1] "Guido Adler, Johannes Brahms. Wirken, Wesen und Stellung," *Studien zur Musikwissenschaft: Beihefte der Denkmäler der Tonkunst in Österreich* 20 (1933): 1–22, receipt of which is noted in Schenker's diary for May 27 (OJ 4/6, 3836). Two copies of this offprint are preserved among Schenker's papers: OJ 48/1 and OC B/444. Adler was editor of the journal at this time.

12
The Photogram Archive

It was Anthony van Hoboken who, at Schenker's urging, in 1927 founded the "Archive for Photograms of Musical Master Manuscripts" (*Archiv für Photogramme musikalischer Meisterhandschriften*). The goal of the "Photogrammarchiv" or "Meisterarchiv," as it was also called for short, was to capture photographically the autograph manuscripts of famous composers from Bach to Brahms, so that they could be made generally available for the purposes of study and preparing editions, without the originals themselves being susceptible to damage. In addition, in the event that the original was lost, at least its photographic reproduction would survive for posterity. The administration of the Archive required a Board of Trustees in which Schenker and the music historian Robert Haas sat under Hoboken's chairmanship. Haas was also the head of the Music Collection of the National Library in Vienna, to which the Archive was attached.

While Schenker acted merely in an advisory capacity, Haas took over the main responsibility for the organizational work. To assist him in this task, Hoboken engaged the services of Julius Kromer, who was responsible for arranging the photograms, and for the bookkeeping and other paperwork. Hoboken himself restricted his involvement largely to providing financial backing, but did so from a position of leadership. He made important decisions and established priorities. In addition, he used his frequent trips abroad and his worldwide contacts to promote the interests of the Archive outside of Austria. Hoboken's private librarian, Otto Erich Deutsch, played an important part also, giving the project his active support from the very beginning.

After the official inauguration of the Archive on October 21, 1927, Hoboken and the Board of Trustees sent out an Appeal (*Aufruf*), in three languages, in order to publicize their intentions.[1] All official research libraries and archives, antiquarian dealers, and private owners of manuscripts were asked for their cooperation in making the manuscripts in their possession available for photographing. The Appeal was followed by several articles in various magazines, which called attention to the new institution.[2] One of the high points of this publicity campaign was the broadcast over Vienna Public Radio ("Radio-Wien") on February 4, 1928, of a twenty-minute lecture by Deutsch, about the goals and intentions of the Archive. The idea for this came from Schenker himself: he used his personal acquaintance with Leopold Richtera, then head of programming at the Austrian Radio Corporation (RAVAG), to secure an agreement to broadcast the lecture.

---

[1] The German Appeal is reprinted in *Das Archiv für Photogramme musikalischer Meisterhandschriften in der Musiksammlung der Österreichischen Nationalbibliothek in Wien* (Vienna: Austrian National Library, 1958), 12–16.

[2] Including Schenker's own "Eine Rettung der klassischen Musik-Texte: Das Archiv für Photogramme in der National-Bibliothek, Wien," *Der Kunstwart* 42 (March 1929): 359–67.

In addition, Schenker undertook a thorough revision of Deutsch's lecture before it was transmitted.

In the years that followed, there were repeated conflicts of interest among the Trustees. Tensions arose, for instance, in connection with the International Schubert Congress of November 1928, organized by Hoboken and Haas under the auspices of the Archive, in which Schenker declined to participate. A collected edition of the works of Carl Philipp Emanuel Bach, planned in 1930, never materialized: Schenker could not be persuaded to act as one of its editors, and Haas wanted to take control of the edition himself, against Hoboken's wishes. There were also differences of opinion about the purpose and scope of the Archive. Whereas Schenker was keen to deposit his collection of Urlinie graphs in the Archive in order to make them accessible to the public, Hoboken was not averse to opening the Archive to the collection of photographs of manuscripts of well-known contemporary composers—something that Schenker had no intention of allowing.

A crisis point was reached in 1932, when Hoboken drastically reduced his annual financial contribution to the enterprise. Nonetheless, the Archive developed into an internationally recognized center for musical documentation, whose holdings steadily increased over time. Well-known conductors such as Wilhelm Furtwängler and Arturo Toscanini used the Archive; and Schenker himself consulted its holdings for the purpose of his own studies. A year after Schenker's death, the space housing the Archive was, of necessity, increased; this event was officially marked by an opening ceremony. In 1957, Hoboken donated the Archive to the Austrian National Library; at this time, the collection comprised about 1,400 works recorded in 37,000 photograms.[3] Today, the principal significance of the collection lies in the fact that it contains reproductions of manuscripts that were lost during World War II.

MARKO DEISINGER

[3] *Katalog des Archivs für Photogramme musikalischer Meisterhandschriften*, Part I (= Museion, new series, series 3: Veröffentlichungen der Musiksammlung 3) (Vienna: Prachner, 1967), xvii.

❧ Deutsch to Schenker (letter), January 8, 1927
OC 54/III

Vienna II,
Böcklinstrasse 26

Highly revered Doctor,

I received your cover letter, together with the copy of the contract (which, strangely, is undated), at the same time as your letter,[1] and I thank you for everything.

Your messages about Dr. Einstein are very informative for me, even though in this case I still cannot share your pessimism. In addition, Drei Masken Verlag accepted our proposal yesterday.

If it is not too much trouble for your wife, I would be grateful for excerpts from the letters from DMV, insofar as they were written after the contract. I am concerned to get copies of the important passages only.[2]

Today I spoke with Dr. Haas about the project of an Archive for Photograms of Musical Master Manuscripts. He is enthusiastic and believes with me that the Archive could easily be housed in the National Library. I would like it to be called the "Hoboken Foundation" (*Stiftung*), and think that you and Haas, together with Mr. Hoboken (who will have to take care of the financial side), should assume the internal functional administration. Haas very much agrees with this.

I discovered by chance that the Beethoven House (the likes of Bonn's patricians are missing from Vienna's Schubert Museum—a failing of our community) is preparing a collection of all of Beethoven's manuscripts in photographic reproduction; something that could also be announced—along with our plan, I hope—at the [Beethoven] Congress. In England, a music scholar is apparently collecting the autograph manuscripts of Bach in this way. Perhaps the ground is already prepared for Handel, too.

Then there remain for us Mozart, Haydn, and Schubert above all. It is, however, in no way to be regarded as a competition if other parties are finally now active in the same direction. This only facilitates our work, and we will of course have [photographic] positives of those pieces that have already been collected elsewhere as negatives.

Our plan, in which I of course play only a motivational role, should remain secret for now. Mr. Hoboken, from whom I expect a valuable increase in activity as a result of this, will probably speak to you about it at the Huberman concert.[3]

Upon my return, although pressed for time on account of lectures, I shall give you at least a brief account of the progress of the Munich dealings.

Please be prepared to receive the proofs from Waldheim in the next few weeks. I gather that your manuscript is so complete that there will be only a little to amend. Should you still have concerns about the Urlinie leaves, it would be advisable for you to go to the printing house yourself, to see that everything is in order.

I am happy to be of practical use for your good cause.

With best regards, from house to house,

    Yours very truly,
    Otto Erich Deutsch

---

[1] Neither letter is known to survive.
[2] That is, passages from the correspondence concerning DMV's reluctance to put the second volume of *The Masterwork in Music* into production.
[3] Bronisław Huberman gave a concert in Vienna, including violin concertos by Bach, Beethoven and Brahms, on January 10, 1927.

ꙮ Schenker to Haas (letter), August 14, 1927
PhA/Ar 56, [1]

Dear Dr. Haas,

Mr. A. van Hoboken has asked me to send you his Appeal.[1] You will no doubt be acquainted with everything else that he has told me as to where matters stand. Things are becoming deadly serious, and I am very glad that I may count on your help in all issues.

Best wishes for the rest of the summer, and greetings from

    Yours very truly,
    H. Schenker

---

[1] Hoboken had sent Schenker the Appeal on August 9, and in a letter to Hoboken of August 12 Schenker stated: "I am just now sending your Appeal to Dr. Haas. As I read it again, I find it very good, as I did the first time. Mr. Deutsch's suggestion in footnote 1 I find excellent. Would it not be advisable for Mr. Deutsch to read out your Appeal on Radio Vienna, and if necessary add a few amplifications? Radio access is always open to Mr. Deutsch, otherwise I could also be of help there with my relationship to Prof. Richtera." (Footnote 1 refers to an agreement with the Beethoven Archive in Bonn not to duplicate photographic work on the Beethoven manuscripts.)

ꙮ Haas to Schenker (letter), August 19, 1927
OJ 11/32, [1]

Highly revered Professor,

With grateful thanks, I acknowledge receipt of the Appeal, which has now taken shape very well. I am quite confident that the final bureaucratic obstacles will in no time at all be surmounted and swept away, and that our wonderful enterprise will be underway. I am delighted to be able to work with you, and consider this project at the same time to be a noble restorative activity.

I kiss the hand of your wife and send greetings from her homeland.

    With best compliments,
    Yours very truly,
    Robert Haas

🎵 Hoboken to Schenker (letter), August 28, 1927
OJ 11/54, [15]

GIGER'S HÔTEL WALDHAUS
    SILS MARIA, ENGADINE

Dear and highly revered Dr. [Schenker],

Last week, I had tea with Mr. Furtwängler. We spoke for a short while beforehand, but what we had was by no means a more detailed discussion. We only touched on the matters. I naturally told him about the Archive. Whether it interested him very much, I cannot even say, and even less whether he will one day put the results into practice. It is difficult to decide this early, when we still have no source-examples. In the course of the winter, when we will be able to show him with reference to reproductions how the editions deviate, will in my opinion be a far more propitious moment than now to urge him toward performances according to the sources in the Archive. But it was gratifying to meet him. He impressed me as relaxed and congenial. We spoke also about Vrieslander and Weisse, and naturally quite a lot about you.

He asked me one question that seems important: he wondered whether the masters, during correction of their first editions, did not at that point make further modifications and improvements which they would not have entered in the manuscript. The question is very complex and can in many cases (Chopin!) even be answered affirmatively. Still, the manuscripts seem to me more important than the first editions, because the latter also include many errors.

I am now invited once more, this time with my wife, to join Mr. Furtwängler for dinner. Then I will immediately speak with him about when he can visit us in Vienna.

Prof. Oppel's plan to teach in Leipzig according to your system is most welcome. Now it will be of interest to see how the students react. Because the Hindemith method of composition, and that of Alban- and Schoen-berg etc. etc., in which one need take neither vertical nor horizontal combinations or situations into consideration, and one only synthesizes one's personal opinion (if such exists) about music, is of course substantially easier than yours.

I am completely amenable concerning the matter of your fee,[1] and will remit to you at the end of September one third of the amount owed for 1927/28, thus thirteen weeks of four lessons each at 50 shillings making 2,600 shillings, and the remainder at the beginning of summer, assuming that to be satisfactory to you.

Concerning the contract with the National Library, I still can report nothing definitive. The Ministry of Education has made all manner of corrections to it. Thus, for example, one may not speak of a "foundation" (*Stiftung*), since all foundations in the Federal State of Vienna stand under supervision of the City Council, and we want to avoid this if possible. Now, I think, it is to be called "dedication" (*Widmung*). And the Ministry of Education also wants to give the National Library's representative on the Board of Trustees only an advisory vote (which, in case Dr. Haas should at some point be replaced by somebody else, can only be welcome to me). But now the financial officer will not sign the draft until Court Counselor Bick[2] has commented on the changes. He will however have to approve them, as the Ministry of Education is after all his superior authority, but he was not yet back from vacation, and so I could not sign the contract before my departure. Dr. Rochlitzer[3] will now do that during my absence. However, I assume that all is in order and am proceeding accordingly, as I have no more time for waiting.

And so I send you herewith the final version of the Appeal. The newly added last sentence in the second section, page 1, goes back to a speech that Hans Pfitzner gave at a special conference on the occasion of the 57th Composers' Festival in Krefeld. How much success he realized by it you can see from the critique of Dr. Alfred Heuss,[4] which I also enclose (I do not need it returned). Footnote 1 is to be inserted at the marked place on page 3 in the text. Mr. Deutsch considered it important. Footnote 2, concerning Beethoven, is to be included as a footnote, provided that Prof. Schiedermair[5] is agreeable. I have also sent him a copy and requested a meeting on September 9. Should the date and time I have suggested be suitable to him, my travel plan for September then would be as follows: depart here on the 4th, one day in Basel, to Frankfurt on the 6th to visit Mr. Koch. Two days there. On the morning of the 9th to Bonn, there a meeting with Prof. Schiedermair, and on to Rotterdam on the same day; on the 13th to England. There I will be in touch with Prof. Dunn. I would very much have liked to take him the new yearbook. Is there a chance that Drei Masken Verlag (<u>one</u> mask would really be enough for this publisher) could have the book ready by then? In Scotland I will also, on the recommendation of Dr. Haas, visit a Prof. [Charles Sanford] Terry in Aberdeen. He is said to have done much work with Bach manuscripts and also certainly to know the location of many important manuscripts, so that a visit there seems to me very important. Then I will spend some time in London and go from there to Paris. There I am also in touch with Mr. Cauchie,[6] who is much interested in the project, and whom I will ask to make the translation of the Appeal into French (the English is already done).

Then, at the Conservatory, I will complete the inventory of the manuscripts that I began in May. I also want to try to have photographs made. But, if I insist on photostats, I foresee difficulties, as the two photographers accredited there work with plates. The Conservatory opens on October 3; I will allow myself two weeks for everything, will thus leave Paris for Vienna on October 15, and thus I hope to come to your lesson for the first time on Tuesday the 18th. A nice plan, isn't it? I am just wondering what will interfere.

The stay here is very pleasant and the air is excellent, especially when one gets reports from down below about tropical temperatures. I assume that the weather is equally nice in Galtür.

With best greetings, to your wife as well, in which I am joined by my wife, I am

   Yours sincerely,
   A. v. Hoboken

PS Will you please send the Appeal directly to Dr. Haas (Music Collection of the National Library, Augustinerbastei 6)?

---

[1] i.e. fee for study with Schenker.

² Josef Bick (1880–1952): Austrian librarian, from 1926 Director of the National Library in Vienna, a Professor of the University of Vienna, and from 1934 Director of the Albertina. He transformed the former Court Library into an international library, and as Inspector General reorganized the Austrian library system.
³ Ludwig Rochlitzer, Hoboken's attorney, chancery Vienna I, Schottenring 35 (PhA/Ar 3, report of the meeting of the Board of Directors of December 2, 1933; *Lehmanns Wohnungsanzeiger 1931*).
⁴ Alfred Valentin Heuss (1877–1934): music critic and writer on music, who was at the time the chief editor of the *Zeitschrift für Musik*, and whose interests lay in early music and Classical and Romantic music, and who saw contemporary music as "un-German."
⁵ Ludwig Schiedermair (1878–1957): German musicologist, professor of music at the University of Bonn from 1920 to 1945, Beethoven scholar and founder of the Beethoven House in Bonn in 1927 and its Director until 1945, during which time it became an international center for Beethoven research, with its major collection of Beethoven autograph manuscripts, sketchbooks, and first editions, as well as photographic copies.
⁶ Maurice Cauchie (1882–1963): French music historian and editor specializing in sixteenth- and seventeenth-century music, notably that of Clément Jannequin, whose five-voice chansons he edited, and François Couperin, of whose works he published a complete edition (1932–33) as well as a thematic index (1949).

❧ Schenker to Hoboken (letter), September 6, 1927
OJ 89/1, [4]

Dear Mr. van Hoboken,
Through the visit of a nephew of mine and also through the preparations for departure and for a visit to my older brother,¹ I was deterred in Galtür in the last days of August from commenting on a few points regarding your visit with Furtwängler. As I finally returned home yesterday, I had planned to follow up today on that intent when your second kind letter (via Galtür) arrived. I must speak openly.

In one place in your excellent Appeal you speak of the significance of the manuscripts and state that even those who examine them are not particularly convinced of their value, since various divergences encountered appear to them to be too trivial. For a moment I felt inclined to encourage you to speak the complete truth, that the editors and musicians can and must say this because they <u>do not know how to read the autograph manuscript</u> in terms of what it means to express. (A moment later I reconsidered, and thought that you were better advised in your Appeal to speak somewhat more discreetly, just as you have in fact done.) The matter stands thus: in the first place one must understand the composition down to the core; second, one must read the autograph manuscript in the spirit of that core content; and third, one must <u>know how to evaluate</u> the differences between first edition and autograph manuscript <u>in relation to the composition</u>; because however certain it is that the composer sometimes makes improvements in the first edition (which however happens <u>very, very, very seldom</u> with the masters), a far more common occurrence is that (apart from such improvements) the autograph manuscript is far from being well enough represented by the first edition. What must be done, then, is to establish this advantage of the autograph manuscript, not only in order to correct the crude errors of the first edition, but also, above and beyond that, to shed light on all that the first edition <u>does not even attempt to reproduce</u>.

As long as I am speaking of this, I hear (from the historians, from the Kinskys[2] and Altmanns, the pianists and conductors) the facile word about the triviality of all of these things, about the superior value of the first edition—but those are all people to whom the composition is completely unknown, and thus to whom the autograph manuscript as well, despite all of its marvels of particular expression, signifies nothing more than a museum piece.

And precisely that this group used to include a Bülow, Liszt, etc., and today includes a Furtwängler—<u>that completes the damage and the pity</u>! Not only that the reproduction in text and performance sounds faulty, childlike, childish, amateurish, and that because of this most irremediable ignorance the danger threatens of the destruction of all manuscripts as allegedly superfluous objects, so that one quite seriously has reason to <u>appreciate the dealers</u> and music lovers who keep the manuscripts just for the purpose of profit so long as possible. More concisely: our Furtwängler understands nothing of all that; when he is offered 3–4,000 dollars, and in Germany so and so many marks per evening, the other things don't go to his heart, and unfortunately also not to his ear! There's the problem, you know: our best people are still much too bad and too ill-suited, and therefore things got so catastrophic—that is no accident, it is the result of causes. Is it not frightening that I have to say that my friend Professor Violin in Hamburg and you hear better (with more refinement, I mean) than our Furtwängler? Just look at the way of the world: you deliberately suppress in your Appeal the stridency that would be called for, I suppress the urge to recommend stridency to you, we restrain ourselves, but the ignorance-begotten monsters practise no restraint whatever, and they oblige us, oblige me here, to take a strident tone. With the best of intentions: stridency cannot be suppressed without betrayal of the cause; one is <u>obliged to use strident language by the people</u> responsible for the damage and whose destructiveness knows no rest. How I would like to take a milder tone, but that would be betrayal. With the sword of truth and of anger it must succeed and it will succeed!

Good luck on your quest and best greetings from us both,

    Yours,
        H. Schenker

---

[1] Hans Guttmann, who was staying in Vienna September 8–18 and visiting the Schenker home each day. Wilhelm Schenker (1862–): Heinrich Schenker's surviving older brother, a medical doctor. In 1927 Wilhelm was living in Sankt Bernhard, near Horn, fifty miles northeast of Vienna, and only fifteen miles from Waidhofen, where their mother, Julia Schenker, was buried. Schenker and Jeanette had just returned from visiting him on September 3–5.

[2] Georg Kinsky (1882–1951): German musicologist, organologist, and iconographer; from 1909 to 1927 curator and director of the Heyer Music-Historical Museum in Cologne, and teacher at the University of Cologne; cataloger of musical instruments, principal compiler of the standard thematic catalog of Beethoven's works, *Das Werk Beethovens* (Munich and Duisburg: Henle, 1955), and author of *Geschichte der Musik in Bildern* (Leipzig: Breitkopf & Härtel, 1929).

Alban Berg to the Board of Trustees of the Photogram Archive (letter), December 11, 1927
ÖNB F21.Berg.3276. Mus

To the Board of Trustees of the Hoboken Dedication,[1]
Vienna I

I welcome your initiative of making photographic copies of manuscripts, and offer you my most cordial congratulations. However, I would not want to let this opportunity go by of <u>supporting</u> you in your intention possibly to photograph <u>contemporary</u> works. <u>In precisely this</u> lies the possibility of preserving them in their <u>original</u> image (at least photographically). You yourself will best know how manuscripts that have to be yielded up for purposes of performances, arrangements, and submissions, and in the process of being printed suffer—indeed how they are defaced. I think only of the scores of Bruckner symphonies, which were <u>altered</u> at the hands of know-all conductors. Such irreverent hands exist in all ages. Even today! Would it not be a worthy task in your dedication in this case, too, to save what there is to save. The danger that threatens <u>these</u> works seems to me even greater than that which threatens the manuscripts of <u>classical</u> music, which are after all—praise god!—mostly in safe keeping.

I take the liberty of offering this advice, confident you will read nothing into it other than a desire to tell you how very much I welcome your efforts "to respect the authoritative meaning of the artwork."

  With kind regards,
  Alban Berg

[1] A reproduction and transcription of this letter appears in *Das Hoboken-Archiv der Musiksammlung der Österreichischen Nationalbibliothek. Eine Ausstellung zum 90. Geburtstag von Anthony van Hoboken, 23. März bis 14. Mai 1977, Augustinerstrasse 1, 1010 Wien* (Vienna: Austrian National Library, 1977), 34–37 (exhibit No. 32a).

Schenker to Hoboken (letter), December 17, 1927
OJ 89/1, [8]

Dear Mr. van Hoboken,

The reply from Government Counselor Prof. Richtera has just arrived and is enclosed here. Mr. Deutsch is thus invited to give a "proper lecture"; concerning the "illustration," a discussion will probably be necessary, if what that means is to give the audience visual information about the damages.[1] As Mr. Deutsch is visiting you today, I wanted to have informed you already. More on Tuesday, right now (10 a.m.–12 noon) I have something to do. Only one thing more: Mr. Alban Berg might have written you in a fit of irony—from Schoenberg one learns more about that than about music. As you have sketched the purpose of the Archive, it stands, if only as a juridical person, for a great artist who says: "only that which I, the Archive, here reproduce is the true art." The Archive in spirit represents what we have seen with Joachim, Messchaert, [etc.], but which regrettably is lacking today. The Archive attains this high artistic and human judicial authority without actually emphasizing that it wants first of all to guard the treasures against decline. Mr. Berg (thus far alone) understands that "new music" would indirectly suffer an injury to its reputation through the Archive,[2] and therefore he gently protests. It wouldn't be a bad idea to tell him that we hope, in one or two hundred years, that a new Hoboken will come along who will guard "new music" against decline – in case . . .![3] etc.

        With best, hastiest greetings,
          Yours,
            H. Schenker

[1] Probably the damage inflicted by printed editions on musical texts as they are presented in the autographs of masters. Deutsch's lecture, "The Photogram Archive of Musical Master Manuscripts in the Music Collection of the Vienna National Library," broadcast February 4, 1928, was supported by an article written by Haas and several photographs of autograph manuscripts as illustrations in the program magazine *Radio-Wien*, 4th year, no. 18 (January 27, 1928): 659 and viii; and no. 19 (February 3, 1928): vii (picture supplement).

[2] That is, through its very existence.

[3] The tacet continuation could probably be filled in as "(in case) new music has survived that long!"

Schenker to Deutsch (letter), January 25, 1928
WSLB 191.560

Dear Mr. Deutsch,

Many thanks for your manuscript![1] The lecture has, in my opinion, the most pleasing structure, despite its casual style, which will suit the spoken word well. Allow a little explanation with the few comments that I take the liberty of suggesting:

The word "scientific" (used twice on p. 1) should especially not escape the lips of us, who are present at the birth of the Archive; may the generation after us have the use of this buzzword. That which is important in reading masterpieces and manuscripts is as little a science as that with which the masters write their works: music is a special art, an extraordinary unity, of voice-leading, counterpoint, form, etc., one and the same, and always only art, which is only ever accessible by inspiration. The separation of the mentioned elements and their special presentation under the title "science" only occurred to allow the school system a convenient point of invasion into the art: one abandons the unity of music (the bunches of grapes hang too high) and adheres to an alleged science that has nothing to do with the music. This laziness is indeed the cause of the decline, the cause of the misery, which the Archive aims to prevent. The "scientists" should now be wrenched from publishing activities! Therefore on p. 1 I have specifically emphasized the artistic on both occasions.

And again on p. 2 I have a few sentences devoted to the same thought, about the decision in your introduction, before entering into the illustrative examples, to outline precisely the ground on which you stand.

p. 4: Please also mention Beethoven's Op. 106, which is among the piano works as the Ninth Symphony is among the symphonies, or the *Missa solemnis*, or the song cycle *An die ferne Geliebte*!

p. 4, below: I brought forward (p. 2) your general point about collected editions, so that the specific remark about Mozart will be better understood at this point as merely one cited example.

p. 5: a small correction was needed, which you will readily appreciate. Likewise

p. 6: as above.

p. 7: Not for the sake of publicity, I ask you to add these words *ad vocem* Schenker.[2] Rather, so that references are given to works in which everyone can get information about these kinds of questions and solutions: my works are already there and can serve as a model for others who come after me, and would have to come before similar tasks. Also, I have added a few clearly paraphrased words to your word "impetus," otherwise the listener might believe that the stimulus occurred in, for example, a private conversation or the like.

Thanks again, and warmest greetings to you and your revered wife.
We hope to see you very soon at our place (for a very long conversation),
    Yours,
        H. Schenker

---

[1] i.e. of Deutsch's lecture, a draft version of which is preserved in the Photogram Archive at the Austrian National Library.

[2] In the draft version of the lecture, Schenker is mentioned once, in the following sentence: "All the more pressing was the act of this Archive, to which Heinrich Schenker gave the impetus and which Robert Haas, the Director of the Music Collection of the National Library, has organized, both active alongside the founder in the Board of Directors."

Schenker to Kromer (letter), June 22, 1928
PhA/Ar 56, [8]

Dear Mr. Kromer,[1]

I send you—as its representative—my most cordial thanks for the greetings telegram[2] from the Photogram Archive. I hear from its revered creator that it is growing by the day, with every new photograph that comes in it celebrates, so to speak, a new day of glory—All in all, the Archive is and will always remain truly the crowning glory of all music collections!

  With kind regards and greetings,
   Yours
    H. Schenker

[1] Julius (Julo) Ritter von Kromer: secretary of the Photogram Archive from 1927 to beyond Schenker's death, after which he kept in touch with Jeanette Schenker by mail, telephone, and visits until at least fall 1939.
[2] In recognition of Schenker's sixtieth birthday on June 19. Schenker recorded in his diary for June 20: "Telegram from the Photogram Archive 'in gratitude and esteem'."

Schenker to Cube (letter), November 20, 1928
OJ 5/7a, [21]

My dear Mr. Cube,

Most cordial wishes and blessings for the 28th.[1] You are making steady progress; keep at it! But, above and beyond this, I should also like to offer you a few words of advice, to harden you for the struggles that stand before you:

You may well remember that I often spoke of my conviction that the path to the truth should be accessible to many, indeed to everyone, if only I could extricate the teachers from the embarrassment, from all anxiety or shame, by extensive publications concerning Urlinien. I used to point to Riemann, who furnished the teachers with sumptuous banquets, provided them with everything so that all they had to do was to take and to eat. For me, however, what mattered above all was the first notion of the Urlinie, the bass figures, and so on. Now that *Free Composition* is essentially complete, resolving all questions in such a thoroughly methodical way (in numbered sections) and so comprehensively, the time has come in which I am also thinking of a folder of Urlinien.[2] It is not yet clear how many Urlinien the volume of music examples of *Free Composition* can embrace, and whether it should be preceded by my analysis of Beethoven's "Eroica" Symphony, with Urlinien, as a separate publication—the elucidatory edition of Beethoven's Op. 106 belongs to Universal Edition, and must likewise be treated in a special way, with Urlinien[3]—in any event I am contemplating the plan of issuing a <u>folder of Urlinien</u> (without text), to provide teachers with a quite substantial amount of material. I have also communicated to Mr. Hoboken that, if things cannot be done any other way, I would entrust my Urlinien in handwritten form to the Photogram Archive, so that I might insist that, in all circumstances, musicians can have access to them in the cheapest and most convenient way possible. We shall see what is possible.

On the 26th [*recte* 25th], the Archive will be officially opened by the Minister; this will be followed by a kind of symposium for Schubert scholars, with further receptions given by the President of the Republic and the Minister.[4] In spite of the services I have given through my very early involvement, and by promoting the Archive in word and deed, in spite of a Trustee's dignity, in spite of all official invitations, in spite of all inclination to "distinguish" myself as highly as possible, in spite of everything I shall firmly keep my distance from these things. I shall stay at home. Our government and our musical profession have too much on their conscience that I should also join with them in their amusements. I shall only take part in the evening with Tautenhayn[5] at Hoboken's (which, moreover, I likewise promoted) on the 26th; there I shall meet up with Vrieslander, Dahms, Oppel (from Leipzig), Kinsky, and others. That is all that I shall do.[6]

Young Albersheim has notified his parents of your intention to visit them in Cologne.[7]

Let me know very soon how things went for you in Cologne.

The "counter-examples" must be conquered <u>slowly</u>! Do not allow yourself to practise any snobbery. First that which is good, then the bad.[8]

And now: take heart. Everything along the path that you take is honorable; every mistake is excused in advance.

        Best wishes and greetings from the two of us
          Yours,
            H. Schenker

---

[1] On November 28, 1928, Cube was to give the first of a series of eight lectures on Schenkerian theory at the Music Hochschule in Cologne.

[2] This project was initially realized as the *Fünf Urlinie-Tafeln* or *Five Analyses in Sketchform* published in 1932 by Universal Edition (Vienna) and the David Mannes Music School (New York). Further "Urlinie-Mappen" were projected but never realized; some draft analyses from these appeared in *Free Composition*.

[3] An elucidatory edition of Beethoven's "Hammerklavier" Sonata, Op. 106, was planned for the 1910s but held up—and eventually abandoned—in part because the autograph manuscript score could not be traced.

[4] The name of the Austrian Minister for Education, Richard Schmitz, is frequently mentioned in the Foreword to the proceedings of the symposium.

[5] Karl (Carl) Hermann Tautenhayn (1871–1949): Austrian bank employee, accordion player and composer, with whom the term Schrammelmusik (Viennese popular music) is associated. As early as the 1890s he founded a trio (accordion, violin

and guitar), which was expanded to a quartet (a second violin) and which toured the United States, Italy, and Germany. In 1922 Tautenhayn formally founded the Tautenhayn Quartet (Old-Viennese Chamber Quartet): Tautenhayn, accordion; Max Weissgärber, first violin; Otto Strasser, second violin; Anton Sonderegger, bass guitar. This remained highly successful until 1945, including the radio performances "Viennese Evenings."

[6] Although Schenker did not contribute to the Schubert symposium, he received a copy of the proceedings, a publication that specifically mentions the support of the Photogram Archive: *Bericht über den internationalen Kongress für Schubertforschung Wien 25. bis 29. November 1928, veranstaltet mit Unterstützung des Archivs für Photogramme musikalischer Meisterhandschriften an der Musiksammlung der Nationalbibliothek in Wien* (Augsburg: Bennor Filser, 1929). The *Bericht* is one of the very few books (other than Schenker's own) that remained among his surviving papers.

[7] Gerhard Albersheim (1902–96): German pianist and writer on music, pupil of Schenker's 1925–29 who later took a PhD from the University of Vienna and emigrated to the USA and later to Switzerland. When Schenker first learned of Cube's plans to go to Cologne, he asked him to visit the parents of Albersheim, who lived there.

[8] Cube had previously written of his intention to include counter-examples in his Cologne lectures, i.e. examples of (contemporary) works that did not give evidence of the clear tonal structure that his teacher's theory insisted upon. Schenker had himself done this twice in the recently published *Masterwork* 2 (dated 1926 but not issued until 1927): an extract from Stravinsky's Piano Concerto and (in an essay devoted to the work and specifically calling it a "counter-example") Reger's Variations and Fugue on a Theme of Bach, Op. 81.

❧ Schenker to Haas (letter), July 6, 1929

PhA/Ar 56, [3]

Highly revered Professor,

Have you read the notice "Expropriation of the Property of the Pürglitz Estate Held in Tail" in the *Neue freie Presse* for July 4?[1] – about the manuscripts of Haydn (Dittersdorf, Kreuzer) surviving in the Pürglitz Library of Prince Fürstenberg? I am informing Mr. Hoboken of it by the same post. Perhaps the Archive could at least inquire which works by Haydn are involved? What do you think? Have the works already been engraved, or are there compositions among them that are still unpublished?

It is possible that this or that Haydn autograph manuscript passed through Dittersdorf's hands as a gift from one small music director to an even smaller music director.

Best wishes to you and your revered wife for the summer from the two of us,

Yours

H. Schenker

[1] "Enteignung des Fideikommissbesitzes Pürglitz," *Neue freie Presse*, no. 23276 (July 4, 1929, morning edition): 6.

❧ Hoboken to Schenker (letter, carbon copy), September 15, 1930
PhA/Ar 36, [1]

Highly revered and dear Dr. [Schenker],
   With today's mail I am sending you a concerto for harpsichord and string orchestra in D major by C. P. E. Bach, no. 11 according to Wotquenne's catalog. I have assembled the score from the parts of the first edition, and have also provided a realization of the thoroughbass. Please check it over if you have time, and discuss it with me in a lesson that I would like to have with you within the time reserved for me at the beginning of October.[1] I shall then bring the originals along too. Unfortunately it was not possible to send these as well because of the many circumstances attendant thereon. I have not yet been able to see the autograph manuscript of the concerto, or the Westphal copy. The latter is said to be in Brussels.
   Which day I will come to you depends on my arrival in Vienna, and I will notify you as soon as the latter is definite. I expect that to be Friday, October 3. I will then remain for only a few days in Vienna, as I want to spend the time up to Christmas in <u>Berlin</u>.
   The work is intended to serve as engraver's copy for the imminent collected edition.[2] I wanted to prepare for this edition several, if not all, harpsichord concertos, but after the work at hand, I do not know whether I will put up with the sheer toil of score-assembly that often.
   With the thoroughbass I had very little trouble, except for measures 7–11 and 86–90 of the second movement, where, in my opinion, I have not hit on the correct realization of the figuring $9 - \frac{8}{6} - \frac{6}{5}$.
   To continue immediately with the collected edition, I cannot conceal my disappointment at your having declined to participate in the general supervision of it. As a result, the situation has arisen for me that my plan to have the Archive take responsibility for its publication can be carried through only with difficulty, if at all. Prof. Haas, to be specific, has already written me a letter containing a draft contract according to which he will serve as editor, referring at the same time to the fact that you have transferred the supervision to him. The Archive—or better, the Board of Trustees—will be mentioned only as the body commissioning the work. The Archive is supposed to take on all financial obligations relative to the edition and back the latter with its name and reputation, while Prof. Haas, as editor, claims all rights—in particular the selection of collaborators—for himself. Naturally I cannot agree to this, and through this alone the presumed commission of the Board of Trustees is therefore null and void, since he certainly cannot commission himself. Where the Archive has to take on so many obligations, it must be given rights as well. In particular over selection of collaborators, but also over other general guidelines for the edition, it must be able to have a decisive voice. I would like now urgently to request that you not deny us your collaboration

on this; you will have nothing to do with editorial matters anyway, except with the theoretical volumes, which you have, to my great pleasure, taken on.

I participated, as Prof. Haas will probably have reported to you, in the preliminary discussions for the collected edition, which were held in mid-July in Leipzig. I did not want to miss out on that, since the edition means a great deal to me, and I plan to be actively involved with it. Even if I should not yet be able to do so at the beginning, I shall nevertheless learn it gradually.

The proprietor of the Bärenreiter publishing company, Mr. Vötterle,[3] impressed me as pleasant and mild-mannered.

Breitkopf, with whom preliminary negotiations had also been conducted, would have liked to usurp the edition for himself, but he set the requirement that we subscribe for sixty copies, and that he be given a free hand. This, however, we did not want to do, and we thought that here we would be in agreement with you. Anyway, it seems to me of importance for the expected success of the edition that Breitkopf was willing to take it without subvention. To be sure, he wanted to block other plans relative to this matter, among others a Vrieslander-Piper plan,[4] of which you probably know more than I. Is that plan also for an edition of the collected works of C. P. E. Bach?

How were things for you during your sojourn in Galtür? Prof. Oppel wrote me that he had visited you. Did you suffer from the bad weather? The summer, you know, is supposed to have been miserable in the Alps, as has been reported to me from all over. Did you, and especially your eyes, nevertheless have a good rest?

Here the weather was still tolerable, and I have nothing to complain about. The house[5] proved comfortable and well built, and has already accommodated many guests. Among them were no musicians at all except for Kleiber,[6] who took meals with us twice. Klemperer[7] also spent his vacation on the island, but I never met him. Recently a request arrived from Mr. Hans Weissbach, the General Music Director of Düsseldorf,[8] who conducts the symphonic concerts in Scheveningen during the summer, for the photogram of the G minor Symphony by Mozart. The item was then sent to him, and he conducted accordingly, as was specifically mentioned in the concert reviews.

I will now stay here until Monday the 2nd, and then go to Holland for a few days. From there by way of Munich to Vienna (by train; I don't have the car with me this year), and will, as mentioned earlier, notify you about the date of my arrival.

For the present I close with friendly greetings from our house to yours as

    Yours most sincerely,
    [*unsigned*]

¹ No such discussion is recorded in Schenker's lessonbook during October–December 1930.
² Hoboken planned a collected edition of the works of C. P. E. Bach under the auspices of the Photogram Archive. The plan was not realized for reasons of finance.
³ Karl Vötterle (1903–75): German music publisher who founded the publishing house of Bärenreiter in 1923.
⁴ By this time Otto Vrieslander had already published a monograph and an article on C. P. E. Bach, and an edition of songs by him. This letter and another from Hoboken of July 2, 1930, clearly suggest that Vrieslander was planning a collected edition with the publisher of his monograph, Piper Verlag of Munich. When Vrieslander's correspondence becomes publicly accessible, more information will doubtless emerge.
⁵ Kliffende: a guesthouse on the island of Sylt, off the west coast of Schleswig-Holstein, much visited by figures in the world of the arts between its foundation in 1923 and the onset of World War II.
⁶ Erich Kleiber (1890–1956): Austrian conductor, at the time General Music Director at the Berlin State Opera (1923–35) and already internationally well known.
⁷ Otto Klemperer (1885–1973): German conductor, at the time music director of the Kroll Opera in Berlin (1927–31), a branch of the State Opera created to focus on new and recent works (Stravinsky, Schoenberg, Janáček, Weill, etc.), and non-traditional performances of repertory works.
⁸ Hans Weisbach (or Weissbach) (1885–1961): German conductor, whose appointment at Düsseldorf extended from 1926 to 1933, and who thereafter served as conductor of the Leipzig Radio Orchestra 1933–39 and then the Vienna Symphony Orchestra (during World War II renamed "City Orchestra") from 1938 to 1944.

❧ Schenker to Haas (letter), November 12, 1930
PhA/Ar 56, [4]

Revered Professor,

By chance, I read in *Velhagen & Klasing's Monatshefte*, the September issue 1930, p. 116,¹ that Prof. Stephan Ley,² Director of the Gymnasium in Linz on the Rhine, had dealings with Prince Ladislaus Odescalchi, who entrusted to him the picture of the Princess Babette Clarissa Odescalchi, born Countess Keglevich,³ for the *Monatshefte*. As is well known, this countess had the benefit of tuition from Beethoven and several dedications. Isn't what is called for to follow the scent? After all, Prince Odescalchi still has some manuscript material about which neither Director Ley nor the Count says anything, perhaps because for them it is not as valuable as the portrait of the Beethoven pupil that Countess Babette has? The collection is all the more important because very little manuscript material exists from Beethoven's early time in Vienna.

I hope to see you very soon. Until then, with cordial greetings on both our behalves

Yours,
H. Schenker

[1] "Eine Schülerin Beethovens," *Velhagen & Klasings Monatshefte*, 45th year, no. 1 (September 1930): 116.

[2] Stephan Ley (1867–1964): German teacher, writer on music, author of six books and numerous articles on Beethoven. He left behind a comprehensive collection of pictorial evidence now housed in the Beethoven House in Bonn.

[3] Princess Odescalchi: member of the Italian aristocratic Odescalchi family and pupil of Beethoven in Vienna, to whom Beethoven dedicated his Piano Sonata in E♭ major, Op. 7, and his first piano concerto.

❧ Haas to Schenker (letter), November 17, 1930

OJ 11/32, [4]

Highly revered Professor,

Your lead on the Beethoven trail is very valuable. I have addressed myself to Professor Ley on behalf of the Archive and will acquaint you with the outcome of this inquiry.

The [C. P. E.] Bach contract is still not concluded. I understand that Mr. Hoboken will be coming to Vienna in the next few days, and I hope then, if not earlier, to see you again. I am pleased to hear that your health is once again improved.

With best regards to you and your wife,
Yours very truly,
Robert Haas

❧ Haas to Schenker (letter), December 11, 1930

OJ 11/32, [7]

Highly revered Professor,

I am astonished that you have <u>only now for the first time</u> learned of the abrupt end of the [C. P. E.] Bach edition. I thought that you had known for a long time.

After efforts lasting many months, and shortly after it was agreed that the publisher would shoulder half the risk, the refusal arrived, pointing to excessively high costs—what's more, an outright rejection. Dr. Schmid[1] was released, but was retained for one further month at my representations on grounds that the continuation of his work in the Archive is inexpensive.

I should very much like to speak with you about matters concerning the Archive. I greatly regretted recently being so to speak prevented from coming to you at the last moment. But my little boy came home suddenly, school having been closed on account of scarlet fever. Fortunately, nothing came of it so far as he was concerned, but you can never know.

With best compliments,
Yours very truly,
Robert Haas

[1] Ernst Fritz Schmid (1904–60): German scholar, active in Vienna from about 1930 as a freelance conductor and musicologist. He had evidently been hired to assist in the aborted C. P. E. Bach collected edition. Between 1954 and his death he was senior editor of the *Neue Mozart-Ausgabe*.

Kromer to Schenker (letter), January 26, 1932
OJ 12/24, [3]

Dear Professor,
  At the end of the year I came across some photograms that were no longer serviceable for the Archive on account of technical defects. Among them are Chopin Op. 40 and the beginning (some twenty pages) of the *Well-tempered Clavier*, Book I. But it now occurs to me that your pupils might perhaps like to acquire these works for study purposes, and thought I should ask of you about this. If there is any interest, please refer those concerned directly to me.
  In hoping to be able to greet you soon in the rooms of the Archive, I remain
>   with kindest regards,
>   Yours very truly,
>   Julo Kromer

Haas to Schenker (letter), September 15, 1932
OJ 11/32, [11]

Highly revered Professor,
  When I came into the office on Monday I found a letter from Mr. Hoboken, which I read confidentially and then answered. He communicates his regrettable decision to leave Vienna,[1] and encloses a proposal regarding the Master Archive that is tantamount to shutting it down. In my reply, I had to make my position clear that I can devote my participation only to something entire, and that I am prepared to place the necessary evidence before the Board of Trustees. For the sake of the cause, I hope for a better understanding and would have liked to speak with you, since as Board members we are in fact all responsible. Perhaps you might stop by here next week (but in that case I ask for prior notification), or I will gladly come to you if that suits you better.
  I have received your postcard regarding Vrieslander by a circuitous route, and the report will go to him once again, though it will also already have been sent to him from the Archive.
>   With cordial compliments and greetings,
>   Yours very truly,
>   Robert Haas

[1] Hoboken had written to Schenker on September 5, stating that he was vacating his apartment in Vienna on November 1, but that this did not mean he would not

return. Since the letter, as well as covering the withdrawal of Haas's honorarium and the reduction of that of Kromer, committed Hoboken to 15,000 shillings for the costs of *Free Composition*, Schenker's reaction was primarily one of relief.

❧ Diary entry, September 21, 1932

From 5–7:30 p.m. Prof. Haas for afternoon coffee. I show him a Hoboken "vitrine": thoroughbass, chorale, Brahms Op. 117, Nos. 1–3, twelve Mazurkas by Chopin—all of this makes him deeply uncomfortable. The non-musician, non-historian rises up against the superiority that strangely threatens him, and seeks diagnosis and therapy constantly from his own area of expertise: letters, letters, catalogs, catalogs is all that he has to say about the protection, about the promotion of the Archive. Just as a joke I put forward my idea of its promotion by means of a course in "manuscript studies" to be attached to the Academy—he warns me, puts the fear of God into me, but will nevertheless "make tentative inquiries." Perhaps he will nonetheless succeed with his cattle-trade politics: already he has reached 6,000 shillings instead of 3,000. He takes Hoboken's tactics merely as "west-European" manners.

❧ Haas to Schenker (letter), September 10, 1933
OJ 11/32, [16]

Highly revered Professor,

Your kind judgment of my book on performance practice[1] makes me truly proud, for I know the value of this judgment! I hope my approach to the subject will be of use, especially since the book is already in the hands of <u>14,000</u> subscribers and has been repeatedly welcomed. (Only in Austria has it been passed over in silence, like my other works.)

My *Mozart*[2] has also now appeared. In it, I was able to sing the praises of the Master Archive.

I am delighted to hear that you have had a restorative summer. We were in Carinthia (Seeboden) and had good weather.

It would be very desirable if Hoboken's collection were installed again[3] (he could do us a lot of good as an expansion of the Master Archive)! If you need anything, I will gladly send it to you via Mr. Kromer—for example, when you are back, the Griesinger.[4] The Archive has done good business and that has pleased even Mr. Hoboken.

Lacking in the Music Collection unfortunately is volume 1 of your *Masterwork*; only volumes 2 and 3 are in our hands. Might I ask whether you by any chance have a copy of <u>volume I</u> surplus to requirements that you could donate to the Collection? I must somehow complete it.[5]

Best wishes to you and your dear wife for the rest of the summer, with most heartfelt greetings,
>Yours,
>Robert Haas

[1] Robert Haas, *Aufführungspraxis der Musik* (Postdam: Athenaion, 1931).
[2] Robert Haas, *W. A. Mozart* (Potsdam: Athenaion, 1933).
[3] Presumably when Hoboken moved out of his apartment in November 1932, his collection of first and early editions (begun in 1919) was moved, too. It had served as a research tool for the work of the Photogram Archive, with which it existed symbiotically. Its removal, if that was the case, must have constituted a loss to the operation of the Archive.
[4] Georg August Griesinger, *Biographische Notizen über Joseph Haydn* (Leipzig: Breitkopf & Härtel, 1810).
[5] Schenker supplied the copy on September 17.

Kromer to Schenker (picture postcard), April 25, 1934
OJ 12/24, [8]

Dear Professor,

This is to inform you as requested that the Archive possesses among the *Songs without Words* of Mendelssohn that in F♯ minor, Op. 30, No. 6 ("Venetian Gondola Song"). If you need it, I will produce a copy of it (two-to-three exposures) for you and send it. Please let me have just a brief note.

>With best greetings,
>Yours very truly,
>Kromer

13
Professorial Sorties: Ludwig Karpath and Wilhelm Furtwängler

THE mode of address to which Schenker was strictly speaking entitled throughout his career was "Doctor," reflecting the doctorate of law that he had received from the University of Vienna in 1889.[1] During the 1890s he was addressed in letters by professional people (e.g. Eduard Hanslick, Ignaz Brüll, Hermann Bahr, Max Graf) as "Dear Doctor," and by publishing houses (Breitkopf & Härtel, Edition Peters, Simrock) as "Dear Sir" or "Dear Mr. Schenker," while closer acquaintances (d'Albert, Busoni) saluted him as "Dear friend." (Schenker, throughout his life, meticulously addressed people as they were due: "Dear Doctor," "Dear Professor," "Dear Court Counselor," "Dear Baron," etc.)

An early change came in a letter from Josef Weinberger dated January 5, 1900, addressed to "Professor Heinrich Schenker, Esq." with the salutation "Dear Professor." At the arrival of Hertzka as director of Universal Edition in 1907, "Dear Professor" became the customary salutation to Schenker by all the UE staff (except in contracts, where he is "Doctor"). Ernst Rudorff switched from "Doctor" to "Professor" in 1910, and it was around that time, by which Schenker's reputation as a theorist and editor, and no doubt as a private teacher, was growing, that the professorial title was more widely accorded to him. By the 1910s, Schenker's pupils were addressing him either as "Professor" or as "Master," as did some of those who wrote to ask advice of him.

"Professor" remained, however, an honorific appellation. The following selection traces two attempts, in 1908 and 1932–33, to obtain a professorship for him in Vienna, and a further one to engage him in Berlin. Between these is included an incident concerning Moriz Violin and Hamburg, which elicited not only a clarification of the Viennese use of the professorial title but also an extraordinary statement by Schenker on his own use of it. Efforts on Schenker's behalf were made elsewhere, as well:

> Through Prof. [Karl] Straube, I found out that Leipzig University considered appointing me last year [1921] but ultimately refrained from doing so in consideration that a purely artistic environment suits me better than the more historically oriented one within the university. How nicely and correctly judged! I do not know whether Straube's efforts to bring me to Leipzig or Berlin will succeed. I believe my pronounced anti-democratic attitude militates against an appointment at the Berlin

---

[1] Schenker received his Doctor Juris on February 1, 1889, having studied law from 1884 to 1888. See Wayne Alpern, "Schenkerian Jurisprudence: Echoes of Schenker's Legal Education in His Musical Thought" (PhD diss.: City University of New York, 2005), 30–35.

Hochschule. "Handcuffs for reactionary types!" as the musicians' collegium with Scheidemann would say.[2]

Two months later Schenker reported that Furtwängler intended to intervene on his behalf in Leipzig,[3] but nothing seems to have come of that. In August 1929 he reported a conversation with his neighbor, a Professor Curtius, "saying that, at the time, on the strength of Furtwängler's recommendation, he recommended me for the professorship at Heidelberg; but the adviser in the Ministry could not agree to this, since he had grounds for disregarding an Austrian candidate."[4] Three months later, he reported that "two universities, Leipzig and Heidelberg, considered appointing me, though I made no effort at all in the matter myself."[5]

MARTIN EYBL & IAN BENT

---

[2] Letter to August Halm, September 25, 1922.
[3] Non-extant letter to Dahms: diary November 29, 1922.
[4] Diary, August 15, 1929.
[5] Letter to Moriz Violin, November 24, 1929.

1908 – Schenker and the Vienna Academy

Karpath to Schenker (postcard), February 10, 1908
OJ 12/9, [1]

Have just come from Wiener.[1] Have tried to reach you by telephone—in vain. Must talk to you and Floriz <u>urgently</u>. [Do you need] tickets for the Concert Society[?][2] <u>Say nothing! Not to anybody</u>!!

  Greetings
  Karpath[3]

---

[1] Karl von Wiener (1863–1945): President of the Vienna Academy from 1909, when the Vienna Conservatory of the Society of the Friends of Music became a state institution, to 1919. Wiener, as an official of the Austrian Ministry of Education, was added to the Society's Board of Directors in 1901, and was a member of the committee appointed in 1907 to oversee the transformation of the Conservatory into a state academy.
[2] Presumably an offer to procure tickets for a concert by the Vienna Concert Society.
[3] Ludwig Karpath (1866–1936: see Plate 36): Budapest-born Austrian singer and writer on music, music critic of the *Neues Wiener Tagblatt* 1914–17, editor of *Der Merker*; friend of Brahms, Mahler, and Richard Strauss. In 1906/07 he was a pupil of Schenker's, and around that time a member of Schenker's circle. He was involved in the transfer to state ownership of the Vienna Conservatory of Music in 1909, the founding and establishment of the Vienna People's Opera, and the building of the Vienna Concert House in 1913, and in the 1930s was Adviser on the Arts to the Ministry of Education.

❧ Diary entries, February 10, 11, 15, 1908

[February 10:] Mr. Karpath alerts me in a postcard open for all to see that the wheels have been set in motion in the Ministry regarding the professorship.

[February 11:] With Floriz at Karpath's place. Chandelier comes crashing down, all the globes dashed to pieces—by the laws of superstition, a most propitious omen. Meaning: I must now go and see Court Counselor Wiener myself.

[February 15:] With Court Counselor Wiener (10–11 a.m.) concerning the Royal and Imperial Professorship in Theory. A difficult interview. I was required to give some idea of my inclinations in the form of a monolog, without which there would be no concrete basis for the negotiations. In the course of this, the objection occurred to me that my method of abstracting theory from the work of art could lead today's youth into acquiring a taste for rulelessness before their minds have been given a track on which to proceed by fixed rules—regardless of whether or not they are actually erroneous! I sought to correct this objection (which only *appears* to be based on reasoning) by arguing that the alleged rulelessness in artworks comes together again in the unities of higher laws, the truth of which is easier to grasp than the untruth of the nonsensical and erroneous rules that are given out today. I venture, said I, without endangering the younger generation, to lay the doctrine of truth, i.e., of genuine art, before these same pupils, from whom people today, on the unanswerable pretext of "youth," expect only inartistic errors. — In the afternoon, report given to Karpath.[1]

---

[1] No further correspondence on this matter is known, and there are no further references in Schenker's diary. However, two years later, in a long letter to Cotta of December 2, 1909, explaining why delivery of his manuscript for the first volume of *Counterpoint* had been delayed, Schenker adds the following statement, which encapsulates the dilemma he felt between on the one hand independence combined with patronage, and on the other state employment with its attendant obligations:

> I may possibly by then [spring 1910] be in a position, even for the first half-volume, to put in front of my name the title of a Royal and Imperial Professor of Composition and Theory at the Vienna Hochschule (Academy). There is a possibility that I may be selected for this leading post, with all the attendant advantages in honor and remuneration, to open up my theories unfettered to the Academy and other such institutions. There are admittedly differences of opinion, also, and whether I can reconcile myself to sacrificing my freedom will depend on the resolution of those difficulties. For, first and foremost, I aspire to take full advantage of the auspiciousness of a fate that sent me a patron, and to complete the work previously begun, namely to publish volume 3 [*Decline of the Art of Composition*], the core of my total work, in the best interests of an artistic renaissance to come. Moreover, so confident am I already of the success of volume 2, *Counterpoint*, indeed even of its success from the secondary, i.e. commercial point of view, that I prefer to suffer economic disadvantage at the personal level and so with some sacrifice continue my work in isolation rather than, with outward honor and wealth, risk imperiling the latter through a whole lot of inescapable friction.

1931 – Moriz Violin and Hamburg

❦ Diary entries, October 21–22, 1931

[October 21:] From Floriz (express letter): perhaps it would be good to have a confirmation of "practice"?[1] — To Karpath (express letter): I agree with Violin: it is a distinction between waiters and prostitutes and people from the circles in which we move, if they confer the title "Professor"! Why [do we have] a "professional regulation" only in music, not in poetry? And I myself? My title, "Professor," is emphatically correct; I have "tested" myself severely enough. (At most, revered Doctor!). Perhaps Wiener could pen a word about "usage"?

[October 22:] Karpath himself will draft something in writing.

---

[1] Moriz Violin had been teaching at the Vogt Conservatory in Hamburg since 1921. In 1931 he had founded the Schenker Institute in the city (see chapter 21). He had perhaps been challenged for using the title "professor," and was defending himself on grounds that he had borne the title while teaching at the Vienna Conservatory 1908–12. When asked to confirm this, Karl von Wiener denied that Violin "had had a professorship." Karpath, to whom Schenker appealed for help, opined that nothing could be done for Violin, hence Violin's request, backed by Schenker, for a statement of practice in the use of the title, and this elicited the following clarifying letter.

❦ Karpath to Schenker (letter), October 23, 1931
OJ 12/9, [30]

COURT COUNSELOR LUDWIG KARPATH
VIENNA IV, PRINZ EUGENSTRASSE 16

Dear friend Schenker,

Are you so out of touch with the world? It seems you are so wrapped up in your own works (and you are right to be!) that you are not even aware that I gave up writing music reviews many years ago. In all probability you don't read any newspapers, which is very sensible. Nowadays I make my living as a freelance writer; but alas I still have to read newspapers, because for the past nine years I have served as Adviser on the Arts to the Minister for Education. Evidently you do already know that, for otherwise you would surely hardly have turned to me on the matter of our mutual friend Violin, from whom I have not heard in a million years.

What Violin is complaining about, in his cry of anguish about which you write to me, is sheer nonsense. Naturally, anyone who worked at the Conservatory of the Society of the Friends of Music (at what is today the State Academy) would be referred to as "Herr Professor." There was not a single teacher who would have protested against it, because he would have had to hang a placard around his neck saying "I am not yet a professor, just a teacher." I know from experience that even the deceased conservatory Directors Perger and Bopp addressed every individual teacher as "Herr Professor," though they themselves must have known better than anyone else that teachers to whom the title "Professor" had not been formally granted were not as of right accorded the professorial title. This can be accounted for as a generally observed practice, to which no one took exception, since in fact ultimately every teacher after a few years' service was, I might almost say automatically, nominated as a professor. Then there is the mode of address on the part of the students! It would have been almost comical if the students, instead of saying "Herr Professor," had said "Herr Lehrer"! Indeed, I am pretty sure that the simple fact that there existed both professors appointed to that rank and also mere teachers was completely unknown to the students. Thus if you are of the opinion that at that time it was the general practice to address all teachers giving instruction at the Conservatory or the later Academy as "Herr Professor," then I would entirely go along with that view.[1]

Were I to be asked this in the Ministry of Education (the section is today entirely filled with new people), I would automatically give the answer that I have given here. I would have no objection to your using these remarks of mine in a suitable fashion; I would just prefer not to be cited in newspapers because I would first have to obtain the permission of my Minister.[2]

  With most cordial greetings,
   Yours truly in old friendship,
    Ludwig Karpath

[1] Violin, to whom Schenker sent Karpath's letter, responded by referring to "the stupidity over titles" as "incomprehensibly tragic" (letter of November 4, 1931).

[2] The self-declared anti-Semite Emmerich Czermak (1885–1965), a member of the Christian Socialist Party, was Minister of Education in three Christian-Socialist-led governments between September 1930 and May 1932.

1932–33 – Schenker and the Vienna Academy or Berlin

Diary entry, November 18, 1932

At Karpath's place: I describe my situation, and give him a year in which to build up a body of support. He knows nothing of any source of money for me and my work, and to whatever I came up with against that, he exclaimed: "Ah yes, the atonalists ...," "Ah yes, Hertzka ...," "Ah yes, the Ministry doesn't have a penny to its name"[1]—yet he is convinced that he can definitely still create a job opening for me. He tells me that Furtwängler was with him for a meal and has declared that he will bring me to Berlin.—This gave Karpath the idea of getting Furtwängler to write a letter about me that he will emphatically publish in the newspaper so as to enlighten Vienna about me; he even asked my dear Lie-Liechen for a list of my successes abroad. In short, never for one minute during this hour did he drop his journalistic antics; it almost seems as if he were wanting to wangle an article about himself; he kept constantly patting me on the back. All this points to his having no wish to give information about my accomplishments either to the Minister or to the Viennese. I rather prefer Departmental Counselor Thomasberger,[2] who openly admitted he was unable to enlighten his superiors about me.—Karpath asserts that he knows more about me than does Furtwängler. We part with the feeling of having been barking up the wrong tree.

[1] Presumably Schenker had raised each of these three entities only to be met with Karpath's vacuous remark in each case.
[2] Konrad Thomasberger (1891–1964): government official in the Ministry of Education.

Furtwängler to Schenker (letter), December 10, 1932
OC 18/37–38

Dear, revered Mr. Schenker,
    Today is the first time I have had a quiet moment in which to answer you. First: as concerns Karpath, I had a similar impression to that which you convey to me, when I visited him on the penultimate day of my stay in Vienna. Namely that he is only trying to divert the whole matter into his journalistic channels, and that that is much more important to him than the matter itself, for which he clearly has no affinity. In addition, his overweening vanity, which came out at every turn during our conversation, this time gave me the impression perhaps of untrustworthiness. It also seems to me that his influence has *de facto* very much diminished in recent times. At any rate, I am thoroughly of one mind with you that a letter from me about you, sent to him for publication, would not seem ultimately, from a practical point of view, to yield the desired outcome. Accordingly, I have not written such a letter.
    I have meanwhile been trying to do some exploration here. Conditions as a result of constant government crises are—or were—very complicated.[1] There seems to me to be at least a possibility that you may be offered a so-called "masterclass" in composition (emanating from the Academy!), which would fall vacant in September 1933.[2] That could have been achieved without more ado, if [Leo] Kestenberg still had his earlier post at the Ministry; to what extent that is the case under the present, altered conditions, I cannot exactly say, but I will try and clarify the matter by Christmas. This could give you a financial basis for existence. Other lectures—either at the Hochschule or with Graener[3] (who declared himself enthusiastic about you)—of the inspiring impact of which I would give sundry assurances should the occasion arise, could then easily be added. I will at any rate soon be able to tell you more than I know now; things may however perhaps not go as fast as we would like, firstly because conditions here are really very unclear at the moment, secondly because I may not always myself have the necessary time.
    I have had a short letter from Weisse. He is doing well, and has clearly—bearing in mind the conditions under which he is working—had much success, which pleases me greatly.

I shall write to you again soon. For today, with most cordial greetings as ever—and to your wife,

  Yours,
   Wilhelm Furtwängler

Enclosed is a review by your pupil Roth from Hamburg.[4] He is also one of those German intellectuals—anyway, a personality in itself not all that benevolent, not devoid of envy—who suddenly pays attention differently when one has the dubious fortune of being "famous." With this last remark, I really mean to say: May the world at long last be enlightened over its false enthusiasm for Furtwängler. And one has to put up with that sort of thing! What he praises is characteristic, too: Fritz Stein as a conductor, and Muck's[5] Bruckner!!

---

[1] 1932 was the last year of the Weimar Republic.

[2] The Academy of Arts in Berlin, which had since 1869 included a Music Hochschule, the Director of which was from 1920 to 1932 Franz Schreker, and from 1932 Georg Schünemann. The idea came to nothing because of residential ineligibility (diary entry March 2, 1933).

[3] Paul Graener (1872–1944): Director of the Berlin Stern Conservatory 1930–33, vice-president of the Imperial Music Chamber 1933–41.

[4] Probably a review by Herman Roth of a concert by Furtwängler mentioning Stein and Muck.

[5] Carl Muck (1859–1940): German conductor, a specialist in Wagner's music dramas and Bruckner's symphonies, at this time conductor of the Hamburg Philharmonic Orchestra.

☙ Karpath to Schenker (postcard), December 23, 1932

OJ 12/9, [3]

Dear Friend,

All the very best for a happy Christmas! But where on earth is Furtwängler's letter, which is the basis of our campaign?

  Most cordial greetings
   And to your dear wife,
    Karpath

☙ Diary entry, December 30, 1932

To Karpath (letter): Am without answers from [Franz] Schmidt and Marx, though they themselves have given occasion for letters and outlay of money and time! But under pressure from Mrs. [Friederike] Hauser and Prof. [Friedrich] Buxbaum, Marx has written. Ought not a *fait accompli* to go ahead?

Karpath to Schenker (letter), December 31, 1932
OC 18/43

Dear Friend,[1]

I must confess that I don't rightly understand your letter. Some of the blame is perhaps to be placed on your rather indecipherable handwriting, and the various interpolations, especially on the last page, which make understanding difficult for me. The Minister[2] is oblivious of your existence, so I would not know what you could put forward to him personally now. That's just why we need the letter from Furtwängler: to prepare him. The particular problem is precisely money; at present no one has any at his disposal.

I can't imagine why the *Neue freie Presse* suppressed your name from the Weisse notice.[3] I don't even remember having read such a notice. Is Weisse in Vienna, then? Why on earth would Marx be subject to pressure from a Mrs. Hauser or a Buxbaum? Marx is precisely one of the few people who know how to value a genuine artist. He is unfortunately a bit lax, and he lets things go by that are otherwise close to his heart. Don't tar everybody with the same brush: I myself am also ill and cannot always do what I should like to do. Kobald,[4] the new President of the Academy, is the man who must take up the cause. To this end, I will come to an understanding with Marx and Schmidt. <u>This</u> is the only way to go if one wants to achieve one's goal. Furtwängler's endorsement would of course be of great importance. So do write to him and say that words [alone] are not enough: he needs finally to provide the stimulus.

With best wishes to you and your dear wife for the New Year, I remain

    Most cordially yours,
    Karpath

---

[1] Schenker's reaction to this letter in his diary is that Karpath is "somewhat daunted; will speak to Schmidt and Marx—ever more stupid."

[2] The Styrian provincial governor Anton Rintelen (1876–1946), member of the Christian Socialist Party, was Minister of Education from May 1932 to May 1933 in the Engelbert Dollfuss government. He supported the attempted Putsch of the National Socialists against Dollfuss on July 25, 1934.

[3] There appears to be nothing in Weisse's letters to Schenker or in the latter's diary to explain this reference.

[4] Karl Kobald (1876–1957): Karl von Wiener was recalled as head of the Academy for 1931/32. Karl Kobald succeeded him as head on December 1, 1932, and then as President on August 22, 1933, serving until March 15, 1938, when he was removed by the National Socialists.

Diary entries, January 20 and 21, 1933

[January 20:] Dictation: letter to Karpath.[1]

[January 21:] The eight-page letter to Karpath mailed off.

[1] The letter is not known to survive. On January 18 Joseph Marx had met with Schenker at the latter's home for three hours to discuss a prospective new edition of his *Theory of Harmony*, including the possibility of adding an appendix on form, for use at the Academy.

Karpath to Schenker (letter), January 23, 1933
OC 18/44

Dear Master Schenker,

Surely you have access to a typewriter. Why don't you use it? What on earth are you doing tiring yourself out with handwritten letters? But now to business: as of now, I know nothing of a Marx administration other than that I recently met him and told him: "You ought to become the Director of the Academy again." Department head Pernter,[1] to whom I reported this, is not very enthusiastic about his candidacy because Marx, when he was still Director, gave him a hard time—but he was not wholly negative. If Kobald proposes him, then he will be appointed. Since Furtwängler has still not written, I myself am writing to him at this time, because there is nothing else that I can do. A man such as Pernter needs the authority of a Furtwängler in order to believe what I could much more easily explain to him. Should Marx really have his turn, I will also be in touch with him; his proposal to appoint you at the Academy would surely be listened to. I will also talk to Kobald. What you accuse Marx of is perhaps his unfamiliarity with the circumstances; he does not know that these days you need the Academy, and will at least learn from your books. I am convinced that it is so. I will close this letter now, solely in order to give myself the time needed for Furtwängler. I must seize every halfway good day in order to influence events wherever influence is possible, before it is too late.

Cordial greetings, and to your dear wife,
Yours truly,
Ludwig Karpath

[1] Hans Pernter (1887–1951): from 1932 to 1934 Section Head for the Arts and Federal Theater in the Ministry of Education, and after this Federal Minister for Education and the Arts in the Austrian fascist government (Czeike, *Historisches Lexikon Wien*, vol. 4 (1995)).

Schenker to Furtwängler (letter), January 24, 1933
OC 18/49

Most revered, dear Dr. Furtwängler,

I have just received a letter from Court Counselor Karpath in which he informs me that he is writing to you at the same time regarding the instruction discussed previously! I deflected his first pressing request by saying that it would perhaps be embarrassing for you to acquaint the Viennese with me first through the newspaper, when I am very well known outside of Vienna (which is indeed the case).

Now, it so happened that Court Counselor Dr. Marx, the Director of our Academy, was with me a few days ago to settle the details of the adaptation of my *Theory of Harmony* (volume 1).[1]—whether or not UE is going to want, or be able, to bear the costs, we shall see. On this occasion, he spoke also of his plan to take other works of mine as the topics of special lectures. Now Dr. Marx knows very well that it is customary for authors of textbooks to be the first to teach their [own] material, and I do not doubt that Marx would agree to follow that custom in my case if he had any inkling that I were prepared today to affiliate myself with the Academy on account of adverse circumstances. But . . . he thinks I am wealthy, independent, and—"Hoboken"!

On the strength of this, I wrote to Karpath that a wholly natural opportunity would present itself for a very honorable appointment, if my theory were to be taken up by the Academy, with my theory of harmony, Urlinie, the theory of connection. At that, Karpath reverted to his hapless idea! The good fellow does not realize that he would do me nothing but harm if he were to drag me through the mire of Viennese pity. And so unnecessarily, what is more, if my theory is in any case already attracting attention.

Perhaps you might escape his clutches if you promise him an article for after the event, in which you express your satisfaction at my appointment.

Dr. Marx actually told me that all appointments come about only by personal contacts, intrigues, and behind-the-scenes string-pulling! Why must I, too, be insulted? It is really only a misunderstanding; the Viennese take me for a rich man. Oh! If I could only do as the English and French do, and take money from the pockets of others, calling it "monetary policy" or some other kind of politicking.

If only I had my lost savings back, I would already be hatching other things. For the time being, *Free Composition* goes on from strength to strength.

And lastly, when Karpath writes "A man such as Pernter (departmental head) needs the authority of a Furtwängler in order to believe that which I could much more easily explain to him," would he not rest content if you were to suggest writing the letter direct to Pernter (thereby avoiding the publicity)? Forgive me for writing so passionately, but Karpath's letter to you drives me to do so!

   With all the best wishes from us both,
    Yours,
     H. Schenker

---

[1] In his obituary for Schenker ("Der Musikforscher Heinrich Schenker," *Neues Wiener Journal*, February 3, 1935, p. 8, repr. in *Betrachtungen eines romantischen Realisten. Gesammelte Aufsätze, Vorträge und Reden über Musik*, ed. Oswald Ortner (Vienna: Gerlach & Wiedling, 1947), 405–09, quotation from 408), Marx recalls: "Some time ago I had visited him and admired his unstinting capacity for work. He was actually thinking of promoting his system by way of several short guides; those principal works were too comprehensive and therefore time-consuming." — See also Robert W. Wason, "From Harmonielehre to Harmony: Schenker's Theory of Harmony and Its Americanization," in *Schenker-Traditionen: Eine Wiener Schule*

der *Musiktheorie und ihre internationale Verbreitung / A Viennese School of Music Theory and Its International Dissemination*, ed. Martin Eybl and Evelyn Fink-Mennel (Vienna: Böhlau, 2006), 171–201.

ଈ Diary entry, January 25, 1933

To Karpath (letter): I share his conviction that Marx would go along with us if he knew the truth. Is it not too early to approach him?—better to be appointed on the strength of my achievements than out of sympathy.

ଈ Furtwängler to Schenker (letter), January 30, 1933
OC 18/50

BERLIN W.35
HOHENZOLLERNSTRASSE 9

Dear, revered Mr. Schenker,
 Enclosed, I send you copies of two letters that I have sent today to Court Counselor Karpath.
 I am just about to set off on my travels, and I just wanted to keep you informed.
   With best greetings,
    ever yours,
     W. Furtwängler

Enclosures

I will write to you about conditions in Berlin—which, as a result of the political developments,[1] are undergoing permanent transformation—after my return from England, later this winter[?]!

---

[1] On January 30, 1933, Adolf Hitler was sworn in in Berlin as Chancellor of the German Reich.

ଈ Furtwängler to Karpath (letter, carbon copy), January 30, 1933
OC 18/46

Dear Mr. Karpath,
 I enclose a letter concerning Dr. Heinrich Schenker. Please make use of it when the opportunity arises.
 I consider it highly desirable that Dr. Schenker be at the very least engaged to give a course on performance at the Academy or similar institution, and would find it—culturally speaking—nothing short of a scandal if for financial reasons difficulties were made for a man who has contributed so much to the wider world in the continuation and completion of his work.

I ask you under no circumstances whatsoever to let the enclosed letter get into the hands of the press, or to make it available to the press.

      With best greetings,
        Yours
         [unsigned]

❧ Furtwängler to Karpath (letter, carbon copy), February 6, 1933
OC 18/47

Dear Mr. Karpath,

In response to your inquiry regarding Dr. Schenker, I should like to reply to you briefly as follows:

I consider Schenker the most important music theorist of the present day, and am of the opinion that his music-theoretical work, which while admittedly not yet concluded is so far advanced that a judgment can certainly be made about it, belongs among the greatest and most significant achievements of our time. I can only express astonishment that in his home city of Vienna so very little notice is taken of the fact that this man has long worked there. If anyone has, then he, who has in truth given greater services to music—as the future will show—than many a currently famous composer, has deserved honorary positions, public distinctions, and expression of gratitude.

      With warmest greetings,
        Yours
         [unsigned]

❧ Karpath to Schenker (letter), February 10, 1933
OC 18/51

Dear Dr. Schenker,

The letter from Furtwängler has at last arrived, but with a prefatory remark that I find very unwelcome: "<u>In response to your inquiry</u> regarding Dr. Schenker, I should like to reply to you briefly as follows …." What then follows is of course very appropriate for drawing attention to you, but the prefatory remark does not give an impression of spontaneity. Notwithstanding, just as soon as I get out of the Cottage Sanatorium[1] I will go and see Kobald with Furtwängler's letter in the next few days. What is more, in Furtwängler's covering letter, he asks me: "under no circumstances whatsoever to let the enclosed letter get into the hands of the press …." That's not much use to me. It is precisely through the publication of Furtwängler's rapturous praise that it would have been possible to catch the attention of the authorities. As soon as I am back home, which will be next Tuesday, I will let you have sight of both [letters]. In the meantime, I send my best greetings,

Yours truly,
Karpath

[1] The Cottage Sanatorium was a luxury convalescent home built in 1908 in the Cottage Quarter in Vienna Districts XVIII (Währing) and XIX (Döbling), where Karpath was evidently a patient (Czeike, *Historisches Lexikon Wien* 1 (1992), 595).

࿓ Karpath to Furtwängler (letter copy), February 15, 1933, with annotation to Schenker
OC 18/52

Dear Dr. Furtwängler,

Only today, on account of illness, do I turn to answer your letter of the 6th of the month. Unfortunately, I cannot make use of your encomium about Schenker. This is because of your prefatory sentence: "In response to your inquiry regarding Dr. Schenker, I should like to reply to you briefly as follows." What I would have wished for in the interests of Schenker would have been a spontaneous outpouring of appreciation on your part, and not an answer to an inquiry. An answer to an inquiry implies that the Academy is actively considering Schenker's appointment and would want to hear the view of an eminent musician such as yourself. But that is absolutely not the case, and so people might rightly ask why I had inquired of you, which is plainly not at all the case. It is a different matter if I show the Academy administration a letter from your pen that represents a spontaneous pronouncement. Thus, if you wish to help us attain our goal, you would have to write me a second letter in which you alert me—as Adviser on the Arts to the Ministry of Education—to Schenker and seek to exhort his appointment. Also the closing sentence: "has given greater services than many a currently famous composer" will not do, for everyone will promptly think of Richard Strauss and that will detract from the force of your recommendation. Please do not misunderstand me. I have no wish to give you a lesson in how to write a letter; but I am accustomed to undertaking only those things that have some prospect of success. With the letter from you that I currently have in my hands, there would be no chance of success.

With warmest greetings,
Yours truly,
L. Karpath

Dear Dr. Schenker,[1]

This is a copy of a letter that I have just addressed to Dr. Furtwängler, about which I should still like to speak to you. In Furtwängler's covering letter it is made clear that his letter of recommendation may not under any circumstance be made public, and as a consequence everything that he says is simply worthless. Within the next week I will ask you to come and see me in order to discuss our future plan of action.

I ask you under no circumstances whatsoever to let the enclosed letter get into the hands of the press, or to make it available to the press.

  With best greetings,
   Yours
    [unsigned]

❧ Furtwängler to Karpath (letter, carbon copy), February 6, 1933
OC 18/47

Dear Mr. Karpath,
 In response to your inquiry regarding Dr. Schenker, I should like to reply to you briefly as follows:
 I consider Schenker the most important music theorist of the present day, and am of the opinion that his music-theoretical work, which while admittedly not yet concluded is so far advanced that a judgment can certainly be made about it, belongs among the greatest and most significant achievements of our time. I can only express astonishment that in his home city of Vienna so very little notice is taken of the fact that this man has long worked there. If anyone has, then he, who has in truth given greater services to music—as the future will show—than many a currently famous composer, has deserved honorary positions, public distinctions, and expression of gratitude.

  With warmest greetings,
   Yours
    [unsigned]

❧ Karpath to Schenker (letter), February 10, 1933
OC 18/51

Dear Dr. Schenker,
 The letter from Furtwängler has at last arrived, but with a prefatory remark that I find very unwelcome: "<u>In response to your inquiry</u> regarding Dr. Schenker, I should like to reply to you briefly as follows …." What then follows is of course very appropriate for drawing attention to you, but the prefatory remark does not give an impression of spontaneity. Notwithstanding, just as soon as I get out of the Cottage Sanatorium[1] I will go and see Kobald with Furtwängler's letter in the next few days. What is more, in Furtwängler's covering letter, he asks me: "under no circumstances whatsoever to let the enclosed letter get into the hands of the press …." That's not much use to me. It is precisely through the publication of Furtwängler's rapturous praise that it would have been possible to catch the attention of the authorities. As soon as I am back home, which will be next Tuesday, I will let you have sight of both [letters]. In the meantime, I send my best greetings,

Yours truly,
Karpath

[1] The Cottage Sanatorium was a luxury convalescent home built in 1908 in the Cottage Quarter in Vienna Districts XVIII (Währing) and XIX (Döbling), where Karpath was evidently a patient (Czeike, *Historisches Lexikon Wien* 1 (1992), 595).

Karpath to Furtwängler (letter copy), February 15, 1933, with annotation to Schenker
OC 18/52

Dear Dr. Furtwängler,

Only today, on account of illness, do I turn to answer your letter of the 6th of the month. Unfortunately, I cannot make use of your encomium about Schenker. This is because of your prefatory sentence: "In response to your inquiry regarding Dr. Schenker, I should like to reply to you briefly as follows." What I would have wished for in the interests of Schenker would have been a spontaneous outpouring of appreciation on your part, and not an answer to an inquiry. An answer to an inquiry implies that the Academy is actively considering Schenker's appointment and would want to hear the view of an eminent musician such as yourself. But that is absolutely not the case, and so people might rightly ask why I had inquired of you, which is plainly not at all the case. It is a different matter if I show the Academy administration a letter from your pen that represents a spontaneous pronouncement. Thus, if you wish to help us attain our goal, you would have to write me a second letter in which you alert me—as Adviser on the Arts to the Ministry of Education—to Schenker and seek to exhort his appointment. Also the closing sentence: "has given greater services than many a currently famous composer" will not do, for everyone will promptly think of Richard Strauss and that will detract from the force of your recommendation. Please do not misunderstand me. I have no wish to give you a lesson in how to write a letter; but I am accustomed to undertaking only those things that have some prospect of success. With the letter from you that I currently have in my hands, there would be no chance of success.

With warmest greetings,
Yours truly,
L. Karpath

Dear Dr. Schenker,[1]

This is a copy of a letter that I have just addressed to Dr. Furtwängler, about which I should still like to speak to you. In Furtwängler's covering letter it is made clear that his letter of recommendation may not under any circumstance be made public, and as a consequence everything that he says is simply worthless. Within the next week I will ask you to come and see me in order to discuss our future plan of action.

In the meantime, I send most cordial greetings,
>Yours truly,
>L. Karpath

[1] In summarizing this letter in his diary, Schenker comments: "incorrigible in his vanity, in his ignorance" (February 16, 1933).

Diary entry, February 16, 1933

To Karpath (letter): Nothing unpleasant ought to be expected from Furtwängler; he is true to me, but not to the Academy.

Karpath to Schenker (letter), February 17, 1933
OC 18/53

Dear Dr. Schenker,
   I don't think that you have lost Furtwängler altogether. I say only that it cannot be done with this letter. I must stand by that. I am happy to help, but I won't take on something that is futile.
   I can of course tell people myself who you are, but they will believe me only if we have Furtwängler. I can use him only as an advocate. But his letter is not an essay in advocacy, merely an unsolicited testimonial. He knows perfectly well why he wrote "In response to your inquiry," but will not do precisely what is needed. I underplay my personal knowledge of you if I use Furtwängler to present you to the authorities. And that I won't do. An advocate who needs a crutch to do the job is no advocate at all. More when we speak face to face.
>Best greetings,
>Yours,
>Karpath

Diary entries February 17–19, 24, 1933

[February 17:] Before supper, to Karpath (letter dictated): I enclose the letter from Hoboken:[1] the judgment of the foreigner Furtwängler [and] the foreigner Hoboken about the scandal—the last morsel is snatched from my mouth. — It takes Lie-Liechen until midnight to write the letter out.

[February 18:] Letter to Karpath sent by express mail. […] The first four pages of a letter to Furtwängler begun.

[February 19:] Furtwängler letter, pp. 5–8. — Letter finished. — Don't give in to Karpath; send me pupils; the Wellesz case. — By the evening exhausted on account of Hoboken's letter and the letters to Karpath and Furtwängler!

[February 24:] To Karpath (express letter): the letters from Weisse.²

[1] There is no obvious surviving letter from Hoboken corresponding to this. The most likely is his letter of November 11, 1932, in which he congratulates Schenker on the fact that Marx was planning to introduce his *Theory of Harmony* into the Academy's curriculum.

[2] The only possible letter that Schenker might have forwarded to Karpath is that which Weisse wrote on February 15 in which he reported his success with a series of twelve lectures on Schenker to a class of just under 90 students (see chapter 26).

❦ Karpath to Schenker (letter), February 24, 1933
OC 18/54

My dear Dr. Schenker,

What is most distressing is that I was unable to succeed with your appointment. I went over it in detail with Kobald, and he explained to me that he knows full well who you are, but that he has no money, and any proposal would be turned down by the two ministries, all the more so as Marx, Schmidt, and a third person whose name I forget are teaching theory at the Academy, and that consequently "no need" can be demonstrated. On the other hand, he and—very intensively—Marx have recommended you for the Austro-American course that is in process of being set up,¹ and you would be sure to get this post. I should like to talk with you about this. Telephone me to let me know when you can call on me.

How about Sunday?

It <u>sincerely</u> pains me not to be able to bring you better news. I have at any rate put every effort into achieving the goal.

        Most cordially yours,
        Karpath

Enclosed: three letters²

[1] Schenker refers to this sardonically in his diary as "the American club." The course seems not to have materialized.

[2] Two letters from Weisse, one from Hoboken.

❦ Joseph Marx to Schenker (letter), February 28, 1933
OC 18/23

Greatly revered Dr. [Schenker],¹

You will by now be taking me for "forgetful" or even "unfaithful," because you have heard nothing from me for so long. There were reasons for that. I did not want to put anything in writing to you without having at least tried something and informing you about it.

First of all, I should like to thank you for your gracious kindness, which I sensed on my first visit, and also for your understanding, which I take as an echo of my personal feeling toward you. It is my hope that this reciprocal effect may grow as time goes by!

In the matter of your theoretical system, there is really not much that can be accomplished at the Academy unless something is decreed from on high. I do not have control over the institution,[2] nor does anybody want to listen to me because others are at work who know how to "behave" better than I; also there are (one or two!) alphabetically-challenged people, as you recently so wittily put it, who lose track of the argument if one switches from cursive to regular script.[3] One has one's hands full with such people. For all that, I have advocated the inclusion of your name in the new school statute as the author of valuable works that should be taken account of in teaching, and it will appear there if it is not struck out by being sanctioned against in the Ministry of Education—something that is not really to be feared. So you at least already figure by name in the official business. For our time—and, moreover, considering that everything at best arrives a hundred years too late—something nevertheless!

I have also succeeded in having Violin's name put down for a teaching position that is about to fall vacant at the Academy. Sadly, this is the best that could be achieved up to now ...[4] Of course, it is as always a matter for debate how this application will be judged at the Ministry—whether it will go through or be denied. I have also spoken with Reitler;[5] but unfortunately he once got into a row with him, and that may now work against him in some way. It's a pity he wasn't in Vienna after the overthrow—that would have made things a lot easier. And Violin's suggestion of going to Istanbul can in good conscience not be supported. There, in oriental isolation, badly paid, and with radically changed living conditions, the fellow would be sure to become depressed in no time at all. We can only hope that in the foreseeable future it will be possible to work something out for him.

Ah well! I have taken up enough of your precious time. I send you my most heartfelt greetings, and likewise ask you to remember me most cordially to your dear wife. I should be delighted if I were to have the opportunity of visiting you in the near future. With kind regards, I remain

Yours very truly,
Marx

---

[1] Schenker's reaction on receipt of this letter was: "long, respectful, suspiciously respectful—Is he after material and information for himself and his students?" (diary, February 28, 1933).

[2] Marx was not elected President; Karl Kobald was elected to that position.

[3] i.e. from the script used by an older generation (*Kurrent*, or *Sütterlinschrift*) to the more modern style of writing (*Lateinschrift*), hence people who are stuck in their "old-fashioned" ways or are unduly affected by mode of presentation.

[4] On January 19, 1933, Schenker had written to Marx saying "I place Violin's fate in your hands." Discussion of Violin's situation had been going on for some time before that. Violin fled Hamburg in May 1933, but no appointment at the Academy was forthcoming.

⁵ Josef Reitler (1883–1948): Viennese newspaper music critic and teacher, studied theory with Schoenberg in Berlin; from 1915 to 1938 Director of the Theodor Kretschmann Music School, which under his leadership became the New Vienna Conservatory.

Diary entry, March 1, 2, 4, 1933

[March 1:] 9 p.m. (express letter): from Karpath: he has spoken with section head Pernter, and now it is up to Furtwängler to put his word in. — To Furtwängler (express letter with Karpath's letter): it would be advisable to follow this lead—invitation.

[March 2:] When we get home, we find a letter from Furtwängler (by messenger): He is coming today at 8 o'clock. — Furtwängler 8.15–11.15: "masterclass" in Berlin impossible, reserved exclusively for "native Germans" (good!); has spoken with Huberman about help, I should remain calm! He several times refers to the University, to which I do not belong. I take up my suggestion of Pernter; I read the article aloud.[1] — He takes exception to the form of words "Music is dead"—the objection is made in his own interests, as once before his objection to Brahms's turn of phrase "a mere conductor"[2] demonstrated.

[March 4:] To Marx (letter): thanks for "putting my name down"—comment on that! Father, son, vengeance—Vienna a sacrifice to that vengeance. Weisse's financial success could be emulated in itself. We look forward to his visit.

[1] Schenker, "Erinnerung an Brahms," *Der Kunstwart* 46 (May 1933): 473–82.
[2] Brahms's verdict about Hans von Bülow.

Diary entry, April 11, 1933

Furtwängler to the Minister: adopts a stance against the theoretical outlawing of the Jews—for the arts, the only criterion is whether bad or good.[1]

[1] On April 11, 1933 there appeared in the *Vossische Zeitung*, Berlin, a letter from Furtwängler addressed to Joseph Goebbels, accompanied by an open reply from the latter as Reich Minister for Propaganda. Furtwängler wrote, among other things: "If this battle being waged against Jewry is directed mainly against those artists who— themselves rootless and destructive—seek to operate through *kitsch* and *empty virtuosity*, then that is all well and good. [...] If this battle is waged against *genuine* artists, then it is not in the interests of cultural life. [...] Accordingly it must be clearly proclaimed that men such as Walter, Klemperer, Reinhardt and others must get a hearing with their artistry in the future in Germany" (quoted from Herbert Haffner, *Furtwängler* (Berlin: Parthas, 2006), 153).

IV
Beethoven's Ninth Symphony

14
Genesis of *Beethoven's Ninth Symphony*

THE idea of a monograph on the Ninth Symphony came about in part fortuitously. On October 16, 1909, Schenker reported to Emil Hertzka that Wilhelm Bopp, Director of the Vienna Academy, wished to arrange a "historical" concert for January or February 1910, the program comprising:

1) Concerto for keyboard and orchestra by C. P. E. Bach
2) Concerto for two keyboards and string orchestra by C. P. E. Bach
3) Cantata by J. S. Bach.

And there might in addition, at my suggestion, be as a fourth work a concerto by Handel for harp and orchestra.

Preparations for this event continued, for in February Schenker visited Hertzka with Moriz Violin to deliver the latter's "modest little manuscript […] intended to serve as a prelude to, but also as the program booklet for the historical concert" (letter to Hertzka, February 15, 1910). Four months later came a howl of rage:

Director Bopp does not keep his word. The planned performance of the two C. P. E. Bach concertos and the two cantatas by J. S. Bach was dropped. So all the tribulation that went into preparing the pieces for the concert, and that I bore so nobly, was for nought. […] In place of the "historical" concert he offers the Ninth Symphony of Beethoven. The result, after forty rehearsals, was the most deplorable in the world! The din of trumpets and drums in the foreground, not to mention (strictly metronomically) the bungling of the priceless content without the remotest sense of its meaning, was intellectual whoredom practised on the younger generation. (diary, June 1910)

In early July Schenker traveled to the Karer Pass, in the Dolomites, for a summer vacation during which he evidently hatched a new project, provisionally dubbed "Pocket Library." From his hotel he wrote to J. G. Cotta, publisher of his New Musical Theories and Fantasies, describing his plan and explaining its relationship to that series. Included in the plan from the start was Beethoven's Ninth Symphony, and within a month a monograph of this work had taken pride of place in his plans.

Was it Bopp's change of heart from the Bach family to Beethoven's Ninth that diverted Schenker into writing his monograph? Or was Schenker already interested in the Ninth Symphony prior to July 1910? Was it a chance remark to Bopp that inadvertently caused the latter to switch his concert plan? It is at any rate a strange coincidence that fourteen years later Schenker was to be involved in a historical reconstruction not just of Beethoven's Ninth but of the entire concert in which that work had been given its first performance (see chapter 15).

Some time early in 1911 Hertzka evidently proposed that a score of the symphony might be incorporated into the monograph, thereby converting it into

IV
Beethoven's Ninth Symphony

14
Genesis of *Beethoven's Ninth Symphony*

THE idea of a monograph on the Ninth Symphony came about in part fortuitously. On October 16, 1909, Schenker reported to Emil Hertzka that Wilhelm Bopp, Director of the Vienna Academy, wished to arrange a "historical" concert for January or February 1910, the program comprising:

1) Concerto for keyboard and orchestra by C. P. E. Bach
2) Concerto for two keyboards and string orchestra by C. P. E. Bach
3) Cantata by J. S. Bach.

And there might in addition, at my suggestion, be as a fourth work a concerto by Handel for harp and orchestra.

Preparations for this event continued, for in February Schenker visited Hertzka with Moriz Violin to deliver the latter's "modest little manuscript […] intended to serve as a prelude to, but also as the program booklet for the historical concert" (letter to Hertzka, February 15, 1910). Four months later came a howl of rage:

Director Bopp does not keep his word. The planned performance of the two C. P. E. Bach concertos and the two cantatas by J. S. Bach was dropped. So all the tribulation that went into preparing the pieces for the concert, and that I bore so nobly, was for nought. […] In place of the "historical" concert he offers the Ninth Symphony of Beethoven. The result, after forty rehearsals, was the most deplorable in the world! The din of trumpets and drums in the foreground, not to mention (strictly metronomically) the bungling of the priceless content without the remotest sense of its meaning, was intellectual whoredom practised on the younger generation. (diary, June 1910)

In early July Schenker traveled to the Karer Pass, in the Dolomites, for a summer vacation during which he evidently hatched a new project, provisionally dubbed "Pocket Library." From his hotel he wrote to J. G. Cotta, publisher of his New Musical Theories and Fantasies, describing his plan and explaining its relationship to that series. Included in the plan from the start was Beethoven's Ninth Symphony, and within a month a monograph of this work had taken pride of place in his plans.

Was it Bopp's change of heart from the Bach family to Beethoven's Ninth that diverted Schenker into writing his monograph? Or was Schenker already interested in the Ninth Symphony prior to July 1910? Was it a chance remark to Bopp that inadvertently caused the latter to switch his concert plan? It is at any rate a strange coincidence that fourteen years later Schenker was to be involved in a historical reconstruction not just of Beethoven's Ninth but of the entire concert in which that work had been given its first performance (see chapter 15).

Some time early in 1911 Hertzka evidently proposed that a score of the symphony might be incorporated into the monograph, thereby converting it into an "elucidatory edition." The idea lingered throughout 1912, and then turned, in 1913, into a proposal for a free-standing, new critical edition of the work. When Hertzka saw the costs that would be incurred by such a plan, he backed away and the idea died.

IAN BENT

Schenker to Cotta (letter), August 19, 1910
CA 118

Dear Sir,
 The fire at the Lake Karer Hotel, which also houses the Imperial-Royal Postal Office for all the hotels in the Pass, prompts me to inquire of you whether by any chance on the 15th of this month the final proof of the Foreword [to *Counterpoint* 1] was among the items sent by post. Please would you be so kind as to let me know this?
 Let me seize this opportunity to inquire also whether there is any possibility of my laying out clearly before you in person in Stuttgart at the end of August or beginning of September the matter of my planned "Pocket Library"[1] (including, for example, the Second, Fifth, and Ninth Symphonies of Beethoven, the "Jupiter" Symphony of Mozart, the four symphonies of Brahms, the last five sonatas of Beethoven, etc.). Hard though it will be for me, I will not shrink from bearing the costs of travel in order to make my way to Stuttgart. The "Pocket Library" conflicts to some extent with volume 2 of my [New Musical] Theories and Fantasies; I must therefore set out precisely my plan and purpose, and get your verdict and thoughts on timing, if the work is to go ahead. Perhaps it might even be possible to bring out a [first] booklet of the "Pocket Library" as early as simultaneously with the second half-volume [of *Counterpoint*]. What a pity it is that the *Chromatic Fantasy and Fugue* by J. S. Bach will not be published until mid-September,[2] or I would otherwise produce a specimen copy. However, even without this I hope to set out for you in person with complete clarity what I would like to do.[3]

 With kind regards,
  Yours truly,
   H. Schenker

---

[1] *Handbibliothek*, literally "hand library." The term usually denotes a "reference library," i.e. one in which the books are within easy reach. *Handbibliothek* is the name given initially to what in the course of 1910 became "Little Library" (*Kleine Bibliothek*), which remained thus until changed in March 1921 to *Der Tonwille*. There is little doubt that Schenker wished to emulate certain series of pocket guides to individual works, such as the Schlesinger Music Library, and Reclam's Elucidations of Great Works of Music: see Ian Bent, ed., *Music Analysis in the Nineteenth Century* 2, *Hermeneutic Approaches* (Cambridge: Cambridge University Press, 1994), 31–33.

² Schenker's elucidatory edition of that work, published by Universal Edition, was released in mid-October 1910.

³ In their first reply, Cotta informed Schenker that their proprietor was due to be away for a long time, and suggested that Schenker put his proposal in writing at the time the *Chromatic Fantasy* was published.

℘ Schenker to Cotta (letter), September 10, 1910
CA 121–122 (=OJ 5/6, [5])

Dear Sir,

In my last letter to you, requesting a meeting in Stuttgart, I may perhaps not have expressed my intentions clearly. At any rate, the title is: "Pocket Library," which is only provisional for now, not definitive. It is, moreover, a "repertory appendix" to volume 3 of my New Musical Theories and Fantasies, the *Decline of the Art of Composition*, already <u>announced</u> several times by me in the forewords to volumes 1 and 2/1.¹ Logically expanded, the latter would have to include in the course of its theoretical discussions the most important examples from the repertory. Since, however, the examples there would have to be kept within all-too-tight limits, and since the force of my teachings would be severely restricted as a result I consider it critically necessary to produce overwhelmingly convincing evidence in the form of an independent repertorial appendix to volume 3 in <u>separate booklets</u>. Each of these little booklets would perhaps bear the general title:

"Repertory Appendix to volume 3 of the New Musical Theories and Fantasies, currently in preparation." (or something similar)

but with each individual booklet bearing a number, as for example:

I.
"Beethoven's Ninth Symphony"

A little booklet of this sort could also be obtained individually, which would be of great advantage not only for the dissemination of my theory but also from a commercial point view.

On the other hand, these little booklets amount to self-contained short <u>monographs</u> in that they can also be profitably read without knowledge of volume 3, hence even <u>before</u> the latter is out! Besides, I am already <u>convinced</u> that they should be published beforehand by the point of view that I advanced in my own Foreword to 2/1, of which I urge you to look up pp. i–viii. I should like to see conclusive evidence as soon as possible backing up this incontrovertible charge— perhaps it might interest you in this connection to examine two letters from Mr. Ernst Rudorff, the well-known Professor and Senator of the Royal Music Hochschule in Berlin.² And in addition, the success of volume 2/1 would be very nicely bolstered by this.

I therefore suggest that you might make your esteemed press available to me again for these little booklets <u>under the conditions agreed for the main work itself</u>, as <u>organic components</u> of that work, so that the "Ninth Symphony" (perhaps the most unappreciated work in our repertory!!), already completed, could appear as the first one as early as this winter. This small volume, as well as those that succeed it, could then of course be purchased at <u>low prices</u> (because published singly).

I shall be sending the newly revised manuscript for 2/2 of Theories and Fantasies shortly.

    Looking forward to an early reply, I remain,
     with kind regards,
      H. Schenker

---

[1] *Decline*: see chapter 6, above; 1 = *Theory of Harmony*; 2/1 = *Counterpoint 1*.
[2] Ernst Rudorff (1840–1916): member of the Brahms circle, professor at the Berlin Hochschule 1867–1910. Rudorff and Schenker corresponded avidly between 1908 and 1912, and shared a belief in a decline in artistic creativity and need for regeneration. The letters referred to here are not known to survive.

Cotta to Schenker (letter), September 14, 1910
OJ 12/27, [12]

Dear Dr. [Schenker],

We gratefully acknowledge receipt of your letter of the 10th of the month, the content and enclosures of which we have noted with interest.

According to this, you envision publishing in separate booklets a musical appendix to volume 3 of your Theories and Fantasies, itself to be published at a later date; and moreover the individual booklets of this musical appendix are to appear <u>before</u> the publication of volume 3, which will presumably still be a considerable time in coming.

On the basis of our experience in publishing, we must advise against the publication of a <u>continuation</u>, of an "<u>appendix</u>" to a main work, before the latter is itself released, as totally inopportune. Such a dislocation of the sequence of publication of main work and appendix would lead to the most undesirable consequences, and would be critically detrimental to the commercial success of both parts. The Preface to volume 2/1, moreover, provides no pressing reason for doing so.

We would in any case not be able to resolve to entertain the adoption of the planned musical appendix into the commissioning publishing house at the present time. On the contrary, we would have to reserve our decision on this until the publication of volume 3.

We herewith return to you with many thanks the two letters of Professor Ernst Rudorff that you most kindly sent us, and remain

    with kind regards,
     Yours very truly.
     p.p. Heirs of J. G. Cotta's Bookdealership
      H. Kurz

PS Publication of volume 2/1 is expected probably on the 23rd of the month.

Association of Viennese Music Critics to Schenker (letter), September 20, 1910
OJ 14/44, [1]

Dear Dr. [Schenker],

At the suggestion of Dr. Robert Hirschfeld, and at the instigation of our colleagues, we take pleasure in extending to you the invitation to give a lecture series on the construction of Beethoven's Ninth Symphony under the auspices of our Association.

So that we can make further arrangements, we would ask you, if your time permits, kindly to join us on Monday, October 3, at 6 p.m. in the Café Imperial.

In any case, we should be grateful for a communication from you (Stauber, [Vienna] IX, Währingerstrasse 31), and we remain,

With kind regards,
ASSOCIATION OF VIENNESE MUSIC CRITICS

| The President: | The Secretary: |
| Th. Antropp | Paul Stauber[1] |

---

[1] Theodor Antropp (1864–1923): theater critic of German nationalist newspaper *Ostdeutsche Rundschau*, pro-Wagner, anti-Mahler; Paul Stauber (1876–1918): Viennese writer on music, music critic of the *Illustrirtes Wiener Extrablatt*, strongly anti-Schoenberg, member of circle around Robert Hirschfeld.

Universal Edition to Schenker (letter), October 14, 1910
OC 52/425

Dear Professor,

Further to your discussion with our Director,[1] we are sending you by postal money order:

100.– kronen

as second payment for the *Chromatic Fantasy & Fugue*. We are also sending you, enclosed, the publication slip for your Lectures on the Ninth Symphony of Beethoven, and would ask you to return it to us signed, after which you will receive a copy.

We remain,
With kind regards,
Hertzka

[1] A meeting had taken place earlier the same day with Emil Hertzka, according to a letter from Schenker to Hertzka on October 21, at which presumably Hertzka took up the idea of publishing the lectures.

❧ Contract between UE and Schenker, November 6, 1910
OC 52/431

Assignment of Copyright[1]

I hereby assign to Universal Edition & Co., Vienna the exclusive, sole, and transferable copyright of my work (monograph)

Lectures on Beethoven's Ninth Symphony

for all impressions, all editions, all countries, all languages, and all means of reproduction.

I undertake not to publish any comparable or similar work in monograph form with any other publishing house, or to collaborate directly or indirectly in any such work.

Universal Edition has the right to arrange for translations into other languages. I assign to it the fixing and subsequent alteration of the purchase price.

Publication must take place within at the latest two years from submission of the manuscript.

In return for the assignment of my copyright I receive 1,000.– (one thousand) kronen, which shall be paid out upon submission of the complete manuscript.

Vienna, November 6, 1910

Dr. Heinrich Schenker m.p.[2]

[1] Universal Edition's standard contract at the time was a printed form with handwritten (or typed) interpolations, establishing an agreement between the two parties. This contract, however, like those for the *Table of Instrumentation* (June 30, 1908) and *Der Tonwille* (March 23, 1920) was custom drafted, and worded as a declaration by Schenker. In a letter of October 19, 1910, Schenker contested hotly the terms of the then current draft of the contract, and most of his suggested alternatives seem to have been accommodated in the text given here, which is, however, still described in Hertzka's letter of November 5 as a "draft contract."

[2] *manu propria* (by his own hand): the signature is typed.

❧ Diary entry, May 18, 1911

The monograph on the Ninth Symphony finally delivered to UE after many months of work.[1] First, and larger-scale, substantively grounded thrust against Richard Wagner at long last brought to fulfillment. What will people now say to the grounds that I have put forward there?

[1] Schenker's letter of May 17 includes the following statement:

> It has, as you will see, become a voluminous work, and I will say it loud and clear to anyone, of whatever persuasion: there has certainly been no truer, more deserving work of this type up to now, nor will any better work succeed it. It will do honor to the publisher and author, provided that you champion the work with the same degree of conviction that you have done, e.g., those by Schoenberg, Mayrhofer, and the rest of them. Soon, soon the day will surely dawn when people will see more clearly whether it is not I who in fact stand for "progress" whereas those scribblers, incapable of writing, represent nothing but the most presumptuous racket of "regress" (admittedly with good warning!).

Hertzka (UE) to Schenker (letter), September 19, 1911
OC 52/492

Most revered Dr. [Schenker],

Having just returned from one of my longer trips, I come upon your esteemed letter of the 14th of the month, to which I hasten to reply.

You are expecting a clear decision from me regarding your edition of the last five sonatas of Beethoven. The situation is that we absolutely cannot decide this without a generous grant from the Academy, given such conditions as you have stipulated. The great value of the work to be undertaken by you is to my mind wholly beyond question. The means at our disposal today, however, still do not permit us to take on the project proposed by you. It may well be that large German publishing firms, the youngest of which are fifty years old, the older ones over a hundred years old, can commit themselves without much deliberation to an investment of perhaps 15,000 marks for the text criticism of the five Beethoven sonatas. I shall be happy if I can nurse our company slowly through its teething troubles, and must use all my powers to husband our resources.

You will receive the proofs of your *Ninth Symphony* in the late fall. As you well know, your delay in delivering the manuscript was so great that for us to accommodate it within our summer work schedule was no longer possible, and the job will now have to be printed in the autumn.

I was delighted to hear that your *Counterpoint* has had such glittering success.[1] I congratulate you most heartily on this.

> In sincere appreciation,
> Yours most truly,
> Hertzka

[1] Schenker had reported the sales figures for *Counterpoint 1*: 114 copies in six weeks.

❧ Schenker to Hertzka (UE) (letter), October 28, 1911
WSLB 83

Dear Director,

Late autumn is not yet here, I admit, but I should like, as the anxious author whom you surely cannot begrudge having an interest in his own work, to ask you to be sure to issue the appropriate orders so that the proofs will reach me at the prescribed time.

I can no longer restrain myself from challenging the reproach, repeatedly made in your letters, that I delivered my manuscript "late" by pointing out that, on the contrary, in submitting it in May I accomplished something the likes of which you could not easily match. Not until the <u>beginning</u> of the season last year did the Association of Viennese Music Critics invite me to give the lectures, and only then, at <u>that</u> time, was the topic of the Ninth Symphony chosen and agreed. Only with my unique degree of preparedness for such things could I promptly consent to this and hope to deal, so to speak, <u>on the fly</u> with the work's great, sublime material in five lectures. Since the contract between you and me on the same topic materialized only soon after that, I of course first had to <u>formulate</u> the latter (since it had had no place in my work plan up to that point).[1] And if, in the course of a season with ten pupils and the near-mortal illness of my almost eighty-year-old mother [Julia Schenker], I completed in the space of <u>five months</u> a work of this magnitude and of such exceptional quality—its value will be publicly revealed to you once the work has appeared!—then any talk of "delay" is in all truth unfair. On the contrary, I should ask who other than I could complete anything like this achievement? I did not correct your turn of phrase immediately because I did not expect to suffer consequences from it; but since these are now arising, it is my duty, in the interests of truth, to put the matter to rights.

   With kind regards,
    Yours truly,
     H. Schenker

---

[1] Schenker is, of course, being disingenuous here: the idea of a "booklet" on the Ninth Symphony arose no later than the summer of 1910, and on September 10 of that year Schenker described the work to Cotta as "almost completed."

❧ Hertzka (UE) to Schenker, March 7[?], 1912
OC 52/432

Highly revered Dr. [Schenker],

It would give me great pleasure to get together with you for half an hour in the course of the next few days. I should like specifically to discuss with you the matter of your Beethoven Ninth Symphony book, in particular in the light of the fact that I have now procured the rights to use the plates of the entire Eulenburg edition orchestral score.[1] The rest when we meet, assuming you can give me a time at which either I can speak with you on neutral territory or you might afford me the pleasure of a visit.

With my compliments,
Kind regards,
Yours truly,
Universal Edition & Co.
Hertzka

[1] This recalls a passing inquiry by Schenker in a letter to Hertzka of June 21, 1911: "A propos the Ninth: I forgot to ask you at our last meeting how matters stand over the conducting score planned by you? Have you given up this idea?"—to which Hertzka did not respond in his reply of June 27.

Schenker to Hertzka (UE) (postcard), March 13, 1912
WSLB 100

Dear Director,

Please very kindly retrieve the remaining gatherings, 17 and on, [while you are] in Leipzig![1] I need them urgently.

Perhaps it would be a good idea to separate the book from the score for ease of study; and let the price indicate only that the two can be had more cheaply if the items are purchased together [rather than] individually. But then, you are more familiar with this [than am I]. Tomorrow, the four paragraphs will be on their way to you.[2]

With kind regards,
Yours truly,
H. Schenker

[1] i.e. from Breitkopf & Härtel's Leipzig printing works. Schenker is referring to page proofs of the monograph.

[2] i.e. additional material for Niloff [= Schenker], *Table of Instrumentation* (1908), of which a new, enlarged edition was about to be published.

Hertzka (UE) to Schenker (letter), May 7, 1912
OC 52/433

We[1] are in receipt of your esteemed communication of May 5, 1912,[2] and have taken careful note of its contents.

We respectfully inform you that our request [for a meeting] in fact concerns the handling of the second movement of the Ninth Symphony in your study. As you should be aware, you begin counting the measures of the Scherzo, the Trio, and the Reprise [of the Scherzo] each time anew, and in so doing you have measure 1 of the Trio begin in one instance as early as measure 426 of the Scherzo, but in the other instance not until measure 428 of the same, thus <u>after</u> the repeat-sign. In the interests of avoiding any confusion, would it not be more practical if you were to number the measures of the entire second movement <u>in a single sequence</u>, so that at the Trio, and also at the Reprise, the necessity for a new measure-numbering would be obviated. Furthermore, you label the Scherzo in its formal diagram "First Main Section" (in the text itself simply "Main Section"), without its being followed by a "Second Main Section," and then again you call its subdivision "First Section." Might this not be changed in the interests of greater comprehensibility?

We look forward with interest to your earliest reply, and remain

>With kind regards, yours truly,
>Universal Edition & Co.
>Hertzka

Dear Professor,
Also I should have liked to hear your final opinion regarding the pocket-score edition of the Ninth Symphony which we plan to bring out as a separate volume 2. Sadly that now becomes impossible, since I leave town on Thursday for eight to ten days.[3]

>Best wishes,
>Hertzka

---

[1] This letter is written, in elegant *Sütterlinschrift*, either in a stenographer's hand, or in Hertzka's own hand—either way uniquely so. The body of the letter is in pen, the signature and postscript, in informal *Lateinschrift*, are in pencil.

[2] Hertzka had invited Schenker to meet him on the morning of May 6; because of teaching, Schenker had asked to meet later in the day. Hertzka was evidently fully scheduled after 12.30.

[3] Schenker's reply of May 11 does not address the matter directly; but his response to the issue about measure numbering, which includes the phrase "for implementation in the miniature score" and a similar remark in a letter of May 24 indicate that he still considered this a live possibility. However, in a letter of June 2 Schenker remarks "If only we had known then that the score was going to have to be dropped" and refers to "the cancellation of the score."

❧ Extract from the Preface to *Beethoven's Ninth Symphony* (1912), issued July 2, 1912

On being invited by the Association of Music Critics in Vienna to present a series of lectures to its members, I selected for the occasion the Ninth Symphony of Beethoven. For reasons that need not be discussed here, the lectures were never presented. This gives me no reason for particular regret, however, as the invitation by my publisher to transform the work into a monograph has provided the opportunity to make it accessible in a significantly expanded and enriched form to a larger public.[1]

---

[1] *Beethoven's Ninth Symphony*, 3 (Ger., [v]), opening paragraph.

Hertzka (UE) to Schenker (letter), December 12, 1913
OC 52/440

Highly revered Dr. [Schenker],

As concerns the edition of the score of the Ninth Symphony on the basis of the original manuscript,[1] matters are technically more complicated than you envision. After careful consideration, in spite of my extraordinarily keen interest in the project, I can still say nothing definite for the time being, for I must first see whether when I am next in Leipzig I can reach an agreement with the firm of Eulenburg that will permit me the part use and alteration of the Eulenburg engraved plates. If this were not possible, then I would have to start from scratch in engraving the pocket score, which properly speaking would cost me a small fortune. Thus, while appreciating the importance and immeasurable value of publishing an orchestral score based on the original manuscript with your elucidations, it is impossible to reach a decision straightaway.

In asking you please to send Kopfermann's letters to me here, I remain

        With heartfelt best wishes,
        Yours very truly,
        Hertzka

---

[1] Schenker had revived this issue in letters of November 12 and December 9, 1913, by proposing that he edit a new score on the basis of the autograph manuscript. He wrote again on January 7, 1914, but after that the matter seems finally to have been dropped.

15
Paul von Klenau and Beethoven

COMPOSER and conductor Paul von Klenau (1883–1946: see Plate 37) was Danish but studied mostly in Germany, his composition teachers being Max Bruch (Berlin), Ludwig Thuille (Munich), and Max von Schillings (Stuttgart). His conducting career took him first to the Civic Theater in Freiburg, next to the Bach Society in Frankfurt, then back as the chief conductor in Freiburg. He spent World War I in Denmark, where in 1920 he co-founded the Danish Philharmonic Society, which he conducted until 1926. From 1922 to 1930 he served as conductor of the Vienna Concert House Society. It was during this period of residency in Vienna that he became acquainted with Schenker. Their correspondence covers September 1923 to December 1924, with one further letter from 1927 (not included below), and there were numerous meetings and other contacts during this period. Although only Klenau's side of the original correspondence is known to survive, two of Schenker's letters and one other document are preserved in fair copies (some indication of the importance Schenker attached to them).[1]

In Schenker's eyes perhaps the most significant act on Klenau's part was his historical reconstruction of the concert that took place in the Kärntnertor Theater on May 7, 1824, at which Beethoven's Ninth Symphony was first performed, together with the Kyrie, Credo and Agnus Dei of the *Missa solemnis*, and the Overture *The Consecration of the House*. This reconstruction was held in the Vienna Concert House on the centenary date, May 7, 1924, in advance of which Schenker was consulted on performance issues. Schenker published a favorable account of this first performance as part of a polemical article on the symphony's historical reception.[2]

Initially Schenker was skeptical of Klenau's abilities to follow his ideas. Ever a hard taskmaster, he readily criticized aspects of Klenau's performances. However, he gave time generously to correcting these, to showing him photographs of autograph sources, and to explaining editorial issues. In the Ninth Symphony performance, he conceded, Klenau had achieved the ultimate goal: that of demonstrating Beethoven's "synthesis." How did Klenau compare in his mind with Furtwängler? In 1924, Furtwängler still stood high in Schenker's estimation, and was regarded as a vehicle for the promotion of Schenker's theories. Moreover, he was prestigious and influential, so had power to promote Schenker's work in official circles. Although Klenau was a more minor figure, his interpretive work

---

[1] Most of Klenau's letters are transcribed in Federhofer (1985) along with many diary entries. The items by Schenker were unavailable at the time that Federhofer compiled his volume, and now add great interest to the exchange. Schenker filed the item dated September 21, 1923, about the *Missa solemnis* in a folder containing analyses of music by Beethoven—a further indication that he valued its contents.

[2] "One Hundred Years of the Ninth Symphony: On the jubilee performance of the Vienna Concert House Society, May 7, 1924," part of "Miscellanea," *Tonwille 8/9*, vol. 2, 121–22 (Ger. orig., 53–54).

publicly validated Schenker's performance principles—undoubtedly Schenker basked in Klenau's success—and Klenau's published articles about Beethoven performance practice promulgated Schenker's ideas about the relationship of text to performance.

Both conductors presented a conflict for Schenker in their promotion of "modern" music. Not only did Klenau give prominence to contemporary music with the Danish Philharmonic Orchestra, but he was a close friend of Alban Berg and was intimate with the Schoenberg circle. Klenau took lessons with Schoenberg shortly after the end of World War I, and this had some influence at least temporarily upon his work as a composer.

First contact between Klenau and Schenker seems to have been the latter's attendance on December 29, 1922 at a concert by the Vienna Symphony Orchestra and several Vienna choirs under Klenau's baton, as recorded in Schenker's diary: "In the evening [Haydn's] *Creation* under Klenau (with Bamberger): tempi mostly correct, especially the arias more relaxed and easier; by contrast, an impermissible abbreviation of the final fugue, which makes a ridiculous effect."

IAN BENT

❧ Klenau to Schenker (letter), September 17, 1923
OJ 12/11, [1]

Greatly revered Mr. Schenker,

Forgive me for writing to you without our being personally acquainted; but I have long so very much harbored the desire to make your acquaintance, and should like to ask you to permit me to visit you. I am—presumptuously—taking it that my name is familiar to you, and am accordingly approaching you without formal introductions. My wish to visit you is not solely a personal one, but also I should like—if you grant my wish—to ask you many things (having read your *Sonata Op. 109* with great admiration) concerning the *Missa* [*solemnis*] and also some questions about the "Eroica" Symphony.

Please, highly revered Mr. Schenker, allow me a visit, and if so grant me an hour of your time on Thursday or Friday.

I am, in greatest admiration,
Yours very truly,
Paul v. Klenau

c/o Director E. Hertzka
Address: Vienna XIX,
Kaasgraben [19]

🕮 Diary entry, September 18, 1923

To Klenau (letter): I ask him to visit on Friday at 10:30.

🕮 Klenau to Schenker (letter), September 19, 1923
OJ 12/11, [2]

Revered Professor,
    Cordial thanks for your kind letter, which I have just received. I look forward most especially to Friday 10.30 a.m. (September 11 [*recte* 21]).
            With best greetings,
                    Yours very truly,
                        Paul v. Klenau

🕮 Record of discussion of *Missa solemnis*, September 21, 1923
OC 82/10[1]

With Paul v. Klenau (September 21, 1923)   Missa solemnis

Tempo of the first movement [Kyrie eleison]: stipulates ¢; immediately the augmentation demands that it proceed by half notes.—Against that, the invocations in clarinet, oboe, and flute, later tenor, soprano, alto, convey the hidden Adagio, but it is not right to bring the Adagio into the half notes, let alone the quarters. After repeated circling around F♯ the cadence is finally reached at the *sf*. —Then the syncopated cries of the chorus, and again the ¢ movement as far as the *f*, then the *cresc.* to the *p*; —the same tempo, hardly at all faster, is carried over into the 3/2 time signature [Christe eleison]. Always seek the upward path in the voices here (notwithstanding the seventh). In general, the dynamics should be followed, as the best guide to the form. At a *f* or *p*, the next *ff* or *sf* should be noted and the sound should be adapted accordingly.

On the Gloria: A more precise reflection of the content is called for, but not a tumult at the expense of precision. Right at the beginning, the twofold ascent to the peak tone A. I draw attention to the parallelisms, as it were antecedent and consequent, to the augmentations in the parallelism, and again to the *sf* as carrier of the sense-accent.

At "pax hominibus" the building up of the triad: the first group extends as far as the modulation into B♭ major ["Gratias agimus"], the third [group] in F major ["Domine Deus"] as far as the D minor Larghetto ["Qui tollis"], the whole governed by a falling third, which undergoes varied imitations at various other intervals, e.g. in the D major section, the passage for solo voices, then the bassoon, as well as at the "Miserere nobis" in the cello and flute, etc., see also the end [of that section] with the falling fifth G♯–C♯. In the fugue ["In gloria Dei Patris"], despite the *ff*, the emphasis occurs on the *sf* in m. 4 of the subject—only in the strings the *sf*, not at all in the winds. On p. 76 of the score [Poco più allegro] the timpani's *sf* as it were divides the fugue into two halves.

The groups of the Credo: a B♭ major section, D minor section at the Adagio ["Et incarnatus est"], score p. 114, then an F major section, p. 125 ["Et resurrexit"], finally B♭—the fugue ["Et vitam venturi"].

Credo as motto. In the last of these [groups] ["Et vitam venturi"], the staccati in the flute and clarinet also indicate the manner in which it is to be sung: do not let the chorus force the tone; moderate tempi, and the dynamic indications are to be followed exactly. The *cresc.* directly before the *f* at p. 142, then new *p* at p. 143, etc. announces the new direction that the form takes. The Allegro con moto, p. 149, really needs no change in tempo since the desired Allegro is already achieved through the greater [rhythmic] animation. Here again aim for the final *sf*: Amen, amen.[2]

[1] OC 82 is a folder of analyses of music by Beethoven. Schenker evidently preserved this document, which is in Jeanette's hand, for possible future use. It is preceded (OC 82/9) by a diagram of the entrances in the fugue "In gloria Dei Patris," marked "first inspection," which might conceivably have formed part of the discussion.

[2] Page numbers cited here do not correspond to the Beethoven Collected Edition (Breitkopf & Härtel). Surviving in neither the Oswald Jonas Memorial Collection nor the Oster Collection, Schenker's own score was most likely sold in the job lot of scores and sheet music, 750 items, offered by the antiquarian bookseller Heinrich Hinterberger in 1935 or 1936.

🕮 Diary entry, September 21, 1923

Paul v. Klenau from 10:45 to 12:30; about various topics, also including personal reflections of Furtwängler and other conductors—he says Furtwängler could today already permit himself to play the role of an aristocratic standard of value—we finally arrive at the actual topic, the *Missa*. I lead him to the score on the piano and outline the basic plan of the entire work, even move on to details, always taking the lead myself, if only in the knowledge that my companion would not even know what to ask; I also don't let myself get bothered by the normal statement " . . that's what I thought, too," and continue—so to speak as if over his head—addressing whatever occurs to me. I see that my comments have the effect of something new, and make a strong impact. It remains questionable whether Klenau will be able to alter his performance accordingly. — At the end, he thanked me repeatedly and most warmly and asked me to visit him once he has moved into his apartment on the Wiedner Hauptstrasse.

Klenau to Schenker (letter), September 25, 1923
OJ 12/11, [3]

Greatly revered, dear Professor,

I <u>must</u> express my most heartfelt thanks to you once again, by this means,[1] for the extraordinarily stimulating hours that I was able to spend with you. Believe me, I shall hold this visit for ever in my memory. And be assured that you have given a human being and musician a precious, lasting gift.

> I am, with sincerest admiration,
> Your cordially and gratefully devoted
> Paul v. Klenau

[1] i.e. by letter rather than in person.

Klenau to Schenker (letter), October 4, 1923
OJ 12/11, [4]

Highly revered, dear Master,

I would prefer to come running to you, because I drive myself so hard and there is no end to my questions and challenges. Yet that is just not possible in our well-mannered way of life. But please write me a few words in a letter about the "Eroica." I have conducted the "Eroica" many, many times, and now discover that I shall never know the symphony completely. That is the nature of this man, who wrote the "Eroica" a few doors from me. A remarkable, incredible man!

First movement: Does not the first theme press forward at a fast tempo? And is that, however, not incorrect, since as a result the theme at [rehearsal letter] C

(Peters Edition)  will

be too fast, and in addition the force of all the accents will be diminished? The metronome marking of ♩. = 60 must surely be wrong: the melody does not indeed call for any great speed, since the tension can easily be conveyed!

Second movement: Is the situation here not precisely the opposite? Does not the tempo marking *Adagio assai* relate to the quarter note rather than to the eighth note? Otherwise it is completely impossible to sustain the tempo throughout—for the fugue really ought not to be too slow; also the passage at [letter] H, if taken at too slow a tempo, loses its coherence. (How lovely the oboe is, and the entry of the clarinet in the seventh and eighth measures after H [mm. 215–16]—an incredible instrumental inspiration!) Is Beethoven's marking of *Maggiore* in general a sign of a new tempo, or is it not rather the case that the entire movement is conceived in <u>one</u> tempo? Is not the flowing movement:

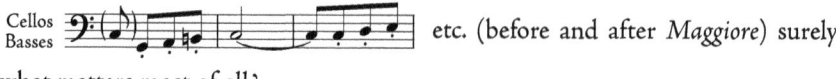 etc. (before and after *Maggiore*) surely what matters most of all?

In the Scherzo (the tempo of which I feel to be <u>very</u> fast), the only question is whether the Trio must really be <u>slower</u>. Should these French horns not rather be rushing along!!! Those romanticized hunting horns, with which—to my annoyance—I have often heard this passage compared, please me so little, if only on account of the main accents, which always fall on the unstressed measure of the period [mm. 166–97]. (Hence they are bad hunting horns, if that is what they are.) Is it wrong to take the Trio at a madcap tempo? I find the momentum (to use an ugly word) exhilarating, if the phrase hurtling along is constructed so as to drive toward the accent. But that is possible only at the fastest tempo. You must give me your expert opinion: please, please!

    I am not finished—because I shall never be finished. But I shall not burden you further.
    Don't be angry. But in the end – – – we sometimes don't have a choice.
              I am, in great admiration,
                   Your grateful
                      Paul v. Klenau

Döblinger Hauptstrasse 60
c/o Marle Vienna XIX

❧ Schenker to Klenau (letter), October 9–10, 1923
OC 54/333–336

Dear Maestro,
    I feel the same way as you. In the meantime, let us journey on, to gaze into this sun; sunburn is no threat to us, only recovery beckons ....

1.) All performance is closely linked to sounding texture (*Tongebung*): a thick, turgid, overblown texture makes for lingering, an airy, lithe texture flows, hurries, etc. In the first movement of the Third Symphony the original metronome marking ♩. = 60 is really not so bad, but woe betide if the cellos immediately slow down and savor their motive, as if the symphony finished at the end of the motive. It cannot be said too often that the cellos alone decide the weal and woe of the movement. But—and here lies the insurmountable difficulty—how can long-range hearing be inculcated into an instrumentalist, an orchestra? In my opinion it is possible to sustain the tempo throughout, including even the passage that you cite from the second subject, and moreover one would be advised to do so. In order to help achieve this completely, one could for practice imagine the main subject in three four-measure groups—<u>one</u> beat per quarter [*recte*: measure]—and, provided that the cellos (approximately indicated) play this:

    [*space left for music example, none entered*]

(which is crucial for what follows), and one maintains a flowing tempo, which itself verily beckons into the distance. The sounding texture that I have in mind guards against an impression of haste. (Haste arises only when thick tones, like pot-bellied people, try to run or are being chased.) Everything in this movement must be on a large scale, the gaiety spacious, even hovering at *ff* passages. Pathos, somberness, calamity here and there must, so to speak, be absorbable. Transcending all the ups and downs is the far-seeing eye of the genius, the hero. A touch of melancholy, of sentimentality there must be—that [too] belongs to genius, nevertheless it remains cheerful! Everything proceeds at that flowing tempo. No haste, thus (only easy-going) at the figures in mm. 65ff. (*p* shadings), just as little in mm. 75ff. Most of the *sf* unconstrainedly expressive, warm (not stabbing), already thus at mm. 40 and 42, but especially in the development section among the basses in the motive at mm. 198ff. The second theme, mm. 83ff., passionate, striving toward the *sf*, equalizing the eighth-note figure m. 90. Fluctuations of the tempo are thus called for, and the conductor will do well to bring out even the individual quarter notes of a measure in many passages, even as early as m. 14, for example.

2.) The metronome marking of the second movement, ♪ = 80 is approximately right in the groups mm. 17ff. in the *Maggiore*, in the fugue, indeed even in the reprise at mm. 173ff. I say approximately: only the opening does not conform: it needs to be about ♪ = 60. In the revised copy at m. 20, I found above the two b♭¹'s in violin I strong wedges (*staccato* wedges): this flinging upward of the b♭ (certainly not to be thrown off coldly, but vehemently sustained) conveys an agitated, active pain, together with long slurs, unknown in our scores these days (!) (At this very moment I am sending the Philharmonic Publishing House corrections to the Fifth Symphony, which has already been published.[1] You would cover your face.) So it seems that Beethoven was not so much aiming to depict a funeral march, as that he was contemplating, suffering sorrow, almost before our very eyes, only after his own manner in broad wellings-up of sorrow. The *pp sotto voce* at the opening seems to confirm that, since these markings promote the gentle pulling of the waves. (We might indeed linger on each 32nd note ". . tarry a while, thou art so beautiful."[2]) However, I believe that we can no longer replicate the beginning as Beethoven may have felt it. By contrast, from m. 17 onward the spirit of the sorrow can be rendered with greater movement. At any rate, the major section moves on faster.

3.) The Scherzo is fast, the metronome marking is just right. The Trio, too. It has a distant goal, the *sf* in m. 70 (of the Trio!). But [there should be] no rushing, especially not in the eighth notes (m. 9 etc.), also not in the French horns in the Trio, which must of course play accordingly.

But, but – – – woe to you if you try to play Beethoven as Beethoven intended. The public [and] musicians cannot match up to his measurements. The speeds of film—yes, these are welcome; but the speeds of the spirit (I am not also referring here to the speeds of tempo)—those are agonizing for them, they cannot abide them.

But now, this could go on for ever, but—even though it is Sunday—I must close.

Yours, with warmest greetings,
H. Schenker

[1] The Philharmonischer Verlag, founded in 1923, brought out a miniature score of Beethoven's Fifth Symphony as the first publication in their Philharmonia series. Having recently completed his essay on the Fifth Symphony for *Der Tonwille*, which included a close reading of the autograph score and first edition, Schenker was sending them—presumably unsolicited—corrections for a revised imprint. Schenker's personal copy of the Philharmonia score contains textual corrections on most of its pages.

[2] Goethe, *Faust*, Part 2, line 1700, also quoted elsewhere in Schenker's correspondence.

Klenau to Schenker (letter), October 21, 1923
OJ 12/11, [5]

Dear Professor,

I wanted to express my thanks to you in person for your splendid letter about the "Eroica." Today once again my wish has been thwarted; I don't want to wait any longer, so am expressing my most cordial thanks by this means. I went to most enormous trouble, but the first performance was not a success. As chance would have it, a week later I conducted the "Eroica" yet again, in place of Ferdinand Löwe, who was ill, and this performance was, I believe, in many respects good. At least, bows were tightened[1]—a few of them! Can I ask for more? I am deeply grateful to you, and believe that much has become clear to me – – – But—it isn't exactly easy.

I shake your hand in admiration and gratitude,

    Your
        Paul v. Klenau

And the Ninth – – ! – ? –

[1] A metaphor perhaps implying that the orchestral players were more attuned to the unfamiliar style of performance, or that the rhythm in the string sections was tighter, more precise.

Klenau to Schenker (letter), December 28, 1923
OJ 12/11, [6]

Dear, greatly revered Professor,

I am currently reading with greatest satisfaction your *Beethoven's Ninth Symphony*—a splendid book, full of life, the product of a lively mind. Your way of looking at things is extraordinarily stimulating. The contents come to life uncannily, and tonality emerges again with full force—as reality. Once we have trodden to its end the road to calvary of the atonal composers, let us hope we will again attain a renaissance—but (Do our views diverge at this point[1]) "one must tread this road," even if it appears dangerous. (This is my personal, relativist viewpoint.)

I frequently regret that I never get to visit you. It saddens me greatly that you were unable to be at my performance of the *Missa solemnis*.[2] I would have loved to hear your verdict. It goes without saying that I am reproached for un-wingèd tempi. Because, for example, the Gloria was of a breadth and weight that astounded even me—every accent crushingly heavy.

But these lines are intended only to wish you a good, productive, creative New Year.

I hope for some stimulating hours with you in the New Year

        In admiration,
        Yours truly
        Paul v. Klenau

---

[1] Klenau is alluding here to his association with Alban Berg and the Schoenberg circle. Klenau incorporated elements of the twelve-tone method into his compositions later in his career.

[2] Two performances, December 8 and 9, 1923, in the large hall of the Concert House with the orchestra of the Vienna State Opera.

ꙮ Schenker to Klenau (letter copy), January 4, 1924
OC 12/249

Dear Mr. v. Klenau,

I reciprocate cordially your kind good wishes, and I thank you no less cordially for your ready approval of my Ninth Symphony monograph. As regards your further remarks on the <u>atonal composers</u> as the Renaissance: If an impotent man were to claim to be <u>a-feminine</u> by reference to a philosophical or some other sort of trend—toward progress, development?—the self-conceit, self-deception, might please the unfortunate man to the core, but women would judge him more accurately. Or from another point of view: Nature is always consistent; that is, to every cause she supplies its logical effect; but that is just why it would be wrong ever to give her consistency another name: progress, history, trend, movement. A humpback, a mule, a mulatto, and all other such things of that sort that Nature has produced from given causes, specifically do not signify any purpose—nothing whatsoever more than a logical consistency. So the atonal composers represent a consistency in Nature and nothing more than that: they had to become atonal, they must remain atonal, because Nature in her usual fashion gives to their incapacity a consequence. But to say of them that they want to be atonal, as they allege, in order to foster development, transition or germination, does not correspond with the true state of affairs. Do not forget: The destroyer—and the atonal composer is just that—fancies himself in a rewarding role: he believes always in starting from scratch. Ah! what a hero he thinks himself for that!

To my mind, there is no such thing as a Renaissance. People take up anew what their predecessors have given up out of incapacity, but with no greater understanding. I do not consider possible—or indeed even desirable—an association of humanity with the great masters. It is always the individual who emerges as a great master, and then again it is only a few who come close, very very slightly so, to achieving this. All the others are merely presumptuous. But enough of all that.

I gladly reiterate that I would be delighted to welcome you once again. I see no pupils on Wednesdays. Perhaps it would suit you to do me the favor of a visit one Wednesday or another. But even in this case I ask for prior notice as a precaution, for it could be that I am going to the Archive, or something of that sort.

With best wishes,
Yours,
Schenker

PS Issue 5 of *Der Tonwille* includes the Fifth Symphony of Beethoven. You may like to take a look at it.

Diary entry, April 30, 1924

2:15 Klenau and Botstiber appear;[1] we soon turn to their questions: Both gentlemen agree to my suggestion of using the original tempo. Botstiber has to go [...], Klenau stays until 4:30. We go through the entire symphony. As he is leaving, he promises to reserve two tickets for the performance. I refuse to participate in the rehearsals, so as not to give the critics any pretext for an attack. [...] Botstiber envies my abstinence from society; he reckons he lacks this ability, so that he loses out on work as well.

[1] Three months' silence had ensued from Klenau. Then on February 26, 1924 Schenker received a letter from Hugo Botstiber asking if he and Klenau might call on Schenker to discuss a forthcoming performance of Beethoven's Ninth Symphony on May 7. Hugo Botstiber (1875–1942): Austrian writer on music, secretary of the Vienna Concert House Society 1913–38.

Diary entry, May 7, 1924

In the evening, the Ninth. In the program there is an explanation by Klenau: elucidation of its historical character, to which end the original tempo and original instrumentation have been restored. First there are sections of the *Missa solemnis*: the tempo at the repetition of the Kyrie is just right, Credo good throughout. The progress is unmistakeable: Klenau leads the massed choir with a sure touch, more securely than Furtwängler. Although the tempo in the first movement of the symphony is good, it is not free enough in the second and third themes—all in all, it leaves something to be desired. The second movement very good in the first part, the Trio too slow. The beginning of the Adagio obviously yielding to tradition, at any rate timid; the violins not yet sufficiently worked through. Toward the end more lively, and more in keeping with the original tempo. The final movement up to the opening recitative good, even very good. Great success for the conductor. The program mentions my *Ninth Symphony* in a footnote.

❧ Klenau to Schenker (calling card), May 13, 1924
OJ 12/11, [7]

Highly revered Professor,
  Could you speak with me for five minutes at any time tomorrow? Please give your answer directly to the servant.

>With cordial and admiring greetings,
> Yours truly,
>   Paul v. Klenau

❧ Diary entry, May 14, 1924

Klenau appears punctually, to offer thanks and to ask about any potential deficiencies. I bring up several passages: I censure the end of the first theme, the tempo of the second theme etc. Klenau talks about difficulties, the resistance of the orchestra, which was broken only when the president and the board of directors intervened. Klenau said he convinced the musicians by reciting a Mörike poem—now they are very pleased! While leaving, Klenau remarked: "I have learned a lot from your guidance in my compositions too, I shall show you them sometime."

❧ Klenau to Schenker (letter), [May 20, 1924]
OJ 12/11, [8]

Dear, highly revered Professor,
  I have promised to write an article for a periodical about the performance of the Ninth Symphony.[1] But since this is based entirely on your insightful explanations, I should not like to submit it for printing without having first asked you whether you approve what I have written. Would you be so very kind as to read through the enclosed manuscript and, where necessary, make annotations if you are <u>not</u> in agreement with anything whatsoever? For simplicity's sake I will collect the manuscript from your place on Wednesday at 12 noon. Would you be so kind as to give me your opinion on that occasion, or to communicate it in a couple of lines? In this case, I cannot proceed without your consent.

>Most cordial greetings from
> Your grateful devotee,
>   Paul v. Klenau

---

[1] "Die 'Klassische' Neunte," *Pult und Taktstock* 4 (July 1924): 55–63.

❧ Diary entry, May 21, 1924

Klenau from 12:00 to 1:00; we discuss the article, move on to several passages in the *St. Matthew Passion*, the very short choral passages at the end; I append the choral fantasy and passages from Mozart's G minor Symphony.

❧ Diary entry, September 17, 1924

At 10:00, Paul von Klenau; he tells [me] that he received a lot of agreement, including letters from [Siegfried] Ochs, Professor Rickert, etc., also one from Weingartner, who raises the question of the metronome marking in the Trio of the Scherzo. I have already answered this question from a motivic perspective in my book,[1] the answer should actually preclude any new question, even if the manuscript and the first print shows a whole note, not a half note. So I again remark, that an internal argument is not at first effective, an external, visible one is desired! I show Klenau Beethoven's letter to Moscheles,[2] in which a half note is also notated and express my willingness to look at the facsimile to see whether an erasure or some other sign indicates Beethoven's wrestling with this passage. We also talk about the Fifth Symphony, which he will be conducting in about three weeks in Copenhagen. I show [him] the corrections I made in the Kalmus score, they fill him with amazement, and he asks whether the corrected score has already been released. I say no and tell him that the absence of the second edition proves how large the [print-run of the] first must have been! Klenau leaves me after an hour, sends me the letter from Rickert and his article on the Ninth right away.

[1] *Beethoven's Ninth Symphony*, 171 (Ger., 177).
[2] March 18, 1827, postscript: Beethoven writes out the metronome markings for the movements (including tempo changes) of the Ninth Symphony, which suggests a *l'istesso tempo* approach to the performance of the Trio: dotted half note (one measure of music) of *Molto vivace* (main section) corresponds to half note (half a measure) of *Presto* (Trio). *Ludwig van Beethoven: Briefwechsel Gesamtausgabe*, ed. Sieghard Brandenburg (Munich: Henle, 1996), vol. 6, 381 (letter 2284), *The Letters of Beethoven*, ed. Emily Anderson (London: Macmillan, 1961), vol. 3, 1344–45 (letter 1566).

❧ Klenau to Schenker (letter), September 17, 1924
OJ 12/11, [9]

Highly revered Professor,
    I send herewith the letter from Rickert, and should be glad to have it back when the occasion arises.

With cordial thanks for the hour (stimulating, as ever) just spent with you.

       In great admiration,
          Yours truly,
            Paul v. Klenau

Jacquingasse 15
Vienna

❧ Diary entry, September 20, 1924

To Klenau (letter): I return the letter from Rickert; the passage in question in the facsimile looked at, an instruction to the copyist found, but I was too hurried because the store was closing; recommend reading through the "Miscellanea" for the eighth issue [of *Der Tonwille*]; I thank [him] for the Rickert letter; music director Lorenz must be mistaken about the overarching connections, since just arbitrarily selected points without evidence of voice-leading do not constitute a connection.[1]

[1] Reference is to Alfred Lorenz, *Das Geheimnis der Form bei Richard Wagner*, 4 vols. (Berlin: Max Hesse, 1924–33), which aimed to discover the "architectonics" of Wagner's massive structures through ascending hierarchical levels of periodicity, harmonic movement, and melody.

❧ Klenau to Schenker (letter), September 23, 1924

OJ 12/11, [10]

Highly revered Professor,

    I take the liberty of enclosing herewith Felix Weingartner's remarks concerning my article, and my response to them. My cordial thanks for your letter. I shall go to Universal Edition today and ask them to show me issue 8 of *Der Tonwille*. May I ask you to be so kind as to return the enclosed to me? I should not like to say anything in connection with this article in print without having conferred with you.

       With warmest compliments
         and most cordial greetings,
           Yours truly,
            Paul v. Klenau

PS On Saturday and Sunday I am again conducting the Ninth in the Concert House. If you should wish to have tickets, please just let me know.

ꙮ Diary entry, September 24, 1924

To Klenau (letter and enclosures returned): the most important thing is to maintain the tempo in the Scherzo throughout the first section and throughout the Trio; I refer [him] to the motivic reason described by me on p. 177, draw to his attention that in the Trio, the fact that there are two instead of three quarter notes to a beat itself gives the impression of a retardation, which is why it is not necessary to play even more slowly than what the notation itself indicates. Aimed in Weingartner's direction: it is a true act of meanness for a music director to make the others out to be musicians who only follow [the notation] literally, while making oneself out to be the one who conducts according to the meaning. I say: if he knew the meaning, he would above all find it especially already present in the literal notation; I ask for two tickets for Saturday (the letter handed over to the concierge myself).

ꙮ Diary entry, September 27, 1924

In the concert: celebration to mark the 20th anniversary of the Concerts for Workers! A disgraceful speech by Dr. Bach from which one could clearly deduce that he does not know whether he is facing an already educated audience or one that first needs to be educated! It begins with two chorale preludes by Bach arranged for instruments by Schoenberg: the first too short, the second very well suited for instrumental arrangement; a symphonic poem by Salmhofer: an overly long nothing put forth with the typical vigor of an untalented youth; at the end the Ninth; the first movement still shows the most flaws, the Scherzo in the first section is too fast, then better. In the Trio, still a slight tendency to drag, the Adagio is superb, including the long bowings by the violins. The last movement is very good.

16
Georg Dohrn and the Ninth Symphony

GEORG Dohrn (1867–1942) was a conductor working in Flensburg, then Munich (1898–1901), then with the Breslau Orchestral and Choral Societies (1901–36). He was an admirer of Schenker's writings, and in 1926 sought the latter's advice, raising points of interpretation on Beethoven's Ninth Symphony that Schenker answered in close detail.

Some time after this correspondence took place, Hellmut Federhofer, while browsing in a bookstore, happened on a used copy of Schenker's *Beethovens neunte Sinfonie*, which he purchased. When he later opened the volume, Schenker's holograph letter to Dohrn fell out of its pages. Federhofer had no way of identifying the addressee, but he nevertheless wrote about the letter, and kindly sent me a copy.

I recognized the text, for Schenker had retained a copy of his own letter, in Jeanette's hand, and I had many years earlier seen this document in the Oster Collection,[1] together with the original letter of inquiry from Dohrn. Through correspondence between Federhofer and myself, we were able to solve certain puzzles: the identity of the recipient was established, and a word in Schenker's letter that had been obscured by an ink-blot in the holograph was revealed by the aforementioned copy to be not *molto*, as in Federhofer's published transcription, but rather *marcato*.

Schenker's reply to Dohrn is, typically, full of the finest artistic touches. A good example is his observation that "at the arpeggiation through kettle drums and horns after the 'ritmo di Quattro battute' [i.e. mm. 248–51 (and 256–69)] the effect approaches that of a *legato* of the head-tones." Perhaps most important of all, however, is Schenker's insistence on the importance of the manuscript as an indispensable source for an accurate text: comparison of the manuscript of this very movement against the scores available in Schenker's time (and most of those still in use) will amply illustrate.

JOHN ROTHGEB

---

[1] Jeanette's handwritten copy shows slight variants from the finished text. The copy was placed in Schenker's file of materials concerning Beethoven's Ninth Symphony– (his diary states "copied into the folder on the 'Ninth'") for future reference. Federhofer's transcription and discussion, "Ein Lehrbrief Heinrich Schenkers," is found in *Festschrift Otto Biba zum 60. Geburtstag*, ed. Ingrid Fuchs (Tutzing: Hans Schneider, 2006), 727–30.

❧ Dohrn to Schenker (letter), April 2, 1926
OC 82/27–28

Breslau Orchestra Society

Breslau,
Steinstrasse 4/6

Dear Dr. Schenker,

    Permit me, please, as one who knows and highly values several of your publications—especially your "Presentation of the Musical Content" of Beethoven's "Ninth"—to pose a question to you to which your answer would be of really special interest to me.

    Facing the prospect of a performance of the Ninth Symphony, I am preparing for it, as always, as though for a sacred act, in which I feel myself obliged anew to decide how the well-known octave-motif of the second movement should be performed—whether, to put it briefly, it should be *staccato* or *non-staccato*, i.e. whether this way: [musical notation] or this: [musical notation].

Beethoven added no performance indications to this measure, but always applied *staccato* dots[1] only to the following measures of the ordinary quarters, so that given the general precision of his markings, one could assume that he did not want the measure with the octave leaps performed with the same kind of *staccato* as that of the measures that succeed it; and that is maintained throughout, in both the principal section and the *Ritmo di tre battute*. Actually, we do play that way from the twenty-first measure after the first *fortissimo*, and in the subsequent sixteen measures *ff* in the great *unisono* the strings completely automatically, as though unconsciously [musical notation]. But conversely, also as though automatically, we hear, in the introductory measures, strings and all winds—probably in order to give expression to the pungency of the tempestuous energy—sound the motif in question in *staccato*, perhaps infected by the collaborating kettle drum, which can play no other way than *staccato*. Now should one regard the kettle drum as setting the standard for this measure throughout the whole movement? That would not seem correct to me already in the sixteen (melodic?) measures following the twenty-first measure after the first *fortissimo*, in which I direct that the first quarter be <u>weakly</u> accented and held. Also from the tenth measure of the heading "*Ritmo di quattro battute*" on, where an exchange occurs between kettle drum and horns, I have thus far not been able to make up my mind to have the horns join in the kettle drum's only possible mode of performance, but have instead always recommended to them to imagine the first quarter exactly as though a *tenuto*-stroke were applied to it, though on the other hand, precisely from the horns, the motif in *staccato* is set off in a most highly characteristic way and joins well with the kettle drum in this mode of performance. By the same token, if one wants to go by the kettle drum, one would have to have the last six measures before the heading "*Ritmo di tre battute*" (a, a♯, b), in their alternation between strings and woodwinds, performed *staccato*, for which, however, I have thus far not been able to make up my mind.

If you would now be so good, in response to my polite request, as to find it possible to take the time to tell me your estimable opinion as to the performance of the measure in question, I should be most sincerely grateful.

In the hope that no inconvenience may thereby be caused you, with kind regards I remain,

   Respectfully,
    Yours sincerely,
     Georg Dohrn

---

[1] Beethoven's autograph score shows strokes rather than dots, but published scores in general—including, no doubt, the one Dohrn was using—show only dots.

Schenker to Dohrn (letter), April 5, 1926
Rothg 1 (= OC 82/29–31 (copy))

Dear Music Director,

Your opinion that it should be played as follows: [musical example] is one with which I concur for many reasons; I agree too that this manner should be maintained in all sections. A clue is provided already by the *sf* in measure 3 and measure 5 (in the kettle drum!): *sf* is (contrary to the usual practice) a warm, heartfelt accent, in contrast to the dry *f* or *marcato*. Something of this *sf* (within *ff*!) clings like dew to all of the head-tones depending on the tempo, the instrumental forces of the orchestra, etc.

Despite the pressure on the head-tone, however, the figure is certainly to be played *non legato*. The violinist makes a longer bow-stroke downward, as with a light, thin pull (*pp*); the reflex motion brings him the two a¹s, the eighth still in the direction of the first bow-stroke, but the quarter upward. The expression, even in the *pp*, is this: [musical example]. But all of it very subtle.

At the arpeggiation through kettle drums and horns after the "*ritmo di Quattro battute*" the effect approaches that of a *legato* of the head-tones.

At this point I call your attention to measures 77ff. (and the later repetitions), to which Beethoven, in the manuscript, expressly adds: "< at its strongest in the fifth measure, from there on weaker."[1] It goes without saying, for measure 81 has the suspension ($\underline{d^3\text{--}c^3}$ then $\underline{c^3\text{--}b^2}$); therefore, because of the suspension, in measure 81 ———— must begin. The [published] scores are incorrect here.

Perhaps I shall be able finally to publish the gleanings from the manuscript in my yearbook *The Masterwork in Music*, of which the first volume, 1925, will appear (somewhat late) in the coming weeks by Drei Masken Verlag, Munich. At the time, UE denied me the funds for photographic imaging; later, when I reached an agreement with Director Kopfermann in Berlin on a modest rate for the images, the war broke out; during the war, I had to bear personally the cost of the images for Opp. 101, 109, 110, and 111, since the publisher was too tight-fisted, and so I was once again deprived of the images of the Ninth Symphony.

I speak of this because the manuscript contains <u>absolutely invaluable directions</u> that the scores reproduce <u>incorrectly</u>.*

The "Philharmonic Publishing House in Vienna" (actually again Universal Edition) a couple of years ago sent me their associate, a conductor, with whom I had a few meetings (for purposes of revision); I then dropped the matter, because I found myself deplorably hoodwinked by the publisher; but the result of the first meetings, [covering] about up to the Reprise in the first movement, was already used for the new edition of the Ninth under the aegis of the Philharmonic Publishing House.

As I say, I hope to be able to return to this very important matter.

In warm gratitude for the expression of your confidence, I am

       Yours sincerely,
       H. Schenker

*I doubt that my monograph on the Fifth Symphony (UE 7646) has come to your attention. There, on pp. 16–17, 43–44, 57–58, [and] 68–69, very substantially base offenses of the score against the (misinterpreted) manuscript are cited.

---

[1] Schenker paraphrases here; Beethoven's exact comment is "NB the ⟨⟩ is strongest at the 5th measure and decreases in strength from there on."

V
Contrary Opinions

17
Expedient Mutuality: Schenker and August Halm

THE correspondence between August Halm and Heinrich Schenker (thirty-six letters and eleven postcards between 1916 and 1927) chronicles the views of self-appointed spokesmen waging campaigns in a cultural conflict between tradition and modernity during the last few years of World War I and the birth and subsequent sociopolitical and economic travails of the Weimar Republic. In some ways the two men are allies under the banner of traditionalism—preserving and deepening appreciation for the German musical canon—but in others they occupy seats on opposite sides of the political, sociological, and music-aesthetic aisle. Their written communication is a mix of mutual affirmation, self-interested opportunism, and open conflict. The letters provide a multifaceted view of the turbulent times from the vantage points of two similarly motivated men struggling with the same problems, but arriving at different understandings of and solutions for them.

This selection includes seventeen items: nine letters from Halm, seven letters and one postcard from Schenker. A short diary entry of March 1914 provides a glimpse of Schenker's tacit critical attitude toward Halm's analytical style. The dialog is on the whole cordial (in 1919 Schenker awarded Halm a stipend: see chapter 10, above), but occasionally quite frank. Often each writes with the goal of gaining some advantage through the other: for Schenker, favorable reviews by a widely-read author in order to expand readership to circles otherwise not attracted to music-analytical writings; for Halm, public endorsement of his music in order to establish legitimacy for his compositions and raise awareness of them. For example, Schenker praises Halm rather over-exuberantly for a favorable review of the elucidatory edition of the late Beethoven piano sonatas,[1] yet six years later calls him "childish" for misguided criticisms of Beethoven and Brahms, and blind worship of Bruckner.[2] Halm frequently sends his compositions to Schenker, or repeatedly offers to send them, and prompts for reactions in hopes of receiving laudatory comments and analytical confirmation of structural soundness (an Urlinie) and genius, neither of which is forthcoming from Schenker's pen.

---

[1] In Schenker's letter dated January 17, 1918.

[2] Diary entry of February 16, 1924. The space devoted to Halm in Federhofer (1985), 133–49, gave recognition to the importance of Halm among the artists, scholars, and writers on music in Schenker's circle. Federhofer had already published an article that includes Halm substantively ("Heinrich Schenkers Bruckner-Verständnis," *Archiv für Musikwissenschaft* 39, no. 3 (1982): 198–217) and subsequently published another article, on the correspondence between Halm and Schenker on the subject of Bruckner ("Anton Bruckner im Briefwechsel von August Halm (1869–1929)–Heinrich Schenker (1868–1935)," in *Anton Bruckner: Studien zu Werk und Wirkung*, ed. Christoph Hellmut Mahling. Mainzer Studien zur Musikwissenschaft 20 (Tutzing: Schneider, 1988), 33–40).

Contrary to Schenker's usual brutal honesty, he silently endures Halm's recurrent angling for validation, but does eventually voice his opinion privately, in a diary entry of November 3, 1927, when he writes "New music from Halm—downright unmusical!"

Halm and Schenker agree on certain issues that are central for both—for instance, on the superiority of German music, particularly Bach and Beethoven. Further, they jointly reject musical modernism in Reger, Schoenberg, and Strauss, and abhor the distortive musical hermeneutics of Hermann Kretzschmar and Paul Bekker, who cheapen masterworks with baseless analytical narratives. However, they disagree fundamentally on certain details in those areas of agreement. While Schenker reveres Brahms as the "last master of German music," Halm considers him a "victim of sonata form." Halm champions Bruckner's symphonies as a "third culture" of music, while Schenker dismisses him for failing to achieve coherent forms because of an inability to coordinate the vertical and horizontal dimensions on a large scale. Other musical issues on which the two men diverge include the music of Berlioz and Wagner, the question of genius in music, and the validity of the Urlinie as a necessary criterion for genius.[3] Finally, their political orientations differ widely—Schenker an arch-conservative monarchist, Halm a moderate Social Democrat; and their sociological outlooks diverge equally widely— Schenker a hardline elitist, Halm a committed populist. For example, one of Schenker's letters (September 25, 1922)—too long for inclusion here—highly self-revealing in content and tone, speaks about his childhood and home, his working relationships with Schoenberg and Maximilian Harden, also reveals his dim view of human nature and society's dull masses, his disdainful attitude toward the French, and his contempt for German democrats.

LEE ROTHFARB

---

[3] As Halm observes in a letter of March 18, 1917, "what differentiates us primarily is your belief in genius and its perfection."

❧ Diary entry, March 19, 1914

Reading Halm's book![1] What peculiar paths do the imagination and pen of a man take who "in obscure impulses" seeks a way to the purely musical but sadly is unable to find it. An absolutely grotesque mixture of technical material and the most far-flung aesthetics. Time and again the purely musical breaks down, and the writer's imagination so often resorts to feelings, philosophizings, in short it interjects surrogates that cast an inadequate light even on the technical aspect. More individualistic and more educated than Mr. [Herman] Roth, at the same time he recalls him in the fatal inadequacy of the purely musical and in the delusion that he has captured it precisely. There is nothing so curious as the execution of Bekker and the physiognomy of the analysis that Halm counterposes to Bekker's.[2] With Halm, too, it ultimately boils down mostly to empty aesthetics.

[1] *Von zwei Kulturen der Musik* (Munich: Georg Müller, 1913).

[2] In ibid., 39–79, Halm attacks Bekker's anthropomorphic interpretation of the opening of Beethoven's "Tempest" Sonata, as given in Bekker's *Beethoven* (Berlin: Schuster und Loeffler, 1911), 118–19; Eng. transl. (London: Dent), 114.

Halm to Schenker (letter), undated [probably November/December 1916]
OJ 11/35, [0]

Stuttgart, Lehenstrasse 21

Dear Professor,

After a brief glance at your Beethoven edition (to which I want to devote more careful study and a review in the *Freie Schulgemeinde*[1]), (a copy will go out to you from Universal Edition), I would like to express to you my delight and gratitude. I am fully aware of the possibility that you have read this and that of mine which you reject.[2] And I do not altogether concur with your assessment of Beethoven. But with respect to our, as I believe, common artistic volition, I think differences in judgment may for now recede behind the fact that we have the same enemies, are nevertheless strongly in the majority, are respected, and thus have power. Allow me the question whether you would be inclined and might find the time in the near future to take a look at an essay of mine about a new type of piano instruction?[3] I am planning a "piano method" for beginners, am looking for a publisher for it, and would request a recommendation for Universal Edition based on your findings.[4]

  Yours respectfully,
  August Halm

I will soon have a volume of piano compositions sent to you by my publisher.

[1] Halm's highly complimentary review, titled "Heinrich Schenker," appeared in *Die freie Schulgemeinde* 8 (1917): 11–15, reprinted in Halm, *Von Form und Sinn der Musik*, ed. Siegfried Schmalzriedt (Wiesbaden: Breitkopf & Härtel, 1978), 271–74, on Schenker's elucidatory editions of *Op. 109*, *Op. 110*, and *Op. 111*.

[2] By 1916, Halm had published three books and over fifty articles, at least thirty of which would have interested Schenker.

[3] i.e. his essay "Bildender Klavierunterricht," *Die Freie Schulgemeinde* 7 (1916/17): 103–18, in *Von Form und Sinn der Musik*, 292–305.

[4] Halm's *Piano Method* ultimately comprised three volumes: vol. 1 (Stuttgart: Zumsteeg, 1918); vol. 2, ed. Willi Apel (a former Wickersdorf student of Halm's), (Kassel: Bärenreiter, 1932); vol. 3 (unpublished).

§ **Schenker to Halm (letter: first draft), [December 29, 1916]**
OC 1B/9

In reply to your cordial letter,[1] for which I warmly thank you, I hasten to confirm that I have known about your works for some time already and have also attentively followed their fate in the press.[2] Further, I concur with you completely when you say that that which unites us must for now be more important than that which divides us. All in all, you will meanwhile have noticed that in principle I take the field against opponents only very unwillingly, and do it only when the opponent manifests a specifically tinged bacterium of error or, in becoming aggressive himself first (I understand here naturally also remaining silent), provokes my weaponry.

My tendency is to think that, in the enormously enlarged circle of art enthusiasts over the last 200–300 years, individuals genuinely able and knowledgeable in voice-leading and harmony can be cultivated and realized, if not in the same relation, then at least in a similar one as still existed, after all, so many centuries ago within the smaller circle. I see the cause of the current disruption, of the predominance of our opponents, of the unceasing babble about progress and the like, solely in the lamentable disparity between the informed and the uninformed.[3] At bottom, therefore, it simply depends on whose concepts of voice-leading and harmony are the correct ones—that is, are more in accordance with the works of our great masters: mine or those of my opponents. In the second [half-]volume of *Counterpoint*, soon to be delivered to the printer, which deals mainly with free composition,[4] I believe I have adduced evidence that tones, just like stars in the firmament, for example, have but few primal laws that remain all the more immutable at their core the more mutably—indeed, bewildering in their mutability—they manifest themselves in individual phenomena. Never—of this at least I am convinced—can a new generation, a new youth, add even a single law to the few primal ones. And awaiting the world will be the exceedingly happy and gratifying business of contenting itself with the endless mutability and working securely within it, instead of ending up in regions where nothing is even perceptible to us. After all this, you will understand that I look forward to the announced essay with genuine interest.

Regarding your plan possibly to submit the piano method to Universal Edition: I cannot conceal from you that I myself am in a tense relationship with the publisher, at least for the time being—as so often occurs—so that, accordingly, even my editing of Opp. 101 and 106 is in question. However, it would be possible—as this too so often happens—that the relationship will presently improve, which I will of course communicate to you, [and am] gladly willing to make the publisher amenable toward you.

[*without valediction or signature*]

---

[1] Halm's letter is not known to survive. This letter draft was dictated to Jeanette, written out by her, then heavily edited by Schenker. Schenker's diary indicates that it was mailed out on December 29, 1916. The reading given here represents Jeanette's

first draft, since it has not been possible to reconstruct Schenker's emendations with certainty.

[2] Schenker may have learned about Halm in 1908 from author and Stuttgart music critic Karl Grunsky, who in a letter to Schenker of September 10 of that year mentions with great emphasis Halm's essay "Melodie, Harmonie und Themenbildung bei Anton Bruckner," *Neue Musikzeitung* 23 (1902): 170–74, 196–98, 211–14, 227–28. He reiterates Halm's importance a few months later in a second letter (November 5, 1908). Halm and Grunsky crossed paths while studying at Tübingen University. See Rothfarb, *August Halm*, 109.

[3] In this formulation Schenker summarizes a basic difference between himself, an elitist addressing a musically and technically highly literate audience, and Halm, a populist addressing musical amateurs, as he says in *Von zwei Kulturen der Musik*, vii, and in *Die Symphonie Anton Bruckners* (Munich: Georg Müller, 2nd edn. 1923), xiv. See Rothfarb, *August Halm*, 72.

[4] See Hedi Siegel, "When 'Freier Satz' was Part of *Kontrapunkt*: A Preliminary Report," in *Schenker Studies* 2, ed. Carl Schachter and Hedi Siegel (Cambridge: Cambridge University Press, 1999), 12–25.

Halm to Schenker (letter), March 18, 1917
OJ 11/35, 4

Dear Professor,

I believe what differentiates us primarily is your belief in genius and its perfection.[1] As often as I grant that you are right when you rebuke a windy attack, I do have the impression that you are tempted actually to censure the attack in itself.—When you write that certain characteristics in Bruckner's symphonies prevent you from granting them the highest rank, I am genuinely eager to find out more precisely what you mean (which you also allude to), but am not further surprised. Only in Beethoven's symphonies could I perhaps find even more than you in Bruckner, let alone Brahms, whose genuine mastery is for me very doubtful—only I cannot speak about it publicly because I do not know his music sufficiently, and I do not want to study just to be able to speak about him. He attracts me only in very occasional works.

On the whole, I believe he was a victim of sonata form and its sovereignty.[2]

But in your Beethoven edition you have made me aware of various things that had escaped me, so that in any case I look forward to your comments with joy and excitement, even though with a different orientation.—Universal Edition does not want anything from me now, and suggests that I inquire again after the war.

I cannot convey your greeting to Dr. Grunsky; some years ago we went our separate ways owing to his taking sides and the manner of his fighting in an internal conflict at Wickersdorf, where I was teaching at the time.[3]

With kind regards and greetings,
August Halm

[1] Halm mentions this difference in "Heinrich Schenker," 14, repr. in *Von Form und Sinn der Musik*, 273.
[2] In a notebook, Halm describes Brahms as victim of sonata form, Bruckner as a master of the symphony (DLA, Halm estate papers, protocol 69.446, folder 3). See Rothfarb, *August Halm*, 95, 147, 159.
[3] Halm, a co-founder in 1906 of the Wickersdorf Freie Schulgemeinde, taught there until 1910, and then again from 1920 until his death in 1929. The "internal conflict" revolved around the issue of reinstating Gustav Wyneken, another Wickersdorf co-founder, to the post of headmaster, from which he had been administratively removed in 1910 because of political disputes.

Schenker to Halm (letter), July 8, 1917
DLA 69.930/1

Seefeld in Tyrol, Guesthouse Wetterstein

Dear Professor,

Your cordial missive [of July 2, 1917] reached me here only circuitously by way of Vienna. However, my reply, which I am sending right away, and which, in addition, has by nature a shorter path to you, will probably take all the shorter a time.

So far as I recall, volume 2 of the Beethoven variations in the Peters edition is not the worst edition and may be much closer to the presumed original than the others.[1] The variations therein are among the less "famous" ones, and in those cases the "famous" editors save themselves the trouble, which is all the better for the pieces. Even the first volume of variations, where the "Diabelli" and "Eroica" Variations have been placed, is questionable. Under all circumstances, I personally prefer the Collected Edition, which makes fewest additions and modifications, even if it fails with respect to the deepest issues of composition and notation.[2] Especially in those variations, the original is likely in large part to match the rendering in the Collected Edition, although I don't want to do anything to underestimate their wonderful artistry, which surely has never been exceeded. I would be interested to find out which variation you chose. Would you provide fingerings for it? It occurs to me what a rewarding, pleasurable task it would be, for example, to bring together into one volume all passages from all of Beethoven's works that have his own fingerings, and to draw conclusions, which could indicate unacademic paths for piano technique.

I look forward with the greatest interest to your cordial review of my Beethoven editions. Recently I saw a review in *Der Kunstwart*, signed by A. Liebscher, who with such genial acknowledgment attributed to me nothing more and nothing less than accusing Bülow of inferior instinct.[3] However, how often have I stressed that I understand it as enjoyable only with respect to Beethoven himself and not to musical aspects generally, and what a tremendous difference that represents! Yes, and because there is such a huge distance from a Bülow to Beethoven, I demand that all of the others may not fall too much behind Bülow.

I am writing to Cotta [*recte* Universal Edition] at the same time that he should have a review copy sent to you without delay.[4] It is simply incomprehensible to me in that regard that he has not already sent you one on his own. The second [half-]volume of *Counterpoint* will appear with Cotta, but I am still putting the finishing touches [to it]. Too bad that the printing takes so long. Volumes 1 and 2/1 have taken two years. But I have patience. Greeting you warmly,

   Yours very truly,
   H. Schenker

---

[1] Halm had remarked: "I would like to incorporate the easier Beethoven variations into my piano method, the ones that appear in volume 2 of the Peters edition—a selection naturally."

[2] Schenker owned a copy of vol. 17 of the collected edition of Beethoven's works (Leipzig: Breitkopf & Härtel, 1862–65), which contains the piano variations.

[3] Artur Liebscher, "Musikalische Urtextausgaben," *Der Kunstwart*, April 1917, on Schenker's elucidatory editions of *Op. 109*, *Op. 110*, *Op. 111*, and *Op. 101*.

[4] On the same date as this letter, Schenker reported to UE that Halm was about to publish a review of the Beethoven editions, and asked that a copy be sent to him when UE received it.

Schenker to Halm (letter), January 17, 1918
DLA 69.930/2

Dear Mr. Halm,

 The first awareness of your essay regarding me, which is extremely dignified and full of character, and which honors you no less than me, I received through a former pupil who lives near Munich.[1] I then waited a while to see whether one of my publishers would send it to me for review. Only when nothing came of that, I requested the essay from that gentleman. The essay came to me as a "galley proof," so that I did not know whether and where it appeared in print, which is why I believed I had to hold off for a while on an answer to you. Almost at the same time I brought the essay to the attention of the Vienna publisher [Universal Edition] who, if I am not mistaken, must have then requested it from you personally, and actually received it. From him, now, from the publisher, your booklet came to me at the end of December (of course without a single word of shared joy), and so I also got to see your "postscript" for the first time.[2]

 Just in the last days of December my mother [Julia Schenker], over ninety years of age, passed away. My pen stalled, and all work in general. Looking back on my accomplishments—after the death of my father,[3] a doctor, poor but highly revered far and wide, barely twenty years old myself, I took in my mother and all the other siblings and sustained them with the yield of poorly paid piano lessons until after extremely difficult years, during which I almost broke down twice under the burden, I finally succeeded in providing for my siblings, and then in devoting myself more undisturbed to my projects. Looking back on that feat, I say, which in the natural course found its end with my mother's last breath, it overwhelmed me completely and severely. As endlessly tragic as those years seemed, I nevertheless thank destiny for that test, for it opened my view into the world, into the shallows of humanity, brought me together with rich and poor, and allowed me to have experiences that alone entitle me to speak to people as I do.

That fateful interruption, too, is now past and I used the first rest—if I can even speak of one—to thank you for your essay, to shake your hand as a gesture. What you managed to do in those few pages only a German can do, above all, and never a Frenchman or an Englishman. That genuine dedication to the task, which in practice means more than all other ideologies, more even than religion, means the "redemption" of humanity, how beautifully and nobly it is articulated in every word that you write! What a sense of well-being, too, for me to know that I am not of further relevance for you other than solely our intersection in the object that it circumscribes—if there were only a more worthy expression for that godhead of humanity! I bear your high praise humbly and serenely, as though I were not even the one whom you have in mind, only truth, meaning the parts of the object which we all must serve from our hearts and with all powers if we are serious about our redemption, about our existence.

But look, is it possible that someone else even among the Germans could write such an essay that does not have your moral and intellectual stature? Certainly not. Unfortunately, unfortunately not. And you yourself say that you do not grasp the reason for my "esoteric approach"?[4] Where you are the most perfect example that one can only speak to a person who himself can "see and hear"? Believe me, it is possible to speak with genuine benefit only from leader to leader, and only that which descends from them belongs to the world—and how precious little that is![5] But here I come upon a subject that caused and causes me immense pain, even intense physical pain, precisely during the war—the subject of "folk," what it appears to be, what it really is, etc. And when I say briefly that I distinguish between Beethoven, who emerged from the folk ("Baron Beethoven" for example would be a farce that would show the dear creator as a frivolous jester), and the folk that remained folk, with that I surely declare my attitude well enough. The delusion that all of the folk is, like Beethoven, capable of the same characteristics in intellectual and moral regard damages humanity. At this very hour we are experiencing the horror where the delusion is inflicting incurable wounds on my and your fatherland. But I also reckon the nobleman, the Junker, the rich person among the "folk", and believe that all salvation comes from genius as the direct intermediary of things and, through those things, as the direct intermediary of God.

And now, after that statement of belief, let me thank you wholeheartedly and express the hope that the second half-volume of *Counterpoint* bonds us yet more. Then I have a plan in mind for which I will also request your cooperation—but everything in its time.

With warm regards,
Yours,
H. Schenker[6]

1. Presumably Otto Vrieslander.
2. The postscript states "It was a Württemberg teacher who made me aware of Schenker, thus not a professional musician, not a professional journal, not his publishing house, nor a music retailer." For the person in question, see Halm's letter of July 28, 1921, below.
3. Johann Schenker, "town doctor" in Podhajce, Galicia, who died at the age of 59 in late 1887.
4. Halm, "Heinrich Schenker," *Von Form und Sinn der Musik*, 274: "It is the strongly esoteric approach of Schenker, who addresses only musicians, the knowledgeable and able, and does not quite seem capable of imagining a musical public or even a following, at least according to my impression."
5. Schenker's effusive praise here for Halm, for recognizing the value of the Beethoven editions, contrasts with his criticisms of Halm in the diary entry of March 19, 1914, included above. It is curious that Schenker would now trust the opinion of someone whose musicality he felt was fatally inadequate, as he charges in the diary entry, and then assert that Halm is one of the few who can "see and hear," someone he can talk to as "leader to leader."
6. At this point, a further sheet appears, partly in Schenker's hand, partly in Jeanette's, the content of which is not included in the letter of January 17, 1918, but the latter part of which is interpolated into a letter of September 25, 1922. It may well have been drafted in 1922.

❧ Schenker to Halm (letter), October 27, 1919
DLA 69.930/8

Dear Professor,

It is truly not easy today for someone in the German-Austrian desert to rescue himself in an intellectual oasis. The way that the entire population is being brutalized in an unheard of manner, the individual must also take a beating. Even I suffer unspeakably severely in the knowledge that people here have no prospect of <u>really</u> coming to terms with themselves about it, which is why it had to turn out this way, and so continues. No one here knows what America, France, England, Italy are, what their ability or permissibility is in the best case. With every hour, we fall deeper into the shame of prostitution by foreign countries, relinquish something better in exchange for something worse, in politics as in art and literature.[1] The entire race cannot learn to see, to think—thus it turns out bitter that, instead of Goethe, Herder, Schiller, Lessing, instead of Bach, Mozart, etc., we put first Herzog, Skovronek, Rolland, Anatole France, first *Tristan* and *Elektra*— and a hundred years after Beethoven we have to throw the Bekkers of this world out the door, and two hundred years after Bach you have to write a *Piano Method*.

It is to your honor the way you open the ears of the deaf with it, the way you provide the fingers with understanding and eyes. That beautiful, genuine German love for the subject matter, for the student as connoisseur of art and as—human beings! How all of that expresses itself in every turn of phrase of the beautiful language, which on its own must elevate the pupil, in the handling of each individual problem presented to him. I almost would like to believe that your *Piano Method* will afford the autodidact more blessing than someone who calls on a teacher. <u>Without blaming the teachers</u>, who struggle so arduously with life, I mean that the qualitative illumination unfortunately cannot keep pace with the quantitative increase of this condition, and I fear that your wonderful work, which relieves the teacher of practically all effort, will nevertheless not be able to overcome the law of the "mass." You have done your duty, however, and must now leave it to the world whether or not they follow.

What appealed to me personally was the way you always keep sight of "diminution." Diminution has brought us to the highest level, such that we must consult it above all when we want to arrive at the primordial kernel.[2] The pupil, too, the connoisseur and aficionado must therefore cover the same distance that the composer, that the music, covered.

But—I speak completely freely to you and in doing so want only to honor our relationship—the reason remains foreign to me why, on the question of phrase markings, you do not follow the original, e.g. Mozart, A major sonata, whose theme of course is considered: ♩ ♪ ♩ ♪ , and not: ♩ ♩ ♪ | ♩ ♩ ♪ |. (It is not like that in my copy either.) As a creative artist, you surely have experienced enough firsthand the trickiness of the issue of articulation not to know that it disconcerts and distresses all musicians. First of all, I say: until that issue has been resolved, loyalty to the original has at least fewer dangers, and in my opinion no pupil should be initially shown a different picture than what the author himself specified.

As appropriate as the idea is to guide pupils even at this stage toward, for example, Bach's preludes and inventions, and as wonderfully as you usually sneak up on those treasures, moving from exercise to exercise as well as from association to association, as little advisable, on the other hand, do I find the method of intervening at some point and bringing the pieces to a conclusion. Even in the case of those composers who, like you, rightly base an art-work on voice-leading, that power has not yet reached ultimate elasticity, as would be necessary to continue the tradition of Bach, since in the meantime the Wagner avalanche has descended, and the paths should be rebuilt. For my part, nothing would be more exciting than to discuss in person with you in particular the status of our current voice-leading. What sort of imponderables might come up for discussion, perhaps less tangible in verbalization than oscillating between the miracle of your neural system and the miracle of my neural system, and nevertheless with conclusiveness the most unimaginable result, in the positive as well as in the less positive!

So, perhaps it will come to such a face-to-face conversation. For I want to leave Vienna in order to move to Germany. At least I am so planning, and have the sense of needing to do it as soon as possible in order to save my life and work. If only I were already done with the second half-volume of *Counterpoint*, so that the other works, which are actually already completed, could move forward!

I send you cordial greetings and look forward in advance to the continuation of the *Piano Method*.

    Yours,
        H. Schenker

1. The Treaty of Versailles (in Schenker's mind "atrocious"), signed on June 28, 1919, was registered with the League of Nations on October 21, 1919, just six days before Schenker wrote this letter.
2. As will become clear in Halm's letter of February 1–6, 1924, and Schenker's of April 3, 1924, the two men conceive of diminution and figuration very differently, and therefore misunderstand each other on the subject. Halm is thinking of local, surface embellishments of simple melodic patterns, while Schenker has in mind levels of figuration (diminutions), beginning with "primal intervals" in the background, that embrace and constitute an entire work.

❧ Halm to Schenker (letter), January 11, 1920
OJ 11/35, 15

Dear Professor,

In response to your letter, I could for the moment give my opinion regarding the business matter. I am very happy that your publisher now accepts that you must have a say, or that he will also fare well if he produces something important and lasting. However, the idea of the *Little Library* does not make me happy to the same degree, that is, not necessarily.[1] I mean typical analyses should suffice; only reluctantly do I imagine an entire second existence of works of art in analyses.[2] Based on my needs, I would wish that you might write a history of music, for which up to now we barely have paltry surrogates; and if that is not possible, individual sections of music history, since things of importance are yet wholly unclarified according to my knowledge or supposition (who first employed the cadence, the sequence, with clear awareness of its functional effect? That issue did not concern authors on music history at all!). What I found in that direction in your books very strongly stirred the wish in me that I want to present to you here. The publisher will eagerly go for it, I think. (I know far too little and cannot consider something of that sort, and who other than you should be able to do it?)

With warm greetings and wishes,
Yours,
A. Halm

It occurs to me, additionally, that if you follow through on the possibility of moving to another country, even if it is only Germany, you should assure yourself of regular proceeds instead of a one-time settlement in Austrian currency, and moreover also a percentage of earnings going to other countries, in the relevant currency, including publishers' (and where possible (?) the retailers') mark-up.

1. *Little Library*: working title from 1910 to 1921 for what became *Der Tonwille* in 1921.
2. In the essay "Musik und Volk," in *Von schwäbischer Scholle. Kalendar für schwäbische Literatur und Kunst* (Heilbronn: Eugen Salzer, 1922), 70, Halm spoke disparagingly—and with unwitting accuracy!—of a "proliferation of such analyses" that would "gradually form a large literature, so that at some point opposite the bookcase with masterworks another would stand with analyses of them." See also Halm's *Die Symphonie Anton Bruckners*, 246.

Schenker to Halm (letter), January 18, 1920
DLA 69.930/9

Revered, dear Professor,

Many, many thanks for your lovely letter and for the two enclosures (which I include here).[1] It was a fortunate idea of yours to enclose the original documents. The visual experience in itself was useful to me and had to be if you consider that in my entire life I have achieved almost no justice in reciprocation from the publisher, and only on my own efforts. I knew precisely that the publisher [Universal Edition] was exploiting me, not that he would have taken me for one of those intellectuals who prostitute themselves, who want to see themselves in print at any price. Rather, he figured out immediately that my willingness to be a victim would give him the opportunity to guarantee his advantages optimally. And again I granted him this capitalistic onanism because I knew only one thing, and in the very last moment had to rescue the material of music, the craftsmanship, the voice-leading as much as was still possible. And still today I seek no advantage. But I must protect myself against the publisher's damaging my work on the basis of greed (in which he is endlessly absorbed) if he does not promote it. To him, what are all my plans and projects that ought to be carried out yet, what is my health as the precondition for the possibility of work in general, if on account of it he loses pleasure in being able to pay, for example, 1,000, 1,200 kronen for an existing work? I therefore have to act myself on behalf of the capital, as does the capitalist, and in order to bring in interest and compound interest for the publisher, defiantly, fighting against his incompetence; I have to extract better working conditions,[2] particularly today, when in an era of world foolishness, notably only the American dollar counts, no longer alongside it the kroner, the mark.

So, for *Op. 101* I satisfied myself with 15,000 kronen (approximately 5,000 marks). That the publisher agreed to it turned out retrospectively to be a ruse, a bait. For with the *Little Library* he planned to reduce his capitalistic "accommodation." But even at 600 kronen per gathering of the *Little Library* (up to 5,000 copies, and then again 600 kronen) I would have agreed in the end for the sake of the project, had I no reason to better protect myself as an object of the publisher's exploitation. For what use to someone obsessed with the bottom line is an author who has fallen ill? And so it is certainly not in the intellectual world as it is in the non-intellectual one, where one who withdraws can be replaced arbitrarily by another. The matter is not yet settled. The publisher has the say.

What you say about the content of the *Little Library* stirred me deeply. As I believe I have already written, the most important thing is the second half-volume of *Counterpoint*, in which the voice-leading of free composition and its complete identity with so-called strict counterpoint is discovered and verified. *Semper idem, sed non eodem modo* illuminates every section.[3] That same motto [applies] to three-voice strict counterpoint, through four- and multi-voice counterpoint, through mixed species to free composition, and again in the sections on scale-steps, composing-out, voice-leading, parallel fifths and octaves, passing tone, suspension, keyboard settings and reductions, figured bass, chorale, and so forth. Solely for the sake of that verification have I been holding back for years material ready for publication in the scope of a book; for, what I do not expect to achieve through any form of argumentation, I do expect to achieve through the purely outward effect of juxtaposing strict and free composition in the same volume. Readers will sooner believe their <u>eyes</u>, and all is won if musicians penetrate with me to the "primordial sources" and encounter there an eternal, more indestructible unity in whose name they will have to cease setting the worlds of strict and free composition in opposition to one another, and speaking of rules and exceptions.

Only from the feeling of such unity do geniuses create endlessness and diversity in the individual. But the rest of the world? The individual element must also close itself off from it [the world] if it does not somehow knock, if ever so gently, at the door of the mystery of primordial laws. Consequently, as you will therefore understand, analyses were and are for me merely <u>examples</u> from that paradise of unity. And with you I share most intimately a certain disinclination to allow musicians to eat too much from the tree of knowledge. At least for us the paradise of art would long remain a paradise once another has been lost to us. However, when I consider that nothing bears guilt for the decline of our art as much as the <u>all too</u> Adam-and-Eve-ness of humanity that enjoyed itself in the Eden of our greatest masters; as much as the <u>rupture</u> in the <u>organ for music</u> that no longer permits the unity of the vertical and horizontal to emerge, then I am involuntarily driven to assist with another and yet another example.... How blissfully could humanity enjoy life and fulfill its divine image if it only knew how to draw the immediate analogy, fashioned by humanity itself, between the continuity of the races and a similar continuity in the intellectual dimension, instead of offending the eternity of primordial laws with the restless addiction to new starting points as ostensible sources of new primordial laws. There would still be enough room in the world of our geniuses for a thousand others, but no! People do not summon the strength to make that connection.[4]

A history of music would above all have to show precisely the unity in the geniuses as well. However, to write it presupposes that the <u>unity</u> has already been verified in the primordial laws, in the material. Completing that precondition is, as you see, my most fervent aspiration, and you can believe me that I would then gladly also like to show the fate of the primordial laws as it was experienced by artists over the course of the centuries. However, will that be granted to me in a world that no longer even proves adequate in the simplest things, and falls into a second "Egyptian" darkness[5] against which the first one was the clearest brightness of summer?

If I were only free from giving lessons, I would attempt anything! The tragedy is that the possibility of leading a life devoted solely to work actually exists, to a certain degree exists <u>readily</u>, but that nevertheless those fail who for reasons of rationality, of decency, also of bloodline, would surely have to let themselves be appointed to what is for them an effortless enterprise.

We shall see.

I share most joyfully in your successes. The purity of your efforts must command respect from anyone, even from an "objective" opponent—though if only such knew how objectivity speaks in your favor. I happily read of the declaration of respect from Furtwängler, who so often comes to Vienna.[6]

Once again, in closing let me express my sincere thanks for your wonderful attitude and add my hearty greetings,

    Yours,
    H. Schenker

---

1. Schenker is referring to Halm's letters of January 5 (not included here) and January 11, 1920. The enclosures were two publishers' contracts, which Schenker was to return soon by registered mail.
2. Schenker means his own circumstances, particularly the need to teach so many private piano students to make a living. He had been pleading for more than a decade for a government subsidy in order to reduce the number of students and devote more time to editing and theoretical work, as expressed in this letter.
3. "Always the same but not in the same way," Schenker's motto, appears on the title pages of *Der Tonwille*, *Free Composition*, and elsewhere.
4. Schenker means the connection (musically) between the horizontal and the vertical as well as between strict and free composition, and by extension (socially) between the propagation of life and intellectual thought.
5. i.e. one of the ten plagues of Egypt (*Exodus* 10:21–22).
6. A lost letter of Halm that mentions Furtwängler, or one from the conductor to Schenker, must have preceded the present one. The first time that Halm mentions Furtwängler in the known letters is on February 10, 1920. There Halm writes, "If only Furtwängler would once perform something of mine. I was actually surprised when you wrote me that he spoke favorably to you about my pieces. When I was once with him, while acknowledging this and that, on the whole he spoke in a, for me, less than hopeful manner. I also played badly, as easily happens to me when I sense resistance."

Halm to Schenker (letter), July 28, 1921
OJ 11/35, 19

Dear and revered Professor,

A Mr. Matthäus Henz, now a senior teacher (title is probably "lecturer") in the teacher's college in Heilbronn on the Neckar, first made me aware of your works, specifically of the Beethoven sonatas, individual editions.[1] He is a scientist and mathematician by profession. He will surely be extraordinarily happy about the intended gift. But I believe that it would be musically more fruitfully placed with my friend Schmid, senior teacher and music director [at the teacher's college] in Nagold (Württemberg).[2]

None of the mentioned items has yet reached me. I no longer live in Esslingen but in Wickersdorf near Saalfeld on the Saale, Thuringia. Did I write you that in May I heard my large C major concerto performed by Fritz Busch in Stuttgart?[3] The success at the concert was very good; in the newspapers, mixed and mostly dull or even less! It was performed in October for the first time in Ulm, where I played the piano part (so that I heard too little of the whole). I am happy that I am here (in the Free School Community). That Cotta is giving up *Counterpoint* makes me sorry insofar as I was happy that the old Swabian publisher was issuing something important and of grand style.[4]

But if that way it is more advantageous for you, then it is naturally also preferable to me. I was rather productive in winter. Maybe I shall also find a publisher soon.

            Cordial greetings from your
            A. Halm

[1] i.e. Schenker's elucidatory editions, likely to have been the "gift" referred to two sentences later.

[2] Theodor Karl Schmid (1876–1963): a long-time friend of Halm, was a major force at the Nagold Teachers' Institute and had a significant impact on the musical life in Nagold (c. 32 miles southwest of Stuttgart). Schmid closely followed Halm's music-educational model.

[3] Fritz Busch (1890–1951): music director at the Stuttgart Opera beginning shortly after the end of World War I. In 1922 he became music director at the Dresden State Opera. Halm's Concerto in C major for large orchestra with obbligato piano was published in 1913 (Stuttgart: Zumsteeg) under the auspices of the Society for the Publication of the Works of August Halm, founded in that year.

[4] See chapter 6.

❦ Halm to Schenker (letter), July 24 and August 19, 1922
OJ 11/35, 20

Dear and revered Professor,

I think of you often when I read something from Vienna (but not only then), and worry about how you might be doing. But when I then look at the postage on Austrian letters, I think that one should not prompt anyone to an avoidable letter. (Which of course also applies to us). I am very happy that I can announce to you a new publication: of three suites for violin, cello, and piano, two of which will appear together in one volume, which you should receive from me immediately after printing.[1] I have already asked the publisher to take care of this. I hope you will receive it before Christmas. The galley proofs have been definitively corrected.

            August 19, 1922

The letter was not ready after all before my little vacation trip. In the meantime I received the second [half]-volume of your *Counterpoint*. I thank you heartily for your valuable gifts. The more I am aware of how little system there was in my works as a whole (I do not mean individually), the more I admire the power of broad conception and, in execution, of the extensive, highly active patience to which your individual works testify, even apart from their great value separately. I do not want to fault myself on that count or to belittle that I mostly just seized on coincidence, and you should certainly not think that in false modesty I am fishing for consolation or a compliment. In principle, I am not dissatisfied with the course of my works, and it is in any case according to my nature. But the sight of a systematic and strong-willed strategist capable of extended breadth is to me the more valuable, since I am simply completely different. And as certain as you feel that, in emerging and then appearing, your works were impeded and delayed by all kinds of external constraints and publishers' stupidity, perhaps also publishers' malice, you can certainly be sure that with your output you grant that exemplary and invigorating perspective to an uncommonly high degree.

Our yellow community school volumes [Die freie Schulgemeinde] are ceasing. I hope to offer one review (short, somewhat in summary, as it will work no other way) in the farewell issue, which however is not altogether assured.

In truth, I have to tell you that your attacks on England and its supporters and your glorification of Germany are distressing to me. First, I find it unjustified that from the perspective of our former enemies (who to some extent continue the enmity contemptuously, to be sure!) we are punished as a people for the [errors] doubtless committed by our government, and moreover that there is in part no end to it. Conversely, it is also not right when we now view the French government (I name it as the main enemy at the time) as the French people. At some point, somewhere, people have to stop this ethnic hatred. And if that should be much more difficult for the conquered and actually betrayed than for the conquerors, then we prove our better quality by making a start nevertheless. And we were and are lied to or misled also from our own side. When I read in Harden[2] (whom I certainly do not like—I was pleased, by the way, by two reviews of yours, on Smetana and Italian opera performances in past issues of Die Zukunft that a colleague gave me to read), a speech by [Aristide] Briand in original wording, for instance: how different, how much more level-headed, more moderate, more educated it sounds than the excerpts and reports in daily newspapers allow one to surmise. In short, if one cannot read the most diverse newspapers all day, especially foreign ones as well, we know far too little to be capable of having a fundamental account for judgment. Second, I value the spirit and the accomplishments of French art far more than you, but do not dispute, and even believe, that German music is in first place. That can mean pre-eminence for German music, but it can also be that it comes at the expense of other music when a genius arises in Germany. So it seems to me, when I think of the Russians, who as a folk strike me as more musical than the Germans, but who do not rise as high with respect to their geniuses. In our case, grand elevations from the deep lowland (which of course does not hold for the Middle Ages). There, and probably also in Italy, the higher plateau.[3] Practically speaking, we of course may not grant that any validity, i.e. we may not sacrifice the educational enterprise, must carry on "as though." And you surely also emphasize openly enough the fact of German lowlands and marshes and foggy regions without holding back. But the calling to a leading role does not follow for Germany from the fact of a larger number of superior geniuses in Germany.

In particular: I do not reckon the song "I Stood in Dark Dreams" as good music, and verification of the Urlinie as well as of many refinements is for me still no proof that I am wrong.[4] But I cannot expound more fully on that now. For me it is similar to the late Beethoven sonatas in A major [Op. 101] (also A♭ major [Op. 110]), which just simply do not fully convince me (emotionally). The Beethoven fugue type ranks very high for me. Beethoven fulfilled it, as I think, only in the "Hammerklavier" Sonata [Op. 106], in the great B♭ major fugue [Op. 133] for string quartet, and probably in the finale of the late D major sonata for cello and piano [Op. 102, No. 2]. Certainly, you have opened my eyes to many good features precisely in those pieces that are internally foreign to me, and I feel gratitude for that, even with some opposition.

Your proposal about what a history of music would have to illuminate meets a need of mine. I have already tried something similar but did not identify so many of the questions, nor the order. And something else: what I wrote above also goes for the announced mailing, in another way. I assume that they (i.e. my suites) will reach you just about at the time when you are in the middle of urgent work. Then don't be disturbed, and wait as long as it suits with writing. That I am not indifferent to what you say about them is surely clear from my whole attitude toward you so that I do not need to give assurances, and even a somewhat less favorable critique coming from you would be for me a sign of a support. We have frequently played the music here [in Wickersdorf]; it is part of the chamber music collection of our school community.

Our publishers are unfortunately not as prudent as Universal Edition, which apparently notices that publications are after all now among the safer and better "securities." My new publisher, G. Kallmeyer, is a dear and decent man, and thinks highly of me. Not very strong in capital, unfortunately, he cannot risk much at one time, otherwise he would publish more from me right away. But I really do not have anything to risk myself, and have no business troubles at all in the matter.

Earlier, you wanted to move to Germany. Have you postponed the plan or given it up altogether? At our school we are still getting along rather well, but no one knows how long we can hold up to the inflation crisis.[5]

       With cordial greetings and wishes,
         Yours,
           August Halm

---

[1] Halm, *Kammermusik*, vols. 2–3 (Wolfenbüttel: Zwissler, 1922), contains piano trios in D major, C major, and B minor. The first suite had already appeared as a supplement in the *Neue Musikzeitung* xl (1919).

[2] Maximilian Harden (Felix Ernst Witkowski, 1861–1927): one of the foremost political journalists in Wilhelmine Germany. He founded the periodical *Die Zukunft*, which appeared 1892–1923, and to which Schenker contributed articles and reviews, and with whom he corresponded 1892–95.

[3] In a lengthy response dated September 25, 1922 (not included here), Schenker followed up on various topics that Halm addresses here, in paragraphs headed "Briand," "Harden," "People's Government," "Things French," and "Higher Plateaux."

[4] Schenker published an analysis of "Ihr Bild" (*Schwanengesang*, No. 9) in *Tonwille* 1, vol. I, 41–43 (Ger. orig., 46–49).

[5] Between June and December 1922 the German currency fell from 320 marks to the dollar to 800 to the dollar. A year later, in November 1923, at the height of hyperinflation in the Weimar Republic, a one-pound loaf of bread cost 3 billion marks, a glass of beer 4 billion, a pound of meat 36 billion.

Halm to Schenker (letter), November 6–10, 1923
OC 12/7–9

Dear and revered Professor,

Your postcard very much delighted me. Just in recent days I gave a Wickersdorf teacher traveling to Vienna a newly published score of a string quartet for you (the score will be delivered to you there); the printing of the parts is not yet finished.[1] I received from friends some "largesse" (as the grand-sounding term puts it) as a gift for the purpose of publishing my music and with it was able to issue volumes 4–6 of *Chamber Music*. That is now done. Gifts for that purpose I accept without hesitation. However, I view the intent of your concert differently, such that I not be considered for it, since for the time being I do not belong to the needy among artists.[2]

To be sure, up to now we often have had difficulties in our Free School Community, but in the end always have been able, more or less well, to overcome them. Our food is nourishing and sufficient, quite good comparatively. We were cold to some degree, but tolerable in order to save our heating reserves for the winter. The newest complications together with plunging currency value caused us worry, but we hope that we can hold out. In spring I am going to give a few lectures in Switzerland. Professor Dr. Ernst Kurth in Bern, who holds my books and my music in high regard, has promoted it.[3]

My small assets, around 30,000 marks in peacetime, have of course become worthless. I don't think about it much. I will continue my projects as long as I can. Currently I am working on the orchestra score of a larger symphony, which is supposed to be performed in fall 1924 in Stuttgart (in the summer I played the sketch for the resident conductor, Leonhardt).[4] My C major concerto and an overture were planned for a concert in Berlin, which, however, apparently will not take place, at least not for the time being.

For our performances of plays here, I have over time written some music that I would like to publish, with small-scale instrumentation (flute, string quartet, piano), accessible for a trained orchestra. *A Midsummer Night's Dream*, *The Winter's Tale*, *Cymbeline*, *The Tempest* (the overture and the reveler's canon from *As You Like It* appeared some time ago in a volume of the now defunct *Freie Schulgemeinde*; I assume that I sent them to you at the time).[5] And additionally music for several pieces by [Martin] Luserke.[6] I think a publisher would not do badly with them—I don't expect any idealism at all from publishers. To my mind, if they understood more about their business and had instinct and knowledge of human nature, both sides would be helped.

I have learned some good things from your volumes of *Der Tonwille*, and I thank you for the enrichment of my knowledge and conception. What you say about Bach's C♯ [*recte* F♯] major Prelude made the biggest impression on me.[7] I do not know whether these theories have achieved any influence on my compositional invention and design. I believe one cannot actually adopt something like that and resolve to think in that manner. Further, I would not accept deriving a final decision from it. Supposing that Bruckner does not possess the Urlinie, I would still leave open whether that is a fault, and accordingly a deficiency in his music, or whether it is the necessary obverse of his virtues—to which I would hold now as before.[8] I would first have to investigate it. In general, I believe we would be outright opponents in narrower but important technical areas if we did not feel the common hate for the rack and ruin (whose dimension certainly first became clear to me in full measure through your writings, above all through your Beethoven editions.).

Only recently I learned that my book on Bruckner's [treatment of the] symphony properly appeared in a new edition last summer (improved in certain places). I had feared that the publisher could have suspended the edition because of inflation. If you are interested, I will have it sent to you. I am lacking some comment from you on my music, but without therefore being annoyed at you because I do know how much you are occupied with urgent projects. Still, over time I have gotten something like a suspicion that you may not exactly be in agreement with these pieces, which would be a shame for me, to be sure, but could in no way alienate me from you and your work. For that reason, however, I have not had further publications sent to you, until (about half a week before the arrival of your postcard) I gave Miss Neumann the newly printed string quartet to take with her on her trip.[9] I thought you might like it. If you are interested in having the intervening publications—I mean, if my music is of some value to you, even if you do not completely agree with it—then just say the word and I will have them sent to you. The parts to the new string quartet (it is, by the way, about three, four, or five years old) are not yet available. Would you like to have the parts? The last thing I had sent to you was, I believe, *Chamber Music* vol. 2 and *Hausmusik* vol. 18 (string trio, score). *Hausmusik* is a supplement to the *Musicians Guild*, various authors in it. Do you have my sonatas for solo violin (*Hausmusik* vols. 9–10)?[10] Kallmeyer, the proprietor of the publishing house I. Zwissler, is a nice and kind man. Unfortunately, he does not have very much money such that he could publish a lot right now. Otherwise he would certainly publish more by me. As I already wrote, *Chamber Music* vols. 4–6 was made possible through gifts, as well as the songs of the fool in *As you Like It*. *Chamber Music* vol. 2 should actually attract string players because those suites, actually duets with piano accompaniment, allow larger gestures for strings than does the style of the classical piano trios in general. Even if accomplished virtuosos do not want to include them in their programs, it would surely be fine material for concert programs of music schools. Last winter we played it in Leipzig, as well as three Serenades for string trio. In between I played the Prelude and Fugue in C minor from my fourth volume of piano music.

Socialism must come, whether we like it or not, as a historical necessity; and if we resist it, it will only come more toxically. So it seems to me. The Bavarians are wreaking havoc, whether they triumph or succumb or retreat.[11] If Germany wants to come apart, then it already no longer exists. One can't glue together a nation.[12]

        With cordial greetings,
           Yours,
              A. Halm

1. Halm's String Quartet in A major, published in *Kammermusik* 6 (Wolfenbüttel: Zwissler, 1923).
2. The reference to a concert organized by Schenker ("your concert") is probably a misunderstanding on Halm's part because there is no indication elsewhere (in Schenker's diary or other letters) of such a concert.
3. Ernst Kurth (1886–1946): Viennese musicologist trained under Guido Adler, author of significant monographs on Bach's "linear counterpoint," Wagner's romantic harmony as modeled in *Tristan und Isolde*, and Bruckner's symphonic form. Numerous letters passed between Halm and Kurth about a lecture or series of invited lectures on Bruckner, going back to December 1920, and then continuing through early 1924. However, the lectures never materialized.
4. Carl Leonhardt (1886–1969): General Music Director of the Württemberg State Theater in Stuttgart, 1922–37, and conducting teacher at the Stuttgart Music Hochschule up until 1945. He was well known as a conductor of Wagner's operas. The symphony, in A major, remains unpublished. A recording appeared in 2004 (Sterling CDS-1064-2).
5. *A Midsummer Night's Dream* (Wolfenbüttel: Zwissler, 1924), *Cymbeline* (Augsburg: Bärenreiter, 1927), *As You Like It* (ibid., 1927).
6. Martin Luserke (1880–1968): novelist and story writer, colleague of Halm's at the Hermann Lietz Country Boarding School in Haubinda, and at Wickersdorf from its founding in 1906.
7. "The Art of Listening", *Tonwille* 3, vol. I, 118–20 (Ger. orig., 22–25), actual publication date January 19, 1923, features the F♯ major Prelude from the *Well-tempered Clavier*, Book I.
8. Halm mentions the Urlinie in connection with Bruckner in *Einführung in die Musik* (Berlin: Deutsche Buch-Gemeinschaft, 1926), 75.
9. Fräulein Neumann: a Wickersdorf colleague.
10. *Kammermusik*, vols. 2–4 (Wolfenbüttel: Zwissler, 1922); *Hausmusik*, vols. 9–10, 18 (ibid., 1921, 1923).
11. Halm is probably referring to the Bierkeller Putsch, November 8, 1923. A march of 3,000 Nazis the next day met with police resistance and led to Hitler being tried and imprisoned.
12. Lee Rothfarb, "Halm and Schenker: Culture, Politics, Aesthetics," in *Festschrift Hellmut Federhofer zum 100. Geburtstag*, ed. Axel Beer (Tutzing: Schneider, 2011), 401–17, discusses political differences between the two men.

🎻 Halm to Schenker (letter), February 1–6, 1924
OC 12/10–12

Don't be startled at the long letter, nothing in it is urgent!

Dear and revered Professor,

I would accept your Beethoven edition with much gratitude. Of them I own the ones that appeared first, sonatas *Op. 109, Op. 110, Op. 111*, and otherwise none. I will send you the second edition of my *Culture* book and the Bruckner book as printed material. You are going to write me yet about what you already have of my chamber music, and whether you are interested in having the parts of the A major string quartet. Up to now, the *Tonwille* volumes have always been sent to me by the publisher.

Improvisation as the foundation and motivation for creativity has long been important to me, and your various discussions and commentaries in that direction have reinforced and illuminated that insight. The awareness, too, that I am deficient in that regard, and that one must also detect it in my music, has not escaped me. Over time, I have learned various things and sometimes I can improvise such that I myself thought that it could be enjoyable. Others thought better of it and said it was some ready-composed piece "by someone." But I know better. Recently, I improvised a fugue (for the second time in my life) so that I was tolerably satisfied. What I at first lacked, and had to laboriously acquire, is good figuration, and it should be no surprise to me if that were still not up to snuff.[1] Oh, but dear Professor, from the start I had difficulties with my role models. In part, I did not understand them and therefore underestimated their artistry in figuration. In part, even now it is for me not yet convincing, in part I was missing that which makes the art of figuration difficult, and sought it on my own. Even today I have not come to terms with the classicists. I can say that I have come to admire them ever more (also very much through you!), and that they have still probably not gotten any closer to me (or I to them) because of it. I have virtually hated Beethoven's Fifth Symphony—no, but, perceived as an adversary, it is to me today entirely alien. And when what you say about it is correct ten times over. For my part, I am prepared (and always was) to find some genius in it. You see, I simply have need for a certain lifestyle, or race in music, corporeality, which for my sensibility is expressed above all in dynamic rhythm.[2] All artistry, even the whole art of voice-leading, does not replace for me what I miss here—does not befriend me when something repels me. I seek to implement this corporeality in my music, and in my judgment have come so close to it that one can see and feel it. That is above all important to me. I try to avoid shortcomings in individual designs, or to remedy them. Some things may inhere in the type itself, thus unavoidable. That is not always easy to distinguish. I believe I am capable of highest candor with regard to my works, and similarly capable of valuing candor from others, even if it is against my music. I assess my musical talent carefully. The simplest things have sometimes been so difficult for me to grasp that I see myself as barely above average (at times it was better).[3] However, regarding my artistic, productive nature—I simply believe in it, and without wavering for some time now. Or rather I believe in the image of music toward which I strive. I do not believe in that of Brahms, to name one example, whether he executed it perfectly or imperfectly (I have not yet pursued that question). Openings such as that of his F major symphony or F minor piano sonata suffice to alienate me completely. His Requiem is to me in great part almost tormenting, in part unbearable.)[4]

That you rank Brahms so highly gave me a rather painful jolt at first, and still today I think: could it be that, in this point, you are looking only at the *natura naturata*, but not at the *natura naturans*?[5] Granted that I see the former here as inadequate, compared to you even as entirely inadequate. But why do I know Brahms so inadequately? Because he does not induce me to pursue him.[6] Beethoven, recently entirely foreign to me, just never lets me go, belongs to my conscience, is for me even more important than Mozart as a standard, was often for me an exhorting (so to speak my evil) conscience. It thus does not have to be mere narrowness, prejudice of my own conception if I do not want to tackle something, or can't want to. Bruckner's musical conception is certainly very different from mine (and I consider it <u>substantially</u> higher than mine!) (By the way: You perhaps heard Bruckner's organ improvisations, which were so renowned. I would like to know whether you also rate them so highly, especially his fugue improvisations, I mean from the technical standpoint. Not as though I would not credit him with something good, and very good, but I do not trust those who have given reports, and would therefore like to ask someone whom I trust.) With that, I come to the subject of pernicious chord progression, even more to that of modulatory succession (both of which I see fulfilled in Bruckner most beautifully and nobly). It is—independent, arbitrary, egotistical, it has become a danger and has destroyed precious things, has introduced outright stupification into music (I cannot call Reger's music overall anything other than stupid, but I know only very little by him. But if he were to have ended up in a different time, would he not have chosen some other stupidity, would he not have made stupid some other good things? Is he the victim of chord progression and not, rather, of his lack of intelligence?)[7] Unfortunately, I know chaotic improvisation from experience with others and myself, where a type of frogspawn comes about through senseless stringing together of progressions (be it even nice ones), and many, alas, also compose that way. The question is whether this historical necessity can mean a transition, whether these forces that came to light can be overcome, utilized, elevated. Simply switching them off, ignoring them, will not work, and wagging your finger does not help much—"you may venture this far, but not this far."[8] I am very much in favor of the clearest balance; one should know what one is perpetrating, where one errs, be it necessary, be it avoidable. And if we could talk in person, I would emphatically request that you indicate to me exactly individual passages as examples of where and how I fail. That is too cumbersome in writing to request that of you. By contrast, I will make a suggestion. If you find in my music (or in [Reinhard] Oppel's or elsewhere) an especially instructive example of failure, rupturing, breakdown, a passage where one can say: the non-genius reveals itself here—if you find such a thing, would you not want to discuss such a passage in an essay in the *Tonwille* volumes? Particularly with music that otherwise comes close to good music, or otherwise <u>would be</u> good music, it would be especially informative. You won't misunderstand this wish, possibly as though I wanted to at least garner public rebuke if I can reap no public praise. I don't think I can accept, i.e. <u>use to advantage</u>, just any rebuke, even if it convinces me. How much have I found to be vulnerable in the great masters, without thinking, therefore, that a correction is possible. Where I have confidence that I can come up with something better, I try it out.

Recently, in the first fugue of my first volume of piano pieces I almost completely reworked the counterpoint, in part awkward, in part bad, that has weighed on my mind for some time, whether with successful results I don't want to decide yet. My suggestion is entirely sincere, and if you also think that you can achieve greater clarity for others (that should certainly be a lot better than if you overtly mention a void as a contrast), then in any case I would like to explain that a rebuke from you is worth serious consideration, that my appreciation of your work would not be tarnished through your qualified acknowledgment, or even through stronger rejection of my music (for me, that would assuredly play a far lesser role than your doubts about Bruckner, your lack of doubts about Brahms, and similar things), and that I am personally almost indifferent about whether my music deserves to have genius or non-genius attributed to it, perhaps even entirely indifferent. What I wish is only that it be known and played, so that its strength, its prospect for value, can at least be put to the test. I am not thinking here of effect "on" but rather of the impact of the conception, the productive power of the idea, so to speak, from which this music springs. However, if according to you I appear to greatly overestimate my own music—which I absolutely assume—then it is perhaps conversely possible that your attitude toward me will be tarnished. I will just have to let that depend, i.e., I would have to show my colors according to your comments (I have not even said everything yet, but still enough). For your support, so valuable to me, should not be based on illusion. It would perhaps even be time now, and could really be of value, if we were to have it out publicly in a debate* (but not about my music!)— but I don't want to publish any more if I don't really have to.

      With cordial greetings,
        Yours,
          A. Halm

Indeed, I have a lot on my mind against you, and I could really be in the mood for a feud in which two opponents want to seek what is right, though without wanting to be proved right.[9] You discuss the opening chord of the Scherzo of Bruckner's Ninth Symphony. Why don't you also look into the continuation? In measure 35 it reappears in second inversion (how wonderfully the first inversion is circumvented, made unrecognizable!)—everything in between is passing, and everything held together through the firmly fixed leading tone, C♯—a case similar (for me, however, nicer) to the beginning of the C minor sonata, Op. III [of Beethoven]. And how many refinements in the harmonic rhythm, then too the complication of the second inversion with apparent reminder of the jolt near the end of the first movement, E♭ minor–D minor chord, still prominent in memory, and the E♭ major chord imposing itself repeatedly right before the final D minor of the first movement.

    Another question: You apparently do not know my book *Of Boundaries and Countries of Music*[10] (collected essays by that very unfortunate title, as reliable people tell me—with it I just wanted to express that I, too, have placed myself on the periphery and, in part, outside of it). I once pointed out to you a discussion about the strange *sforzatos* (which on first glance are in the wrong place) in the Finale of the [Beethoven] D minor Sonata, Op. 31. Or do you actually have the book?[11] I don't have any more copies, but would arrange for my publisher to send it to you. You will surely get angry about some things in it.

    Brahms: You don't simply take me to be blind and deaf. How gladly I admire the first tonal exposition in the C minor Quartet. But the <u>gesture</u> of the theme! No, and ten times no. And not a bit of Yes mixed in. The gesture, the gesture, the lacking corporeality! With Beethoven, [the gesture] is for me also frequently inimical—but certainly even there, it is convincing, natural, "how existing!"[12]

Then another request: read in the Bruckner book (second edition—even if you are already familiar with the first edition) first the analysis on p. 147 etc. [of the Finale of Bruckner's Second Symphony], which I have significantly improved. Then, the likewise improved section, p. 173 etc. [of the opening of Bruckner's Fourth Symphony, and the Finale and Adagio of the Seventh], then the Afterword (p. 242).[13]

This letter has taken on the disordered character of a diary. I want to consider one more point. You see, almost all of our great masters could not play the violin, and I detect that. Mozart could <u>also</u> play the violin. He was probably capable of a lot, Haydn presumably the same—but both "part time." Beethoven could barely play the violin (I know, I know). Handel could play, yes, but Bach alone could <u>really</u> play, with whole heart and family lineage. I am convinced that he played his solo sonatas with pleasure and with superiority. Should I be deceiving myself in that matter, it isn't of greatest importance. In any case, those sonatas arise idiomatically for the violin like nothing else in the entire literature. Bach alone felt (besides what others also felt) the youthful vitality, the <u>surging</u> force of the violin tone (next to him, it seems to me, comes Haydn, but at a very, very large gap removed from him). (Parenthetically, it is a <u>great comfort</u> to me that you speak often and with so much fondness of Haydn. I sometimes wished to write about him. That is among the things I deny myself.) When you speak of improvisation, you probably think of the piano or perhaps the organ. When I have improvised on the piano, as I said, I was usually dissatisfied with myself. But it seemed to me really lame when I tried it on the violin (it has gotten better with violin but the relationship of the one to the other gave me a lot to think about). Have you noticed that violinists, when they try out an instrument, almost without exception "fantasize" in a minor key (to my recollection I have not yet encountered an exception)? That it is usually D minor has a technical reason, because they can slide so beautifully over the fourth A–D on the G-string (or even more beautifully A–C♯ with the first finger). But the fact that it is minor: yes, because no melodic material is prescribed for them, therefore pathos and tragedy are churned out into the void. The violin is the sternest touchstone for melodic gold. Viewed differently: do you seriously believe that Beethoven, indeed even Mozart, could have written an entire sonata for solo violin? I don't. I even believe definitely that they could not have done it—unless after a prior act of penance, indeed only after pronounced repentance (μετάνοια, change of mind/heart). So that there is no error: my sonatas for solo violin are small-scale, modest music, intended in no way to compete. Those of Reger are, as far as I know them, a misunderstanding.

---

[1] In this and the following paragraphs we see again how differently from Schenker Halm conceives of improvisation. Schenker clearly recognizes the marked difference and addresses it, accordingly, in his letter of April 3, 1924. Halm is thinking of local, surface-level melodic embellishments, not the deep, subsurface diminutions of primal intervals that Schenker has in mind.

2 On corporeality, see Halm, *Die Symphonie Anton Bruckners*, 14, 166, *Einführung in die Musik*, 39–40, and "Musikalische Erziehung III," in *Von Form und Sinn der Musik*, 210; also Lee Rothfarb, "August Halm on Body and Spirit in Music," *19th-Century Music* 29, no. 2 (2005): 123–25, and *August Halm*, 95, 128, 244.

3 On Halm's decidedly modest self-assessment, see Rothfarb, *August Halm*, 38, 209.

4 Halm was mercilessly critical of Brahms, e.g. in "Anton Bruckner," *Musikblätter des 'Neuen Österreich'* 2, no. 4 [1917], where Brahms is "the classicist with a bad conscience," or "the bad conscience of the classicists" (*Von Form und Sinn der Musik*, 176). Further, "What wannabe openings, indeed, that of the F minor sonata and F major symphony of Brahms! Clattering is a part of the trade, they say. What—is the sonata supposed to have become a trade?" (*Von Form und Sinn der Musik*, 177).

5 On Halm's references to the notions of *natura naturata* and *natura naturans*, see Rothfarb, *August Halm*, 117–19, 128, 173, 241 fn. 57, as well as Alexander Rehding's essay, "August Halm's Two Cultures as Nature," in *Music Theory and Natural Order from the Renaissance to the Early Twentieth Century*, ed. Suzannah Clark and Alexander Rehding (Cambridge: Cambridge University Press, 2001), 159.

6 In "Triviality and Mastery" (*Der Kunstwart* 40, no. 2 [1927]: 148), Halm says Brahms is a case of involuntary self-exposure, blindsided by his otherwise suppressed natural instincts, which are disposed toward triviality and banality. However, he is also "disposed toward cultivated, conscious taste, and elevated aspiration." Such composers may reach a "true peak in art," but they sometimes forget themselves and show their true face, as in Brahms's "Holder klingt der Vogelsang," Op. 71, No. 5.

7 Halm criticized Reger's music harshly in various publications, among them "Der Führer Max Reger und die Ästhetik," *Süddeutsche Zeitung*, March 6, 1914 (insert), reproduced in *Von Form und Sinn der Musik*, 275–77. See also ibid., 179, 246, 252, 256; Halm, *Beethoven* (Berlin: Max Hesse Verlag, 1927), 193.

8 It is curious that Halm argues on behalf of modernist composers, or at least in favor of tolerance toward them, in light of his staunchly anti-modernist essays, one of 1924, the year of this letter, titled "Fortschrittler oder Altgläuber: Ein Gespräch" [Progressivist or Traditionalist: A Conversation], *Die Musikantengilde* 2 (1924): 61–70; the other one year later, "Müssen wir mitmachen? Gedanken über Musik und Zeit" [Do We Have to Join In? Thoughts about Music and Time], *Die Grüne Fahne* 2 (1925): 18–26. The two appear in Halm's *Einführung in die Musik* (Berlin: Deutsche Buch-Gemeinschaft, 1926), 310–34, with the title word "Fortschrittler" changed to "Neutöner." The "Neutöner" essay is reprinted in *Von Form und Sinn der Musik*, 319–27.

9 In a diary entry of February 16, 1924, a no doubt bemused Schenker calls Halm "childish" for his futile struggles and defiance in this letter against the music of Beethoven and Brahms, and advocacy of Bruckner.

10 Halm, *Von Grenzen und Ländern der Musik* (Munich: Georg Müller, 1916).

11 Halm refers here to a discussion in his anthology of essays, *Von Grenzen und Ländern der Musik*, 158–62, of parts of the last movement of Beethoven's "Tempest" Sonata, Op. 31, No. 2.

12 "Wie seiend!" is a phrase from Goethe's *Italian Journey*, Part 1, Venice (October 9, 1786), where Goethe expresses his deep admiration for animal life at the seashore: "A living creature is such an exquisite, magnificent thing! How adapted to its condition, how true, how existing!"

13 In the Afterword of the 2nd edn. (1923), 243–44, Halm discusses Schenker's negative view of Bruckner because of lacking large-scale synthesis. In defense, Halm

concludes that Bruckner does not need classical-style figurations. "He does not think in figurations, or only seldom; and he does not perchance replace meaningful figurations of the classicists (not always evident there either) with meaningless and empty ones."

🙢 Halm to Schenker (letter), March 15 and April 1, 1924
OC 12/13–14

Dear, revered Professor,

I will begin my letter on the offensive, that is, on the defensive. At the next opportunity I plan to refute what you write about Berlioz in issue 5 of *Der Tonwille*, would like first and initially, however, to express personally my feeling that such derogatory condemnation is not permissible without specifying precisely what is meant or, if you mean the entirety of Berlioz's melodic practice, without saying that explicitly.[1] Examples would be necessary here, and they should be <u>discussed</u>, the failures should be presented. And even then one should consider whether the same clarity cannot be achieved with less harsh language. You can believe that I find some silly things in Brahms if I give in to my natural disinclination toward him. I would rather not do that publicly if it is not absolutely necessary—and it isn't, because I do see his life's work in the background.

If Berlioz is clumsy, it is nevertheless more to my liking than the tiresome fluency of Mendelssohn.[2] And I say of a part of my melodic practice that the best of it derives from Berlioz. For some time, I believe that I am the first to have noticed that we can learn from Berlioz particularly in melodic practice and, if that is correct, I will be proud of it. Moreover, in Berlioz there are such unique, inimitable elements that I cannot think of him without immense gratitude. Where he appears weak to me, I certainly do not forget those passages, but they do not tarnish my opinion.

Additionally, as soon as I can I especially want to study more carefully what you say about Beethoven's Fifth Symphony in that issue, first out of a sense of fairness and, so to speak, for my own education and assessment, because that symphony is for me the most alien, the inimical one among Beethoven's symphonies. I received the piano sonatas, four volumes, and very much thank you that you arranged for this valuable gift to be sent to me.[3] In your [next] letter I hope soon to find your wishes with regard to my music. I particularly like sending it to you (even if you don't think as well of it as I do). My music for *A Midsummer Night's Dream* is currently being engraved. In the next few days the music for *The Winter's Tale* is to follow. All of my theater music is written for small instrumentation, i.e. for our school orchestra.

   With cordial greetings,
    Yours,
     A. Halm

You will also write me whether you would like to have the <u>parts</u> for my A major quartet, right?

PS April 1, 1924 You know, one should of course in the end say what one considers to be true, but in a way that communicates something by it. Such ideals will not lead devotees of Berlioz (by the way, are there in fact so many of them that a wave of proselytizing is necessary, even with your view?) to quiet examination of their viewpoint.

As I said, without question I concede one and another weakness in Berlioz. But to me he is vain, smug—I find these traits sometimes in Brahms. And then, is a melody like "Rosen brach ich nachts mir" [Op. 94, No. 4]; "Holder klingt der Vogelsang" [Op. 71, No. 5] perchance less silly than the failed melody of Berlioz?[4]

[1] Schenker's remark about Berlioz appears in *Tonwille* 5, vol. 1, 189 (Ger. orig., 18–19), published about three weeks before Halm began this letter: "Berlioz, because he believed that the entire wonder of Beethoven's effect (rather like Wagner) was contained in the simple triadic unfolding of his principal themes, felt himself induced to follow Beethoven in this respect; which bestowed upon him no more than the most feeble, misconceived, unspeakably awkward and childish melodies."

[2] Mendelssohn is another composer on whom Schenker and Halm disagreed, as Halm points out in his 1917 review of Schenker's Beethoven edition ("Heinrich Schenker," in *Von Form und Sinn der Musik*, 273). Gustav Wyneken, Halm's colleague at Wickersdorf, notes that the institution was proud of its musical one-sidedness, focusing on Bach, Beethoven, and Bruckner, while avoiding Mendelssohn, Schumann, and Brahms; Wyneken, *Wickersdorf* (Lauenburg: Adolf Saal, 1922), 108.

[3] *L. van Beethoven: Klaviersonaten, nach den Autographen und Erstdrucken rekonstruiert*, 4 vols., ed. H. Schenker (Vienna: UE, 1921–23).

[4] In a review of a performance by the New Stuttgart Trio (November 4, 1913), Halm was severely critical of Brahms's "Holder klingt der Vogelsang," whose main melody he characterizes as "trivial," strongly reminiscent of a waltz tune, and "off target ... a true misunderstanding of the Lied" ("Chamber Music Evening of the New Stuttgart Trio," *Süddeutsche Zeitung Stuttgart*).

❧ Schenker to Halm (letter), April 3 and 4, 1924
DLA 69.930/12

Dear, revered Professor,

The moment I started writing, your second letter arrived,[1] for which I thank you cordially, as for everything from you. Issue 6, which was due in January 1924,[2] suddenly ended up in a type of preliminary stage again. Engraved plates (already approved for printing) got lost, an [exceptionally?] large plate for Schubert had to be reengraved,[3] and above all issue 7 (Beethoven's complete Op. 57, Beethoven's letter regarding his quartet Op. 127, and the recitative for alto, "Erbarm dich Gott!"[sic] from the *St. Matthew Passion*—by way of Furtwängler's indirect inquiry)—had to be assured.[4] On top of that, at the half-yearly statement there was the need to fend off the thievery of the publisher, who in order to limit my already very modest proceeds from the sonata edition (more for the future than for today) contrary to the contract threw his old editions in huge quantities on to the market, who served up lies in the accounting, who diverted a portion of royalties from me to his nephew[5] without my knowledge for further cost-free exploitation, who once as a shop assistant sold collars[?][6] and now as a publisher of the "moderns" [has] accumulated fabulous wealth, but outwardly and inwardly has—despite his cosmopolitan, pacifistic declarations, accentuated by long hair, long beard—remained a shop assistant. Even up to the present hour the matter of the aforementioned royalties is still not settled, but after these many irritating weeks I am entering a better mood.

Your first letter is lying in front of me, and I will take up the pages and questions in order, which, still trembling from pain, is easiest for me.

Yes. The art of figuration of the so-called classicists is the sum total of music generally. Thus historically it happened, and history will confirm, that the lack of consciousness of the art of figuration was music's downfall. But what is to be understood by figuration? Arpeggios, melodic embellishments perhaps? No. The newly discovered "linear counterpoint" with its up and down?[7] What child would not see, exactly as does Kurth, that these notes (in Bach) ascend, these descend, but child and Kurth must say <u>why only up to this height, this depth</u>. (On that point, see *Tonwille 8*. I know that you are well disposed toward Kurth, but I also know that your quest for truth will pass this test too.) I mean that art of figuration alone which is built on the narrowest shoulders of a few primal intervals, thus that powerful foreground (romping about in chords, scale-steps, keys), which, arising from the middle and background, is *all in all itself figure* before the primal intervals—not, therefore, the figures in the foreground but rather <u>the whole as—figure</u>! Where the whole is not figure, all figures sound merely pasted on like an instance of an ornament, like earrings, noserings. The whole as figuration is, however, an organism. Figure is then synthesis, so that whole, <u>synthesis</u>, <u>organism</u>, <u>figure</u> are *synonyms*! Just as human beings, animals, plants are figurations that arise from the smallest seed, so are pieces by geniuses figurations of a few intervals. Perhaps the stars are also figurations of something considerably simpler. All religious feeling, all philosophy and science, urges toward the briefest formulation of the world, and a similar religious tendency allows me to hear a piece of music as "figuration" of a kernel. That, therefore, is the "art of figuration" of our masters, that is music, that alone is also <u>improvisation</u>!

We don't understand each other yet because we are using the same words while thinking different things. With our masters, if the whole were not figuration we would still have no music. Figuration of sections and passages does not produce a whole. Therefore my devotion to them, which somehow still alienates you. At home at the piano, I once asked Furtwängler why Beethoven ascends to the high register in the development section of the first movement of Op. 109 (m. 21) and abruptly leaps away.[8] He admitted that he was always puzzled by that passage. I referred him to 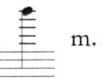 m. 42, but he couldn't make anything of that either. I then laid it out:

A *cover tone* in the upbeat: b^1 (over $g\sharp^1$), which could justifiably be eliminated, plays such a powerful role in Beethoven's imagination. We really have to think of the cunning of burglars and such riffraff when we see how in the development section he first moves separately from g♯ to b, then ultimately couples them at the beginning of the recapitulation, as in the upbeat, etc., etc. And yet this trait is a final detail in the figuration of the whole! After I showed Furtwängler so many figurations (in my sense),[9] among them also Brahms's Third Symphony, for example, I proclaimed: "I was still much too cowardly. I said far too little about our geniuses, and still say too little. But I want to make up for the cowardliness." And Furtwängler and the other guests broke out laughing owing to deep emotion and agitation. They laughed so heartily that I behave so cowardly. But that is surely the case!!

I said too little about what these masters represent, about what music was to them, about what their illustriousness (precisely of genius) as the *closest connection of kernel and unfolding*, what their elasticity, ubiquity are.

April 4
You mention your feeling (against Beethoven, Brahms, for Bruckner: "corporeality, race, etc."). It is not my business to contend with feelings. I would think Halm and Schenker had to wrestle first with facts of musical language since most everyone is still completely in the dark about the incalculable depth of genius. If you dispute what I present as facts, then there is a fruitful debate about the truth, at least that. Don't forget, dear Professor Halm, that you surely also bore Beethoven in your heart in your youth. Perhaps that "feeling" will yet return at some point?

I heard Bruckner improvising. But he couldn't do it. He was too much a foreground designer. More accurately, he knew only one dimension, a space of at most twenty measures, even that viewed merely two-dimensionally. That space did not arise for him from a depth, where space links to space, belonging together, like bones, muscles, joints of my body. For him, it stood for itself. Consequently, his manner of underscoring every space with scale-step I and an opening on the downbeat, which however over the long term is as little appealing in the language of tones as in that of words. You are a person of responsibility and therefore I will relate, for example, the following to you.

In class, Bruckner once called me to the piano. "Listen, Mr. Schenker," he says, and plays just one passage, which plainly represents an escalation. "Do you think that's enough already, or should I continue?" He didn't allow me to hear what came before or after the escalation. Later, I was able to determine that it was a passage in the Seventh Symphony, which he was working on.[10] But how could he ask about something like that? According to what could the listener have oriented himself, and according to what did he orient himself if he could ask that way? Read Friedrich Eckstein's memories of Bruckner and the assignments related there.[11] In that condition they are not strict composition, not free composition, the usual obscure domain. If I hadn't had obligatory respect for so many marvelous pieces of music and above all for his genuine religiosity, I would have laughed sixty minutes through every class, such impossible things did he present. In addition, he was deeply pained that a professorship for composition was withheld from him—he was allowed to teach only harmony and counterpoint.[12] In any case, he put forth real effort to present the few students in good shape in the final examinations, with the expectation that the board of directors would offer him a composition class based on favorable results. So what did the good, poor Bruckner do? Since he knew that director Hellmesberger[13] or the professors of piano or violin, etc.—the entire "commission"—did not enjoy getting involved in theory, he gave each one of us the fugue subject in advance, worked through it with each of us, and then came the comedy of the examination. "Would the director like to provide a subject!!, asked Bruckner. The director replied quickly, "Please, Professor, assign one yourself." And then everything went off as rehearsed. A trifle, but I do not trust whoever tells me he heard Bruckner improvising wonderfully, because Bruckner could very well have prepared the improvisation. Whether he did or not, by improvisation I understand more, the figuration of a deeply perceived kernel which—in the manner of seminal filaments—follows a path with inexplicable power. I also witnessed (there was actually more to see than hear) Bruckner's first inspiration for the Ninth Symphony. Fiery red-faced, he came into the class—6 in the evening—and shouted and shouted: "Now I've got the theme for a new symphony," ran to the piano and repeatedly pounded the same few measures, ran out of the classroom into a neighboring one, where Professor Schenner, one of his most avid devotees who was giving a piano lesson, brought him into our class and played the same few measures over and over again.[14] I believe I have already written you how he labored to coordinate his figurations with the harmony. Whether he does it that way in all manuscripts I don't know. Since then I haven't seen any more.

I return to Reger. I am asked from many sides to show what in Reger appears faulty to me. But to keep pace with that impatience is neither objectively allowed nor technically possible. How it pains me that the fourth volume, the main volume, *Free Composition*, is not yet out. How cumbersomely I have to manage in *Der Tonwille* and yet how much better it has become since volumes 1 and 2/1–2 are out! Further, if I were to go after merely that which I call errors, on what would I support my proofs, since no one would even know what I'm talking about! And this too: Do you believe that my publisher would put up with the degradation of his products?[15] Do you have any idea what martyrdom issues 1–6 [of *Tonwille*] have suffered, how out of fear of me, contrary to the publishing firm and other endless assurances, the publisher himself obstructs the volumes. How often have German musicians brought to my attention the many damages that the publisher intentionally inflicts on me. Furtwängler and many others frequently expressed the opinion that Director Hertzka especially set the snare of the contracts in order to render me harmless to his business. Today we are supposed to be at issue 20 (and beyond). Look where I am. What has just happened to me urges me more than ever to extreme caution. I can only offer material that will not be disadvantaged through delay tactics. I will take care to continue the Short Preludes of Bach [and] the sonatas of Beethoven,[16] since I have been hindered by the publisher from letting them achieve their impact; only a quick settlement, even a joint settlement (the contract stipulates <u>monographs</u>) will give them the treatment they deserve.[17] The young Reger, the young Strauss, who Universal Edition bought from Aibl in Munich, are his main source of income, which he will not allow to be choked off. He has paid as much as nothing for Bruckner, Mahler, for Reger and Strauss only a few marks. Those are—business deals! cheaply purchased, acquired in vain, merely expensively sold. How the hearts of the Jews Hertzka, Kalmus and brother [?], etc., do wallow! Every line that you read in *Der Tonwille* has been bought with blood. And I will yet return to Reger. I planned for issue 8 Mozart's A major sonata theme and variations, Brahms's Handel Variations, and Reger's Bach Variations.[18] But if issue 7 is delayed, I will have to arrange the material otherwise.[19] Indeed, I had long since decided to forgo my 20 percent for the benefit of the publisher, but even then he would not print any sooner because the content is in opposition to his interests. Do you perhaps think, for example, that your Zwissler would want to print just the Short Preludes—the little booklet would have fifty to sixty pages with Urlinie analyses—even if I wanted to give it to him as a gift, if the typesetting and printing costs, at most, five million of our kronen? I am having appalling difficulties, of which my readers have no idea.

A transition? A historical necessity? Nothing of either. A regression, a collapse, because of inability for figuration of the whole and of the parts. Today people write as well as live where art and life mean different things. People "may" live life as it suits them, as it veers off track. But art doesn't tolerate veering off track. More accurately, the artists are veering off track but don't want to accept it. They appeal to the fact that no one has the right to decree prohibitions. Consequently, however, that is the standpoint of life that forbids nothing. On the contrary, art forbids things, even if no placard is hung over its mouth saying "but not this far."

A public forum between the two of us would only mean a loss of time and work. In music, listeners have not yet come so far that we could accept them as a court of justice. Recently, I was supposed to give an informal lecture at the piano in a Hamburg home before house guests, which would have brought me a very nice sum of money. I declined because I still saw no way to reach the audience. The Hamburg musicians might also have shown up and for professional reasons brought their antagonism with them, since they usually feel the effects in their pocketbook. Further, it is not necessary that I make your or Oppel's compositions the object of my line of reasoning. Perhaps I will get enough leisure time to put together for you a letter of my own about your compositions and to identify the passages, etc. If only the path of *Der Tonwille* were somewhat smoother, I would just lose less time because of obstacles. In any case, however, I will very soon justify myself to you in *Der Tonwille* on account of some misunderstandings, which, with regard to me, I gather from your most recently arrived works. You may expect that the zeal for art and truth will surely provide me the best form for the purpose. Then, no matter how this or that issue may still divide us, we are both living pure of heart and of good intention, honest before ourselves and others. How could it be that I would not honestly respect you on account of such rare qualities, [and] that we would strive against one another rather than [striving] for art with united strengths wherever possible?

Regarding the quartet, I will lay out various things in the separate letter. Please send me the parts. It might be possible that a string quartet here will soon rehearse it.

I don't know *Of Boundaries and Countries of Music*. If possible, have that work sent to me, too. You will receive from Universal Edition *Op. 101*. Many, many thanks.

In conclusion, yet a brief comment. It is not impossible that I could send you a contribution for your purposes. My only wish would be that our currency (which nowadays is just crumbling domestically) doesn't deteriorate yet more. In any case, I will ask you at the appropriate time whether the contribution is acceptable to you. It would have been twice as much if in the interim the kroner catastrophe had not occurred. Now, though, an end. Students, *Tonwille*, volume 4, etc., are calling me.

      With cordial greetings to you,
         Yours,
            H. Schenker

---

[1] March 15 and April 1, 1924, the first being February 1–6, 1924. Schenker answers both letters in this response.

[2] *Tonwille* 6 (1923), actual publication date April 29, 1924 (see above, p. 119).

[3] Referring to the table preceding p. 3 of issue 6, belonging to the article "Schubert's *Gretchen am Spinnrade*: Latest Results of a Manuscript Study," vol. 2, 3–7 (which contained errors, corrected in this Eng. transl.). The implication may be that Schenker had prepared a larger chart which the publisher thought too unwieldy and insisted be reduced, and that the reengraving delayed publication.

[4] "Beethoven's Sonata in F minor, Op. 57," *Tonwille* 7 (= 4/1), vol. 2, 41–64 (Ger. orig., 3–33); "The Recitative 'Erbarm es Gott' from Bach's *St. Matthew Passion*," ibid., 65–68 (Ger. orig., 34–38), "Beethoven on his Quartet Op. 127," ibid., 69–71 (Ger. orig., 39–41), actual publication date August 25, 1924.

[5] Alfred Kalmus, the second son of Erwine Fuchs (wife of Jacques Kalmus), was the (step?)-sister of Hertzka's wife Jella (Fuchs).

[6] Diverse previous careers have been attributed to Hertzka; according to Hans Heinsheimer, in *Best Regards to Aida* (New York: Knopf, 1968), 10, he had worked "in the textile business."

[7] Ernst Kurth, *Grundlagen des linearen Kontrapunkts: Einführung in Stil und Technik von Bach's melodischer Polyphonie* (Bern: M. Drechsel, 1917).

[8] On October 22, 1922, Schenker recorded in his diary: "made magnificent discovery in Op. 109: for the Urlinie, beginning and end of first movement and development: g♯–b! … Golden Sunday!" He subsequently reported the discovery in "On the Organic Nature of Fugue as demonstrated in the C minor Fugue from Bach's *Well-tempered Clavier*, Book I," *Masterwork* 2, 28 (Ger., 51).

[9] In light of Schenker's recognition in this letter that he and Halm use the same words but understand something different by them, the phrase "in my sense," referring to the word figuration, is revealing.

10. The Seventh Symphony was written 1881–83. Bruckner was either revising it in the period of Schenker's study with him (1887/88 and 1888/89), or Schenker means the Eighth Symphony (1884–87, recomposed with Schalk 1889–90).
11. Friedrich Eckstein, *Erinnerungen an Anton Bruckner* (Vienna: UE, 1923).
12. Bruckner taught organ, harmony, and counterpoint (1868–90). The composition teachers at that time were Robert Fuchs (harmony, counterpoint, composition, 1874–1912) and Franz Krenn (theory, composition, 1869–91).
13. Joseph Hellmesberger (1828–93): Austrian violinst and conductor, founder of the Hellmesberger String Quartet (1849), director of the Vienna Conservatory 1851–93.
14. Wilhelm Schenner (1839–1913): Austrian concert pianist and organist, professor of piano at the Vienna Conservatory 1864–1904.
15. As Schenker points out shortly, UE had taken over publication of Reger's compositions.
16. Schenker had already published studies of five of Bach's Short Preludes in *Tonwille* 4, vol. 1, 141–45 (Ger. orig., 3–7) (Nos. 1–2) and *Tonwille* 5, vol. 1, 171–81 (Ger. orig., 3–9) (Nos. 3–5), so this remark refers to his intention to publish studies of the entire set. Ultimately he published studies of Nos. 6, 7, and 12 in *Masterwork* 1, 54–66 (Ger., 101–05, 109–13, 117–23), leaving five not done. Regarding Beethoven piano sonatas, since Schenker's edition was completed in 1923, the reference here is to his elucidatory editions of *Op. 109*, *Op. 110*, *Op. 111*, *Op. 101* (1913–20), with Op. 106 still outstanding because the autograph manuscript was unavailable.
17. The only contract to specify monographic publication ("Monographie … monographisches Werk," entirely at Schenker's insistence: letter to UE of October 19, 1910) was that for *Beethoven's Ninth Symphony* (1912). The contract for *The Last Five Sonatas of Beethoven* (August 25, 1912) makes no such specification; nor does that for *Der Tonwille* (March 23, 1920). It is therefore unclear what is at issue here.
18. *Tonwille* 8–9 (= 4/2–3), vol. 2, 77–114 (Ger. orig., 3–46), appeared just before November 18, 1924, hence months after this letter. It contains no essay on the Mozart A major sonata, though the piece is briefly discussed in "True Performance," *Tonwille* 6, vol. 2, 32–33 (Ger. orig., 38–39). The article on Reger, "A Counter-example: Max Reger's Variations and Fugue on a Theme by Bach, Op. 81, for Piano," appeared in *Masterwork* 2, 106–17 (Ger., 171–92).
19. *Tonwille* 7 appeared just before August 25, 1924, thus after this letter.

❧ Halm to Schenker (letter), April 7, April 14 and May 6, 1924
OC 12/15–17

Dear and revered Professor,

I didn't mean it that way with the [debate in] public, that the readership should count as a court of appeal, but rather that it should see how a respectably conducted dispute looks in which an opponent is sometimes gladly in the wrong, i.e., is grateful when he admits better insight. However, if you take the trouble to show me in a letter one or another passage where I got off track and the lack of genius in my music reveals itself, that's all right with me too. It is not necessary to point out many instances, for I suppose from the start that I lack what you mean, or I do consider it very possible.

"Foreground music"—a good expression which, depending on the findings, I would surely also accept for my music with much modesty as well as some pride. That is, I have long since believed that the foreground, or surface, has been neglected at the expense of the background and foundation, corporeality at the expense of spirituality.[1] You counter: everything is merely a body and therein lies the quality of genius. Granted, but certainly not, therefore, on that account beauty. That is something! Unattractive physiognomy, body parts are biologically just as much a wonder as beautiful ones. Feeling: I won't dismiss it by any means, but I talk about it only in private, as it should be. Knowledge that demonstrates facts is surely also guided by feeling. One presents facts in the hope—or relying on luck—that they will guide the reader to feelings, to relish them. Regarding facts, I have always said: I consider irrefutable what I write about Beethoven's music. On the other hand, I am constantly aware that yet other weights can be tossed onto the scales. Their rise and fall is not definitive. What you adduce about Beethoven is almost all valuable to me. I admire it; in part, it elates me, for example precisely the passage you mentioned in your last letter.

Regarding religious feeling vis-à-vis music: specifically on account of such feeling I think music is spiritual in itself, and one doesn't have to spiritualize it yet further. The immediate phenomenon, the foreground, is therefore so important to me. Bruckner regained innocence (the classicists were too much in a hurry). His downbeat quality, his solidity (opening with tonic harmony) I accredit him as greatness. What you recount (about the escalation) seems at first of deep concern but does not confuse me. (Simplest explanation: he respected you and wanted to show you a nice passage and did it under an awkward pretense.) I see too much structure and awareness, will and ability. I have hauled out a fairly full bag of facts here, and could fill yet quite a few sheets of paper. But even if it were just a matter of "wonderful musical images"—that is of course above all what was needed after the classicists; music purely of the present. But as I said, I dispute that it is merely that, and believe to have proved the opposite.

Regarding Dr. Kurth, I think he certainly said a bit more than how you present it, and that More seems important to me. The "blow" that you struck has thus not overthrown his image for me. But you need not worry that I cannot abide such things. What someone can overthrow for me may merely fall down, my own music as well as its support and assistance. I am always delighted when my music pleases someone. If one were to prove to me that he understands nothing, it is for me a pleasure to bring him joy. (It is certainly possible that my music pleases someone who understands little of music, even someone who does not understand my music in particular.) For some time, already at my first acquaintance with your writings, I noticed the difference; you are much more esoteric than I am.

I will soon be sending you the quartet parts.[2] If you listen in on a rehearsal, do try to influence the players, as far as you can, not to rush. In general I find that players always take a faster tempo than I intend (surrogate for spiritedness!). I will have *Of Boundaries and Countries* sent to you by the publisher. You have still not written me what items of my chamber music you do not have (volume 4, 5?). Most preferably, I would have the parts sent together with the other volumes, so write me soon about it.

I will gladly accept a contribution for printing if you have an appropriate foundation at your disposal. I may surely conclude from the offer (if such comes under consideration at some point) that you wish to see my music published, and that you are not familiar with other music that in your opinion deserves it more than mine. Should you have decided [about a contribution], I still think you should publish something from your writings when publishers don't come through or even stand in the way. (I read with regret and sincere sympathy about your difficulties with that bunch of people, and can readily imagine that you have opened only a small slit in the curtain on a very sullied commercial stage.) It can be no other way than for you to consider your writings more important for music than my music, and you would have to make decisions and act accordingly. In truth, that would truly not be egotism.

You write that you had already told me "how Bruckner laboriously coordinated the figurations with the harmony." That has not happened yet. It would very much interest me, very much, and I ask that you write me about it, or mention an example of it in a volume of *Der Tonwille*, even if you will then assume that I will not be budged thereby from my viewpoint. For ultimately it depends on the outcome of the labor; as with Beethoven, who also sometimes seems (April 14, 1924) unexpectedly awkward to me in his sketches.

Back to the beginning: After what I have observed (occasionally, for I don't study my pieces as I do others'), I still consider it possible that a beautiful Urlinie could be demonstrated in them. The opposite may also be possible. My actual, conscious work (as the painter makes composition studies of a picture) mainly applies to harmony. The remainder I search out until I find something that satisfies me—without such intensive work as with the harmony. However, since with respect to line I am also very sensitive (you say I am insufficiently sensitive, insufficiently aurally aware—I won't try to force my opinion on you on that point, and mean this now purely from a practical viewpoint: I am indeed sensitive, whether I sense incorrectly or correctly) to unsatisfactory [linear] continuation, I suspect, then, that some kind of synthesis must exist, perhaps the Urlinie, perhaps an unknown type.

Op. 101 arrived the day before yesterday. Cordial thanks.

May 6, 1924

An Easter trip intervened. Four evenings were devoted to my music at a youth convention in Hildesheim, which Dr. Wyneken directed; before that, I had various things to do with preparations. I do now have other things to say, but the letter should finally be off.

        I express to you cordial greetings.
           Yours,
              A. Halm.

Reger: I mean, there is so much to say against him (and to my knowledge none of his devotees has said anything tangible or concrete for him), that to me it almost seems unnecessary that you have to deal with it. The Nearly would be more interesting, enlightening. I understand that according to your attitude this Nearly must mean a difference in nature, i.e. a huge gap.

[1] Neither "vordergründlich" nor "oberflächig" —the latter very deliberately used— is proper German: "vordergründig" and "oberflächlich" would be correct. Halm rejected the latter because of its negative connotation (superficial), and coined "oberflächig" to signify surface detail. Similarly, Halm writes "vordergründlich" because "vordergründig" means superficial, simplistic.

[2] The parts of Halm's A major String Quartet.

❧ Schenker to Halm (postcard), January 22, 1927
DLA 69.930/14

Dear, revered Professor Halm,

Many thanks for your new book.[1] Because of the proofs for the second yearbook, I could give it only a cursory glance, but will read [it] all the more carefully once my duty has been done.[2] Each time I see a work of yours, the feeling comes over me that we two, despite all, would find ourselves in close accord if only we could first speak with one another (instead of writing). However, I hope to get back to your book soon, then I will say more.

   With best wishes,
   Yours,
    H. Schenker

[1] Halm, *Beethoven*, on which Schenker comments in his letter of July 11, 1927.

[2] Schenker's manuscript of *Masterwork* 2 was sent to the printer on January 18, 1927, and on January 21 proofs of the text and music examples were promised simultaneously. Proofing occupied Schenker from February to August, and the volume was released in September.

❧ Schenker to Halm (letter), July 11, 1927
DLA 69.930/15

                Galtür, Tyrol

Most revered and dear Professor Halm,

Here in the Tyrol I am only now getting around to thanking you cordially for your *Beethoven*, and to wishing you luck on contracting with Hesse's publishing house and with the [German] Book Society.[1] Now you won't lack for the dissemination of your ideas.

Your Beethoven book also gives me the opportunity to say that the misunderstandings prevailing between us can surely be removed, that in a certain sense it is a shame if we don't join forces. In that regard, *Free Composition*, whose turn it now is, will perhaps bring about some change. For the time being, the second yearbook, with which I finish off *Der Tonwille*, comes first (October at the latest) so that I can be master of my time and of my energy for work. It just so happens that my second yearbook likewise includes the first C minor fugue of the *Well-tempered Clavier*, specifically as evidence for organicism also in the fugue. Contrary to Jöde's, Werker's, [and] Graeser's undertakings with Bach, the brief essay may perhaps initially convey little.[2] But if a Bach fares so badly with those brutes, why should I expect anything better? Four to five years ago I would not have ventured to assume such a deterioration in the understanding of Bach, although for thirty years I too have prepared myself for the worst in my readers.

Only if Schoenberg attempts a rebuttal would I publish a short essay to substantiate statements against him presented in my second yearbook. Otherwise I will stick to *Free Composition* and continue on that work without interruption up to its conclusion.

I did not participate at all in the Beethoven festival in Vienna.[3] It revolved too much around Romain Rolland, Casals, etc., not to mention Herriot and colleagues.[4] I sidestepped titles and elevated honors, and just wrote a little essay for the *General-Anzeiger für Bonn und Umgegend* titled "Beethoven and his Descendants."[5]

Hindemith wrote me some well-intentioned words; I replied with something well-intentioned;[6] however, events in music and in music literature are unfolding like a genuine tragedy. Each person wants and can do as he is compelled, all are against all, everyone against everyone else, and that will produce a tragic end: music will go down the drain.

All the better for you if you expect anything better. I stick with the view that people have not yet looked the art of music in the eyes, although it has so wonderfully opened them.

Let me hear from you soon, please, and accept best greetings
      from your
          H. Schenker

---

[1] The Deutsche Buch-Gemeinschaft published Halm's *Einführung in die Musik* (1926).

[2] Fritz Jöde (1887–1970): German music educator, author of *Die Kunst Bachs* (1926) (not mentioned in "The Organic Nature of Fugue," perhaps because the book was too recent to come to Schenker's attention in time for that article). Wilhelm Werker, *Studien über die Symmetrie im Bau der Fugen und die motivische Zusammengehörigkeit der Präludien und Fugen des "Wohtemperierten Klaviers" von Johann Sebastian Bach* (Leipzig: Breitkopf & Härtel, 1922), discussed in "The Organic Nature of Fugue," 45–47 (Ger., 81–84). Wolfgang Graeser, "Bachs 'Kunst der Fuge'," *Bach-Jahrbuch* 21 (1924): 1–104, and the supplementary volume 48 of the Bach-Gesellschaft edition, discussed in "The Organic Nature of Fugue," 47–48 (Ger., 84).

[3] The centenary of Beethoven's death, 1927, was celebrated with a major centennial festival and exhibition in Vienna (see chapter 11).

[4] Romain Rolland (1866–1944): French novelist, dramatist, Nobel Prize winner in 1915; author of, among other things, *Beethoven* (Paris, 1903, 1927) and a six-volume study *Beethoven: les grandes époques créatrices* (Paris: Éditions du Sablier, 1928–45). He was also a member of the Clarté group, much criticized by Schenker, notably in "The Mission of German Genius," *Tonwille 1*, vol. 1, 14–15 (Ger. orig., 14–15). Pablo Casals (1876–1973): Catalan cellist, conductor, composer. Edouard Herriot (1872–1957): author of the popular biography *La vie de Beethoven* (Paris, 1929), and radical French politician, three times premièr of France between 1924 and 1932.

[5] "Beethoven und seine Nachfahren," *General-Anzeiger für Bonn und Umgegend*, special supplement "Zum 100. Todestage Beethovens" (March 26, 1927): 3–4.

[6] See chapter 19.

18

Expectations Unfulfilled: Schenker and Furtwängler

ONE would expect remarkable insights from an exchange such as this between a sophisticated intellectual and an aspiring conductor. But their conversation never got off the ground: the radical theorist and the artistically open-minded musician failed to come to terms. This makes their exchange not in the least uninteresting. It follows two different characters and outlooks in their ups and downs over one and a half decades, and it covers a wide range of topics. However, it all stems from a small number of fundamental principles that form a constant background to the unfolding of ideas.

These principles are visible even in the earliest documents. When they first met, Furtwängler was already aware of Schenker's writings. Yet he was not prepared to fully subscribe to their theoretical foundations and aesthetic consequences, as proven by their opposing estimation of Bruckner's music. Schenker found Furtwängler's conducting impressive in its craftsmanship and his "beautiful gesture," but lacking musical insight. When Furtwängler declared himself willing "to serve a timely mission" and "to lead the youth of today," Schenker drew the conclusion that he might teach him and thus provide the missing intellectual background. Their carefully worded letters aimed to please, but their different expectations were hard to overlook. Schenker's pedagogical aim stood against Furtwängler's approach to accept his analytical superiority without delving into the technical, aesthetic, and political implications of his musical world view. When Schenker sought an exponent for his ideas and a translator for the concert audience who subordinated himself to the theorist as he envisioned in his "Art of Performance," Furtwängler rather enjoyed his company, his analytical coaching, and his broad intellectual outlook. However, he integrated Schenker's findings into an eclectic aesthetics as opposed to their original conception.

Such issues remained virulent over the years. Not to speak of their ideas about Jewishness, including Furtwängler's alleged anti-Semitism, or of Paul Bekker or contemporary culture, Schenker and Furtwängler never even agreed in their evaluation of Bruckner and Wagner. Their apparently firm common ground in Beethoven and Brahms proved slippery as well. Schenker's accusations were severe; he claimed that Furtwängler "does not know sonata form at all," that he had no knowledge of textual matters, that he replied "nonsense" when Schenker presented his analytical findings, that he was "far too ill-prepared" for serious discussion. Thus he implied that Furtwängler's understanding of classical music was shallow, that he therefore got lost in superficial detail and lacked "synthesis." Although Furtwängler wrote diligently that he studied Schenker's latest writings, Schenker's letter from November 1931 contained an overview of his theory condensed to fundamentals—as much an apologetic text as a didactic one to finally make Furtwängler understand, interspersed with wild imaginations of the role he would play in a post-apocalyptic musical life newly organized according to Schenkerian doctrine.

Schenker increasingly took issue with what he regarded as Furtwängler's lukewarm standpoints, finally—with a touch of irony—congratulating him that he "after all resolved to pin [his] colors to the mast" in August 1932. More so, he accused him of vanity and avarice as driving forces behind this eclectic attitude. But he never stopped hoping for a change—hoping to coax Furtwängler into becoming his disciple and follower. So the exchange stayed ambiguous to the last. Amidst all failed expectations, Schenker conceded that Furtwängler was "the first and foremost conductor of the day." And although Furtwängler never delved deep into Schenker's theoretical approach, he remembered him fondly in an essay written after Schenker's death: There he singled out the concept of "long-range hearing" (*Fernhören*), thereby retaining vestiges of Schenker's ideas in his own view of music perception.

CHRISTOPH HUST

Diary entry (extract), May 4, 1919

Around 8 p.m. to Director Hammerschlag.[1] Furtwängler turns up after me, a man thirty years of age; the conversation while at table at first goes only very sluggishly on minor political matters, Adolf Busch[2] etc. (during supper Breisach and concertmaster Rothschild[3] turn up); over black coffee, the conversation was already becoming more intimate and substantive. Furtwängler recounts that he got to know my book[4] six years ago in Lübeck and shows himself entirely well-informed on my links with Germany. Anyhow, he expressed himself ready and willing to serve a timely mission. In the meantime, Dr. Mandyczewski,[5] too, turned up, but he remained in the salon, since as a nonsmoker he could not join us. Later we join him in the salon, and the conversation again becomes guarded, since people may have been afraid of hurting one another, or embarrassing them, on matters of general interest. [...]

Soon Dr. Mandyczewski left, and now the questioning caught fire all the more. Bruckner was principal topic. Furtwängler has a soft spot for the "beautiful themes," and to my astonishment also a soft spot for his symphonic style. I pushed a battering ram quite gently in the direction of the others, and, ultimately playing upon personal vanity, put forward the opinion that it is not good, for the sake of details whose beauty is not to be underrated, to surrender oneself to a composer in this way when harm would be done to the soul if, in abandoning itself to details, it would cause itself, so to speak, to disintegrate into atoms. I expressed the opinion that if the younger generation of today in any case suffers so severely from a lack of long-distance vision, it would be utterly unpardonable to pass on this infection still further by bringing to the fore composers who themselves suffer from this lack. On Mahler I declined to speak, which those present, amidst laughter, took anyway to be a judgment. It was noticeable finally that the man of the house stressed the dishonorableness of Kalbeck and the ill-will of Dr. Hirschfeld—value judgments that must surely have cost him very dear when one considers his relationships to those two men. Furtwängler, Rothschild, and Breisach accompanied me home, and on the street I took the opportunity to redraw the picture of Bruckner, Mahler, and Hugo Wolf in still more stringent terms. And again and again I emphasized our duty to lead the youth of today toward the masters of organization, the masters of synthesis.

[1] Paul Hammerschlag: Director of the Austrian Credit Bank for Trade and Business; member of Schenker's circle from at least 1906. A letter of May 2, 1919, from Hammerschlag to Schenker reads: "Yesterday evening, Mr. Furtwängler was at my place and spoke in the warmest terms about you and your work, in the course of which he expressed a keen desire to make your acquaintance. I take the liberty of asking whether you might grant me the pleasure of a visit on Sunday at 8.30 for a frugal supper. I think you might perhaps be interested to get to know this excellent musician and admirer of your theories."

[2] Adolph Busch (1891–1952): German violinist, from 1912 concertmaster of the Vienna Concert Society, founder in 1919 and first violin of the Busch Quartet, founder in the 1930s of the Busch Chamber Players, which played Baroque music with small forces.

[3] Paul Breisach (1896–1952): Austrian conductor, pupil of Bruno Walter and Franz Schreker. He studied with Schenker 1913–18, was later accompanist of Lotte Lehmann and Elisabeth Schumann, conducted in several opera houses before becoming conductor at the Berlin Opera in 1930, emigrating to the USA in 1939 and pursuing a successful career there. The Rothschild referred to here is not his former pupil Alphons von Rothschild.

[4] *Beethoven's Ninth Symphony*. Furtwängler's 1947 essay "Heinrich Schenker: Ein zeitgemässes Problem," in *Ton und Wort: Aufsätze und Vorträge 1918 bis 1954* (Wiesbaden: Brockhaus, 1958), 199–200, confirms this identification. The paragraph in question begins: "The first work that brought Schenker's name to a wider public was a monograph on Beethoven's Ninth Symphony. This book came into my hands by chance in 1911 [sic] in Lübeck when as a minor concert conductor I was on the brink of my career, and it instantly aroused my most impassioned interest."

[5] Eusebius Mandyczewski (1857–1929): Rumanian-born Austrian musicologist. He studied with Hanslick at Vienna University, was a friend of Brahms, from 1887 he was archivist of the Society of the Friends of Music in Vienna (of which he published a history in 1912), he also taught choral music, history, harmony, counterpoint, and organology at the Vienna Conservatory/Academy from 1894–1924, as Professor from 1892. He edited ten volumes of the Schubert collected edition (1895–97), and contributed also to collected editions of Haydn, Beethoven, and Brahms.

❧ Diary entry, November 4, 1919

To Furtwängler concert; "Egmont" music with Wüllner: the violins' irritatingly long bowing before a *sf* rendered the passages rather ponderous. Fifth Symphony performed in a very round, logical form, the conductor's gestures at first glance appropriate, often surprisingly happily pictorial, for example especially in the C major section in the Scherzo, and, in general, the way the orchestra was handled left nothing at all to be desired. On the other hand, it also became instantly apparent to me that the conductor was not familiar with certain innermost secrets of the composition, which is why they were necessarily lacking in the performance as well; even the first two fermatas were simply coordinated, and not, as the author intended, matched with one another such that they would coalesce to form a four-measure period. The performance of the second theme of the first movement was random and irritating; the three-measure group in the development section was lacking. The tempo in the Andante was fluid and natural, but violins did not correctly perform the *crescendo* group starting at m. 15. Some of the fermatas or rests were grossly exaggerated, which did create a certain dramatic tension, which was, on the other hand, achieved too cheaply. In the Scherzo the tempo and the rendering of the two-measure upbeat were off the mark. The last movement was very good as a whole and in detail. There is no doubt that the young conductor is superior to Weingartner, Nikisch, and Strauss, which leaves it all the more regrettable that he has not yet penetrated more deeply into the composition. — Floriz sees us from the parterre and arranges to meet us; Lie-Liechen actually finds him and I inform him that I would rather not speak with Furtwängler in the green room, and will send a letter to him immediately.

❦ Schenker to Furtwängler (letter), November 5, 1919
Sbb 55 Nachl 13, [1]

Dear Mr. Furtwängler,

Anyone with a normal complement of obligations, with a normal work output, must find himself these days in flagrant contradiction to other people, who throng the theaters and concert halls from as early as 3 o'clock, or 5 o'clock, or 6 o'clock onward. Who on earth are these people, and how do they otherwise spend their time in the afternoons? The fact that I got to hear you for the first time yesterday was thanks, so to speak, to surgery—not life-threatening, and known about a week in advance—undergone by one of my pupils; in short, I was able to hear you, and to take heartfelt pleasure in your accomplishment.

At long last, we have a magnificent counterweight to the fatal "Wine Bower,"[1] to the Strauss foxtrot (applied to Beethoven, Brahms, Mozart), to the execrable lack of temperament that fancies itself to be "temperament" if it merely hurtles along with a one-and-a-two for a hundred measures at a time in the same haste and lack of differentiation. I persuaded myself yesterday that you had already totally won over the pernicious Viennese to your side; however, I don't think any the better of the Viennese for your new following, since these childish people in fact suffer more from "temperament" in the imagination than in reality and so might easily tomorrow evening turn to the "piquant rhythms" of the world demimondaine of Geneva,[2] which matches their aridness to a tee. The Viennese simply love rejoicing, and even more do they indulge in this quality, which in itself is truly trivial. Reason plays no part in it—today's reason may flatly contradict that of tomorrow—so long as it somehow provides an occasion for rejoicing.

Things have already almost reached the point at which, although you have been in action for so short a while, you are accorded the mantle and authority of Mahler, as a result of which, of course, your situation has become a serious matter for the Viennese. To be sure, you yourself could do nothing better than to eradicate the barbarisms of the "celebrities" of yesterday, and I do not need to dwell at length on how great a cause I myself have for joy at that.

I would have liked to shake your hand in the artists' dressing room yesterday; but because I had something to say that could not have been said there, I had to resort to the alternative of writing this letter. You may have become acquainted at Mrs. Hauser's house with her teacher-friend Professor <u>Moriz Violin</u>, who has been a faithful friend to me, too, since earliest days. Mr. Violin would like to go to Hamburg in order to give concerts etc. there. Consequently, a day or so ago he asked me if I could put in a good word for him to you, such that you might be in a position, if the occasion arises, to recommend him to Hausegger.[3] To be brief, most of what you need to know is: He has an ear such as very few musicians of today possess. In keeping with the quality of his ear and of his intellect, he really should be in a permanent position, but fighting is not his forte, although, as is so often Nature's way, he himself believes that he has the fighting spirit. He was Professor of the <u>senior</u> training class at our <u>Academy</u>, but is so no longer. Regarding that, you will hear only the most honorable things from him himself or from any other quarter you may choose, as for example, why he has not found a home at the Academy again since the end of the war.[4]

As I have already said, his ear is unique, a masterstroke of Nature, exactly what is needed for the connoisseur these days.

Enough in writing. Perhaps it may be possible, if need be, to take the matter a little further in person, if, as I very much hope, the occasion should arise.

    Finally, I send you my best wishes,
     Yours,
      H. Schenker

One last word: I have examined your conducting in minute detail, arm motion by arm motion, and it occurs to me that, if you could make contact with Ebert,[5] and Renner[6] and <u>teach them</u> a certain baton <u>gesture</u> [that says]: "Get out of here, you pack of French and Anglo-Saxon vermin," the gesture would be bound to have an irresistible effect, and we would immediately be rid of the ten plagues!

---

[1] "'Wein-Garten'lauben": this is a double play on words, on Weingartner's name, and on: *Weingarten* = "vineyard"; *Gartenlaube* = "arbor", "bower."

[2] i.e. Igor Stravinsky, who lived in Swiss exile from 1914 to 1920. He had several connections to Geneva in 1919.

[3] Siegmund von Hausegger (1872–1948): Austrian conductor, teacher, and writer on music, from 1920 Director, later President, of the Academy of Music in Munich, from 1925 President of the Allgemeiner Deutscher Musikverein.

[4] Schenker is skirting round the fact that Violin mounted opposition to, and published a pamphlet against, the Academy's President and Director in 1912, and left

the Academy's faculty after that opposition failed. It is notable that Schenker says nothing about Violin's piano technique or interpretation.

[5] The Social Democrat Friedrich Ebert (1871–1925) had been elected the first Imperial President of the Weimar Republic in February 1919.

[6] Karl Renner (1870–1950): Social Democrat politician, Austrian State Chancellor from 1918 to 1920.

Furtwängler to Schenker (letter), [November 19, 1919]
OJ 11/16, [1]

Dear Mr. Schenker,

I must admit that no testimony to the approval of my work, from whichever quarter it may come, could afford me greater pleasure than yours—as that of a man who, like scarcely any other today, <u>knows</u> about the true greatness of the masters, of a Beethoven etc.; of a man with whom I am in perfect harmony in the type of relationship to precisely these great masters (just as in many other cases resulting from it). As far as your characterization of the Viennese and so on goes, it confirms me in my mistrust of Vienna and Viennese "successes." And it is still completely unclear to me how far fate wishes me to play any more decisive a role whatsoever in the practical musical life of Vienna, this city richly endowed yet full of corruption.

I shall probably be remaining here until the end of November, when I still have two concerts,[1] and should like to express the hope that we can in the meantime see each other some time and talk. I have become acquainted with Violin, and will, insofar as it is in my power, try to be of assistance to him.

Meanwhile, I send you my best wishes,

    Yours truly,
    Wilhelm Furtwängler

Perhaps we could get together one evening next week?

[1] Furtwängler was conductor of the Autumn Concerts played by the Wiener Tonkünstler-Orchester, founded in 1913.

Furtwängler to Schenker (letter), November 27, [1919]
OJ 11/16, [2]

Vienna I, Universitätsstrasse [2]

Dear Mr. Schenker,

If it suits you, let us meet on Saturday evening at 8:15 (I have a concert first) in a guesthouse. I know only the "Stadt Brünn," but if you know a better one, that is fine by me. In any case, that is—unfortunately—the only evening that I still have free. So, in the hope that we will meet soon.

With cordial greetings, and also to your wife, though I have never met her.
Yours,
Wilhelm Furtwängler

Diary entry, November 29, 1919

Since there is no number for Mrs. Hauser in the telephone book and we do not trust a messenger, we personally make the trip to Universitätsstrasse 2, where I accept the proposed time and place on a calling card. [...] To the restaurant in the company of Julian,[1] where Furtwängler is waiting for us; we chat about Bruckner, Brahms, about the circles around both, about individual works; from the restaurant to the coffeehouse Pucher, where we continue the conversation. The idea of a Schenker Institute does not make so good an impression on him; the proposal of giving lectures at the Academy, about which he will talk to Straube, makes a better impression. We bid cordial farewells.

[1] Julian ("Julko") Guttmann, son of Schenker's sister Sophie (Shifre), hence Schenker's nephew, who was at this time attending an Export Academy, hence perhaps roughly twenty years of age.

Diary entries, April 16 and 24, 1920

[April 16:] To Furtwängler (letter): I ask when and where we shall meet again, suggest Meisl restaurant and ask for tickets to the Ninth Symphony.

[April 24:] With Furtwängler and Floriz at Meisl and in Café Vindobona[1] in the evening; no real results; the situation with Straube and me fades away immediately, and the same with Violin and Hausegger. I attempt to examine more closely Furtwängler's knowledge and mention that I noticed the passage in the modulation section of the first movement in his interpretation of [Beethoven's] Fifth Symphony; I succeed in drawing out an admission from him that he himself instigated the new articulation and had it written in. He defends himself against my objection citing the supposed greater effect. My polemic is again discussed and I note that Furtwängler has once again changed his position; it sounds as though he feels affected as well and this makes me even more irritated: I represent and support my right to polemic as passionately as ever and on the way into the coffeehouse I get worked up enough to say that I feel the need to strike my opponents dead. "There we have it," Furtwängler said, "why are you then surprised that the others defend themselves." In the coffeehouse there is much more talk about autograph manuscripts and especially about Op. 101. On this point as well, Furtwängler acts as if he had thought so all along, *post festum*, which in this case means: as though he had paralleled the autograph manuscript. He must certainly be credited with an extraordinary memory which enables him to speak about every individual passage, which he cannot possibly be prepared for.

[1] Vindobona: the name of the Roman military base (previously a Celtic settlement) on this site, hence the Latin name for Vienna; coffeehouse on the Schwarzenbergplatz.

Furtwängler to Schenker (letter), November 26, 1920
OJ 11/16, [3]

Dear Mr. Schenker,
   Would it suit you if we were to get together on Tuesday evening (somewhere in a restaurant of your choice)? Perhaps you could respond with a few lines (c/o Mrs. Hauser, Universitätsstrasse 2) letting me know what you think about this. With most cordial greetings.
   Yours truly,
   Wilhelm Furtwängler

Diary entry, November 30, 1920

With Furtwängler in Café Vindobona: about [Beethoven's] Fifth Symphony, Bruckner, Berlioz, Schoenberg, [Paul] Bekker; says he is giving concerts in Stockholm in order to provide for his mother.

Diary entries, November 15 and 19, 1922

[Nov 15:] Furtwängler asks me into his artist's dressing room; may come on Thursday. — At the concert: most of the *crescendi* are bad, reaching their goal too early, the tempi are also bad; only individual passages are developed, lacking connection. In Furtwängler's dressing room for just a minute; he commits to Sunday 7:30, since he is departing at 5 a.m. on Monday.

[Nov 19:] 8:00 Furtwängler, 8:30 Weisse and his wife; ample meal! Furtwängler praises my unconditionality, contrasting with his conditionality stemming from his profession! I show him the Urlinie of Brahms's Third Symphony and of Bach's Short Preludes, of [Beethoven] Op. 109 and the "Appassionata"; he also expresses the opinion that Hertzka is "sabotaging" me and voluntarily expresses his willingness to inquire in Leipzig with Peters and Breitkopf & Härtel. He expects Schuster will really print the article, and not out of mere sympathy because I am considered obstinate in Berlin, but rather out of clear objectivity that occasionally also lets someone who thinks differently have a word; stays until 11:00, we invite him.

※ Furtwängler to Schenker (postcard), October 3, 1923
OJ 11/16, [4]

Dear Mr. Schenker,
   Would it be possible for us to get together tomorrow evening (Thursday)? It is my last evening.

   With best wishes,
       Yours in haste,
           Wilhelm Furtwängler

※ Diary entry, October 4, 1923

Around 11 a.m., express postcard from Furtwängler: would like to see me, today [being] the last possibility. —I request Miss Elias[1] to telephone him and ask him to come to the Café Vindobona (around 9 p.m.). — [...] Evening at the Café Vindobona, Furtwängler does not get there until 9:30 p. m.—we stay together until midnight. The conversation yields almost no results. He has his hands full just meeting the demands of the public, and even considers it important that he make the selection so that the public gets something satisfying out of it! He rightly feels hurt by the way the executive committee conducts itself, and appears to want to hold on only to the Society [of the Friends of Music] concerts. He reasserts the increasing worth of my name, advises me to go to Leipzig, and also, with reservation, to confess my faith in Bruckner and Wagner so that it is manifest to everybody how greatly I rate the individual features of their works. I find it strange that he knows little or nothing at all of precisely the best of Mendelssohn. I call his attention to Brahms's arrangements. A guest at the coffeehouse sends him a bunch of carnations by the hand of the waiter. The contemporary world binds garlands about the actor's head.[2] A musician who at one time played under Furtwängler speaks to him; it turns out that he now plays light music in the band at the coffeehouse—he invites Furtwängler.

---

[1] Angi Elias (1882–1944): pupil of Schenker's from c. 1905 to 1935. Heavily involved in preparing and copying voice-leading graphs for Schenker's work (numerous examples survive), she functioned as his unofficial personal assistant. She also gave or offered Schenker financial support at several points.

[2] Quotation from Schiller's *Wallenstein*, Prologue: "Art is difficult, its reward is transitory, posterity binds no garlands about the actor's head" (Schwer ist die Kunst, vergänglich ist ihr Preis, Dem Mimen flicht die Nachwelt keine Kränze).

※ Diary entry, November 20, 1923

Evening: *Samson* under Furtwängler: selection of the numbers bad, when the work in any case lacks dramatic effect. Wind and strings do not blend with one another, the tempi often too slow, then again in some cases too fast. The monotonous rhythm creates an unmistakably leaden effect—and yet the work contains Handelian features of high—of the highest—quality.

🎵 Furtwängler to Schenker (postcard), November 25, 1923
OJ 11/16, [5]

Dear Mr. Schenker,

I was hoping, since I was previously so much preoccupied with the rehearsals for *Samson*, to be able to speak with you at the performance. Now, subsequently, it occurs to me that you said a while ago that you did not have a ticket for it. I totally forgot that, and am only sorry that under these circumstances you have not heard this beautiful work. The next concerts (December): Stravinsky and the Ninth Symphony will probably interest you less?

At any rate, I hope to see you in person then, and send my cordial greetings in the meantime to you and your wife.

Yours,
Wilhelm Furtwängler

🎵 Diary entry, November 29, 1923

To Furtwängler (postcard): I have heard *Samson*; about my mental blockage with Handel, when we talk.

🎵 Diary entry, December 13, 1923

At Bamberger's in the evening; I play the Haydn C major trio, the Mozart E major Trio, and the Beethoven "Ghost" Trio with Pollak[1] and [Friedrich] Buxbaum. Furtwängler shows up for the last piece. Weisse with his wife and other innocuous guests are present. Furtwängler criticizes the excessive freedom in the performance of the Adagio subject. I counter, sitting at the piano, but notice very quickly that he is far too ill-prepared for a dispute of this type. He talks about the whole but does not take any notice at all of rests that last whole measures, and when he puts his hand on the piano keys, I see that he would like to perform the ornamentation much too broadly and pretentiously. He refers back to the listener, talks a lot about personal sense, "brace your arms!", finds few words, in short: the moment was not exactly pleasant—but we soon move on from that, even play another Haydn trio (E major). Buxbaum asks a few questions, about the [Beethoven] string quartets Op. 59, No. 2, etc. Not home until 2:30!

---

[1] Robert Pollak (1880–1962): violinist, taught at the New Vienna Conservatory 1919–26, first violinist of the Buxbaum Quartet.

❧ Diary entry, December 20, 1923

With Furtwängler in the restaurant "zum Krautstopel"; he excuses his wife, who is purportedly ill. Appears totally uncertain, but has all the ingenuity needed to find a bridge to me in any case, as often as he sees his position endangered. I explain to him candidly that he is wallowing and getting lost in over-lyricism. He is vain enough to ask whether that is the result of ageing. I describe it as temporary. However, I speak about this for the sole purpose of holding him back from the interpretation of the Brahms symphonies, about which he had spoken to Bamberger and on which apparently the overly slow tempo is based. Oddly enough, he dares to admit that he lost the tempo of the Ninth in this case, that he is improvising more these days in general, rather than introducing a predetermined tempo! I see through the pretense: he apparently wants to win an excuse in case a critique dares to be launched against his tempo. He ultimately says, on the way to the streetcar, that he wants to give up conducting. I don't believe that; and when he praises the unconditional way I live, I reply quite suggestively—and then I boarded the streetcar right away—: that comes about because I am not concerned about money!

❧ Diary entry, December 14, 1924

At the Spieglers' place from 8:00 to 11:30; Furtwängler and his wife are also there; his wife makes a good impression on Lie-Liechen; for my part, I am not yet sure what to make of her. Furtwängler arrives very late! We remain cautious in our conversation. I have always found it awkward to set someone right in front of his wife; it is difficult enough to ensure that truth prevails, and this is doubly difficult in the presence of someone's wife—in those circumstances, two people rise up in opposition. As it is, the conversation centers around Brahms's loneliness, Brahms–Hanslick (whether press obsequiousness?), Brahms–Wagner (why no programmatic expression from Brahms?), finally around Bruckner. A bit about composition technique—in passing also touched on Halm. The food offered was disgusting, the cakes actually moldy, Lie-Liechen spits it out and stops Mrs. Furtwängler from eating it, Furtwängler notices it and also refrains, only I—not without suspicion, but on the other hand in fear of sending something back that is good—take three pieces of it straight off. No butter is served with the cheese, and also no black coffee. Furtwängler makes insinuations: he notices that the Spiegler family is enjoying a chocolate gateau and passing around the rancid cake and demands, caustically enough, a piece of the gateau for himself as well. We will not enter the house again.

❧ Diary entry, April 11, 1925

Furtwängler in the evening: from 8:30 to 12:45. Weisse turns up soon after him and brings his String Quartet Op. 4. During the meal, some technical questions are touched on, primarily regarding the sonata. Furtwängler's lack of knowledge becomes apparent, and to a degree not previously suspected! He doesn't know sonata form at all!! Argues for Bruckner by considering me an opponent—a condition in which he himself does not believe. Since he is also lacking insight into the higher demands and achievements, he believes he has to argue for Bruckner as he would for a composer who has something to say. It is of no use to try to make it clear to him that perfection includes all the more a mind which, like Bruckner, has something to say. In Furtwängler's opinion, it is as if personality and perfection were mutually exclusive—in short, Furtwängler speaks like a dilettante and both of us, Weisse and I, found it difficult to have an artistic discussion with him at all. How disheartening to have to say that he nevertheless is and remains the best conductor of the day! After the meal we went into the music room, where the Bruckner debate was continued. In the course of the conversation, he openly revealed himself as an anti-Semite, not without reason, yes, I had to agree with the reasons, but did not refrain from emphasizing my strong position in adhering to Judaism.

Furtwängler to Schenker (letter), [December 13, 1925?]
OJ 11/16, [C]

HOTEL IMPERIAL VIENNA

Dear, revered Mr. Schenker,
  Is it all right with you if I come to visit you and your wife today (Sunday) (after supper) at 9 p.m.? If I hear nothing to the contrary, I will be at your door at 9 p.m.!
  With cordial greetings,
    Yours,
      Wilhelm Furtwängler

Diary entry, December 13, 1925

From 8:30 to 11 Furtwängler; Weisse and his wife came somewhat later. Weisse appeared at the very moment at which Furtwängler began to weaken Weisse's objections concerning aristocratism in the conducting business. I have always agreed with Furtwängler, because the dependent position of a conductor requires him to offer to his audience all the things about which it is always curious. It is another matter if the exceptional position of a conductor—e.g. Bülow's with the Duke of Meiningen, or Safonoff's at the head of his own orchestra—permits him to present works for which he campaigns with a certain missionary zeal. We also spoke about the bowings in Weingartner's edition of Haydn; and before he had a chance to understand what I meant he recounted (or, rather, repeated) that he went through the bowings in Brahms's symphonies with the concertmasters, and changed them! Only afterwards does he notice that he finds himself in contradiction to me, but also no less in contradiction to himself, since he had previously declared himself in agreement with my position and set great store on the original text. The conversation also turned to my polemics, which he wished were more tactful! Now, I am in no doubt that he feels attacked by them and would gladly be treated as an exceptional case in my writings. Finally we talked about the organic nature of fugue, from the lead essay in the second yearbook, also about Shaw's *St. Joan*.

ꙮ Schenker to Furtwängler (letter), July 3, 1927
Sbb 55 Nachl 13, [2]

Most revered Dr. Furtwängler,

Not long ago I read in a Berlin newspaper that you, of all people, inexplicably, still did not hold the oft-bestowed title of Professor. Now, with your most recent title you have, in my opinion, surpassed that of Professor,[1] and now—what will people do with you next? There is no further to go in the realm of human distinctions...

The purpose of these few lines is, however, not to lament the shortcomings of the system of awarding distinctions, but to draw to your attention a four-voice Mass in the Olden Style by Professor Oppel[2] (Kiel, now in Leipzig if I am not mistaken). If Mr. Oppel were to send you this work and you were to cast an eye over it, you would find the work rewarding. Professor Oppel promised to visit me here in Galtür—[he is] an artist and person of great character.

In addition, I should like to take this opportunity of apprising you of the visit of Mr. Anthony van Hoboken, who is staying in Sils Maria.[3] Despite his glittering wealth, he is heart and soul a splendid musician—for just that reason, I am very happy to give him my assistance—not only has he the merit of having created an utterly first-class collection of first editions, but also history is greatly indebted to him for a foundation in which are being assembled absolutely all the manuscripts of the great [composers] in photographic reproductions, by means of which many will be rescued, and almost all will be available for establishing an accurate model text.[4] If you are going to be with us in the fall or winter, you ought to see Mr. van Hoboken's library some time—he will certainly invite you—, and then I will come along as well, and we can perhaps have a good chat about many delightful and useful matters in his artistically congenial house.

All the best to you and your wife from me and my wife,
Yours,
H. Schenker

Galtür, Tyrol

---

[1] In 1927 Furtwängler was installed as conductor of the Vienna Philharmonic Orchestra, but perhaps Schenker had already heard that he was to become General Music Director in Berlin in 1928, too.

[2] *Messe für Vierstimmigen Chor*, Op. 32, SATB a cappella (1926).

[3] Sils Maria, in the Engadin Valley, eastern Switzerland: Hoboken's summer address that year.

[4] See chapter 12.

Furtwängler to Schenker, St. Moritz (letter), July 18, 1927
OJ 11/16, [6]

St. Moritz

Most revered Dr. Schenker,

I shall be seeing Mr. Hoboken, who had meanwhile written to me directly, in a day or so. I have not had sight of Oppel, or more to the point his four-voice Mass in Olden Style. If not now, then that can perhaps be rectified in Leipzig if, as you tell me in your letter, he is now moving there. I do in fact know of and about him from hearsay, but only by way of Kiel.

Also, I very much hope to be able in Vienna at long last again to speak with you at leisure and in detail. I hear occasionally about you and your projects from third parties (Weisse etc.; the young Bamberger was also with me a few days ago). Have you read Halm's book about Beethoven?[1] What do you say about that?!

I envision remaining here as long as possible (certainly until September 20). I hope that you are having a good and enjoyable summer. My very best regards, and from my wife, too, and to yours, and best wishes

Yours,
Wilhelm Furtwängler

[1] August Halm, *Beethoven* (Berlin: Hesse, 1927).

Diary entry, December 8, 1927

From 8 until 11:45, at Hoboken's, with Furtwängler a foursome. He appears to be looking at first editions for the first time ever; he admits to not having a library and says with a smile, pointing to his forehead, "I've got everything up here!" With all due credit to his truly excellent memory, the memory of a library is worth a good deal more; it is not right always to remain within oneself. I show him the corrections to my newly revised edition of Schubert's B minor Symphony[1] and refer specifically to new discoveries in the autograph manuscript, which even Brahms and Mandyczewski have overlooked. Among other things, we speak also about metrics. He recounts that Heuss found one too many measures right at the beginning of the first movement of the "Pastoral." On closer examination this proved to be a mistake on the part of Heuss who, in the hitherto customary way, mistakenly reckons the periods of four-plus-four measures also in an expansion. In the Scherzo of Beethoven's Seventh Symphony, Furtwängler says that the first two measures are an introduction and the real m. 1 begins with f^2, from which point it is possible to count regular periods. I show him, on the contrary, the octave coupling f^1-f^2, g^1-g^2, a^1-a^2 as the leading factor, and also decisive for the rhythm. I explain the path to the root $\underline{A}$ from the progression of the bass: $\underline{F}-\underline{A}-\underline{C}-\underline{F}$. We speak at length about the Trio section of the Scherzo. He still continues to play it too slowly, I say, on the basis of the reports of others, and I refer to the metronome marking. At this moment Hoboken comes to my aid, by setting up a metronome.

I begin to play, the metronome follows, and now it is demonstrated that the beats agree perfectly with my playing. Furtwängler, however, defends his position on the basis of the horns' needs, and similar nonsense. He has the kindest things to say about Halm, from personal acquaintance; further, that in Berlin people are no longer satisfied with Schreker[2] and that no one at all wants to learn—that Straube is indeed a highly educated man but basically no musician. I repeatedly ask him about the program of his Sunday concert, and he speaks all the time only of Schubert and of Tchaikovsky's E minor Symphony.

[1] With Otto Erich Deutsch, Schenker prepared a revised edition of Schubert's Symphony in B minor ("Unfinished") for the Philharmonia series of miniature scores. The two men met on October 19, 1927, and worked through the facsimile edition of the score with Schenker's copy of changes that had been noted by Brahms. The new score was published in April 1928, with a note formulated by Deutsch: "New edition (1927), based on a recent comparison with the autograph manuscript." The publishers credited neither Schenker nor Deutsch with the editorial improvements.

[2] Schreker was Director of the Berlin Music Hochschule 1920–32.

Furtwängler to Schenker (letter), August 30, 1929
OJ 11/16, [7]

St. Moritz (Engadin)

Dear Mr. Schenker,

I am delighted to hear from you so unexpectedly. You will no doubt have heard more, and in greater detail than I can say, from Professor Curtius on the Heidelberg story.[1] I have recommended you here, as also elsewhere, as much as in my judgment I consider it my duty. That nothing positive has ever materialized for you has been a constant source of great regret to me. Whether you would then have accepted it, and would have preferred a regular position to your free existence as a writer, would have been a matter for you to decide. At any rate, it is certain that by those means you will obtain a hearing both for yourself and for the great cause that you represent.[2]

We all of us have good reason to rejoice at a monograph on the "Eroica." I am sorry to hear that you have sometimes had difficulties over my Vienna concerts—which at any rate I shall still be doing next year. By the way, I had no idea whatsoever that you attend concerts with any degree of regularity. I have missed getting together with you throughout the whole winter, and this time shall, as soon as I have time, definitely get in contact with you. (I have stayed the whole year round at the Hotel Imperial, and shall for the time being continue to do so.) So perhaps I can say "until we meet" in the fall! With warmest greetings, and to your wife as well, and from mine. I remain

Cordially,
Yours,
Wilhelm Furtwängler

¹ Probably Ludwig Michael Curtius, who had been teaching in Heidelberg since 1920. Perhaps Schenker had hoped, with Furtwängler's help, to procure a regular appointment in Heidelberg, but had been disappointed.

² See chapter 13.

❧ Furtwängler to Schenker (letter), December 16, 1929
OJ 11/16, [8]

Most revered Mr. Schenker,
Since I am in Vienna this week passing through, my long-cherished desire to get together with you once more for an evening might perhaps become a reality. I am staying now at Hamburgerstrasse 11 (entrance 6). Perhaps you could send word to me whether we could see one another on <u>Thursday</u> evening.[1] My telephone number is A 35081. (You evidently do not have one?)
With all the best greetings, and to your revered wife, too.

   Yours,
     Wilhelm Furtwängler

¹ The meeting, for December 19, was agreed, but Furtwängler canceled on the day because he had a fever.

❧ Diary entry, March 18, 20, and 21, 1930

[March 18:] From Furtwängler (letter): would Friday evening be convenient for us? [...] To Furtwängler (letter): we shall expect him on Friday.

[March 20:] Lie-Liechen begins preparing for the Furtwängler evening.

[March 21:] 8:15–12 Furtwängler! Lie-Liechen prepared a fine, perhaps too opulent, meal; we speak about Beethoven's *Missa solemnis*, regarding the insurmountable difficulties in the Gloria and Credo; I show him the passages in the first edition of Schindler, the passage that refers to Op. 14, Nos 1 and 2; we also touch upon the Jewish question, then I give him an outline of Rameau[1] up to today (in the third yearbook); concerning Weisse's Octet, I speak very appreciatively, and Furtwängler promises on his own volition to write to Hase[2] concerning its publication. He agrees to help me, too, by writing to Hase and expects that I will be asked for the work. We were strangely touched by his communication that, though he earns a great deal of money, he must support many persons who are close to him, so that he actually has nothing in the event of a serious career disruption. He leaves 1.50 shillings for the maid.

¹ Schenker, "Rameau or Beethoven? Creeping Paralysis or Spiritual Potency in Music?", *Masterwork* 3, 1–9 (Ger., 11–24).

² Hellmuth von Hase (1891–1979): an official at Breitkopf & Härtel whom Furtwängler had undertaken to approach about possible publication of either the "Eroica" Symphony study or *Masterwork 3*.

❧ Schenker to Furtwängler (draft letter), November 11–16, 1931
OJ 5/11, [1]

[*This letter was dictated, heavily edited, and then a final copy made that is not known to survive. The text below represents Schenker's final intentions as far as they can be determined from the amended draft.*¹]

Your gesture of sympathy gave me great pleasure. This summer, I followed the instructions of my doctors, who strenuously demanded that I give my eyes a rest. My battle over the "Eroica" had been waged rather too heroically on my part. Insufficient time! I was obliged to do only very little writing and reading, no matter how hard this was for me, as someone who has experienced no let-up in work since my thirteenth year of life. I held myself to this injunction, and see myself amply rewarded by the restoration of my eyesight. (There is still room for caution.)

Our dear Dr. Weisse's successes really do exceed all expectations. Even just immediately before his departure,² he spoke once at the Music Pedagogical Association in Vienna [and] enthused his colleagues, without being able to carry them off as he would have liked, for their own sakes, to be able to do. Weisse then also spoke in the concert hall in Hamburg with dazzling success. As evidence of his success in Hamburg I am enclosing herewith a review by Herman Roth,³ who has taken over [Ferdinand] Pfohl's place at the *Hamburger Nachrichten*, because I seem to recall that you have been acquainted with Roth since Munich days.

I very much give Roth credit that after a lull of so many years he has, as in former times, very agreeably become active once again in my cause. Only the gaffe at the end of the article, where even he speaks erroneously of an "abstraction," obliged me to write him a letter setting him straight. It is really incomprehensible to me how musicians with the examples of my right thinking available to them can attribute such "abstraction" to me! Never and nowhere have I ever said that all good composing always takes the Ursatz and its 3rd-, 5th- or octave-progression as its point of departure, and that it then continues to propagate itself through the diminutions of the layers until, hey presto!, you finish up with, e.g., a new "Eroica" Symphony! That is not the way it is. The image of the Ursatz and its layers that I offer has its logic only in the connection to a content, whereby it is completely immaterial whether one views it as moving from the simplest thing in the background to the most colorful thing in the foreground, or conversely from the most colorful in the foreground to the simplest in the background. That indicates at the same time that the background is present always and everywhere in the foreground, i.e. the background proceeds always in tandem with the foreground.

But the "chronological dimension" of actual creation is quite another matter. This absolutely does not comply with that "logical" progression as fully as the image in the mind of the person who has misunderstood it seems to say. Rather, in the context of a gift for improvisation, the composer's imagination is secretly set on fire by some kind of sweeping intuitive move. The latter can be whatever he wishes; the only crucial thing is that at the very moment a growth process gets underway, what is burgeoning submits itself to that selfsame "logic" that adheres to my image: It is as if a masterwork composed itself into the spaces of third, fifth, or octave! Artists who work with language can also confirm this process from their own creative activity. They, too, operate with a certain something that causes the foreground to grow in conformity with the simplest foundation. This feeling is definitively no "abstraction" if it expresses itself in tangible form in the composition.

The incapacity of today's composers to create a true masterwork can be explained in historical terms precisely in that they have lost that "something." Through increasing complicity, through commercialization, and above all through false teaching, the improvisatory impulse, hitherto greatly cherished, has been killed off—that impulse which bears as if effortlessly the brunt of the work of creation and spares the composer, so to speak, the labor of combining the small components. Perforce, he confined himself accordingly within the temporal dimension to inventing short "motives"—the master composers know nothing of this sort of motive—which he then for the first time extended by means of mechancial repetition occupying himself with "fashioning" through augmentation, diminution, inversion, etc. With this dreary mechanical working, the eye for the larger-scale interconnections was lost, in his own creativity as sadly also for such interconnections that are inscribed in the masterworks!

Now back to Weisse's successes. In New York he managed in no time at all to win over the entire teaching faculty of the Mannes Conservatory to his way of thinking and to my cause. All the teachers, most notably the previous theory professor in the post,[4] are familiarizing themselves with the new theory in regular lessons under his direction. Even Mr. Wedge, the Director of the Institute of Musical Art,[5] who was teaching according to my books at an even earlier stage, has allied himself with him. I venture now to say that a "Schenker Institute" like that in Hamburg[6] (which was the first of its kind in the world) has been opened in the USA.

I endorse your opinion that all is up with modern music (are you perhaps familiar with the article by Stravinsky in the *Baseler National Zeitung* of November 3, 1931?[7]), and thus the articles that you published during the summer and fall in the *Neue freie Presse*. It gladdens my heart that you have after all resolved to pin your colors to the mast and show confused musicians and friends the way of music.

Your call to <u>Wagner</u>[8] is really in keeping with the times. Certainly it ought to and must be stated in criticism of this giant spirit from the loftier vantage-point of the yet greater masters of instrumental music in all seriousness that "leitmotive" = "motive," see above. Thus, for example, the disadvantages of a motive-based technique (see above) recur also in his leitmotive technique. Leitmotives work counter to any synthesis, even the synthesis of a "music drama"! (One might almost see in Wagner's leitmotives an anticipation of the flashbacks used in film so copiously these days.) But none of this enters the heads of today's generation, for even in his own day it [i.e. Wagner's work] was given only once and will never be given again.

In Verdi's entire output, I would not know eight measures that I would like to make a fuss about—although one could still do so, perhaps, in Smetana, Dvořák, and others. Even today he barely satisfies the banal appetite for "melody" of Werfel[9] and his comrades. What the earliest Italian composers wrote still benefited even our masters, whereas Verdi is by contrast of no artistic value.

You yourself (as also Huberman) have finally declared in the full blaze of publicity that the musical community is in the process of disintegration. You have also quite excellently adduced the cause of that, insofar as it is to be sought in the nature of radio and recordings.

But an even more important cause seems to me to lie in the lack of relationship to the production of our great masters that has been going on now for 200 years.[10] Centuries of music were required before the emergence of Handel and Bach! It would have been impossible for these two geniuses to appear, for example, as early as the third or fourth century of our era. The feeling for the linear progressions had first to gain strength in the practice of the art, in order that they could shoulder the even greater freights of diminution. Thereafter, the new belief for the first time attained its edifying full power—the belief to which people just could not pay sufficient service with the most noble art!

But today! There, above all, lies the grievous error, which in itself alone testifies against any talent whatsoever on the part of today's younger generation: the latter considers a genius from the past as fundamentally a long-lost entry in the ledger of history instead of understanding it as something also enduringly valid for the future, as an immutable goal to strive for. A genius from the world of religion such as Moses is truly not dead when still today in his name millions of orthodox Jews stand fast against a whole world. There is no doubt that the Jews fundamentally misunderstand the Bible—this is exactly the misunderstanding from which Jesus wanted to free them—and yet, the error itself, through which they are chained to Moses, redounded—and still redounds—to their benefit. That is how strong the blessing of a genius is! (This is why I place this example first here.)

Is it possible for Jesus to be surpassed? Does he not remain the goal of all men, even into the remotest future? Is it possible for Plato to be surpassed? However much successive ages may take the substrate of these geniuses, there remains in their work a godlike element that disdains each age! Of this godlike indestructibility the world has not the remotest inkling! I am in no doubt whatsoever that there will be nothing left for Germans in future centuries to do other than to cherish the musical geniuses with exactly that godlike honor with which the Jews wander through the ages with the Old Testament. But how the pursuits of today's German world contradict that, especially in the so assiduously Americanized cities! From year to year, new geniuses are proclaimed, for whom people try to make room so that the old geniuses can be declared superannuated and packed off into retirement. — But then, you know all this, too — —

What remains unanswered to this day, however, is the question: What now? What should and ought to happen now that "modern" music has been ruinously mismanaged, in the vacuum, the first such ever in the history of music? If nothing happens—soon it will not be possible for anything to happen at all—the total extinction of music will be sealed. That a people of the power of genius of the Germans has literally within the space of a few years discarded its greatest musical spirits is all the more inconceivable since it, out of material (to say nothing whatsoever of spiritual) instinct, and overtaken by such great material need, ought already to have contemplated the unparalleled monetary value of the master-repertory—and cultivation!!

I dare to assert that all the industries in the world do not compare with the German industry of genius. Once that is recognized, then this industry, too, must again be recapitalized, just as banks and other monetary values are being recapitalized today! It is imperative that the German people do not themselves undermine the "credit"—I make progress in adapting to the expressions of the monetary era—which German music has enjoyed throughout the world up to now. They have the duty to stand up with all their might for the greatness of that spiritual currency. But is there still any possibility of this happening? I say: Yes! Only it must not be the ?—people who make the decisions on this, for they know nothing about these matters.

So, for example, nothing would be simpler than to begin as early as the lowest school classes with teaching and listening for third-, fourth-, and octave-progressions in folksong, chorale melodies, in small exercises—Dussek, Clementi, and others. This would equate with the method whereby language is taught in schools on the basis of grammatical concepts and relationships. Thousands of children, who are otherwise lost to music, could be won over anew to it in this way and form the artistic humus[11] that you, too, obviously seek. If music were not simply the poorest and most misunderstood of all the arts, outlawed for everyone, do you not think that I might long ago have been called upon by the Berlin or Vienna Ministry as a consultant? After all, I am, as my life's work attests, one of the very few Morgans[12] in today's music—does one not consult Morgans in all times of need? Why is this or that person too cowardly to seek advice from me; are they afraid that I might demand something of them that they could not fulfill?

In short, all practices that seek to help out the banks ought to be valid also for music. A stop must at last be put to the "Amstel Bank" people![13]

For Vienna in particular I would have in mind a glittering recapitalization, without Geneva, Basel, or Paris.[14] I have often put my suggestion forward in the past (in *Der Tonwille*, before Hammerschlag[15] and others). Instead of clinging desperately, for example, to some particular death date, it would be far more profitable, even for the foreign tourist industry, if Vienna were to build a "Festival Playhouse" for its musical gods along the lines of Bayreuth in which, annually, a hand-picked orchestra made up of the best instrumentalists in the world were to present their great works in canonical fashion. One such as yourself ought to open the series and take care of its subsequent growth, so that the tradition would continue to be effective over time! People throughout the world would then know: only in Vienna can one hear the masterworks to best advantage! Salzburg would retain its own particular Mozartian character, which it would no longer ever need to falsify, because Vienna would be taking over part of the task.

And there would still be many another way of recapitalizing music! What has to be made clear is this: just as monetary calamities can be recapitalized only through money, so also a musical calamity can be recapitalized only through music. (Homoepathic cures!) No Pan-Europe, no politics—only the *restitutio in integrum*[16] of our great art can help!

Have you heard that, for example, people wanted to convert a Gothic cathedral into a "modern" church because today's interpretation of religious or architectural matters has changed? Every proud Gothic cathedral stands as a witness for the past, and no less also for its own time. What right do interpretations, changing, falsifying, have to tinker with the Gothic cathedrals of Music?!

[*in Heinrich Schenker's hand:*] Do not neglect to let me know whenever you are in Vienna! Then we can talk more about this matter.

Most cordial greetings from us both to you and your wife,

Yours,

H. Schenker

---

[1] The creation of this letter is recorded in detail in Schenker's diary: November 11th: first part dictated to Jeanette; 12th: dictation completed; 13th: first draft [18 pages] written up by Jeanette; 14th–15th: corrections made [with redraftings on some versos]; 15th–16th: 18-page fair copy made by Jeanette; 17th: letter sent registered mail.

[2] In September 1931.

[3] Presumably "Bekenntnis zu Heinrich Schenker," *Hamburger Nachrichten*, September 17, 1931, a clipping of which is preserved in Schenker's scrapbook.

[4] Presumably Leopold Mannes, son of the Mannes School's co-founders, David and Clara Mannes.

[5] Institute of Musical Art: music conservatory founded by Frank Damrosch in New York in 1905, which in 1926 merged with the graduate school of the Juilliard Music Foundation to form the Juilliard School of Music.

[6] Moriz Violin's ill-fated Schenker Institute, founded in 1931: see chapter 21.

[7] Igor Stravinsky, "Moderne Musikauffassung," *National-Zeitung* (Basel), November 3, 1931.

[8] Wilhelm Furtwängler, "Der verkannte Wagner" and "Die Lebenskraft der Musik," in *Ton und Wort: Aufsätze und Vorträge 1918 bis 1954* (Wiesbaden: Brockhaus, 1958), 31–32, 33–39, extracted in part from "Ueberdruss an der Musik: Zur Krise des Konzertlebens," *Neue freie Presse* no. 24114 (November 1, 1931): 31, no. 24116 (November 3, 1931): 12.

[9] Franz Werfel (1890–1945): Austrian poet and writer, author of *Verdi: Roman der Oper* (Vienna: Zsolnay, 1923) and articles on Verdi, German translator of three Verdi librettos.

[10] Perhaps an oblique reference to Jean-Philippe Rameau's *Traité de l'harmonie* (Paris: Ballard, 1722) (thus approximately two hundred years prior to 1931), about which Schenker had written an antagonistic article in *Masterwork* 3, 1–9 (Ger., 11–24.)

[11] Schenker uses the concept of "humus" notably in "The Mission of German Genius," *Tonwille 1*, vol. 1, 3–20 (Ger. orig., 3–21).

[12] John Pierpont Morgan, Jr. (1867–1943): American financier, son of the investment banker, art collector, philanthropist, and contributor to the New York Metropolitan Museum of Art. John Pierpont Morgan, Sr. (1837–1913): creator in 1924 of the Pierpont Morgan Library in New York in memory of his father and to house the latter's library and collection, and philanthropist in his own right. This is part of the larger financial metaphor that Schenker is creating in this section of the letter.

[13] The Amstel Bank was founded in the Netherlands in 1921. It had ties to the Österreichische Credit-Anstalt, the bank founded by the Rothschild family.

[14] The allusion of all three locations is perhaps to Stravinsky, although that of Paris could refer to Debussy or Ravel; or perhaps all three are meant as banking centers.

[15] Possibly János Hammerschlag (1885–1954), Hungarian composer, music critic, and pioneering early music specialist, who founded the chamber music ensemble Musik der Vergangenheit in 1923, and taught composition, music history, and organ at the National Conservatory in Budapest.

[16] *restitutio in integrum*: legal term (shades of Schenker's legal training), the restoration of something to its previous (or original) condition, a principle of Roman Law enshrined in the *Corpus Juris Civilis* (Justinian I, 529–34), one of the primary guiding principles behind the awarding of damages in common law negligence claims.

❧ Furtwängler to Schenker (letter), dated April 5, 1932
OJ 11/16, [10]

BERLIN W. 10
HOHENZOLLERNSTRASSE

Dear, revered Mr. Schenker,
Such a present,[1] coming from you, I accept with pleasure. I will limit myself here to thanking you briefly and cordially. —
May I visit you and your wife on Friday evening? Perhaps you could send word to me at the Hotel Imperial.

With all good wishes to you both,
most cordially,
Yours in haste,
Wilhelm Furtwängler

[1] A copy of Brahms's arrangement of Handel's oratorio *Saul*, as promised in Schenker's invitation. Federhofer (1985), 128, assumes that the gift was a sign of gratitude for Furtwängler's funding of *Masterwork 3*. Evidently it was part of a plan to persuade Furtwängler to perform the work; the matter is discussed in letters from Schenker to Oswald Jonas of April 9 and July 18, 1932.

❧ Diary entry, April 8, 1932

8:30 p.m. to midnight: Furtwängler. The evening passes very congenially. The meal that Lie-Liechen provides is the most delightful overture! Lots of conversation about art and artists, Haydn, Brahms, about critics. After the meal, I present the gift and explain it concisely. Finally, a little Haydn celebration: I show him the development section of the E♭ major sonata,[1] and play little pieces from sonatas. Lastly, I speak of my wish regarding thoroughbass and show him the little book of J. S. Bach,[2] of which he is completely unaware. It was nice that he reminisced on his first encounter with me in my *Ninth Symphony* in Lübeck! He consoled me over the absence of comment, saying that my cause is in fact spreading far and wide. So many people speak [about music] in my terms without being aware of where they have got it from; he has recently caught himself committing plagiarism in an article for the *Vossische Zeitung*.

> [1] Piano Sonata in E♭ major, Hob. XVI:49, for which an analysis of the development section of the first movement appears in *Five Analyses in Sketchform*.
>
> [2] J. S. Bach, *Vorschriften und Grundsätze zum vierstimmigen Spielen des General-Bass oder Accompagnement* (1738), which survives in an error-ridden copy by Johann Peter Kellner.

❧ Diary entry, July 22, 1932

To Furtwängler (letter): I send the Urlinie graphs;[1] invite him; congratulate him on Bayreuth:[2] but [there is a] Marian cult—*mulier taciat in ecclesia*[3]—even in the Wagner church, women must remain silent!

> [1] *Five Analyses in Sketchform*.
>
> [2] Furtwängler first conducted at Bayreuth in 1930; it is unclear precisely what this remark refers to.
>
> [3] Latin: "Woman should remain silent in church."

❧ Furtwängler to Schenker (letter), August 2, 1932
OJ 11/16, [11]

Seebad Bansin

Dear, revered Mr. Schenker,

Your missive, and now—by a roundabout route—also the Urlinie graphs, have reached me here. I can't tell you how delighted and grateful I am for them. It always gives me special pleasure when I see your handwriting once again. Among other things, it is particularly my consciousness of how closely related our strivings are, and how much they have in common—strivings that, despite each individual particular instance, might in your words appropriately be called the fight against mankind for genius. And for me, as the younger man, your passionate undertaking is a mainstay for, an affirmation of, the undying and indestructibly incessant operation and vitality of vibrant genius!

Your suggestion that I visit you in Igls is for me very tempting. Sadly, however, at this moment it is a very remote possibility; but I do have in mind at any rate to go to Switzerland in the late winter and perhaps it could be combined with that! Just send me word <u>how long</u> you intend to stay there.

Have you heard anything from Weisse? Do you know where he is, what his address is? I know little or nothing of him since he has been in America.

Cordial best wishes, and also to your esteemed wife,
every yours truly,
Wilhelm Furtwängler

🎵 Furtwängler to Schenker (letter), November 16, 1932
OJ 11/16, [13]

Dear, revered Mr. Schenker,

I have been in Vienna since yesterday evening. Might it be possible for us to get together this evening? i.e. that, if it is convenient for your wife, I might call on you today at around 7:30, have supper with you, and spend the evening with you?

Please drop me a line via the bearer of this—in the affirmative, I hope.

In hopes of seeing you soon,
with cordial greetings, and to your wife, too,
[unsigned]

🎵 Diary entry, November 16, 1932

Furtwängler from 8:00 [p.m.] to 12:30 [a.m.]: he talks also about his piano concerto, will perhaps play it to me on Saturday. Later, I speak of my difficulties. — Furtwängler will do what he can to help.[1] He speaks about his position vis-à-vis the public and critics, etc.

---

[1] See chapter 13.

19

Open Disagreement: Schenker and Paul Hindemith

THIS material is the only known exchange in writing between Schenker and a leading contemporary composer to address technical and aesthetic matters. Hindemith had begun his professional life as an orchestral violinist in 1915, and was soon composing prolifically. From 1923 he focused his performing activities on the Amar Quartet, which played only contemporary music, and on composing. In 1927 he became a teacher of composition in Berlin, and began to develop the interest in music pedagogy that intensified after his move to the United States in 1937 and resulted in several theoretical texts. His letter to Schenker is an early indication of his thinking about tonality and, with that, his views on the teaching and practice of composition.

Aged 31 in October 1926, Hindemith was responding to this comment by Schenker, published just four months earlier:

> A theory teacher writes: "If Beethoven were alive and composing today, his musical style would resemble that of a Hindemith more closely than that of a Clementi." It comes as a shock to see Beethoven, Hindemith and Clementi in collision with one another like this! Be it so!—but there is a far simpler solution to the matter. Supposing Beethoven wrote music "today" like Hindemith—well then, he would be bad like him.[1]

It is no surprise that Hindemith's blithe rhetorical ploy of asserting basic affinities between their views on music failed to break down the well-practised Schenkerian resistance to the blandishments of committed modernists. Even if Schenker had lived long enough to study Hindemith's *Craft of Musical Composition*[2] and heard such major compositions as *Mathis der Maler* and *Ludus Tonalis*, it is unlikely that he would have changed his mind. Despite Hindemith's claim in his letter that "the fundamentals of musical activity [...] are every as bit as important for our music of today as for that of times gone by," his eventual proposition, according to Robert Wason, that "all chords have 'roots' (determined by the root of their lowest, most 'consonant' interval),"[3] was scarcely compatible with a theory owing more to Fuxian counterpoint than to the fundamental bass.

---

[1] "Miscellanea," *Masterwork 1*, 121 (Ger., 219). The volume was not published until June 21, 1926.

[2] Paul Hindemith, *Craft of Musical Composition*, transl. Arthur Mendel (New York: Associated Music, vol. 1, 1942; vol. 2, 1941; Ger. orig. *Unterweisung im Tonsatz*: vol. 1, 1937; vol. 2, 1939; vol. 3, 1970).

[3] Robert W. Wason, "*Musica practica*: Music Theory as Pedagogy," in *The Cambridge History of Western Music Theory*, ed. Thomas Christensen (Cambridge: Cambridge University Press, 2002), 46–77, esp. 69–70.

Matthew Brown has argued that "Schenker was extremely flexible in his handling of highly chromatic music," and "claimed that composers can never write too chromatically in tonal contexts."[4] But Hindemith's aspiration "to obviate distinctions between diatonicism and chromaticism by invoking various distinctions of tonal relations based upon acoustical grounds"[5] has more in common with post-Riemannian attempts to extend or even suspend tonality along lines explored by theorists such as Ernst Kurth and Arnold Schoenberg than with Schenker.

Hindemith's recommendation that "if the tonality is well thought through and clearly presented by means of several harmonic pillars placed in wisely calculated positions, then the harmonic construction in between can be somewhat looser, the tonality worked out in weak, even the weakest, form"[6] might be thought to fit with the kind of Schenkerian understanding of chromaticism presented by Brown. Yet what David Neumeyer defines as Hindemith's understanding of "the diatonic as a special case of the fully chromatic"[7] underlines the latter's remoteness from Schenkerian theory. Summarizing the relative impact of Schenker and Hindemith in the USA after 1960, Wason judges that "Schenkerian theory gained an increased following such that Hindemith's pedagogical program soon became little more than a historical curiosity."[8] Even the recent prominence of neo-Riemannian routines and "sonata theory" seems not to have brought any renewed interest in Hindemith's thinking about chordal construction and analysis in its wake.

ARNOLD WHITTALL

---

[4] Matthew Brown, *Explaining Tonality: Schenkerian Theory and Beyond* (Rochester, NY: University of Rochester Press, 2005), 180.

[5] Wason, loc. cit.

[6] Cited and translated from *Unterweisung im Tonsatz* 3, Übungsbuch für den dreistimmigen Satz (Mainz: Schott, 1970), in David Neumeyer, *The Music of Paul Hindemith* (New Haven: Yale University Press, 1986), 42.

[7] Neumeyer, op. cit., 25.

[8] Wason, op. cit., 69–70.

❧ Hindemith to Schenker (letter), October 25, 1926
OJ 11/51, [1]

FRANKFURT am MAIN,
GROSSE RITTERGASSE 118

Greatly revered Professor Schenker,

On the last page of your first yearbook I have come across my name and the word "bad." As our dear Lord has seen fit to put me on Earth at this time, I am prompted by this to send you a few lines—(I had been meaning to do so for some time). Not, I should say, that I am vexed: I am not. Since you know that I am bad, I am bound to infer that you know something of my music, and about that I certainly cannot be vexed. Of myself I can tell you that I am an ardent and delighted reader of your books. Delighted because they correctly state for the first time what a good musician hears, feels and understands when occupied with music; because in them are revealed the fundamentals of creative musical activity—fundamentals that, as you so rightly say again and again, had validity from time immemorial and will be valid for evermore. And they are every bit as important for our music of today as for that of times gone by. Believe me when I say that, long before I read so much as a sentence of your writings, I have always—please don't laugh at this—striven to fulfill these fundamental demands. For sure, these strivings have in part miscarried: in many pieces they are perhaps not fully apparent, in others they are possibly submerged under a tangle of surface elements. (It takes time before one is able to express correctly what one wants to say.)

I am enclosing with this letter scores of two of my quartets.[1] If after overcoming some initial and lingering discomfort you will vouchsafe them the same meticulous and profound treatment that you do a Scarlatti sonata,[2] then I am convinced that you will find the "Urlinie" in this music, too, hence musical reason and logic, and the confirmation of your teachings. I cannot presume to compare myself to Schubert, but I do wonder whether I cannot modify the last sentence on p. 200 of your yearbook[3] in such a way that the guilt need not rest unconditionally upon me alone if contrary to expectations you reject this music as lacking any meaning. I do not share your opinion that music died with Brahms; nor am I yet old enough to believe that the present era is worse than any previous one—for I would be putting myself in the position of someone who readily grants to a train that it should move forward while at the same time demanding that it do so with the aid of four legs since wheels are not to be found in Nature. Only one thing is perhaps worse: that the best minds occupy themselves with moaning that things are no longer what they used to be. One only describes, discusses: but where is the positive work? Is it not better to try to produce music, even at the risk of going astray ninety-nine times out of a hundred, rather than merely writing about it?

Please, I beg you, do not think that I profess myself a follower of your theories for some dishonest reasons. Do not fear, either, that your teachings are misunderstood or distorted by me as a result of a superficial enthusiasm. Rest assured that, in these works as in all the music that I write or play, I strive for nothing other than clarity and integrity. Even if we completely fail to reach agreement in words or notes, I hope that by playing a Bach violin sonata[4] to you I can not only afford you some pleasure but also prove to you that there are still musicians around even today. Finally, I ask you not to read this letter more intemperately than the spirit in which it was written. Try to exercise the peace of mind that permits fellow-men not to despise, above all not to hate, one another. That peace and that boundless love of music [are what] induce me to undertake everything—even this epistolary attempt, doomed to failure as it perhaps is—that can serve to clear away misunderstandings, smooth over roughnesses, and promote a manner of working together, not against one another.

With greatest respect and cordial greetings, I am
Your devoted
Paul Hindemith

¹ Hindemith had written six string quartets by 1926: those in C major (1915) and E minor (1917), now lost, and No. 1 in F minor, Op. 10 (1919), No. 2 in C major, Op. 16 (1921), No. 3, Op. 22 (1922), and No. 4, Op. 32 (1923). A week after receiving this letter, Schenker discussed the quartet with two of his students: November 2 (Hoboken): "Hindemith's Quartet"; November 4 (Elias): "the Steckel Quartet and the Hindemith Quartet that was sent."

² Allusion is to the two studies of Scarlatti sonatas included in *Masterwork 1*, 67–74, 75–80 (Ger., 125–35, 137–43).

³ "Further Considerations of the Urlinie: 1," *Masterwork 1*, 111 (Ger., 200): "It follows from all of this that Schubert has committed no error of declamation at all in measure 2; if the author of the essay in question nevertheless senses a difference between Wagner's declamation and Schubert's, he will have to account for it in some other way than by an error on Schubert's part."

⁴ Allusion is presumably to the two studies of Bach solo violin sonata movements included in *Masterwork 1*, 31–53 (Ger., 61–98). Hindemith is suggesting that Schenker would find his performance musical, even if he cannot concede that his compositions are.

❧ Diary entry, October 30, 1926

From Hindemith (letter and score): he feels hurt by my recent remark in the yearbook; he seeks to find a way to me in which he—not without some offensive remarks (which contradict the rest of the content of his letter)—wants to convince himself and me that he had always agreed and would continue to agree with my demands, including the Urlinie. He invites me to read the letter without animosity and to act constructively, instead of contrarily!

❧ Schenker to Hindemith (draft letter), [November 10, 1926]
OJ 5/17, [1] (Plate 4)

[*This letter was dictated by Schenker to Jeanette on November 3. It occupies fifteen pages. On November 10 the draft was amended in Schenker's hand with copious redraftings on the versos of several pages, and Jeanette copied up the final version. That version, mailed on November 13, is not known to survive. The text below represents Schenker's final intentions as far as they can be determined from the amended draft.*]

My most cordial thanks to you for your friendly letter and score—only one score was enclosed. I am in the agreeable position of being able to reply that I am familiar with your works and actually have several of them in my possession,¹ hence we were not at all unknown to one another when your letter arrived.

I would much prefer to take you at your word and have the pleasure of a visit from you next time you are in Vienna. I am not talking so much of a Bach performance by you—there is really no need for such a thing in order for me to concur wholeheartedly with your artistic self-awareness—a conversation on its own would provide the opportunity to discuss in this way the questions that you have raised. But for now, please permit me to tackle your ideas in the order in which your letter presented them to me.

Your "good musician" is a self-delusion. He always bides his time until the opinion of others is available in print, then makes out that it was his opinion too (indeed, that he thought of it first). Why does he not hit upon the opinion sooner on his own? Time and again, musicians have ingratiated themselves with me as such "good musicians" who had the same opinions as me—mostly behind my back, more rarely to my face—but I have never taken that as anything other than a subterfuge resorted to by characters who cannot elicit approval from people by any other means than by flattering them with the fantasy that they, too, had had that very same thought. Leaving aside evidence to the contrary in word and deed, just how does is it come about that the good musician coexisted and coexists with the likes of myself, and of Marx, Riemann, Thuille, Kurth, Lorenz and dozens of others, too? With whom ultimately does he side, if all those with whom he thinks and feels alike come into conflict with one another, as is ever the case? You see, most highly revered Mr. Hindemith, that I take a quite different view of this matter than do you: I go so far as to posit that things in the realm of artistic property are just as they are in that of material property. Just as in the material sphere the difference between my property and yours is deeply ingrained in us[2]—we do not really possess what belongs to the other—so also in the intellectual sphere the adoption of the opinions of others is only illusory, and everyone abides by his own possession.

You were kind enough to pronounce my ideas about "music of the past" valid also for the "music of today." I myself do not find that so, and take the view that you, too, ought rather to have the courage to say that today's music is completely new, rather than seeking to anchor the latter in some way in that of the past; or—to stick with your metaphor—passing off so-called "new music" as a train and simultaneously as a horse-drawn carriage. In the course of conversation, Schoenberg used to ask me whether it *has* to be and to remain exactly as the masters write. —Thereupon, he bluntly rejected the latter root and branch, while at the same time not disdaining to claim J. S. Bach as his forebear, albeit as someone who constituted a beginning that aimed towards the peak of Schoenberg. That the masters have never been able to express themselves as well as the musicians of today is a claim that you, too, have no doubt heard.

However, you suggest that it could be my fault if I do not keep abreast of today's music. For a start: I would have to agree with you, were it true that today's music had any connection with the art of the masters. Incidentally, is it not a contradiction for you to assert that my ideas about art are valid also for present-day art, while I utterly deny any understanding of the latter? However, not only do I refute that connection, but what is more, I can easily prove that the art of today is no longer art at all, in the sense of the art of earlier times. Consequently, may I take the liberty of responding to your objection in the manner in which I have repeatedly done hitherto? Plainly, it is more likely the case that you have never listened properly to the art of the masters, although you profess that art to be the prerequisite for your own creative work. You personally exhibit modesty in your unwillingness to speak your name in the same breath as that of Schubert;

but a certain Munich theorist,³ against whom my remarks in the yearbook were directed, compares you with Beethoven.

As regards your ideas on the future of music, on the character of the music of our time, I should like to say:

I am not so ambitious as to want to improve on Nature, and I bow to her when she dictates to mankind that any achievement, be it even in the form only of destruction, is wrung from him by means of none other than a belief in progress and perfection. It is Nature herself that instills this illusion into man in order to impel him to work, i.e. to life, to action. The passage of history teaches us that there are, among the generations just as among individuals, those who have destructive tendencies. It is not only material possessions that are squandered by those who inherit them, but intellectual ones as well. The outlook is not always for growth toward material or intellectual prosperity. It is above all on this point that we are not of one mind, and precisely there lies the root of our remaining disagreement. What remains, other than for each of us from our own side to profess the most noble intentions for art and mankind? If you have your views, permit me also to have mine.

You are right to stress above all the need for creativity. Thus it is that someone constituted like me can potentially become important, which leads me to think that when it comes to the secrets of creativity I know a thing or two from experience.

As you can see, therefore, I am not prepared to apologize to the world of today for the fact that I live, work, and claim the right to express myself just as my nature dictates. So then: Is what I have uttered here hatred, revenge, intemperance? Not in the least! You discount my services [to art] in favor of the unknown good musician; you discount also my ear, although you proclaim its usefulness; and despite everything, you think yourself kind and humane. Ought I not to fear that my reply, solely because it is a reply, will appear to you all the more as proof of humane and artistic deficiency?

And yet, motivated by the same sincerity, we want to grant each other the right to his own views. — It is surely the case that your creative work can no longer be allied with that of the masters.

[without valediction and signature]

---

1 Schenker must be referring to Hindemith scores, since the composer did not start producing books until 1937. Whether Hindemith scores were in Schenker's library at the time of his death cannot be ascertained because the catalog for that sale, which was in the form of a card index, has not been traced.

2 more literally "Mine and Thine is deeply felt here" ("hier ist Mein u. Dein gut durchempfunden").

3 "Munich theorist": unidentified: cf. Schenker's diary for August 28, 1924: "From Reygersberg (letter): Quotes a daily newspaper in which, he claims, a professor of theory in Munich wrote: Beethoven would compose like Hindemith [if he were alive] today!".

VI
Advancing the Cause

20
Fighting the Propaganda War: Walter Dahms

A BERLIN-BASED freelance writer and composer, Walter Dahms earned his living primarily as a music critic and as author of composer biographies.[1] Dahms was an active voice in the German press during the 1910s and 20s, writing regular concert reviews and editorials for the *Neue Preussische Kreuz-Zeitung*, the *Kleines Journal*, the *Berliner Börsen-Zeitung*, and the *Magdeburgische Zeitung*; he also wrote more extended articles for theater and music periodicals such as *Bühne und Welt*, *Die Musik*, and the *Allgemeine Musikzeitung*. Dahms was, above all, an outspoken critic of modern music and a conservative voice of his time. His writings in the press had embroiled him in a number of controversies, most notably with supporters of Arnold Schoenberg.[2] But beyond his everyday contributions as a critic, Dahms also wrote extensively on Italian opera and *bel canto* singing, and he had a deep affinity for the writings of Friedrich Nietzsche.

In light of its contents, the selection given here might well have been placed in the preceding section of this volume. Having himself served on the Eastern Front during World War I, Dahms was outraged at Germany's handling of the war and distraught over its post-war politics. His hatred of the Kaiser and the entire officer class of the German army and navy, which spills over in his letter of September 26, 1919, is searing; his conversation with Schenker on August 27th of that year might have become a full-blown row had it not been for the watchful eye of Jeanette. After spending nearly thirteen years in self-exile in Italy and in France (1921–34), Dahms ultimately renounced his German citizenship, changed his name to Gualtério Armando, and moved to Portugal with his second wife, Margarete Ohmann. There, he continued to write books and to compose music until his death in 1973.

However, there was much more agreement than disagreement between the two men. Through all the unrest of the war and postwar years Dahms maintained an unwavering devotion to Schenker. Having first heard of him in 1913, he quickly became one of Schenker's strongest advocates. In the years that followed, Dahms would use his position in the German press to write reviews

---

[1] As Walter Dahms, *Schubert* (Berlin: Schuster & Loeffler, 1912); *Schumann* (Berlin: ibid., 1916); *Mendelssohn* (Berlin: ibid., 1919); *Bach* (Munich: Musarion, 1924); *Chopin* (Munich: Otto Halbreiter, 1924). As Walter Gualterio Armando, *Paganini* (Hamburg: Rütten & Loening, 1960); *Liszt* (Hamburg: ibid., 1961); *Wagner* (Hamburg: ibid., 1963); *Mozart* (unpublished manuscript).

[2] See Walter Dahms, "Offener Brief an den Komponisten Arnold Schönberg," *Das kleine Journal*, February 26, 1912. Reprinted in *Musikblätter des Anbruch*, 6 (1924): 323–24.

promoting Schenker's publications and to write a number of other Schenker-inspired essays advancing the latter's cause.[3]

> The genius is always ahead of his time and stands in conflict with it. Today we also have a master who, though not productive [i.e. compositionally], but rather pathbreaking, demolishing, and constructive, prepares the way for a better art, for better artists. I am referring to the Viennese music theorist Heinrich Schenker, who [...] carries out the work of a musical reformer.

In two books Dahms gave Schenker's ideas a more philosophical orientation by connecting them to the writings of Nietzsche: *The Revelation of Music: An Apotheosis of Friedrich Nietzsche* (1922); and *Music of the South* (1923).[4] In 1926 he even attempted to start a publishing company through which he could fight the Schenkerian propaganda war (as he called it) and do battle with the musical modernists. This project, however, saw just one publication, *Der Musikus Almanach*, edited by Dahms, with the imprint of Panorama, Berlin in 1927, and then fell apart through lack of finances.

Although Dahms's initial plans to study with Schenker never materialized and although they met only once, on a four-day sojourn in Altenmarkt in August 1919, the two men corresponded extensively over a period of eighteen years, from 1913 to 1931. In total, 106 separate items related to their correspondence survive, all of which come from Dahms's side (with the exception of one letter fragment from Schenker to Dahms, presented here). In his diaries Schenker evinced both sympathy and respect for Dahms, even as he expressed some reservations about his ideas about music and his philosophical outlook. And while they shared many political and cultural viewpoints, Dahms and Schenker disagreed bitterly about Germany's handling of the war (as shown again in the letter of September 26, 1919).

This selection contains ten separate items from the correspondence, with supporting entries from Schenker's diaries, spanning the years 1914 to 1923. Some of these items can in fact be seen to form the basis for many ideas Schenker expressed in his published writings—not his considerations of analysis, counterpoint, and harmony, but rather his thoughts on topics of musical genius, music criticism, modern composers, culture and politics. The selected correspondence and diary entries are thus aimed at foregrounding the intimate relationship between these two figures while illuminating a period of immense turmoil.

JOHN KOSLOVSKY

---

[3] Examples include reviews of the Beethoven elucidatory editions, *Der Tonwille*, and *The Masterwork in Music*, and also articles with titles such as "Basic Musical Principles," "The Power of Genius," "Musical Biology," and "Heinrich Schenker's Personality." The quotation is from "Musikalischer Fortschritt," *Neue Preussische Kreuz-Zeitung*, April 9, 1914.

[4] Walter Dahms, *Die Offenbarung der Musik: Eine Apotheose Friedrich Nietzsche* (Munich: Musarion, 1922); *Musik des Südens* (Stuttgart: Deutsche Verlags-Anstalt, 1923).

Dahms to Schenker (letter), March 27, 1914
OJ 10/1, [2]

Charlottenburg 5
Friedbergstrasse 23

Dear Dr. [Schenker],

Out of a personal motivation I am taking the liberty of writing to you to ask for advice. As you fully know, and as I have already told you, I am currently active as a music critic in Berlin; I am actually employed at the *Kreuz-Zeitung*. My greatest wish is to pursue theoretical studies once again from the ground up. My education has been the usual—one learns pure four-part voice-leading, does exercises in counterpoint, and fumbles a couple of fugues together. As I go to work, when my burning urge to compose propels me, I notice that the mastery of musical material (in the sense of our great models) is lacking in all respects. When I open the two volumes of your Musical Theories and Fantasies again, I can see exactly what I am lacking in pure black and white.

Amidst all of this, what I have composed up to now—for the most part songs—I would like to leave behind and enroll once again in school—your school.

Since moving to Vienna is dependent upon a number of factors, I would first like to ask you a question: Do you know anyone in Berlin with whom I could study the "foundations" (in your sense of the word) of music theory? Even though I have spent nearly twenty-seven years of my life here, I do not know a single person to whom I could entrust myself with theory.

Believe me, I truly would have restarted these studies earlier if life in the past seven years had not thrown me to the floor with all its weight.

I would gladly leave this place and come to Vienna if only I could find employment there as a music critic at perhaps some newspaper. Therefore I turn to another question for you: To whom must I express my desire for working in Vienna as a music critic? Do you happen to have any connections whom you could make known to me for an opportunity? It really would be my most ardent wish to come there.

Please excuse me if I have bothered you with so many questions. I simply have no one to whom I can turn.

Asking for your gracious response I remain, with the greatest respect and admiration,

Your most devoted
Walter Dahms

Dahms to Schenker (letter), July 15, 1914
OJ 10/1, [6]

Muggenbrunn

Dear Dr. Schenker,

Your kind letter has thoroughly revitalized me in my hermitage. The recovery of heart and nerves progresses daily, and nothing is more beautiful than this feeling of strength with which one can await what is to come and take delight in the greatest difficulties and adversities with the greatest fighter. Every line of yours continues to sharpen the picture of our time to me a few shades. But most splendid of all is the awareness and joy of being able to contribute a little stone to the dam against the flow of mud and wickedness of less worthy people (above all: the disingenuous). Now you have the blessed certainty that your work is spreading, that slowly but inexorably the effects are disseminating, that friends from all parts come with fiery hearts and the desire to help, and that your work pierces ever more sharply the eyes of the dishonest, these demented art degenerates. Even Vienna will come to this realization. If there are at first but a few who spring from your well then it will continue to grow, and a knighthood of the holy grail (but not a pitiful or teary-eyed, rather a bold and fierce one) will arise, which will uproot the modern magic garden.[1] Triumph!

Your experience with the Vienna Concert House Society yet again speaks volumes. What a pitiful, stupid bunch of people. The best part of it, though, is your position, with which you outmatched all the pettiness and the bitterness. How one will later lament! To all of us the consoling awareness remains, that the Strausses, Regers and Mahlers, despite all the imaginable "advances," and despite all the desperate praise and monuments and titles and gold medallions, will shortly be pushed aside. History is hard and unerring. The truth will be instructive for later generations; but they will stand by their great masters just as blindly as they do today and as they always have. I have just read Schopenhauer on "Fame, Criticism, etc."[2] and found everything so clear and necessary, that greatness even requires time and that the house of cards of quotidian fame collapses on itself when the winds blows in.

Words are flowing into this letter and everything is so endlessly immersed in beauty, that something wholly wonderful and mildly conciliatory gathers around the heart. But we can really only ally ourselves with beauty and good friendship, therefore the fight goes on if we wish to be once again in the place where our foes dwell and squander.

Wishing you the best recovery and renewal of vigor, I remain with the warmest greetings and thanks,

Your
Walter Dahms

---

[1] It is clear from this last sentence that Dahms is contrasting Schenker's circle to the Wagnerian circle, given the allusion to *Parsifal*.

[2] Arthur Schopenhauer, *Parerga und Paralipomena* (1851), Part 2, chapter 15, section 20, "Über Urteil, Kritik, Beifall und Ruhm" (On Judgment, Criticism, Applause, and Fame).

❧ Dahms to Schenker (field postcard), April 25, 1915

OJ 10/1, [8]

Walter Dahms, Armaments soldier
20th Army Corps, 43rd Armaments Battalion,
4th Company, 6th Corporal,
currently Willudden, near Lötzen/East Prussia

Highly revered Dr. Schenker,

 Cordial thanks for your lovely postcard, which made me very happy. The mail is—unfortunately—the only contact with a better and more spiritual world, it beautifies the wasteland for us. But despite all deprivation, the thought remains that it is for our glorious homeland, the mood in particular, which recognizes deeper connections at marvelous heights. You are correct about the wonderful "voice-leading" of Hindenburg.[1] Even here we find the eternal laws of the beautiful and practical in agreement with one another. In Berlin I had the opportunity to hear Hindenburg's brother, who said that the great general is really an artist of Nature in the most elevated sense.

 Please write to me once again, when your work time allows you. I have often reflected upon what I have experienced here and have thereby felt ardent gratitude for you.

   Warm greetings,
    Your true devotee,
     Walter Dahms

---

[1] Paul von Hindenburg (1847–1934): German Field Marshal during World War I and second President of the Weimar Republic 1925–34.

❧ Diary entry, May 5, 1915

Postcard from Dahms from Willudden near Lötzen with touching declaration of gratitude for the advantages he has drawn from my works. Basically unsurpassable experiences, which afford me hope of the best outcome for the later effect of my publications.

❧ Dahms to Schenker (letter), June 15, 1916

OJ 10/1, [20]

                Grunewald-Berlin
                Warmbrunnerstrasse 4

Dear Dr. [Schenker],

 That I am only now replying to your kind postcard from the end of May has to do with my existence in the military. Around the turn of the month I had to pass all sorts of medical examinations. My period of time to stay at the recovery home was lengthened a little. But one always has the feeling of a reprieve. In the meantime I am frantically seeking employment in Berlin with a military office, in order to at least hold a position that is useful for the State and for myself. But I have not been able to achieve this anywhere. At the war press office, only officers are given such positions for the most part, on account of discipline. And at other offices one prefers to take on five dull intellectual tasks with unusual energy rather than a single task, just in order to carry out this service easily. Now it has not been ruled out that I will be sent to Vilnius in the German administration.[1] That is not as nice as Berlin, but much better than cleaning barracks and peeling potatoes in the garrison, whereby one also unfortunately uses up intellectual energies in Germany.

If I were to describe my suffering for what it is, I would say it is war psychosis. A dreadful mental pressure weighs down on me; valuable time goes by; my health erodes more and more; and at every attempt to work my nerves fall to pieces. I have the greatest trouble reading a worthwhile book. Melancholy becomes ever stronger, to the point that I cannot even tell my doctor what is actually wrong with me. I am not a person, but a soldier. A bitter truth for one who is more mentally than physically ill.

I have written a few lines about *Op. 111* in the *Kreuz-Zeitung*;[2] unfortunately I <u>could</u> not write about your work in a more dignified way. That will happen later.

May I shake your hand on your upcoming birthday and wish that the next one is a more "peaceful" one? –

      With cordial greetings,
        and in all devotion,
          Your,
            Walter Dahms

I wish above all that at least you may remain free from direct participation in the war, in order to continue working.

---

[1] Vilnius: capital of Lithuania, which prior to World War I was part of the Russian Empire, was occupied by the German Army from 1915 to 1918, and granted independence in 1918.

[2] Walter Dahms, "Neue Musikliteratur," *Neue Preussische Kreuz-Zeitung*, June 14, 1916, a review of Schenker's elucidatory edition of *Op. 111*, released on March 31, 1916; a clipping is preserved in Schenker's scrapbook.

❧ Diary entry, June 17, 1916

Letter from Dahms with enclosed review from the *Kreuz-Zeitung* of June 14, 1916, both very pleasing. It was with particular gratification that I found he had in his review quoted and emphasized my political allusion.[1] May it as always speak to each reader as it was conceived and articulated by me, and may the reader be transported by it into that atmosphere in which I alone can bring about an awareness of that which is truly German in a Beethovenian genius, a consciousness both of the specific profundity as also of his specifically German essence. If the recognition of a folk-like character as a natural disposition is as imperative as in another respect also the recognition of errors, then may it be of such errors as the German has perpetrated against the most German of Germans. And another thing, too: For all that I place little value on it, it still gives me pleasure that Mr. Dahms remembered my birthday at a time when it seems to have escaped even my closest family and friends, and my pupils male and female. It is, moreover, also the very first sign that a stranger has spoken out about me in this way.

[1] Dahms quotes from Schenker's polemical Foreword, then proceeds: "Schenker is unsparing in the harshness of the fighter for truth […], in the so necessary polemic against the falsifiers and parasites. With passionate conviction he chases the money-changers and hagglers out of the temple of art. Again and again he preaches reverence for the genius. He guides us toward the true understanding of Beethoven in the course of establishing proof, with the aid of the work itself, of the errors of all the editors, improvers, and explainers of the master, and accords us deep insight into Beethoven's spiritual workshop." (Cf. Matthew 21:12; Mark 11:15–16; John 2:14–15).

❧ Dahms to Schenker (letter), July 10, 1917
OJ 10/1, [30]

Vilnius

Dear, revered Master,

Your kind and long letter reached me yesterday. I sincerely look forward to the results of your recent research, especially that you can now complete *Counterpoint 2* in the mountains undisturbed. My Berlin affairs are still "dangling." There are many complicated layers of jurisdiction to pass through before the travel orders come to me. But I hope that they will come ultimately. Waiting around has been the most grueling experience of all in this war. I have some bad weeks behind me, both physically and emotionally; but I hold myself together with all remaining strength.

Less pleasant is what is now happening to the country. One can no longer halt the delirium of democracy and the surrender of our public life to the mammonism and loudmouth behavior of the Parliament. But I firmly believe that, precisely through the partial egalitarianism of people in war, afterwards individualism will take shape in an all-the-more limitless capacity than ever before seen. Many, many people who are now forced down to the level of every minion will embrace an excessive yet equally justified aristocratism. The inner revolt of better and more intellectual people will be very strong against the rotten spell of democracy and will bear its fruit. Now everything reeks of despair. I just read Hölderlin's *Hyperion* and found the following sentence: "For he who suffers in extremity, extremity is for him righteous."[1] —One may not yet speak about the chapter "The Hatred of the Germans" (so long as it is not exclusively about the hatred of the Entente against us). But after the war there will be some things to say and I think they will not be very pleasant things. What you say about the great error of overestimating the common man as a state-preserving element is deeply true. How telling is the demobilization plan previously released by the German government, which makes no mention of intellectuals, scholars, or artists, but instead speaks only about laborers, business people, and public servants. Likewise for the senselessly blind undervaluation of the true—or better—the only bearers of culture with whom they pretend to want to build a new and better Germany. I read about the draft of the electoral law for a proportional electoral system in Prussia from a conservative writer in the ultra-German newspaper *Deutschlands Erneuerung*, where again scholars and artists are completely passed over. Yes, strangely divergent are the views about "culture." The only means by which to live without disgust after the war will be to live in Nature, far away from the metropolis and without newspapers. Could it be so far away??

Wishing you all the best for recovery and strength to work, I remain,

with best greetings,
Your
Walter Dahms

---

[1] Friedrich Hölderlin, *Hyperion*, vol. 2, Book 1 (1798).

Diary entry, August 27, 1919

We chat in Dahms's room for a while,[1] and see a rainbow out of his window, the likes of which we have never seen before: a double rainbow with very strong colors spanning the entire valley. Soon the group[2] enters my room, where I again take a seat at the piano to play this and that, e.g., the Adagio from Beethoven's Sonata in D major, Op. 7.[3] In the evening, Weisse delivers a few sayings by Goethe, but Dahms and I slip into a political controversy; namely, he, while affected by the war, is deeply resentful of those formerly in power and the army generals, apostrophizing Hindenburg as a sergeant, Ludendorff as a felon—no doubt that this betrays a certain limitation, which does not exactly lead one to hope for the best for his artistic development. But I avoid pushing it to the limit, given that Lie-Liechen is also watching to see that we do not slip too deeply into differences of opinion or dare to advance too far into politics; but I always indicate strongly enough how differently I think about all of these issues.

---

[1] This and the following diary entry relate to Dahms's visit to the Schenkers in Altenmarkt in the Pongau (Salzburg region).
[2] The "group" included Hans Weisse, and also Mr. Klammerth, the owner of the castle, Schloss Tantalier, where the Schenkers were staying, and the latter's son, who was currently a pupil of Schenker's.
[3] More likely Sonata No. 7 in D major, Op. 10, No. 3, than the Sonata No. 4 in E♭ major, Op. 7.

ቈ Diary entry, August 29, 1919

Now alone with Dahms. He immediately brings up the issue that has been weighing on his mind for so many years: he describes the lessons with Vrieslander,[1] what material he has covered so far, and asks me for help for the upcoming year. He also mentions his family situation, his divorce from his first wife and living together freely with his second. I then break in to outline a broad plan of study suitable to occupy him for over a year. I remark that, although he has to enjoy species counterpoint without setting his sights on free composition since Vrieslander himself has been inadequately prepared for this method by me, this deficiency can be overcome later. I only all the more urgently recommend the study of thoroughbass of Bach, father as well as son, explain the fundamental differences between the two methods, and tell him that he must study especially C. P. E. Bach's book on thoroughbass to acquire the organ for that unspeakably fine sense of voice-leading, which no musician should lack. Finally, I bring to his attention that there is also a lot he has to read and listen to, if only to stimulate questions in his own mind, which will make him all the more open to the answers that he receives from others. We take the opportunity to talk a lot about Vrieslander's supposed pessimism, about resignation, about the right of talent and half-talent, and I do not tire of repeatedly emphasizing that Vrieslander draws incorrect conclusions from my teaching when he believes he should understand especially from my sermon on genius[2] that no one other than a genius has the right to compose. I clear up the misunderstanding and again emphasize that I only wish to see poor composition and dishonesty banned from art, and incidentally also gladly honor talent when it is aware of its distance from genius, since this is very crucial for mankind as a whole as well as for every individual.

[1] Dahms had been taking lessons with Otto Vrieslander in 1919 and perhaps 1920.
[2] Schenker may be referring either to an article he wrote in August 1914 entitled "German Genius in Battle and Victory," submitted to the *Frankfurter Zeitung* but rejected by that newspaper (surviving as OJ 21/2, [1]), or to a draft of the leading article in *Tonwille* 1, "The Mission of German Genius."

ቈ Diary entry, September 16, 1919

To Dahms (letter): I put up defense against his psychosis; – Nietzsche is better replaced by other leaders.

Dahms to Schenker (letter), September 26, 1919
OJ 10/1, [45]

Wasserburg am Inn

Dear, revered Master,

I received your very detailed letter as I came home from a wonderful hike in the Bavarian Alps. So much sunshine—that was the most beautiful part of it.

Never for a moment have I wanted to suggest that Germany in 1914 was the instigator of everything that was brutal. In times past, brutality was the way of supporters of militarism <u>of all</u> peoples, because these groups never knew of other weapons than their own murderous instruments. Therefore (because for the militarists it will always be as it was, like a lingering "spirit") there is no such thing as military <u>genius</u>, and when one calls it that, it is but a guise accompanying some momentary and mindless bliss, perhaps talent in their line of work. Even Alexander the Great, Caesar, Hannibal, and Napoleon (to say nothing of Hindenburg, who would be prohibited right away from being counted among putative "geniuses") were only talented. Their work has crumbled; nothing other than perhaps their talk of bloodbaths "honors" their memory. They were <u>not</u> productive, they could not even be considered as approaching genius, since the very basis of their existence is destruction. A million Riemanns and Bülows cannot destroy Beethoven's work, whereas it takes only a few politicians (on top of everything a bunch of idiots) to leave the so-called "work" of the militarist in ruins.

It begs the questions: Should mankind again and again allow blood to be shed at the behest of such madcap and criminal types? Should people, whose weapon is spirit, become slaves once again to such ruffians? My answer is: No! For four years I experienced for myself the slavery and tyranny that such "geniuses" and their accomplices carried out for <u>their own</u> ambitions and aspirations without ever being involved themselves.

There is no longer any doubt today that Germany bears just as much guilt for the World War as do the Entente powers. One can no longer speak solely of aggression against us. <u>To me</u> personally it was irrelevant whether or not the Austrian heir to the throne was murdered in Sarajevo. I never had a Frenchman or an Englishman as an enemy, nor have I ever had any bad feelings toward them— thus I remained from the start completely uninterested in the war. Nevertheless I was called for duty, first of all because otherwise (how grotesque!) I would have been thrown into prison, and second because I was caught up in the wave of hazy notions and the torrent of lies with which the German state flooded the German people; in such a short period of time the opinion became that everything German would be attacked. And now I come to the question of my German "brothers."

Yes, most revered master, we were brothers as we pulled on our field-gray military garb; but scarcely were we clad in it when it was made clear to us that, on the contrary, we were not brothers. There were certain men who everyday drank wine, earned 200,000 German marks per year, and for whom others did their dirty work, without themselves ever firing a single shot (I'm referring of course to the high generals). Then came the grand army officers, whom <u>we brothers</u> (as you said) <u>had to obey unconditionally</u>.

There are still people today who approve of blind obedience, of "discipline." For those people only a four-year cure from Prussian militarism can be hoped. "Obedience" is so wonderful when it serves ulterior motives. Then came an army of torturers, slavedrivers, and hangmen who were supposed to "train" us. They did so, however, not as one instructs men and citizens in their hour of danger in how to use weapons, but rather through the application of the most scandalous nastiness, brutality, and baseness—we were treated like slaves, criminals, and prisoners by <u>our own brothers</u>. For four years. No, a million times no, everything I have ever known about brutality, baseness, the most scandalous nastiness I have learned <u>from my German brothers</u>. And all in the name of the King,[1] who is responsible for this, just as he is accountable to a court of law for surpassing all depravity, corruption, and lack of principle—everything imaginable. You have no idea at all what German militarism means, or that in Germany (in stark contrast to England) every loafer, every lump of an official has the <u>right</u> to meddle in the private affairs of a citizen. What's more, he has the <u>duty</u> to do it. This is simply the straw that breaks the back of Germany, when everyone claims someone else to be nastier than him. Every German genius is a single enormous denunciation of Germany—against his "brothers."

You write: "Do you think it would be possible among the French or the English that, standing before the enemy, they would treat each other as enemies?" That is precisely my accusation against Germany: Why were we not all treated like brothers, why were we made into helpless, powerless slaves of dehumanized, bestial, sadistic, and brutal criminals (officers and military doctors by proxy)? Why did these depraved individuals not come and join us, the rank and file, as brothers? Germany would have been invincible!! No, dear Master, that German refinement in military garb had to walk and stand to attention on the excrement-covered embankments, while the officer riffraff and their whores took the footpaths---that is a <u>symbol</u> of <u>German brotherhood</u>, of which <u>we were not</u> guilty. Never should a pardon be granted, nor should people ever forget!! Never!! Germany must be dragged through the mud just as the high command dragged us through the mud. That is the only satisfaction that we have for what we had to endure ourselves with clenched teeth for four years.

Blockade? The most revolting act?[2] What's more revolting was the starvation of the Germans by their own countrymen. You know that Rathenau's[3] war commission had <u>deliberately</u> allowed vast quantities of food supplies to become spoiled in order to raise the price. And even today? The English give supplies, while the shady profiteers control the prices?

And now even Bismarck?! <u>Who</u> consciously and deliberately destroyed his work? Who kicked the creator of the "Reich" out in order to replace him with a bunch of cretins? None other than Wilhelm II. This man had the nerve to demand of those who were <u>innocent</u> of his crimes that they sacrifice their lives for him and his syphilitic household, for his and Krupp's[4] millions, for the whole vermin of grocers and industrialists etc. while he himself (this revolting loudmouth) makes his cowardly escape and is thus too cowardly to end his disgraceful life with a bullet. But I believe, from my pure and just conviction, that the bullet itself would struggle to penetrate this monster, a bullet of <u>our million curses</u>, from the men stuck in the barracks, the bunkers, and the shell holes.

I stay away from all political parties. I associate only with the party of German spirit—Goethe, Jean Paul, Schopenhauer, Beethoven, etc.—of the German spirit that was besmeared in wartime. Not by the Entente powers, who hardly stand up to the likes of Goethe and others. No, they were besmeared by our own dictators. What did Wilhelm II, Ludendorff,[5] Hindenburg, Tirpitz,[6] and all the valiant heroes of the main headquarters have to do with the "German spirit"?? These wretched people, who never even heard a single Beethoven symphony. The German spirit lies in those who were crushed not by their enemies, but by their own brothers. The German dictators, the officers, the military doctors, the war profiteers, the extortionists—they all discredited the German spirit so that it must depart this world with limbs that have become stiff from all the standing to attention and from blind obedience. Germany became the victim of its own character, its all-too-boastful discipline (the means of scoundrels always prevails over defenseless ones).

I don't even believe that the Germans are <u>only</u> angels and the English <u>only</u> scoundrels. I believe they each hold themselves to their own morals, the difference being that in Germany (as I already said) every scoundrel official and every porter has the right and the duty to concern himself with the affairs of others, while this is not so in England. How Mendelssohn, who certainly had a very acute sense for nastiness and baseness, would have had to suffer and struggle in Germany if England had not smoothed the way for him? What a difference in treatment the master experienced from every single Englishman, in contrast to scandalous nastiness, know-it-all, and true Prussian vileness and deceitfulness that he as a mature man of the world had to endure from the riff-raff in Berlin. He himself clearly spoke of such things in his wonderful letters.

How could I be mistaken about something that I experienced and suffered at first hand, what I for four bitter years, every day, every hour felt with my own body and with my own soul. <u>Where has there ever once been raised a voice of compassion for the innocent and murdered millions upon millions of unlucky ones—the elderly, women, and children?</u>? The farewell scenes at the train station, the curses of the slaves, who had to go away yet again, what was called in the disgraceful press the "field of honor"—unforgettable memories for me. The appalling, nervously exhausting hope for the end prepared the ground for the question that is becoming ever-more turbulent: for whom? Here is where the peace process began and I took part in it. Because every person who could still be rescued from being massacred "for the honor of the Krupp and Hohenzollern corporation" (as we the soldiers called it) was of more worth than all the rubbish of the "Fatherland" and the "national honor" (and other such phrases). Now (and not because of hunger) the humiliation of the German dictators was resolved and secured. I feel pride when I think that it was the soldiers who chased away Hohenzollern and had the epaulets of the officers and their pests stripped. I wanted to keep working, to be at home once again, without superiors, without uniform. I had a right to that and they who prevented me from having it deserve my hatred. We tout our national honor; if we could only have our human dignity once again. You write to me that I do not want to pardon any person or any idea. You concede that the people affected have something to pardon, that a crime has been committed against them. An appalling crime, the robbery of youth, the zest for life, hopes, goodness, trust, labor—in short, everything that has made our lives worthwhile. And <u>that</u> we are supposed to pardon?? Perhaps in Christian good-shepherdly fashion we should let ourselves be robbed of the other half of our lives by our German brothers?? —Right away the thought comes to me of abandoning Goethe, Jean Paul, Herder, Lessing, and Beethoven; they and their spirits have been trespassed upon. Never should this noble German spirit, which I would call the spirit of the world because of its all-encompassing greatness, be identified today with the Germans of 1914, this barbarous mob, devoid of even the slightest breath of compassion for one's own brothers. I will cheer when my wife and I can shake the dust of Germany from our feet—Germany, which has besmirched, dishonored, and humiliated me for four years. You want to call this hatred towards Germany a psychosis. Whom do I have to thank for such a thing? Not the Entente powers, but only Wilhelm II and his "brothers." And we are a million in number. The misdeeds that have been done to us are so boundless that the earth would have to burst asunder for a pardon to be granted.

I ask only one thing: that you do not confuse me with Bahr[7] and his associates. These men were not Prussian soldiers, so they have no idea what crime and punishment really mean.

You do not believe how greatly we both lust to be free of Germany. Rather, we can't even begin to think about a recovery. Where we may be happy people once again, then can we think of ourselves as being in a homeland. When we no longer hear the language of the past four years, which has been nothing but talk of detachment, renunciation, orders, humiliation, and killing people.

This is a chaotic letter. I had already written two others, but my indignation towards the "brotherhood" had gone too far, so I had to rip them up. When will one be able to think about things more important, better, and of greater worth—about music? I am now getting down to *Op. 110* and am immersing myself in your wonderful work. How infinitely more elevated that is than England and Germany and all the talk about these concerns. I owe you many thanks for it. I will attempt to pay this debt of gratitude back with tireless work for as long as my decimated powers hold up. Tomorrow I will visit Vrieslander. Then the dreadful politicizing will begin again. Only the two of us are of the same opinion as to the war and to Germany. Stay balanced, my dear Master.

    Your ever faithful and thankful,
    Walter Dahms

Most sincere greetings also to your wife, and from my wife, too.

---

[1] Kaiser Wilhelm II (1859–1941): the last Emperor of Germany and King of Prussia, of the Hohenzollern dynasty, who had been installed June 15, 1888, and would abdicate on December 2, 1919.

[2] Probably the alleged blockade by the Hungarians of foodstuffs discussed in "The Mission of German Genius," *Tonwille* 1, vol. 1, 6 (Ger. orig., 6).

[3] Walter Rathenau (1850–1922): prominent Jewish industrialist, liberal thinker and politician. He was especially active in the early years of the Weimar Republic, until his assassination in 1922 by right-wing extremists. He was author, among other works, of *Von kommenden Dingen* (1917).

4   Krupp A. G.: German company manufacturing steel, ammunition, and armaments. Krupp was an arms manufacturer in World Wars I and II.
5   Erich Ludendorff (1865–1937): alongside Paul von Hindenburg, the leading general of World War I. He was joint commander of the Third Supreme Command.
6   Alfred von Tirpitz (1849–1930): Grand Admiral of the German Navy and Secretary of State of the German Imperial Naval Office before and during World War I.
7   Based on the context, Dahms is most likely referring to Hermann Bahr (1863–1934), an Austrian playwright, novelist, and critic. A member of the Viennese avant-garde and a champion of modernism, Bahr was also active in the press. Among his numerous literary and critical publications, Bahr and his associates published a commentary on Dostoyevsky in 1914, to which Dahms could be referring here.

Diary entry, December 15, 1919

To Dahms (letter): I recommend Koch over Halm and give reasons for doing so. I reiterate the advice I gave him at Tantalier of examining any old work (e.g., Richter—just so long as it is not Riemann) by way of introduction, and then reading Marpurg,[1] but simultaneously pursuing studies on his own in the *Well-tempered Clavier*: Here, among the geniuses, in addition to finding conventional practice, inimitable freedoms are also present, the likes of which conventional practitioners have never so much as seen! I cite the exposition of the Bach C♯ major Fugue and the Brahms B♭ major Fugue [from his "Handel" Variations, Op. 24] as examples, in both of which the entries of the exposition follow each other directly without episodes—the "intellectual future" of these geniuses allows them to leave the conventional practitioners' prescriptions behind and to trust in their innate ability such that a little later they can make up for what was neglected with a longer and more interesting episode.

1   Presumably Friedrich Wilhelm Marpurg, *Abhandlung von der Fuge, nach dem Grundsätzen und Exempeln der besten deutschen und ausländischen Meister* (Berlin: Haude & Spener, 1753–54; new edn. Leipzig; Kühnel, 1806), of which Schenker possessed the 1806 edition.

Diary entry, December 27, 1920

To Dahms (registered letter): picture sent: to the valiant fighter for German musical genius.

❧ Dahms to Schenker (letter), December 29, 1920
OJ 10/1, [60]

Grossgmain

Dear Master,

Many thanks for your long letter, which was for me the greatest joy at Christmas. Thank you as well for your gracious assessment of my books, which I wrote in the spirit of what you now say.[1] I wanted nothing else than to serve genius in a form and manner intelligible to wider circles. Needless to say, such "discussions of works" can never claim to have the character of an analysis or the like. They should not be this way, but should only give casual advice on this or that feature of the work in question.

You were so very kind as to ask about my latest work! I am to write a book on Nietzsche and music for a publishing house in Munich that aims to produce a series of books on Nietzsche in connection with the complete edition of the philosopher. At first I resisted such a thing; then later this work gained a great appeal to me, since the theme deals so closely with questions of world perspective. Perhaps it would interest you to get a sense of the arrangement of my work. I will briefly offer one here:

> The Revelation of Music: An Apotheosis of Friedrich Nietzsche

Preface:
Point of departure is Stendhal's statement that the democratization of people signifies the demise of the fine arts.

Chapter I: Stages of Knowledge
Connection of the philosopher to music from Socrates to Nietzsche. Final stage: Heinrich Schenker

Chapter II: The Dionysian Enthusiast
The experience of music

Chapter III: The Artist and the World
The creative genius is the highest instance of humanity. The genius is the sole measure of art.

Chapter IV: The Old Ideals
Development of music from Palestrina to Beethoven.

Chapter V: The Magic Garden
Musical romanticism. The old ideals are obliterated.

Chapter VI: Dramma Eroico
Wagner. Attempt at a representation of the relationship between Wagner and Nietzsche. Wagner as a symptom of decline.

Chapter VII: Dies Irae
Music after Wagner. The complete decline. Not merely decadence but rottenness.

Chapter VIII: <u>The Great Style</u>
Attempt at a representation of what one understands as "great style."

Chapter IX: <u>Idyll, or Banter and Deep Meaning</u>
The case of Bizet; at the same time a discussion of the essence of opera in general.

Chapter X: <u>David's Harp</u>
Nietzsche and Peter Gast. (A matter perforce to be handled).

Chapter XI: <u>Ariadne</u>
May we hope that our yearning for a new, pure, great art will find fulfillment? —The future of music.

In the course of the book I cite Nietzsche, without, however, always following him or proving him right. The whole book is actually nothing more than a sketch. As I write it down I feel how many thoughts would still allow themselves to form in different ways and perpetuate themselves. These I will reserve for a later work, which is to reveal a more complete and independent character, thanks to the insights that have come to me in part through you.

I am extremely eager for the publication of your new work; I hope to find an appropriate opportunity straight away to be able to draw attention to it befittingly. Above all I am delighted at the interpretation of "Urlinie" in the first volume of the *Little Library*.

I will definitely not be coming to Berlin, nor will I go to Munich to complete the "thoroughbass" studies with Vrieslander. I have not heard an orchestra for a long time now; however, on November 28 I was in Dessau for the première of the opera *Magda Maria* by Oscar von Chelius, to which the composer, the former adjutant of the German Emperor, had invited me. Certainly I would have preferred to listen to *Fidelio* or *Don Giovanni*.

Now once again: a healthy, joyfully productive and successful New Year to you and your revered wife.

       Your ever-true devotee and thankful,
       Walter Dahms and wife

---

[1] Dahms is referring here to his biographies of Schubert, Schumann, and Mendelssohn. See Introduction, above.

❦ Diary entry, August 30, 1922

To Dahms (letter): about our worries; about the Germans' politically and intellectually incorrect attitude; about his book: Nietzsche only suspects, but knows little; the core of all questions is synthesis.

Schenker to Dahms (letter fragment), November 29, 1922
OC 12/91–92

[*the beginning is lacking*]¹

I also know that if the German of ordinary talent and aural capacity does not grasp the depth of his own masters, regardless of whether it comes from a second source or from myself, and despite expert proof, he will never learn to understand such depths—an eternal chasm—and in this matter, which will be the undoing of the races and the peoples, again only the law [of the tones] can effect change, and one day the asinine modern-day fighters of the future, who sell out genius with foreign unscrupulousness and feebleness, will be thrown on to the scrap heap. Today's new clique will again be overtaken by the next race of jackasses, which will be of its own making in the future. Only different! This law will judge today's criminals. In the meantime the greats can wait, since they are of all time. They would think in tones and not about the future, or about their role, or about other human affairs of the day. Even the immediate outpouring of tonal motion in their brains cannot be understood, but it must remain for all times <u>the future of all failed races</u>. The genius does not perish at the hands of mankind, it is the other way around: the human race perishes at the hands of the genius (this by the way goes against Spengler's² formulation).

America and England are unmusical; while our masters preclude any competition with these people, by virtue of the law of communicating vessels their lack of musicality has today become world famous; Universal Edition also brings Germany's lack of musicality over there, and likewise the publishers there sell their junk to us. Under the masters Germany stood in first place; under the sign of dotage, all people have become equal. And all the dandies are recognized in the exchange.

The self-fashioned German intellectuals bear the guilt, who as half-educated people do not understand genius (even from the outside), but who also as Germans out of their lack of understanding, if it is only something foreign, wish to betray nation, soil, art, and school. Today even the *Frankfurter Zeitung* asked whether "the other Frenchness" was not simply a German fiction? Yes, it is! Not only a <u>revision</u> of the Versailles Diktat, but also a revision of world history would have to come from Germany and that would be more than Luther's task, to free the world from the lies, from the commoners, from the rapacity of the West, which seeks to enslave all peoples with idleness and the most base ostentatiousness. That would have to be Germany's future.

[*in Schenker's hand:*] (On behalf of genius)

---

¹ Many of the ideas in this letter, which is written in Jeanette Schenker's hand, found their way into the "Miscellanea" of *Tonwille* 4, vol. I, 160–63 (Ger. orig., 22–26).

² Oswald Spengler (1880–1936): German writer and historian, famous for his two-volume work *The Decline of the West* (1918/1922), to which Schenker is most likely referring.

Diary entry, November 29, 1922

To Dahms (letter, some of which put in the *Tonwille* folder for safekeeping!): about my fees; "Vrieslander–Bekker" in the *Anbruch*; about the boycott on the part of Hertzka; about Furtwängler's intention to intervene in Leipzig; about the article for *Die Musik*[1] as a test of endurance. The law of the "other" will ultimately swallow up those of "today" while the big ones wait; about Germany's self-defacement; Halm's agreement to Briand; Furtwängler's definition as "city dweller," etc.

---

[1] Heinrich Schenker, "Joh. Seb. Bach: Wohltemperiertes Klavier, Band 1, Präludium c-moll," *Die Musik* 6, no. 9 (June 1923): 641–51. This essay was reprinted in *Masterwork* 2 as an appendix to the analysis of its companion fugue.

Margarete and Walter Dahms to Schenker (letter), December 27, 1922
OJ 10/1, [73]

Rome (Monteverde)
via Alberto Mario 21

Dear, revered Master,

Please forgive me that I write to you on the typewriter. But my hands are numb, we have to manage completely without heat, and while it is so beautiful during the day in the sun, inside one's room one freezes. Furthermore the housing profiteers always rent the worst rooms illegally, so that they can live in the nicest ones themselves free of charge. But one cannot change that now. One cannot push the profiteers with spirit, because spirit is a luxury item that "one" can happily renounce. Let us quietly continue to expand, for it will bring "glorious times." I saw from your lovely letter that you at least have become master of the present difficult situation. And I hope that this will remain so. I have been fighting a genuine struggle of despair for some time now with publishers, in order to improve my conditions and to adjust to the food prices. But I arrive at an insurmountable difficulty, as I still have to overcome the gap in foreign currency exchange. And that is simply not possible. <u>One</u> consolation remains: that in Germany, thanks to the famed German justice system, we would have it much, much worse and more difficult than we have it here, where at least we can enjoy personal freedom like decent people, while in Germany we were chased literally out of house and home.[1] Seen in this way, we live happily here, the fight to earn a living is a necessity, and since we are internally at peace we can enjoy the sunshine. There is just one thing, and that one thing has to do with money: the possibility to work more. We have been in our new room since October 15 and in these ten weeks I have not written ten pages of a manuscript. From seven o'clock in the morning until midnight there is the most vulgar Italian noise, making any work impossible. Even as I write now on the typewriter I still have to hear an antiphonal chorus in my ear, the faint noise from the corridor, the uninterrupted screaming and singing, phone calls, and doors slamming. Better dwellings are more expensive. And this is one of the so-called "better families"—imagine how the others are. In the German colonies there are diversely cheap and splendid homes available. But these are made available only to officials, who have a monthly income of at least 2,500 lire. I have had strange experiences here and can only say that the Germans have learned nothing, absolutely nothing from the war. The same methods as in the war. In fact even now coming again from people of the bottom and middle rung of Nature. The ambassador himself is a splendid man, of whom I am fond.

But enough of that! It is boring. The pitiful concert season has begun here. It is again <u>dominated</u> by Beethoven, Wagner, Strauss, etc. One is more or less openly infuriated by this, but one cannot manage a musical season without German predominance. One criticizes practising German artists, when they appear here, superior and proud; but one cannot get on without them. Furtwängler also had to survive it. For here one "knows" Beethoven!! You can hardly imagine the vanity.

I hope next to have the opportunity to be able to write expressly about your teachings. Unfortunately it did not go through with *Die Musik*. I had to fight Schuster's[2] unjustifiable position toward me, even if it meant breaking some hearts. Also the terror of Bekker etc. there naturally works, and I am truly astonished that Schuster wants to publish your contribution. I think therefore that he will have to put up with certain things. Recently I came upon an article by Bekker in the *Frankfurter Zeitung* on "Physiological Hearing." Ah, the despondency from what is said there! They are all at the end still just fighting against admission of the truth, and I fear that now comes the great trial of fraud! To think that Universal Edition would sabotage you seems at first glance highly tempting and very probable. But one reservation: does such a crafty character as Hertzka really believe he can hold you down when the ideas continue to gain ground? I fear it would have the same appearance to every other large publisher. Because in my opinion the deeper reason lies much more in the hostility of the predominant majority of critics and musicians who feel threatened by the existence of someone like you. I am of the opinion that Hertzka thinks without any further concern for anything other than the direction of his own business. And if the ban of silence were to be lifted, which is imposed on your work thanks to every criminal society of critics, then even the sanctions would tear off as from a warm bread roll, and Hertzka would glow.

No, dear Master, if all of those who learned from you and have you to thank for your musical insights would openly attest to this, then even at UE it would be out of the question to sabotage your work. Why does Furtwängler not come out publicly and ardently for your cause, and others with him??? Here is the root of the problem! The world craves names! It may be all the "highly respectable musicians," as you call them, who are speaking of sabotage at Universal Edition, but it could also be all these musicians who attest to you and your work!! Why do they not do it? I have asked Furtwängler this before; he avoided my question. But there is only courage or cowardice. I like Furtwängler very much. But either one plays Mahler, Schoenberg, or some other filth and makes his reputation through compromises, or one shows his allegiance to Heinrich Schenker. One cannot do both without either being disingenuous to one side or at least being ambiguous. I would know of no other publisher who would do it better than Universal Edition. At this moment, if you were a business—and you would be a much greater business than

Schoenberg, Mahler, Schreker, or Bekker ever could be, even if Hertzka does not know it but surely suspects it and takes it into consideration—Hertzka would let out his servitude with a calm placidity and build his Schenker business. And this moment begins as soon as all the highly respected musicians speak up for you in a determined and ardent way, without regard for themselves. It simply is and remains a matter of personal courage like any important matter. And have faith—one day they will be forced to confess [their error]. If we were thirty or forty extremely determined people, then in ten years the entire musical world would be fundamentally turned around. And if those who know better nevertheless conduct Schoenberg and Mahler(?!), then Germany also would be saved—not through fascist mimicry—but rather through spirit, through religion, because our great affair is religion.[3] How it hits the mark on what you wrote: that now, where commoners have become the measure of all things, all people can compete with Germany.

I have already obtained *Counterpoint 2* and, as far as I remember, I wrote to you soon afterwards at length about what pleasure the work gives me. I am still not at the end, for the above-mentioned reasons. But I will, as I said, talk about it in more detail, which I wish to do more than anything else.

I am still working on the end of my book, *Music of the South*. Here I go further with the ideas laid out in *The Revelation*, as I hope to make them clearer, more openly fervid, and stronger.

To try to get more money for future works, I am arranging a deluxe edition of 100 copies of *Music of the South*, sumptuously presented. The German Publishing House in Stuttgart,[4] combined with Schuster, will publish the book. I will put my honorarium from the public edition into the costs of this subscription edition and will thus receive the entire earnings from the hundred copies. The leather-bound book should cost 100 Swiss francs, and the vellum-bound book 80 Swiss francs. It is very difficult to get 100 subscribers. But I have to try. Were all 100 copies accounted for, the profits would make possible another year of work. What you do think: should I solicit Hertzka by sending a prospectus of the subscription edition? It would be a real temptation for this profit-driven man, for whom even I—if one wants to express it as he would—have done such a "pleasure." My studies now deal with a vocal topic—the history and nature of *bel canto*—and it is my wish and endeavor with this to give a supplementary study to your pure teachings of counterpoint, a contribution to its reconstruction.

December 28

Last night I was told the following typical incident: on the 26th the opera season at the Costanzi Theatre opened with *Siegfried*. For this reason Mussolini had declined to come to the performance, which from his point of view one can understand very well. The director of the performance was Mr. Otto Klemperer from Cologne. What did this very clever man do? When the house went dark, some prince and princess entered the royal loge. Mr. Klemperer seized the moment and immediately played the royal march. Fine, a bow of sorts, which is rather common here. But, as if this were not enough, he then followed the Emperor's march with the fascist hymn "Giovinezza,"[5] which was completely out of place. Just a bending over of sorts, and the success left nothing else to be desired: his new

Siegfried overture ensured him success with the public and the press. Even artists like Furtwängler really do not understand it. But that is the reality of art today.

Now, dear and revered Master, we wish you and your dear wife all the best for 1923, above all for progress in work and we think of you with the most cordial greetings,

   Your ever devoted,
   Margarete and Walter Dahms

---

1. As mentioned in the diary entry for August 29, 1919 (above), Dahms had left his first wife, Agnes Matulke, during the 1910s and had been living openly with Margarete Ohmann in Berlin, evidently attracting at the very least disapproval. Dahms was unable to obtain a divorce from Agnes until 1929, and he and Margarete could not marry until 1931.
2. Dahms is referring to a review that he wrote and submitted to the journal *Die Musik* about *Tonwille 1*; Schuster & Loeffler were the publisher of *Die Musik*.
3. What Dahms seems to be suggesting here is that, in spite of his and Schenker's hypothetical victory over the moderns, there would still be those who, although they know (or ought to know) better, nonetheless continue to perform the music of Schoenberg and Mahler. Even so, that victory would be one for not only the world of music, but also for the entire German nation.
4. Deutsche Verlags-Anstalt, which published *Musik des Südens*.
5. *Giovinezza* (Youth), the official hymn of the Italian National Socialist Party between 1924 and 1943, played and sung at all kinds of events.

❧ Dahms to Schenker (letter), February 9, 1923
OJ 10/1, [74]

     New address: Rome
     via Sardegna 79

Dear revered Master,

Many thanks for your kind letter, which reached me at a moment of great turbulence. After a period of long waiting and endless probing I have finally found admittance to the German community home. The Italian rental prices were simply no longer manageable and now new unbearable increases are looming. We paid 400 lire for two small, shoddy, and unheated rooms (unusable for work), and we lived so far away that we had to pay over 100 lire for the tram each month. It was no longer bearable, it was affecting our very livelihood. Since November I have been playing organ on Sundays in the new evangelical German church, and because of these "connections" I have obtained for us in the community home a furnished attic room, which is to cost between 60 and 80 lire per month. For this reason we are saved, so to speak. But today nothing comes free: my wife has not felt well recently, and despite being active her condition has worsened such that she had to undergo a small operation, which had already been recommended to her for a long time. In those same days I moved—we have to lodge provisionally in an entrance hallway before we are able to move into our Olympic room. By the middle of next week we will be at peace. My wife is doing much better, but she just feels terribly weak. There are some very nice people who are caring for her recovery, namely Princess Bülow (my wife handles the private correspondence of the Prince)[1] and other friends. So we are well taken care of and hope now for prosperity under advantageous connections.

Following your advice I sent a prospectus to Hertzka, and with the appropriate words in the accompanying letter it was not left out that for him the decision will be made easier. But, dear Master, for the thought that you would like a paid subscription [to *Music of the South*], I must express my deepest thanks. I want to declare right away that I decline your subscription. That would be even better! Such a thing is only for war profiteers and profiteers of revolution, in short for "democrats," who especially will not feel flattered, should any of them actually read the book. If you casually and incidentally happen to hear from someone who is ready and able to subscribe, your advice in this case would be the only thing that I would accept from you. —The promotion now begins; I feel my way through step by step and from one address to the next. The first subscriber was Ibach in Barmen,[2] who without hesitation in the most noble form wrote: "with pleasure I fulfill this obligation." Now prospectuses are swimming to America, etc.

By the way: in America there is now a friend of mine, Dr. Penzoldt,[3] who accompanied his wife there, the singer Sigrid Onegin.[4] He is so interested in my affairs that he has set all the wheels in motion to help me (insofar as his position as a German and not as a "beggar" allows him). He has put me in contact with a certain Mr. Sonneck,[5] who is the editor of a *Musical Quarterly* in New York. Mr. Sonneck has invited me to work with him and I will first try to write a longer essay for his journal.[6] In it I will also come to speak about your work, so that the Americans, who for the most part hear only of European decadence, also experience in the meantime that whole other powers are at work to wipe out this decadence as a hideous and defacing stain. My entire collaborative work depends on whether I am able to write in a manner that can be translated without pain or difficulty into English. The "American mentality," which my friend pointed out to me as an especially dangerous cliff, prepares me for fewer worries. This American mentality, which ignorantly consumes so much filth, will digest just as ignorantly a pure and good idea. It is then—and this is my only concern—that even over there in the leading positions of publisher and editorial staff the spiritual and business brethren of our publishers and editorial heroes sit and practise censorship.

The "*Bel canto*" is arranged in two volumes;[7] one volume is of a purely historical nature: it deals with the history of the art of singing and of art song, both its development and its decline, and it surveys publications up to the present day; it will also represent the experiences and observations of the most prominent singers, collected and presented in essential formulas. The other volume is dedicated to the essence of vocality. Beginning with vocal principles, I describe the anchoring of vocalization in composition and vice versa, and compare the use of the "art of *bel canto*" in song to the use of counterpoint in composition: that is, *bel canto* as an experimental stage to actual art song. Here the essence of all so-called "methods" will be worked out. It should, therefore, if somehow possible, become a complete picture and as I hope, a new picture, new above all not insofar as a "singer" or a "vocal pedagogue" is concerned, but rather as a disciple of Heinrich Schenker, who grapples with things from another point of view, namely the musical one.

I devoured *Tonwille* 3 immediately after receiving it; I have only postponed the Haydn sonata for the coming days. Everything, every word is to be underlined. Even in the "Miscellanea" there is not a single ambiguous point. Either/or! A third one does not exist. But here much misunderstanding will begin. Perhaps, dear Master, you can declare in your clear, convincing voice at the next opportunity once again in no uncertain terms and in detail, that "democratic" is not a political but rather a <u>cultural</u> concept. (I know from my own experience that one must first <u>attain</u> clarity about such things). You thereby knock from the hand of opponents not a dangerous but an unpleasant and debilitating weapon.

I would like to speak with you about so many things, things that may not be written. Let us hope that destiny will one day take a turn for the better. Politically speaking everything is so hopeless, because it is all just politics and nothing else. Years will still go by, dreadful years for Germany, until the most damned "citizen" and "worker" vanishes and the "German" becomes a docile tool for a larger man and leader. How long will the current "resolve" last? asks the ever-nurtured, unconquerable mistrust. Already Mr. Wirth[8] puts on his top hat again and waits for Cuno's[9] collapse. Then again it will be negotiations, betrayal, bartering away – – – –

With the most cordial greetings to you and your dear, revered wife—also from my wife,

Your thankful devotee,
Walter Dahms

---

[1] Dahms is most likely referring to Prince Bernhard von Bülow (1849–1929) and his wife Princess Maria von Bülow (1848–1929), who resided in Rome during this time.

[2] Ibach: German manufacturer of pianos and organs.

[3] Fritz Penzoldt (1888–1959): husband of Sigrid Onégin and the author of numerous books, including the biography *Sigrid Onégin* (Magdeburg: K.J. Sander, 1939), which was later republished as *Alt-Rhapsodie: Sigrid Onégin, Leben und Werk* (Neustadt an der Aisch: Degener, 1953).

[4] Sigrid Onégin (1889–1943, *née* Lilly Hoffmann): renowned German contralto active between 1911 and 1938. Between 1922 and 1924 Onégin was on the roster at the New York Metropolitan Opera.

[5] Oscar Sonneck (1873–1928): American musicologist, librarian, first editor of *The Musical Quarterly*.

[6] Dahms published two articles for *The Musical Quarterly*: "The Biology of Music," *The Musical Quarterly* 11, no. 1 (1925): 36–54, and "The 'Gallant' Style of Music," ibid., no. 3 (1925): 356–72.

[7] As suggested in this letter and elsewhere, Dahms intended to write a book on *bel canto*, but this book never came to fruition.

[8] (Karl) Joseph Wirth (1879–1956): German politician of the Catholic Center Party, Chancellor under the Weimar Republic (1921–22).

[9] Wilhelm Cuno (1876–1933): German politician and business leader, Chancellor of the Weimar Republic 1922–23.

Diary entry, August 19, 1923

To Dahms (postcard): How is he? Of Krehls's invitation; whether the fourth issue [of *Der Tonwille*] is in his hands; promise to return to a point for which up until now only he showed understanding, I mean the inadequacy vis-à-vis the genius, which is the root of all evil.

Diary entry, October 21, 1923

To Dahms (letter): about the quarterly publication [of future issues of *Der Tonwille*], the search for his article, about which Furtwängler and Hertzka spoke; express my happiness about his agreement on the genius question. Belief in genius, like belief in God, apparently rests on original grace; what it granted me and through me the world. Belief in genius is needed more now than ever before, all authority is exhausted; mankind is split into two groups: the larger group will wriggle free of the forced labor imposed by Nature and suspend itself in the brains and money bags of the smaller group; the latter is too impotent to improve Nature—there is no practical solution, only belief in authority can provide relief!

21
Hamburg and Moriz Violin

THE letters that Moriz Violin and Schenker exchanged between the years 1922 and 1933, when Violin was living in Hamburg, are of special significance because they record the activity of both musicians in considerable detail and also document Violin's extensive involvement in Schenker's cause. Violin's letters paint a portrait of Hamburg as a pleasant but culturally conservative city; they also describe aspects of the political situation in Germany, including the "Jewish question." A considerable stretch of letters and postcards from 1923–24 are directly related to Schenker's controversy with Emil Hertzka over the content, publication, and distribution of *Der Tonwille*; around the time of his legal dispute with Universal Edition, Schenker enlisted Violin's help in boosting the sales of the publication beyond Austria's borders.

Not only do Schenker's letters to Violin refer to events and people also mentioned in his diaries, they often expand upon them in greater detail, including character portraits—often unflattering ones—of members of Schenker's close circle, including Otto Vrieslander, Anthony van Hoboken, and Hans Weisse.

One thread that runs throughout this part of the correspondence is the childhood illness of Violin's son Karl (1913–31), and of his vain efforts to have it treated successfully. For a time (1927) Violin was hoping for a position in a newly created *Hochschule* (Music Hochschule) in Frankfurt, partly to spare his son the extreme dampness of Hamburg; Schenker wrote to acquaintances to enlist their help in this endeavor, but to no avail.

The correspondence also reveals Violin's efforts to keep pace with the latest developments in Schenkerian theory by reading all of his friend's publications as soon as they appeared. While his remarks on Beethoven's "Appassionata" Sonata show considerable musical sensitivity, his efforts at a voice-leading sketch of Bach's Two-part Invention in C major fall far short of what the new theory was capable of showing. Nonetheless, Schenker's letters to Violin include two middleground reductions of Bach inventions (in C and E♭), and a sophisticated reading of the introduction to Mozart's "Dissonance" Quartet. The latter appears in a letter with numerous briefer analytical notations, all intended as the basis for a refutation of Schoenberg's apparently fraudulent invocation of the works of the great German masters as harbingers of musical modernism—a response to a journal article which Schenker had hoped his friend would write.

WILLIAM DRABKIN

Schenker to Violin (postcard), October 16, 1920
OJ 8/3, [91]

Floriz,

Your last postcard took from September 29 to October 5 to arrive.

Let us hope that your guiding star remains true to you. I know [Ferdinand] Pfohl from his writings on Wagner and his reviews. He has undoubted influence as critic for the *Hamburger Nachrichten* and in other respects in Germany, too. But I am very curious to see how you get on with him. Should the contrast between his and your ways of looking at things bring you somehow closer together, or at least result in propriety concerning your interactions, then such a thing would by no means be exceptional (there were, and are, quite a few examples of this). Is there a conservatory there, and are you serious about securing a teaching post? In my view, it should be possible for you to succeed in finding in Hamburg whatever is achievable by the likes of us today. Write to me about your encounters with the musicians in rehearsals and in conversations!

From my side: Vrieslander has finally delivered the manuscript [of *Counterpoint 2*] to Cotta; he reports that Guido Adler recently inveighed against me furiously in private company in Munich. Here he is purely a supporter and friend—oh, the coward!—I cannot help but laugh! The continuation of Halm's article is not yet published. Tomorrow I shall vote for Ottokar Czernin, who is fighting valiantly against the Reds.[1] I give voice to my own opinions in the Foreword to *Op. 101* and the first issue of the *Little Library* in favor of the aristocracy, as you will read.[2]

Tomorrow we were wanting to visit your Vally,[3] but again it was not possible. Definitely next Sunday, however, as I have written to her. Schreier[4] has spoken of you to me in most enthusiastic terms—he is very nice. Mrs. Hauser recommended Mr. Bamberger to me today.

We send you our sincere greetings,
Your Heinrich and Lie-Lie

---

[1] Ottokar Czernin (1872–1932): conservative Austrian politician, Foreign Minister during World War I who sought to prevent the dissolution of the Austro-Hungarian monarchy and to preserve ties between Germany and Austria.

[2] "The Mission of German Genius," Schenker's longest and most widely read political essay, was published as the lead article in the *Little Library*, i.e. the first issue of *Der Tonwille*.

[3] Valerie ("Vally," "Wally") Violin, Moriz's wife.

[4] Probably the Otto Schreier (1901–29) who was a pupil of Violin's in Hamburg before being appointed Professor of Mathematics at the University of Rostock.

Schenker to Violin (postcard), February 6, 1921
OJ 8/4, [2]

Floriz,

A truly colossal pile of work prevented me from conveying my joy about your forthcoming concerts. Above all, the start of your employment at the Conservatory,[1] which is definitely fixed, makes my joy full and complete. May this, finally, be the long-awaited foundation for your continued success and security in life. Your wife was so kind to look us up shortly after your departure, in order to recommend your apartment to us—against your own interest. We promised to come for a meal one Sunday, but then the printers came with a number of tasks that had to be dealt with quickly, and in the last few days Lie-Liechen suffered another difficult bout of obstipation, which required us to go today—on Sunday—to the doctor. Next Sunday we should be able to come out.

We are eagerly awaiting the edition of *Op. 101*, the first volume of the *Little Library*, both editions of the "Moonlight" Sonata, etc.;[2] nothing stands in their way any longer. We have still not had a decision from Cotta; a pity that the publication [of *Counterpoint 2*] has been delayed. If only I could be preparing the next volume, the "most important of all"![3] At the moment, the second volume is occupying my attention: Brahms's Intermezzo in E♭ major from Op. 117, Mozart's Sonata in A minor [K. 310], Beethoven's Sonata in F minor, Op. 2, No. 1, the conclusion of the first movement of Beethoven's Fifth Symphony, and the "Miscellanea."[4] How I envy you being in Germany!

    Your Heinrich

---

[1] A teaching post at a conservatory in Hamburg; the name is not specified in the correspondence.

[2] The numerous publications from 1921 include the elucidatory edition of *Op. 101*; the first volume in the *Little Library*, i.e. *Der Tonwille*; the facsimile edition of the "Moonlight" Sonata in Universal Edition's series of Musikalische Seltenheiten (Musical Rarities); and individual editions of the Beethoven piano sonatas for Universal Edition, among them the "Moonlight."

[3] *Free Counterpoint*, at that time conceived as the third and final volume of *Counterpoint*. The word in quotation marks is one of Schenker's neologisms: *derjenigste*, a double superlative of "derjenige," i.e. the one that will change the face of music theory.

[4] This is nearly a complete and accurate list of the contents of the second issue of *Der Tonwille*: the analysis of Brahms's Intermezzo in E♭, Op. 117, No. 1, remained unpublished, though there are sketches for it in the Oster Collection, together with the text in Jeanette's hand (OC 34/83–105).

Schenker to Violin (letter), January 29, 1922
OJ 6/7, [2]

Floriz,

You are surprised that you are not yet in possession of the package. The delay can be explained by the pressure that the printers are applying with regard to the second issue of *Der Tonwille*, and to the edition of the [Beethoven] sonatas. Now, on a Saturday evening, I can finally take a break, and Lie-Liechen is packing for you:

1. Concerto in A minor, score and <u>parts</u> (I can no longer find the cadenzas);[1]

2. <u>Double</u> Concerto (without the parts: are these not perhaps in your library? Otherwise they <u>would have</u> to be in mine!)[2]

In Hamburg itself, the city of Carl Philipp Emanuel Bach, this would be a rare, worthy salute. I have cast my eyes at the scores, and find that they remain wonderful and full of surprises, as I found them the <u>first day</u>, at the <u>first evening</u> performance. May your plan succeed, for Bach's honor and yours.

From the Landesmanns[3] (who were kind enough to take care of a chandelier at our place) I have heard several things, about a child prodigy, etc. Perhaps you will find the time in the summer, after all the work you have done this winter, to write something of a chapter on music in Hamburg. From your previous reports I have indeed already begun to form a picture, but one question—is Hamburg in the clutches of the most brazen [composers], or is it more conservative than Vienna?—is something I am unable to answer. According to official reports it seems also to smell of marshland, but that might simply be aggressive [negative] publicity, while good musical respectability prevails at home. I can almost imagine that to be the case. For it has been shown that in Berlin, and Vienna, it is principally Jewish families that spearhead the "new movement," while the Aryan sector deals less in this trade.

How is your wife? And how do the little ones find themselves in their new surroundings? Are they already talking with a northern accent, or have they remained linguistically Viennese?

Weisse told me a few days ago that he thought it better to withdraw his lecture. I must accept his arguments, even though I concede that he will perhaps never be offered a suitable opportunity.[4] But that is his matter. Dahms wrote two long and very, very beautifully articles, in the Grünig music journal (Stuttgart, November 17, 1921) and in a Berlin music journal, about me in general and *Der Tonwille* in particular. And in a letter from Rome he adds the following, by way of explanation: he has evidence that there is "an incredible amount of Schenkerizing," and that the Schrekers and Busonis of the world only have to cease and my work will be unstoppable. Evidence of this comes, moreover, by way of Universal Edition: a reprinting of my edition of the *Chromatic Fantasy and Fugue* is followed now by a reprinting of the elucidatory edition of *Op. 109*; that is already saying a lot. In a publicity notice for *Der Tonwille* in *Der Anbruch* Hertzka could go so far as to say: "known and read throughout the world," "world-famous," from which enough remains even if one allows for the fact that it is an advertisement. In the end, even in such a notice, a publisher would not venture to say so much if there were no basis for doing so. (From Ludendorff, to whom I sent a copy of the first issue, I received <u>by return of post</u> (!!) a very charming letter, in which he thanks me for so much new stimulation. He congratulates me for what I have done, etc.)[5]

Already fourteen of the Beethoven sonatas are in print: they will <u>all</u> be sent to you (what have you got so far?). I shall soon have finished volume 1, which comprises Opp. 2 (Nos. 1–3), 7, and 10 (Nos. 1–3), and afterward I shall add to the remaining volumes: Opp. 26 (A♭ major), 27 (No. 2), 28, 31 (No. 2), 81a (and 101, 109–11)[6] are, moreover, also completed.

The second issue of *Tonwille* will include:

1) Laws of Music
2) History of Music
3) Yet Another Word About the Urlinie
4) Mozart's Sonata in A minor   (in both cases, the
5) Beethoven's Sonata in F minor, Op. 2, No. 1   complete sonata)

6) Miscellanea (very, very <u>varied</u>)

The third issue will include:

1) Haydn's great Sonata in E♭ major [Hob. XVI:52]
2) Beethoven's Fifth Symphony (continued)
3) Brahms's Variations on a Theme of Handel

4) Miscellanea[7]

([This issue will comprise] merely 2 gatherings)

In February, the second volume of *Counterpoint* should also be completed. For now, we are stopping at the eleventh gathering. If only I could make progress during the summer! The last two summers I could no longer push myself to work continuously; in September I got stuck. I raised my fees from 4,000 to 10,000 kronen per lesson (Elias and Bamberger pay 120,000 monthly), but good pupils left me when I raised my fees previously, and I am teaching the likes of Hupka and Kahn almost without charge, so that even in spite of the increase, the prospects for the summer, when viewed in terms of the exchange rate, seem bleak. Mozio does not ask after me, does not seem to care—is it not even a wonder that we are alive and working so frightfully hard?—he is afraid: he is better off not asking, and I too am silent. From Universal Edition I have not seen so much as a penny, despite having worked for 1¾ years. The first payment will be made in July 1922. Whatever else I may have had to say shall follow soon.

Please confirm the arrival of the package.

                Best greetings to you and yours!
                Your Heinrich

[1] [Schenker's note:] In my notebook that carefully records names of people and the works they borrow from me, there is an entry: "Floriz: cadenzas to the A minor Concerto," which has not been crossed out! If necessary, you can write something yourself. [Of Bach's keyboard concertos in A minor, Wq. 26 (Helm 430) had been published by C. F. Kahnt, Leipzig, in the early 20th century.]

[2] The work in question is either the Double Concerto in F, Wq. 46 (Helm 408), or in E♭, Wq. 47 (Helm 479); both had been published in the mid-1910s by Steingräber in Leipzig.

[3] Presumably a Viennese family, who were friends of the Violins.

[4] This remark probably refers to a lecture on Schenker's work, which Hans Weisse was supposed to give at the conservatory in Hamburg where Violin was teaching.

[5] Ludendorff's reply, dated November 19, 1921, reads: "Dear Dr. Schenker, Please accept my warmest thanks for sending me your publication *Der Tonwille*. Your presentation gave me much that was new and much encouragement. I congratulate you on the way in which you observe art for us, in order to rescue us from the Marxist democratic morass. — With faithful German salute, Ludendorff." (OJ 24/10–11). Schenker received a second letter from Ludendorff, dated January 21, 1922 (OC 24/13).

[6] The last four are those that had already appeared as the elucidatory edition of 1913–20.

[7] The contents of *Tonwille* 2 and 3 ended up somewhat different. No Miscellanea were published in *Tonwille* 2, the first continuation of the long study of Beethoven's Fifth Symphony did not appear until issue 5, and the Brahms analysis was held up until the double issue 8/9.

❦ Violin to Schenker (letter), February 2, 1922
OJ 14/45, [13]

Dearest Heinrich,

First of all, many thanks for the communication! It arrived yesterday, and in the evening I combed my entire collection of scores. I looked high and low and found—nothing!! I remember only that you once asked at my place for the return of the Concerto in A minor, and that I gave it back to you. Now, having looked, it is a mystery as to how it could have gone missing. The parts to the Double Concerto are in any event an unfortunate loss, but with money they can be regained. For me, it is dreadful to think that your cadenzas could have gone missing. They had, so to speak, become attached to my heart, as true models of such pieces, that it would be difficult for me to succeed in composing new ones. In addition, I still remember them quite precisely. I could indicate to you the construction of the first cadenza from memory; could you then reconstruct it? The cadenza to the Andante was a gem: unfortunately, I cannot remember it well.

Hans Weisse <u>most certainly</u> did not cancel [the lectures] that I arranged. He merely wrote to me to say that he would not like to give the lectures in apparent connection with the performance of his music, for reasons known to you. I replied to him, saying that I accepted his arguments, that I only wanted to give him the pleasure of being able hear his pieces and that was the reason we wanted to postpone the lectures; and I asked him <u>again</u> how much he would want to be paid [for giving the lectures]. If this modesty conceals a certain cowardice, this was not immediately discernible. I shall uncover the complete truth in the matter!

The silly case of the Landesmanns' chit-chat was very painful to me. His information must have come fourth-hand. For, firstly, I have not written to the Landesmanns at all and, secondly, I do not have any child prodigies, other than my own two. Apparently Fanny[1] told them that current patrons have arranged for the education of a thirteen-year-old boy, and that I am providing the piano tuition.

Until now I did not want to write anything to you, since all my work is devoted to sustaining my existence. By chance, this has made considerable progress in the last two weeks. I now have seven private lessons a week; in the near future there will be three or four more. I receive 50 marks per lesson, from one pupil as much as 70 marks per lesson. Apart from my marginal earnings at the conservatory, I shall thus be earning 2,000 marks per month. That is not enough; but in the course of the year it shall increase significantly. Vally is already earning a few thousand from selling crocheted hats; perhaps she will even be able to start up a business. I am writing all this to you today because I am in much better spirits and I have the secure conviction that, by the uniting of our powers, we will be able to have a modest but secure existence. The acquisition of a piano cost me a lot of effort. <u>Today</u> I received confirmation from Steinway that they will furnish me with an instrument in the new apartment. Think, then, about my goals, my as yet unrealized plans, and you will understand that I was not happy to have you share in my <u>fruitless efforts</u>.

The musical public in Hamburg is, I believe, thoroughly conservative, apart from the newspaper criticism, which is, however, still entirely inexperienced with respect to "modern" music. In part it could not care less, because the Hamburg public will walk out of the concert hall when an excessively [modern] work is performed; in part it behaves audaciously, because in Berlin "modern music" is where the "business" is. We have an outstanding organist here, by the name of Sittard.[2] It is difficult to offer a prognosis for Hamburg: In <u>every</u> respect it is conservative and progressive in the good <u>and</u> bad senses of the terms. There is a strong *Rheeder* element. The only <u>positive</u> feature is the public's uncorrupted taste. They love everything up to and including Brahms. Otherwise, things here look like they did in Vienna thirty years ago. As soon as one of my intentions is realized, I shall write you something cleverer and more valuable. That is what counts the most with respect to all my thoughts.[3]

    Heartfelt greetings from us to you,
    Your Floriz

---

[1] Fanny Violin: Moriz's sister, a frequent visitor to the Schenkers' home.

[2] Alfred Sittard (1878–1942): organist at the church of St. Michael, Hamburg, 1912–25; he left Hamburg to take up the organ professorship at the Music Hochschule in Berlin.

[3] The edge of the paper is crumpled, or torn, and one or two words at the beginning of the sentence are illegible.

Schenker to Violin (letter), December 21, 1922
OJ 6/7, [4]

Floriz,[1]
    As with you, so have things gone with me. I kept meaning to ask after your good little boy Karl, but was tossed "from cliff to cliff" (Hölderlin-Brahms),[2] so that it was impossible for me to live up to my reputation as a virtuoso letter- and postcard-writer and get over to my desk. (Newspaper clippings that are two to three months old lie on my desk, even unread.) Now you have beaten me to it, and with doubled pleasure I set this sheet of paper in motion, better in the course of the day.
    On the very day that your short letter arrived, I went over to Eduard's[3] to give him the luxury edition of the "Moonlight" Sonata facsimile edition. I am recounting this on account of Hertzka, about whose actions you inquire. The copy was old and scuffed, even with something glued onto the title page; and it was charged to my account, with a mere 25 percent reduction, as a new copy: to me, who at any rate may claim one copy as stipulated in my contract. But since I wanted to give Eduard a piece [of my work], I showed him all these faults myself without mentioning the matters concerning Universal Edition's discounts to friends and [important] persons. The matter becomes ever more drawn out. Always more of the businessman's same idiotic joke, treating others as if they were even stupider; one tires of "the return of the same thing" by these millions of people—so bereft of talent!
    I have happier news to report these days concerning *Tonwille 3*. After a long delay (which prevented it from appearing before Christmas, as had been hoped), the first proofs arrived, which I sent back by return of post (within a matter of hours). Nonetheless, another delay of a month, and finally the day before yesterday I could give the *imprimatur*. You may be in possession, as early as the beginning of January, of the issue in which the stolen "Miscellanea" will be restored. I do not know if I told you that Furtwängler, when he was last with me, offered on his own initiative to inquire of C. F. Peters or Breitkopf & Härtel whether they would like to free me of Hertzka. Recently I received through Bamberger a preliminary "letter" from Furtwängler, that Peters would be like "leaping out of the frying-pan into the fire." And, it so happened that, practically at the same time, [Herman] Roth wrote to me from Karlsruhe about "leaping out of the frying-pan into the fire." He, the child of the publishing-house Peters. (He has warned me.) So I shall be sending the fourth issue to Hertzka in the coming days, and insist ahead of time on a present of one hundred copies for one hundred schools.
    If I could find the support of someone with a few millions in his back pocket, I would stage a "St. Bartholomew's Day Massacre"[4] against the moderns within a year's time. Not a stone would remain standing, not a single name; but these damn millions always turn up in someone else's hands. *Der Tonwille* is doing a good business, as Hertzka assumed; but it does not suit him from a modern business standpoint. Nonetheless I have means to put pressure on him.
    He delays and causes damage; I shall delay even more (in the preparation of the edition of the Beethoven sonatas!) and cause damage to him in terms of bookshop

orders. I shall waste not a single word more; the action will speak. He needs a good beating from time to time—he shall have one.

Those who heard you here found your playing wondrously beautiful, which it indeed was. The newspapers "are silent in the forest"[5]—today you, too, leave them speechless. Eduard spoke of a concert tour—is it? I am near to embarking on one myself: in *Der Anbruch*, in the *Zeitschrift für internationale Musikwissenschaft*, even in Prague I shall be performed [i.e. my writings will be discussed]; Roth has guaranteed me an edition of C. P. E. Bach with C. F. Peters. But the main task is the last volume [of the New Musical Theories and Fantasies], *Free Composition*. I am proceeding with the Urlinie Edition of the Short Preludes by J. S. Bach (all eighteen pieces, quite exquisite).[6]

What is your wife up to? My Lie-Liechen is taking a "holiday" in the apartment, all sorts of counterpoint, inversion of the furniture, braided bread—the Jew is singing: "Ma nish tanu?"[7] So, most cordial greetings to the two of you—you and Vally—from the two of us. And may your children receive from Uncle and Auntie the most beautiful blessings.

        Your Heinrich

Hupka has just given up a career as a concert pianist. He has been appointed rehearsal accompanist at the Frankfurt Opera House. So why did he "bite the bullet"? This comes from his Jewish elbows, which can never take the place of [real] work.

---

[1] This letter is written on paper with the printed letterhead of the *Tonwille* publishing house (Tonwille-Flugblätterverlag).

[2] Hölderlin-Brahms: a reference to the last lines of the Friederich Hölderlin's poem "Hyperion's Song of Fate," set by Brahms as the *Schicksalslied*, Op. 54: "But it is our lot never to stay peacefully in one place: suffering, helpless blind beings, we disappear and fall from hour to hour, like water tossed from cliff to cliff for years on end, into the unknown below."

[3] Eduard Violin (died 1925): Moriz's brother, a medical doctor.

[4] In the night of St. Bartholomew's Day (August 24) in 1572 there was Catholic uprising against the Huguenots in Paris, which spread in the following weeks to the French countryside and was responsible for the deaths of thousands of Huguenots.

[5] "Die Vöglein schweigen im Walde": a line from Goethe's well-known poem *Wanderers Nachtlied*.

[6] Short analyses of eight of these keyboard works were published, together with voice-leading graphs, in groups of two or three in *Tonwille* 4 and 5 and *Masterwork 1*.

[7] The first words of the Four Questions, "Why is this night different from all other nights?", a passage from the *Haggadah* (Jewish Passover service).

Violin to Schenker (letter), May 31, 1923
OJ 14/45, [22]

My dearest Heinrich,

I greet you and Lie-Lie in somber mood. For the time being, I didn't want to answer the question in your last letter as to what impact the current state of Germany was having, because first of all you will only go and upset yourself with speculations, and secondly you will be able to think out from your own experience the economic consequences. But what would perhaps get you even more worked up is the pitiful way in which the Germans are inviting their own ruin and shamefully bringing it about. In the first place, "intelligence." Such talk as: the Germans are idiots, we have lost the war, we must pay, we have only ill will, the French are right to have everything on the Ruhr, every foreigner the same – – – – – – such talk can make one crazy. I now look at such spokesmen with dismay and say just: I hope you will be the first to realize the injustice that you are perpetrating. – – – – – – – You would not believe how magnificent the masses of the people show themselves to be at heart. Only now are they being led by their "leaders" into deprivation.

Among the people, hatred of France, England, etc. is intense. The villainous, intellectual "righteous" ones, the "objective" ones, condemn the hatred to powerlessness. I almost regard the matter as "Jewish." Among those who want to stand up for Germany, you will find no Jews. Among the "oratorical" ones, who consider themselves "above the matter," only Jews.

    Forgive the anti-Jewish Jew.
    Floriz

All of us send heartfelt greetings.
The little lad[1] is making slow progress.

---

[1] Karl ("Karli") Violin, Moriz Violin's son.

Schenker to Violin (postcard), June 11, 1923
OJ 8/4, [23]

Floriz,

I shall get back to you on the leading-tone matter (nicely asked and written), but not until I am in Galtür, from where you will be the first to receive a letter. It simply is not possible just now. But I feel compelled to say in the interim in response to your most recent letter that I am absolutely of one mind with you. The German is like the Jew in intellectual consumption, and has all the disadvantages of his superficial education (which, in the case of millions, can certainly never be a full education): inner turmoil, partisanship, etc. Everyone "knows" everything, everyone reads, writes.—By chance, I read in the *Deutsche Allgemeine Zeitung* for June 10 (Sunday issue) the very same argument (which, incidentally, I had already previously written to Dahms, as I did in *Tonwille* 4, which will reach you one of these days). Frenssen, too, in his *Letters from America* published by Grote,[1] puts it excellently when he reveals the nations in their animality and cries: "Strike down those in your midst who are soft-hearted, who talk of belief and trust. Strike them down, for their talk signifies children crippled with tuberculosis, corroded with narrowness and hopelessness, sinking morality and shame. … Germany is ruled by animals! By nothing but animals! You have experienced it." A pastor speaks in this way: then strike [them] down! If only superficial German education knew what a totally uneducated rabble the English, French, and Italians are, and above all the Americans, things would instantly be better, but it has too much respect for these animals.

On Wednesday we shall, I hope, be at Eduard's place for dinner. Much more from Galtür. Departure on the 24th.

Warmest greetings to you, your wife, and the little ones, from Lie-Liechen and myself.

Your Heinrich

(How are things with the dear little Karl?)

---

[1] Gustav Frenssen, *Briefe aus Amerika* (Berlin: Grote'sche Verlagsbuchhandlung, 1923).

ꞌ Violin to Schenker (letter), July 14, 1923
OJ 14/45, [24]

My dearest, good Heinrich,

You shall now quickly become acquainted with my intentions, and the start of my activity [on your behalf].

Let me ask you: Is Hertzka contractually obliged to publish four issues a year of *Der Tonwille*? If so, then, on grounds of it being to your artistic and financial detriment, you are in a position to dissolve the contract, which I consider would be for the best. For no manner of inducements will return this cavalier to good faith. He will happily put himself in your good favor by knowing that he is in a position to circumvent even these new conditions. I am utterly and entirely enraged by the fact that your struggle with Hertzka has gotten the better of your nerves and threatened your work.

Yesterday I spoke with a Mr. Temming,[1] a wealthy music enthusiast. I laid out for him your whole plight, and told him that it is not in the least a matter of creating financial advantages for you, but of putting your work on a secure and firm foundation. Mr. Temming is willing to take out as many annual subscriptions as would be necessary to supply every German university and conservatory with a free copy. (Research libraries probably first and foremost!) All you would have to do in this regard is to explain your preferences and wishes. In private circles, I shall still arrange as many subscriptions as possible. If there were, in addition, an efficient practice [of this sort] in Munich or Vienna,—why should it not be possible to a create a firm base that would enable you to do exactly as you wish?

The Schoenberg and Hindemith etc., etc. journal issues—see how important they are!!! Write to tell me immediately your opinion of my idea. Mr. Temming leaves on August 1 for three to four weeks. Hans Weisse messed up my plans a while ago.² <u>You</u> – – could give as many recitals as you want here and would get whatever honorarium you wanted. Unfortunately, I imagine that does not fit into your work plan!

Things are much worse with price rises here than in Austria and – – earning a living is even more difficult. If Vally were not also capable of earning a good income, we could not cope at all, despite my giving four or five private lessons daily during the season.

If, as it seems, the cost of a vacation in Galtür is unattractive, I shall probably not be able to come, especially as something must surely be done about my little boy next fall.

Fanny arrives tomorrow.

For today, most heartfelt greetings from us to the two of you!

  Your faithful
  Floriz

---

[1] Max Temming: a Hamburg industrialist and patron of the arts, the owner of a cotton bleachery, flax processing and papermaking plant founded in 1911 in Glückstadt near Hamburg.

[2] This remark probably refers to Weisse's decision not to give any lectures on Schenker's theory at the Vogt Conservatory in Hamburg, where Violin was teaching.

❧ Schenker to Violin (letter), July 20, 1923

OJ 6/7, [6]

Floriz,

Between the lettercard and your present letter, suddenly and for some unknown reason (perhaps unwisely choosing a drink that was too cold after a three-hour-long walk in extreme heat, or something of that sort) a Theme and Fifteen Variations¹ crept in, which overcame me within a day and rendered me so weak that I could not eat anything, still less put pen to paper. "Sentendo nuova forza" (in Beethoven's words),² the first thing I am doing is to make good on my promise.

I do indeed call that which you are offering me through your music enthusiast³ timely and ingenious. Many, many thanks. Thanking the man himself should be reserved for the moment at which I shall be able to make use of his generosity, and I hope we will get to that point. As soon as my lessons ended in June, I told my pupils that they must each secure fifty subscribers [to *Der Tonwille*] for between two and <u>four issues a year</u>, which will make up between 24,000 and 48,000 kronen a year—Hertzka reckons [a cost of] 12,000 kronen per issue. (Once this scheme is in full swing, it will actually make more <u>by itself</u>.) What is more, most of these subscribers will surely have their own book dealers, who give them discounts, so that even the basic sum of 48,000 kronen will probably be reduced to little more than 40,000 kronen. But the principal point that I directed at my pupils (cried out in pain and fury, for I was ashamed that it should ever have been necessary to say it), was: "Were you the pupils of Schoenberg, or Schreker, or Busoni, or anyone else who similarly cannot hear properly or teach correctly, you would be standing on your heads, running into the streets, through every town and society, parting with your money in order to be with them and to support them; but so touched are you by the truth that you sleep and snore in the broadest daylight, as though I were giving you opium rather than the truth." And I cried out to them with an even louder voice, saying: "Say to all those to whom you will turn, in my name, that they should not dare to raise the objection that they understand nothing in *Der Tonwille*, for they surely have in their libraries works that they have never read—or, if they have read them, they have not understood that, for the sake of the cultural discipline, it is necessary also to include *Der Tonwille* in their libraries, unread or uncomprehended, if only in the secret hope that ultimately their children's children will profitably take to them." I saw very clearly how my protestations disturbed their slumber, but I had to do it. I really cannot go on in such a way that I have to take care of everything almost entirely on my own, 1) preparation for the work (and how much of that there is!!), 2) the writing of the work, and 3) the promotion of the work (instead of leaving this to the publisher and the schools)—that is too much, above all while so much work remains to be done, above all volume 4, which languishes half finished, the culmination of the whole, the brightest light of the volumes.[4] My pupils promise to do it; even Weisse, this very troublesome boy, who in my name has such an extraordinarily large following (six pupils a day), was finally in a position to stipulate 10,000 kronen per lesson, and—something I myself still cannot manage today—to reserve the mornings for his own work, and to teach only in the afternoons, who despite everything steps to one side at the crucial moments (thus he has turned down writing the essay about me for Hertzka in the *Anbruch* but also the independent monograph [about me] that Hertzka was—and still is—prepared to publish, always referring to Haydn, Mozart, Beethoven, Schubert, and Brahms, who also did not write about music, in disregard of the lineage of C. P. E. Bach and Schumann, among others, who wrote about music alongside composing; even Weisse, I tell you, promised it most explicitly. Miss Elias is, unfortunately, highly unskilled and lacking all social connections; she will nonetheless certainly and willingly exert herself. She promptly took one copy to Haslinger's[5] and asked them in my name to display it in their shop window—Hertzka sends them only the *Anbruch*, never *Der Tonwille*! —Haslinger did so, but by the next day it was already gone: the idiot had sold it. Elias went back to them and repeated her request, notwithstanding the fact that it was self-evident that the copy that had been presented was not for sale; they promised to honor her request, but whether or not they kept their word I cannot say. On another occasion, Lie-Liechen and I took a copy to Rosé's shop (now owned by Kern)[6] and ask him to put it on display. Lie-Liechen makes it clear to him, in the most polite manner, that the issue can no longer be for sale since she has underlined things here and there, and has unfolded the Urlinie graph. Suddenly Kern, with the most charming laugh and sensing a big deal in sight(!?!), says in a Jewish accent: "I will sell that easily!" Which is the greater, the stupidity or the greed? Or are the two in equal measure? At any rate, however, I hope to be able to build up a number of subscribers, by means of which the undertaking would from now on unfailingly bring in for <u>any publisher</u> a precisely calculable clear profit, and that is to be the basis on which I operate. To Vrieslander I have likewise directed the question as to what he could expect to achieve in Munich. But now to the question of Leipzig:[7]

Shall I give the requested lecture to the congress? Is it worthwhile abandoning the great work over which I am at present toiling, absorbing the loss of lessons and the travel costs, risking contact with "colleagues" (perhaps only the one time); or is it not better to work out of the Keilgasse, as I have been doing up to now. Finally, I can say [what I have to say] far better and more freely in *Der Tonwille* than in front of those thin-skinned liver-sausages. And what you once very rightly said holds true: these people will certainly not understand me. For to these secrets, the penultimate ones (for the ultimate ones reside in God and are unfathomable, not even to the one who penetrates these mysteries himself), belong our two ears, which is more than these people have among them — Floriz, you need not blush in modesty; I am not ashamed to write this: in short, should I go to Leipzig, or not?

If you can get here, then I will show you all manner of interesting things. Provisionally, then, to you and all yours, most cordial greetings from me and from the ever-writing Lie-Liechen. From the two of us to the five of you[8] (including Fanny),

       Your Heinrich

Issue 5 includes the Andante, Scherzo, and Finale of Beethoven's Fifth Symphony, <u>i.e. complete</u>!

Issue 6: Brahms's Handel Variations, J. S. Bach's solo pieces for violin and cello, *contra* Kurth's *Linearer Kontrapunkt*.

Issue 7: Mozart's G minor Symphony, Haydn's D major, or Brahms's Third.

<u>If Hertzka grants me the freedom</u>, I shall immediately have it out with Reger, with Wagner![9]

---

[1] Schenker is referring to a digestive disorder of some sort. At the same time, there is an allusion to Beethoven's Fifteen Variations and Fugue on an Original Theme, Op. 35, the so-called "Eroica" Variations.

[2] Another Beethoven reference: in the third movement of his A minor Quartet, Op. 132, the "Heiliger Dankgesang", Beethoven wrote above the faster middle sections (Andante) "Neue Kraft fühlend (Sentendo nuova forza)."

[3] The Hamburg industrialist Max Temming, with whom Violin had become acquainted earlier in 1923.

[4] *Free Composition*.

[5] Probably the heirs of the publishing house of Tobias (later Carl) Haslinger, situated near the Graben in first district of Vienna.

[6] Alexander Rosé was a dealer in sheet music and books at Vienna I, Kärntnerring 11 in 1905; the business was later taken over by Ludwig Kern.

⁷ This probably refers to a conference of musicologists scheduled for the fall of 1924.
⁸ Schenker uses the shorthand "2 : 5".
⁹ Most of the works listed in this postscript were the subjects of published articles, some of which appeared in *Masterwork* 1 and 2 (1925, 1926). There was, however, no analysis of a Haydn or Brahms symphony, and Schenker's opposition to Wagner is aired only briefly.

Violin to Schenker (letter), March 16, 1924
OJ 14/45, [31]

Dearest Heinrich,

Today I finally have enough time to write to you about so many things. First of all: my relationship to Mr. Temming is entirely dispassionate, so long as I can appeal to the paramount importance of your working necessities. That I reserve him only for you is something that you should be so kind as to recognize. Since, however, I turned down *Der Tonwille*, and then the "Performance" study, I do not wish to approach him straightaway, as this could be misinterpreted as, say, a roundabout way of not saying immediately what I intended. At any rate, I shall keep to this pause, for the sake of decency.

I was more than amply showered in gifts by the receipt of *Tonwille* 5 and the Beethoven sonatas. I read through everything [in the issue of *Der Tonwille*] first, so that I might formulate my thanks to you in a more informed way. Now I have read it, and I must believe myself to appear wretched were I to make space here to express my enthusiasm. The main thing: as soon as I have time, I shall get down to it. I must admit that I found the studies of the Bach preludes more difficult than anything I had previously encountered. The act of hearing, at least concerning the first layer of these voice-leading graphs, requires an imagination several degrees greater than for that of any of the others.

I shall be able to write to Bamberger in the next two to three days and, I hope, optimistically. I was not able to speak with Pollak¹ until yesterday, as he was unwell. Pollak said "yes," but he must still speak with the director. I myself do not understand the younger generation. To them, difficult matters always seem so clear in their eyes that even the most sensible advice ricochets off them.

May I take the opportunity of asking you whether I am hearing the following detail in Beethoven's Sonata in F minor, Op. 57, incorrectly? A pupil of mine asked me to explain why measures 94–100 in the first movement are different from measures 24–30. At first sight, it seemed that an explanation of the difference merely as a variation (for sake of diversity) was too superficial, since elsewhere the movement does not give evidence of this type of change. And so I said to him: The first time (measures 24–30) the descending motion in fact represents only the establishment of the falling figure, since the falling figure on its own cannot be understood rhythmically. In measures 94–100 the descending motion would reach too low; the chord would become too thick to fulfill a purely rhythmic role. For this reason, apparently, the ascending motion, which however no longer has <u>merely</u> the innocent task of establishing the rhythm but also a secondary, motivic role whose sudden appearance here would likewise not make sense were it not for the fact that Beethoven had incorporated the motivic idea earlier, at

 etc.

All this occurred to me so spontaneously that I am almost inclined to think that it is correct.

Are you and Lie-Lie in good health? Here, everything is in the best of order in terms of health and finances! Which makes the purpose of life all the more pointless.

   Ever faithfully,
    Your Floriz

---

[1] Egon Pollak (1879–1933): German-Czech conductor, from 1917 General Music Director of the city of Hamburg.

❦ Schenker to Max Temming (draft note), October 10, 1924
OJ 14/45, [35]

My very good Sir,
 You were so very kind as to make an initiative of my friend, Professor Moriz Violin, your own, and to help the youth who are dedicated to the study of music in musicology departments[1] with continuous access to my quarterly publication *Der Tonwille*. For this, my dear Sir, I express to you my warmest thanks; and my feelings of gratitude are surely shared by all youth who have, directly or indirectly, taken advantage of the help you have given to the art.

---

[1] In a letter to Violin (October 16, 1924), Schenker indicated the names of the ten cities whose universities were to receive copies of *Der Tonwille*: Berlin, Bonn, Breslau, Frankfurt am Main, Freiburg im Breisgau, Göttingen, Halle, Königsberg, Leipzig, and Munich.

❦ Violin to Schenker (letter), January 19, 1925
OJ 14/45, [41]

Dearest Heinrich,
 Just a few pieces of good news!
 The concert went absolutely magnificently. I say <u>absolutely</u> magnificently, because I can describe it as a success of a kind that I have never experienced "outwardly," one that would have been worthy of a Selma Kurz.[1] There was so much foot-stomping, as well as cries of "Bravo," especially for the soloist.[2] The

close relationship with the Klinglers,[3] who were very cordial, is the most important thing for me. In spite of a good audience, it was an expensive pleasure.

Many thousand thanks for issue 10 [of *Der Tonwille*]. Now I shall have free time in which to study it carefully. Looking through it for the first time brought back happy memories of Galtür, i.e. on account of Schubert's [*Moment musical* in] F minor.

How do things stand with the publisher? You still owe me advice regarding the Becker case, which I sent you (hesitation over compensation for price of 2 marks).[4]

Hans Weisse sent me his Vocal Quartets at Christmas. They are really extraordinary. I cannot help but feel a certain impoverishment in him. It is puzzling to me how one who is thus handicapped can compose so well. For me this is the first example of it in music. I understand that he himself suffers on account of it.

In the next few days I shall go to Mr. Temming. Perhaps I will then send you a report of how he feels about things. I received letters of confirmation [of the receipt of *Der Tonwille*] from only four universities; these were, at any rate, most cordial. If they are of interest to you, I shall forward them to you.

   Accept our most intimate greetings.
   Your faithful
   Floriz

---

[1] The comparison is to Selma Kurz (1874–1933), one of the outstanding sopranos of the early twentieth century, who was based at the Vienna State Opera.

[2] By "soloist," Violin is referring to himself as the featured instrumentalist in the piano quintet ensemble or, more probably, as the performer of a solo work during the concert. (From his letters of November 6, 1924, and January 24, 1925, one can infer that Schenker assumed the work in question to be the Passacaglia by the Hamburg-based composer Robert Müller-Hartmann.)

[3] String quartet founded by Karl Klingler (1879–1971), a pupil of Joachim, and widely regarded as successor to the Joachim quartet 1905–35. In 1925 the other members of the quartet were Richard Heber, Fridolin Klingler, and Max Baldner.

[4] In previous correspondence Violin reported that his pupil Agnes Becker had been overcharged for an issue of *Der Tonwille* by the Leipzig branch of Universal Edition.

Violin to Schenker (postcard), December 5, 1925
OJ 14/45, [110] (Plate 7)

Dearest Heinrich,

I only want to get in touch! I was ill for a week. I am dogged by the summer wherever I go. Concert halls have been booked here and in Berlin for the end of January and February 1. I hope that our goal is successfully realized. Program: Brahms C major, Beethoven E♭ major, Schubert B♭ major.[1] Are you happy with this? Also with the order of the pieces? How are you? How are things? Has the first yearbook appeared yet? Where are the notices, advertisements, etc.?? Perhaps you will be so kind as to write me a line?!

Most cordial, intimate greetings from us to you!

   Your Floriz

---

[1] A program of piano trios, performed with the Dutch violinist Maurits van den Berg and the Austrian cellist Friedrich Buxbaum.

❧ Schenker to Violin (postcard), December 21, 1925
OJ 8/4, [40]

Floriz,

I have <u>nearly got to the end of all</u> corrections,[1] but will insert between them my most cordial Christmas greetings to you and your family, and to add a few notes. Your sister[2] was with us last Wednesday (evening). Your concert program is, of course, an interesting one; in particular the Beethoven E♭ [Trio] will reveal a certain aspect of your playing that indeed distinguishes you. Yesterday I heard Buxbaum and Berg again; you too will have very great joy. Berg justified the greatest hopes, somewhat more up to the task [than Buxbaum] in late Beethoven; and we may speak of a "Joachim reborn" in chamber music; his right-hand technique and bowing style are first-rate.

The yearbook ought to appear at the end of January, and then the announcements will come. With Universal Edition, a "settlement" was struck;[3] as you can imagine, I came out the victim. Dr. Baumgarten[4] betrayed me too much, purely to satisfy his hunger for settlements and because of his cowardly obsequiousness toward his opponent. About this I shall say more <u>in a letter</u>. Write me a line about the Hammer portrait as soon as it has reached you.

Now back to my tasks!

Many, many best wishes from me and Lie-Liechen.

   Your Heinrich

---

[1] At this time Schenker was correcting the proofs of the first yearbook of *The Masterwork in Music*.

[2] Fanny Violin.

[3] See chapter 8.

[4] Theodor Baumgarten, Schenker's lawyer during negotiations with Universal Edition in the mid-1920s.

Schenker to Violin (letter), December 29, 1927
OJ 6/7, [36]

Floriz,

From your lovely note received today, I can perceive your old sense of humor and am delighted about it! May you live more peacefully now, too! Your fate has, for sure, "gone off the rails" enough already; it is high time that it plays cleanly once again, on fully resonant strings. May this time begin with the year 1928. Your concert (<u>what</u> are you playing?) and the Vienna trip of your dear little Karl are the best preparations. For your greetings, we send you our most intimate thanks!

What you write about Vrieslander is only too well-known to me. You are completely right in every respect, only you would have as little advice in these matters as I myself. I found out about the prospectus only when it was shown to me; of the forthcoming monograph about me I do not yet know a single word. In short, I must take <u>everything from everyone as it comes</u>, as they write it, they sign their own names—the main thing, as you write, is that my work is published. With this in mind, I continue ...

Of course Weisse could have done this more solidly; perhaps he will yet come around to it, for—listen and be amazed:

Recently he appeared at my place and informed me that he and his pupils Dr. Jonas and Dr. Salzer (from the Wittgenstein family) have decided to establish a <u>monthly periodical</u> entitled *Die Tonkunst*, placed exclusively in the service of my ideas. He was already in a position to give the titles of the articles, mainly his own, and assured me of some further collaborators—you will also be invited— etc. It might therefore be possible that Weisse still renders outstanding service [to my cause]. But what if Weisse departs for New York to teach at the Damrosch Conservatory? Then what would become of the periodical? The publisher is an uncle of Dr. Jonas,[1] who already runs a publishing house; he has calculated that 700 copies sold at two shillings each will cover a monthly print-run of 2,000 copies.[2]

All this in the greatest of haste, so that everything is done in time for New Year's Eve. A happy holiday we wish you and your whole dear family! And Dr. Brünauer is coming in two or three minutes.

In fact, he has just rung the doorbell!

In the evening: My pupils have gone, and I send you greetings and best wishes in Lie-Liechen's name, and in my own, both a sort of *perpetuum mobile* greeting,

Your Heinrich

---

[1] Fritz Ungar: a cousin of Oswald Jonas.

[2] Like many projects of the late 1920s devised to promote Schenker's work, *Die Tonkunst* never materialized. After Schenker's death, however, Jonas and Salzer revived the idea of a monthly periodical, renamed *Der Dreiklang*, of which nine issues were published by Krystall-Verlag, Vienna, between April 1937 and March 1938; repr. in one vol. by Georg Olms, Hildesheim, 1989.

Violin to Schenker (letter), July 18, 1928
OJ 14/45, [71]

Sanatorium Schierke
Schierke in the Harz

My dearest Heinrich,

 I was hoping to answer your lovely postcard, concerning Prof. [Fritz] Stein, by return of post. But I was suddenly overcome by a complete breakdown. In deepest desperation, Vally wrote to her brother Julo, who wired me the money with which I have been able to get myself sorted out here, as necessary. Things will turn out all right. I look at all things in the way I must look at them and am therefore also quite at peace; and I hope that this communication will not dampen your spirits for a moment, either.

 My relationship with Prof. Stein is the same as I would have with any puffed-up being. You have no idea <u>how</u> he pursued me, so that 1) he could, with my help, put your Handel materials in order, and 2) use me to help promote a possible performance. Immediately after I returned from Vienna, I wrote a letter <u>and</u> a postcard about the entire matter – – – <u>To this day</u> I have not received a reply. Somehow I'll catch up with the fellow. With regard to your manuscript, I shall not write until <u>August</u>, curtly and insistently. By then he should have returned, like everyone else, from his summer holiday. At this moment, it would be too easy for him to fiddle things with the forwarding; and I will give him an opportunity to return the manuscript only on the basis of a request from me. On this you will surely be in agreement.

 Shorly before the holidays, I had a very nice experience; and the communication of it was likewise delayed by my illness.

 I have a pupil by the name of Harry Hahn, with whom I have been for a year speaking in his lessons only about art and less about his not exactly promising piano playing. He is the leader of a worker's community of the local society of composers. Within this community, he babbled his wisdom about Riemann, Kurth, aesthetics, pedagogy, youth movement, and death and damnation. I gave him a good talking-to, and encouraged him most intensively in the study of your works. Suddenly he surprised me, saying that he would be giving a lecture on June 27 about the Urlinie in the workers' community. I threw my hands up in horror and asked him how he could imagine doing such a thing. I could not prevent him, since your published works are available to all, and so they are indeed – – fair game. At his invitation, I went to the lecture, behaving like the American observer at the League of Nations. As limited as it naturally was, I was pleasantly surprised by how <u>skillfully</u> he managed to do this from the conceptual point of view, something that I was able to confirm from the fact that <u>very</u> intelligent questions were asked by members of the audience. In the autumn, they want to go further. "Let them go ahead," as we say here: I find it very gratifying. He took a Bach prelude and a Schubert waltz from your source of Urlinie graphs and had them enlarged to the dimensions of a schoolroom blackboard. These looked very attractive. I shall send you these two clear examples to Galtür in August.

 Enough for now; above all, unfortunately, for me!

Most intimate greetings to the two of you.
All good wishes!
Your faithful
Floriz

Schenker to Violin (postcard), October 9, 1928
OJ 8/4, [58]

Floriz,

Many thanks for the gratifying news that your relapse had itself suffered a relapse and that you are striving to regain normal health! And how is dear little Karl? We have not yet been able to see your sister, since the start of the season gives us both a great deal to do. From Mr. Hahn I received a very sweet letter and a <u>very good</u> essay and the truly inspired graphs! I am writing also to him at the same time. Many thanks to you for kindly arranging this. To all of you, best greetings.

Your Heinrich

Schenker to Violin (postcard), October 22, 1928
OJ 8/4, [59]

Floriz,

I showed several pupils and guests the beautiful graphs of Mr. Hahn; I need not tell you that they were met with the greatest enthusiasm. I was asked merely why Mr. Hahn does not use a projection apparatus, to make things easier. As I hear, such equipment is readily lent to schools and sanatoriums, if they are not already available; that is, they do not have to be purchased. As Mr. Hahn wrote that he is preparing the so-called "Appassionata" Sonata, perhaps this suggestion, which is well intended, will be helpful, as it is intended to be.

How are you, dear little Karl, your wife, and little girl?[1] I am steamed up in work, likewise my Lie-Liechen.

From the two of us to all of you,
Best greetings and wishes,
Your
Heinrich and Lie-Lie

---

[1] Genoveva (Eva) Violin (1916–2013): daughter of Moriz and Valerie Violin.

Violin to Schenker (letter), October 25, 1928
OJ 14/45, [73]

Dearest Heinrich,

A thousand thanks for your postcard! I have an enormous amount to do and hope that I shall continue to have the strength for all the work.

I do not entirely understand that projection idea. Surely it can work only on the basis of the projection of light, in which case one can use it only in the evening, right? But these lectures take place during the day!!??

Most recently, I struck up a delightful acquaintance with an organist and teacher in Hamburg by the name of Hahnemann.[1] It turns out that he teaches only in accordance with your theory. He told me that you are the only musical fact-giver, and he is burning with curiosity to hear more about you at our next get-together, which we also discussed. Otherwise, nothing new!

Are you about to publish the last volume?[2] Will it appear soon? Otherwise, everything is in good order with us!

        Accept most intimate greetings, in faith,
          from your
            Floriz

---

[1] Almost certainly Carl Friedrich Wilhelm Hannemann (1890–1945), a Hamburg organist and teacher. He taught at the Schule Kileortallee and was a part-time organist until 1925, when he took up a full-time post as organist of the main church in Altona. Hannemann exchanged letters with Schenker for a brief period following Violin's encounter with him. (We are grateful to Alexander Odefey for making this identification, and providing details about Hannemann's life.)

[2] The last volume of the New Musical Theories and Fantasies, i.e. *Free Composition*.

Violin to Schenker (letter), March 3, 1929
OJ 14/45, [76]

Dearest Heinrich,

A thousand thanks for your letter! I am now going to the "Riviera" with Julo towards the middle of March: quotation marks, because I am thinking more about my health than about the Noblesse! It is possible that I shall travel via Vienna. What a joy it would be to be able to see the two of you for an hour or so!!?!?!

In the meantime, I shall let you in on a little folly of mine today, which concerns you. Behind it lie so many discussions and arguments that it is hardly possible to explain the background to this folly. Please write merely on a postcard: wrong, not far off, correct. If completely wrong, please give a hint. But all this only if you can find a quarter of an hour . I am sending you what I believe to be the high points of the first Two-part Invention by Bach:

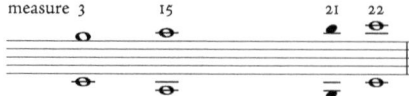

I am sending you only these points; if they are wrong then everything that I found between them must by implication be wrong!

    Your incorrigible
    Floriz

❧ Schenker to Violin (letter), March 7, 1929
OJ 6/7, [42] (Plate 2)

Floriz,

  Without waiting to see whether you will pass through Vienna—something which, of course, would delight us greatly—I am sending you by return of post the reading of and solution to Invention No. 1 in its most concise form:

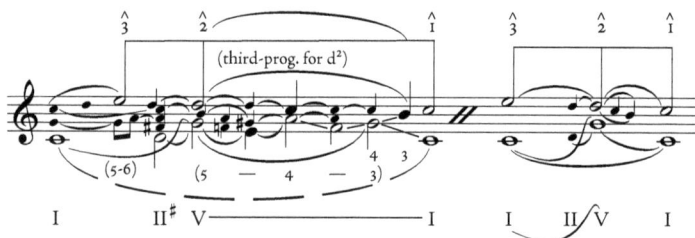

  In your honor, I shall include the <u>intricate</u> and difficult voice-leading of this example, which is indeed all that matters, in *Free Composition*, where all "connoisseurs and amateurs,"[1] as well as my opponents, will be able to look at it.[2] "Riviera today, Riviera tomorrow," the main thing is that you are not going there to see Frenchmen, or even French women, but to enjoy <u>the</u> sun and <u>the</u> air, to the delight of us all. We shall be with you in spirit.

  To your, dear Vally, dear little Karl and your little girl, best greetings and wishes from the two of us.

    Your Heinrich

Have you already received my article in *Der Kunstwart*?[3]

---

[1] A reference to the title of C. P. E. Bach's later keyboard works, published with the subtitle "für Kenner und Liebhaber."

[2] Schenker did not, however, include this example in *Free Composition*. In his reply of March 20, 1929, Violin confesses not to have made sense of it: "I did not understand the voice-leading of your sketch. It would have been so important to me to tell you what I thought about it and to hear how you discovered the correct solution. Perhaps in the summer?"

[3] "Eine Rettung der klassischen Musik-Texte," *Der Kunstwart* 42 (March 1929): 359–67.

Schenker to Violin (letter), November 24, 1929
OJ 6/7, [44]

evening–night

Floriz,

Above all: that you were able to mount the podium, in spite of everything, and won new joy for yourself, was as brave as it was beautiful. Such self-help is worth more than help from outside, which at any rate cannot ever be counted upon: may it serve you well!

I have a slip of paper with notes; I shall attempt to work my way through them:

What you say about Mozio[1] is correct, indeed observed with a poetic beauty. I bear him no ill-will for his error; I was actually in Baden with him in his darkest hours, more than once; now I am also teaching his son the third year of theory and piano (without pay, it goes without saying)—if I could again reclaim the money that I left in his care! With great difficulty, I managed to get him to repay me half of it; I am still waiting for the other half. Given his present material situation, we do not know exactly … .

That you are thinking of leading me to a publisher is extremely kind; perhaps your lucky hand will once again touch me! You must make it explicit to the good man that I command today—almost undisputedly—first place; that Furtwängler has described me in a letter as the first musical brain in history; that two universities, Leipzig and Heidelberg, thought of appointing me, though I did not trouble myself at all in the matter; that I have left Universal Edition because Hertzka betrayed me, lied to me, and concealed from me. (Thus, for example, he concealed from me for three years that *Harmony* had been completely "out of print"; to every inquirer, he offers this explanation unreservedly; it is just to me, the author, that he says nothing though he was obliged to: he causes me damage, even financially, even when the demand [for my work] increases.) For a year Hertzka has delayed me with regard to the "Eroica"; how happy would I be if I could place this work elsewhere. Perhaps I can then even publish my principal work, *Free Composition*, elsewhere. Hertzka is poison for my work and my health. (Dr. Halberstam[2] has himself remarked on this.)

In the November 5, 1929, issue of the *Deutsche Tonkünstler-Zeitung* (Berlin), which is the Society's official organ, an article by W. Schmid,[3] also about me; have a look, the article can if necessary perform a useful service with the publisher. My works are all in print, are selling well, in spite of Hertzka's lack of love and professional care.

If you should happen to have that issue to hand, you should also read the first article, by Schoenberg: a ridiculous ass and rogue, almost disarming. If it really were not beneath my dignity to publish a reply to his examples, I would not let his nonsense go unpublished. I am enclosing the answers; perhaps you will have the opportunity of somehow taking the mickey out of Schoenberg:

In the Prelude in C♯ minor from the *Well-tempered Clavier*, Book 1, Schoenberg gapes at the b♯ and b♮ in measure 29; he hears them—in order to lend support to his unmusical theories—vertically ("new harmonies"—he is indeed looking for them), instead of horizontally, thus:

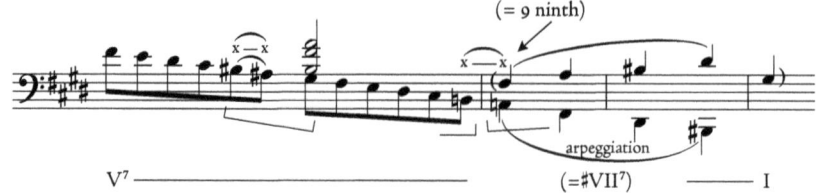

In measure 30, the A is made the seventh and the starting point of an inverted arpeggiation. One should not write:

but rather

and thus the A in measure 30 retrospectively required B as the last eighth note in measure 29. (B♯ to A, B♯ to A♯ [across the bar line]: both were impossible, not permitted.)

To waste a word on this is actually a scandal. Since music began to breathe, its voices have known such an independence of movement—counterpoint shows and teaches this, too—but of course when Schoenberg forces the voices that want to pass near each other, against each other, into a harmonic-vertical bind, then he should be sent to a school desk, if necessary to a reform school. Where are such things not found? There are millions of examples! In this regard, the most recent composers wrote exactly like the first, a similar example may be found in C. P. E. Bach's instructions in thoroughbass:

d is an upper suspension (8–7), but this does not involve the bass at all: the suspension is a "private garden" of the seventh, C.

Another example is Beethoven's Seventh Symphony, last movement:

and so on. Schoenberg could today just as well discover the German alphabet as "new"! If that is everything that raises the masters above Schoenberg!! The youngster, out of folly, takes the far too easy way out.

*

In Mozart's String Quartet, the voice-leading does not conceal such difficult puzzles (for Schoenberg, of course, they are insoluble):

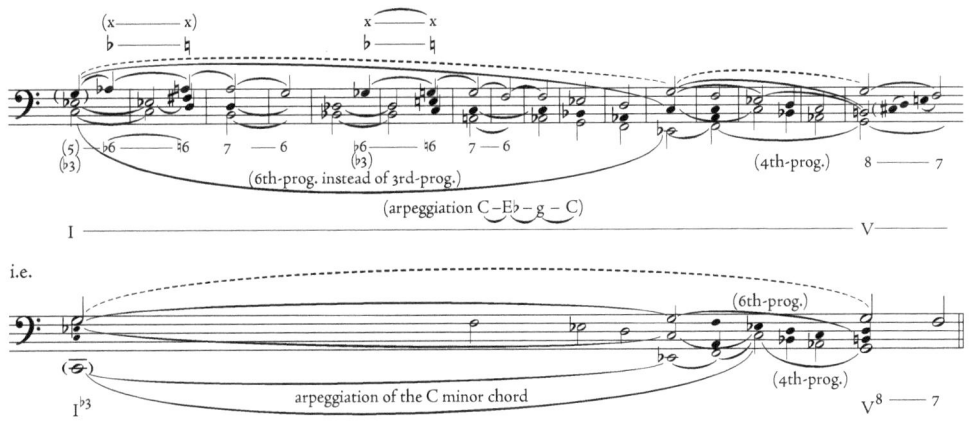

Mozart, String Quartet in C major [K. 465], introduction

NB: I will gladly keep the fee low, if it has to be that way. Should I come out with this now?

Many greetings to each and every one of you, from me and Lie-Liechen.

    Your Heinrich

---

[1] In June 1929 Schenker had demanded to withdraw the money invested for him by his younger brother Moriz (1874–1936) so that he could himself invest it in dollars. His son Georg Schenker, whom Schenker taught 1927–30, was a cellist and played with the Vienna Symphony Orchestra until its disbanding in 1944.

[2] Julius Halberstam: medical doctor at the Löw Sanatorium, whom Schenker had been consulting at the instigation of Eduard Violin.

[3] Waldemar Schmid, "Seminarleiter in Kiel"; this article is cited on page 79 of Schenker's scrapbook (OC file 2). Schmid had probably been a protégé of Reinhard Oppel at the University of Kiel.

Schenker to Violin (letter), March 2, 1930
OJ 6/7, [47]

Floriz,

I am rather late in sending you my thanks for your kind message. In the meantime, I had been so dreadfully overworked—since October, I have not had any free time: not on Sundays or holidays, not on Christmas or New Year's, etc.—until I was compelled by my doctor to take a short break. I am feeling better again.

I am hoping that I can soon hand over the music illustrations for the "Eroica" for engraving by Waldheim & Eberle, who can indeed do this best of all. Concerning a publisher, I shall let you know later. For the time being, I thank you most sincerely for ever-kind intentions.

How did the trip to Berlin turn out? Did you bring home the hoped-for fruits?

At the moment, I am wrestling with that scurrilous boy Mozio for my savings, specifically the second half, which I desperately need now. I am prepared to take the extreme step of legal action in the light of his inconsiderateness (which is well known to you), as I went through a lawyer already once before, in a matter concerning my dear mother. He has actually kept them for two years now, even saying untruths. He is indeed an—idiot!

Recently I heard Hans Weisse's new Octet. Furtwängler, too, had heard it a few days earlier, and it pleases me, for Furtwängler's sake, that he (Furtwängler) spoke out with a genuine flood of emotion, as Hans reported to me: "I would not have thought it possible that something like this can be written today." He is right: viewed in terms of its overall production, the Octet is a <u>colossus of invention and realization</u>. Your ears would really be torn open by the last movement, a passacaglia! The essential features are, naturally, Brahmsian, which is something that Hans would not happily admit. His natural gift is the same as it has always been, i.e. limited; but what he is able to come up with in its absence is all the more astonishing. At the end of September last year he played me his Six Bagatelles for Piano, which are supposed to represent an essay in ingratiating himself with the world of dissonance. He wanted specifically to demonstrate, so he told me, how one can compose well even using fourths and suchlike. I did not keep my opinions to myself. I was all the more pleased, then, to hear the Octet proceed with good voice-leading. Furtwängler promised to intervene on his behalf in connection with publication by Breitkopf & Härtel.

It is also very gratifying to report that a pupil of Hans's, Dr. Salzer (a member of the Wittgenstein family), took care of the very, very considerable costs of <u>fourteen</u> rehearsals with <u>eight</u> musicians (<u>two</u> of whom are concertmasters), and for the provision of food and drink for about 100 guests on two evenings. Things of that sort do not happen to me. I have the incomparably wealthier Hoboken at my side, a real nabob; and in spite of all the trouble that I take, I cannot gain his material support for my life's work. He simply will not listen; he takes the view that, by paying me his <u>hourly</u> fee, he is my "benefactor"—that is literally how he puts it—though I charge him the same amount as my Viennese pupils, instead of asking for twice as much! If I am not mistaken, Hoboken has, however, made himself very unpopular in Vienna on account of his improper behavior. He is not to be helped. For the time being, do not say anything further about it.

How are you otherwise?

Many greetings to all of you from me and Lie-Liechen.

    Your HSch

❧ Schenker to Violin (letter), November 26, 1930
OJ 6/7, [52]

dictated[1]

Floriz,

Weisse has just informed me that you are in fact going to Berlin.[2] The content of this letter will spare me any further explanation or justification.

The passion of my very own being has had the effect that several of my pupils have, so to speak, drawn strength from my effort and flown further than was, or is, something that I welcome, for their own sake. As much joy as it gives me to see them so filled with my passion, so saddened am I, on the other hand, that they have exceeded the boundary and, in so doing, damaged their own being. These people have less of life's wisdom than I. It was to me that the awesome task fell: of assembling the work, of formulating it, and—of living it. I can, indeed, be satisfied with the result. My pupils, however, have not toiled with the material and, being spared this burden, they believe that they may be permitted to grope further, all the more since they are indeed deafened in this day and age by the call to "progress."

Prof. von Cube and Albersheim, for example, have stayed at all times within their limits. But already poor Vrieslander has had to pay with his being, since, without having understood me, he had the vanity to introduce to the world the concept of "Urtöne"! (I have never corrected him in this matter!) Further, Prof. Roth, in his textbook on counterpoint, simply expropriated my most attractive ideas as his own—to put it in Jewish terms: when threatened with bankruptcy, he transferred the business to his wife's name—, simply by transferring them to himself and giving me credit only for trivial matters, though he has, to be sure, written with a great deal of character and support for me in the *Stuttgarter Zeitung*.

And even Dr. Jonas has had the temerity to write to me that he gave a lecture in Munich in which he mentioned my work as a "point of departure." Recently he asked me to write a letter of recommendation to Furtwängler; naturally I had to refuse him, as I had no inkling whither he was steering himself from the "point of departure" that I provided for him.

And now, too, our dear Hans Weisse! He was plagued by an impulse toward progress that was far too intellectual. Thus he asked "Must I, in fact, continue?" His successes in composition—I mean his inherent successes—increased his appetite to move on, but in so doing he falsified the true picture. As strange as it may sound to you, Weisse never once brought me a voice-leading graph, and openly acknowledged, "I do not know why: either I am timid or too stupid." He asked me to improvise these things in front of him, but nothing brought him out of his reticence! It was only last year that he presented me with a graph of a work by Brahms, which was truly lamentable. It was even more lamentable for me to learn that he had spent the entire year making all sorts of plans, which were likewise spoiled by things that were too strongly intellectual being mixed in with them; then he immediately betrayed to me the fact that he was not entirely at home with my work. His own facility with words deceives him; but I had the task, at almost every encounter, of opening his eyes to the basic principles of my theory. He came, for instance, and said: "Master, I know it, indeed, but how am I supposed to explain it to my pupils?" And now he asks me whether the Urlinie might not also consist of just—a neighbor note, for instance, e–f♯–e in [the Prelude to] Bach's E major Partita [for solo violin] ([second] Yearbook). Until last year he did not understand the Urlinie clearly enough as the tonal space of a piece; or he believed that it was supposed to give a subordinate meaning to the form, etc. I set all these misconceptions aright, but I am concerned as to whether he will stick to the proper boundaries in his lecture. He actually appears—this is the best I can hope for—to want to impose a certain amount of restraint in his presentations of voice-leading graphs, for he remarked that he would have come to grief in his polemic against Prof. [Alfred] Lorenz had I not shown him the correct path. Thus he appears, for sake of prudence, to provide his listeners only with the score, and to leave the rest to improvised talk, which does not bind him [to a particular interpretation]. This is the way I see things. It is possible, however, that he will explain the matter correctly, and also with character, which will give me pleasure for his sake. I have no doubt, however, that he will never achieve my level of reading; and at present he has no idea of what will be contained in *Free Composition*, in spite of all that he has already heard from me, in lessons and letters. And for this reason I would be sorry, for his sake, if the path leading back to the truth were to be blocked by a false appetite. [It is true] that the young people have learned a great deal from me, but not the very thing that is most important: to apply themselves fully and solely to the theory itself, without any peripheral intentions. Would I have achieved so much had I wanted to go beyond Beethoven, Brahms, and Mozart?

Very well, then: I am writing to you about this so that you might listen carefully and give me your impression as to whether he lectured more about himself or about me! Weisse will be reading his lectures to me and my pupils, so I will be able to form a view of them here, too.[3] Whether, in the heat of battle, he might commit an error of judgment is something I would like you to communicate to me. Oppel will be coming to Berlin; perhaps Cube, too, from Duisburg.

You may have already received a copy of *Masterwork 3* by that time. Please send my greetings to Furtwängler, Oppel, and other acquaintances.

How are your dear wife Vally and the children? I hope that you have a safe journey and bring good news home with you!

  Your

    Heinrich

whose <u>lovely</u>, <u>lovely</u>, <u>Lie-lie-lie</u>chen was concerned to spare his eyes.[4]

[1] The letter is in Jeanette's hand.
[2] Violin had said that he would be going to Berlin to hear Hans Weisse's lecture on Schenker's theories at the Central Institute for Music Pedagogy. A written version of this lecture, "What is Counterpoint?," is preserved in OC/17.
[3] Weisse's talk at Schenker's apartment took place on Friday, December 5, from 6:30 to 9:15 in the evening. (An account of it is given in Schenker's diary, on pp. 3551–53.)
[4] Valediction, signature, and this postscript are in Schenker's hand.

Schenker to Violin (postcard), dated December 2, 1930
OJ 8/5, [1]

Floriz,

Many thanks for your note. If I am not deceiving myself, Weisse's lecture should lead to a professorship in Berlin. "On the urgent recommendation of Dr. W.

Furtwängler," at the beginning of [Leo] Kestenberg's first letter to Weisse, suggests as much. Furtwängler behaved in true conviction of Weisse's worth: he heard him speak about the material for three hours in St. Moritz (Edwin Fischer[1] was also there); in the spring of this year he heard the Octet, which rightly impressed him. Thus Furtwängler does well in promoting Hans. The Viennese scene is becoming ever more barren (also for me, it goes without saying), so Hans would really wish to obtain a professorial post in Berlin. He himself (in such cases, secretively) did not express this thought.

Have a pleasant journey; to all, most affectionate greetings from

Your Heinrich

[1] Edwin Fischer (1886–1960): Swiss pianist, conductor of the Munich Bach Society 1928–32. In 1931 he succeeded Artur Schnabel at the Music Hochschule, Berlin.

🎼 Schenker to Violin (letter), January 9, 1931
OJ 6/8, [1]

Floriz,

As I told your sister Fanny, who was at our place the day before yesterday, it must be thus: I cannot sit down to write you a letter until I have cleared everything else from my mind; collectedness and devotion are conditions that should lead me to you … .

The economic troubles are unparalleled; my losses are no smaller than yours. Everyone who writes to me from afar complains! Brünauer—in his twenty-eighth year [with me]!—was the very first who—merely from the usual flaunting of his niggardliness—had withdrawn from one of his two weekly lessons even last summer! That gave me a sharp pain, whose consequences I still feel. New pupils can hardly be expected: the [last] four years' worth of youth, who today would be between sixteen and twenty years old, are simply non-existent![1] And who would want to study music, without any prospects!

It is a devilish trait: the innate musical inadequacy of the world is joined by an economic one: man would like to lower himself to the level of beast, without realizing that this transformation will in the end threaten him with starvation and death, as enticing as it may be as relief from intellectual or physical effort.

With regard to Weisse: that you were so kind as to go to Berlin, and to write to me, are things that I shall treasure in my heart as signs of an ineradicable bonding of our souls and fates. He gave a talk at my place, a thoroughly excellent one. Already at home I have gained the impression that he has set aside all his hysteria about "progress" and is doing his best to remain faithful to his "Papa." He has even taken my advice not to look for absolute certainty, as he had been doing for years, but rather to express his wisdom in just the way that he possesses it. That addiction to "certainty" (fear of subsequent disgrace) he referred to, very clumsily, as his "inhibition"; and since he spoke about it in connection with me— in front of me and also in front of others—we all had the impression that he was blaming me for tyrannizing him. Today he defines the meaning of his "inhibition" almost cynically: "I used to have so many inhibitions; now I see that one can say anything and everything to people to their faces: as <u>they</u> speak, so too do <u>I</u>, without fear." Following the lines of my advice, it was therefore also a question of concealing from him (as I had hitherto done) the fact that, without exception <u>each and every</u> presentation of evidence is <u>false</u>. I praised him with the most genuine conviction since—and this is what it amounts to these days, for us all—the insight must be publicized, and proclaimed from every rooftop: that music has its <u>own coherence</u>, whatever it may be and whatever it may be called—except that it is <u>not</u> what is taught in schools! And Hans has fulfilled this responsibility in <u>the most excellent possible way</u>: his formulations (which are, of course, also my own) were and are splendid; his language and its delivery are captivating, inspiring, inspired.

It was only the Invention in E♭ that he set in front of me, asking for help with it; and it turns out that he himself committed the very mistake that he accused Prof. Lorenz of having made. He erroneously had [identified the primary tone as] a $\hat{3}$, which I corrected to $\hat{5}$. Unfortunately, he was pressed for time and did not understand my little sketch,

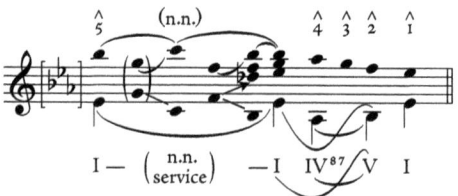

[and] the expansion by the neighbor note c^2, which holds back the course of events until finally the progression $\hat{4}$–$\hat{1}$ arrives. He accepted the $\hat{5}$ but did not understand the bass, and created a real mish-mash.

Until now I had withheld my interpretation from Weisse. Was I not right to have done so? And now, too? No one observed the mistake; but the audience would have had something to listen out for, which they would otherwise not have heard. Oh, if only the time would return where I could, for example, at a table in a coffeehouse, or at your place or mine, show you the relevant improvements in writing, as in the past!

My suspicions turned out to be correct. I am in no doubt that Weisse appealed to Furtwängler; now he will <u>surely go to Berlin</u> next year (in Vienna he has, unfortunately, no further prospects!). Furtwängler wrote to him from St. Moritz, to say that he had a meeting with Kestenberg, Schünemann[2] and Schreker[3] at the beginning of January, where the offer of an appointment for Weisse would be on the agenda. Weisse is looking to him to find a permanent job (on account of his children, and also on account of his advancing years); if he does not obtain an official position, he will go to America and there, with Warburg's help, … .[4] I believe, however, that he will carve a path for himself in Berlin; with or without a position, he will establish a seminar. (The cost of enrolling in a seminar is low, enabling a great number to take part.) He is thinking about a Schenker institute, which would give employment to all who are currently displaced (as is, for example, also Dr. Salzer). Now would be the time for me to let you in on another secret, but my eyesight is beginning to fail: I shall certainly not forget to return to it in my next letter … .

Let me add merely that the editor of *Der Kunstwart* in Munich, the journal founded by Avenarius,[5] enjoyed my "Miscellanea" so much that he filled nine pages with extracts from it. In Kiel, the Conservatory newsletter reprinted ["The Mission of German Genius" from] *Tonwille* 1 (1920).

Just now, at 9:30 in the morning, your letter arrived with the sensational news: what a surprise![6] Professor von Cube (Duisburg) should be considered ahead of Oppel; Vrieslander would be quite excellent for counterpoint and thoroughbass.[7] But you cannot found a school on the basis of giving due notice to these disciplines, to say nothing of devoting time and money to them. Perhaps Weisse will pitch in; that would be—hitting the bull's eye! I fear that he will want to leave [Germany], specifically to earn money to provide for himself and his children. If you were here, I myself would take the theory position, for the sake of our own secure footing. For—in the same post—a letter arrived from my solicitor, who is taking action against Mozio on account of 14,000 shillings, which I handed over to him in cash. I had been counting on this money when, amid difficulties with my eyes and under severe time pressure, I paid 7,000 shillings out of my own pocket for the printing of the third yearbook! This was a betrayal of my Lie-Liechen who, however, did not bat an eyelash over it; an act of suicide![8] Should I have killed myself on account of my eyes (just take a look at the music illustrations for the "Eroica"!)?! Hertzka deceived me for a whole year. Furtwängler learned of this directly from me, did all that he could, managed to get Breitkopf & Härtel at my disposal; but, owing to despair about my eyes I was already committed to Drei Masken Verlag and feared—correctly, I am sure—that Breitkopf & Härtel would have held up the publication for years, on account of the current situation, and would cause me a great financial loss, insofar as I would not have been able to work on *Free Composition*. I expected that Furtwängler would have relieved some filthy rich Berlin Jewess of 3,000 marks, but he cannot do so. I must take care of it, until Mozio gives me back my money! A veritable crucifixion, which has made me ill.

Keep the secret to yourself. I have at least managed to be able to continue work. For the eternal frictions with the publishing houses rob me of my life and work. In the last ten years I have established the concept of "Urlinie," published ten issues of *Der Tonwille*, three yearbooks, and the Beethoven [piano sonata] collected edition, and prepared *Free Composition*. Who can compare his accomplishments with these? And finally, in addition to my work, I also had to give the world my life savings. For this reason I would even today accept a position; I know, however, that this is not possible.

Vrieslander should be considered first of all. But my most serious piece of advice is this: Save yourself and your family, do not concern yourself with theory; leave the class to some person who would teach the children in any old way— according to Thuille, or Riemann, or Richter: it makes no difference which one of these[9]—think only of yourself! And if you are fortunate, which is something I wish from the bottom of my heart, then you may be so kind as to help me once more with *Free Composition*, as you have so often done in the past. What would I be today without the three yearbooks? What would Weisse be? But to be freed from Hertzka, which in fact made it possible for me to work, is something for which I have you and the Hamburg gentleman[10] to thank.

Vrieslander's address is, in any event: Locarno-Solduno, Villa Olga, Ticino, Switzerland.

The best, the very best of luck!!! In the end, the skies will also brighten over all of us.

Best wishes and greetings to you and your lovely family from me and Lie-Liechen.

Your Heinrich

---

[1] Schenker is apparently writing off the four wartime years (1914–18) as a time when very few children were conceived, 1915 marking the first year in which few children were born on Austria. But he seems to have counted in the wrong direction: children born during the period 1915–19 would be between twelve and sixteen, not between sixteen and twenty.

[2] Georg Schünemann (1884–1945), German musicologist and educator, Deputy Director of the Music Hochschule, Berlin, from 1920, its Director 1922–34.

[3] Franz Schreker (1878–1934): Austrian composer, most notably of operas, Director of the Music Hochschule, Berlin, 1920–32. Schenker disapproved of his music for its modernist tendencies, and also resented what he saw as the higher level of publicity that Universal Edition afforded Schreker's work than his own.

[4] Gerald F. Warburg (1902–71): American cellist, pupil of Weisse in the 1920s. The ellipsis suggests that Schenker believed that Warburg was enthusiastic about bringing Weisse to New York. Weisse did, in fact, emigrate to the USA and take up a teaching post at the David Mannes Music School in the autumn of 1931.

[5] Ferdinand Avenarius (1856–1923): lyric poet, a leading representative of the culture reform movement of his time, and the first to popularize the Sylt dialect.

[6] This must have been the news of Violin's intention to found a music institute dedicated to the promotion of Schenker's work and teaching.

[7] [Schenker's footnote:] It goes without saying that the "Urlinie" would be well covered by him; thus he is in fact the only one under consideration who will have an impact!!

[8] From the diary, one learns that the 7,000 shillings came from Jeanette Schenker's personal savings.

[9] That is, a quite ordinary teacher could be brought in to teach from one of the standard set books in use in the early twentieth century, by Hugo Riemann, Ludwig Thuille, or Ernst Friedrich Richter.

[10] Schenker is thinking of the generosity of the Hamburg industrialist Max Temming, and of Violin's untiring efforts to help with the sale and distribution of *Der Tonwille* in 1924, as a means of putting pressure on Hertzka at Universal Edition.

❧ Schenker to Violin (postcard), June 6, 1931
OJ 8/5, [4]

Floriz,

Miracles do happen. Yesterday evening Hans brought me 3,000 marks (as remuneration for my last work[1]), which Furtwängler provided him. He will now continue to make an effort with respect to *Free Composition*, and it seems certain that *Free Composition* will thereby be entirely <u>secured</u>. Hans has rendered <u>great service in these matters</u>; I am very, very pleased also by Furtwängler's contribution. Now you can share in my joy! We are leaving on June 14; it will then be a question of completing *Free Composition*. How are you, your lovely family. In respect of health, and otherwise? Many greetings and kisses from the two of us.

        Your Heinrich

Five pupils of Hans will continue the seminar exercises, to spare my eyes.[2]

---

[1] *Masterwork 3*, which was in effect a monograph on Beethoven's "Eroica" Symphony.
[2] The seminar comprised Felix Salzer, Trude Kral, Greta Kraus, Manfred Willfort (all former pupils of Weisse), and Angi Elias. (See chapter 25.)

❧ Schenker to Violin (letter), September 6, 1931
OJ 6/8, [5]

HOTEL ÖSTERREICHISCHER HOF
SALZBURG

dictated[1]

Floriz, my dearest Florizello,

For a long time I have delayed—on account of a suggestion from Cube—thanking your for your beautiful deed.[2] It was only a letter from your dear Fanny, which reached us here in Salzburg (where we have stopped for a while longer), in which she announces her forthcoming trip to Hamburg, which gave me the courage to send you a few words that cannot dispense with a certain amount of mysticism, although I am convinced that they are anchored firmly in the most vivid reality.

To begin with, a few words on current events. In Galtür I made the acquaintance—unintentionally—of Prof. Dr. Kestner of Hamburg, whose sixteen-year-old daughter is taking piano lessons from Müller-Hartmann. I gave him a copy of the prospectus [for the Schenker Institute]. To myself he did an extraordinary kindness, in that he found me to be in relatively "excellent" shape for a man of my age.

My eyes improved in Galtür, apart from the flickering; the constant inflammation has subsided, also the trembling of the eyelids, but as you can see I still avoid writing at length.

Since on the same day the [Paznau] Valley doctor assured me most particularly that my constitution (my heart included!) does not have the slightest flaw, that it is entirely normal and healthy, and enables me to continue with my work—of course, in sensible measures—I am holding myself at the ready for *Free Composition*, all the more since ...

On the very same day, the mail brought me a letter from a Viennese industrialist,[3] whose wife has been a pupil of Weisse's; informed furthermore [about my work] by his wife, he will place 5,000 shillings at my disposal on October 15, as a contribution towards [the production costs of] *Free Composition*! That is indeed a miracle! I have indeed paid for it dearly, with fear for my life and work, but the miracle has occurred. And where there are already 5,000 shillings, further shillings will be found; nonetheless I hope that, just with this sum I shall be able to find a publishing house that will be willing to cover the rest from its own resources. The crucial lesson of the last few years, however, has been this: It is only since I have had the support of Furtwängler, and now this Viennese industrialist, that my inner being has been opened to the form that *Free Composition* is to take, in the most intimate way, and I found it as if at a stroke. Thus I could have already presented *Free Composition* years ago, if the financial assistance had been secured; without this, the form of the work was not to be achieved. Now, of course, I understand this so well!

Finally the mystical words that I promised:

One day, Universal Edition called upon me to work with them. I chose Carl Philipp Emanuel Bach as my theme. What was it that drove me to this master? With my edition [of his keyboard works] and *A Contribution to the Study of Ornamentation*, I brought the master to life for the second time; and never again will he be so thoroughly forgotten, as he was after his death!

You, too, have loved this master, marveled at him, played his music;[4] and one day you made your way to Hamburg, to the very Hamburg where Emanuel Bach was employed. You see, Emanuel Bach accompanies us like a star; he leads me, leads you! In his constellation we are, as your new Institute demonstrates, joined together again in our work, as we were once in Vienna. Our two lives are, at the beginning and at the end, entwined in the same way. It is just as if I, too, were living in Hamburg, so that my words (which Vrieslander, too, later adopted and often published) have been confirmed: there is only one book in music literature, and that is Emanuel Bach's book; everything written before is meaningless, also [everything] written since, until my life's work, which represents as it were the second book in music literature. It is truly not presumptuous to say that Emanuel Bach and I belong together, and only the two of us. In this sense, I am, like him, a citizen of Hamburg! And now I shall indulge myself in a little improvisation:

It would be nice if you, in the name of this union of two spirits,[5] could gain a measure of civic support for your Institute so that, being twice blessed by Emanuel Bach, it could also embrace a Schenker Museum, with materials that would be appropriate for such a museum.

For the [Schenker Institute] prospectus, of which I first received news by way of Vrieslander, I thank you cordially; it gave me great pleasure. I understood quite well your apparent reserve, for sake of caution with respect to colleagues who might wish you ill. (You will become aware that already many reviewers have recognized my work at a higher level.) The text is very good, well written; I should like to note just one ill-devised formulation, which might be explained and corrected orally. I realize, of course, that the two of you, yourself and Cube, are aiming in the right direction with the words "receptive genius" (*rezeptives Genie*), for my compositional output plays no role in the historical mission that has been assigned to me; but if I consider that, for example, Joachim, Messchaert, and now Nathan Milstein cannot be described in any other way than as receptive geniuses, then this description, when applied to me, is less apposite; otherwise it would be necessary for you to say that the term "genius" should altogether be avoided with regard to these artists. In my great achievement, specifically in my unified conception of the theory of harmony, counterpoint and structural levels—and ultimately in the crowning by the Urlinie—there is so much that is creative, uniquely creative, that the epithet "receptive genius" would ill serve the cause! It will be Cube's task, in his lectures, to refer to this, i.e. to say what he meant by it! Vrieslander used to joke: "The most extraordinary thing about your case is that you have accomplished such an act of synthesis despite the fact that you are a Jew; the Jews dissolve, destroy things, but a Jew with [capacity for] synthesis is non-existent!!"

Weisse will visit you while in transit; I have asked him to do so.[6]

I shall keep you informed about the work of my miniature seminar, as I have already written to Cube.

Turning to *Free Composition* will no longer permit me to consider Galtür as a place in which to spend my summers. The trip is too long, too dear, too strenuous; we want to stay nearer to Vienna, where we will be able to complete the work more easily. This little picture shall be for us a souvenir of Galtür; in this spirit, we are also sending it to you.[7] Depending on the weather, we shall stay here another two or three days; then: back to work!

Most cordial greetings to all of you from the two of us.

    Your
        Heinrich

---

[1] This letter is written in Jeanette's hand, with only the signature and second date in Schenker's hand.

[2] The establishment of a Schenker Institute in Hamburg.

[3] Paul Khuner.

[4] Violin performed a Piano Concerto in A minor, and a concerto for two pianos, by Bach soon after arriving in Hamburg; but he may have also performed one or both of these works in Vienna, since Schenker made a note of his friend having borrowed the cadenzas to the solo concerto.

[5] *Zwei-Einheit*: a play on the word *Dreieinigkeit* = Holy Trinity.

[6] On September 18, 1931, Weisse boarded a ship in Hamburg bound for New York, where he was appointed to teach at the David Mannes Music School. The day before he set sail, he gave a public lecture in Hamburg on Schenker's theories; he was assisted at the piano by Cube.

[7] Probably OJ 72/15, photograph no. 10, which shows Schenker and Jeanette outside their hotel in Galtür. The reverse side is marked "summer 1931, Lie Lie and Heinrich"; the name "Floriz" is pencilled in the upper-left-hand corner.

❧ Schenker to Moriz and Valerie Violin (letter), [c. January 24, 1933]
OJ 6/8, [21]

My dear friends,

Although in the grip of the Angel of Death since his childhood days, your poor boy has also seen for himself God's light and wonder.[1] It is only that his time was given such a short measure that enrages our feelings even against God! Still, He has not once strayed from his course: Nature, herself alone, has become a sinner, a murderer to Him! You all loved him—what joy for a child!—and helped him with joy in your hearts, as much as you could: that raises you above cruel Nature! May God remain at your side!

From me and Lie-Liechen, most heartfelt greetings and kisses in old faithfulness!

Your Heinrich

---

[1] Karl Violin had just died, having been ill since 1922 and bedridden for many months before his death.

❧ Schenker to Violin (postcard), February 26, 1933
OJ 8/5, [16]

Floriz,

In the midst of our sorrows, a piece of good news will provide a welcome elixir. So listen to this: Hans writes from New York that he is giving a course about me—twelve hours, spread over three months—to which already 90 (ninety) musicians and teachers have already subscribed. They are all taking it with unprecedented fanaticism; he is also addressing the [*Five*] *Analyses in Sketchform*. Even Hertha[1] was moved to write me a note of effusive gratitude. 90 × $5 = $450! For me, an hour's lesson for three persons brings in 15 shillings—and were I to attempt to announce a course, no musician, no teacher would turn up.

[Joseph] Marx is a quite ordinary rascal, out of ignorance, on account of *moral insanity* a veritably frantic Ajax; he contradicts himself from one week to the next, in speech and in writing, in his letters and articles; he steals like a raven, conceals things, etc. More about this on another occasion.

To you and your dear family, most heartfelt greetings from the two of us.

Your Heinrich

---

[1] Hertha (Herta) Weisse, Hans Weisse's wife.

22

Further Inroads into Germany: Felix-Eberhard von Cube

FELIX-EBERHARD von Cube (1903–87) was the son of a Munich-based architect who had married into the Sternheim family. For a time Gustav von Cube's family lived on the estate of his brother-in-law, the poet and playwright Carl Sternheim, for whom he had built Schloss Bellemaison. It was here that young Felix studied the piano with Sternheim's private librarian Otto Vrieslander, on whose recommendation the boy went to Vienna in 1923 to study with Schenker. (It was after one of his first lessons with Schenker that Cube made a pencil drawing of himself seated at the piano, while Schenker ranted about "Litfasskreaturen" who ought to be locked away: see Plate 10.)

Although the lessons lasted for just two and a half years—Gustav was unwilling to provide his son with further financial help, and Schenker had to chase him for unpaid fees—they had a lasting effect on Cube, who raised the Schenkerian flag wherever he taught, occupying himself with voice-leading analysis and tonal composition for the rest of his life.

Cube obtained a secure position at the Rhineland Music Seminar in Duisburg in 1927, where his father was now working. He stayed there for five years, also giving guest lectures in the nearby cities of Düsseldorf and Cologne; in 1927 he visited the Schenkers in Galtür, where he made photographic portraits of Heinrich and Jeanette (see Plates 12, 18). The following summer he persuaded the owners of the Duisburg bookseller Scheuermann to mount a shop-window display of Schenker's writings and editions, on the occasion of his teacher's sixtieth birthday; he also wrote a vivid appreciation of Schenker's life and work, which was published in two local newspapers.

In September 1931 Cube left the relative security of Duisburg to become the theory teacher at Moriz Violin's newly founded Schenker Institute in Hamburg (see chapter 21). Although the Institute closed down in 1934, barely a year after the National Socialists came to power in Germany, Cube reopened it after World War II as the Heinrich Schenker Academy, and it enjoyed mixed fortunes as a private music school for about fifteen years; an unpublished *Lehrbuch der musikalischen Kunstgesetze*, a kind of textbook, contains numerous voice-leading graphs of teaching works, "counter-examples" of bad composition, and of Cube's own works.

Nearly 100 items of correspondence between Schenker and Cube survive, and these furnish a near-complete record of the exchanges between them over a period of a decade. In them we find a greater proportion of musical discussion than anywhere else in the correspondence. There are copious exchanges over Bach's Prelude in C major from the *Well-tempered Clavier*, Book I, a graphic analysis of which appeared in Schenker's *Five Analyses in Sketchform* (1932), and of the opening theme from Beethoven's Sonata in A♭ major, Op. 26, which was to form part of a second such set of published analyses (see also chapter 25). In both cases, the choice of work was Cube's. There are detailed observations from Schenker about Cube's early piano sonatas, and from Cube a schematic representation of the tonal system and a sketch for a further prelude from the *Well-tempered Clavier* (the D major from Book I) that testifies to his own skill as an analyst at the dawn of the age of the voice-leading graph.

In his letters, Schenker showed an almost paternal fondness for Cube; and his name appears in the list of pupils in the entry on Schenker in *Riemanns Musiklexikon* in 1929. Like Furtwängler, however, he chose to remain in Germany during the Nazi period, believing that he could do his teacher's cause more good there than by emigrating to the USA. He had become estranged from Violin in the 1930s over a financial dispute; later, he alienated Oswald Jonas by objecting to the latter's political sanitizing of Schenker's texts. As a result of his abiding German nationalist feelings and tendency to go his own way, he had little influence after the war as a proponent of Schenkerian theory.

WILLIAM DRABKIN

❧ Cube to Schenker (letter), January 30, 1928
OJ 9/34, [10]

Duisburg, Rhineland
Pulverweg 41

Most revered Master,

Gradually—slowly, but all the more surely—the anchors that I have thrown out are reaching quite firm ground. The third theory class will probably start up sometime in February. The other two have pressed on as far as the modal-mixture rows.[1] We work slowly, without rushing things, and solidly, very solidly!

Because it is carnival season, the performance of my sonata has been delayed. It will probably take place <u>after</u> Ash Wednesday. The programme will probably include Scriabin and a second Duisburg composer, Paul Strüve. I am trying to get the Scriabin replaced by my Variations, the Tarantella and several preludes.

The number of my private pupils has risen to three. This means that my [monthly] income, reckoned in shillings, stands already at 380. Nothing to be ashamed of!

Recently, at a successful winter festival at which 400 invited guests were present, I played Scarlatti, Brahms, and pieces of my own with real success. That sort of thing is the best advertisement.

My lecture[2] is scheduled for March 3; I will send you the manuscript afterwards, as you requested. In order to help fulfill an urgent need, I was elected as junior member of the local committee at the last general meeting of the Imperial Association. This is the first rung on the ladder to becoming a "specialist advisor" in the Ministry of Culture.

On the occasion of your birthday this year,[3] I have made contact with the largest bookstores in Duisburg and Essen for the purpose of a collective exposition of your works. Would it be possible for us to borrow two of the Hammer engravings from the relevant Viennese art publishing house?

I have not yet heard anything about Hoboken's Appeal (though I did receive a very sweet letter from our friend Otto Vrieslander), but I would be very interested to know how far the enterprise has progressed.[4]

Otherwise, my "linear progressions" maintain my calm and sense of direction (the "Urlinie" belongs only to the master);[5] I am grateful for the congeniality of good people, and—I eat quite a lot!

For now, most affectionate greetings to you and your wife

from your
Cube

Until now, I have had no news from Frankfurt.[6]

---

[1] *Mischungsreihen*: these are scales based on a combination of tones taken from the major and minor scales, as discussed in Schenker's *Theory of Harmony*, §§41–47.

[2] In an earlier letter (October 9, 1927) Cube mentioned a lecture that he was to give to the Imperial Association for German Musicians and Music Teachers.

[3] June 19, 1928, was the date of Schenker's sixtieth birthday.

[4] The Appeal of November 1927, a leaflet appealing to archives and collectors to deposit copies of composer autographs in the Austrian National Library (see chapter 12).

[5] Here Cube is aping Schenker's habit of using his own terminology in a metaphorical sense.

[6] The previous year, Cube had offered to find out more about a teaching position at the newly created Frankfurt Hochschule, on behalf of Moriz Violin.

❧ Schenker to Cube (letter), February 12, 1928
OJ 5/7a, [13]

Dear Mr. von Cube,

Your note brought great joy to me. There is almost an alpine sense of excitement in your upward climb; indeed, I share even the intellectual joy of your pupils. Putting my teachings into the form of a "school" is nothing short of squaring the circle. If you have made just a few steps in that direction, that already signifies a great deal. Admittedly, you will have an easier time achieving this with private pupils, and I very much hope, for your sake, that you will get more and more of them. You appear indeed to have the skill to deal with "officials," which is necessary to survive in an institution. To be able to support yourself with private pupils, however, also signifies an advantage, insofar as that you are thereby able to keep yourself artistically clean for as long as possible. You have made a start; may you continue to prosper!

I had the Appeal sent to you straight away. Have you seen Vrieslander's "prospectus" for volume 2 of *The Masterwork in Music*? If not, please send me a line, and I will write to him, unless you prefer to write to him yourself.

For some weeks, a plan has developed among Dr. Weisse's students for a monthly musical periodical, *Die Tonkunst*, which is to be devoted exclusively to the cultivation and application of my theories. If the financial support is sufficient, I will recommend that you, too, contribute to the writing, as you write very well.

I thank you most kindly for your thoughtful intentions to get the book dealers to offer me their support. If the dealers are really so far along as to grant your wishes, I shall be glad to arrange for two engravings to be sent. Vrieslander's article in *Die Musik*[1] would also be entirely advantageous for such a demonstration. I shall await a further reminder from you, in case the booksellers really want to go ahead with this.

My best wishes for your next undertakings in performance and lecturing. Does your radio receiver occasionally reach Vienna?

I am stuck into work, work, work on *Free Composition*, and all the noteheads are rejoicing with me; for soon, soon they will be released.

The two of us send our most cordial greetings. Write again.

Yours,
H. Schenker

---

[1] Otto Vrieslander, "Heinrich Schenker," published in the October 1926 issue of *Die Musik*, included a reproduction of Hammer's mezzotint.

❧ Cube to Schenker (letter), April 24, 1928
OJ 9/34, [11]

Most revered Master,

I seem to have survived this winter, too, and spring has just about arrived. Not, of course, one that can be compared with the Viennese: in the shadow of the blast furnaces no almond trees thrive; and where the steam-hammers thunder, all tenderer sounds are silent. But if one walks a bit further on, one finds a few nice places where one can always pursue contemplation.

The struggle for existence is, however, no empty phrase! My dear colleagues are slowly recognizing that I have not come here merely to say "good day" to them. They take up their well-tested little tricks, and make my work as unpleasant as they possibly can. And if, further, one adds to this the bad state of the economy, then the picture that emerges is not an especially rosy one. I have lost pupils, and am back to where I was half a year ago. Well, things will get better again.

My sonata was, naturally, not performed. It is better to rely only on oneself! The second sonata is approaching completion. I believe that it is very good; when it is finished, I will simply play them both in November myself, and that will be it.

The intrigues began after my lecture. (The material is at present still in Düsseldorf, but as soon as I get it back I shall send it to you; it includes several analyses that I completed myself.) I had an audience of 50 persons, including many local teachers, and a fair number of seminar pupils. Standing at a large blackboard, I spent more than an hour and a half demonstrating with coloured chalk. The result: vague recognition alongside great enthusiasm among the vast minority;[1] in the other camp, sympathetic smiles from the grayed oxen yoked to pedagogical honor. The breath from the land of genius had not reached them.

Yes, and now the "matter of editions." My God, I had stirred up a fine hornets' nest! The entire swarm fell upon me with their stings. By way of reply, I posted my "Table of the best editions" in the theory lecture room, as Luther did with his theses in days of yore. The saga continues.

<u>One</u> good thing did come out of the entire affair, and perhaps I can make it <u>the one</u> good thing to come out of it. The administration had no choice but to continue the discussion, and so I am supposed to give a lecture on Urlinie and editions at the seminar in a short time. I hope that the "chef" will not reconsider this again.

The bookstores Scheuermann in Duisburg and Schmemann in Essen are putting on a special exhibit in their shop windows.[2] I would be very grateful if you would let me use the two Hammer engravings. Perhaps they could even be sold here. We will exhibit everything of yours. (I suppose that *Free Composition* is not yet ready?)

At the same time it would be useful if we could include a few autograph [reproductions] in the display. Is something ready yet? I wanted to contact Hoboken myself, but find that I don't have an address for him. (Is it true that he has divorced again?)

Then I shall write a meaty newspaper article:[3] in short, we shall make a proper campaign, to which I am already looking forward!

How do things stand with Dr. Weisse's journal? Did you read Vrieslander's article in the Association's journal?[4]

With affectionate greetings to you and your wife,

    Yours,
        Cube

PS My five-valve radio receiver can reach Vienna; but it is often more difficult to get good reception from there than from Madrid or St. Petersburg.

---

[1] überwiegende Minderheit: an ironic play on words, suggesting that only a small part of the audience showed much interest in Cube's presentation.

[2] In the event, only Scheuermann took up the suggestion of a shop-window exhibit.

[3] Two versions of this article were published, in the *Rhein- und Ruhr-Zeitung* on June 24, 1928, and the *Duisburger General-Anzeiger* on June 28.

[4] A one-page article by Vrieslander entitled "Heinrich Schenker," written in connection with the publication of *Masterwork 2*, appeared in the *Deutscher Tonkünstler-Zeitung*, March 5, 1928; a copy of this is pasted into Schenker's scrapbook.

Schenker to Cube (letter), April 29, 1928
OJ 5/7a, [14]

Dear Mr. von Cube,

The first Sunday morning gives me the opportunity of replying to you. The hostilities you encounter from the teachers, the "class" of people who decide in this matter, are all too understandable. They feel that, with the new things, they can no longer proceed with such businesslike smoothness as they can with the authorized harmony textbooks, "with keys" to the assignment book; they can no longer reel off [the answers] with such idiotic convenience—B♭ major, C major, F♯ major, E♭ major,[1] F minor, G♯ major, and so on—but that their heads will have to join in the conversation, and moreover a very special head, stripped down to the purest music, with a thousand musical ears. The "feeling" [for music], so obsessively practised by their dear selves, which is set against the so-called "reflection" even of a Beethoven or Brahms—whereby it is merely surprising that it is the reflective masters who are capable of the symphonic where as they, who are capable of having feelings, are incapable of the symphonic (though in principle the opposite ought to have been the case!)—this high-handed feeling should be rejected as superstition, [but] that is more than the teachers are willing to accept. Had I, of course, laid the table for these men exactly as the business-wise Mr. Riemann had done for their sake, in his countless "catechisms" with the Ollendorf question-and-answer game,[2] in his "great" and "short" composition textbooks (for every occasion), had I saved them each and every embarrassment by explaining the entire collected literature [of music], then, yes, then I would long ago have won the place that was owing to me, even among them![3] For now, things must drag on and, in fact, my death will be the first precondition [of the recognition of my theories]. The cause, however, is making magnificent progress .... .

Now for the matter at hand. You will receive from the art gallery Artaria two [copies of my portrait by] Hammer in at most a week. (The earlier series was sold out; Artaria has to order a new one, hence the short delay.) Of these two, please be so kind as to keep one for yourself, to remind you of the struggles of your youth; the other, however, I ask you to return to me, as it is not expected to be sold.

On Friday, Vrieslander came with a request from you; I took this on myself in order to expedite matters.

You will find a few things [about me] in Riemann's *Lexikon*, and in Kürschner.[4] I am afraid I haven't seen the latest editions [of Riemann], and thus do not know whether Einstein has shortened my entry further in order to gain a few lines for some up-and-coming jazz star. Yet I believe that a basic outline may be found there—apart from the date of death, which is not yet known.[5]

I can say that I had to overcome all unending difficulties, right from my twenties, since I had to take care of a family of five which was left to me by [the death of] my father,[6] a highly respected country doctor, and that, in the further course [of my life], these were further surpassed by the difficulties that people, i.e. publishers, created for my works. However incomparable my human achievement may have been, with regard to the former difficulties, the completion of my work may nevertheless be reckoned as the greater accomplishment. I received no help anywhere, I had to overcome resistance in struggles that lasted many years. Even the life-long contract (with Universal Edition) did not protect me. Thus it turned out that several series of work have had to remain incomplete to this day: The *Last Five Sonatas of Beethoven* is missing the most important volume, on Op. 106; the editions of the sonatas of Mozart and Haydn, to which I had a contractual right, could not be realized; *Der Tonwille* suffered the most extreme opposition from my own publishers (breach of contract and sabotage), and so on. This loss of work, of fulfillment of tasks, which I alone was able to master (as its discoverer), has remained the most painful thing for me, since it can no longer be made good. Had the publishing house granted me the time for work which it instead took up in these stubborn struggles, I would have accomplished even more of value for the good of everyone, publisher included.

In my life, I was certainly not short of invitations and assignments on the part of various organizations, which would have brought honor to me. But everything fell through in the moment at which I gave notice of how I would realize them, since there was too much and this exceeded the expectations of the promoters. It was less a question of my cause, which was indeed an entirely closed book for them, than rather a cheap realization (cheap in every respect), to be accomplished only to confer distinction and the honor upon themselves, the clients. I came away empty-handed, and so it came about that I also preferred to keep clear even of the institutions of learning. I realized that I would have to wage the battle from a neutral position.

To have endured the most extreme poverty was a blessing for me; I am very proud to have thus been marked out by fate, for it became my happy duty to set a spiritual plus against the material minus. (Never did poverty reduce me to becoming a democrat, still less a social democrat. In the name of the eternal aristocratic spirit, I have, since childhood, always held my head high above the mob.) Only by serving the spirit faithfully and selflessly was I able to find what was granted from above for me to find.

Further blessings of my life: Joachim, Messchaert as models of the very difficult art of performance. The concert tour with Messchaert furnished me with insight into the utterly and uniquely subtle workshop of this singer, whom I readily acknowledge to be the greatest singers of all times and places. He towers above the proudest Italian examples of all centuries, including Caruso;[7] unfortunately the world knows nothing of his rank, nor could they understand anything, since Messchaert never sang in the opera house, which is the only artistic trough[8] from which the masses feed.

And that I was able to experience Brahms late in life, to see him, to hear him speak, perform, is a joy about which I would have to write tears, if I were able to. I always knew that he was the last master, that music is dead is something I understood long, long before the others were forced to admit this. (See the Preface to *Counterpoint 1*.) This pain concerning the dying art drove me to work feverishly (day and night), I threw my ideas on to paper in the midst of a most threatened material existence, I struggled with publishers, with readers; and now I finally see—success.

In Brahms I saw the twilight sky of art; since this glow has been extinguished it has become totally dark over the world—forever. The world has never enjoyed, never understood, never shown its gratitude for the higher blessing of the great masters, and thus the art of music has gone from them.

I must close: these thoughts are painful to me. Perhaps you can nevertheless make some use of what I have thrown down.

One question: did Universal Edition make my works available to you? From where, then, will you get these??

This year Prof. Dunn, Prof. Oppel, and Vrieslander (with Klaus:[9] his first trip to the mountains) are coming to Galtür. Will you be there? That would be very nice. This time I am leaving Vienna exceptionally early, on June 15, and will travel slowly, in stages, to Galtür.

With most affectionate greetings from me and my wife,

    Yours,

        H. Schenker

---

[1] Schenker writes "Mies^{dur}," possibly in jest at the name of Mies ("Mi" is the solmization syllable for E, and "Es" is German for E♭), possibly in error. The chord sequence is entirely made up.

[2] This appears to be an allusion to the *Nouveau cours de langue anglaise, selon la méthode d'Ollendorf* (1906), which used the method of the catechism.

[3] The idea of a substantial collection of theory books by a single author as a "meal," to be consumed by musicians or teachers, is something Schenker returns to in his letter of November 20, 1928, where he compares his various types of composition—theory books, analyses, editions, Urlinie graphs—as a banquet similar to that provided by Riemann.

[4] "Schenker, Heinrich," *Kürschners Deutscher Literatur-Kalender auf das Jahr 1928*, ed. Gerhard Lüdtke (Berlin, Leipzig: De Gruyter, 1928), col. 998.

[5] Schenker is joking about the fact that, though he has an entry in an important dictionary of music, he is still alive.

[6] When Johann Schenker died in 1887, five of his six children were alive. The eldest daughter, Rebecka, died two years later; she would probably have been in her mid-twenties at the time, though no birth certificates were issued for the first five Schenker children. At the time of his father's death, Heinrich Schenker was just nineteen years old.

[7] Schenker's admiration for the artistry of the Italian tenor Enrico Caruso (1873–1921) is noted in a diary entry of February 17, 1928, i.e. just two months earlier.

[8] *Kunsttrog* ("art-trough"), a derogatory neologism that likens opera audiences to herds of cattle.

[9] Vrieslander's son.

Cube to Schenker (letter), May 24, 1928
OJ 9/34, [12]

Most revered Master,

The Hammer engravings arrived, and are already under glass and in frames, in order that they may serve their purpose.

That I may be permitted to keep one of them is one of the rarest joys of my life, and adds to my great thankfulness to you in a new and no less beautiful or profound way!

I shall give my lecture now also in the Conservatory of the City of Düsseldorf, in front of what is expected to be a large audience. I had to change it a bit, as I had anticipated an extra measure of intellectual alertness among the listeners.

My activity at the local conservatory is growing. As an immediate consequence of my theory instruction, I may reckon among my new pupils a few "transfers": a situation that is not likely to win the sympathies of my dear colleagues who have thus been injured.

At the end of June I shall speak for an entire morning to all the pupils and teachers in the Seminar about your theories, the Urlinie, and the true art of playing the piano.[1]

The bookstore Scheuermann will mount the exhibition immediately after a Reger festival that is taking place here, so long as the spirits are still musically excited. The firm wrote to the archive of the National Library in Vienna, but did not receive any reply at all. I would love to know if we can therefore count on making available several copies of manuscripts of Duisburg's musicians. Interest and expectation are in sufficient supply. Hoboken's Appeal did not go amiss.

The third movement (the finale) of my second sonata is in progress; both sonatas will take part in the composers' competition this coming winter.

> For today, my best greetings to you and your wife
> from your
> Cube

---

[1] A quotation from the title of C. P. E. Bach's *Versuch über die wahre Art, das Clavier zu spielen*; for Schenker, Bach's *Versuch* was the most important treatise on music yet written.

Schenker to Cube (postcard), May 28, 1928
OJ 5/7a, [15]

Dear Mr. von Cube,

Moved as I was by your recently announced plan regarding Düsseldorf, I am sending you at the same time, as printed matter, an essay of mine printed in Bonn for the Beethoven festival (1927).[1] Perhaps you will enjoy the connection (Bonn/Düsseldorf); perhaps the the musicians of Düsseldorf will be somewhat more amenable when they learn how much Professor Schiedermair[2] has sung my praises in Bonn. And in general you would do well to mention to your German colleagues not only Prof. Dunn, who plans to visit me in Galtür, but also the American (English-speaking) teachers in New York and San Francisco who have been teaching the Urlinie in their schools for some time. For next year Dr. Weisse has had acceptances from another [two older[?]][3] professors who want to learn about the "line." Since the Germans are so keen on all things American, they ought to study the example of the studious Americans!

We are leaving Vienna on June 15 (exceptionally) and will make our way slowly towards Galtür, where we shall arrive at the end of June. Best wishes for your plan, and for your successes, and also most cordial greetings from the two of us.

  Yours,

  H. Schenker

---

[1] "Beethoven und seine Nachfahren," *General-Anzeiger für Bonn und Umgegend*, March 26, 1927, 3–4.

[2] Ludwig Schiedermair (1876–1957): German musicologist, Professor of Music at Bonn University 1920–45. His interest in Beethoven brought about the establishment of the Beethoven Archive Research Institute (containing originals and photostatic copies of manuscripts, sketches, and early editions of Beethoven's works) in 1927 (the centenary year of Beethoven's death) in conjunction with the Beethoven House, Bonn; Schiedermaier was the Archive's first director. He had recently published *Der junge Beethoven* (Leipzig: Quelle & Meyer, 1925).

[3] The edge of the card cannot be read for certain.

❧ Cube to Schenker (letter), July 6, 1928
OJ 9/34, [13]

Most revered Master,

 It was certainly wrong of me to delay with news for so long; but it had been my intention to wait for all the consequences of the matter, so that I could prepare an all the more complete report. Here it is.

 The exhibition ran for two weeks at Scheuermann's bookshop, of which I spoke. Apart from *Der Tonwille*, all of your work was available in multiple copies. In the big shop window stood Hammer's engraving, surrounded by books and editions of music. (Niloff's *Table of Instrumentation* functioned for two days as backcloth.) In addition, a few photocopies of autograph manuscripts were on display at all times. For Chopin's Scherzo, Op. 54, and Beethoven's "Moonlight" Sonata we additionally placed good and bad editions side by side, for comparison.

 My biographical article appeared in Duisburg's most widely read newspaper. (A few other papers turned it down, without giving reasons.) This article was my first essay of this kind. I made an effort to hit upon what was right. I hope it meets with your approval. I have sent copies to "prominent" people, thus also to Damrosch[1] and J. P. Dunn. I enclose two replies; please be so kind as to return them to me. I will work on the Cologne project with all seriousness; perhaps something good for me can come out of it.

There has been much talk here about the exhibition [of your work], and a few things have been sold: mainly the [New Musical] Theories [and Fantasies] and your edition of the Beethoven sonatas. The municipal library has, for the present, acquired the monographs on the Ninth and Fifth Symphonies, the *Contribution* [*to the Study of Ornamentation*], the sonata edition, and the yearbooks for its music section. More will follow. The director of the library, Dr. Sallenthin, has, moreover, beautiful first editions from the period of Haydn, Mozart, and others, and also the "second edition" of [Carl Philipp Emanuel Bach's] *Versuch*, though unfortunately without the test pieces. Since these are missing from most copies, might I suggest that this supplement to the *Versuch* be included in the holdings of the Archive? Better as a photographic reproduction than not at all.

My last activity before the holidays, I shall speak at the Conservatory for an entire morning about your theories, about the Urlinie (with many examples), and about the question of editions. The number of converts is still limited, though reliable—that lies in the nature of the subject. The following Tuesday I shall probably proselytize a few more conservatory students.

In Düsseldorf, I was invited to give a lecture. Ten listeners appeared. And so I postponed the lecture. The organizer was disappointed by this, but he promised me a sizeable audience the next time.

Here a big composers' competition has been announced, which I shall enter with two sonatas. There is still something missing from the last movement of the second, but that will be finished by the October deadline.

The second engraving was not used: I could not devote myself sufficiently to the bookshop in Essen. Shall I send it to you in Galtür, or would you prefer a different address?

It is very unlikely that I shall be able to come this summer. Business is again in crisis, the consequence of which is that my pupils are leaving in droves. But they will come again. As a matter of principle, I am not lowering the rate for my lessons, which currently stands at 10 marks.

I therefore send you all the more heartfelt thoughts and wishes to Galtür, and will be present in spirit at your table by the window with *Luftbrot*, whipped cream and gigantic cutlets. I also send my warmest greetings to the Türtscher family.[2] Nor am I forgetting your servant-Kapellmeister, and the marmot who eats sweets.

    To you and your wife,
        Cordial greetings from your
            Cube

---

[1] It is not clear whether Cube means the conductor Walter Damrosch or his brother Frank, both of whom had illustrious careers in America. Frank Damrosch founded the Institute of Musical Art which, in 1926, became part of the Juilliard School of Music. (Their sister Clara married David Mannes, founder of the David Mannes Music School.)

[2] The Türtscher family: owners of two small hotels in Galtür, of which the Schenkers stayed in the Alpenhaus Fluchthorn, and also of the local car service, which the Schenkers used. Cube is reminiscing about his visit to Galtür the previous summer.

Schenker to Cube (letter), July 13, 1928
OJ 5/7a, [17]

My dear Mr. von Cube,

Now things have gone as you had planned! The fact that there were just ten in the audience in Düsseldorf does not change things in the slightest. For instance, Dehn[1] had such an audience of ten in Vienna (I myself had fewer than ten, at times), and Liszt, Ysaÿe[2] and others often enough. Your troubles were rewarded, and you have made great contributions to music in Düsseldorf, however little the people in Duisburg themselves have an idea of them: all contributions look alike, indeed insofar as the profiteers observe nothing for a long time, either large or small, regardless of the material. Moreover, the profiteers are unlikely, because of their character, to be the first to rise and offer thanks.

The two of us do not belong to the profiteers; precisely for this reason I—merely as the guardian of my ideas—thank you, too, as guardian, for the thousandfold efforts for bringing them to light, as man to man, as artist to artist.

Your essay, like the earlier one, shows a lightly agile way of thinking and writing. The imprecision regarding Joachim and Brahms ("collaboration") is something for which I take responsibility, since you probably had difficulty reading my handwriting.[3] I meant merely: with regard to Joachim, he was always my model in matters of performance (I did not know him personally); and with regard to Brahms, his manifestation in general, as the bearer of such a magnificent artistic sum (my first Brahms symphony was already his third, which Bülow brought with the Meiningen [Orchestra] to Vienna for its first performance!)[4] The Brahms peak was already crowned for all eternity when I first began to see him, to hear him!: the priceless remarks on music, which I had the good fortune to hear from his mouth.

The word "collaboration" is thus an overstatement. To put this right is something I owed to you. From time to time, of course, you can come up with the right interpretation yourself, depending upon whom you are on conversational terms with, but that is not necessary. It was just a misunderstanding that could happen at any time, and everyone knows that I am not reckoned among those who ingratiate myself with Joachim or Brahms simply because they are dead and cannot contradict me. Vienna is swarming today with "friends" of Brahms! Your account of the opportunity of working with Messchaert is absolutely correct.

In spite of this, I find your article attractive and comprehensive, well-grouped[5] and vividly illuminating. Many, many thanks! I can affirm, with joy, that you are testing and proving your powers.

Your proposal regarding the book of music examples for C. P. E. Bach is something I find very commendable. I shall go through it with Hoboken.

Please send the second Hammer portrait to Vienna, but not until October!

Professor Oppel is coming again to Galtür. A pity that you could not be there.

My wife, who shares my joy in what you have accomplished, sends her most affectionate greetings, as also do I.

Yours,
H. Schenker

¹ *die Dehn*: possibly the violinist Bertha Dehn (1881–1953).
² Eugène Ysaÿe (1858–1931): celebrated Belgian violinist and conductor.
³ Cube's article for the *Duisburger General-Anzeiger* speaks of "collaboration" with Brahms and Joachim.
⁴ The first performance of Brahms's Third Symphony took place on December 2, 1883; Schenker was then fifteen years old.
⁵ *gut gruppiert*: Schenker is alluding to the *Gruppenbildung*, the putting together of large sections of a cyclic form from a variety of contrasting ideas.

Cube to Schenker (letter), January 2, 1930
OJ 9/34, [20]

Most revered Master,
First of all, my best greetings and wishes for the New Year. As it is at the same time a new decade, the concept of time is involuntarily extended and I become aware of how little, and yet how much, of the infinite has once again rushed passed me. I imagine myself to be like the frog in the shallow pool by the river bank: outside the great current marches on, and I cast a furtive glance at my hind legs, wondering whether they will succeed in coming along with me.¹

At the moment my mood is somewhat philosophical. The overstraining of the stomach and gut at Christmas might well have something to do with this. On the other hand, things have been quite peaceful around me. Apparently, fate also furnishes occasional periods of rest for its children. This may be very advantageous for my nerves; in the meantime I am already beginning to suspect that my energy is perhaps adjusting itself to the new situation to make me lazy and indolent without my realizing it. As things appear, I have my livelihood and am able to earn my daily schnitzel, with a bit of salad on the side, without overexerting myself. That's not too much of a task, if one is reasonably frugal. But the visible stations of success are getting further and further apart. And so I think keenly about new assignments on which I can test my powers. The Conservatory is running now like a well-oiled machine. Private teaching offers somewhat more from an artistic point of view, but of the many there are only two with whom I can speak that language which, I am afraid, will remain hieroglyphics for the majority of people. For the *Deutsche Tonkünstler-Zeitung* I am working on an article "Urlinie and Piano Teaching" or "A Lesson with Bach," and for this purpose I have chosen the first C major prelude from *The Well-tempered Clavier*. I hope I have read it correctly.

The Urlinie moves in the space of a third, $e^2-d^2-c^2$; the harmonic degrees of the background are I–V–I. The V is preceded by a ♯IV, which supports the chromatic passing note eb^2 in the upper voice. The development [of harmonic degree I] shows an octave-progression, e^2-e^1, which in a certain sense is divided into two tetrachord-like fourth-progressions, which enable the harmonic affirmation II[♯]–V (in measures 10–11) and V–I (measures 18–19) at their end. By this means, the voice-leading arrives in a lower register; only at the very end, again with help from a figuration against a stationary bass, is it brought to its conclusion in the appropriate high register with $\hat{2}\,\hat{1}$. With the help of three Cs— namely c^1, c and C— the bass encompasses two octaves (coupling). That is what I have been able to read from the score, naturally in broad outline. From this I would like to write a short piece, for the interest and benefit of the reader, though not without asking whether I should send it to you before I publish it.[2]

With regard to composition, all sorts of things are going around in my head. Until now, something for string quartet seems to be shaping up most of all; this naturally would have as a consequence long and strenuous special studies, and much reading and listening. There remain— alas!—all too large holes to fill up, and time is constantly slipping through my fingers. Perhaps my Piano Sonata in A♭ major will be performed by a master pupil at one of the next Conservatory concerts; that would be another small quantity of water passing through the mill of public opinion, which we must—for professional reasons—continue to keep in working order. I have not reached the point at which the little children come to me; at present I am still at the acquisitive stage and make an effort to keep ahead of the competition.

Alongside this, I read the latest philosophical works, for instance Edgar Daqué's *Nature and Soul*,[3] and have discovered within me an aptitude for billiards. I'm also beginning to get stronger, slowly and by the kilogram, which has a beneficial effect on my general health and a detrimental effect on my tailoring costs. Apart from our chamber music evenings, I have begun a new "sport": jazz on two pianos. (I cannot help myself!) All in all, I am as satisfied as one can safely expect to be in these times.

With most affectionate greetings to you and your wife, I am

Yours,
Cube

---

[1] The entire paragraph is written in neutral terms (with the German *man* as the subject), but Cube is referring to himself, imagining his situation to be not so very different from other people's.

[2] The *Deutsche Tonkünstler-Zeitung* did publish a letter of Cube's in 1930, but the essay on Bach's C major Prelude never materialized. Instead, Schenker went over the content of the analysis carefully with him. Cube made a new voice-leading graph of the Prelude in October 1931, and again Schenker provided a critique. In the end, the final form of the voice-leading graph was published—under Schenker's name, without acknowledgement of Cube's involvement, and without verbal commentary—in the *Five Analyses in Sketchform*.

[3] Edgar Daqué (1878–1945), German paleontologist and mystic philosopher. His publications included *Urwelt, Sage und Menschheit* (Munich: Oldenbourg Verlag, 1924), *Natur und Seele* (Munich, 1927), and *Organische Morphologie und Palaeontologie* (1935).

Schenker to Cube (letter), January 12, 1930
OJ 5/7a, [28]

Dear Mr. von Cube,
  To begin with, a simple graph for purposes of confirmation and correction:[1]

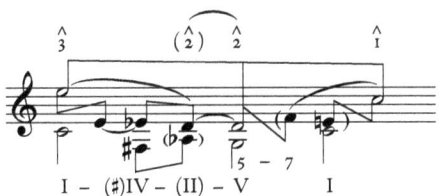

The first descending register transfer proceeds in parallel tenths:

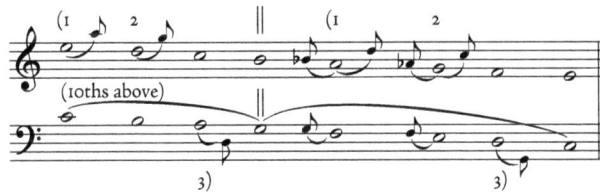

at which the diminution plays all sorts of tricks: inner parts are brought to the fore, above; voice-exchange (measures 12–13 and 14–15): (b♭–a, a♭–g closely positioned near the bass, rather than in a higher register, etc.
  The bass leads, supporting parallel tenths, divided into c^1–g c. Wonderful parallelisms in the upper part in the midst of the trickery. Twice [the inner part] is thrown above, e–a^2 and d–g^2, then with a single response in the bass, a–d; then similarly a–d^2, g–c^2 and d–G in the bass. The $\hat{2}$ is taken by d^1.
  Finally, the most difficult problem: completing the obligatory register from d^1 to c (but in which octave?) as $\hat{1}$, back into the register of the $\hat{3}$, by means of:

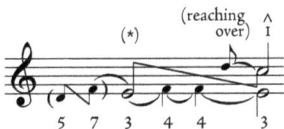

an arpeggiation from e^1 to c^2, combined with 3–4 4–3.
  But in order to gain e^1 (see above example), Bach hones the d^1 (= $\hat{2}$) by means of d^1–f^1, [thus] leading to the seventh, which urgently demands resolution to e^1!
  Have a look, on p. 204 in the [Bach] collected edition (at the back of the volume), at Forkel's version of the piece, so that you will understand the value of that exquisite diminution.[2]
  Read the Berlin *Tonkünstler-Zeitung* of November 5[, 1929]. You will find there an (indescribably bumbling) article by Schoenberg,[3] and one from Kiel, which also refers to me:[4] the author thanks me, indeed, for freeing him from Riemann, but—these books should on no account be put in the hands of today's youth; [the present] system [is the] rubbish heap of the Inquisition—ludicrous, today, when victory is so very nearly within our reach, ridiculous! I speak of these

things because you may possibly have arrived at a view of the quality of the Berlin *Tonkünstler-Zeitung*. And yet, if I remember correctly, Vrieslander published an article about <u>me</u> there.⁵ Your article would be somewhat different, and therefore <u>would have to be</u> suitable: it concerns a question of pedagogy, and is not specifically about me. Take courage. In any event, you should find it easy to publish your essay in any other music journal.

Your joy in life brings joy also to me. Do not rest. Many thanks for your sweet letter.

With best wishes from the two of us,

Yours,

H. Schenker

I should be grateful to read your article <u>before</u> you submit it; I hope that will be all right.

PS. (in opposition to Riemann and other writers)
<u>Rhythmic-metric analysis:</u>

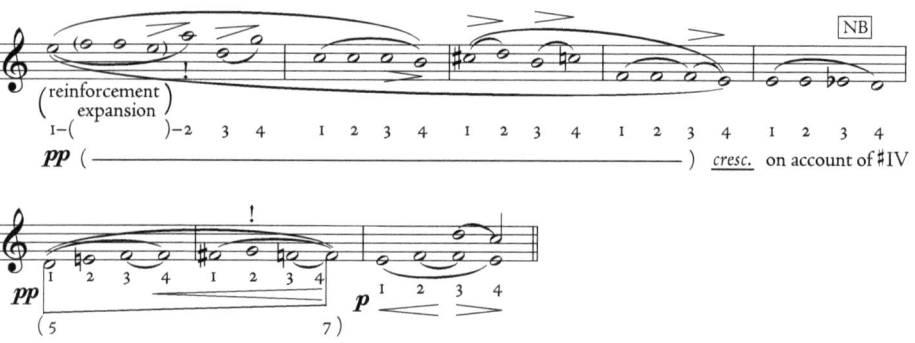

NB: the measure with the 6/4 chord inserted between the e♭¹ and the d¹ is not by Bach.

Dynamics (<u>performance</u>) are in accordance with example 4; they are <u>incorrectly</u> given everywhere (see the Peters edition, Czerny, etc.).

The dissonances in the left hand should always be played <u>louder</u> than the consonances, thus for example

The difference between a $\frac{4}{2}$ chord and a $\frac{4}{3}$ chord will clarify the shading of those magnificent parallelisms.

Bach deliberately writes

in order to avoid a "naked" repetition in the upper voice.

---

[1] This letter offers an extensive commentary on Cube's provisional reading of the same prelude as discussed in his letter to Schenker of January 2, 1930. The details of Schenker's analysis are very close to those in the graphic analysis of the prelude in the *Five Analyses in Sketchform*; the main difference here is the prominence of the bass F♯ supporting a diminished seventh (in the published analysis the F♯ is a passing note between F (supporting a major seventh) and G (the structural dominant). For further commentary on this letter (and a facsimile of pages 1–2 and 5–6) see William Drabkin, "A Lesson in Analysis with Heinrich Schenker," *Music Analysis* 4 (1985): 241–58.

[2] The Bach-Gesellschaft edition (vol. 14) includes in its text-critical report—on p. 205, not p. 204—a version of the Prelude attributed to Johann Forkel (the so-called "Forkel'sche Gestalt"), which appeared in the later eighteenth-century printings of Hofmeister's edition of the *Well-tempered Clavier*. It is only twenty-four measures long, and lacking in many of the contrapuntal features discussed in this letter. (A further abbreviated version, twenty-eight measures long, appears in the Notebook for Wilhelm Friedemann Bach.)

[3] Arnold Schoenberg, "Zur Frage des modernen Kompositionsunterrichtes," in *Deutsche Tonkünstler-Zeitung*, November 5, 1929; Eng. transl. "On the Question of Modern Composition Teaching," in *Style and Idea*, transl. Leo Black (London: Faber & Faber, 1975), 373–76. Schenker made extensive analytical notes about various works by Bach, Mozart, and Beethoven, for a response to Schoenberg's article; he included them in a letter to Moriz Violin (see chapter 21).

[4] On p. 79 of Schenker's scrapbook Jeanette has written the note: "Waldemar Schmid, director of the Conservatory in Kiel, cites Schenker alongside Kurth," *Deutsche Tonkünstler-Zeitung*, November 5, 1929.

[5] Schenker's scrapbook contains Vrieslander's "Heinrich Schenker" from the *Deutsche Tonkünstler-Zeitung* of March 5, 1928, written on the occasion of the delayed publication of *Masterwork 2*.

❧ Cube to Schenker (letter), February 10, 1931
OJ 9/34, [23]

Most revered Master,

First of all, many thanks for forwarding the latest issue of *Der Kunstwart*,[1] about which I shall presently have a few things to tell you. But before that, the most important matter. The enclosed letter gives you information about the present state of my Cologne plans. In fact I wrote a mile-long letter to Braunfels[2] about the necessity, which continues to make its way into the foreground of pedagogical interest, of establishing a state-sanctioned basis for Schenkerian teaching in the Rhineland. The progress that has taken place in the country, and also the symposium in Berlin, were duly mentioned. Braunfels's answer, which actually raises only <u>one</u> legitimate argument against it at the present time, can be understood as having two meanings: a real one and a political one. Real, in so far as the finances of the Hochschule are indeed particularly bad; and politically one can imagine that even Braunfels fears the malevolent influence of the "chained pedagogues" in Berlin (in spite of Kestenberg!), and, with extraordinary politeness, prefers the diplomatic tactic of waiting to stirring a hornets' nest. Personally, I regard the first of these interpretations as highly probable!

So as to leave no voice-leading stone unturned, so to speak, might I in the meantime ask for your advice, possibly even your good word in the matter that I shall amplify in the following way:

The creation of a regulated program of Schenkerian instruction at the Cologne Hochschule would signify a truly palpable step forward! Your world of ideas would be made accessible to all the western provinces, which have hitherto been untouched. And the involvement of the Hochschule might lead to other musical institutions being persuaded to set up similar programs. I am thinking here of the great difficulties that have been created for me, and will continue to be created, by the authorities of the Folkwang School in Essen,[3] who are simply unteachable, and those in my own sphere of influence!

The Hochschule ought to be in and of itself ready to get to work on the matter immediately. I am waiting, not far away, to concentrate all my strength in a place whose undertakings will be regarded, talked about and imitated in the widest imaginable area. What is still missing from the complete triad is a sum of money—and, I might add, a relatively small sum—which would make possible the establishment of one or several classes in harmony, counterpoint, Urlinie, etc!

In this connection, one naturally thinks of a man who has, in the most generous way, enabled cultural projects to be realized by providing financial assistance that was certainly more substantial than the purposes described above would require. Do you believe, my dear Professor, that there may be good reasons to approach Mr. Anthony van Hoboken in this instance, and to ask him to provide assistance for this plan, which can surely be <u>only</u> a profitable one? As I said, it would not amount to a great deal of money, and only for one or two years; for I am convinced that by this time, perhaps even sooner, a seriously mounted program of studies at the Hochschule would of itself become obligatory, and could win and assert its place in the "balance sheet" of the school administration.

There is the further question as to whether I should write immediately to Mr. van Hoboken myself, or whether you would like to deal with him personally, on the basis of my letter and that of Braunfels. Possibly one could even strive for an agreement with the Hochschule, to the extent that it provides at least a <u>part</u> of the necessary funds itself! In my view, an agreement <u>in principle</u> from Mr. van Hoboken would be enough to persuade the Hochschule to make the necessary concessions. Regarding the <u>form</u> of the assistance—whether it is to be a trust fund, a grant, or a repayable loan—would naturally have to await direct negotiations with the Hochschule. I myself wait in agony for the moment that gives me the opportunity to stand in the foremost line of battle. Although I wanted to write yet more, I must close now. Very soon I shall report to you about my other experiences, opinions, and attempts. For today, best greetings to you and your wife, and most devoted regards to Mr. van Hoboken, also to Dr. Weisse.

>   Your
>   Cube

---

[1] The January 1931 issue of *Der Kunstwart*, 44, no. 4, contained a notice of Schenker's *Masterwork 3* by Otto Vrieslander.

[2] Walter Braunfels: professor of theory at the Cologne Music Hochschule, who had given support to Cube's efforts to promote Schenkerian theory in northern Germany.

[3] The Folkwang-Schule in Werden, near Essen, was founded in 1927 as an interdisciplinary school devoted to music, dance and speech. In 1963 it gained the status of a Hochschule, and today there are four Folkwang-Hochschulen in the Ruhr region: Essen-Werden, Duisburg, Bochum, and Dortmund. Cube had gone there three years before in the hope of introducing Schenker's approach, but he encountered mainly "folk-dancing and chorale singing" and made little headway with the young musicians there.

❧ Schenker to Cube (letter), March 28, 1931
OJ 5/7a, [35]

Dear Professor von Cube,
  Now you should learn the true sequence of events.
  After you wrote me your first letter about the opportunity in Cologne, I informed Hoboken immediately that I had received an important letter from you; but I thought it unnecessary to reveal its content just then, since you might possibly not undertake anything further. For us to engage in a secret deal would have been the most unbearable thing for him, if by some chance he gained knowledge about it. Now you write that the matter is thus [still] open. The first words that sprang to his lips, after he communicated to me the content of your letter [to him] were: "What am I supposed to do about this? If Braunfels wants, he can certainly get rid of others and employ Cube." As I said nothing in response to this statement—it deliberately avoided the entire matter—the small-minded man came up with the following: "Might I ask you for some advice?" I saw straight through the scoundrel: merely the fact that he had been called upon was enough to satisfy his snobbism, his materialism. For him, this satisfaction—as we have all experienced here, to our horror—takes the place of doing something. He will even agree, for my sake; but then he lets everyone wait—without even so much as apologizing.
  This is how he took the collected edition of the works of C. P. E. Bach upon himself, bringing countless people together, arranging trips to publishers, to solicitors (I was summoned from my sick-bed to the meetings!); finally he writes to Professor Haas: "Emanuel Bach is a German master, why should I, a foreigner, be involved in the collected edition?" Is that not an outrageous thing to say?[1] Not once did he apologize to the publishers, to any of us—the rascal! And we all have similar private experiences to recount. He is completely untrustworthy, shabby, usurious, a fiendish liar; in short, he guards his money like ten dragons, except

that he cannot help ingratiating himself everywhere, <u>running after everyone in order to accrue a little honor for himself</u>!

I replied to the rogue: "You know that I agree to any help that you can give Cube; do it, then; I merely ask you not to assess this offer of help as a gesture also in respect of <u>my</u> life's work. It would indeed by grotesque for me to recommend Cube if you stood in opposition to me." He would have gladly obliged you and me, made a "gesture," without coughing up a single mark. We know what he is like. After some moments he said, "I'll talk the matter over with my wife"(!)—she is in Berlin—there you have it, the retreat from the gesture was already on the way ... Within the hour he had withdrawn it entirely, for suddenly (though he had prepared for it long before, for he is a sly one beyond all measure) explained: "No, I shall write recommendations for Cube, etc." His first words contained the truth. Today he rattles his money in Berlin, he plays with the people to whom he becomes attached, giving them the illusion that everything is possible, then, having sized them up, he betrays them all and goes off elsewhere, rattling his money; that satisfies him.

  With best greetings from me and my wife,
   Yours,
    H. Schenker

[1] *Entsetzen Sie sich nicht?*: a variant of a common German play on words: "setzen Sie sich!" (sit down) / "entsetzen Sie sich!" (be outraged).

Cube to Schenker (letter), October 20, 1931
OJ 9/34, [29] (Plate 5)

       Hamburg, Beneckestrasse 2, c/o Alexander Schmidt

Most revered Master,

Enclosed is the attempted reading, as announced.[1] What is of interest to me is determining the distance between my previous and my present capability of hearing, and also my ability in writing things up. The first sketch[2] included the space of a third, the bass arpeggiation, and the descending register transfer, even though this had still been clumsily expressed. Of the rest, there was not much present. You referred me at the time in particular to the parallelism:

and also 3–4–4–3 in the [opening and] closing measures.

Now for the questions:[3] In a.), should I place the $\hat{2}$ already above the II in the bass?[4] In b.) the holding-over, which creates a seventh chord above F in the bass, is shown clearly. I assumed the exchange [of d^1 for e^1] on account of [consecutive fifths]:

In c.), I introduce first of all the neighbor-note motions above the third,[5] and a further exchange, but still without the descending register transfer and still in four-part harmony, in order to clarify the former for itself, along with a few chromatic parallelisms.

At d.) the octave-progression, divided into two parts, and the five-part harmony come to the fore; at the 3–4–4–3 at the start and at the end I attempted to show the yielding of the voices[6] above [each] accompanying fourth-progression. Thus I saved the play of registers in the final arpeggiations for e.). e.) is intended additionally to show merely the avoidance of consecutive fifths and octaves by means of 6–5, 6–5 and the throwing of the inner voice [into the highest/lowest voice], which additionally creates the parallelisms. The differing treatment of the two fourths that make up the octave-progression is something I see as founded in the openings, where the leap of a fourth from e to a is transformed into a filled-in third-progression b–c♯–d. In addition, the 6–5, 6–5 is reversed.

The chromatic passing tones surely originate in the original passing tones shown in a.). Does all this seem a more or less sensible reading? Or have I gone entirely wide of the mark? What do you think of my choice of notation? I should be greatly indebted to you for a new correction.

With most cordial greetings,

    Yours,

        Cube

---

[1] In a letter written four days earlier (October 16, 1931) Cube had explained that a new graph of the Prelude in C major from Bach's *Well-tempered Clavier*, Book I, would soon be ready. The graph is not with the letter, and is not known to survive.

[2] This is a graph dating from nearly two years earlier, and included in Cube's letter of January 2, 1930. (The graph is not known to survive.)

[3] In fact, there is more in the way of explanation than "questions" in what follows: each layer of the graph is explained in some detail. There are, in fact, many more layers than the three that are used for the graph of the Prelude in the *Five Analyses in Sketchform* (and for the graphs in Cube's unpublished *Lehrbuch der musikalischen Kunstgesetzte*).

[4] In the piece itself, the definitive $\hat{2}$ of the Urlinie, d^2, arrives after the final C major has appeared in the bass; Cube is asking whether this should be shown at the "highest" level in the analysis.

[5] That is, the 3–4–4–3 in measures 1–4 and 32–35.

[6] *Stimmenzedierung*: i.e. their gradual progression to the lower register in the course of the octave-progression in the bass.

Schenker to Cube (letter), October 29, 1931
OJ 5/7a, [40]

My dear Professor von Cube,

At my request, Miss Elias has made a fair copy of the work,[1] which I completed with her during her lessons. This version is nearly ready for publication; nevertheless I will use the opportunity of revision perhaps still to "savor" the graph in my little seminar group,[2] and to further ennoble and clarify matters here and there (possibly!), so that the picture can "speak" even without text. You may now, without further ado, place Miss Elias's work in the service of your teaching!

Now, I have a favor to ask of you. Make a fair copy of this page, which I can use as a model in my seminar. Perhaps your model will remain the final version and will be printed or photo-reproduced, or …

In the end, Professor Violin will receive the model (along with Chopin's Op. 10, No. 12), and we shall begin consultation about the form of the publication and how it will be used.

Please send a few words of thanks to Miss Elias (Frl. Angi Elias, Vienna I, Gölsdorfstrasse 4). Perhaps she will have the occasion to render yet other services, with the models that she has prepared in her lessons, even if these are not entirely ready for publication.

Pay closer attention to the slurs!

F♯ appears in the bass in measure 22 only because of e♭^{1} in the upper voice (as support for the flatted seventh: f♯ is better *per se* than f♮). As soon as e♭^{1} has proceeded to d^1, the f has once again become important if ⌒7 is to follow. In accordance with C. P. E. Bach's principle, that "the keys should already be lying beneath the hand," f belongs in the left hand. For this reason, f♯ in the bass versus f in the middle voice does not signify a cross relation: each note has its own reason for being there; the succession does not represent any connection between the two notes. Finally: the second d^1–c^1 in the 6/5 above A♭, being a second, does not permit an elaboration of the sort that occurred earlier. For this reason, and only this reason, Bach pretends that there is the space of a third between b and d^1, to produce something similar. (This happens frequently in the music of Bach, and others.)[3]

You will learn from Professor Violin the content of Weisse's letter. It is indeed most encouraging.[4] For sake of simplicity I am putting all letters and additional material together.

With best wishes from the two of us,

Yours,
H. Schenker

---

[1] Although the present letter is undated, it is clearly a response to Cube's letter of October 20, 1931, and the graph of the Bach prelude that he had recently prepared, not the graph of the same prelude sent to Schenker on January 2, 1930.

[2] For the weekly seminar that Schenker held from 1931 to 1934 (see chapter 25).

[3] Schenker is probably thinking of Bach's Violin Concerto in E major, first movement, mm. 23–24, where the interval of a third in the bass is similarly filled in by passing

tone and the diminution has "a life of its own"; see *Masterwork 1*, 64 (Ger., 120), Fig. 2. The example is repeated in *Free Composition* (Fig. 119/16a).

4 By this time, Hans Weisse had arrived in New York and had begun his duties as a theory and composition teacher at the David Mannes Music School. Schenker is most likely referring to Weisse's letter of October 15, 1931 (see chapter 26).

❧ Cube to Schenker (letter), July 2, 1932
OJ 9/34, [33]

Hamburg 37, Innocentiastrasse 11

Most revered, dear Master,

This letter will probably be rather long, so I will get to the heart of the matter immediately: it concerns a chain of thought that I should like to amplify for you, in order to learn whether it is logical enough to be worth pursuing further. The cardinal points are [tonal] system and modal mixture! And still further: the concept of tonality resulting from both. In what follows, I shall outline my ideas in broad terms here, so that you yourself can best see that they are entirely consistent with your theory and also whether, and where, any mistakes in reasoning or listening may be hidden.

The limitations of human hearing and the capacity for abstraction result in three principal requirements of the musical system: a) an unbroken series of fifths, b) a closed-up circle of fifths, c) differentiation of the resultant intervals in a diatonic projection (as ordered by relative pitch).[1]

The system of twelve fifths is the only imaginable one that can fulfill all three demands. In the systems of fifty-three and forty-one fifths, the intervals of the resultant "scale" would no longer be distinguishable.[2] A system of twenty-four fifths (i.e. a quarter-tone system) cannot be tempered, and is not closed in itself. (The current quarter-tone systems are made up of two unconnected circles of twelve fifths, a quarter-tone apart.) NB: if there were another possibility than the system we have, the geniuses would certainly have made use of it!

From the chaotic superabundance of natural possibilities, it was, rather, preferable to take the "perceivable" series of fifths, which corresponded to limits of our capacity for abstraction,

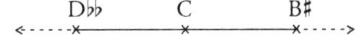

which could be represented as a spiral   and close it up to form a circle

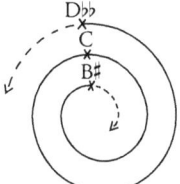   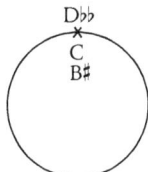

With intellectual and chronological logic, a path to the system of twelve fifths (not to be confused with Schoenberg or Hindemith!) made its way in slow strides

via the systems of five and seven fifths (in which the music of most other cultural groups has remained fixed, with the exception of polyphony). The smallest closable circle is that of seven fifths; this cannot, however, be tempered, since the resultant median values for third and fifth would differ too greatly from the natural ones; in addition, a relation between a tempered system of twelve fifths and one of seven cannot be achieved. <u>For this reason</u> the "false" fifth[3] was thrown into the bargain, and the system of twelve fifths was used for the circle of keys while the system of seven – its exact half[4] – was used as the system of harmonic degrees! Two birds killed with one stone! The system of seven fifths gave us the minor third, the "dominants," and the correlation between chromaticism and diatonicism: our best "artistic concepts"!

Moreover, the system of seven fifths is like a chameleon in its diversity. Depending on how one turns it round, it reveals new and usable features, and the masters have, in truth, not left any of its possible transformations unused. Indeed, it seems to me of late that the principle of <u>modal mixture</u>, which you discovered, is an <u>eternal</u> compositional principle, which is by no means restricted merely to major and minor! Consider the possible projections of the system of seven fifths:

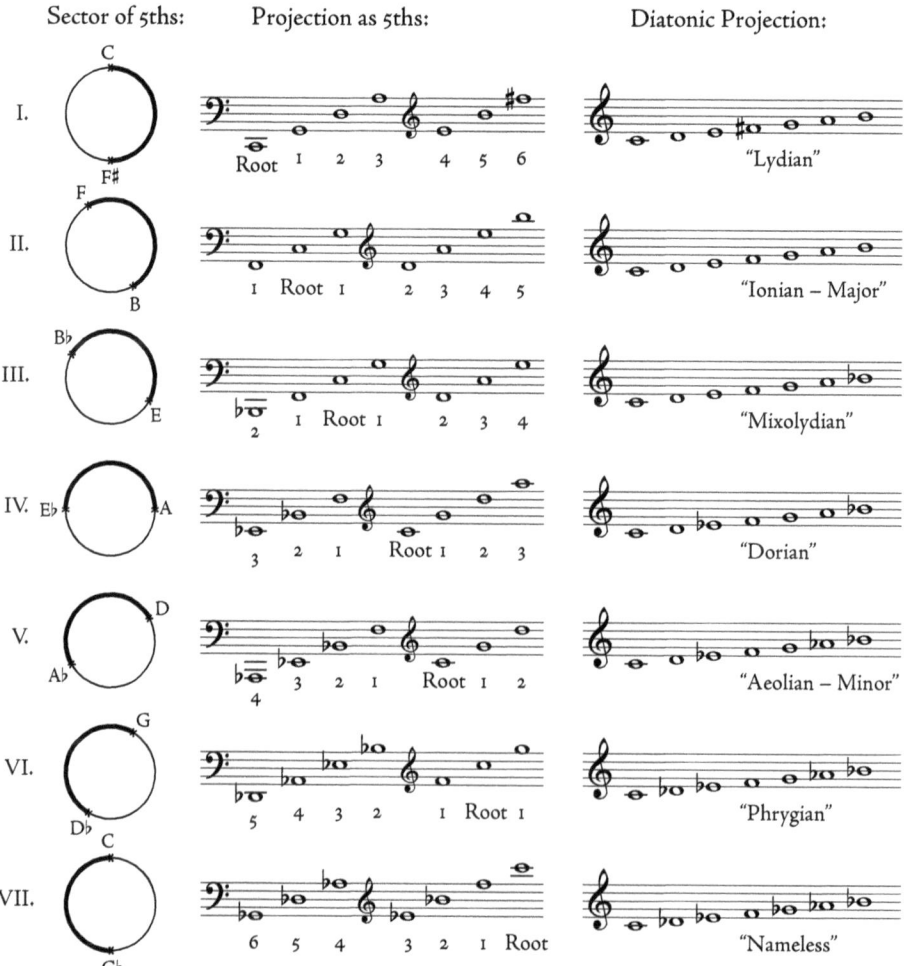

And now I ask: why, in developing your principle of modal mixture do you <u>stop</u> precisely at the fifth upper-fifth and the fourth lower-fifth?[5] By a continuation and broadening of the <u>principle</u> of modal mixture, right to the <u>boundaries</u> of the system of seven fifths, surely <u>no damage at all, per se</u>, will be done to the compositional precedence of major and minor that resides in the fact that the triads on the principal scale degrees have the same quality?[6] Would it not be <u>entirely sensible</u> to bring the "Phrygian ♭II" and the ♯IV, with or without ♭7, into the same general nomenclature, as all the other manifestations gained previously for the <u>total tonality</u> by the principle of mixture? Would it compromise the importance of the <u>motive</u>, or of the <u>passing tone</u>, if one regards the region in which they operate in the overall tonal system as merely extended right up to the natural boundaries of the system of seven fifths? Is it not also possible for the altered chord to be given its due place in the overall tonal system, alongside the diminished third and augmented sixth, without robbing it of its iridescent ambiguity?

If the former theory can have a two-fold harmonic basis:

and if we now recognize the basis of modal mixture:

why can it not, finally, be extended, as follows:

whereby, of course, f♯/g♭ – as the "enharmonic point" – cannot function, say, as a "diminished second" or an "augmented 7th", but of course represents the closed barrier to chromaticism!

As you may easily understand, I am eager for your response. With most cordial greetings to you and your wife,

    Your
        Cube

---

[1] By "diatonic projection" Cube means the reordering of notes initially determined by a cycle of fifths to form a stepwise series, i.e. a scale.

[2] Cycles of forty-one and fifty-three "pure" fifths (i.e. an exact frequency ratio of 3:2) will come nearer to closing the tonal circle than a cycle of twelve fifths, i.e. the end point will be more nearly an exact multiple of an octave. But when either of these sequences is reconfigured as a series of ascending tones, the distance between them is barely perceptible as an interval.

[3] The doubly augmented fourth or diminished sixth required to close the tonal circle, e.g. C♭–F♯ or B–G♭.

[4] That is, any seven fifths, e.g. F–C–G–D–A–E–B will take up exactly 180°, or half, of the complete circle of twelve fifths.

⁵ Cube is referring to the discussion of modes and modal mixture in Schenker's *Theory of Harmony*, §§38–52, especially Figure 75 and Table III.

⁶ By this Cube means that the triads on the principal harmonic degrees, I, IV, and V, are all major triads in the major (Ionian) system and all minor in the minor (Aeolian) system.

℘ Cube to Schenker (letter), June 2, 1934
OJ 9/34, [40]

> Everyone thinks the game is up,
> But, no, there's life in them yet!
> (Wilhelm Busch.)¹

Most revered, dear Master,

I have growled and flashed my teeth in many directions, and again been active and at work on other fronts to enlighten and convince, with the result that I have driven a solid hook into the crumbling wall of obstinacy, on to which I may be able to rope myself once more.²

A letter, which I received from the provincial leader of the Imperial Music Chamber,³ reads as follows:

"Dear Mr. von Cube,

This is to let you know that I shall inform myself directly concerning the grounds of your dismissal from the German Conservatory. An opinion concerning "Schenkerian theory" seems to me at this time entirely unnecessary, and I cannot understand why you were dismissed on grounds of that sort …"

There then follow remarks about the extent to which the Imperial Music Chamber exerts an influence over employment contracts. After receiving this letter I spoke face to face with the administration, saying that the reason for my dismissal was a lame pretext for shady business dealings (for I also know now who my successor is!), whereupon we had the fiercest row and I was categorically thrown out! Nonetheless, it is I who wears the clean shirt, and the administration which has a black mark for conduct! This is at any rate for me an honorable, though unfortunately not a material, substitute for the lost sources of income. A few brave pupils went with me "into banishment." But the outlines of a new possibility for work are rising only hazily on the horizon. Now the summer holidays are intervening, and in the midst of this the new member of our family, so that all of my hairs are standing up like mountains and I have issued an S.O.S. to our relatives. But will that help???

I have also enclosed for you the review of a lecture that I gave recently, with the courage of despair. It seemed to me the only possible way of giving voice to the truth, without meeting an *a priori* objection. The success exceeded my expectation, and even the review—lightly drawing inspiration from me—shows that there are still people who are prepared to bear intellectual responsibility. Strangely enough, the lecture received an echo from, of all places, Frankfurt! From there a Professor Alfred Hoehn (do you know him?)⁴ wrote to me, saying that he wanted to learn more about these things. I shall send him a few related notices and a "self-drawn" Urlinie.

In the Bach Prelude,⁵ I have arrived at the following Ursatz:

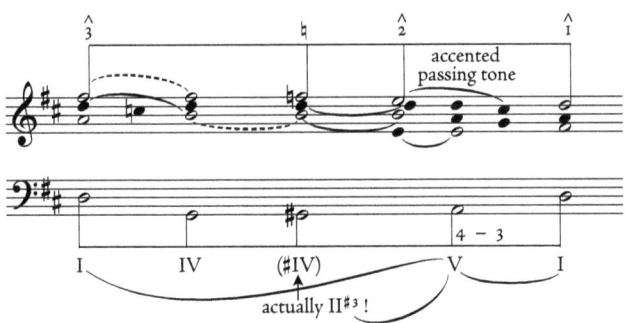

[You may take this,] of course, with a pinch of salt! Now I am also working on the fugue.⁶ This is very similar. Otherwise, I am busy "building a nest," painting my furniture, papering the walls, and building tables and wardrobes, since paying a builder is impossible and, in addition, my self-esteem is thereby increased.

May God and my belief in the eternity of everything German—even in the new Germany—help me further!

With many cordial greetings from the two of us to you and your dear wife, I am always

    Your
      Cube

PS: What is Hans Wolf up to?⁷

Oh, yes: Furtwängler will get in touch with me in the middle of June!

---

[1] Wilhelm Busch (1832–1908): artist and poet, most famous for his picture stories, among which *Max und Moritz* (1865) became a children's classic.

[2] *Haken* (a thin wedge driven into a rockface, used as a safety device in mountaineering) and *anseilen* (to tie into a rope) are terms that Schenker, a keen Alpine hiker, would not only have understood but also have been pleased to see used metaphorically.

[3] *Reichsmusikkammer* (Imperial Music Chamber): the body controlling music throughout Germany during the period of National Socialism, itself subdivided into departments for composition, soloists, orchestras, entertainment music, music education, choral music, church music, concert agencies, etc., and thirty-one regional offices. It was one of seven sub-chambers of the *Reichskulturkammer* (Imperial Culture Chamber), founded in 1933, the year that Hitler came to power, under the authority of the Propaganda Minister Joseph Goebbels. Its President for the first two years was Richard Strauss.

[4] Alfred Hoehn (1887–1945): teacher of piano at the Frankfurt Conservatory.

[5] This is a follow-up graph to an analysis sent with Cube's previous letter to Schenker of April 29, 1934.

[6] Voice-leading graphs of both the Prelude and the Fugue in D major from the *Well-tempered Clavier*, Book I, are included in Cube's unpublished *Lehrbuch der musikalischen Kunstgesetze*. (They are dated 1956 and 1957, respectively.)

⁷ Hans Wolf (1912–2005): German conductor. He was a pupil of Schenker's 1934–35, and published an account of this experience in "Schenkers Persönlichkeit im Unterricht," *Der Dreiklang* 7 (1937): 176–84.

❧ Cube to Schenker (letter), October 4, 1934
OJ 9/34, [42]

Most revered Master,
 It is time to give you once again a comprehensive report. To begin with, the facts: there are several things that are new and of interest. Here is a copy of a letter from Furtwängler:

"My esteemed Mr. von Cube,
 As a result of my numerous trips during the last months, I am only now able to answer your letter of May 4.
 Whether it is really true that you were dismissed in Hamburg solely because of your adherence to Schenker's theory is something I am unable to judge. I know only that today a great number of people are dismissed for personal motives, i.e. because somehow someone else ought to, or must, have the post in question (my post is now taken by the deputy leader of the Provincial Music Society of the Northern Mark), and that the material grounds that are advanced on such occasions are often merely used as a pretext.
 As concerns Schenker and his theory, I am of course prepared at all times to tell you, and anyone else who wants to hear it, my opinion: that we are concerned here with a matter of the <u>greatest consequence</u>, which, because it is anchored in the essence of nature and the great masterworks, has a future in itself, unlike so many other theories of music that have been pulled out of thin air for their own sake, and that Schenker himself, although racially a Jew, must be regarded as one of the greatest and most powerful defenders and exponents of <u>German</u> musical genius and musical spirit.
 I am just on the point of going on holiday; perhaps you will tell me, when you have a chance, how things develop further for you.
 With my best regards, I am
   Yours,
    Wilhelm Furtwängler"

 I received this letter eight weeks ago. I sent it immediately to the director of the one and only institute here from which I have any hope of receiving any sort of work, since not only does he desire to test the pedagogical values of your theory but also he is personally well acquainted with me. This gentleman returned recently from holiday and declared himself—visibly influenced by Furtwängler's letter—prepared to arrange a half-year course for his seminar students and trainee teachers on a temporary basis. It is entirely indicative and, <u>in spite of</u> all the Furtwängler letters and proclamations from the Imperial Music Chamber, characteristic of the entire situation at the moment that, in a text written by me for the purpose of publicity, your name, together with those of Halm and Kurth, were crossed out! I had imposed this constellation, which will seem paradoxical to you, only as a formality and for the purpose of avoiding a repeat of the false accusations from that mind-set which is constantly bothering me here. It is possible that you will misinterpret this likewise, as you did the incriminating passage from that review,[1] but many things are incomprehensible to someone who is not involved, who has not experienced it himself. Thus it occurs, for example, Handel's settings of [Old Testament] texts (*Judas Maccabaeus*, for instance) are turned down(!) Of course Halm and Kurth would have, of necessity, been removed as comparators;[2] this is now, to be sure, no longer necessary, but I am once again forbidden to speak your name aloud. (Thus one can, if necessary, talk me out of this: [my] teaching is not officially identified with your theory!) That one day your name may be mentioned without the least fear is something to which I can once again devote myself, temporarily, over the next half year!

In the meantime I have not been lazy, and have given the director of the Provincial Music Association a copy of your essay "The Mission of German Genius" to read (it will be the first thing of yours that he will have read). I do not, at any rate, have much hope that he will express his opinions in less general terms; nonetheless, I am happy that he has the time to read just this essay. It will at least help a little. More cheering is the last chapter of a work, *Outline History of Music Aesthetics* by Dr. Rudolf Schäfke,[3] in which—not without every apostrophizing—there is otherwise a very thorough account of your work, and above all it is said that the methods of contemplation that you have evolved have secured a future for themselves. My own activities, in addition to tiresome hours of teaching, extend to my chosen special field, intellectual speculation about Western tonal systems. I can already say this much today, that many more conceptual bridges may be found leading to Nature, in all its effectiveness, than we had imagined. Nature appears to lead the pen of the gifted musical visionary to the place (I should almost like to say "to the precise place") where we most admire "art"! Translated into geometrical terms, a web of conformities to natural laws is revealed, for example, such that one does not know in which manifestation God's wonders are best to be admired. The seven diatonic steps of a tonality yield a sum of 360°, their regions of a fifth rotate by 180°, major and minor (the second and fifth diatonic step)[4] are vertically aligned, differing by 90°, thus explaining their mirror-image similarity, the "false fifths"[5] (each the radius of the tonal circle) turn and move with every tonicization and modulation, or merely with the transition to the diatonic system with the same note names, e.g. Phrygian (No. 6) and provide the ear the greatest encouragement to orient itself to a new progression of fifths, and so on and so forth. The harmonic path and the Urlinie go their separate ways, albeit by laws of the sort that one finds in polygons, and in interaction with one another. (It is only fitting, I note entirely in passing, that Schoenberg's twelve-tone circle may be conclusively shown to lead to an absurdity!) That the church modes are still viable (and not merely on account of modal mixture)[6] is likewise demonstrable, as is the fact that major and minor assume—or, rather, must assume—a position of limited advantage. And thus it goes on with hundreds of things, so that one cannot keep up with the tasks of observing, describing, and codifying. I shall, however, send you a few test pieces the next time I write, although I do not yet know how these things will turn out for me. In this matter I shall adhere deliberately to the principle that the ear is king, reason his minister! Otherwise one can become only too easily confused: look at the writings of Werker, Lorenz, and others.[7]

Now for the human, and the all-too-human:[8] I am enclosing a small picture of my wife and son—I call him "Opus 1" and believe that he is the best thing that I have produced to date. (In writing the forgoing, I forgot to note that a new sonata is also being composed!) The young boy is the joy of my life, a comfort in all adversities. Our existence is meager. There is hardly enough food. Even with the new course (1.50 marks per person per month!) things will hardly get better. Gradually one grows indifferent and hardened to such things. Unfortunately, one's features become correspondingly gray and rough-edged. The all-too-human has also reached me: there are rumors going around Hamburg! I do not know who has been circulating them, but if I ever catch anyone I shall break his spine <u>with my own hands</u>! People are saying that I damaged Mr. Violin financially, or cheated him, for that matter—it has gone so far that it is said that Mr. Violin has, on my account, been "left out of pocket" a sum of money. I am firmly convinced that Mr. Violin would, in such a case, have turned to me, or directly to the appropriate tribunal, and I would be very sorry if, instead of doing this, he had given the opportunity, through some unguarded remarks, for a few "female beings" to hatch a tale of such dimensions as to dangerously tarnish my honor. Even here I would quote Bismarck, saying: *Nescio quid mihi magis farcimentum esset!*[9]. The matter has in the end gone so far that these female beings, purely because of "personal distaste" for me (for the reasons expressed above), have engaged another teacher from Berlin, whose idea of "collaboration" we had the occasion to learn about all too well back in the days of the Schenker Institute. I can keep my composure in the face of these things because the prospects of that man increasing his circle of activity in Hamburg do not appear to be all that great. But I am recounting these things to you, because I have reason to believe that your judgment of my character and of my standing with you were or are exposed to influences which I, standing in the front line for you here and doing the fighting (while others draw advantages from it), am not willing to tolerate under any circumstances.

I shall therefore tell you in <u>confidence</u>: I am of the opinion that Mr. Violin, in spite of all of his laudable and endearing qualities, is unfortunately disposed to feeling trodden on by <u>everyone</u>, and because of this complex picks an argument with <u>everyone</u> sooner, but always being of the view that it is <u>he</u> who has been unfairly treated. I can understand that a high degree of subjectivity can also have its negative aspects. When I was in Hamburg in May 1931, Mr. Violin presented me with a calculation [of my likely income] that I subsequently discovered to be <u>so much</u> at variance with the conditions I found, that he simply could not lay the blame here on the "times," but must rather have been drifting into fields of fantasy and illusion. Yet one ought not subject any business partners to this! In commerical life, this sort of optimism would not have been imaginable. When viewed from <u>that</u> angle, then it is I who has been "left out of pocket," in an entirely different way, and I am still out of pocket, and in a city in which I do not have a single friend. If one reckons on sources of income that later prove to be utterly unrealizable to start with, and still later not even halfway realizable, then <u>it is hardly surprising</u> to find the ghosts that one summons cost money from one's own pockets, which afterwards cannot be regained through employment.

One can be despondent about this, but one should not allow the seeds of discord to germinate, as was the case here! I am not demanding any compensation on my part. One should not dig up old dirt. But I was merely so annoyed that the waves of this gossip reverberated as far as you. Thus it was my obligation to make myself—in spite of the danger of "who excuses himself accuses himself"—understood with you!

So: now it is about 1:30 in the morning. Time to sleep. My wife and I thank you most cordially for the congratulations we received from you and your wife!

>With best wishes I am
>Ever your
>Cube

PS Has the second series of Urlinie graphs already been published? When will *Free Composition* appear?

PPS Please give the enclosed note to Mr. Violin, with the remark that the steps I took in this direction proved useless.

---

[1] A review of a lecture given by Cube, on the basis of which Schenker (in a letter of June 5, 1934, which does not survive) had censured his former pupil for misappropriating his ideas; Cube responded vigorously to this in a letter of June 7, 1934.

[2] Cube would have known of Schenker's antipathy toward Kurth from his critique of the *Grundlagen des linearen Kontrapunkts*, in *Masterwork 1*. He may not have been aware that, in spite of a generally dismissive attitude toward August Halm as a musical thinker (and especially for championing of the music of Anton Bruckner), Schenker and Halm remained on good terms until the latter's death in 1929 (see chapter 17).

[3] Rudolf Schäfke, *Geschichte der Musikästhetik in Umrissen* (Berlin: Max Hesse, 1934); a second (1964) and third edition (1982) were published by Hans Schneider, Tutzing.

[4] If one arranges the steps of the diatonic scale as an ascending series of perfect fifths, e.g. F–C–G–D–A–E–B, the keynote of the major scale is the second note (C), that of the minor scale (A) the fifth.

[5] False fifths are the doubly diminished sixths or doubly augmented fourths made by joining the "ends" of the circle of fifths, e.g. F♯ to D♭, or G♭ to C♯.

[6] The relationship of the church modes to Schenker's concept of "mixture" is first discussed in *Theory of Harmony*; see especially §§38–52.

[7] i.e., writers who become trapped by the complexities of their own systems. The first of these is Wilhelm Werker (1873–1948), whose *Studien über die Symmetrie im Bau der Fugen und die motivische Zusammengehörigkeit der Präludien un Fugen des 'Wohltemperierten Klaviers' von Johann Sebastian Bach* (Leipzig: Breitkopf & Härtel, 1922) was roundly dismissed by Schenker in his essay on fugue (*Masterwork 2*, 45; Ger., 81) for its pseudo-scientific approach.

[8] A reference to Friedrich Nietzsche's *Menschlich, allzu menschlich* (1878).

[9] "I no longer know what a sausage might be to me."

23
Collecting Sources: Anthony van Hoboken

THE correspondence between Schenker and his pupil Anthony van Hoboken comprises 114 letters and postcards written from 1924 until shortly before Schenker's death in January, 1935. Of these items, seventy-four are by Hoboken, fifty-six by Schenker. The letters here selected span the period beginning with Hoboken's enthusiastic acknowledgment of Schenker's acceptance of him as a pupil until 1932. They provide insight into the character and interests, both professional and nonprofessional, not only of the correspondents but also of other members of the wider Schenker circle.

Regarding Anthony van Hoboken himself, the letters document above all his quest for photographs of manuscripts for the Photogram Archive, which he established at the Austrian National Library—a quest that took him to most of the major cities of Europe. A "side-trip" is documented here as well: Hoboken at one point sought the services of Professor R. M. Breithaupt, a piano pedagogue in Berlin, who prescribed therapy for the hand- and arm-pain that Hoboken experienced in playing the piano. Schenker's response to Hoboken's report reveals much about his own view of the relation of piano technique to masterworks of the keyboard repertory.

An interesting perspective on Schenker's view of his own teaching—which aspects he considered indispensable to it, and what else could possibly be handled with more leeway—emerges from his correspondence with Hoboken concerning the latter's comparative study of Brahms's Three Intermezzos, Op. 117. Hoboken concedes in one letter (September 27, 1931) that he has not studied the works extensively in terms of the Urlinie, "which requires so infinitely much more inner peace of mind and concentration" than piano playing. Schenker's response advises his pupil not to take matters about the Urlinie all too seriously; it is only the linear progressions that cannot be neglected, for without them, there is no hearing, no performance.

Finally, Schenker's high esteem for his pupil must be noted. His praise of Hoboken's ear and general musicality is expressed too often in the correspondence to be regarded as merely idle flattery.

JOHN ROTHGEB

❧ Hoboken to Schenker (letter), June 10, 1925
OJ 11/54, [3]

Paris

Dear Professor,

Your cordial lines of June 4 reached me here, and I thank you very much for their content. I am greatly pleased to become your pupil, and will try to place all my powers in the service of art.

In addition, I should be settled in Vienna on October 1. I have immediately begun to inquire about lodgings.

Naturally I am also quite agreeable concerning the fee.

I think that to begin with, three lessons per week should be sufficient. In case it should happen that I can manage more, we could perhaps still change the arrangement. For the rest, I hope to stay with you for at least two winters.

With respectful greetings, and warmest felicitations as well to your wife, I remain, along with my wife,

> Yours very truly,
> A. v. Hoboken

❧ Hoboken to Schenker (letter), January 3, 1926
OJ 11/54, [60]

CENTRAL HOTEL
40 RUE DU LOUVRE PARIS

Dear Professor,

Allow me first of all to wish you and your wife a really good New Year, a wish in which my wife joins me.

Here I immediately took steps toward getting access to the autograph of Op. 57.[1] From a friend I obtained an introduction to Henri Prunières,[2] the editor of the *Revue musicale*, and through him I reached Mr. Expert,[3] the librarian (I believe) of the Conservatory. I am going there on Monday and he will there show me the manuscript of the "Appassionata" and many other autographs as well. For example, an autograph of Chopin's Ballade in F Major[4] is said to be there, which differs significantly in various points from the version we know of this Ballade.

Nothing would be easier than to have Op. 57 photographed, since Mr. Expert is an ardent advocate of this, for, as he rightly commented, the manuscripts can so easily be destroyed by fire, and then we would have nothing left had they not been photographed. But he believes that the autograph has already been photographed per order of Dr. Einstein, Munich, who also had the whole autograph of *Don Giovanni* photographed. —

I have reserved my place in the sleeping car for Wednesday. Thus I shall arrive Thursday evening in Vienna and join you on Saturday[5] at the usual time.

> With warmest greetings,
> Yours sincerely,
> A. v. Hoboken

[1] Beethoven, Piano Sonata in F minor ("Appassionata"), Op. 57. The autograph manuscript was acquired by the Paris Conservatory in 1889, and is now at the Bibliothèque Nationale. A facsimile of it was published in 1927, and reissued in 1970.

[2] Henri Prunières (1886–1942): French musicologist, founder of the *Revue musicale* and its editor 1920–39, specialist in seventeenth-century music, author of books on Lully, Monteverdi, and Cavalli, editor of *J.-B. Lully: Ouevres complètes* (1930–39, incomplete).

[3] Henry Expert (1863–1952): French musicologist, editor of fifteenth- and sixteenth-century French music; deputy librarian of the library of the Paris Conservatory 1909–20, senior librarian 1920–33.

[4] Chopin, Ballade No. 2, in F major / A minor, Op. 38.

[5] Wednesday was January 6, and Saturday January 9: Hoboken's first lesson for January is recorded in Schenker's lessonbook for 1925/26 as having taken place on Thursday January 14.

❧ Hoboken to Schenker (letter), January 28, 1927
OJ 11/54, [12]

Savoy Hotel,
London WC2

Dear Professor,

One of the purposes of my journey could not be achieved: the visit to Prof. Dunn in Edinburgh had to be canceled, because yesterday I was in bed with a fever and therefore could not travel in the evening. This was certainly a great pity. I had written him, and had received a letter of reply from him from which I could see that he still is greatly interested in your works. I will probably visit him this summer as I want to return to England then. Here I can obtain introductions to various private collections, and I don't want to fail to do that.

I have been to the British Museum. Which important manuscripts are held there can be seen from the catalog. Everything can be photographed. I have not yet discussed the price for this.

The Handel manuscripts are private property of the King of England, who reserves all rights, including that of copying. But I am told that I would probably also receive the necessary permission there. I cannot, however, photograph all of them at one time! Besides, a catalog of this collection is to appear soon.

On Tuesday I meet with Mr. Expert in Paris. I hope that it will be possible for me at least to bring home a few photocopies of the Chopin Ballade. The system of photography there is the same as in Vienna and also just as cheap. In London I am not so sure of that.

For the rest, I have purchased several things here. For example, Part 4 of the *Clavier-Übung* of J. S. Bach in the first edition. Likewise for a mass by Palestrina and two Purcell pieces.

The weather is not very inviting for travel, and I believe that in this season if possible I will make no further trip. Especially not to cities where influenza is prevalent. Today it is very stormy, which does not make the crossing to France tomorrow very inviting.

I need not write you anything further about the Munich discussions; you will no doubt already have heard everything.

With a request that you remember me to your wife, I am,

    Yours very truly,
       A. v. Hoboken

I hope to be back in Vienna on Sunday, February 6.

Schenker to Hoboken (letter), July 3, 1927
OJ 89/1, [1]

Dear Mr. van Hoboken,

From Dr. Weisse, who last Friday made a farewell visit to us before our departure,[1] I learned Furtwängler's summer address. As you will go soon or very soon to Sils Maria,[2] I will give it to you: Moriz-Dorf, acla silva. Later today or tomorrow I will write to Furtwängler to enlist him for Oppel's Mass;[3] I am glad to do it, though I know that Furtwängler in such cases would rather be the tenth or fifteenth conductor than the first. In this letter I will take the liberty of mentioning your visit, which however places you under no obligation. But I should not fail to mention the advantages that a visit to Furtwängler could yield: I envision the possibility of enlisting him for the artistic realization of the purposes that you associate with your extremely historically important foundation. If you could spin a few threads already in your first visit, or even invite him to your house in Vienna, where I could also take part, who knows whether it would not be possible to get him to spearhead the movement among conductors who would perform the masterworks according to the manuscripts, and to bring about the "new mode," so to speak, which would be definitive for successors. Perhaps it would be vanity, or ambition, or even the love of art, that would incline him in our direction—it seems to me in any case worth trying.

At the last lesson Mrs. Pairamall[4] showed me the first edition of Schindler's Beethoven biography, which she obtained from Dr. Haas for a security deposit:[5] the first edition includes performance instructions, which are lacking in the reprint.[6]

From our trip, the following mini-report. Listen and marvel: in the Hotel Post Landeck there are now rooms with hot and cold running water, even with bathtub! The most typical Americans, so the hotelier told us, were astonished at this progress in a one-horse town.

In conclusion, a communication that I believe I owe you without delay:

I think at one time I told you or even wrote to you that the fee of $5 has already been in effect for five years. The pupils from earliest times have always voluntarily compensated for my passivity in fee matters, and you too were so kind as to make the adjustments yourself. As I know today, it was not out of bad faith that several other pupils failed to think of adjustment; it was only inattention. In any case, with the number of years and lessons the shortfall has now increased, so that, partly at the instigation of Mrs. Pairamall, I have had to reconsider.

In the last days I have first been in touch with the Viennese pupils, whom I owe consideration for very many reasons, and whom I must take as the standard, since I prefer to maintain uniformity, with the exception of cases in which, for humanitarian reasons, I provide free instruction. From oral and written transactions, the possibility arose for me, with all due respect to the League of Nations, in the face of the financial reconstruction (which I would have been ordered to credit) regarding the dollar to replace the five-dollar amount with an amount in [Austrian] shillings.[7] In the war I lost a great deal because of my personal policy, and no less in the post-war period through my faith in the reconstruction; in short, I cannot continue this way. I have known for a long time that even Dr. Weisse had surpassed me, not to speak of the "prominent" teachers. I let matters slide, because I know no "prestige" in money matters. But the damage grew out of control and that obliged me to a reorganization: with the oldest pupils I have arrived at a fee of 50 shillings per lesson and I am counting on your kind consent to this arrangement too. The mode of payment remains the same, except that instead of $5 or $6 the sum of 50 shillings will apply. If this suits you, you can continue to pay in dollars, or in some other form, as you wish.

It could have easily happened that you had learned of this by coincidence from some other source—not because the fee would cause talk of its being "abnormal" (with the new one I am still lower than "non-prominents")—and so I simply considered it my duty to let you know at once.

Two essays are enclosed[8] which I request that you read and, if possible, keep for me.

Have you already made the tour to Gmunden?

How is your dear wife?

Don't forget to visit Lake Hallstatt,[9] but only in sunny weather!

As our car entered Ischgl, we ran into snow, a real winter snowfall, which quite got us down. Today, admittedly, spring is here, but not that dependably so. Whether winter or spring outside, we still have much sleeping and idling to do in order first to rest up from the hard work of the season. But it goes without saying that the mind is already at work.

I had a letter from Vrieslander in which he announces his visit to Vienna.

Our best wishes to you and your wife for your summer!

    Yours,

        H. Schenker

---

[1] Weisse had visited on June 24, and the Schenkers had departed Vienna for Galtür on June 25, for their summer vacation.

[2] Sils Maria: municipality in the Upper Engadin Valley, in the Swiss canton of Graubünden, famous for winter sports; situated between the Lake Sils and the Lake Silvaplana.

[3] Reinhard Oppel, Music for Four-Voice Choir, Op 32, SATB a cappella (1926).

[4] Evelina Pairamall (1870–??): wealthy Polish landowner. She was a pupil of Schenker's from at latest 1912 to his death, and student at the Schenker Institute

of the New Vienna Conservatory in 1935–36. Nothing is known of her after 1938. She claimed in 1929 that she had influenced Schenker in the policy of collecting photographs of autograph manuscripts that led to the Photogram Archive.

[5] Anton Schindler, *Biographie Ludwig van Beethovens* (Münster, 1840; 2nd edn. 1845; 3rd edn. 1860). The Austrian National Library is not a lending library, but Dr. Haas apparently made an exception in consideration of Mrs. Pairamall's deposit.

[6] Schenker's notes on these performance instructions (or, more exactly, reports by Schindler on Beethoven's playing) were published posthumously. See Heinrich Schenker, "Ein Kommentar zu Schindler, Beethovens Spiel betreffend," *Der Dreiklang* 8/9 (November 1937 / February 1938): 190–99. See also Oswald Jonas, "Nachtrag zu Schenkers Aufsatz über Schindler," ibid., 200–07.

[7] According to Schenker's diary of November 7, 1925, $1 = 7.08 Austrian shillings.

[8] These enclosures are not preserved with the letter.

[9] Hallstatt: small town and lake 10 miles south of Bad Ischl, in the Salzkammergut.

Hoboken to Schenker (letter), August 7, 1927
OJ 11/54, [14]

GIGER'S HÔTEL WALDHAUS
SILS MARIA, ENGADINE

Dear and revered Doctor,

I feel very guilty toward you, having thus far not sent a single syllable in answer to your gracious letter of July 3. I must say in advance that it reached me only on July 18. I found it on the day in Gmunden when I returned there from an automobile trip through the Salzkammergut (on which I also passed through the delightful Hallstatt and spent four days in Salzburg, with my wife). I then traveled ahead on that same day to Linz, and on the next day to Vienna.

I thus arrived there in time to witness the exemplary outbreak of "proletarian liberty," which played out on the 15th.[1] The Socis[2] were irate that somebody had let a crowd be fired upon who had set fire to the Palace of Justice! And so now, as the single positive achievement of the unrest, they have brought about the establishment of a dedicated guard that is to see to it that in the future, when similar "peaceful demonstrators" for example try to set fire to the University and/or the Parliament, they will no longer be fired on! And the government "most humbly asks" Seitz[3] only that this special guard . . . . etc. etc. What is one supposed to say about such an incompetence? Is it any wonder that the Social Democrats get a big head?

But to the main topic.

At home I naturally found all kinds of minutiae, which took a lot of my time. I can't complain about it, because, among other reasons, I stayed in Vienna during the month of July in order to dispose of such things, so that I wouldn't be bothered any more by them in the fall.

Meanwhile I have used every available moment to index my Haydn editions, and I feel at least the satisfaction of having progressed as far with that as I had planned—that is, everything is in the boxes, the index cards are written (and other little cards too for my personal use in respect to the planned chronological catalog of Haydn's works[4]), excepting those for the songs.

Thus I postponed replying to your letter (for which I did want to take time) longer and longer, until on August 1 I left Vienna without getting to it.

Only today I return to it and beg you not to be annoyed about it.

I want in the coming days to get in touch with Furtwängler and ask him when my visit would be convenient.[5]

If the second yearbook were to be ready on time, that would be very nice. I would just like to ask you to inscribe in the copy that I plan to take to Prof. Dunn a dedication to him. The last stop on which the book can reach me is on September 14 at the Savoy Hotel in London.

I forgot to mention in my previous letter the important purchase of Beethoven first editions, which I made shortly before my departure. It involves 138 first editions that I lacked, and then also many early editions, which were better preserved there than my copies. Deutsch says that my Beethoven first-edition collection now ranks among the best that exist.

I received a report from Vrieslander. He complains bitterly about the dry heat in Naples.

Here it is exactly the opposite. Recently we even had a whole day of snow.

With best greetings,

    Yours very truly,
    A. v. Hoboken

---

[1] The Vienna riots of July 15, 1927, in which a mob set fire to the Palace of Justice, with the loss of many of its records.

[2] Members of the Austrian Workers' Social Democratic Party (SDAPÖ), who on July 15 formed demonstrations to protest against the judgment in early July in the Schattendorf trial.

[3] Karl Seitz: mayor of Vienna at the time.

[4] Hoboken's published catalog would not be completed until thirty-six years later: *Joseph Haydn: Thematisch-bibliographisches Werkverzeichnis* (Mainz: Schott, 1957–71), vol. 1, *Instrumentalwerke*; vol. 2, *Vokalwerke*.

[5] The meeting took place during the week of August 21–27, 1927.

Schenker to Hoboken (letter), August 20, 1927
OJ 89/1, [3]

Dear Mr. van Hoboken,

With today's mail—and simultaneously with a reply from Mr. Furtwängler, which states in the very first sentence that he will see you soon—there arrived the final page proofs [of *Masterwork 2*], which I will now finally approve. On Monday I return the proofs; now the yearbook can be printed and bound. It is conceivable that you may receive a copy, and I would urgently request that the publisher send one to you on the desired date.[1] In any case please let me know where the copy could be sent. I do of course have your itinerary on hand, but I would not trust myself to go by that. Perhaps you will give me a clue; I repeat, however, it depends only on the good will of the publisher, or, to say the same thing, on the right timing.

Furtwängler hopes to have another meeting in Vienna. That suits us perfectly. In the setting of your beautiful home we can discuss the matter, provided that you are in Vienna at the same time; indeed, we can even speak quite plainly, since we are, so to speak, intellectually among friends. (Furtwängler goes along with the moderns only for business reasons: it's not a pretty thing, but basically he keeps faith with the masters.)

Young Cube was here, stayed ten days, and left just today at noon.

We both hope that you and your dear wife have survived or slept through the "earthquake" nicely and are otherwise well, and we send our best greetings.

Yours,
H. Schenker

[1] In time, that is, for presentation as a gift to John Petrie Dunn.

Schenker to Hoboken (letter), March 16, 1928
OJ 89/2, [4]

Dear Mr. van Hoboken,

Illness and unexpected difficulties[1]—a bit too much aggravation for a man who is about to make a grand contribution.[2] Well, you seem to have recovered completely from the illness—nature takes care of this with wisdom and generosity—; but the other difficulties come from men, who are less wise and generous than Nature. And above all when it is a matter of something lofty that doesn't quite make sense to them! Listen, just recently I visited Dr. Haas and had them show me a copy that Beethoven's pupil the Archduke (and Archbishop) Rudolph made for himself directly from the manuscript of the Sonata Op. 90[3]—you must have them show you the item, how neat it is, scrupulous, dedicated, excellent in devotion and execution!—; it is only a copy and yet it showed me things that could not be guessed from the original edition. Even if we never get hold of the [autograph] manuscript, I would confidently rely on this copy alone to make a revision of my edition—inclusion of a photogram of the copy in your Archive too, as a substitute for the manuscript, would be most advisable!—yet another experience, then, that shows in practical terms the urgency of your task. Thus I also have no doubt that we both must also speak out to indicate and demonstrate the most important corrections—then the work will be a credit to the master.[4]

Once you have survived your difficulties, you too will certainly find a form for such communications (Dr. Haas [and Mr.] Deutsch have suggestions and plans ready for you); I will help with the greatest pleasure, and above all you must take up the pen; you are twenty years younger than I and you have to become heir to this art. Your ear is excellent, your writing is to the point; practice will help you, as will I. We must not worry about contemporaries, we must rather spruce ourselves up in grand style for posterity. In the end, renown in posterity, which is derided by skeptics, is not worse than renown among contemporaries—in fact, it is instead better—much, much better.

In the interim two important essays have arrived, by Dahms and Vrieslander,[5] both published in Berlin (it's best if I show them to you in Vienna, don't you think?).

Did you know that also in the interim you have become the fortunate owner of the Gebethner collected edition of Chopin?[6] Mr. Deutsch found it in Graz.

Will you come to Vienna on the 23rd or celebrate your birthday in Paris this time? Here or there, I will be thinking of you with true happiness!

Our warmest greetings to both,

   Yours,
   H. Schenker

Furtwängler apparently will take over opera and concert in Vienna, and may *remain* here altogether.

---

[1] Hoboken had been delayed for ten days in Munich by a severe cold.

[2] i.e. to found the Photogram Archive.

[3] The first page of this copy is reproduced in *Ludwig van Beethoven, Klaviersonate e-Moll op. 90, Faksimile des Autographs*, edited with commentary by Michael Ladenburger (Bonn: Beethoven House, 1993), 36.

[4] The last six words are a slight modification of line 7 from the first stanza of Schiller's *Lied von der Glocke* (1799): "soll das Werk den Meister loben."

[5] Presumably Walter Dahms, "Das Meisterwerk in der Musik," *Allgemeine Musikzeitung*, February 3, 1928, and Otto Vrieslander, "Heinrich Schenker," *Deutsche Tonkünstler-Zeitung*, March 5, 1928 (copies of both of which are preserved in Schenker's scrapbook).

[6] Chopin collected edition published by Gebethner & Wolff (vol. 1, 18??; vol. 2, 1882).

Schenker to Hoboken (letter), March 26, 1928
OJ 89/2, [5]

Dear Mr. van Hoboken,

Warmest thanks for your nice diligent note![1] After receiving it I immediately wrote to Mr. Deutsch. When he visited me, he told me too about the matter, but without any intent concerning the Archive. It was, however, surely his conviction that Schubert's [melodic] lines, which he used to write out without any setting, would for the sake of better salability have to have some kind of setting by an arranger, from which I concluded that he was dealing in this matter with a publisher. This thought was all the more plausible as Mr. Deutsch now has actually secured a prominent press for Schubertiana that remain unpublished in part. But

I in any case repeated the basic thought that your Archive is not concerned with sketches.

A word about your difficulties in Paris. As you expressed the plan in the small meeting to use leverage in Paris to bring Berlin and other cities to heel, I immediately felt a small misgiving. Paris does indeed seem to have learned <u>through you for the first time</u> of the enduring <u>artistic</u> value—beyond everything material—of the masters' manuscripts (just as for example our dear good Furtwängler likewise saw original editions and such things for the first time in your company), but the new knowledge immediately made Paris cautious: she doesn't want to waive her rights to such values, and especially not in favor of Vienna. (That is a slight touch of the political, as you will read about here and there in letters of Mozart and still better of Mendelssohn (from Paris)). If I am mistaken, all the better for the project, and I am prepared to apologize.

Should things not work out as you wish, however, would it not be possible to urge that Paris itself establish such an archive, with which you could enter into an exchange? Or, which seems to me still better: You come out with the first issue of your "News,"[2] in which you, I, or also Haas and Deutsch, to the extent that they may have material, <u>legitimize</u> ourselves through citations of errors in the pieces, i. e. <u>through the corrections</u>, as the only ones in the world for now who are qualified to discuss these decisive questions connected to the deepest secrets of the composition. We will then take the booklet to Altmann and ask his advocacy with <u>Harnack</u>,[3] unless we prefer to approach Harnack directly. (He was already very friendly to me once; we can hope he will be again.)

These are only suggestions. Perhaps Vrieslander, Haas, [and] Deutsch will have better ones—all the nicer.

I have heard of Prof. Steinhof[4] often through Hammer, but have never met him.

I recently heard lieder by Berg here. We'll talk about that. —I am very eager to hear about Santini's collection!![5]

Best wishes for your further endeavors, and kindest regards to you and your good wife from us both.

    Yours,
    H. Schenker

---

[1] Hoboken had written from Paris on March 21, 1928, lauding the city, but reporting that he was making no headway with the French authorities over permissions to photograph musical sources. He also reported a letter he had received from Otto Erich Deutsch about sketches by Schubert for a Symphony in E of which Deutsch had hopes of publishing a facsimile—a plan that Hoboken asked Schenker to quash as contrary to the principles of the Photogram Archive.

[2] *Mitteilungen*: newsletter, to be issued by the Photogram Archive, planned at this time but never realized.

[3] Adolf von Harnack (1851–1930), German theologian and historian, general director of the Royal Library (Prussian State Library), Berlin 1905–21, co-founder and first president of the Kaiser Wilhelm Society for the Advancement of Science.

[4] In a letter of March 21 from Paris Hoboken reported meeting Steinhof, whose wife was a music historian. She had expressed an interest in giving a lecture to mark Schenker's sixtieth birthday, and had asked for material on him.

[5] Santini Collection: comprehensive collection of sources of Italian music of the sixteenth to nineteenth centuries belonging to the Diocesan Library, Münster. It contained some 4,500 manuscripts and 1,200 printed editions constituting some 20,000 titles in all.

Schenker to Hoboken (letter), June 22, 1928
OJ 89/2, [6]

My dear Mr. van Hoboken,

I hear your very nice and prodding birthday-cheer[1] with joy and greatest thanks! Yes, I will and must finish my work: *Free Composition*, *Theory of Form*, *Theory of Performance* (on the methodological foundation of *Free Composition*), *Decline of the Art of Composition*, etc. You shake your youthful head and ask: when will the "old man" get around to these things? It is less a question of me than of the publishers, who steal not only your work but also your time. But—*Free Composition* must be ready at some point, and today I want to thank you again and again most warmly for your very courageous outlook! I see and feel exactly how heroically you fight for the Archive, and no less for that which your ear has identified as the only right thing. Do these deeds not speak louder than words?

You know how highly I value the Archive. Even the highest commemoration fails to do justice to the service provided by its founding! Such a deed is properly recognized only by the commemoration that is intrinsic to it. You therefore did right to refuse the honor intended for you, for all that the thought you expressed is correct in itself that in the eyes of the world such an honor also reflects back onto the work itself. If I understand you correctly, your heart commanded you to strike up high comradeship with me and to prefer to refuse rather than to suffer and support an injustice (as you considered it) to me. This is not the first time I have seen you stand up so bravely for me, but that has an intrinsic reward which is better than could be found in my words—henceforth, no more talk of it: I see, feel, and am thankful continuously.

Any commemoration, by the way, is good only for the briefest first moment. Within the first ten years it departs from the person, and only the work speaks, in proportion to its inner strength. Not even the lexica take notice of this bluff. We, however, can confidently depend on the centuries; our cause is not of the day.

A propos of the lexica I can tell you that a note from Einstein has reached me here (printed form) with the request to supplement the existing entry from the Riemann *Lexikon*.[2] I read the entry for the first time and found it curious: it lacks *Counterpoint 2*, the "collected edition" of the piano sonatas of Beethoven, even the title *The Masterwork in Music* (though these Yearbooks and Drei Masken Verlag have already been mentioned!!)

Well, I have provided the supplements, and improved so many other things—am curious, though, how Einstein will handle it. Einstein himself has mentioned the "Urlinie," and I must really marvel at the weight this new (but certainly not understood) concept has carried, just on the strength of *Der Tonwille*, which the fine fellow Hertzka has shunted onto a sidetrack, shortened by half in the printing through breach of contract, and otherwise sabotaged.³ Against all opposition, the first issues and the first readers carried the day. Our dear Vrieslander certainly underestimates the number of my readers; there are certainly far, far more of them than of purchasers (just consider Furtwängler, who knows of all the things, but doesn't buy the book; I think of the many, many young musicians who I <u>know</u> read me but are unable to buy). It is a certainty that UE has found good business in me; I have no doubt that Drei Masken too will get their money's worth, but slowly, I'll warrant. Thus I cannot speak of a state of "isolation," so I understand you in your kindness and enthusiastic participation when you wish only that we could have a bit more outwardly visible success. I would indeed like it myself, but—the "management," with which I have nothing to do, stands in the way. On the contrary, I count myself as lucky to have extricated so many young musicians from the pitiful milieu of our academies and conservatories, and to have shown them art from the perspective of the geniuses; it's not my fault that they haven't made more of it.

Concerning the happenings in Berlin I was already informed even before your nice lines arrived.

How delighted I am about the increase in both places, in the Archive and in your collection! Now it will soon be time to give the outside world an accounting of the progress.

From Prof. Dunn I received his picture and a very nice note with it.

From Weisse and his seminar a very beautiful "address" arrived, etc. etc.

Vrieslander as always, selfless, cheerful, and also spreading cheer! Mr. Deutsch's kindness was touching, also that of Dr. Haas, and the telegram from the Archive⁴ was a special lift: this noble little bell will ring far and wide. Many, many thanks to you.

Now I, and with me my wife as well, fervently wish you the most wonderful holiday on the journey and also at the destination.

    Yours most sincerely,
    H. Schenker

---

[1] Schenker had celebrated his sixtieth birthday on June 19, 1928. Hoboken's letter of congratulation is not known to survive, but Schenker recorded its contents in his diary: "Congratulations; Hoboken tells me that he was proposed for the honor—I also; however, he has insisted that a higher honor [is due?] to me—on that point the whole thing disintegrated"). What the honor referred to is unknown; perhaps that of the rank of Court Counselor (*Hofrat*).

[2] The request was for update information for *Hugo Riemanns Musiklexikon*, 11th edn., edited by Alfred Einstein, 2 vols. (Berlin: Max Hesse, 1929). Schenker comments here on the entry on him in the 9th edn. (1919).

[3] See chapter 8.

[4] See chapter 12.

❧ Hoboken to Schenker (letter), August 27, 1928
OJ 11/54, [24]

Highly revered and dear Dr. [Schenker],
Before the summer reaches its end and we meet in Vienna, I would like to send a few more lines.

To wit: we have survived the automobile tour well, have visited and viewed many beautiful places in Germany, and had good weather all the while. We were also in Weimar, where Goethe's residence made an unforgettable impression on us. In Nuremberg we visited the Dürer exhibition, which was very beautiful and provided a good survey of this master's work. There, in the Hotel, we met Mr. Waltershausen,[1] the Munich music-Mussolini, with whom we bandied a few trivial words. I drove my wife to Kyffhäuser, so that she too could learn of the pilgrimage places of the bygone German Empire, which cannot easily be surpassed in tastelessness. Further to the north we encountered the great heat, which did not bother us much, however.

After an eleven-day journey we arrived at Sylt. We are staying in a nice small house and go for meals over to Kliffende,[2] which belongs to a friend of mine, who runs it with his wife in an exemplary fashion. He has assembled a nice assortment of guests including several luminaries, of whom the leading member is Thomas Mann, who has settled in here for several weeks with his biological and intellectual family circle. He is friendly and relaxed, tactful and unpretentious, but all, so to speak, from his Olympian heights. Another matter, though, is his wife, who watches everything like a hawk so as to miss nothing, and meddles where she has no business. I believe she thus functions somehow as the poet's ear-horn, and it would not surprise me if in no time, along with the "Magic Mountain,"[3] which is indeed playing in Arosa, there should appear a "Magic Lake" playing here. General Music Director Kleiber[4] was here several times as well, but I have never met him personally. Bruno Walter is to come later. Music publishers too were represented in the person of Dr. Strecker, co-proprietor of the firm M.[recte B.] Schott & Sons, Mainz. He is not exactly a shining light (on one occasion he was unable to distinguish piano playing from a phonograph), and when you talk with him about music, he is visibly embarrassed, the reason being that he may have taken to the business of being a publisher.[5]

But it is not only greats in the field of Art that are present here; no, they are not lacking in other areas either. Mr. Gustav Mayer, proprietor of the world's most important art dealership in London, and incidentally a great wine connoisseur, was here, and now Mr. Borchardt, from the famous gourmand emporium in Berlin, has arrived.

The sea air here is very good and the landscape quite beautiful; it is very reminiscent of the Dutch dune landscape, except that there is no tidal land in our area, also no heath, as here. But in any case we are so enthusiastic about nature here that we have bought a lot on which to build a summer house. Pity only that the weather here is not good. Completely different from the Alpine region, where this year it is said to be especially beautiful, here there is always too much wind, too many clouds, and often rain.

We want to stay here about three more weeks and then begin the journey back by automobile. This time it will take us through western Germany and specifically through Westphalia, Cologne, the Eifel range along the Mosel, to Strassburg and Colmar, by way of Freiburg through the Black Forest to Constance, and from there over the Arlbergs to Vienna. I hope to meet Vrieslander along the way and bring him with us to Vienna. I would like to be back there mid-October.

I hope that you have enjoyed a good summer, or rather will still have fine days to enjoy in Galtür, and greet you, and your wife as well, on behalf of my wife, as

        Yours most sincerely,
        A. v. Hoboken

Dr. Haas has received a distinction: the Silver Medal.[6]

---

[1] Hermann Wolfgang Waltershausen (1882–1954): German composer of operas, Lieder, and orchestral works, author of books on opera and dramaturgy. He was a progressive educator, professor at the Munich State Music Hochschule from 1920, its director 1922–33, and founder in 1933 of the Seminar for Private Music Teachers.
[2] Guesthouse on the island of Sylt, off Schleswig-Hostein, which became an artists' refuge in the 1920s and 1930s.
[3] Thomas Mann's novel *The Magic Mountain* (1924).
[4] Erich Kleiber (1890–1956): at the time General Music Director of the Berlin State Opera.
[5] Untranslatable play on words in which the root word "verleg-" has entirely different meanings in its three manifestations (verlegen ... (sich) verlegt ... Verleger).
[6] The Silberne Medaille: awarded for services to the Republic of Austria.

࿋ Schenker to Hoboken (letter), September 5, 1928
OJ 89/2, [7]

Please forgive the unprepossessing form. Ink has just been poured; we are <u>only starting to unpack</u>...

Dear Mr. van Hoboken,

It is my hope still to reach you in Kliffende, as you mentioned in your last letter (for which I thank you very much) your plan to extend the sojourn by three more weeks. The fantastic nature of your travels from Sylt seduced me to even greater fantasies: I thought, who knows where you and your dear wife might meander, just on a whim, with your complete automobile independence. I asked Vrieslander too at one point, but he had no information to give.

The bad weather, as I gather from your note, has not been able to cramp your style: you have kept your senses[sic] of humor in observing and depicting. The gallery of your Sylt personalities looks amusing. Alas, the "personalities" of today: today's word and idea, unfortunately also only today's—value. Do you also know *Tristan* by Thomas Mann?[1] (Reklam booklet.) Have a good laugh on the trip home.

In Galtür we had +50° in the sun, up to 30° in the shade—continuously clear skies, an intensity of air and heat that finished off eyes and nerves. The oldest man in Galtür, aged 90, cannot recall such an excess in Galtür on Nature's part. I had to use the very first daylight hours (starting at 5 a.m.) for *Free Composition*— that's how strangely the day took shape. At the end of July Prof. Oppel arrived with two boys, and stayed with us five days. Then visits followed, until on the 29th we departed and made a stop in Salzburg. It was a magnificent world that Mozart first glimpsed there, but for the youth it soon became intolerably—well, narrow; for the sake of his genius, he had to go out into the wide world, though it may have been uglier than the world of Salzburg. Once out in the big world, he carried along his own world, which however was still bigger (and certainly more beautiful as well). Mozart as hotel waiter, as music waiter—that I cannot imagine. How beautiful it was in Salzburg twenty-five years ago, when Mahler suddenly appeared (with Andrade, Farrar,[2] etc.), and nobody had yet dreamed of the "festivals"! This endless exploitation of helpless Art!

I look forward with great pleasure to your return. Much is planned.

A string quartet by Oppel has been published by Peters. He will come to Vienna in October.

I have congratulated Dr. Haas. With all my personal antipathy toward the contemporary hail of honors I was truly happy that the Ministry for once has looked where our president couldn't even see cow pies.

We are in the midst of unpacking—we send warmest greetings to you and your spouse, and wish a speedy, most carefree journey home!

   Yours sincerely,
   H. Schenker

---

[1] Thomas Mann's novella *Tristan* (1903).

[2] Francisco de Andrade (1859–1921): Portuguese baritone, mentioned favorably in Schenker's essay on Mozart's G minor Symphony (*Masterwork* 2). Geraldine Farrar (1882–1967): American soprano.

Hoboken to Schenker (letter, carbon copy), March 19, 1930
OJ 89/4, [2]

Dear and revered Dr. [Schenker],

The two performances of the *Missa solemnis* are over. The one under Furtwängler was in my opinion the better by far. The work sounded here even better than recently in Vienna, but the orchestra in places covered the voices somewhat too heavily, especially in the Benedictus, where—probably because of a too slow tempo among other things—the violin solo was too little heard. This is a problem in general, and I wonder why they don't hire a prominent solo violinist. The average concertmaster simply cannot do justice to the score. The Kyrie was too sluggish here as well, although Furtwängler gradually attained the correct tempo. Only in the Dona [nobis pacem] did he appear uneasy to me. But the whole sounded supple and musical under his direction, and that was perhaps the most important contrast to the performance under Klemperer, whose overall approach was hard and angular. Certainly he several times hit on the correct tempo better than Furtwängler, but on the other hand he mostly started the individual sections with such excitement that he sacrificed from the outset any opportunity for intensification. His shadings, too, sounded too forceful; it seemed to me that he took the performance markings too literally. He seems on the whole not very flexible. He still has a great following here and probably, if he should give up the Opera on the Square of the Republic,[1] will take over from Kleiber at the State Opera Unter den Linden. His followers praise him most of all for conducting "differently" (I cannot express it any better), while they accuse Furtwängler of emotional torpor and poor programming, unfortunately not without justification.

I notified you by telegram on Monday that I cannot now yet return to Vienna. The reason derives from the fact that I have undertaken something here that detains me until the end of the month, and of which I owe you an explanation.

You remember that a short while ago I complained about pains in the arm, which I considered a consequence of too much playing. I began medical treatment, was X-rayed and received the advice to take a break from piano playing for four weeks and then slowly, along with massage and the like, to begin again, at which point I would always be exposed to the danger of having the pains reoccur. None of this was pleasing to me. I had the feeling that I should continue playing despite the pains, but in the correct manner. As I discussed that here with my wife, she advised me to talk about it with Breithaupt,[2] who as a piano pedagogue has the reputation of having successfully treated many arms suffering from overplaying. I have done that, but have at the same time arranged for five lessons with him, and, these now being finished, for five more.

Breithaupt teaches me to realize what you have often remarked about my piano playing. To cite an example at once: you always told me "relax the thumb!" Breithaupt has shown me, now, how I am to get the thumb relaxed. He considers the stiff thumb altogether the primary obstacle to my piano playing and attributes the [pains from] overplaying to that as well. And he seems to be right about this, for, although I play regularly, the pain is easing significantly. He shows me gradually the movements that I lack and that I need to play as comfortably as possible. He demonstrates them with Beethoven's C minor Variations, Mendelssohn's *Variations sérieuses*, and Schumann's Symphonic Etudes.

I have not hesitated to seize this opportunity, especially in consideration that everything you tell me about phrasing and performance cannot benefit me so long as I cannot play the piano. Besides, I cannot expect you, with your comprehensive theoretical and other works, to be my piano pedagogue. You have better things to do and have anyway told me recently that for you it is a precondition that one be able to play the piano. It seems now that I understand Breithaupt's method of playing, and thus I have, after the first five lessons, immediately asked for five more. Later, then, I will always go to him now and then for a few lessons, although I foresee conflicts in this, for then the musical interpretation will also be discussed, and it will probably differ strongly from what I learn from you. But I should really be happy about that!

I have had to go on so long about this and in such detail to avoid awakening the impression on your part of a disloyalty as a result of my action. Nothing is further from my mind, and I think that as I already enjoy the privilege of being instructed in music by you, there will be no talk of giving up that instruction, even if I were to work on the playing for half a year with Breithaupt.

I have also been active for the Archive in the meantime, and have today obtained permission to order photography of the Trio Op. 70, No. 1 (the "Ghost" Trio), by Beethoven. The piece is here with Friedländer Bros.[3] I hope, though, to achieve still more. I have not yet thought further about the journal,[4] though its publication would probably be of importance for the Archive's reputation in the outside world. But I am in no hurry, and want first to finish the work (or actually: *your* work) on Brahms's Op. 117.[5]

For my personal collection I obtained the very rare Op. 40 by Beethoven (the first of the violin romances) in original print of the parts, a still complete, uncut copy.

I continue work on the Urlinien of the Bach-Roth lieder, but I don't work on them especially often, for Berlin, in contrast to Vienna, is home to many of my acquaintances, and where in Vienna I almost never meet people, here I see very many—sometimes even *too* many! But there is no harm in that.

I want now to return (with my wife) to Vienna on Sunday the 30th. But we remain only until April 12, and then we will travel, by invitation of my relatives, to Holland, from there to join on the maiden voyage of a new steamer to Marseille. From the beginning of May then I will be again in Vienna (alone) for six or seven weeks.

With best greetings from our house to yours, I am

> Yours truly,
> [unsigned]

---

[1] Staatsoper am Platz der Republik, Berlin: a branch of the Berlin Staatsoper established in 1927 and closed in 1931. It operated in the Kroll Theater, hence was also known as the Kroll Oper. Klemperer was its artistic director throughout its four seasons, performances including operas by Hindemith, Janáček, Schoenberg, Stravinsky, and Weill.

[2] Rudolf Breithaupt (1873–1945): German pianist and teacher who taught at the Berlin Music Hochschule, author of *Die natürliche Klaviertechnik* (Leipzig: Kahnt, 1905).

[3] Presumably R. Friedländer & Sohn, Berlin bookseller. The manuscript was in the possession of the German musicologist Max Friedländer until his death in 1934; it is now in the Cary Collection of the Pierpont Morgan Library, New York.

[4] Hoboken is referring to a series of *Mitteilungen* (Communications) or *Jahrbücher* (Yearbooks) issued by the Photogram Archive, which were to inform readers about its development and include articles on manuscripts and the significance of original readings for the understanding of musical works. The idea of such a publication collapsed early in 1931.

[5] Brahms, Three Intermezzos, Op. 117, which Hoboken studied in lessons with Schenker between October 5, 1929 and April 8, 1930 (lessonbook 1929/1930). A typescript survives of a study by Hoboken of Op. 117, No. 1 (OC 14/2).

Schenker to Hoboken (letter), [March 23, 1930]
OJ 89/4, [3]

Dear Mr. van Hoboken,[1]

Many thanks for your nice letter. What you say about Furtwängler (who visited us the day before yesterday, by the way) and Klemperer is really well formulated. But you may write such things only to me—a newspaper would not take the bait of such "criticism"; a good thing for you that you thus are spared the life of a "critic"...

Regarding your Breithaupt therapy I would basically need to say nothing at all, as you yourself clearly express everything that needs to be said about it. That I always admonish you: "don't force!" you know very well; thus I am happy <u>as a person</u> to acknowledge the validity of your enterprise; it brings you diversion, variety, occupation, satisfaction of a curiosity, etc. And even if it were only a whim, why shouldn't you yield to it? That I as an <u>artist</u> think differently about it <u>professionally</u>, however, and that I need not alter the view that I have publicly expressed these thirty years, however, you yourself actually reiterate in your letter. One trains children in the use of the fingers as a general presupposition of piano-playing, but at the same time spares them the knowledge of content and performance for which they would not be sufficiently mature. With Dussek, Field, Clementi, Kuhlau, that certain training-in of the hand and finger apparatus, as a certain "technique *per se*," occurs propitiously, because logically, from the proper source. Everything changes, though, as soon as one confronts Haydn, Mozart, Bach, Beethoven, etc.: there the content as well makes its demands, especially as meanwhile the child has grown into an adult person. And I still insist that these contents have their own individual techniques—not the ones that are suitable for Dussek, Clementi, Czerny, etc. How often <u>you</u> justly censured the performance of even the most renowned performer, because you found the content to be impaired! For <u>you</u> it was after all not enough that these men were in possession already since childhood of the most polished *per se* technique. Now our great masters were gifted by heaven with the invention of the work as well as simultaneously with the ever-varying performance; <u>they</u> did not need to <u>learn</u> performance, but all others of the human ilk have first to laboriously master performance, and therefore <u>I insist that everybody learn piano-playing</u>. That I say daily, and write year after year. (The formulation that you give this idea could mislead an uninitiated person to misunderstanding.)

For your kind disposition toward me I express my special thanks. I relate it actually not to my person and my teaching, only to you yourself: you thus commit yourself to a beautiful loyalty in turn to yourself, to your inborn, so clairvoyant instinct. I believe, <u>with you</u>, that your nature will not change on this point. I congratulate you on your happy acquisition! Best greetings from both of us to you and your good wife.

   Yours,
   H. Schenker

PS The mixture that characterizes you: <u>indisputable superiority</u> of your musical aptitude (from now purified and strengthened by me), a superiority thousands of musicians may envy; and on the other side a purely mechanical inferiority (don't forget, though, that even Joseph Haydn and Wagner could play only very indifferently), suggest for you a correspondingly characteristic life-course as a compelling logical result. But since it is a question of the secret of a life-course, I must remain silent. May it be granted you to hit upon this line on your own as the happiest fulfillment of your hopes and dreams.

---

[1] This letter is undated, but can be dated precisely from Schenker's diary.

Hoboken to Schenker (letter), September 27, 1931
OJ 11/54, [36]

HOTEL FOUR SEASONS
RESTAURANT WALTERSPIEL
MUNICH

Dear and revered Dr. [Schenker],

I take the liberty of sending you enclosed your fee in the form of a check. It is figured on the basis of 60 shillings per lesson, for three months = thirteen weeks, three lessons per week. I don't expect to be back in Vienna yet by October 1, but would like you to have the money punctually.

I am only moderately satisfied with the summer months that have just passed. True, I have practised the piano a lot, and quite systematically, but, except for considerable reading, that is all that I can claim in good conscience. I have applied myself only little to Urlinie studies, though that actually is not correctly expressed. But I have tended to shy away from written work in the area. This is not at all the fault of your theory itself, still less that I am no longer convinced of its validity. But the pressure exerted by my capabilities leads me just now more toward piano-playing than to that work, which requires so infinitely much more inner peace of mind and concentration. Naturally you will answer that through continuous application to the material the peace of mind will indeed come. I myself believe that too; this summer, however, it just hasn't worked out that way. I know, however, that one day I must come to this work and will do so, because otherwise it is impossible for me to grasp musical pieces in their full meaning, and also because only on this basis will I be able critically to appraise other analytical works.

For example in Königsberg I happened upon a new small work, *Form und Linie in der Musik* by Hans Meyer, in which he attempts to interpret Beethoven's sonata Op. 57 by counting the notes of the motives, counting the measure-groups, counting the measures—in short, counting everything in order to prove that the sonata is based throughout on the same numerical relationship (10:16, I believe). In the process he naturally counts wrongly and arbitrarily and divides the groups according to the pianistic figures. He cites you, incidentally, but in such a way that one sees immediately that he has not read your works.

A work of this kind, though, is not difficult to refute. More difficult is the one by Cassirer,[1] who wants to lend expression to his ambivalent feelings by means of still more ambivalent words. What can one seriously protest when, for example, at the end of the "Appassionata" he cries: "Homunculi, that will coagulate and sink everything!" What is supposed to coagulate and sink? His ideas? The ideas of the player, or of the reader? But certainly not those of Beethoven, which in the sonata, to the contrary, lie before us perfectly coagulated and sunken! Then what? But he is prized and cited as the one whose accomplishment it is to have discovered the "uni-motivic," as it is called today, in the works of Beethoven, while on the other hand [Alfred] Lorenz is admired as the first (!!) to have revealed that Beethoven developments are not composed without a system. And so on and on! You will know well enough about all of that; I am just now finding out about it.

The weather in the north was miserable, and in the mountains, I am told, it has not been much better. Have you also had so little sun, and have you nevertheless had a good vacation?

I will return to Vienna some time this week, but prefer not to commit to a particular day. Back home, if experience is any guide, much library work and other matters will be waiting, so that I prefer not to come for the lesson until Tuesday the 13th.

I look forward to seeing you again and greet you, with the warmest felicitations to your wife, as

Yours truly,
A. v. Hoboken

[1] Fritz Cassirer (1871–1926): German conductor, author of *Beethoven und die Gestalt: ein Kommentar* (Stuttgart: Deutsche Verlags-Anstalt, 1925).

Schenker to Hoboken (letter), September 29, 1931
OJ 89/5, [7]

My dear Mr. van Hoboken,

Many thanks for your nice letter with the check.

What you report about your summer applies to us as well. There is nothing for all of us to do but only now to—make up for it with a true vacation.

What you write about your musical activity during the summer is understandable. In Vienna I will have more to say about that, here only a few words.

Please, don't take all the Urlinie matters too seriously. You can bear me out that I have gladly spared you that. What I cannot let pass are only the "linear progressions"; without a feeling (or knowledge) of these there is no hearing, no performance, whatever the "method" may be etc. Thus even in chorale studies and the fugue I must unfortunately make you consider the linear progressions. As for the rest, you will soon—how fast a nine-month course does fly by!—you will soon be finished with all of that. (The reason for diffidence about the Urlinie among musicians lies in a completely different place than they suppose; such things bother me not in the least.) I am convinced that we will do just as well this year as in the previous one: you had every reason to be satisfied with yourself. And finally, we have at hand the possibility of making simplifications, as we often did last year. I carry in my heart the principle: no forcing, no stress may be allowed to barricade the approach to Art; serene and calm (as by inspiration from above, with eyes uplifted to heaven's grace), I would say: in a lazy, Bohemian manner (if you understand me correctly), and I stand by that.

Till we soon meet again, then!

With best greetings from both of us,

   Yours,
    H. Schenker

❧ Schenker to Hoboken (letter), February 27, 1932
OJ 89/5, [1]

My dear Mr. van Hoboken,

I hasten to thank you most heartily and in writing for the letter that you were so good yesterday as to give me personally.[1] I have immediately placed it along with my testament, so that in case my time should come, God forfend, during the printing, my widow will know where to look for the aid in fulfilling the commitments I made to the publisher or the printer at the time of the order. But I persist in the hope that we all will live to witness in best spirits the publication of the large work, which without doubt is destined, in terms of time and value, to be the premier text on music. Along with this work—this is by no means envious boastfulness; today I have the feeling that I can say this with your agreement—only two works maintain eternal value: the thoroughbass books of Bach father and son, and not a single other work of the literature. I thank you especially that the sum allotted will make it possible for me to be more liberal with the examples. But on the other hand I will take extra care that the work not unnecessarily exceed limits, that it remain easily affordable also for less affluent musicians and amateurs. Let us be sincere in not begrudging the masses, who otherwise love the dark, participation according to their abilities in the light of day that beams from the work!

And once again: thank you, thank you, thank you!

With best greetings,

   Yours,
    H. Schenker

---

[1] Hoboken's letter is not known to survive, but it evidently gave a commitment to funding the printing costs of *Free Composition*.

Hoboken to Schenker (letter), July 29, 1932
OJ 11/54, [40]

Partenkirchen, at Dr. W. Grahl's

Dear and revered Dr. Schenker,

Many thanks for your cordial postcard of July 15 and for sending the program-books. I already knew several pieces, to be sure, since I have heard a few concerts of this musical-rubbish festival. I must acknowledge to my satisfaction that the public no longer unconditionally accepts such music. Only on the evening when the *Music to Accompany a Film Scene* by Schoenberg and *Der Wein* by Alban Berg were performed did it bestow—especially after the second piece—frenetic approval.[1] The reason for that is, without doubt, a riddle to me, for if people constantly repeat that Berg is "serious" in his work (no doubt in contrast to the other musicians of today, who thus do not appear to be "serious"), the piece still fails to rise above the level of a line-by-line programmatic work. By that I mean that in the beautiful poem by Baudelaire, which in the translation by Stefan George first of all loses its capitalization and punctuation, each line has been somehow tone-painted, but the meaning of the whole has not been grasped. Unfortunately the program book of precisely this concert is missing, since Deutsch was not present; I didn't save mine either, otherwise I would have been glad to send it to you.

The new Chopin edition by Édouard Ganche[2] contains at first glance many good things that other editions lack. Unfortunately it is nowhere made clear which pieces have been revised according to the autograph manuscript and which according to the original edition. Regarding the Mazurkas, Op. 24, however, I was already able to discover that they are revised according to the Schlesinger original edition. They include all of its errors and a few more. The manuscript, which of course resides in the Breitkopf archive, Ganche appears not to have seen, and a superficial inspection supports my assumption that he has examined none of the manuscripts from that archive. Did he not receive them? In any case, he knows perfectly well which of them are there.

It is interesting, though, that he was able to examine the French original edition from the collection of Miss [Jane] Stirling, in which Chopin entered comments and improvements in the course of teaching. Thus in the C minor Prelude, a flat sign before the e^1 in the fourth quarter of measure 3, where according to the printed text one is actually supposed to play e^1 (while I have always played $e♭^1$ at that point), and also a very noteworthy alteration in the G♯ minor Etude from Op. 25, where in measure 42 he is supposed to have changed the two occurrences of $c♯^1$ in the left hand in the sixth and seventh eighths to c, thus really to b♯.

The Foreword is unfortunately very arrogant; especially the comment that the French original editions, despite their errors, are always better than the German, is not accurate. I hope, when I should visit you some time, to be able to bring along a volume to you; I am just now in process of comparing with the new edition the information that we gained in the lesson from comparison of the photograms with the original editions.

How are you faring in Igls? Is it not too fashionable there for you? You will probably have the same weather as we here, thus mostly rain and little sunshine.

Perhaps I shall after all come, with Miss Boy, to see you once more; it is really not very far. What time of day are you usually in?

With best greetings, also to your wife, I am, as always,

        Yours most truly,
        A. v. Hoboken

---

[1] On June 21, 1932, *Der Wein* and *Music to Accompany a Film Scene* were performed at a Worker's Concert, by the Vienna Symphony Orchestra with Růžena Herlinger, soprano, under Anton Webern, together with Schoenberg's *Friede auf Erden*, in the large music hall of the Musikverein Building, as part of the ISCM Festival of that year, which was held in Vienna (*Neue freie Presse*, no. 24343 (June 21, 1932): 14).

[2] Édouard Ganche's edition of Chopin's works (London: Oxford University Press, 1928–32).

24
Edinburgh Outpost: John Petrie Dunn

JOHN Petrie Dunn (1878–1931) was the son of a Scottish school inspector. He attended the University of Edinburgh from 1896 to 1899, where he was among the outstanding students of Frederick Niecks; a Bucher Scholarship enabled him to continue his studies abroad. At the Stuttgart Conservatory he had piano lessons from Max Pauer and studied theory with Samuel de Lange; later he joined the teaching staff there. In 1909 he moved to Kiel, as Professor of piano and, subsequently, as Vice-Principal of the Conservatory, where his first book, *Das Geheimnis der Handführung beim Klavierspiel*, was written; it is probably in Kiel that he met his future wife, Aline, who was a pupil of his there and is described in a letter from Hoboken to Schenker (see below) as "much younger." After serving in the Royal Scots during the War, he settled in Edinburgh, first as a private piano teacher and, from 1920, as lecturer in music at the University, where he worked alongside—and somewhat in the shadow of—Niecks's successor, Donald Francis Tovey. In spite of inordinate classroom and private teaching duties, Dunn published two further books, *Ornamentation in the Works of Chopin* (1921) and *A Student's Guide to Orchestration* (in 1928, the year he received a DMA from Edinburgh). He was also active as a performer, both as a soloist and with his wife, Aline; Tovey, in an "Appreciation" to the obituary of Dunn published in *The Scotsman* (February 6, 1931), singled out two works—Beethoven's Op. 109 and Brahms's Paganini Variations—in which he showed consummate technical mastery and profound musical understanding.

It was during the later part of his time at Edinburgh that Dunn began corresponding with Schenker, initially to inquire after *Free Composition* (a local bookshop had told him that it was "out of print"!). He was among the earliest English-speaking music teachers—almost certainly the first in the United Kingdom—to pursue an active interest in Schenker's theoretical project of the 1920s, which led him to prepare an English version of sections from *Counterpoint 2* (1927), and to include an excerpt from Schenker's Ninth Symphony monograph in his *Orchestration*. Schenker readily admitted Dunn into his circle; he asked Hoboken to visit him in Edinburgh, and Dunn's name is listed among Schenker's disciples in the eleventh edition of *Riemanns Musiklexikon* (1929). The city of Edinburgh also heads the list of outposts of Schenkerian theory enumerated in a letter from Schenker to Cube of June 1, 1927.

The two men corresponded regularly for five years; Dunn (a great fan of Wagner) and his wife spoke of their hopes of combining a visit to the Schenkers with a trip to Bayreuth, or to Aline's family in Leipzig, but this did not materialize.

WILLIAM DRABKIN

❧ Dunn to Schenker (letter), April 18, 1926
OJ 10/13, [1]

42, Murrayfield Avenue,
Edinburgh

Highly revered Sir,

Permit me to direct a question to you. For some time now, I have been in search of volume 2/3 (*Free Composition*), of your incomparably valuable New Musical Theories and Fantasies.[1] Now the foremost music shop in town tells me that the work is "out of print." Is this true? If so, could you possibly give me an idea, how and where I might get hold of a copy of it? For a year, I have in fact been studying volumes 1, 2/1, and 2/2 with ever growing joy, and for the most splendid gain to my understanding of theory; must I now forgo the pleasure of the last volume, in which, so I understand, the ultimate secrets of the "progression of degrees" is revealed?

If you could give me a possible supplier who would help me out of this difficult situation, I would be most exceedingly indebted to you.

With my greatest respect, and profound thanks, I remain

Yours most devotedly,
John Petrie Dunn

---

[1] By the mid-1920s, "Freier Satz" (as it was then called) had been advertised as being in preparation for several years; Dunn's fear that the book—as yet unwritten—might be out of print and difficult to obtain are, therefore, entirely understandable.

❧ Dunn to Schenker (lettercard), May 13, 1926
OJ 10/13, [2]

Highly revered Mr. Schenker,

For your recent, informative lines, I offer you my most heartfelt thanks. I must admit that your news, that the fourth volume of the New Musical Theories and Fantasies has not yet appeared, comes as a bitter disappointment. Please publish it as soon as possible! Consider, after all, that it represents the logical continuation of the masterly volumes that have already appeared, which will crown the work as a whole. For my part, I regard your Theories and Fantasies as of even greater significance than your splendid Beethoven [sonata] commentaries.

Please forgive my forthright manner, but in all seriousness it means infinitely much to me to possess this final volume in particular.

You will perhaps be pleased if I tell you that I have prepared a condensed English version of your second volume. I shall have several copies of it reproduced on a typewriter and distributed it to my students this autumn. The Foreword will contain a reference to your book. I shall tell you more about this later.

Your very devoted
John Petrie Dunn

❧ Dunn to Schenker (lettercard), June 27, 1926
OJ 10/13, [3]

Highly revered Mr. Schenker,
    Above all, I express my most heartfelt thanks for the joy, and the honor, you have conferred upon me in sending me your [first] yearbook. You have undertaken a work which has never before been attempted with such thoroughness, and for this reason I wish you the very best success in completing the last volume. The veil has indeed been lifted!
    As concerns the adaptation of *Counterpoint*, I have to battle against an evil enemy: <u>chronic lack of time</u>. Moreover, you will readily understand that the purely mechanical difficulties of making multiple copies led to a stark curtailment of the scope of the work. If I take the opportunity of presenting you with a copy, you will take it for a very thin potion compared with the original! I regret that it could not be done any other way. The adaptation of two-part counterpoint is now complete, and will be copied with the typewriter. Then the music examples will have to be entered by hand. But since the verso of every leaf is empty, I shall add remarks, amendments and clarifications from time to time. For the moment, what is of principal importance, for reasons which I shall explain to you later, is that we provide a solid foundation for the study of counterpoint. More about this later.

        With cordial thanks,
        Your most devoted
        J. P. Dunn

❧ Dunn to Schenker (letter), February 1, 1927
OJ 10/13, [4]

Dear Mr. Schenker,
    You will probably have wondered why I have been silent for such a long time; but the work that I undertook was much more strenuous than I had expected. It is, however, finally completed, and I have sent the fruits of my labours to you today, specifically in the form of an abbreviated adaptation and translation of Parts 3 and 4 of volume 2/2, of your New Musical Theories and Fantasies. I hope that you will be pleased by my modest achievement, the preparation of multiple copies of which cost me and also my wife a great deal of time and effort. Translating your book was especially difficult, for its conceptual content is, for the most part, new and profound and makes no small demands on the reader's musical instinct and powers of imagination. From a linguistic point of view as well, it was enormously difficult.
    The most difficult of all—for example, the justification for the downward resolution of the suspension—I was forced to omit. In addition, I took the liberty of weaving in a few elementary elucidations, to make it easier for our young students to understand; and I hope that I have done this in a manner that is compatible with your ideas.

We were extremely sorry not to be able to see Mr. van Hoboken at our house, on account of his illness.[1] But we hope that we will have this pleasure at a later time.

I would be most grateful if Mr. van Hoboken could inform us in good time of his next visit, since it might be possible for me to speak with him in London, as I shall have to spend a week in London on account of a radio lecture on Beethoven.

In the hope that I shall hear from you again soon, I send you my most respectful greetings.

Your ever devoted
John Petrie Dunn

[1] See chapter 23, letter of January 28, 1927.

Diary entry, February 13, 1927

To Dunn (letter): thanks for the book; I give my preference to his work above that of Roth, on account of its greater precision.[1] In return, I send him my picture[2] as a present. Hoboken will get in touch.

[1] Schenker's initial reaction is similar: "It makes a better impression than the one by Roth" (diary, February 4, 1927). He regarded Herman Roth's *Elemente der Stimmführung* (Stuttgart, 1926) as partly plagiarized from his own *Counterpoint*.
[2] From Dunn's reply (February 22, 1927) it may be inferred that this was a copy of Hammer's mezzotint portrait of Schenker, executed in 1925. This portrait is a frequent topic of discussion in chapter 2, above.

Dunn to Schenker (letter), February 22, 1927
OJ 10/13, [5]

Highly revered Professor,

I express my most heartfelt thanks to you for sending me your picture. It is a most exquisite work of art and, at the same time, a sign of your amicable feelings toward me, which I value to an extraordinarily high degree.

I am uncommonly pleased that you are satisfied with my translation of your book. After I have taken care of a few other smaller pieces of work, I shall likewise translate the section entitled "Bridges to Free Counterpoint." Already the students have even begged me to do this! Now I do not expect this assignment to be quite as difficult as the earlier one.

I shall report to you later on the realization of these plans. For the time being, I am inundated with work.

With my most cordial thanks for your kindness and attention,

>   I remain
>   Your most devoted
>   John Petrie Dunn

PS I take the liberty of sending my most cordial greetings to your wife, though I do not know her.

❦ Anthony van Hoboken to Schenker (letter), September 18, 1927
OJ 11/54, [18]

The Royal Hotel, Edinburgh
53 Princess Street

Dear Dr. [Schenker],

Yesterday I joined Mr. Dunn for dinner.[1] He is a sturdy and healthy-looking man who shows his age of 49. Very vigorous too. His wife, who was also there, is much younger; she is German, and was his pupil when she married him. He studied at the time in Stuttgart: piano with Max Pauer and theory with Samuel de Lange.[2] In 1914 he gave a concert in Vienna for which he is said to have had very good reviews. He came to your works only later, and in fact by way of the elucidatory editions of the last five sonatas of Beethoven, where you do always cite your other works. He ordered them one by one and knows all of them, from the *Contribution to the Study of Ornamentation* up to the first yearbook, including the *Tonwille* volumes. He may well have been astonished by the first issue, but today has been willing to overlook the political statements in favor of the musical ones.

Acquaintance with your theories was a revelation for him and he is, along with Vrieslander, the most thoroughly convinced disciple of them that I have met so far. He is unswervingly faithful to them and does his part to disseminate them. This "part" of his, however, is unfortunately somewhat limited. He is not Professor of Music at the University; this position is occupied by Mr. Tovey, a dreamy, absent-minded musician; a "will-o'-the-wisp," as Dunn calls him. Dunn is his assistant; he has, however, primary responsibility for counterpoint instruction, and the students are loyal to him, and thus, at the same time, to you. But so long as Tovey teaches the more advanced composition classes, your method cannot be fully applied there, though the students would prefer to be instructed according to it. But the Professor will not do that; and even if he knew all of your writings and were ever so convinced of their validity, he would not—as Dunn represents the situation—be in a position to teach accordingly. And a Professor in Scotland sits more securely on his Chair than a king on his throne.

A second obstacle is that the teacher who has responsibility for the elementary instruction is said to be an old pedant, who dispenses instruction in "harmony" according to the old method, etc.—in short, does everything that you so rightly denounce. Thus our Mr. Dunn sits between a jackass and a romantic, and drops the seed that he sows in large part on rocky plots.

Dunn is completely without means and gets by for the rest with the proceeds from private teaching of piano playing. He has also published two small works on this topic: *Usage of the Hand in Piano Playing*[3] and *Ornamentation in the Works of*

Frederick Chopin.[4] The latter, written in English, he will give me as a present; the former, published in German by Kahnt in Leipzig, I will order.

From several discussions on this theme I got the impression that in this area he still has very much to learn from you. But that was only an impression, just as I request that you regard all of these reports likewise as first impressions.

Today I join him again for tea. Tomorrow I will go from here to Aberdeen (that is again somewhat closer to the North Pole than Edinburgh) for a visit with Dr. [Charles Sanford] Terry, with whom I have business concerning the Archive. (Dunn, incidentally, was very enthusiastic about the Archive plan.) I am happy that my trip now has finally borne fruit to the extent that my musical plans can be combined with it. In Switzerland I was not very happy this time, though I like to tell myself that the sojourn in those high elevations has strengthened body and spirit very much.

From Furtwängler, who promised faithfully to invite me again, I have heard nothing, though I met him once more, at which time he repeated his promise. Is he not interested in our project? Well, it will proceed without him too. But it would be a shame.

With best wishes to your good wife, I am, as ever,

> Yours most sincerely,
> A. v. Hoboken

---

[1] Hoboken had planned to visit Dunn in January 1927, but canceled at the last minute on account of illness.

[2] Max von Pauer (1866–1945): German pianist, son of Ernst Pauer, who taught from 1897 to the early 1920s at the Stuttgart Conservatory, was then director of the Leipzig Conservatory 1924–32, then of the Mannheim Conservatory 1933–34. Samuel de Lange, Jr. (1840–1911): Dutch virtuoso organist and pianist, who taught at the Stuttgart Royal Conservatory in the 1890s and became the institution's director 1900–08.

[3] *Das Geheimnis der Handführung beim Klavierspiel* (Leipzig: Kahnt, 1914).

[4] *Ornamentation in the Works of Frederick Chopin* (London: Novello, [1921]).

❧ Dunn to Schenker (letter), November 14, 1927

OJ 10/13, [6]

Highly revered Mr. Schenker,

I cannot thank you enough for sending me the second yearbook; you have thereby conferred a great honor upon me. I have only just got around to writing to you today, as I had not wanted to thank you for your priceless gift until I had carefully gone through at least one complete chapter of the yearbook. This I have done this morning (Sunday); I have read through, word for word, line for line, your analysis of the C minor fugue by Bach. The impression that I gathered from it was precisely this: that never has the "organic" quality of a Bach fugue appeared before my eyes so convincingly, and with such clarity. No less valuable was the recognition that each fugue by Bach has its own laws which the composer must obey—along the lines of the Goethe quotation[1]—notwithstanding that which he is required to do in another fugue and in a different construction of the Urlinie, the harmonic degrees, etc.

I hope you will make allowances for my laziness as a correspondent on particular grounds: here in my home town I have an enormous practice; for all sorts of people, from near and far, who are afflicted with crippled fingers or some other bodily or intellectual shortcomings, regard me to a certain extent as their rock. As things turn out, I am reading the yearbook today, tomorrow I shall speak about "tonicalization" (an entirely new English word), and the day after tomorrow I shall be drumming a Clementi sonatina into someone's head! My wife constantly complains that I must teach unceasingly and can devote so little time to my own studies but this can be attributed simply to the difficult circumstances of today: one must forge the iron while it is hot. Well, the two of us are hoping for better times; moreover, I do actually succeed, by and large, in making ends meet.

What it is about your writings that touches me personally, to such beneficial effect, is that they agree so completely with my instinctive feeling. I had always felt that Riemann was not convincing, that Debussy and Ravel are shallow, that Reger is partly good, partly bad, etc. etc. Now you come along and prove all of this. Having received this impression, I got hold of your books as soon as the war ended. There I found precisely that which I had expected, and I am not a little proud of my good instinct.

It is time to close. I have a very strenuous day ahead of me tomorrow. I would only like to say further that my wife and I have gradually arrived at the point at which we believe that all this writing is of no use, and that we should get to know each other personally. As my wife comes from Leipzig, then a much less significant occasion would suffice for her (and me) to make a slight detour to Austria! (In the late summer, of course.)

With most cordial greetings, also to your wife, and with my deepest thanks,

    Your entirely devoted
    John Petrie Dunn

---

[1] i.e. the distinction Goethe makes, in an aphorism in *Über Kunst und Altertum*, between treating the specific case on the one hand merely as an instance of a general principle and, on the other, seeking to understand the general principle by "vividly grasp[ing] the specific," which he takes to be the essence of poetry. Schenker quotes this toward the end of his essay, where he ponders the question of whether Bach himself was aware of the things that Schenker has been discussing (*Masterwork* 2, 52; Ger., 92).

❧ Dunn to Schenker (letter), June 16, 1928
OJ 10/13, [7]

Highly revered Mr. Schenker,

Allow me to express my most cordial wishes to you for your birthday and, at the same time, give expression to the hope that it may be granted that you remain active for many, many years to come!

I take the liberty of enclosing one of the most recent photographs of myself,[1] and ask you to regard it as a modest sign of my feelings of gratitude toward you.

It will probably interest you to learn that I am at present writing a book on orchestration ("Aspects of Orchestration," which may be rendered in German as "Gesichtspunkte der Orchestrierung"). In a section on "clarity" (i.e. of the melodic line) I permitted myself to reproduce, in English translation, an extended passage from your book on the Ninth Symphony, from p. 47 ("Thus I cannot remember ever …") to p. 49 ("… unnecessary degree of clarity").[2]

How, where, and when the book will appear I cannot possibly say.[3] Perhaps I will be utterly unable to find a publisher who will take it. The market is flooded with wretched little instrument handbooks, which all offer the same thing, each one repeating what the others say. My book presupposes a knowledge of the individual instruments and is concerned only with the leading aspects of the classical art of orchestration, viz. the doubling of voices; the transformation of a filler voice into a true one, and vice versa; tonal color, mixing of colors and register; balance, and synthetic hearing; how one should listen; the role of the three principal groups of instruments in orchestral composition; clarity, etc.

Should the book ever appear in print, I shall request of you, i.e. of your publisher, permission to cite the passage in question.

The translation of your *Counterpoint* was made available to my students by the distribution of many copies. All of them expressed their satisfaction with it. It is, however, impossible for me to exert my influence in this direction as widely as I would like, for the very subject of strict counterpoint is taught not by me but by a colleague of mine. This man commits precisely the same mistakes that you speak out against. He flirts, in fact, with free counterpoint and forbids, for instance,

because these progressions appear to be disguised 6/4 harmonies! As a consequence, the pupils regard strict counterpoint as a test that has to be passed in obligatory dimness. Many of the students are of the view that I should take over the elementary education, since they would then receive the correct understanding of it; unfortunately that is not possible.

I should frightfully like to get together with you and discuss all manner of problems. This year I am going with my wife for a fortnight to Spiekeroog (near Norderney).[4] Next summer, however, we are definitely going to Bayreuth. Perhaps we will then have the opportunity to discuss things face to face.

With the most cordial greetings from us to you, I remain
>Your entirely devoted
>John Petrie Dunn

---

[1] Preserved as OJ 72/4, No. 1, with holograph inscription to Schenker dated June 19, 1928. Photographer: Moffat, Edinburgh. Dunn must have dated it not according to the date of his letter but to that of Schenker's birthday.

[2] *Beethoven's Ninth Symphony*, 67–68. The extract concerns the first eight measures of Beethoven's Eighth Symphony. Wagner criticizes Beethoven's lack of melodic clarity, by allowing the first oboe (in measure 6) and first flute (measure 8) to enter "unthematically." Schenker sees no problem with this: Beethoven's use of the oboe first as a filler part (measures 6–7), then as a reinforcement of the melodic line (measures 7–8) is for Schenker no lack of clarity, but is rather a more subtle approach to orchestration than a theater-orientated composer such as Wagner could have understood.

[3] Dunn presented this work to the University of Edinburgh in partial fulfillment of the DMus in 1928. It was published as *A Student's Guide to Orchestration* (London: Novello, 1930), with a dedication to Donald Francis Tovey; a review appeared in *The Musical Times* 71 (1930): 611. True to his word, Dunn included the extract from Schenker's *Beethoven's Ninth Symphony* concerning the opening measures of the Eighth, in a chapter on "Lucidity" (see pp. 79–80). Dunn quotes Schenker approvingly, and recommends many of his writings in the Preface (the first three volumes of the New Musical Theories and Fantasies, the first two *Masterwork* yearbooks, and the monograph on the Ninth), but is careful not to expose Schenker as an outright anti-Wagnerian:

> It would here be explained that Schenker's words are not intended as an endorsement of the charge of "noisiness" so often leveled at Wagner by the ignorant layman. His meaning rather is that Wagner underestimated and consequently disdained those very refinements of orchestral treatment which contribute towards making Beethoven's instrumental style the supreme artistic achievement that it is.

[4] Spiekeroog, Norderney: two islands in the North Sea, off the coast of Lower Saxony.

❧ Schenker to Dunn (draft or copy of letter), July 8, 1928
OC 30/122–124

Galtür

Revered Professor Dunn,

For the thoughtfulness of your kind words of commemoration, but especially for sending me your picture, I express my warmest thanks to you. Now you stand before my eyes, too, and cheer my heart as a brave compatriot on the front against an age that has probably deteriorated beyond hope. That our struggle and victory, which of course cannot fail, will change the face of future generations and beyond, of precisely this I harbor not the slightest doubt; we may even today rejoice in their future happiness, in opposition to those who live today in darkness, even if we do not find comfort and joy in ourselves.

What you recount about your colleague points to the heart of the disease. The spirit of strict counterpoint, which in former times determined the reality of musical composition in a very substantial way (even if this was not fully understood, from a theoretical point of view), has become a ghost in the school. We do not know whether strict counterpoint is even alive: we recognize it neither in the background nor in the foreground [of today's music], though it ought to be visible everywhere as something forever immutable in spite of all that changes. But, have patience, *Free Composition* will also be of help here. How happy your colleague would feel—would indeed have to feel—if he understood that free counterpoint often enough conceals itself, so to speak, behind the eternally blissful innocence of strict counterpoint for the sake of a better elaboration: thus to give

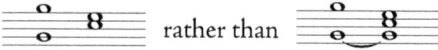

without worrying whether in the first case, too, the ear is inclined to perceive a merely roundabout expression of the 6/4 chord. This is indeed the meaning and the purpose of counterpoint: to present a succession of intervals as though it were disconnected from all interpretation. One pretends to be stupid, writing one interval after the next along the lines of [strict] counterpoint, and imagines that one does not know what their succession means. But this beautiful pretence is something that is derived from counterpoint itself, which in fact truly refuses all interpretation. For the elaboration, how much more convenient, in fact, is the succession 8–3, whereby the octave and the third can both be treated independently and be subjected to rich elaboration—and this, and only this, is the point—in comparison with the rigidity of their summation as a 6/4 chord, which swallows up what was once an octave and a third. This ploy is the source of the entire storytelling art of our masters: they always write, so to speak, their counterpoint, nothing more; it is our job to find out what it is saying, though counterpoint behaves as if it did nothing else but generate intervals.

The work that you have in mind is something that I would welcome with the greatest joy. The content that you outlined is very rich and to the point. For ten years I have been repeatedly telling one of our illustrious conductors[1] that the treatment of the orchestra by contemporary composers is abysmal, and in no way reaches the level of the classical masters, let alone exceeding it (in spite of appearances to the contrary). He simply does not believe it since, being a champion of Wagner, Bruckner, and Hugo Wolf, he cannot accept my reasoning. But one day—after ten years had passed—he suddenly admitted to me, over lunch, that he felt happy when he had a score by Brahms to conduct, for the more recent scores were simply unbearable (Brahms used to be regarded as incapable of writing for the orchestra). Moreover, time is on your side: get your book published and, as it happened with the one conductor in my case, the important people in the musical world will come to recognize their errors.

With the prospect that you offer me and my wife, by which I mean the prospect of a get-together in your Bayreuth year, you have provided us with the greatest pleasure. We shall urge you [to make good your intention]. And so, with the very best greetings from us to you,

>Your most devoted
>H. S.

[1] Almost certainly Wilhelm Furtwängler.

Dunn to Schenker (letter), December 30, 1930
OJ 10/13, [8]

Highly revered Dr. [Schenker],
For the magnificent third volume of your book,[1] which you were so kind as to send me, I express my most heartfelt thanks. At the same time, however, I should like to thank you most cordially for the instruction that you have provided me from time to time in your valuable letters. I am forever regretting the fact that our home towns lie so far apart; there are so many pedagogical questions for which I would like to hear your advice and thoughts in live conversation, rather than via an arduous, written path. Perhaps, one fine day, that will be possible.

Your "Thoughts"[2] have been written from my soul. I envy you your sharp eloquence, your sarcasm and Faustian humor! Thank God that you have put jazz in its place, that festering sore which is responsible for the sickness in today's musical life. The American who invented this and similar things ought to be condemned to having to jazz-dance on hot coals until he drops dead![3]

I shall get deeply into your analysis of the "Eroica" Symphony as soon as possible. For the time being, with most cordial greetings for the new year, also from my wife to yours, I remain

>Your most devoted
>John Petrie Dunn

[enclosure: printed recital program by John Petrie Dunn (4pp.)]

[1] *Masterwork* 3, released on December 9, 1930. Since December 1928 the only contact between the two men had been Dunn's sending of a recital program by his students and his book on orchestration, with no surviving letter. Schenker invited Dunn to visit them in Galtür in the summer of 1930, but that did not materialize.

[2] "Thoughts on Art and Its Relation to the General Scheme of Things," subtitle of the "Miscellanea" section of the *Masterwork* yearbooks.

[3] Schenker's disparagement of jazz and Negro music in *Masterwork* 3, 77–78 (Ger., 118–19).

❧ Aline Dunn to Schenker (letter), February 19, 1931
OJ 10/12, [1]

Dear Dr. [Schenker],

Although I do not myself entirely understand what I am writing to you, I feel that I must communicate the unimaginable to you, being someone for whom my husband had boundless admiration.

On February 4, at 11 o'clock in the evening, my husband was hit by a car and, without regaining consciousness, died in hospital at 11.40.

What has befallen me is so frightful that I hardly believe that I shall be able to endure it.[1]

> With silent greetings,
> Yours truly,
> Aline Petrie Dunn

[1] Schenker's reaction to this news: "There can be no doubt that I have lost a devoted companion, from whom I could have hoped for more" (diary, February 21, 1931). He sent his condolences on February 23, 1931.

❧ Aline Dunn to Schenker (letter), April 28, 1931
OJ 10/12, [2]

> Sophienstrasse 30
> Leipzig

Dear Dr. [Schenker],

As you have always taken such a friendly interest in my husband, I take the liberty of sending you the article from *The Scotsman*, written by Professor Tovey,[1] and a small photograph taken on our last visit to Marienbad, last summer.[2]

For your compassionate letter, once again my most cordial thanks. I have just spent a month in Italy with my mother, but next week I shall return to Edinburgh and try to resume my work. The frightful experience of February 4 still weighs so heavily upon me, and I cannot come to terms with it at all. On February 3 we were practising Bach's C major Concerto, which we were to play with orchestral accompaniment on February 15, and my husband was also booked to give a piano recital on March 24. And now he is silent; struck down, he lay there like a tree that had been felled. It is too horrible to contemplate.

The orchestra played the Allegretto from Beethoven's Seventh Symphony for him; the audience stood.

> With friendly greetings,
> Your very devoted
> Aline Petrie Dunn

[1] An obituary of John Petrie Dunn, together with "An Appreciation" (signed D. F. T. = Donald Francis Tovey), appeared in *The Scotsman* on February 6, 1931. German translations of both were made (there is a minor emendation in Aline's hand); Schenker kept them, and the original clipping from *The Scotsman*, with the Dunns' letters to him.

[2] See Plate 39.

25
The Seminar Years: Felix Salzer

FELIX Salzer was born in Vienna into the Wittgenstein family (his mother, Helene Salzer, was the sister of the philosopher Ludwig Wittgenstein and the pianist Paul Wittgenstein). By the time he became Schenker's pupil in the fall of 1931 he had already, in 1926, completed his doctorate in musicology at the University of Vienna with Guido Adler and had published two articles, the first based on his dissertation, "Sonata Form in Franz Schubert."[1]

The present selection of the correspondence[2] begins in 1930 with a letter concerning Salzer's second published article, an essay on the meaning of the ornaments in C. P. E. Bach's keyboard works that clearly was influenced by Schenker's *A Contribution to the Study of Ornamentation*. Salzer had become familiar with Schenker's approach while still in his teens, when he began studying theory and analysis with Schenker's pupil Hans Weisse. The selection offers insight also into the private seminar of which Salzer was a member, initially convened by Weisse but taken over by Schenker when Weisse left for New York in the fall of 1931. When the seminar was dissolved in 1934, Salzer began private study with Schenker. The *Five Analyses in Sketchform*, which the seminar helped to prepare, also figures in the correspondence, as does Schenker's progress on *Free Composition* and Salzer's work on his first book, *The Meaning and Essence of Western Polyphony*.[3] He went on to produce influential publications, including two books, and to co-edit a major periodical[4] and spearhead the spread of Schenkerian thought in the United States and beyond.

Salzer was one of the first theorists to extend the scope of Schenkerian analysis back to music of the Middle Ages and Renaissance and forward to twentieth-century works.[5] His interest in such repertory dates back to his student years; letters show that Schenker supported his independent work in the field of early music, and even ventured into modern times by recommending a Bartók recording. The correspondence gives proof of the personal interest Schenker took in Salzer's career and traces the warm and mutually respectful friendship that developed between teacher and pupil.

HEDI SIEGEL

---

[1] Felix Salzer, "Die Sonatenform bei Franz Schubert," *Studien zur Musikwissenschaft* 15 (1928): 86–125.

[2] The extant correspondence between the two men consists of twenty-seven items from Schenker to Salzer (1930–34) and five from Salzer to Schenker (1932, 1934); see Hedi Siegel, "Schenker's Letters to Felix Salzer: A Nod to the Future," in *Essays from the Fourth International Schenker Symposium*, vol. 2, ed. L. Poundie Burstein, Lynne Rogers, and Karen M. Bottge (Hildesheim: Georg Olms, 2013), 73–83.

[1] An obituary of John Petrie Dunn, together with "An Appreciation" (signed D. F. T. = Donald Francis Tovey), appeared in *The Scotsman* on February 6, 1931. German translations of both were made (there is a minor emendation in Aline's hand); Schenker kept them, and the original clipping from *The Scotsman*, with the Dunns' letters to him.

[2] See Plate 39.

25
The Seminar Years: Felix Salzer

FELIX Salzer was born in Vienna into the Wittgenstein family (his mother, Helene Salzer, was the sister of the philosopher Ludwig Wittgenstein and the pianist Paul Wittgenstein). By the time he became Schenker's pupil in the fall of 1931 he had already, in 1926, completed his doctorate in musicology at the University of Vienna with Guido Adler and had published two articles, the first based on his dissertation, "Sonata Form in Franz Schubert."[1]

The present selection of the correspondence[2] begins in 1930 with a letter concerning Salzer's second published article, an essay on the meaning of the ornaments in C. P. E. Bach's keyboard works that clearly was influenced by Schenker's *A Contribution to the Study of Ornamentation*. Salzer had become familiar with Schenker's approach while still in his teens, when he began studying theory and analysis with Schenker's pupil Hans Weisse. The selection offers insight also into the private seminar of which Salzer was a member, initially convened by Weisse but taken over by Schenker when Weisse left for New York in the fall of 1931. When the seminar was dissolved in 1934, Salzer began private study with Schenker. The *Five Analyses in Sketchform*, which the seminar helped to prepare, also figures in the correspondence, as does Schenker's progress on *Free Composition* and Salzer's work on his first book, *The Meaning and Essence of Western Polyphony*.[3] He went on to produce influential publications, including two books, and to co-edit a major periodical[4] and spearhead the spread of Schenkerian thought in the United States and beyond.

Salzer was one of the first theorists to extend the scope of Schenkerian analysis back to music of the Middle Ages and Renaissance and forward to twentieth-century works.[5] His interest in such repertory dates back to his student years; letters show that Schenker supported his independent work in the field of early music, and even ventured into modern times by recommending a Bartók recording. The correspondence gives proof of the personal interest Schenker took in Salzer's career and traces the warm and mutually respectful friendship that developed between teacher and pupil.

HEDI SIEGEL

---

[1] Felix Salzer, "Die Sonatenform bei Franz Schubert," *Studien zur Musikwissenschaft* 15 (1928): 86–125.

[2] The extant correspondence between the two men consists of twenty-seven items from Schenker to Salzer (1930–34) and five from Salzer to Schenker (1932, 1934); see Hedi Siegel, "Schenker's Letters to Felix Salzer: A Nod to the Future," in *Essays from the Fourth International Schenker Symposium*, vol. 2, ed. L. Poundie Burstein, Lynne Rogers, and Karen M. Bottge (Hildesheim: Georg Olms, 2013), 73–83.

[3] *Sinn und Wesen der abendländischen Mehrstimmigkeit* (Vienna: Saturn Verlag, 1935). The translation of the title of Salzer's book is as given in John Koslovsky's detailed study of the work, "*Primäre Klangformen, Linearität, oder Auskomponierung?*: The Analysis of Medieval Polyphony and the Critique of Musicology in the Early Work of Felix Salzer," *Journal of Schenkerian Studies* 4 (2010): 187–206. See also Koslovsky, "From *Sinn und Wesen* to *Structural Hearing*: The Development of Felix Salzer's Ideas in Interwar Vienna and Their Transmission in Post-War United States" (PhD diss., Eastman School of Music, 2009), 158–302.

[4] *Structural Hearing: Tonal Coherence in Music* (New York: Charles Boni, 1952; repr. New York: Dover, 1962 and 1982); (with Carl Schachter), *Counterpoint in Composition: The Study of Voice Leading* (New York: McGraw-Hill, 1969; repr. New York: Columbia University Press, 1989); *The Music Forum*, ed. William J. Mitchell, Felix Salzer, and Carl Schachter, 6 vols. (New York: Columbia University Press, 1967–87).

[5] See Carl Schachter, "Felix Salzer (1904–1986)," in *Schenker-Traditionen: Eine Wiener Schule der Musiktheorie und ihre internationale Verbreitung / A Viennese School of Music Theory and Its International Dissemination*, ed. Martin Eybl and Evelyn Fink-Mennel (Vienna: Böhlau, 2006), 105–11.

Schenker to Salzer (letter), May 26, 1930
FS 40/1, [2]

Dear Dr. Salzer,

Many thanks for your "offprint."[1] Let me repeat what I said to Dr. Weisse:[2] You took the best path, namely the one that leads to music as an art and not as a "science"; indeed, I would not have expected otherwise. I wonder, do you have any idea of the difficulties that await you: a future of educating musicians and music lovers who are neither artists nor scholars?

Even so, they will all have to come to us, in their hunger for truth.

    Best wishes to you and your dear wife,
    Yours,
        H. Schenker

[1] Salzer had sent Schenker an offprint of his article "Über die Bedeutung der Ornamente in Philipp Emanuel Bachs Klavierwerken," *Zeitschrift für Musikwissenschaft* 12, no. 7 (April 1930): 398–418; Eng. transl. Mark Stevens as "The Significance of the Ornaments in Carl Philipp Emanuel Bach's Keyboard Works," *Theory and Practice* 11 (1986): 15–42.

[2] At this time, Salzer was still a pupil of Hans Weisse, with whom he had been studying since the 1920s.

Schenker to Salzer (letter), April 19, 1932
FS 40/1, [8]

My dear Dr. Salzer,

Yesterday, a very detailed letter arrived from dear Hans Weisse[1] regarding his efforts on behalf of the *Urlinie-Tafeln* at the Mannes School; they are to be issued as "Publications of the M. School."[2] Mr. Mannes would also like my assurance for the next installment.[3]

Enclosed with the letter was the interview;[4] may I ask you on Friday[5] to tell me what it says. I rather like "Ear-line."[6]

With best regards to you and your dear wife,
Yours,
H. Schenker

[1] Weisse's letter, which is not known to survive, had been sent from New York, where Weisse (who had left Vienna on September 17, 1931) was teaching at the David Mannes Music School.

[2] The publication appeared in the summer of 1932 as *Fünf Urlinie-Tafeln / Five Analyses in Sketchform* with the imprint "Published by the David Mannes Music School, New York." The analyses were prepared in association with Schenker's seminar.

[3] Schenker clearly intended to prepare further sets of analyses with the seminar. An account of the work of the seminar, including a facsimile of Schenker's list of the works to be studied, is given in Salzer's introduction to the reprint *Five Graphic Music Analyses* (New York: Dover, 1969), 17–21. The planned second set never came to fruition; on August 2, 1934, Schenker wrote to Jonas about his disappointment at being unable to complete it with the seminar.

[4] A one-page clipping of a column headed "Music" that appeared in *Arts Weekly*, March 26, 1932, 51. It was written by the music critic Irving Kolodin and was based on a conversation with Weisse. The clipping survives in Schenker's scrapbook; a German translation (translator unidentified) is preserved with it. A detailed discussion of the interview is given in David Carson Berry, "Hans Weisse and the Dawn of American Schenkerism," *Journal of Musicology* 20, no. 1 (Winter 2003): 136–42.

[5] Schenker saw Salzer every Friday, the day the seminar met in Schenker's apartment.

[6] In his column, Kolodin uses "Ear-line" as a rendering of "Urlinie." Berry (p. 137, fn. 79) suggests that Kolodin, being unfamiliar with Schenker's term, may have thought Weisse was saying "Ohr-Linie" when he was in fact saying "Urlinie."

Schenker to Salzer (letter), [June 11, 1932]
FS 40/1, [9]

My dear Dr. Salzer,

Both of us thank you and your dear wife for your friendly wishes for the summer and cordially reciprocate them.

I reiterate my expectation that things will look better in the fall than in the 31/32 season. In any case, as long as I am in good health, I want to continue the work on the volumes,[1] but for sure just based on the plan of the first one, i.e., without sidelong glances at the American "mentality," therefore without including the Mannes School on the title page, as I discussed in the last lesson.[2] I don't doubt that the first volume will win acclaim from the Americans, and so the next volumes will find friends there too, with the content to be kept in line with that of the existing one, for practical and pedagogical reasons.[3]

   So until we see each other again!
    In greatest haste,
     Your
    sender of best wishes to you and your dear wife
     H. Schenker

[1] The "volumes" are the further sets of analyses Schenker planned to issue as a continuation of the *Five Analyses in Sketchform* (1932).

[2] In the diary entry for June 10, 1932, the day before this letter was written, Schenker records what he said to the members of the seminar: "Enlighten the seminarians regarding the Urlinie-Tafeln in order to forestall devaluation of their achievement: I reject things American, all too American!"). Schenker is probably alluding to the title of Friedrich Nietzsche's book *Human, All Too Human* (1878).

[3] This letter was most probably the one referred to by Salzer in his introduction to the reprint *Five Graphic Music Analyses* (New York: Dover, 1969), 21: "Schenker, in a letter to me, explicitly stated his intention to issue publications in similar form containing analyses of some of the works on the seminar's list."

Schenker to Salzer (postcard), July 16, 1932
FS 40/1, [10]

My dear Dr. Salzer,

In a few days you should receive from Waldheim & Eberle four copies of the *Five Analyses in Sketchform*—my inscription must of course wait until Vienna.[1] I ask you to keep one copy for yourself, and to hold the remaining ones for the two ladies and Mr. Willfort[2] (you could notify them, if you wish). The folios are of the noblest beauty,[3] a new *unicum* as a publication, quite apart from the content. To express appreciation of the external appearance and the content every reader must become—a poet.

   Best regards to you and your dear wife from us both,
    Yours,
     H. Schenker

[1] Schenker's diary for July 16, 1932, includes the entry: "To Waldheim (registered letter): imprimatur given to everything. Addresses: New York 800, UE 180 and 20 copies to my close associates." These figures are the apportionment of the print-run

between the Mannes Music School and UE, since the UE publications register for the work records the copies received by UE from the printers as "1932 | July 25, | 180."

[2] The other members of Schenker's seminar: Trude Kral, Greta Kraus, and Manfred H. Willfort.

[3] Schenker recorded in his diary for July 14, 1932: "From Waldheim (letter): report and request for directives: the first proofs of the graphs are picture-perfect!"

Salzer to Schenker (letter), November 14, 1932
OJ 14/1, [1]

Vienna XIII, Maxingstrasse 12

Highly revered Dr. [Schenker],

I just wanted to tell you that I recently heard, in a private venue, a performance of Bach's Sixth Brandenburg Concerto conducted by Carl Bamberger. I found the performance marvelous; it was music-making in the very best sense, so that the work, in its full glory, made an unbelievable impression on me. Bamberger's achievement was extraordinary, and I think that you too, esteemed Doctor, would have been pleased with your former student.

On that evening I had to think of you once again with a grateful heart—you have newly awakened in all of us, through your wonderful theory, the capacity to enter into the creative world of the masters, thereby making it possible for their works to be recreated in a meaningful way, just as Carl Bamberger recently succeeded in doing so beautifully.

Your devoted and grateful
Felix Salzer

Schenker to Salzer (postcard), November 15, [1932]
FS 40/1, [14]

My dear Dr. Salzer,

You gave me real pleasure today with your kind lines! <u>This</u> sets the tone for our task—for the reawakening of the artistic spirit. The tone arose from music: <u>The tone will create music again</u> (to hint at a well-known saying!).[1] I expect you for sure on Friday for the manuscript of the *Egmont* score.[2]

With best greetings,
Yours,
H. Schenker

[1] Schenker is most likely referring to the saying "der Ton macht die Musik" ("it's the tone [of voice] that makes the music"), often rendered as "it's not what you say, but how you say it."

[2] This may be a reference to a photocopy Schenker had borrowed from the Photogram Archive; an incomplete manuscript score—lacking the overture—of

Beethoven's incidental music to Goethe's *Egmont* is listed as No. 365 in Agnes Ziffer, *Katalog des Archivs für Photogramme musikalischer Meisterhandschriften* (Vienna: Prachner, 1967), vol. 1, 61–62.

Diary entry, December 31, 1932

From Salzer (letter): Best wishes and cordial thanks.

Schenker to Salzer (letter), December 31, 1932
FS 40/1, [15]

My dear Dr. Salzer,
 We reciprocate your kind greetings in sending you and your dear wife our sincerest wishes!
 You give me great joy with your joy; in you, as if by a miracle, the spirit *de dato* before 1914 has been saved! The explanation lies in the fact that you will have published your first-born[1] before the onset of a phase marked by the most rampant dissipation—but it is no more than a phase—so I need only add:
 Onward! Your first-born calls, art calls, the next generation calls, mankind calls—best of luck!
 I received a letter from Bamberger telling me about his triumphs. He took his artistry to Russia and back,[2] returning home more victoriously than Napoleon himself.

>Now best wishes to you and your dear wife,
> Until we see each other,
> Yours,
>   H. Schenker

[1] Possibly a reference to Salzer's first book, *Sinn und Wesen der abendländischen Mehrstimmigkeit* (Vienna: Saturn Verlag, 1935), on which work had begun.
[2] Bamberger worked in Russia from 1931 to 1935.

Diary entry, December 30, 1933

From Dr. Salzer (letter): sends best wishes, too, on behalf of his wife, and thanks me for the great troubles I took over the "Fridays."

🎼 **Schenker to Salzer (letter), [December 31, 1933]**
FS 40/1, [19]

My dear Dr. Salzer,
We most cordially reciprocate your friendly wishes for 1934 and send greetings to you and your dear wife! We are still in the fortunate position of being able to wish each other "everything that is good and beautiful"—we already have it!—, but what about those people who still have no inner understanding of such things? (as their wishes show)!

Let me take this opportunity to make a strong recommendation to you, as a collector of recordings:

Col. IX 31, "Hungarian Folk Tunes" for violin and piano, played by Szigeti and Bartók, composed by Béla Bartók.[1] For the first time this is something by Bartók that commands downright – – respect: different from Liszt and Brahms and others, and yet in regard to the line, beautiful, very beautiful!

I am very much looking forward to the Toscanini recording.

        With best regards to both of you from both of us,
        Yours,
        H. Schenker

---

[1] The recording is listed in the *Gramophone Shop Encyclopedia of Recorded Music*, comp. R. D. Darrell (New York: The Gramophone Shop, 1936). It is identified as a twelve-inch 78 rpm record: *Seven Hungarian Folk Songs* by Béla Bartók, arranged for violin and piano by Joseph Szigeti, performed by Szigeti and Bartók, a Columbia recording with the European catalog number C–LX31. (In the catalog number given by Schenker, the Roman numeral LX is written as IX.) The work on the recording is Szigeti's arrangement of seven piano pieces (Nos. 28, 18, 42, 33, 6, 13, and 38) from Bartók's *For Children* (1908–09): Bartók–Szigeti, *Ungarische Volksweisen / Hungarian Folk Tunes* for violin and piano (Vienna: UE, 1927), UE No. 8784. For a comprehensive discussion of this work that draws on the comments Schenker made in his letter, see John Koslovsky, "Tonal Prolongations in Bartók's Hungarian Folktunes for Violin and Piano: A Case Study," *Theory and Practice* 37/38 (2012–13): 139–83.

🎼 **Schenker to Salzer (letter), [January 8, 1934]**
FS 40/1, [20]

My dear Dr. Salzer,
If you and your dear wife could come on Sunday the 14th or 21st to have tea with us with Mozart à la Toscanini on the gramophone, you need only whisper a word in my ear on Friday the 12th—it would be a great pleasure to see you both here.

I finished *Free Composition* yesterday at 11 o'clock, more when we talk.

With kindest greetings from us to both of you,
Yours,
H. Schenker

[PS] Don't forget to bring the essay.

❧ Diary entry, January 14, 1934

5–7:30, Salzer and his wife [...] The Toscanini recording demonstrates the inadequacy of the conductor, of course—only to me.

❧ Handwritten letter from Schenker to Salzer (letter), March 25, 1934
FS 40/1, [21]

My dear Dr. Salzer,

Only to allow my very exhausted body to recover from the strenuous work on what are truly the last pages and examples, I, too, want to—or it would perhaps be more correct to say: I, too, must—take advantage of the "Easter holidays." I am already informing you of this today, to make it easier for you to make Easter plans in time. I will most certainly finish "Form"[1] and thus the entire work this week. Tomay[2] is already in sight!

What arrangements did we make regarding your manuscript?[3] That I am very anxious to see your first attempt at true music-historical writing should not surprise you; that is, I would very much like to read it. Be assured, however, that of course nothing will be done on my part that could hinder you in the pursuit of a superhumanly lofty goal. If you can spare the pages, please give them to me. Should we fix a date for this or do you have some other idea? I promise to read *prestissimo* so I won't cause any delay. Our give-and-take will remain confidential, simply for the sake of discretion, which has to be part of such mysterious things.

I received a very long letter yesterday from dear Hans [Weisse]. New compositions are also on their way. You will be astonished to hear how Dr. Kalmus has tried to draw dear Hans, too, into the business of the English edition of volume 1;[4] the producer "of the song and dance" was none other than Kalmus, who acted oh so innocent when he was with me... The nephew doesn't fall far from the uncle (Hertzka), etc.[5]

I wish you and your esteemed wife a happy holiday, in both our names.

Yours,
H. Schenker

---

[1] "Form," Part 3, chapter 5, of *Free Composition* (1935).
[2] Georg Tomay: autographer/calligrapher of Schenker's late publications.
[3] i.e. the manuscript of Salzer's first book.
[4] *Theory of Harmony* (1906).

[5] Schenker is parodying the proverb "Der Apfel fällt nicht weit vom Stamm" or "Der Apfel fällt nicht weit vom Baum" ("The apple doesn't fall far from the tree"). Kalmus was Hertzka's nephew; he was the son of Erwine Fuchs (wife of Jacques Kalmus), the (step?)-sister of Hertzka's wife Jella (Fuchs).

❦ Schenker to Salzer (letter), June 6, 1934

FS 40/1, [22]

My dear Dr. Salzer,

With Mr. Willfort and Miss Kraus I have had experiences—by this I definitely do not mean their inability to pay, but many other things—which I have encountered for the first time, however I have no desire, no intention, to continue.[1] The association with you, though, has been a very welcome artistic-personal one; I am therefore delighted to make myself available to you, for purposes which for this or that reason might better suit you personally (of course, at the same rates as before). Don't let me frighten you away and do take advantage of my offer, provided you have the time and the desire, and no other obstacles are posed by the Academy, etc.[2]

If you let me know of your decision by September 9–15 at the latest, that will suffice.

With best greetings,
Yours,
H. Schenker

[1] Writing to Oswald Jonas on August 2, 1934, Schenker expressed his dissatisfaction with Willfort and Kraus: "I had much aggravation with them (not with Dr. Salzer)."

[2] Salzer was studying conducting with Oswald Kabasta (1896–1946), principal conductor of the Vienna Symphony Orchestra, at the Vienna Academy; he received his diploma in 1935.

❦ Schenker to Salzer (letter), June 11, 1934

FS 40/1, [23]

My dear Dr. Salzer,

Let us hope the Terror-brothers will let us pass safely; in any case we want to stay prepared for a departure on the 15th, in order to avoid Saturday, Sunday, etc.[1] This time we are too tired to wait around in Vienna longer than necessary.

Furtwängler was here yesterday evening; many nice things came up (not everything can be set to paper); he also broached the prospect of his visit in summer; he does his own driving and wants to come by car on some occasion to Bad Gastein.

He praised Dr. Jonas as a person and artist so warmly, ardently, that it was touching to hear these words of recognition.[2]

The rest to follow when we talk. I do hope to see you, if not now then in the fall. In any case, best wishes for the summer to you and your esteemed wife from both of us.

  Yours,
   H. Schenker

---

[1] The Schenkers traveled without inconvenience by train to Böckstein on June 15 at the beginning of their summer vacation.

[2] The diary entry for June 10, 1934, records: "Furtwängler arrives at 9:30 [p.m.], stays until 11; conversation about Wagner, Strauss, about his job, political matters; of all my pupils, he praises Jonas the most, wants to write 'in general terms' about me, to visit me in the summer, and to show me compositions."

Schenker to Salzer (picture postcard), [June 18, 1934]
FS 40/1, [24]

My dear Dr. Salzer,

The first letter I found waiting for me here was from our dear Hans Weisse; it put me in good spirits which I gladly pass on to you: he is staying at the Atlantic Ocean in <u>Tenants Harbor, Maine</u>; he owns a car which both of them can drive! Perhaps even the little ones can also do it?

Best wishes to you and your dear wife from us both,

  Yours,
   H. Schenker

Salzer to Schenker (letter), July 16, 1934
OJ 14/1, [2]

Highly revered Dr. [Schenker],

Eight days after your departure from Vienna I received a call from Dr. [Fritz] Ungar (of Saturn Verlag) requesting me to visit him to discuss the publication of my work. So I went to see him a few days later and after somewhat lengthy negotiations signed a contract with Saturn Verlag at the end of last week. All of this, as you can understand, now actually happened much faster than I had imagined. But the work had in fact been completed, and the reason I had not taken care of its publication long before now lay in a fear of this final and decisive step. So during the summer I will carefully go over the work again and send it to the publisher in installments. The work, with the title "<u>The Meaning and Essence of Western Polyphony</u>," should appear in mid-October. I am already more than eager to hear your opinion of it. I owe everything to your inspired theory, of which I may truly consider myself a faithful disciple.

Besides, I must tell you and your wife that my wife and I, on mature consideration, have in complete mutual agreement decided to end our marriage.

We will be living apart from now on; the legal divorce can take place only after one year. At the end of next week I will be moving to my new apartment: [Vienna] VI, Laimgrubengasse 4. I will be leaving for Grundlsee in the last week of July, most probably for two weeks. I am already very tired and quite worn out and am looking forward to leaving Vienna.

>Wishing you and your wife a really good vacation, I remain, with
>best regards,
>Your grateful and faithful
>Felix Salzer

❧ Schenker to Salzer (letter), July 18, 1934
FS 40/1, [25]

>Böckstein

My dear Dr. Salzer,

By return post I congratulate you on the signing of the contract, so, now it's right! Only one other thing: spend another 500 shillings or more to make the engraving larger and clearer than you find it in Jonas's book. Your examples are for the reader more difficult to approach (motets!), much more inaccessible, than those of Jonas, which are taken from generally known works. Jonas's book should have long been in your hands.[1] An extraordinarily adept book, capable unto the last fiber, in each insight surprising, intelligent, and the beautiful polemics: he just slightly curls his lip and right away the opponent is dispatched. We may all be proud of Jonas's achievement, also something which extends to the "practicality" of my theory, even if, for natural reasons, it must decline to assign every student to a "genius"-regiment. A book like that of Jonas is simply unimaginable as a product of the other theories, although it only aspires to be an echo.

Your experience on the book prepares you to understand my experiences on *Free Composition*: the three-year labor has thoroughly exhausted me; how good it is that I am already on vacation.

You too will achieve a vacation, so I wish you the best for summer!

>With the warmest greetings from us both,
>Yours,
>H. Schenker

---

[1] Oswald Jonas, *Das Wesen des musikalischen Kunstwerks: Eine Einführung in die Lehre Heinrich Schenkers*, also published by Saturn Verlag, released on July 3, 1934. Salzer's name appears on the list of prepublication subscribers Jonas sent to Schenker in his letter of November 10, 1932. Salzer had spoken of this during his visit to Schenker on September 16, 1932; Schenker noted in his diary that Salzer told him he had "ordered thirty copies from Jonas!!"

26
Letters from America: Hans Weisse

Of all Schenker's pupils and disciples, none was as important for the dissemination of his teachings as Hans Weisse. Weisse seems to be at the forefront of every initiative to promote his teacher's work, whether as a private tutor, a public lecturer, or an ambassador of music theory. It was Weisse who created a little seminar in analysis at his home in the late 1920s, which Schenker himself was later to take over. He introduced American musicians to Schenker's approach to musical structure and gave the first public lectures in Schenkerian theory to the German and Austrian music-pedagogical establishment in the winter of 1930–31. His projected *Die Tonkunst*, a monthly periodical dedicated to Schenkerian concepts but authored mainly by Schenker's pupils, never got off the ground; nonetheless it provided the model for *Der Dreiklang* of 1937–38, edited by Oswald Jonas and Felix Salzer, a precursor of the *Music Forum*. And, famously, he was offered and accepted a teaching post at the David Mannes School of Music in New York (and, later, at Columbia University), and so planted the seeds of Schenkerism in America.

The correspondence shows that Weisse had a facility for engaging with people, something which his teacher could only have envied. He was on friendly terms with Wilhelm Furtwängler, and sometimes escorted the conductor to the theorist's apartment. He had enormous success in raising money and was able to keep Schenker from relying entirely on the patronage of Anthony van Hoboken in later years: it was as a result of Weisse's intercession that Furtwängler offered 3,000 marks toward the costs of printing the "Eroica" Symphony analysis, i.e. *Masterwork 3*; and this was soon followed by a second sizeable donation, from the husband of one of Weisse's piano pupils. He made every effort to ensure that the early success of Schenkerian theory in America brought some financial reward to its originator; and, as late as 1935, he successfully implemented a scheme whereby many of his American pupils contributed to a kind of pension fund for Schenker's widow.

The ease with which Weisse made friends is reflected in a number of his earlier letters to Schenker. In a letter of September 13, 1913, two years before being called up for military service, we read of a street-corner conversation with the baritone Franz Steiner (1876–1954) in the resort of Bad Ischl, from whom he learned that Richard Strauss had expressed an interest in Schenker's writings and in meeting the man himself. His thesis supervisor at the University of Vienna, Guido Adler, must also have recognized Weisse's interpersonal skills when he suggested the possibility of teaching at a school in India established by the Nobel prizewinning philosopher Rabindranath Tagore—this in spite of Weisse's lack of training in English at the time (letter of July 20, 1921). Most importantly, he struck up a friendship with the American cellist Gerald F. Warburg in 1925, which eventually led to his appointment at Mannes in 1931 and, several years later, to Oswald Jonas's emigration to the USA. It was Weisse, moreover, who established the dispassionate, polemics-free tone of Schenkerian pedagogy in America; although his veneration of Schenker—his "dear, revered Master" and "spiritual father"—hardly wavered, he insisted that the teaching of Schenkerian concepts remain grounded in objective listening, never on blind faith in the canon of primary Schenkerian literature.[1]

More than 200 items of correspondence from Weisse to Schenker survive; to date, none of the letters sent by Schenker has turned up, and only a tiny handful exist in draft form. As Weisse and Schenker lived in the same city until 1931, most of their intellectual exchanges were made face-to-face. Many of the numerous postcards dating from before his departure to America are concerned with such matters as arranging when or where to meet, and the supply of brief factual information that would have saved Weisse a trip to Schenker's apartment.

As this selection of a dozen late letters indicates, Weisse's veneration of his teacher did not prevent him from expressing criticism of many in his circle: Otto Vrieslander above all, but also Hoboken and Jonas, and Moriz Violin to a lesser extent. They also reveal a distancing in the relationship between pupil and master: as Weisse gains experience and confidence as a classroom teacher, so he becomes more sharply critical of the uncompromising nature of Schenker's writings. His attack upon *Free Composition* as a weakly formulated expression of the final theory—reiterated in more than one letter of 1935 to Schenker's widow—may have been tactless, but it is characteristic of the way he understood his position at the forefront of second-generation Schenkerism.

WILLIAM DRABKIN

---

[1] For a detailed account of Weisse's teaching plans in America, see especially David Carson Berry, "Hans Weisse and the Dawn of American Schenkerism," *Journal of Musicology* 20, no. 1 (2003): 104–56.

❧ Weisse to Schenker (letter), October 15, 1931
OJ 15/16, [82] (Plate 6)

New York,
170 East 79th Street
c/o Mrs. Freeman

Dear, revered Master,

I am now so well settled in that I believe I may be allowed to report to you without my judgments going too far astray. Moreover, I must report first of all about my work and my working environment; and here I believe I am able to say that things could not have gone better. The spirit that has been instilled in the teaching staff by the two directors of the school, Mr. and Mrs. Mannes,[1] was the best preparation for that which I had to offer them.

Last week, before the school was in session, a gathering was arranged in my honor, and I gave my debut with a presentation of twenty-five to thirty minutes' duration about the relationship of a theory teacher to the other teachers in a music school—in English. The effect, apart from the personal success, was that ten teachers applied to work with me, and to get together once a week in order to learn the new concepts. Further: the second theory teacher, a man about fifteen years older than myself, receives regular tuition from me so that he can eventually teach everyone who must study theory as a subsidiary subject in the same way and from the same point of view as I do. I myself have two different classes with six pupils in each, a composition class with three pupils, and a further five or six private pupils who study with me for two hours: all in all about twenty-two pupils at present. Their faces all light up, even when I lay the foundation stones of the concepts "counterpoint" and "harmony"; and I am convinced that the news of the introduction of the new theory will spread like a brush fire.

Tomorrow I am meeting Mr. [George] Wedge, the Dean of the Institute of Musical Art, who has already been teaching from your books for a considerable time and who is keenly looking forward to meeting me, in order to find out more.

Everything else actually fits into place: anyone who lives strongly within himself will find that his external surroundings are not so bewildering. In any event, I felt at home from the first day; the only thing that I had to get used to was the street noise.

Everything else, however, I can bear; and above all I take joy from the friendship of Mr. and Mrs. Mannes, who look after me as parents, in whose home a thoroughly European atmosphere reigns, and with whom collaboration is an unalloyed pleasure.

So much for today. About Hamburg[2] you will have learned more than I, for I have not heard a thing. Please write soon.

        To you and your wife, all good wishes from your
           Hans

---

[1] David Mannes (1866–1959): American violinist. Together with his wife Clara (1869–1948), the daughter of the German-American conductor Leopold Damrosch, he founded the David Mannes Music School in 1916; later named the Mannes College of Music, it was to become the leading center of Schenkerian analysis in the United States.

[2] That is, news about the newly inaugurated Schenker Institute in Hamburg, established by Moriz Violin. Weisse gave a lecture there on September 17, 1931, the day before he set sail for America (see chapter 21).

Weisse to Schenker (letter), November 28, 1932
OC 18/32–33

Dear, revered Master,

I intentionally held a bit back from my first report, because I thought I should see how things are unfolding before writing to you. Not much has happened yet, but I should like to express my delight in hearing that now [Joseph] Marx has found his way to you, and I am very curious to learn of the results to which your investigation has led. It is of course ludicrous, when one considers all that you have accomplished in the meantime, but it is only now that people have found that correct yardstick, so that one can imagine that those who today are propounding your *Theory of Harmony* will perhaps be able to read the "Eroica" (i.e. *your* "Eroica"!) in thirty years' time.[1] The prospects do not seem so bad after all.

Regarding the gentleman from Brooklyn,[2] I recall that he attended my lectures last year. You wrote to me that you replied to him, on the advice of [Alfred] Kalmus; what you said is something I would only too gladly like to know, for the following reason:

Here, another pupil of mine (who just began this year) has written to say that he would also like to translate.[3] Many things, especially the later terms like Ursatz, Urlinie and Übergreifstechnik, simply cannot be translated, and the danger arises that, the more people who are involved in translating, the more the interpretations, versions and technical terms could proliferate; this is something which, in my view, would not be good for the clarity of the theory and could have an unfavorable effect upon it. Now, I am the first person to teach your theory in public: would it not be better to arrange through the publisher that all those who appear with translation contracts be required to apply to me, so that we can come to an agreement, through reciprocal study, about the translation of specific terms in your theory, thus being able to secure the unity of the terminology also in the English language? That is something that seems very important for the translation of your writings.

I am most certainly not insisting that the translators must always adopt my expressions and translations; on the contrary I am conscious of having translated much only in a provisional manner. In any event, I would be happy if I could learn something from them—although I don't expect that I will. But the cause would surely be served if, at the very outset, one could face the problem of unity of terminology also for the translation [of your work].

As to Vrieslander, I have in the meantime been in contact with him myself. After the ominous correspondence during the war (concerning the Festschrift planned for you), I had not heard anything more from him. His bitterness, which is palpable in every word that he writes, is only too understandable. He sent me a copy of his songs and Ländler.[4]

How things are going with *Free Composition* is something that I am most keen to learn.

Yesterday I heard the news that [Paul] Khuner died; I have not, however, heard anything from his family. I am truly very sorry for the dear, worthy man that he was. Have you already received the money from him?

It gives me great joy to be able to report to you that your flag has also been hoisted over university territory:[5] I have a class of twenty there. The people are all intensely involved with everything: I mean that they seem quite attracted to it (as far as I can see), which is all the more impressive, given that they have already reached the diploma stage. (My class is a so-called "postgraduate class.")

New York and America have changed radically since last year. The suffering is boundless, wherever one looks and listens, the same as with us.[6] The collapse has affected the length and breadth of the country, and because of the previous state of prosperity the situation is much more brutal than it is with us. The number of pupils attending schools, everything is in a frightful decline—one can hardly compare things with the previous year.

And yet we are still faring very well. Hertha is beginning to acclimatize herself. Getting things done is so much more agreeable and easier. We have a nice German girl, who sees to the house in the morning and looks after the children in the evening. The children themselves are thriving and spend time every day, to their great delight, in the beautiful Central Park, where there are swings and slides, and similar things.

At Mannes, I shall not begin my official lectures until January. One of my courses is to be dedicated entirely to your theory: whether it materializes will, however, depend on the number of subscribers. My contractually agreed number of hours at the Mannes School is not full, but I am occupied approximately seventeen hours per week.

I hope I shall hear again soon from you. To both of you my most cordial greetings, also from Hertha!

    Your

    Hans

---

[1] Nearly thirty years had passed since Schenker's *Theory of Harmony* was first published; Weisse is hoping that, thirty years from now, people will have read and understood Schenker's analysis of the "Eroica" Symphony, recently published as *Masterwork 3*.

[2] Frederick E. Auslander (1910–81): a pupil of Weisse's at the Mannes School; in a letter to Schenker from January 5, 1933, Auslander offers to translate and adapt the *Theory of Harmony* for the English-speaking world. See Wason (2008).

[3] Probably Arthur Waldeck (1899–1965), a keen advocate of Schenker's work, co-author (with Nathan Broder) of "Musical Synthesis as Expounded by Heinrich Schenker," *Musical Mercury* 2 (1935): 56–64. He was one of the early translators of the *Theory of Harmony*.

[4] Weisse was evidently never on good terms with Vrieslander. His unqualified opposition to a "Festschrift," to be put together by Vrieslander in celebration of Schenker's fiftieth birthday, is articulated in a letter to Schenker of February 26, 1918. He was also harsh in his criticism of Vrieslander as a composer, as can be seen in his letters of February 15 and March 30, 1933; in this respect he took opposition to Schenker's adulation of Vrieslander's music, as expressed for instance in "Eine Anzeige und eine Selbstanzeige," *Der Kunstwart* 46 (December 1932): 194–96.

[5] i.e. Columbia University in New York City.

[6] Weisse is referring to his (and Schenker's) homeland, Austria.

Hans and Hertha Weisse to Schenker (two letters), February 15, 1933
OJ 15/16, [88]–[89]

My dear, revered Master,

I must thank you immediately for two letters. In the first, you sent me the announcement and the self-declaration.[1] With regard to Vrieslander, I have now received the songs from him and have written him a twelve-page letter about them.[2] I must confess that I cannot align myself entirely to your opinion of them; as much as I understand your praise, from your standpoint, and although I believe I have recognized the technical assets of his composition, there is nevertheless something very important that is missing, and I do not think that this is a question of "taste"—yet I would like to speak about it with you. I hope that Vrieslander did not take my letter badly; he ought to have gathered, from the comprehensiveness with which I wrote to him, how seriously and in what detail I studied his works.

Mr. Waldeck is coming to see me next Sunday. With regard to Auslander, I believe that he will still need to study for a good while before he can be contracted to prepare a translation of any of your works. I also have some doubts as to whether he is so competent in German that he truly understands what you write. But about all this I shall write to you at some later date in greater detail.

Today I should like merely to transmit to you one piece of news, in which I take great pleasure. From the enclosed announcement you will see that I have begun a series of twelve lectures about you, and I may be permitted to say, with honest pleasure, that they have had the greatest success. I have an audience of a little fewer than ninety, and I have taken them so far as to ensure that they will follow me through thick and thin. After a first introductory lecture, I began the second immediately, with the sketches to hand, with Bach's Prelude in C major. <u>The success, the impression made by the analysis, was astonishing</u>. I explained the sketch in terms of the title of my lectures, "Re-creation," i.e. creating anew. I then played the piece and had recordings of two pianists that demonstrated how unwittingly the world has disregarded those things to which you have verily opened their ears. I am very happy about this fact, all the more so as there are nothing but musicians and teachers in my audience. That all of them have purchased the sketches[3] will also contribute to the dissemination of your theory.

I am now living in a terrible hustle and bustle, and ask your forgiveness for closing this letter so abruptly. I just did not want to remain silent any longer, but will write to you again, in greater detail.

To both of you, our most cordial and affectionate wishes!

  Your
   Hans

Dear, revered Dr. [Schenker],

Whenever I hear Hans speak about your work, either at Columbia University every Monday or at the Mannes School every Wednesday, my heart swells with gratitude and contentment. How restorative, how comforting is the spirit that you have brought to life in these times and, I believe, for all times. Surely no one can lose his hold of this spirit: I see this in the listeners. There reigns an alertness, a solemn peace, and the faces light up with joy and everyone has the need to express thanks afterwards. There are nothing but mature people—musicians, teachers, even concert artists—at the lectures, also at Columbia University. They are all deeply interested and want to make a start with it: not merely because it is new but because it is something interesting. I am delighted that your work has found a footing here, too. Knowing that nothing here has a permanent shape, and that all that is good can eventually gain a place, I love New York.

Our two little ones are also developing well here; they have joy and fun the whole day long. This year they will return to Europe, still as thoroughly German children. At home we speak only German. We employ a Swiss girl, and the children have learned rather more Swiss-German.

I often think with joy of the few occasions that I was invited to your place last year. Although I am not a musician, I am eager to know about your work, because it represents the spirit that should penetrate our whole life. I have even begun to re-study the piano, so that I might in time be able to get nearer to your work.

A part of this letter is also addressed to Lie-Lie, whom I greet most cordially. I hope that she, and you, are in very good health.

   With deep respect,
    Your
     Hertha Weisse

[1] The article in *Der Kunstwart*: this short essay is in effect a review of songs by Vrieslander published by Emil Grunert in Leipzig in the early 1930s.

[2] Vrieslander had mentioned this letter, in passing, in a letter to Schenker dated February 1, 1933: "From Dr. Weisse I received a long letter of a highly idiosyncratic nature concerning my junk; to give an account of it would take up too much time and energy. With all respect for his personality: a strange pious man!"

[3] The *Fünf Urlinie-Tafeln / Five Analyses in Sketchform*: the publication (1932) was overseen by Alfred Kalmus at the New York office of UE. The first Prelude from the *Well-tempered Clavier*, Book 1, is featured in this folder of graphic analyses.

❧ Weisse to Schenker (letter), March 17, 1933
OJ 15/16, [90]

Dear, revered Master,

With the greatest pleasure, I should like at least to inform you again here, in a few words, of the unbelievable success of my lectures, which are concerned only with your work, and thus with the immense success of your work. The people come, even in the worst weather—and that, for Americans, is saying a lot. They bring new people with them, and I am convinced that even more will come next year if I continue the lecture series. I am planning a cycle of ten or twelve lectures for next year, my preferred topic being "The 'Eroica' Symphony in Light of Schenkerian Theory." And so I shall ask you to answer the following question of mine as quickly and precisely as possible. We need the sketches for this. Is it possible to have 150 copies of the sketches from your book[1] printed separately, for this specific purpose? And what should the price be? I have a feeling that it should be very cheap to reproduce them, so long as the original plates still exist. We could sell them here for 75 cents or $1 each. I would advise you that we do this on our own, so that the net proceeds, however small they may be, immediately fall to you alone. Could you not in fact contemplate the possibility of doing this with other sketches from *Der Tonwille* and *The Masterwork in Music*?

In my seminar on criticism at [Columbia] University, my fourteen pupils, with whom I spent six hours working through the C minor fugue with reference to your sketch,[2] recently practised their criticism with reference to the way in which the work is played by Harold Samuel, who is regarded here as the "best performer of Bach."[3] I used a record player, and the result was: devastating! I play the role of a true agitator, and the record player is a wonderful aid: after people have learned to hear a piece as you understand it—and that is no longer so very difficult—and afterwards one plays it on the equipment, the result is usually: a success that makes everyone laugh! It is even my intention, therefore, to use this technique to make the celebrated piano virtuosos almost impossible [to take seriously]. Word will get around, and in the end they too (the celebrated piano virtuosos) will also come to these lectures.

Whether I shall have to arrange these lectures privately is, at present, an unresolved question. For Mr. and Mrs. Mannes, under the pressure of the financial situation, have offered me a poorer contract for next season, exactly $1,000 less. Now I do understand their situation and will accept their contract—I have no other choice in these times—but I am not inclined to prepare twelve lectures for a fee of $200. Here, it is easy to arrange lectures for a private circle, and I am considering this as a possibility.

The most important thing I am asking about is thus: to determine precisely whether, and at what price, 150 copies of the "Eroica" sketches could be produced. With regard to other sketches, I ask you to take these also into account and to name the possible sums of money involved. On the material side of things, I imagine that we could work out the costs of reproduction together, so long as they are not great, so that the net gain would come to you alone, and immediately after the sketches have been sold.

In my last lecture, I wrote out the sketch of the exposition of the Haydn sonata (No. 49 in the collected edition) on three large sheets, in different colors, and next Monday (that is already the seventh lecture) I will do the development section with reference to your sketch.[4]

The general situation here is very critical. Yet things appear to be turning toward the better. What can one, after all, foretell in these times? I am wondering whether, given the present conditions, there is any point at all in coming to Europe, as I had actually intended.

In your *Theory of Harmony*, so much seems to me to require such thorough revision that I ask myself: how can Vrieslander undertake this? The concept of scale-step belongs above all to the middleground and background. The scale-steps in the foreground (in fact, you yourself usually indicate these, in parentheses) are only illusory scale-steps. Your *Theory of Harmony*, however, makes no distinction whatever in this regard.⁵ I would almost say that your *Theory of Harmony* is no longer yours. And precisely now, to invoke this very book for use in schools! It's a real tragedy. Only those in the know will be able to recognize, with a special emotion, the passages in *Theory of Harmony* in which the seeds of your entire theory took root.

All of us send you our most cordial greetings, and hope that you are both well.

   Your
    Hans

---

¹ *Masterwork 3*, which is in effect a monograph on the "Eroica" Symphony.

² The graph of the C minor fugue in Bach's *Well-tempered Clavier*, Book 1; Schenker's analysis of this piece forms the major part of the essay "The Organic Nature of Fugue" in *Masterwork 2*, 31–54 (Ger., 55–95).

³ Harold Samuel (1879–1937): English pianist, who was among the first soloists to make the keyboard works of Bach—in their original form, not arrangements—a major part of his concert repertory. From the mid-1920s he toured the USA regularly, with Bach dominating the programs; this may be the reason for his reputation in America as the "best Bach player."

⁴ The development section of Haydn's Sonata in E♭, Hob. XVI:49, first movement, appears in the *Five Analyses in Sketchform* of 1932. The graph of the exposition was evidently Weisse's own.

⁵ This is not quite true: in his analysis of the opening ritornello of the aria "Buss' und Reu'" in F♯ minor from the *St. Matthew Passion*, Ex. 119 (153 in the original Ger. edn.), Schenker made an important distinction between the C♯ major chords in measures 10 and 11, assigning the notion of scale-step only to the second of these because of its function in the perfect cadence.

❧ Weisse to Schenker (letter), March 30, 1933
OJ 15/16, [91]

My dear, revered Master,

To my deep dismay I have heard (from another source) that Vrieslander, from whom I have in the meantime received a letter that I find more than disappointing, has behaved like a schoolboy in spite of his fifty-three years (which he waves at me in his defense) and, when he feels attacked, cannot think of anything cleverer than to cry: "Please, Teacher, Weisse said … ."

My observation, that your favorable judgment of his works may be explained by your considering the works of your pupils from a teacher's point of view and being inclined to pronounce them good, is something that I regard as appropriate and find neither regrettable for nor damaging to you.

Having been transmitted by him, you must have, admittedly, found this observation irritating, and one that put me in an unfavorable light; and I believe that it was Vrieslander's intention to shake your faith in me and my adherence to the cause, and I therefore regard his behavior as more than indiscreet: I regard it as almost dishonest.

In order, however, to clear up the matter between ourselves, I should like merely to remind you of one thing. When you wrote me a letter of recommendation for America,[1] you referred to me in it as a "Viennese master." And I returned your letter with the request not to misuse a word that has a special meaning when it comes from you. The purity of the concept of "master," in your unique conception of it, along with "the cause," meant more to me than any personal advantage. I believe that I convinced you of this. I recognized and treasured, from your original action, your goodness and friendship, and your obedience to your feelings, but it was also clear to me that you had gone too far. And this personal experience had certainly affected me in what I had to say to Vrieslander. I admit that, however much you might perhaps do so, I would never allow you to refer to any of my works in the way in which you have proclaimed Vrieslander's songs.[2] In my opinion, such an expression coming from you damages the world of ideas that you inhabit more than it can serve the one to whom it applies. You have done this, for sure, in complete conviction; viewed from the outside, however, it is and remains an expression that must appear self-conscious if one is aware of the relationship in which you stand to Vrieslander. What would you wish to make of such an opinion as voiced by Schoenberg about Webern? In addition, I remain thoroughly convinced that Vrieslander's songs, though you refer to positive traits and suchlike in them, have merely the value of imitations, not of original work; and so I find that such a far-reaching statement from you would already create a certain amount of confusion in your circle of adherents, to say nothing about how they will be interpreted by that circle which your work, I am most firmly convinced, is still destined to reach and access.

I blush at the mere thought that you could believe that envy or jealousy could have led me to make such a statement. Nevertheless, I cannot and will not believe that you could let any suspicion of this sort arise <u>in you</u>.

I believe that the entire course of my life and my artistic development demonstrate that I live for nothing else but your world, and for your cause which, by the grace of Heaven, has also become very much my own. Such a statement is to be understood not against you but rather <u>for</u> you, even if it is your opinion that I am, moreoever, entirely wrong in my judgment of Vrieslander. The greatness of your work resides in the notion that your judgment, where it concerns the great composers, is irrefutable; I am thus all the more troubled by a statement by you to the effect that "these songs will soon be on the lips of every singer," which will simply be contradicted by the world of facts. If the unfortunate situation should arise whereby Vrieslander succeeds in arousing suspicion in you against me, then these few lines are intended neither more nor less than to convince you that nothing is more important for me than your work and your accomplishment.

Now a bit more about Vrieslander. My amicable relationship with [Viktor] Hammer acquainted me with a generosity in the exchange of opinions that places objectivity over all things personal. There is nothing that we cannot say to each other, even the strongest, most severe criticism. Criticism that is concerned with the subject is indeed the only sort that is useful in the world. When I wrote to Vrieslander, I cherished the hope that here it might be possible to effect an exchange of viewpoints, one that could unite two musicians from the same school to a common purpose. In conclusion, I need not tell you how lonely I feel among all who call themselves musicians. You have experienced this yourself, and will know that this loneliness is a legacy of my adherence to you. It was no other thought than this that guided me when I began writing Vrieslander a fourteen-page letter. The opinion that I expressed awaited an expression of opinion, in return, that should have been concerned with the object alone; instead of this, I received a reply in which every word was used in order to wound me personally. This intention was so obvious that it had to fail to have any effect. I am only sorry for him, for anyone who has so little <u>faith</u> in an amicable criticism that concerns an objective matter suffers from an intellectual and spiritual calcification, from which nothing genuine can any longer emanate. Anyone who answers active participation with poison, inner openness with small-minded suspicion (as if I were arrogant or conceited), will be unfruitful in the roots of his being. Moreover, I know that my personal opinion of Vrieslander is entirely worthless in your eyes; I spell this out because I want <u>you</u> to know (even if he cannot understand) the grounds that motivated me to discuss his work with such thoroughness.

To my last letter I must still add what I forgot to say: Would it perhaps be possible to consider the reproduction merely of the <u>graphs of the Urlinie</u> of the "Eroica"? The other sketches[3] I could easily arrange to have written on large sheets.

With the most cordial and heartfelt greetings to the two of you, from all of us, I remain, in old and immutable faithfulness,

 Your
  Hans

---

[1] In a letter of April 15, 1931, Weisse had asked Schenker to change the wording "famous Viennese master of music" in a letter of reference to the David Mannes Music School. Schenker evidently obliged: on the same day, he drafted a new letter of reference:

> The musical youth of America can consider themselves fortunate in being able to undertake their studies under the direction of the well-known Viennese musician, Dr. Hans Weisse. Dr. Weisse is, in spite of his youth, a true personality, creatively and pedagogically an artist of the highest rank. His musical works justify his teaching composition most particularly; and as an exponent of my new theory, I can think of no one better.

[2] Schenker did indeed express his admiration for Vrieslander's songs, not only in his article "Eine Anzeige und eine Selbstanzeige," but also in private (see Federhofer (1985), 215–16.

[3] i.e. the forty-nine *Figuren*, which were published on loose sheets. Weisse is asking only for additional reproductions of the four graphs (*Bilder*) which were published as a thirty-five-page booklet.

Weisse to Schenker (letter), March 15, 1934
OJ 15/16, [94]

Dear, revered Master,

It pains me endlessly when I consider that you have heard absolutely nothing from me this year, all the more so because, all appearances to the contrary, I have felt myself tied to you in thought so very much, and so often. Not only have I thought much about you during the unrest and in the face of the political and financial situation—no, I have you to thank, as always, for my best hours; whenever I was granted no more than a deeper insight into the essence of music, I was aware of your worth and your significance. That I, nevertheless, was unable to bring myself to write a letter now seems almost incomprehensible to me, and can only be explained in connection with the deep depression that gripped me after returning to New York City from the country last fall.

I had enjoyed a great success the previous year with my twelve lectures about you and your world of ideas—and of hearing—and when the new academic year began I expected a reaction, in the form of a new audience. The School had undertaken to make it easier for the people and announced that courses would be organized, at especially reasonable prices, that would introduce those who were interested in a deeper and more comprehensive study of your way of hearing music. Not a single person subscribed. This was my first great disappointment, and I admit that the first three winter months were thoroughly ruined for me as a result. I began to hate this land and my surroundings, and felt extremely unhappy. That which brought me back, gradually, into equilibrium was simply the joy in my own work, and the satisfaction that I felt as I rehearsed my Variations and Fugue for two pianos. There followed my new lectures, and an efficient piece of work that I had to get through as a result. The last of the six lectures takes place next Monday; I shall speak about my variations, in the expectation of having them performed there. The idea that motivated me to speak about a piece of my own was the question that constantly arises: How does the knowledge gained from you apply in practice for a composer? In five lectures, I therefore showed how the notion of *semper idem sed non eodem modo*[1] affects the attitude of a composer, and I now want to draw the conclusions, as I have raised the knowledge gained to the level of a credo for a creative musician.

In the same post, I am sending you a copy of my Violin Sonata, which has finally reached its conclusion in the form of a private publication after a great deal of trouble and in spite of very high costs, which I had to pay for from my own pocket. Here, too, the indolence of the circle of people who were involved dealt me a hefty blow. I have sold at the school, which announced the publication in 250 printed cards, a single(!!) copy to date. On top of all this, the reduction in my income from the Mannes School, brought about by the general financial situation, has placed me in circumstances that I had never before experienced: it was not possible to put away a sufficient amount of money to sustain me during the following summer, so that I could dedicate myself to my work. I see myself obliged to appeal to the conscience of other people and to ask for money. As little as I perceive this as a humiliation, which it in fact is, it is sufficient to put one in a bitter frame of mind. And I hope that you will forgive my reluctance to write, now that you know the reasons.

From what I have heard, you have received the article about you by the young American composer Israel Citkowitz.[2] He is now working with me. And I count it as the major success of this year that your theory has broken through the front of the radical-modern American youth. It is a beginning that promises much. At any rate, however, I believe that it is more important to win over the youth than to convince the older generations, who are so wrapped up in their own prejudices that they simply are unwilling and unable to understand.

My lectures at Columbia University, into which I "smuggle" your theory, so to speak, are things I regard as very important. Every year I make a hundred more people prick up their ears—for the most part with my lectures, of course—and I bury their false sense of security. And however unsatisfactory that may often appear to be, I do not give up the hope that the effect will, in the long run, not be lost.

Susi[3] had the measles. The children were not at all well this winter, but now they are better.

With deep regret, I must accept the decision once again to abandon a trip to Europe. Apart from the political uncertainty, my finances can on no account permit me to undertake such a costly trip. I will thus stay in America again this summer and, if it is at all possible, strive to continue my work somewhere at the seaside. I plan the completion of a string quartet, of which I wrote the first half in score last summer; the scoring of a chamber cantata on a text by Hölderlin, of which I have completed a draft; and a work for orchestra.

I now come to the most important point of my letter, and this concerns the abbreviated schools version of your *Theory of Harmony*. Recently I received a message from Associated Music Publishers Inc., a branch of Universal Edition,[4] from which it is clear that Universal Edition is disposed towards the publication of your *Theory of Harmony* in abbreviated form (in English), for school purposes.

The story behind this is not entirely clear to me; and I would gladly know what you make of it and, above all, what you think about an abbreviated schools edition. Moreover, I do not understand why two people should be undertaking the same work at the same time, especially as Vrieslander, as Universal Edition reports, is occupied with this work.

Would it not be simplest for Vrieslander to take care of the work and simply to have it translated here? He has, for certain, placed himself in complete agreement with you about this, and he understands your intentions in the most precise way. It is entirely unclear to me how Universal Edition can assume that I am occupied with such a task, or that I have ever expressed the intention of incorporating parts of *Counterpoint* into the *Theory of Harmony*.

The misunderstanding seems to have arisen from a certain Mr. Cobb,[5] who was briefly a pupil of mine and who has been in touch with Associated Music Publishers without saying anything about this to me, by proposing to you the idea of Americanizing the *Theory of Harmony*. The person concerned is no longer my pupil, and the little that he showed me had so little to do with your work that I would never have allowed or advised him to undertake this task. About his relationship to the publisher, I know absolutely nothing.

Can you even imagine that I would take on this sort of thing on my own, without first having spoken to you personally about it? Kalmus never spoke to me about it directly, and I can only remain speechless about this publication house wheeling-and-dealing, regarding which—if I understand the correspondence that was sent to me yesterday—I am at an utter loss to explain how the honorarium that is accruing to me ever existed, as I have never given this slightest suggestion about a translation on which I was working!! Or, for that matter, on an assignment of any sort.

Can you, perhaps, shed any light on this matter?

All that Kalmus mentioned to me was the abbreviated schools version planned for the Conservatory,[6] and he mentioned at the same time that Universal Edition could not provide the necessary funds for such an edition. This he explained when he visited me, and I was merely struck by the fact that he was so certain that he could not undertake this, at a time when I could gather from the comments in your letters that you were sure that a schools edition would come about.

How things stand with *Free Composition* is a burning question for me, and I hope to hear from you that we will soon have it before our eyes.

On account of the enormous copying costs here, I shall have to make the fair copy of the Variations myself, and I hope that I can send them to you next autumn.

In conclusion, I should like to thank you also for the kind, touching words you sent me on the occasion of the death of my father,[7] which was the last direct sign of life from you to me.

Hertha and I send you and your wife our very best and most cordial greetings and hope that you both enjoy the best of health.

        In old devotion and faith,
        Ever your
        Hans

---

[1] "Always the same, but not in the same way": Schenker's artistic motto, which was placed at the head of most of his publications from the 1921 onward.

[2] Israel Citkowitz (1909–74): American composer, author of "The Role of Heinrich Schenker," *Modern Music* 11 (1933): 18–23.

[3] Susannah, the Weisses' first child.

[4] Associated Music Publishers, described here as a branch of UE, was acquired by the music publishing house of G. Schirmer in 1964.

[5] The name of Cobb is not known to appear elsewhere in the Schenker correspondence.

[6] That is, the Vienna Academy for Music and Performing Arts.

[7] Adolf Weisse (1856–1933): distinguished character actor and theater director in Vienna.

❧ Weisse to Schenker (letter), September 23, 1934
OJ 15/16, [95]

Tenants Harbor [Maine]

Dear, revered Master,

I have, unfortunately, received no reply to the letter I sent you from here this summer. I could only gather from your letter to Lytle,[1] who visited me here, that you stayed in the vicinity of Gastein,[2] and I hope that you and your wife have had a good summer and replenished the necessary reserves of strength and intellect to survive the coming winter.

How much I thirst for the publication of *Free Composition* is something I surely do not have to emphasize: it has now become a necessity, I believe, for every one of the many people who follow your work and want to put it into practice themselves. I imagine that you have been swamped by questions of this sort and are now yourself quite impatient to see them answered by action. Are you already correcting the proofs? Yes, I dare to ask you: What are you planning to do next, after *Free Composition* is published?

The receipt of Jonas's book, which arrived last week, was a cause for celebration, even though I feel that it does not fully deserve the subtitle "Introduction to the Theory."[3] It reproduces too much, instead of introducing things in a preparatory and explanatory way. It does not sufficiently smooth the path of access for the average musician, which I think it was especially intended to do. My feeling is that it has too little inspirational value, which could have documented your creative achievements by enlightening and explaining them. I believe that I shall later be in a better position to explain what I mean. Yet I can hardly imagine that you do not understand precisely what I mean; I am sure that similar thoughts went through your head. It goes without saying that I shall express myself in this way about it to no one but yourself. And, to be sure, Jonas has been successful in a number of respects.

I have an especially happy summer behind me. Seldom have I enjoyed such peace, such isolation in splendid, unspoiled nature, looking out on to the infinite from the immediate vicinity of the sea. The air is as pure and as strong as mountain air. Bathing in the sea is, every time, a new elixir of life. The coast, which is elevated to a Romantic quality by the rocks and fir tree forests, gives the illusion of a mountainous region, and one thus feels that one is enriched by the harmony of several types of landscapes, in a way that cannot be expressed. I shall bring two completed scores back to New York with me: a cycle of five madrigals for six voices, on epigrams and elegies by Goethe; and a new four-movement string quartet.

I was deeply overcome by the news, which reached me by telegraph yesterday, of the death of my mother, from whom I had received a letter two days earlier which spoke of her suffering from inflammation of the gall bladder. I wrote my string quartet in memory of my father, and was so deeply gripped by the conception of death. At the time I was writing it, it seemed to me like a memory; and now I am to understand that it was also a premonition!

I can still hardly comprehend it: and as little as the concept of death means something inimical to me, yet there dawns within me that uncanny feeling that informs everyone when, from the death of both parents, all bridges to the past are severed; and with the expiration of the mother's womb as the beginning of life, the "whence," comes the start of one's "being alone" in the world, as a foreboding of one's own death.

That I should write these lines to you this very day, still under the numbing effect of reality, should come as no surprise to you, whom I have often called my spiritual father. It is to you that I owe my entry into a real world; and it is thanks to you that this moment appears to "have become ingrained" in me.

My children have developed magnificently, and Hertha, too, has found a new home in this wonderful landscape. To be honest, the world here makes it in part more difficult, in part easier, to return to New York. For we rejoice in the time that is granted us to gaze at all this magnificence. Can one even contemplate returning to Europe, under the given circumstances? How glad I would be to see you again, and to talk about so many things which can hardly be expressed clearly in letters!

We shall return to New York at the end of next week, where my address will be the same: 1 West 64th Street.

From the two of us, our love and good wishes to you both!

    Most cordially,
    Ever your
    Hans

---

[1] Victor Vaughn Lytle (1884–1969): American organist and academic, who came to Vienna to learn about Schenker's theories and spent two years studying with Weisse.

[2] Bad Gastein: a resort in the Gastein Valley, about 60 miles south of Salzburg.

[3] Oswald Jonas, *Das Wesen des musikalischen Kunstwerks: Einführung in die Lehre Heinrich Schenkers* (Vienna: Saturn Verlag, 1934). For the second edition of this work (1972), the title and subtitle were reversed.

❦ Weisse to Jeanette Schenker (letter), February 21, 1935
OJ 15/16, [97]

Worthy, revered, dear Lie-Lie!

Your two letters distressed me greatly; from the second of these, in particular, I gathered that the beloved master cannot have been in good health for some years. I can only marvel at the expenditure of all his life's strength, which thus enabled him to bring to a conclusion what, I suppose, is his greatest work. He, who was able to grasp the heroism of the great composers as no one before him, was himself a hero, a great man. I had always understood what it meant for you to live with him and through him. And only now can I gauge what it means for you to live after him, to survive him. May it be granted to you to find the strength to do so, and may the day dawn for you, and for all of us with you, on which he begins to live again in the consciousness of those to whom he spoke, as the man that he was.

It comforts me greatly that you, having been trained in collaboration over a period of many years, and being the person most trustworthy to carry out his intentions, wish to, and will, undertake the correction of *Free Composition* and the music illustrations that belong to it. Do I even need to say that, whenever you need my help, you may be sure to have it? The proofreading of the text, and the reading of the examples against the text, are things that I would be only too glad to take on, if you are not deterred by the great distance between us and can put your faith in the postal service. I am convinced that Jonas will do his best and prove to be very conscientious and trustworthy. But if it would give you greater peace of mind, why should not the three of us—you, Jonas, and I— undertake this together? You can deal with me alone, if you feel that this is necessary.

When you, dearest Frau Lie-Lie, consider what it means to me to have lost in the past two years not only both parents but also my spiritual father, you will then understand that nothing draws me back to Europe, specifically to Vienna. Nevertheless, I feel obliged to stress that I would have come for your sake if it were in any way possible. But I cannot contemplate it because—this must of course be kept entirely between ourselves (I have written to nobody in Vienna about it)— the Mannes School has halved my guaranteed employment, in consequence of which I am compelled to seek further employment elsewhere for next year. If I am unable to find any, then I must seek to win the trust of those concerned by new artistic production. I must, therefore, devote the summer entirely to my own creative work. For two reasons, then, the way to Europe is blocked for me, and I am unable to offer my modest assistance in the form of personal attendance.

If I ask you now for something from the master's possession as a memento, then you will understand what moves me to do so, without my having to justify it at length. What I would most like would be simply a modest article, used by the most beloved and revered man. Things are of course nothing in themselves, but the emotions they arouse in us make them so much more than what they are.

I would most particularly like to know, after you are able see things more clearly for yourself, which of the master's [unpublished analytical] sketches you intend to have published. There will certainly be a great deal of this available, which should not be withheld from all of us who live in the master's world of ideas.

I must of course leave to your own judgment how far you wish to rely on me in such matters.

I think of you often, very often, in affectionate and intimate friendship.

  Your faithful and true
  Hans Weisse

❧ Weisse to Jeanette Schenker (letter), May 26, 1935
OJ 15/16, [98]

Dear, revered Frau Lie-Lie,
 Your letter made me feel very sad, since it confirmed the thoughts that had already occurred to me frequently about your financial situation. Your comment, that there is no publisher who would give you 200 shillings per month, soon awakened in me an idea that I immediately turned into a reality. This letter will communicate the result of it.

My idea was the following: Why should it not be possible, with the assistance of my pupils here, to secure for you, for <u>one year</u> in the first instance, the sum of 2,400 shillings, i.e. 200 shillings per month? As a matter of principle, I approached only those pupils of mine who were thoroughly conscious of the worth of our beloved, irreplaceable master. My thoughts did not deceive me: every one of them followed the example I set, committing themselves in writing to a monthly contribution, and considered the fact of my proposal as a commendation of me. The collection from the twenty-two subscribers resulted in the desired sum of $489, which at the current exchange rate is somewhat higher than 2,400 shillings. Murmurs about possible inflation led me to suggest to my pupils that they come up with four months' payment immediately. Some paid the full amount; some could pay only the first two months initially; but most were able to agree to my request. I now have a sum of $182 set aside, whose value in shillings I have had my bank make out to you in the form of checks and which I am enclosing with this letter. If the sum is somewhat more than four times 200 shillings, that is because one female pupil paid the full amount at once, another paid half the sum indicated. The money that I send you will not, therefore, always be exactly the same. I will, of course, arrange to send you the next two or three months' worth in October, if possible, so that you do not lose too much in the event of a further fall in the value of the dollar. But I have not approached two of my pupils; they have been excused from this round, so that their possible contribution at a later date might restore balance to the full in the event that inflation results in a shortfall.

The collection will cover the period from June 1935 to June 1936. What happens after that is something I cannot say at the present moment. You too will understand that, given the uncertainty of the financial situation here in this country, it would have been a psychological mistake to bind people beyond the duration of one year. And yet I hope that you will have faith in my conviction and goodwill: I will then strive once again to do what is in my power. I am glad thus to have dispatched the business part of this letter. I have of course been a bit ponderous and hope that you do not take that amiss.

Concerning the commentary to C. P. E. Bach's thoroughbass theory,[1] I would be very interested to see it and would like to know whether making a copy of it would give you too much trouble. I spoke recently with a musician by the name of Kirkpatrick, who is planning a translation of the *Essay* into English;[2] and I wondered whether a commentary from the master might not make a particularly desirable appendix to it (in English, of course). The lack of English translations of Schenker's books is already being lamented in wider circles; something will surely have to be done about this. I hope that, when *Free Composition* appears, you will not have forgotten to instruct the publishers to have a copy sent to me. Not only am I burning to see the work at last, but I cannot carry out and realize my plan of writing an account of Schenkerian theory in the English language, for use in <u>schools</u>, until I have seen and studied the definitive theoretical formulation of the basic principles in the original language.

Regarding your kind intention of passing on to me the master's inkwell, I thank you from the bottom of my heart—likewise the sheet of paper you sent me in which I could only sense the play on words "erlauben–erleben" without actually understanding its ultimate meaning. Mrs. Jella Pessel Lobotka will look you up on my behalf and, in the event that the inkwell is not too large, bring it back to New York for me. Please be so good as to entrust it to her.

We have experienced the most frightening things concerning our children. Both underwent operations: Monika on her middle ear, Susannah on a difficult abscess resulting from chicken pox. Moni has not yet recovered; she has been in the hospital (for the second time) for three weeks now, and the worst is now to come: we will be leaving for the country and will have to leave her in the hospital. For how long is something we do not know. Hertha will not be able to collect her from New York until she is completely recovered.

Our summer address remains the same: Tenants Harbor, Maine, USA. We plan to leave on the 29th, so your next communication will reach me there.

Hertha sends her most heartfelt greetings. You know, dearest lady, how <u>very much</u> we think of you and how very much we imagine your loss. Hertha is currently so occupied that, at this moment, she cannot write; but she will certainly write to you later.

Please accept the most cordial greetings from the two of us. I hope to hear from you soon.

      Your faithful
      Dr. Hans Weisse

---

[1] Part 2 of Bach's *Essay on The True Art of Playing Keyboard Instruments*. In the Oswald Jonas Memorial Collection is a manuscript entitled "Generalbasslehre. Prepared by Felix Salzer from a manuscript work by Schenker." One part of Salzer's work is described as a typewritten "commentary on the *Essay*."

[2] Possibly the American harpsichordist and Scarlatti scholar Ralph Kirkpatrick (1911–83), who had recently returned from periods of study in Europe. (An English translation of Bach's *Essay* prepared by Weisse's pupil William J. Mitchell did not appear until 1949.)

❧ Weisse to Jeanette Schenker (letter), July 14, 1935
OJ 15/16, [99]

Dear Frau Lie-Lie,

It is only today that I affirm receipt of your lovely letter of June 9, and thank you cordially for sending *Free Composition*. We had so much more anxiety here concerning Monika's ear (she was operated on twice, and was released from the hospital only yesterday evening, finally—we hope—on the way to complete recovery), that I was unable to do anything.

I have already <u>read</u> through *Free Composition*, but will now only begin to <u>work</u> through it properly. For now, I should like to refrain from making any further comments about the work. Its conception is magnificent, the fullness therein is enormous; and if on first reading there is much that appears unclear or confusing to the reader, or contradictory or questionable in any way, then the problem is more likely to lie with the reader than with the author. Precisely because of this, I would like to keep silent for now. When I have succeeded in working through the material thoroughly, I will send you a precise account of my impressions and a detailed list of mistakes, of which I have already encountered a large number. The only thing that I would add here, apart from noting the awesome impression made by the work as a whole, is that the end of the Foreword is more than a little alienating, in that it gives the illusion that the publication of the book was due entirely to Anthony van Hoboken; and [Paul] Khuner does not get so much as a syllable's worth of thanks. I must admit that this touched me most painfully.

I am very curious to learn what Saturn Verlag has decided with regard to the collection of aphorisms that they were thinking of publishing.[1]

Your idea of leaving the master's scores and books to the [Photogram] Archive seems to me to be right and laudable. For the photograph I give you my heartfelt thanks; I find it very beautiful and I like it better as a portrait than the one that I received from Hoboken immediately after receiving your letter. Your intention, to give each of my pupils who contributed to the collection a copy of it, is touching and will certainly bring the greatest joy to each of them. If you wish to fulfill your intention, I thank you for this in advance and I ask you to send the pictures at such a time that they will arrive at my address in New York (1 West 64th Street) at the beginning of October.

In sending me the photographs of Schenker's death mask and hand, you will give me only the greatest joy.

Regarding my own work, I can, unfortunately, report absolutely nothing at present, other than that my many concerns about my child and my future have occupied me until this moment. How much Hertha has had to suffer is something that you can easily imagine. The child was in the hospital four times in the space of four months! And she has gone through three operations under an anesthetic.

I am not sure whether you are still in Hofgastein, and so I am sending you these lines to your Vienna address instead, in the hope that they will be forwarded to you immediately.

With my most cordial wishes, also from Hertha, and with the assurance of our continued interest in all that concerns you, and with our most amicable thoughts, I remain

Your

Dr. Hans Weisse

---

[1] Some of Schenker's aphorisms were indeed published in Der Dreiklang (1937–38), edited by Oswald Jonas and Felix Salzer and published by Saturn Verlag.

❧ Weisse to Jeanette Schenker, September 18, 1935
OJ 15/16, [100]

Dear Frau Lie-Lie,

The death mask moved me most deeply, and I thank you for sending me the photographs of it. The slight, almost youthful features seemed very strange, and I will not deny that a shiver runs down my spine every time I look at them.

I believe I can definitely say that Dr. Salzer has no knowledge of the initiative taken by me and my pupils. In any event, I have said nothing to him about it.

Your idea of selling the master's surviving papers is something that I can understand; yet I hope that you will not take offense at the observation that I should like to add here. It is a different case if the manuscripts of a deceased composer are sold. They come into the possession of foreign hands as something complete and, where sketch-like ideas are concerned, no longer to be completed. The situation appears different with our beloved master's papers: the material gathered here is entirely <u>usable</u>, and the question arises as to whether intellectual property may be sold. After serious reflection, it seemed to me more purposeful to sell his library, but to add the unpublished music illustrations and writings to the [Photogram] Archive as a single collection, not to be dispersed.[1]

You wrote, among other things, in your last letter: "It would be a pity if the surviving papers were assessed not by their value but by my needs." Well, it is unfortunately only too true that intellectual treasures cannot, in this world, be harmoniously reckoned in monetary terms. It is difficult enough to assign a value to intellect by intellectual means, but impossible to put a monetary value on them. Yet these are surely thoughts that have already occurred to you and I probably do not need to fear that you will regard my remarks as a tiresome meddling into things that are of no concern to me.

During the summer I have immersed myself thoroughly in *Free Composition*, and I have studied it as thoroughly as I could, given the limited musical material here. I shall of course work once again through all the examples that I did not have to hand here. Especially with regard to the music examples, there are unfortunately numerous disturbing mistakes in the book, which will cause many readers to rack their brains when working through it. I shall send you a detailed list of mistakes later. In one case the supplementary volume [of music examples] is missing the example that is referred to in the text.

Whenever I take the book in my hands, two things pain me most deeply in my soul. One of these is the formulation of thanks to Hoboken, which is something you already know about; and its verbal formulation marks it out as an alien element in the book, which it in fact is.[2] The expressions "idealistic" and "for all time" indeed betray the fact that the words do not come from the pen of an author who would have compromised the awareness of his own importance in the formulation of an expression of gratitude by pairing words of thanks with expressions of self-esteem.

This brings me now to the subtitle of the book, "the first textbook about music": It is simply and <u>utterly inconceivable</u> to me that Schenker could ever have come up with this. You will surely agree with me that anyone who catches sight of it will lay the emphasis of its meaning on the word "first": in which case one would have to rule out Schenker's *Theory of Harmony* and *Counterpoint*, and C. P. E. Bach's *Essay* (which, indeed, also have to do with music) as belonging to the category of textbook. Apart from the fact that the [sub]title does not correspond to the truth, it is so damaging, which is something that the truth should never be permitted to be in order to be able to assert itself. What was probably intended was that the autocratic operation of music, as an art form, had never before been explained in a written work in this way: in this case, the title is most unfortunate and disastrous, because of its ambiguity. "A textbook of music" or "music's first textbook" (for sure that would not be proper German) would already have allowed less uncertainty to arise. But now:

Any book, if it is to qualify as a "textbook," must be understood as presenting its material methodically in such a way that the user, having thought through and grasped its contents thoroughly, can use the material in its entirety as <u>the author</u> understood and conceived it. It follows that all so-called harmony textbooks are true textbooks; it is just that *Free Composition* is <u>not one</u>. For even the most understanding readers of *Free Composition* will be at a loss to know what to do when it comes to the <u>explanation</u> of a new work of music, in spite of the innumerable terms introduced in *Free Composition*, knowledge of which will not be nearly enough to enable them to be put it into practice. Explaining music is a creative process, and no textbook can fathom the mysteries of creativity. For this reason, *Free Composition* is neither the first textbook of music, nor a textbook at all. You will ask: Okay, then what is it? To which I answer, neither more nor less than "Free Composition," which did not need a subtitle: a subtitle by which the author exposes himself, in the eyes of ignoramuses, to the suspicion of a conceitedness bordering on megalomania; by which the world of facts is distorted; and by which the entire work hinges on a single point, the defense of which even the most convinced Schenkerian will find impossible.

This is not, as one could easily assume, merely word-collection. It is very penetrating and far-reaching, for precisely because *Free Composition* announces itself as a textbook, which is something it can never be, it offers those who will criticize it the easiest points from which it can be attacked. That the master can have made such a disastrous mistake in his most treasured work is something that I regard as one of the most regrettable things.

With this last sentence I have already indicated to you that I have a high regard for *Free Composition*, though I must, for the sake of the truth, add this qualifying remark: that one is more likely to be intuitively conscious of the greatness of the work than to be able to grasp that greatness in every sentence and thought process. This may, in large part, be explained by the fact that language cannot adequately account for listening processes. The supplementary volume, with its aids that appeal to the eye and the ear, is a much more convincing document than the text itself. As a literary accomplishment, *Free Composition* is the weakest of all of Schenker's works; as an auditory accomplishment it is his greatest. Almost none of the many concepts is actually <u>defined</u>; they are merely introduced and illustrated; and so it comes about that, in spite of the subdivision into paragraphs, the whole makes an imprecise impression, and the whole, as well as the individual parts, seem forever to be knocking the reader off course. Contradictions in the use of technical terms contribute to this lack of clarity. I doubt that the book can, <u>on its own</u>, convert intelligent people to adherents of the theory.

Everything that I am merely referring to here I will, first of all, attempt to present, in a thoroughly comprehensive manner, in the form of objective criticism. A commentary is certainly indispensable, but this should surely not follow the style and argument of Jonas's book. Anyone who seeks to make this book his own will, like myself, not escape being tossed and turned about between the two opposing emotional poles of "praising it to the sky" and "feeling saddened to the point of death" ... It is perhaps an immutable law of fate that the whole truth will be revealed to no mortal being, and the Veil of Maya[3] is our inescapable destiny.

What I have to say in the way of "free sentences about Schenker's *Free Composition*" will probably be directed in the first instance only to my pupils and those most interested in the matter, and is not intended for publication. I intend thereby no more than to retain answers that will spur people on to read and think through. It is only as a result of a seminar that I intend to give on *Free Composition*[4] that the guidelines for a commentary will become clearer.

Monika is now fully recovered, and we have been living in peace for the last month and a half. From October 1 we are in New York (1 West 64th Street). The number of photographs for my pupils amounts to twenty-one.[5]

With most cordial greetings from the two of us,

    Yours faithfully,
    Dr. Hans Weisse

---

[1] Schenker's books on music, and separately his scores and sheet music, were sold c. 1936 by an antiquarian dealer: see *Musik und Theater, enthaltend die Bibliothek des Herrn Dr. Heinrich Schenker, Wien* (Vienna: Heinrich Hinterberger). Of the remaining materials, including his diaries, correspondence, analyses, and sketches, unpublished works, some scores, copies of his own music, photographs, and other items, a portion was purchased from Jeanette by Felix Salzer in 1936, and the remainder passed for safe keeping by her to Ernst Oster and Erwin Ratz before she was deported to Theresienstadt. The first two of these were eventually deposited at the New York Public Library, as part of the Felix Salzer Papers and as the Oster Collection, and the Ratz materials went to the University of California at Riverside as the Oswald Jonas Memorial Collection.

[2] "That a work as idealistic as this could have made its way into the world at all, in these godless times, is something for which the author, and indeed anyone who is interested in music, is grateful to the generous act of patronage on the part of an inspired musician, a true and convinced disciple and friend of the new theory. His name, *Antony van Hoboken*, will for all time be inseparably connected with this work; and the [music] lover for whom Philipp Emanuel Bach once wrote his *Essay* will celebrate his resurrection in that man." — This paragraph appears on p. 10 of the original German edition. It was cut from Jonas's revised edition of *Free Composition* and does not appear among the "Omissions from the Original German Edition," Appendix 4 of Ernst Oster's 1979 English translation.

[3] A concept of Hindu philosophy: to "pierce the veil" of Maya is to gain a glimpse of transcendent truth.

[4] A "seminar on Schenker's *Free Composition*" is, indeed, announced in the Mannes College prospectus, but not until the academic year 1937–38; see David Carson Berry, "Hans Weisse and the Dawn of American Schenkerism," *Journal of Musicology* 20 (2003): 104–56.

[5] The pupils who contributed to an annuity fund for Jeanette were each to receive, as a token of thanks, a photograph of her late husband.

Weisse to Moriz Violin (letter), December 21, 1935
OJ 70/46, [12]

Dear friend,[1]

As I have been so overwhelmed by work in the past months, it is only now that I find the time to answer your November letter. Thus I should like to declare at the outset that the delay in my reply is in no way the result of any sensitivity on my part. On the contrary your letter, on account of its sincerity, touched me only sympathetically, as a faithful proof of your friendship; I regret only that, apparently as a result of my imprecise intimations, misunderstandings of this sort have had to surface.

I therefore shall stress here, before I go into the details of your letter, that I—then and now, and more than ever—am convinced of the greatness of the Schenkerian idea,[2] that I regard the principal mission in my life to disseminate it, and that I am doing everything that appears necessary to me in this respect. I am giving two seminars here about *Free Composition*, in which a total of thirty-seven persons are taking part. On December 31, in Philadelphia, I shall make the Music Teachers' Association of America aware of the epochal significance of Schenker in an address that, in my opinion, will be among the strongest I have ever uttered.

In view of these facts, it appears to me highly unjust of you, and also of Mrs. Schenker, to express doubts about my intentions at all. In particular, the suggestions in Mrs. Schenker's letter about the "immutable faith" of Oppel, Vrieslander, etc., are highly inappropriate, as they harbored concealed references to my "change of heart." I am conscious of the full import of the situation. It is up to us to pass on Schenker's work in its fullest purity and clarity. I can only tell you that, since *Free Composition* arrived in my hands, I have put everything else to one side and have taken possession of this work alone, in six to eight hours of daily study. I have not merely "read" each of its sentences, but rather thought them through; I have not merely "looked at" every one of its examples, but rather listened to what they were saying. That which I have gained in understanding and absorption from this exhausting study of *Free Composition* is something that I alone know. The clarity toward which I advance is for me the best proof of my thorough study and understanding, and I must rebut all accusations about my judgments that are related to this, if they should be attacked—as for example by you here, or by Mrs. Schenker—as being premature, over-hasty, or imprudent. I am addressing my reply only to you, because I do not believe that Mrs. Schenker has the competence to take an objective position with regard to the work. It is clear that Mrs. Schenker can only be emotionally disposed, and I can understand that my comments may have hurt her; and I shall not hold this against her any more; but I have no intention of getting involved in an objective discussion with her, since the matters in question can be thoroughly appreciated, understood, and objectively considered only by a musician.

Whether you, dear friend, have made *Free Composition* entirely your own is something I do not know; I do not know how deeply your study of the work has progressed; that is something that you must account for yourself. I only believe that you must grant not only yourself, but everyone who occupies himself with the work intensively, the right to demand complete clarity of the work. Of course, it cannot only be the fault of a book that this or that reader does not understand it. But precisely in my case you should not have drawn this easy-going conclusion, i.e. if you took me and my efforts at all "seriously." Your letter mentions a letter from me to the Master,[3] and Mrs. Schenker's letter quotes it verbatim: it concerned my complete recognition of basic concepts. This very letter should have been the guarantee for the two of you that I had made these basic concepts my own (I could say even much better things about them today), and that my criticisms could never refer to these principles. Instead, the two of you assumed (how could you have done so?) that I had become "regressive" and are treating me like a small immature boy, whom one has a right to warn with raised index finger: "You didn't understand then, perhaps you misunderstand again now! Let this be a lesson to you!" That, my friend, is decidedly too complacent—I hope that you too will not take my candor amiss. Instead of merely being angry, you ought on the contrary to have invited me to speak out, and to bring out all of my arguments, for the sake of the idea that we cherish. Instead of this, Mrs. Schenker has outspokenly declared that it would now be better for me to write "nothing yet" about *Free Composition*, as if she would gladly spare me humiliation.

If I should really now desist from making observations about *Free Composition* that seem to me extremely important, I do so not because I fear being "exposed" but rather because I gather from your reaction that the time for this is <u>too soon</u>. I deduce from this reaction of yours that you yourself, and probably all those whom you say stand with you 100 percent, have not gotten so far in your work on the material as to realize that Schenker's exposition is self-contradictory in many places, leaves much that is unclear and imprecise, and cannot be used in its present form as the basis of a teaching method. I know that the time will come in which concerns will be made palpable, even in your circle, that are inevitable for anyone who attempts to penetrate to the ultimate depths of the Schenkerian idea. Only one who <u>suffers</u> from the imperfections of *Free Composition* will understand the urgency with which much needs to be said in order for the full greatness and the momentousness of the work to achieve its purest effect.

I therefore stress that it was not my intention to offer a superfluous critique of the book, to somehow attack or cast doubt upon the basic concepts of Ursatz and prolongation. All I wanted—in the interest of the idea and the <u>unification of the theory</u>, which has become our most sacred legacy—was to refer to all those points that needed to be clarified and made precise. (And there are many of these in *Free Composition*.) By comparison, the translating of Schenkerian terms into English is a secondary problem; and yet I believe I have solved it as well as possible.

To your comment about Kant, I can only add that it supports precisely what I intend: that Kant decidedly did not call the *Critique of Pure Reason* "the first textbook of philosophy"! To explain why he did not do so would be beyond the scope of this letter; but I ask you to reflect on this a bit before you apply it to the case of Schenker.

What I intend with these lines is <u>simply</u> to make my standpoint clear to you: that Schenker means everything to me—as he does to you—and that I most willingly put everything on the line for his idea; that nothing is further from my mind than to flirt with the notion that I would be able to "develop his theory further"—as if it needed this!!; but that as a teacher of this idea I must strive for a clarity that does not always find expression in Schenker's verbal and conceptual formulation. What I must perform is to clarify meaning, but to do so without in the least departing from Schenker's ideas and concepts—that is all!

You are thus making a fatal mistake in criticizing me as an apostate, where I am most deeply conscious of my apostolicism. Faithfulness to the Master today is even less than ever a "personal" affair; it consists of the deepest grasp of his idea and in the feeling of responsibility with respect to this idea. The idea itself cannot and will not succeed in gaining general recognition of its own accord, it is not disseminated. It is up to us to work out how and to what extent we help it rally to victory. And because it is up to us, we must appropriate the idea uncorrupted. It has not been placed in the world by Schenker faultlessly, even though I, like yourself, know that inwardly Schenker heard and saw it in its pure form. In this way I have, I hope, clearly outlined our own mission; and I hope, for my sake and yours that you might be agreed upon it. In this letter I have intentionally avoided enumerating the individual points that I believe require clarification; I would like to postpone that discussion until the moment in which they force themselves upon you. That you will then find me willing to elaborate on each of these points, down to the last detail, is something that I surely need not say outright.

And now, farewell, and once again thanks for your letter! Accept my most cordial wishes for your Schenker Institute.

If you have become convinced that I, too, am in all modesty doing my part over here, then these lines will have fulfilled their purpose.

Happy New Year. With most cordial greetings from my family to yours, in old and unaltered friendship,

Ever your
Dr. Hans Weisse

---

[1] Though he is not named, and the salutation is uncharacteristic (Weisse normally addresses him as "lieber Herr Professor"), the recipient can only have been Moriz Violin: a marginal comment is in Violin's handwriting, and there is a reference to the Schenker Institute in Hamburg; moreover, it is one of eleven letters and postcards that survive among Violin's papers. — Later in the letter Weisse seems unaware, or to have forgotten, that Violin had fled Hamburg soon after the Nazis seized power in Germany and that the Institute, provisionally left in the care of Felix-Eberhard von Cube, had closed in 1934. — The letter from Violin to Weisse to which this responds is not known to survive.

[2] Here, and throughout the letter, Weisse refers to the *Idee*, i.e. Schenker's concept of musical structure, as opposed to *Sache*, the term most often found in discussions of Schenker's mission, including those in Weisse's letters to Schenker. This seems a deliberate change of tack, from crusading for an ideological cause to promoting a concept of musical understanding in a rational, pedagogically accessible manner.

[3] Probably the letter of March 30, 1933.

Select Bibliography

[*This is primarily a bibliography of English-language writings; it includes only a few German-language items that were considered indispensable. In the case of an English translation, the title and date of the German edition or unpublished work are given in square brackets immediately after the English title. For each item frequently cited in the volume, the short-title form is given in square brackets after the entry.*]

Schenker's Writings in English Translation

"A Contribution to the Study of Ornamentation" [*Ein Beitrag zur Ornamentik*, 1903; 2nd edn. 1908]. Translated by Hedi Siegel. *The Music Forum* 4 (1976): 1–139. [*Ornamentation*]

Harmony [*Harmonielehre*, 1906]. Vol. 1 of *New Musical Theories and Fantasies*. Edited and annotated by Oswald Jonas. Translated by Elisabeth Mann Borgese. Chicago: University of Chicago Press, 1954. [1906: *Theory of Harmony*; 1954: *Harmony*]

"The Decline of the Art of Composition: A Technical-Critical Study" ["Über den Niedergang der Kompositionskunst: eine technisch-kritische Untersuchung," c. 1906–09]. Translated by William Drabkin. *Music Analysis* 24, nos. 1–2 (March–July 2005): 33–129. ["Decline"]

Counterpoint: A Translation of Kontrapunkt by Heinrich Schenker [*Kontrapunkt*, 1910, 1922.] Vol. 2 of *New Musical Theories and Fantasies*. Translated by John Rothgeb and Jürgen Thym. Edited by John Rothgeb. 2 volumes. New York: Schirmer Books, 1987. [*Counterpoint 1, 2*]

J. S. Bach's Chromatic Fantasy and Fugue: Critical Edition and Commentary [*Chromatische Fantasie und Fuge D moll von Joh. Seb. Bach: kritische Ausgabe mit Anhang*, 1910]. Translated and edited by Hedi Siegel. New York: Longman, 1969. [*Chromatic Fantasy and Fugue*]

"The Art of Performance" ["Die Kunst des Vortrags," 1911 and later]. Edited by Heribert Esser. Translated by Irene Schreier Scott. New York: Oxford University Press, 2000.

Beethoven's Ninth Symphony: A Portrayal of Its Musical Content, with Running Commentary on Performance and Literature As Well [*Beethovens neunte Sinfonie: eine Darstellung des musikalischen Inhaltes unter fortlaufender Berücksichtigung auch des Vortrages und der Literatur*, 1912]. Translated and edited by John Rothgeb. New Haven: Yale University Press, 1992. [*Beethoven's Ninth Symphony*]

Beethoven's Last Piano Sonatas [*Die letzten fünf Sonaten von Beethoven: kritische Ausgabe mit Einführung und Erläuterung*, 1913–21]. Translated and edited by John Rothgeb. 4 volumes. New York: Oxford University Press, forthcoming. [*Op. 101, Op. 109, Op. 110, Op. 111*]

Der Tonwille: Pamphlets / Quarterly Publication in Witness of the Immutable Laws of Music [*Der Tonwille: Flugblätter / Vierteljahrschrift zum Zeugnis unwandelbarer Gesetze der Tonkunst*, 1921–24]. Edited by William Drabkin. Translated by Ian Bent et al. 2 volumes. New York: Oxford University Press, 2004–05. [*Tonwille* 1, 2, 3, 4, 5, 6, 7, 8/9, 10]

The Masterwork in Music [*Das Meisterwerk in der Musik*, 1925–30] Edited by William Drabkin. Translated by Ian Bent et al. 3 volumes. Cambridge: Cambridge University Press, 1994–97. [*Masterwork* 1, 2, 3]

Five Analyses in Sketchform (Fünf Urlinie-Tafeln) [*Fünf Urlinie-Tafeln* [–] *Five Analyses in Sketchform*, 1932]. New York: David Mannes Music School, 1932. Reprinted with a new introduction and glossary by Felix Salzer. New York: Dover Publications, 1969.

"Brahms's Study, Octaven u. Quinten u. A. with Schenker's Commentary" ["Johannes Brahms, Oktaven und Quinten u. A., aus dem Nachlass herausgegeben und erläutert," 1933]. Translated by Paul Mast. *The Music Forum* 5 (1980): 1–196.

Free Composition [*Der freie Satz*, 1935]. Vol. 3 of New Musical Theories and Fantasies. Translated and edited by Ernst Oster. 2 volumes. New York: Longman, 1979. [*Free Composition*]

Works by Other Early Authors

Cube, Felix-Eberhard von. *The Book of the Musical Artwork: An Interpretation of the Musical Theories of Heinrich Schenker* [1934–53]. Translated by David Neumeyer, George R. Boyd, and Scott Harris. Lewiston: The Edwin Mellen Press, 1988.

Jonas, Oswald. *Introduction to the Theory of Heinrich Schenker: The Nature of the Musical Work of Art* [1934]. Translated and edited by John Rothgeb. 1st edn. New York: Longman, 1982. 2nd edn. Ann Arbor: Musicalia Press, 2005.

Salzer, Felix. *Sinn und Wesen der abendländischen Mehrstimmigkeit*. Vienna: Saturn Verlag, 1935.

———. *Structural Hearing: Tonal Coherence in Music*. 2 volumes. New York: Charles Boni, 1952. Reprinted by Dover Publications, 1962.

Catalogs, Finding Lists

Kosovsky, Robert, comp. *The Oster Collection: Papers of Heinrich Schenker: A Finding List*. New York: New York Public Library, 1990.

Lang, Robert, and JoAn Kunselman, eds. *Heinrich Schenker, Oswald Jonas, Moriz Violin: A Checklist of Manuscripts and Other Papers in the Oswald Jonas Memorial Collection*. Berkeley: University of California Press, 1994.

[Online] Guide to the Oswald Jonas Memorial Collection. http://www.oac.cdlib.org/findaid/ark:/13030/tf4j49n9zc/

Koslovsky, John, comp. [Online Guide to the] Felix Salzer Papers. http://archives.nypl.org/mus/20415

Rast, Nicholas, ed. "A Checklist of Essays and Reviews by Heinrich Schenker." *Music Analysis* 7, no. 2 (July 1988): 121–32.

Bibliographical Guides

Ayotte, Benjamin McKay, ed. *Heinrich Schenker: A Guide to Research*. Routledge Music Bibliographies. New York: Routledge, 2004.

Berry, David Carson, ed. *A Topical Guide to Schenkerian Literature: An Annotated Bibliography with Indices*. Hillsdale, NY: Pendragon Press, 2004.

Collective Volumes

Beer, Axel, ed., with Gernot Gruber and Herbert Schneider. *Festschrift Hellmut Federhofer zum 100. Geburtstag*. Tutzing: Hans Schneider, 2011.

Burstein, L. Poundie, Lynne Rogers, and Karen M. Bottge, eds. Vol. 2 of *Essays from the Fourth International Schenker Symposium*. Hildesheim: Georg Olms, 2013.

Cadwallader, Allen, ed., with John Patrick Connolly. Vol. 1 of *Essays from the Fourth International Schenker Symposium*. Hildesheim: Georg Olms, 2008.

Eybl, Martin, and Evelyn Fink-Mennel, eds. *Schenker-Traditionen: Eine Wiener Schule der Musiktheorie und ihre internationale Verbreitung / A Viennese School of Music Theory and Its International Dissemination*. Vienna: Böhlau, 2006.

Schachter, Carl. *Unfoldings: Essays in Schenkerian Theory and Analysis*. Edited by Joseph N. Straus. Oxford: Oxford University Press, 1999.

Schachter, Carl, and Hedi Siegel, eds. *Schenker Studies 2*. Cambridge: Cambridge University Press, 1999.

Siegel, Hedi, ed. *Schenker Studies*. Cambridge: Cambridge University Press, 1990.

Secondary Literature

Alpern, Wayne. "Schenkerian Jurisprudence: Echoes of Schenker's Legal Education and His Musical Thought". PhD diss., City University of New York, 2005.

———. "The Triad of the True, the Good, and the Beautiful: Schenker's Moralization of Music and his Legal Studies with Robert Zimmermann and Georg Jellinek." In *Essays from the Fourth Schenker Symposium*, vol. 2, ed. L. Poundie Burstein et al., 7–48.

Bent, Ian. "Heinrich Schenker and Robert Brünauer: Relations with a Musical Industrialist." In *Festschrift Hellmut Federhofer*, ed. Axel Beer, 25–37.

———. "'Niemals also ist der Verleger ein "Mäzen" des Künstlers': Schenker and the Music World." In *Essays from the Fourth International Schenker Symposium*, vol. 2, ed. L. Poundie Burstein, Lynne Rogers, and Karen M. Bottge, 121–33.

———. "Schenker and the *Well-tempered Clavier*." In *Essays from the Fourth International Schenker Symposium* , vol. 1, ed. Allen Cadwallader with Patrick Connolly, 197–211.

———. "Schenker as Teacher: The Case of Gerhard Albersheim." *Journal of Schenkerian Studies* 4 (2010): 35–68.

———. "'That Bright New Light': Schenker, Universal Edition, and the Origins of the Erläuterung Series, 1901–1910." *Journal of the American Musicological Society* 58, no. 1 (Spring 2005): 69–138.

Berry, David Carson. "Hans Weisse (1892–1940)." In *Schenker-Traditionen*, ed. Martin Eybl and Evelyn Fink-Mennel, 91–103.

———. "Hans Weisse and the Dawn of American Schenkerism." *Journal of Musicology* 20, no. 1 (Winter 2003): 104–56.

Blasius, Leslie David. *Schenker's Argument and the Claims of Music Theory*. Cambridge: Cambridge University Press, 1996.

Botstein, Leon. "Music and the Critique of Culture: Arnold Schoenberg, Heinrich Schenker, and the Emergence of Modernism in Fin de Siècle Vienna." In *Constructive Dissonance: Arnold Schoenberg and the Transformations of Twentieth-Century Culture*, ed. Juliane Brand and Christopher Hailey. Berkeley: University of California Press, 1997, 3–22.

———. "Schenker the Regressive: Observations on the Historical Schenker." *The Musical Quarterly* 86 (2002): 239–47.

Cadwallader, Allen, and William Pastille. "Schenker's Unpublished Work with the Music of Johannes Brahms." In *Schenker Studies 2*, ed. Carl Schachter and Hedi Siegel, 26–46.

Cook, Nicholas. "The Editor and the Virtuoso, or Schenker versus Bülow." *Journal of the Royal Musical Association* 116 (1991): 78–95.

———. "Heinrich Schenker, Polemicist: A Reading of the Ninth Symphony Monograph." *Music Analysis* 14, no. 1 (March 1995): 89–105.

———. *The Schenker Project: Culture, Race, and Music Theory in Fin-de-Siècle Vienna*. New York: Oxford University Press, 2007.

Deisinger, Marko. "Heinrich Schenker as Reflected in His Diaries of 1918: Living Conditions and World View in a Time of Political and Social Upheaval." *Journal of Schenkerian Studies* 4 (2010): 15–34.

Drabkin, William. "An Autobiographical Letter of Schenker's from 1928." In *Essays from the Fourth International Schenker Symposium*, vol. 2, ed. L. Poundie Burstein, Lynne Rogers, and Karen M. Bottge, 103–19.

———. "Felix-Eberhard von Cube and the North-German Tradition of Schenkerism." *Proceedings of the Royal Musical Association* 111 (1984–85): 180–207.

———. "Heinrich Schenker." In *The Cambridge History of Western Music Theory*, ed. Thomas Christensen. Cambridge: Cambridge University Press, 2002, 812–43.

———. "Heinrich Schenker and Moriz Violin in the 1920s." In *Festschrift Hellmut Federhofer*, ed. Axel Beer, 51–61.

———. "A Lesson in Analysis from Heinrich Schenker: The C major Prelude from Bach's Well-tempered Clavier, Book I." *Music Analysis* 4, no. 3 (October 1985): 241–58.

———. "Hans Weisse in Correspondence with Schenker and His Circle." *Journal of Schenkerian Studies* 4 (2010): 69–85.

———. "Schenker's 'Decline': An Introduction." *Music Analysis* 24, nos. 1–2 (March–July 2005): 3–31.

———. "Schenker, the Consonant Passing Note, and the First-Movement Theme of Beethoven's Sonata Op. 26." *Music Analysis* 15, nos. 2–3 (July–October 1996): 149–89.

Dunsby, Jonathan. "Schoenberg and the Writings of Schenker." *Journal of the Arnold Schoenberg Institute* 2, no. 1 (October 1977): 26–33.

Erwin, Charlotte E., and Bryan R. Simms. "Schoenberg's Correspondence with Heinrich Schenker." *Journal of the Arnold Schoenberg Institute* 5, no. 1 (June 1981): 23–43.

Eybl, Martin. "Schopenhauer, Freud, and the Concept of Deep Structure in Music." In *Schenker-Traditionen*, ed. Martin Eybl and Evelyn Fink-Mennel, 51–58.

Federhofer, Hellmut, ed. *Heinrich Schenker als Essayist und Kritiker: Gesammelte Aufsätze, Rezensionen und kleinere Berichte aus den Jahren 1891–1901*. Hildesheim: Georg Olms, 1990. [Federhofer (1990)]

———. "Heinrich Schenkers Bruckner-Verständnis." *Archiv für Musikwissenschaft* 39, no. 3 (1982): 198–217.

———. "Anton Bruckner im Briefwechsel von August Halm (1869–1929) – Heinrich Schenker (1868–1935)." In *Anton Bruckner: Studien zu Werk und Wirkung*, ed. Christoph Hellmut Mahling. Vol. 20 of Mainzer Studien zur Musikwissenschaft. Tutzing: Hans Schneider, 1988, 33–40.

———. *Heinrich Schenker nach Tagebüchern und Briefen in der Oswald Jonas Memorial Collection, University of California, Riverside*. Hildesheim: Georg Olms, 1985. [Federhofer (1985)]

———. "Heinrich Schenkers Verhältnis zu Arnold Schönberg." *Mitteilungen der Kommission für Musikforschung* 33 (1981): 369–90.

Hailey, Christopher. "Anbruch and Tonwille: The Verlagspolitik of Universal Edition." In *Schenker-Traditionen*, ed. Martin Eybl and Evelyn Fink-Mennel, 59–67.

Hust, Christoph. "'How desolating to have to say that he is and will be the premier conductor of our time!' Heinrich Schenker and Wilhelm Furtwängler." *Journal of Schenkerian Studies* 4 (2010): 3–14.

Jackson, Timothy L. "*Punctus Contra Punctus*—A Counterpoint of Schenkerian and Weissian Analysis and Hans Weisse's Counterpoint Studies with Heinrich Schenker." *Journal of Schenkerian Studies* 4 (2010): 87–186.

———. "Heinrich Schenker as Composition Teacher: The Schenker–Oppel Exchange." *Music Analysis* 20, no. 1 (March 2001): 1–115.

Karnes, Kevin C. *Music, Criticism, and the Challenge of History: Shaping Modern Musical Thought in Late Nineteenth-Century Vienna*. New York: Oxford University Press, 2008.

Kassler, Jamie Croy. "Heinrich Schenker's Epistemology and Philosophy of Music: An Essay on the Relations between Evolutionary Theory and Music Theory." In *The Wider Domain of Evolutionary Thought*, ed. David Olroyd and Ian Langham. Dordrecht: D. Reidel, 1983, 221–60.

Koslovsky, John. "From *Sinn und Wesen* to *Structural Hearing*: The Development of Felix Salzer's Ideas in Interwar Vienna and Their Transmission in Postwar United States." PhD diss., Eastman School of Music, 2009.

———. "*Primäre Klangformen, Linearität, oder Auskomponierung?*: The Analysis of Medieval Polyphony and the Critique of Musicology in the Early Work of Felix Salzer." *Journal of Schenkerian Studies* 4 (2010): 187–206.

———. "Tonal Prolongations in Bartók's Hungarian Folktunes for Violin and Piano: A Case Study." *Theory and Practice* 37/38 (2012–13): 139–83.

Kosovsky, Robert. "Levels of Understanding: An Introduction to Schenker's *Nachlass*." In *Schenker Studies 2*, ed. Carl Schachter and Hedi Siegel, 3–11.

Marston, Nicholas. *Heinrich Schenker and Beethoven's "Hammerklavier" Sonata*. Royal Musical Association Monographs 23. Farnham: Ashgate, 2013.

———. "Schenker's Concept of a Beethoven Sonata Edition." In *Essays from the Fourth International Schenker Symposium*, vol. 2, ed. L. Poundie Burstein, Lynne Rogers, and Karen M. Bottge, 91–101.

Neff, Severine. "Schenker, Schoenberg, and Goethe: Visions of the Organic Artwork." In *Schenker-Traditionen*, ed. Martin Eybl and Evelyn Fink-Mennel, 29–50.

Pastille, William. "Aesthetic Education: On the Origins of Schenker's Musical Politics." In *Essays from the Fourth International Schenker Symposium*, vol. 1, ed. Allen Cadwallader with Patrick Connolly, 183–93.

———. "Music and Morphology: Goethe's Influence on Schenker's Thought." In *Schenker Studies*, ed. Hedi Siegel, 29–44.

———. "Heinrich Schenker, Anti-Organicist." *19th-Century Music* 8, no. 1 (Summer 1984): 29–36.

Reiter, Andrea. "'Von der Sendung des deutschen Genies': The Music Theorist Heinrich Schenker (1868–1935) and Cultural Conservatism." In *Resounding Concerns*, ed. Rüdiger Görner. London German Studies 8. Munich: iudicium, 2003, 135–59.

Rothfarb, Lee. *August Halm: A Critical and Creative Life in Music*. Rochester, NY: University of Rochester Press, 2009. [Rothfarb, *August Halm*]

———. "August Halm on Body and Spirit in Music." *19th-Century Music* 29, no. 2 (Fall 2005): 121–41.

———. "Halm and Schenker: Culture, Politics, Aesthetics." In *Festschrift Hellmut Federhofer*, ed. Axel Beer, 401–17.

———. "Heinrich Schenker and Ibn Ezra: Literal and Interpretive Meaning in Music." *Musiktheorie* 29, no. 1 (2014): 33–49.

Rothgeb, John. "The Schenker–Jonas Correspondence in the Oswald Jonas Memorial Collection." In *Essays from the Fourth International Schenker Symposium*, vol. 2, ed. L. Poundie Burstein, Lynne Rogers, and Karen M. Bottge, 85–90.

———. "Schenkerian Theory and Manuscript Studies: Modes of Interaction." In *Schenker Studies*, ed. Hedi Siegel, 4–14.

Rothstein, William. "The Americanization of Heinrich Schenker." *In Theory Only* 9, no. 1 (1986): 5–17. Revised and reprinted in *Schenker Studies*, ed. Hedi Siegel, 193–203.

———. "Heinrich Schenker as an Interpreter of Beethoven's Piano Sonatas." *19th-Century Music* 8, no. 1 (Summer 1984): 3–28.

Schachter, Carl. "Elephants, Crocodiles, and Beethoven: Schenker's Politics and the Pedagogy of Schenkerian Analysis." *Theory and Practice* 26 (2001): 1–20.

———. "Felix Salzer (1904–1986)." In *Schenker-Traditionen*, ed. Martin Eybl and Evelyn Fink-Mennel, 105–11.

Siegel, Hedi. "Looking at the Urlinie." In *Structure and Meaning in Tonal Music: Festschrift in Honor of Carl Schachter*, ed. L. Poundie Burstein and David Gagné. Hillsdale, NY: Pendragon, 2006, 79–99.

———. "The Pictures and Words of an Artist ('von einem Künstler'): Heinrich Schenker's Fünf Urlinie-Tafeln." In *Schenker-Traditionen*, ed. Martin Eybl and Evelyn Fink-Mennel, 203–19.

———. "Schenker's Letters to Felix Salzer: A Nod to the Future." In *Essays from the Fourth International Schenker Symposium*, vol. 2, ed. L. Poundie Burstein, Lynne Rogers, and Karen M. Bottge, 73–83.

———. "When 'Freier Satz' was part of *Kontrapunkt*: A Preliminary Report." In *Schenker Studies 2*, ed. Carl Schachter and Hedi Siegel, 12–25.

Simms, Bryan R. "Schoenberg, Schenker, and the Metier of Music Theory." In *Schenker-Traditionen*, ed. Martin Eybl and Evelyn Fink-Mennel, 19–27.

Snarrenberg, Robert. *Schenker's Interpretive Practice*. Cambridge: Cambridge University Press, 1997.

Wason, Robert W. "From *Harmonielehre* to *Harmony*: Schenker's Theory of Harmony and Its Americanization. In *Essays from the Fourth International Schenker Symposium*, vol. 1, ed. Allen Cadwallader with Patrick Connolly, 213–58.

Transcription and Translation Credits

I THE EARLY CAREER

1 Schenker as Composer

OJ 5/19, [6] transcr. and transl. William Pastille; OJ 9/6, [12], [14] transcr. William Pastille and Ian Bent, transl. Ian Bent; OJ 5/9, [3], [4], [7]; OJ 9/6, [18], [28]; OJ 9/20, [5], [8]–[11], [13], [14], [18], [26], [30]; OJ 9/23, [1], [9], [10]; OJ 9/27, [1]–[3], [5]–[8]; OJ 12/40, [2]; OJ 14/24, [2], [5], [6]; OJ 35/5, [1]; Sbb B II 4413, 4415–4419, 4422, 4423, 4426; diary entries transcr. and transl. Ian Bent

2 Schoenberg and Schenker's *Syrian Dances*

OC 52/11; OJ 5/9, [8]; OJ 9/20, [19]; OJ 9/23, [4]; OJ 9/27, [9], [11]–[13]; OJ 15/12, [5]–[8]; OJ 35/5, [14–19], [38–47]; diary entry transcr. and transl. Ian Bent; OJ 14/15, [1]–[7] transcr. and transl. Arnold Whittall; Sbb B II 3549, 3550, 4429 transcr. Ian Bent and William Drabkin, transl. Ian Bent

3 Johannes Messchaert and Performance

JM/Ar, [1]; OJ 12/54, [1], [A]; OJ 12/54, [2]–[10] transcr. and transl. John Koslovsky; OJ 35/5, items 52–54 transcr. and transl. Ian Bent

4 The Society for Creative Musicians and Schoenberg's Music

OJ 14/15, [8]–[15] transcr. & transl. Arnold Whittall; diary entries transcr. and transl. Ian Bent

5 Julius Röntgen: Editing and Ornamentation

NMI C 176-01, 176-02, 176-03; OJ 5/18, [A]; OJ 13/27, [1], [2], [4]–[8] transcr. and transl. Kevin Karnes

II SCHENKER AND HIS PUBLISHERS

6 Cotta and the New Musical Theories and Fantasies

CA 1–2, 3, 4, 5–6, 7–8, 12–13, 25, 26, 27, 28, 41–42, 43, 54–55, 57, 181–182, 183–184, 185–187, 188, 189–190; OJ 9/31, [1]–[4], [8], [9], [13], [45], [46]; OJ 12/27, [1]; diary entries transcr. and transl. Ian Bent

7 Otto Erich Deutsch and the "Moonlight" Sonata Facsimile

OC 24/22; OC 52/485; OJ 10/3, [5], [7], [8], [10], [13]–[17], [20]–[26] transcr. and transl. David Bretherton; diary entry transcr. Marko Deisinger, transl. William Drabkin

8 Universal Edition and the *Tonwille* Dispute

OC 52/312–313, 512, 520, 538, 561, 564–565, 568, 569, 574, 577–579, 588, 601, 605, 609, 610, 657, 658–659, 682–683; WSLB 322, 333, 344, 345, 348, 362 transcr. and transl. Ian Bent; diary entries transcr. Marko Deisinger, transl. Scott Witmer, Stephen Ferguson, William Drabkin, and Ian Bent

9 Drei Masken Verlag and *The Masterwork in Music*

OC 54/2, 5–7, 12, 16–18, 33, 37, 56, 79, 88, 91–92, 95, 96–99, 109, 116, 119, 129, 132, 137, 193, 199–200, 203, 218, 224, 230, 278 transcr. Kirstie Hewlett, transl. William Drabkin; OC 54/298 transcr. and transl. William Drabkin

III SCHENKER AND THE INSTITUTIONS

10 The Sofie Deutsch Bequest and the Vienna Academy

OC 1B/19–20, 23, 34r; OC 16/29r, 28v, 27v, 30v, 31v, 33v, 37v–36v; OJ 5/4, [1], [3], [4]; OJ 9/4, [1]–[3]; OJ 10/4, [1]; OJ 12/31, [1]–[3]; OJ 12/51, [1]; OJ 12/52, [1]; OJ 14/40a-b; OJ 15/31, [1]; UfMdK Z 641 D/1925, [1], Z 767 D/1926, [1], [4], Z 767/D/1927, [2] transcr. and transl. Ian Bent; diary entries 1917 transcr. and transl. Ian Bent and William Drabkin; 1920– transcr. Marko Deisinger, transl. Scott Witmer; DLA 69.930/4 transcr. Ian Bent and Lee Rothfarb, transl. Lee Rothfarb; UfMdK Z 641/1924, [1] transcr. and transl. Ian Bent and Martin Eybl

11 Invitations to Serve: Guido Adler

OJ 9/3, [1]–[6]; OJ 5/3, [1]; UG 32/5, [2] transcr. and transl. Kevin C. Karnes; OJ 11/1, [1]; OJ 12/26, [2]; OJ 11/58, [1] transcr. and transl. Ian Bent; diary entries 1916 transcr. and transl. Ian Bent; diary entries 1926–27 transcr. Marko Deisinger, transl. William Drabkin

12 The Photogram Archive

OC 54/111 transcr. and transl. David Bretherton; OJ 5/7a, [21] transcr. and transl. William Drabkin; OJ 11/32, [1] transcr. and transl. Ian Bent; OJ 11/54, [15] transcr. John Rothgeb & Heribert Esser, transl. John Rothgeb; OJ 89/1, [4], [8] transcr. and transl. John Rothgeb; OJ 11/32, [4], [7], [11], [16]; OJ 12/24, [3], [8]; PhA/Ar 56, [1], [3], [4], [8]; ÖNB F21.Berg.3276. Mus transcr. Marko Deisinger, transl. Ian Bent; PhA/Ar 36, [1] transcr. Marko Deisinger, transl. John Rothgeb and Heribert Esser; WSLB 191.560 transcr. and transl. David Bretherton; diary entry transcr. and transl. Ian Bent

13 Professorial Sorties: Ludwig Karpath and Wilhelm Furtwängler

OJ 12/9, [1], [3], [30] transcr. Martin Eybl, transl. Ian Bent; OC 18/23 transcr. Ian Bent, transl. Ian Bent and Martin Eybl; OC 18/37–38, 43, 44, 46, 47 49, 50, 51, 52, 53, 54 transcr. Christoph Hust, transl. Ian Bent; diary entries transcr. and transl. Ian Bent

IV BEETHOVEN'S NINTH SYMPHONY

14 Genesis of *Beethoven's Ninth Symphony*

CA 118, 121-122; OJ 5/6, [5]; OJ 12/27, [12]; OJ 14/44, [1]; OC 52/425, 431, 432, 433, 440, 492; WSLB 83, 100; diary entry transcr. and transl. Ian Bent; Preface to *Beethoven's Ninth Symphony* transl. John Rothgeb

15 Paul von Klenau and Beethoven

OC 54/333-336; OC 82/10 transcr. and transl. Ian Bent and William Drabkin; OC 12/249; OJ 12/11, [1]–[11] transcr. and transl. Ian Bent; diary entries transcr. Mark Deisinger, transl. Scott Wittmer, Stephen Ferguson, and William Drabkin

16 Georg Dohrn and the Ninth Symphony

OC 82/27–28; Rothg 1 transcr. John Rothgeb, transl. John Rothgeb and Heribert Esser

V CONTRARY OPINIONS

17 Expedient Mutuality: Schenker and August Halm

DLA 69.930/1, 2, 8, 9, 12, 14, 15; OC 1B/9 transcr. Ian Bent and Lee Rothfarb, transl. Lee Rothfarb; OC 12/7-17; OJ 11/35, [0], 4, 15, 19, 20 transcr. and transl. Lee Rothfarb; diary entries: transcr. and transl. Ian Bent

18 Expectations Unfulfilled: Schenker and Furtwängler

OJ 5/11, [1]; OJ 11/16, [1]–[8], [10], [11], [13], [C]; Sbb 55 Nachl 13, [1], [2] transcr. Christoph Hust, transl. Ian Bent; diary entries May 1919 and 1932– transcr. and transl. Ian Bent; diary entries November 1919–April 1925 transcr. Marko Deisinger, transl. Scott Witmer; diary entries December 1925– transcr. Marko Deisinger, transl. William Drabkin

19 Open Disagreement: Schenker and Paul Hindemith

OJ 5/17, [1]; OJ 11/51, [1] transcr. and transl. Ian Bent; diary entry transcr. Marko Deisinger, transl. William Drabkin

VI ADVANCING THE CAUSE

20 Fighting the Propaganda War: Walter Dahms

OC 12/91-92; OJ 10/1, [2], [6], [8], [20], [30], [45], [60], [73], [74] transcr. and transl. John Koslovsky; diary entries 1915–16 transcr. and transl. Ian Bent; diary entries 1919–23 transcr. Mark Deisinger, transl. Scott Witmer

21 Hamburg and Moriz Violin

OJ 5/7a, [13]–[15], [17], [28], [35], [40]; OJ 9/34, [10]–[13], [20], [23], [29], [33], [40], [42] transcr. and transl. William Drabkin

22 Further Inroads into Germany: Felix-Eberhard von Cube

OJ 6/7, [2], [4], [36], [42], [44], [47], [52]; OJ 8/4, [2], [40], [58], [59]; OJ 6/8, [1], [5], [21]; OJ 8/5, [1], [4], [16]; OJ 14/45, [13], [31], [35], [41], [71], [73], [76], [110] transcr. and transl. William Drabkin; OJ 6/7, [6]; OJ 8/3, [91]; OJ 8/4, [23]; OJ 14/45, [22], [24] transcr. and transl. Ian Bent and William Drabkin

23 Collecting Sources: Anthony van Hoboken

OJ 11/54, [3], [14], [24]; OJ 89/1, [1], [3]; OJ 89/2, [4], [7] transcr. John Rothgeb and Heribert Esser, transl. John Rothgeb; OJ 11/54, [6], [12], [36], [40]; OJ 89/2, [5], [6]; OJ 89/4, [2], [3]; OJ 89/5, [1], [7] transcr. and transl. John Rothgeb

24 Edinburgh Outpost: John Petrie Dunn

OJ 10/12, [1]–[2]; OJ 10/13, [1]–[8]; OC 30/122–124 transcr. and transl. William Drabkin; OJ 11/54, [18] transcr. and transl. John Rothgeb; diary entry transcr. Marko Deisinger, transl. William Drabkin

25 The Seminar Years: Felix Salzer

FS 40/1, [2], [8]–[10], [14], [15], [19]–[24]; OJ 14/1, [1], [2] transcr. and transl. Hedi Siegel; FS 40/1, [25] transcr. and transl. John Rothgeb; diary entries transcr. and transl. Ian Bent

26 Letters from America: Hans Weisse

OC 18/32–33; OJ 15/16, [82], [88]–[91], [94]–[95], [97]–[100]; OJ 70/46, [12] transcr. and transl. William Drabkin

Index

Ranges in bold type refer to chapters or passages focusing in whole or part on that subject.

Aberdeen, 192, 446
Academic Union for Art and Literature, 54*n*
Adler, Guido, xxi, xxxvii, 158, 164&*n*, **179–86**, 275*n*, 351, 454, 465
Adler, Oscar, 58
aesthetics, 256–57, 294, 318, 369
Aibl, Joseph (publisher), 10, 14, 286
Albersheim, Gerhard, 199, 200*n*, 377
Alberti, C., 134–35
Allgemeine Musikzeitung, 145, 326
Allgemeiner Deutscher Musikverein, 296*n*
Altenmarkt, 327, 333*n*
Altmann, Wilhelm, xxi, 144, 194, 427
Altona, Hamburg, xli
Amar Quartet, 318
America, *see* United States of America
Amstel Bank, 313, 315*n*
Amsterdam, 48, 66, 68, 145
  Conservatory, 44, 67*n*, 69, 70*n*
Anchor Bread, 153, 156, 172
Andrade, Francisco de, 432&*n*
Andriessen, Hendrik, 70*n*
Andriessen, Jurriaan, 70*n*
Andriessen, Louis, 70*n*
Andriessen, Willem, 69, 70*n*, 72
Ansorge, Conrad, 54*n*
Ansorge Society, 53, 54&*n*, 55
anti-Semitism, 212*n*, 224&*n*, 294, 305, 414; *see also* Jews and Judaism *and* Jewishness *under* Schenker, Heinrich
Antropp, Theodor, 230&*n*
Armando, Gualtério, 326; *see also* Dahms, Walter
Artaria (publisher), 392
Arts Weekly, 456*n*
Associated Music Publishers, 477, 478*n*
Association for the Feeding and Clothing of Hungry Schoolchildren (Vienna), **152–78**
Association of Viennese Music Critics, xxxviii, 230, 233, 235
augmentation, 239, 311
Augsburg, 145
Auslander, Frederick E., 469*n*, 470

Aussig, xi, 46
Austria, 50, 54*n*, 60, 93, 157, 160, 164, 166, 175*n*, 187, 206, 216*n*, 264, 270, 335, 350, 351*n*, 361, 382*n*, 431*n*, 447, 469*n*
  annexation, 179
  economics, 89–91, 96, 174, 177, 361, 379
Austrian Ministry of Education, *see* Ministry of Education (Austria)
Austrian National Library (Vienna), xiv, 144, 184–85, 187–89, 191–92, 193*n*, 196*n*, 197*n*, 198*n*, 395, 389*n*, 395, 418, 423*n*
Austrian Workers' Social Democratic Party (SDAPÖ), 424*n*
Avenarius, Ferdinand, 381, 382*n*

Bach, Carl Philipp Emanuel, xxxiii–xxxv, xl, xliii, 32*n*, 35, 62, 67, 69, 70*n*, 75, 91, 133, 188, 201–02, 203*n*, 204, 205*n*, 334, 353, 358, 362, 372*n*, 374, 384, 398, 405, 408, 434, 438, 454, 482
  Essay on the True Art of Playing Keyboard Instruments (*Versuch über die wahre Art, das Clavier zu spielen*), xxxiii, 395*n*, 397 483*n*, 485, 487*n*
  keyboard sonatas, xxxiv, 62*n*, 70*n*
  keyboard concertos, xxxiv, 226, 353, 355&*n*, 385*n*
    Double Concerto in E♭ (Wq. 47, Helm 479), 355*n*
    Double Concerto in F (Wq. 46, Helm 408), 355*n*
    Keyboard Concerto in A minor (Wq. 26, Helm 430), 353, 355&*n*, 385*n*
Bach, David Josef, 145, 250
Bach, Johann Sebastian, xxxiii, xxxviii*n*, 46, 59, 61–62, 65, 67, 69, 116, 133, 187, 189, 192, 257, 264–65, 275*n*, 279, 282*n*, 283, 292, 312, 315, 321–22, 334, 363, 369, 399, 401–02, 403*n*, 408&*n*, 413, 434–35, 438, 447&*n*, 472, 473*n*
  Brandenburg Concerto No. 6, 458
  cantatas, 266
  Chromatic Fantasy and Fugue in D minor, xxxiii*n*, xxxiv, 66*n*, 227, 228*n*, 230, 353

Bach, Johann Sebastian, *continued*
  Clavier-Übungen, 66n, 420
  Concerto for Two Keyboards in C major (BWV 1061), 452
  English Suites, xxxiiin, 66n
  French Suites, xxxiiin, 66n
  Italian Concerto, xxxiiin, 66n
  Keyboard Concerto in D minor, 66n
  Little ("Short") Preludes and Fugues, 66n, 286, 288n, 301, 358, 364
  Partitas for Keyboard, xxxiiin, 66n
  St. Matthew Passion, 44, 248, 282, 473n
  Two- and Three-Part Inventions, xxxiiin, 65, 66n, 265, 350, 371–72, 380
  violin concertos, 189n
    Violin Concerto in E major, 408
  violin sonatas, 320, 321n
    Six Sonatas and Partitas for Solo Violin (BWV 1001–1006), 377
    Six Violin Sonatas (BWV 1014–1019), 61
  Well-tempered Clavier, xxxiiin, 339
    Book I, 205
      Prelude and Fugue in C major, xlii, 387, 399, 400n, 401–02, 403&n, 407n, 470, 471n
      Prelude and Fugue in C minor, 287n, 291–92, 373, 446, 472, 473n
      Prelude and Fugue C♯ major, 339
      Prelude and Fugue C♯ minor, 8n
      Prelude and Fugue in D major, 388, 413&n
      Prelude and Fugue E♭ major, 8n
      Prelude and Fugue in F♯ major, 273, 275n
Bach, Wilhelm Friedemann, 403n
background, 266n, 283, 289, 310, 399, 450, 472
Bad Gastein, 462, 479, 480n
Bahr, Hermann, 71, 208, 338, 339n
Baldner, Max, 366n
Balkans, the, 60
Bamberger, Carl, xxi, 238, 303–04, 307, 351, 354, 357, 364, 458, 459&n
Bärenreiter (publisher), 202, 203n
Barth, Karl Heinrich, 60, 61n
Bartók, Béla, xliv, 454, 460&n
Basel, 48, 145, 313
Basler Nachrichten, 145
bass arpeggiation, 406
Baudelaire, Charles Pierre, 439
Baumgarten, Theodor, 122n, 127n, 128&n, 129, 367&n

Bavaria, 51, 95, 274
Bayreuth, 313, 316&n, 441, 448, 450
Becker, Agnes, 366&n
Becker, Hugo, 64, 65n
Beethoven, Ludwig van, xxxviii&n, xxxix, 6, 17n, 25, 51, 60, 82, 84, 94n, 95, 101, 110n, 112, 133, 143, 158n, 183–84, 189–90, 192, 193n, 195n, 203, 204&n, 237–50, 253n, 254n, 256–57, 258&n, 261, 262n, 263–64, 271, 276, 279, 280n, 282n, 284, 289–92, 294, 296n, 297, 299, 307, 318, 323&n, 331, 332n, 335, 337–38, 340, 344, 361–62, 367, 378, 392, 396n, 403n, 421, 423n, 424–25, 435, 437, 444, 449n
  An die ferne Geliebte, 197
  Cello Sonata in D major (Op. 102, No. 2), 272
  centenary, xxxvii, 101, 104n, 179, 183–86, 189, 292&n, 395, 396n
  Consecration of the House, The (Op. 124), 237
  Egmont, 296, 458, 459n
  Fidelio, 341
  Grosse Fuge (Op. 133), 272
  Missa solemnis, xxxix, 197, 237&n, 238–40, 245–46, 309, 432
  Piano Concerto No. 1 in C minor (Op. 15), 204n
  piano sonatas, xxxi, xxxiv–xxxvi, xxxix, 62n, 75, 91, 93–96, 101, 108, 109n, 117, 121, 128, 134, 227, 256, 258, 260–61, 262n, 264n, 269, 274–75, 286, 288n, 352n, 353–54, 357, 364, 381, 393, 397, 428, 442, 445
  Piano Sonata in A major (Op. 2, No. 2), 354
  Piano Sonata in A major (Op. 101), 93, 96, 97n, 110n, 254, 259, 262n, 267, 271, 287, 288n, 290, 300, 351, 352&n, 354
  Piano Sonata in A♭ major (Op. 26), xlii, 95n, 354, 387
  Piano Sonata in A♭ major (Op. 110), 93, 96, 97n, 254, 258n, 262n, 271, 275, 288n, 338, 354
  Piano Sonata in B♭ major ("Hammerklavier," Op. 106), 96, 197, 199&n, 259, 272, 288n, 393
  Piano Sonata in C major (Op. 2, No. 3), 354
  Piano Sonata in C minor (Op. 10, No. 1), 354
  Piano Sonata in C minor (Op. 111), 93, 94n, 96, 97n, 101, 254, 258n, 262n, 275, 278, 288n, 331&n, 354

Beethoven, Ludwig van, *continued*
piano sonatas, *continued*
Piano Sonata in C♯ minor ("Moonlight," Op. 27, No. 2), xxxv, xli, **93–105**, 128, 352&n, 354, 357, 396
Piano Sonata in D major (Op. 10, No. 3), 333n, 354
Piano Sonata in D major ("Pastoral," Op. 28), 96, 97n, 354
Piano Sonata in D minor ("Tempest," Op. 31, No. 2), 258n, 278, 280n, 354
Piano Sonata in E major (Op. 14, No. 1), 309
Piano Sonata in E major (Op. 109), 93, 96, 97n, 109n, 238, 254, 258n, 262n, 275, 283, 287n, 288n, 301, 353–54, 441
Piano Sonata in E minor (Op. 90), 64, 425, 426n
Piano Sonata in E♭ major (Op. 7), 204n, 333n, 354
Piano Sonata in E♭ major ("Les adieux," Op. 81a), 354
Piano Sonata in F major (Op. 10, No. 2), 354
Piano Sonata in F minor (Op. 2, No. 1), 109n, 352, 354
Piano Sonata in F minor ("Appassionata," Op. 57), 94n, 119, 136&n, 282, 301, 350, 364–65, 370, 419, 420n, 436–37
Piano Sonata in F♯ major (Op. 78), 94n
Piano Sonata in G major (Op. 14, No. 2), 309
piano trios
Piano Trio in D major ("Ghost," Op. 70, No. 1), 303, 434
Piano Trio in E♭ major (Op. 70, No. 2), 366–67
Romance for Violin and Orchestra in G major (Op. 40), 434
string quartets, 303
String Quartet in A minor (Op. 132), 363n
String Quartet in E minor (Op. 59, No. 2), 303
String Quartet in E♭ major (Op. 127), 282
symphonies, xxxix, 132, 197, 260, 281, 337
Symphony No. 2 in D major (Op. 36), 227
Symphony No. 3 in E♭ major ("Eroica," Op. 55), xxxvii, xxxix–xl, xliv, 130–31, 132n, 199, 238, 241–42, 244, 308, 310&n, 373, 375, 381, 383n, 451, 465, 468, 469n, 471–72, 473n, 475

Beethoven, Ludwig van, *continued*
Symphony No. 5 in C minor (Op. 67), xxxix, 106, 108, 109n, 117, 118n, 119, 129&n, 227, 243, 244n, 246, 248, 254, 276, 281, 296, 300–01, 352, 354, 355n, 363, 397
Symphony No. 6 in F major ("Pastoral," Op. 68), 307
Symphony No. 7 in A major (Op. 92), 307, 374, 452
Symphony No. 8 in F major (Op. 93), 449n
Symphony No. 9 in D minor (Op. 125), xxxviii–xxxix, xliii, 75, 91, 94n, 111, 134, 197, **225–54**, 288n, 296n, 300, 303–04, 397, 441, 448, 449n
variations, 261, 262n
Fifteen Variations and Fugue on an Original Theme ("Eroica," Op. 35), 261, 363n
Thirty-three Variations on a Waltz by Anton Diabelli (Op. 120), 261
Thirty-two Variations in C minor (WoO 80), 433
Violin Concerto in D major (Op. 61), 189n
Beethoven Archive (Bonn), 190n, 396n
Beethoven House (Bonn), 96, 97&n, 98, 101n, 189, 193n, 204n, 396n
Beethoven-Saal (Berlin), 42
Bekker, Paul, xxi, xxxvi, xxxix, 110n, 111–12, 113n, 114, 115&n, 116, 257, 258n, 264, 294, 301, 343–45
Bellermann, Heinrich, 88
Bellini, Vincenzo: *Norma*, 19n
Benedikt, Moriz, 160
Bent, Ian, 4, 75, 106, 153, 209, 227, 238
Berg, Alban, 58, 191, 195–96, 238, 245n, 427, 439
Der Wein, 439, 440n
Berg, Maurits van den, 367&n
Berlin, xxxii, xxxvii, 5, 11n, 22–23, 25, 29n, 30, 32, 35n, 36, 42&n, 43n 62–63, 84, 144, 145&n, 158&n, 161&n, 163, 170, 174, 208, 212, 218&n, 224&n, 237, 253, 273, 306&n, 308, 313, 326, 328, 330–32, 337, 346n, 353, 356, 366, 375–76, 378&n, 379–81, 404, 406, 416, 418, 426–27, 429–30, 434
Academy of Arts, 213, 214n
Central Bank, 170
Kroll Opera, 55n, 203n, 434n
Music Hochschule, 61n, 65n, 169n, 208–09, 228, 229n, 308, 356n, 379n, 382n, 434n
Philharmonic Orchestra, 147n

Berlin, *continued*
  State Opera, 203n, 431n, 433, 434n
  Stern Conservatory, *see* Stern Conservatory (Berlin)
  University, 365n
Berliner Börsen-Courier, 145
Berliner Börsen-Zeitung, 145, 326
Berliner Lokalanzeiger, 145
Berliner Tageblatt, 17, 145
Berlioz, Hector, 31, 257, 281, 282&n, 301
  Trojans, The, 42
Bern, 145, 273
Berrsche, Alexander, 145
Beyle, Marie-Henri, *see* Stendhal
Bick, Josef, 191, 193n
Bienenfeld, Elsa, 145
Bienerth, Anka, 152
Bismarck, Otto von, 336, 416
Bizet, Georges, 341
Bocca, Fratelli, 145
Bochum, 405n
Böhme, Alfred, 135–37
Bonaparte, Napoleon, 335, 459
Bonn, 101–02, 189, 190n, 192, 395–96
  University, 193n, 365n, 396n
Bopp, Wilhelm, 212, 226
Borchardt, Mr., 430
Bösendorfer, Ludwig, 50&n
Bösendorfer-Saal, 17n, 34, 36, 49n, 50&n, 72
Botstiber, Hugo, 246&n
Boy, Miss, 440
Brahms, Johannes, xxxviii&n, xl, xliv, 4, 8, 10–11, 28n, 32, 44, 51, 63, 67, 71–72, 84, 93n, 112, 132, 152, 186–87, 209n, 224, 229n, 256–57, 260, 261n, 276, 278, 280n, 281, 282&n, 284, 294, 296n, 297, 300, 302, 304, 307, 308n, 315&n, 320, 355n, 356–57, 358n, 362, 376, 377–78, 388, 392–93, 398, 399n, 450, 460
  "Feldeinsamkeit" (Op. 86, No. 2), 46
  "Minnelied" ("Holder klingt der Vogelsang") (Op. 71, No. 5), 280n, 282&n
  "Oktaven und Quinten," xxxi, 128n
  Piano Concerto No. 1 in D minor (Op. 15), 10&n
  Piano Sonata No. 3 in F minor (Op. 5), 276, 280n
  Piano Trio in C major (Op. 87), 366
  Rhapsody in G minor (Op. 79, No. 2), xxxiv, 64
  "Sapphische Ode" ("Rosen brach ich nachts mir") (Op. 94, No. 4), 282

Brahms, Johannes, *continued*
  Schicksalslied (Op. 54), 358n
  symphonies, 132, 227, 304–05, 364n
  Symphony No. 3 in F major (Op. 90), 117, 118n, 276, 280n, 284, 301, 363, 398, 399n
  Three Intermezzos (Op. 117), xlii&n, 206, 352&n, 418, 434&n
  Variations and Fugue on a Theme by G. F. Handel (Op. 24), 18, 125n, 286, 339, 354, 363
  Variations on a Theme of Paganini (Op. 35), 441
  Violin Concerto in D major (Op. 77), 189n
Braunfels, Walter, 403–04, 405&n
Breisach, Paul, 295, 296&n
Breithaupt, Rudolf M., 418, 433, 434&n, 435
Breitkopf & Härtel (publisher), xxxvii, 3–5, 13–17, 19–24, 26&n, 27–31, 46n, 60, 62, 75, 76n, 80n, 114, 130, 146&n, 147, 202, 208, 234n, 240n, 301, 357, 376, 381, 439
Breslau, 168
  Choral Society, 251
  Orchestral Society, xxxix, 251–52
  University, 365n
Bretherton, David, 94
Briand, Aristide, xxi, 271, 272n, 343
British Museum, 420
Brno, 45
Broder, Nathan, 469n
Brown, Matthew, 319
Bruch, Max, 237
Bruckner, Anton, xxxii, xxxv, xl, 2, 6n, 76&n, 214, 256&n, 273, 275&n, 277–79, 280n, 281n, 282n, 284–86, 288n, 289–90, 294–96, 300–02, 304–05, 417n, 450; *see also* Bruckner, with *under* education *under* Schenker, Heinrich
  symphonies, 195, 214n, 257, 260, 261n, 274, 275n
  Symphony No. 2 in C minor, 279
  Symphony No. 4 in E♭ major ("Romantic"), 279
  Symphony No. 7 in E major, 279, 284, 288n
  Symphony No. 8 in C minor, 288n
  Symphony No. 9 in D minor, 278, 285
Brüll, Eugen, 26n
Brüll, Ignaz, xxi, 4, 7, 21, 25, 30, 33, 208; Plate 20
  "Abschied, Der," 34
  "Trinklied," 34
Brünauer, Robert Albrecht, 368, 379

Brünn, see Brno
Brussels, 201
　Conservatory, 70n
Budapest, 45–46, 48n, 209n
　Conservatory, 315n
Bühne und Welt, 326
Bülow, Prince Bernhard von, 347, 348n
Bülow, Hans von, 61, 62&n, 63, 69, 70n, 160, 194, 224n, 261, 305, 335, 398
Bülow, Princess Maria von, 347, 348n
Bund, Der, 145
Bund österreichischer Frauenvereine, 152n
Busch, Adolf, 295, 296n
Busch, Fritz, 269, 270n
Busch, Wilhelm, 412, 413n
Busch Chamber Players, 296n
Busch Quartet, 296n
Busoni, Ferruccio, xxii, xxxii, 3–4, 8&n, 9, 11, 12&n, 13–15, 17–18, 19n, 20–23, 24n, 25, 30, 32&n, 33&n, 35&n, 36–37, 38&n, 39&n, 41&n 42&n, 43, 208, 353, 362; Plate 22
Buxbaum, Friedrich, xxii, 214–15, 303, 367&n
Buxbaum Quartet, 303n

Café Vindobona (Vienna), 300, 301&n, 302
Cambridge, 99, 100&n, 101
Carl Theater, 55n, 63
Caruso, Enrico, xxxiii, 45, 393, 394n
Casals, Pablo, 292&n
Cassirer, Fritz, 436, 437n
Catholic Center Party (Germany), 348n
Cauchie, Maurice, 192, 193n
Cavalli, Francesco, 420n
Central Institute for Music Pedagogy (Berlin), 131, 378
Chelius, Oscar von: *Magda Maria*, 341
Cherubini, Luigi, 88
chromaticism, 63–64, 319, 399, 407, 410–11
Chomutov [Komotau], 145&n
Chopin, Frederic, 17n, 46, 51, 112, 143, 191, 426&n, 439, 440n
　Ballade No. 2 in F major/A minor (Op. 38), 419, 420&n
　etudes, 132&n
　　Op. 10, 132; No. 12 in C minor, 408
　　Op. 25, No. 6 in G♯ minor, 439
　mazurkas, 206
　　Mazurkas (Op. 24), 439
　Prelude in C minor (Op. 28, No. 20), 439
　Scherzo in E major (Op. 54), 396
　Two Polonaises (Op. 40), 205

Christian Socialism, 212n, 215n
circle of fifths, 409, 417n
Citkowitz, Israel, 477, 478n
Clementi, Muzio, 313, 318, 435, 447
Cobb, Mr., 477, 478n
Cologne, xlii, 101, 145, 199, 200n, 345, 387, 396, 403, 405
　Conservatory, 67n
　Music Hochschule, xliii, 199n, 404, 405n
　University, 195n
Columbia University (New York), xliv, 465, 469n, 470–72, 477
Conne, Paul de, 64n
consecutive fifths, *see* parallel fifths
consecutive octaves, *see* parallel octaves
Copenhagen, 95, 248
Costanzi Theatre (Rome), 345
Cotta, J. G. (publisher), xivn, xxxiv–xxxv, xxxvii–xxxviii, 61, 69, **74–92**, 107&n, 158n, 160, 210n, 226–27, 228&n, 229, 233n, 262, 269, 351–52
　"Instruktive Ausgabe klassischer Klavierwerke," 62n
Cottage Sanatorium (Vienna), 219, 220n
counterpoint, xxxii, xl–xli, 2, 30, 58, 75, 88, 197, 267, 275n, 277, 283, 285, 288n, 296, 318, 327–28, 334, 345, 347, 374, 377, 378n, 381, 385, 404, 443, 445, 448, 450, 467; *see also* Counterpoint *under* New Musical Theories and Fantasies *under* theoretical, critical and pedagogical works *under* Schenker, Heinrich
Couperin, François, 193n
cover tone, 284
Cube, Felix-Eberhard von, xivn, xxii, xxxii, xl–xliii, 44, 45n, 198, 199n, 200n, 377–78, 381, 383, 385&n, **387–417**, 425, 441, 490n; Plates 5, 10, 41
　compositions, 388
　　Piano Sonata No. 1 in A♭ major (Op. 3), 390, 400
　　Piano Sonata No. 2, 390
　　Tarantella, 388
　　Thema and Variations (Op. 1), 388
　Lehrbuch der musikalischen Kunstgesetze, 387, 407n, 413n
　tonal theory, xlii, 388, 409–11, 415
Cube, Gustav von, xivn, xlii, 387
Cuno, Wilhelm, 348&n
Curtius, Ludwig Michael, 209, 308, 309n

Czermak, Emmerich, 212*n*
Czernin, Ottokar, 351&*n*
Czerny, Carl, 402, 435

Dahlhaus, Carl, 31
Dahms, Walter, xxii, xxix, xxxix, xli, 158&*n*, 161&*n*, 163*n*, 168, 199, 209*n*, **326–49**, 353, 359, 426; Plate 38
   Music of the South, 327, 345, 347
   Musikus Almanach, Der, 327
   Revelation of Music: An Apotheosis of Friedrich Nietzsche, The, 327, 340–41, 345
d'Albert, Eugen, xxi, xxxii, xxxv, 3–5, 6&*n*, 7, 8&*n*, 9, 11, 15–16, 17&*n*, 18–20, 45, 46&*n*, 64, 65*n*, 67*n*, 77–78, 87*n*, 208; Plate 19
   Abreise, Die (1898), 6&*n*
   Gernot (1897), 5&*n*, 7, 11
   Ghismonda (1895), 5, 6*n*
Damrosch, Frank, 314*n*, 397*n*
Damrosch, Leopold, 467*n*
Damrosch, Walter, 397*n*
Damrosch Conservatory, *see* Institute of Musical Art (New York)
Danish Philharmonic Orchestra Society, 237–38
Danzig, 145
Daqué, Edgar, 400&*n*
David Mannes Music School (New York), xliv, 199*n*, 311, 314*n*, 382*n*, 385*n*, 397*n*, 409*n*, 456&*n*, 457, 458*n*, **465–90**
Debussy, Claude Achille, 315*n*, 447
   Prelude to the Afternoon of a Faun, 42
Decsey, Ernst, 145
Dehmel, Richard, 57*n*
Dehn, Bertha, 399*n*
Deisinger, Marko, 188
Demblin, August, 130–33, 137–39, 141, 146, 149–50
Denmark, 68, 237
Dessau, 341
Detoni, Josef Anton, 118, 119*n*
Deutsch, Franz Peter, 93
Deutsch, Heinrich, 163*n*
Deutsch, Otto Erich, xxii, xxxv–xxxvii, xlii, **93–105**, 130–31, 140, 141&*n*, 142–44, 146–47, 149–50, 153, 184, 187–89, 190*n*, 192, 196&*n*, 197*n*, 308*n*, 424–26, 427&*n*, 429, 439; Plates 8, 26
Deutsch, Sofie [Sophie], xxx*n*, xxxvii–xxxviii, 93&*n*, **152–78**

Deutsche Akademiker-Zeitung, 145
Deutsche Allgemeine Zeitung, 145, 359
Deutsche Buch-Gemeinschaft (German Book Society), 291, 292*n*
Deutsche Tageszeitung, 145
Deutsche Tonkünstler-Zeitung, 373, 391*n*, 399, 400*n*, 401–02, 403*n*
Deutsche Verlags-Anstalt, 346*n*
Deutsche Warte, 42*n*
Deutschlands Erneuerung, 333
diminution, 265, 266*n*, 279*n*, 310–12
d'Indy, Vincent
   Songs and Dances (Op. 50), 57
   Stranger, The, 42
Dittersdorf, Carl Ditters von, 200
Doblinger, Ludwig (publisher), xxxiii&*n*, 121
Dohnányi, Ernő, 71
Dohrn, Georg, xxxix, **251–54**
Dollfuss, Engelbert, 215*n*
Door, Anton, 6*n*
Dortmund, 405*n*
Dostoyevsky, Fyodor Mikhailovich, 339*n*
Drabkin, William, 131, 350, 388, 441, 466
Drei Masken Verlag, xii, xxxiv, xxxvi–xxxvii, 74, 94*n*, 126*n*, **130–50**, 189&*n*, 192, 253, 381, 428–29
Dreiklang, Der, 368*n*, 465, 484*n*
Dreililien Verlag, 30
Dresden, 5, 6*n*
   Conservatory, 61*n*
   State Opera, 270*n*
Duisburg, xli–xlii, 378, 381, 387–88, 391, 395–96, 398, 405*n*
Duisburger General-Anzeiger, 391*n*, 399*n*
Dunn, Aline, 441, 452, 453*n*; Plate 39
Dunn, John Petrie, xxii, xxix, xli, xliii, 118*n*, 143, 192, 394, 396, 420, 424, 425*n*, 429, **441–53**; Plate 39
   Geheimnis der Handführung beim Klavierspiel, Das (Usage of the Hand in Piano Playing), 441, 445, 446*n*
   Ornamentation in the Works of Chopin, 441, 445–46
   Student's Guide to Orchestration, A, xliii, 441, 449*n*
Dussek, Jan Ladislav, 313, 435
Düsseldorf, xlii, 202, 203*n*, 387, 390, 395, 397–98
   Conservatory, 395
Dvořák, Antonín, 71, 312

Ebert, Friedrich, 298, 299*n*
Eckstein, Friedrich, 285
Edinburgh, xliii, 420, **441–53**
　University, xli, xliii, 441, 445, 449*n*
Edition Peters, *see* Peters, C.F. (publisher)
Ehrbar, Friedrich, 29
Einstein, Alfred, xxii, xxxvi, 130–33, 140, 142–43, 189, 392, 419, 428, 429*n*; Plate 28
Eissler, Jenny [Jenni], xxx*n*, 13*n*, 161*n*
Eissler, Moritz B., 13*n*, 160, 161*n*
Eitelberger, Rudolf, 179
Eldering, Bram, 67&*n*
Elias, Angi, xxx*n*, 161*n*, 164*n*, 302&*n*, 321*n*, 354, 362, 383*n*, 408
England, 8, 60, 93, 143, 189, 192, 218, 264, 271, 336–38, 342, 359, 420
enharmonicism, 63–64, 411
Epstein, Julius, 3
Essen, xlii, 388, 391, 397, 405*n*
　Folkwang School (Werden-Essen), 404, 405*n*
Esslingen, 269
Eulenburg Edition, 233, 236
Expert, Henry, 419, 420&*n*
Eybl, Martin, 209

Farrar, Geraldine, 432&*n*
Federhofer, Hellmut, xiii, 33*n*, 237*n*, 251&*n*, 256*n*, 315*n*
Felix Salzer Papers (New York Public Library), xiii, 487*n*
Field, John, 435
Figdor, Karl, 163*n*
Figdor, Richard, 163*n*
Figdor family, 163*n*, 166
figuration, 266*n*, 276, 281*n*, 283–86, 287*n*, 290, 399
figured bass, *see* thoroughbass
Fischer, Edwin, 379&*n*
Fischhof, Robert, 5, 6*n*
Fitzwilliam Museum, Cambridge, 99–101
Flensburg, 251
Folkwang-Hochschulen, 405*n*
Foodstuffs Headquarters (Vienna), 154, 155&*n*, 156
foreground, xxxvii, xliv, 31, 283–84, 289, 310–11, 450, 472
Forkel, Johann, 401, 403*n*
form, 197, 216*n*, 239–40, 377, 399*n*, 461&*n*;
　see also sonata form
France, 60, 116, 264, 292*n*, 326, 359

France, Anatole, 264
Franck, César: *The Djinns*, 42
Frankfurt-am-Main, xxxvi, 6&*n*, 8*n*, 44, 64, 65*n*, 95, 96*n*, 97*n*, 121&*n*, 192, 319, 389, 412
　Bach Society, 237
　Hoch Conservatory, 65*n*, 413*n*
　Hochschule, 350, 389*n*
　Opera, 65*n*, 358
　University, 365*n*
Frankfurter Zeitung, 110*n*, 112, 334, 342, 344
Franz, Robert
　"Auf dem Meere," 34
　"Ständchen," 34
　"Vergessen," 34
　"Wenn der Frühling auf die Berge steigt," 34
Freiburg im Breisgau, University of, 365*n*
Freie Schulgemeinde (Free School Community; Wickersdorf), 261*n*, 269, 271, 273, 275*n*, 282*n*
Frenssen, Gustav: *Letters from America*, 360
Friedberg, 145
Friedländer, Max, 434*n*
Friedländer & Sohn (publisher), 434&*n*
Friedmann, Hugo, 153, 156–57, 159, 161, 163, 165*n*, 166, 170
Friedrich Hofmeister Musikverlag, 403*n*
Frimmel, Theodor, 98, 102
Frotscher, Dr., 145
Fuchs, Erwine, 287*n*, 462*n*
Fuchs, Hans, *see* Fuchs, Johann Nepomuk
Fuchs, Jella, 287*n*, 462*n*
Fuchs, Johann Nepomuk, 2
Fuchs, Robert, 288*n*
Fürstenberg, Prince, 200
Furtwängler, Wilhelm, xl&*n*, 114, 130–31, 147&*n*, 150, 188, 191, 193–94, **208–24**, 237, 240, 246, 268, 269*n*, 282–85, **294–317**, 343–44, 346, 349, 357, 373, 376–81, 383–84, 388, 413–14, 421, 424–27, 429, 432–33, 435, 446, 451*n*, 462, 463*n*, 465
Fux, Johann Joseph, xl, 318

Gál, Hans, 97
Galsworthy, John: *Loyalties*, 184
Galtür, 116, 148, 170, 193, 291, 306, 359–61, 366, 369, 383, 385&*n*, 387, 394, 396, 397&*n*, 398, 422*n*, 431–32, 449, 451*n*
Ganche, Édouard, 439, 440*n*
Gärtner, Eduard, xxxii*i*, 3, 34, 63, 64*n*, 65*n*
Gast, Peter, 341

Geiger, Heinrich, 58
General-Anzeiger für Bonn und Umgegend, 292
Geneva, 297, 298n, 313
George, Stefan, 439
German Charles-Ferdinand University (Prague), 179
German Conservatory (Deutsches Konservatorium) on the Alster (Hamburg), 412
Germany, xl–xliv, 8n, 51, 54&n, 60, 71, 84, 117, 157, 160, 179, 224n, 237, 264–66, 271, 272&n, 274, 295, 326–27, 333, 335–37, 338&n, 342–43, 345, 348, 350, 351&n, 359–60, 381, **387–417**, 490n
Gesellschaft der Musikfreunde, see Society of the Friends of Music (Gesellschaft der Musikfreunde) *under* Vienna
Goebbels, Joseph, 224n, 413n
Goethe, Johann Wolfgang von, 46n, 74, 264, 333, 337–38, 430, 447&n, 479
  Egmont, 459n
  Faust, 120n, 244n
  Italian Journey, 280n
  Über Kunst und Altertum, 447n
  Wanderers Nachtlied, 358n
Goldbaum, Wilhelm, 75, 76&n, 83, 85
Goldmark, Karl, 7–8, 9&n, 10, 14, 17, 71, 87n
Göttingen, University of, 365n
Graedener, Hermann, 50n
Graedener, Irene, *see* Mayerhofer, Irene
Graener, Paul, 213, 214n
Graeser, Wolfgang, 292&n
Graf, Max, 87n, 208
Graz, 45, 108, 426
Greef, Arthur de, 70&n
Grieg, Edvard: "Mit einer Wasserlilie," "Wiegenlied," 46
Griesinger, Georg August, 206
Grote'sche Verlagsbuchhandlung, 360
Grube, Gustav, 55
Grunert, Emil, 471n
Grünfeld, Alfred, 158, 181
Grünfeld, Ludwig, 48&n, 50–51
Grunsky, Karl, 76n, 260&n
Gutheil, Gustav, 54, 55n
Gutmann, Albert J., 6, 64, 65n, 66, 67n, 70, 108n, 122
Guttmann, Hans, 194n
Guttmann, Julian [Julko], 300&n
Guttmann, Sophie [Schifre], xxxi, 300n

Haas, Robert, xxiii, 143, 187–89, 190&n, 191–92, 196n, 198n, 200–05, 206&n, 207, 405, 421, 423n, 425, 427, 429, 431–32
Hahn, Harry, xli, 369–70
Hainisch, Michael, 183
Halberstam, Julius, 373, 375n
Halle, University of, 365n
Halm, August, xxiii, xl–xli, 144, 163&n, 165n, 182n, 209n, **256–93**, 304, 307–08, 339, 343, 351, 414–15, 417n; Plate 30
  compositions
    As You Like It, 273–74
    Chamber Music, 272, 273–74
      String Quartet in A major, 275n, 276, 281, 291n
      Concerto in C Major for Large Orchestra with Obligato Piano, 269, 270n, 273
    Cymbeline, 273
    Hausmusik, 274
    Midsummer Night's Dream, A, 273, 281
    piano works, 274, 277
    string quartet, 274
    Symphony in A major (unpublished), 275n
    Tempest, The, 273
    Winter's Tale, The, 273, 281
  pedagogy, 258–59, 262n, 264–65, 270n
  Society for the Publication of the Works of August Halm, 270n
  Von Grenzen und Ländern der Musik, 278, 280n, 287, 289
  Von zwei Kulturen der Musik, 275
Hamburg, xli–xlii, xliv, 63, 121n, 144–45, 194, 208, 211&n, 214, 223n, 286, 298, 310–11, **350–86**, 387, 414, 416, 467&n, 490n
  Philharmonic Orchestra, 214n
Hamburger freie Presse, 20
Hamburger Nachrichten, 310, 351
Hammer, Viktor [Victor], xxiii, xxxi&n, 367, 389, 390n, 391–92, 395–96, 398, 427, 444n, 474
Hammerschlag, János, 313, 315n
Hammerschlag, Paul, 295, 296n
Handel, George Frideric, xxxiii, xxxviiin, 94, 143, 189, 226, 279, 303, 312, 315n, 369, 415, 420
  Judas Maccabaeus, 415
  Samson, 302–03
  Saul, 315n

Hannemann, Carl Friedrich Wilhelm, xli, 371&*n*
Hanslick, Eduard, 179, 208, 296*n*, 304
Harden, Maximilian, 8, 10, 14–15, 63, 257, 271, 272*n*; *see also Zukunft, Die*
harmony, xxxii, xxxiv, 2, 30, 75, 217, 259, 275*n*, 285, 288*n*, 289–90, 296*n*, 327, 385, 392, 404, 407, 445, 467, 486; *see also Theory of Harmony (Harmonielehre) under* New Musical Theories and Fantasies *under* theoretical, critical and pedagogical works *under* Schenker, Heinrich
Harnack, Adolf von, 427&*n*
Hase, Hellmuth von, 309, 310*n*
Haslinger, Carl, 363*n*
Haslinger, Tobias, 363*n*
Haslinger's bookshop (Vienna), 121, 362
Hausegger, Siegmund von, 168, 170, 298&*n*, 300
Hauser, Friederike, xxiii, 214, 215, 298, 300, 301, 351
Haydn, Franz Joseph, xxxviii*n*, 91&*n*, 93*n*, 95&*n*, 132, 143–44, 189, 200, 279, 296*n*, 305, 315, 362–63, 364*n*, 397, 423–24, 435–36, 472
 Creation, The, 49, 142–44, 238
 piano sonatas, 91&*n*, 348, 393
  Piano Sonata in E♭ major (Hob. XVI:49), 315, 316*n*, 473*n*
  Piano Sonata in E♭ major (Hob. XVI:52), 354
 piano trios, 303
Hebel, Johann Peter, 74
Heber, Richard, 366*n*
Heidelberg, 7, 8*n*, 9, 308, 309*n*
 University, 209, 309*n*, 373
Heilbronn, 269
Heinrich Schenker Academy (Hamburg), 387
Heinsheimer, Hans, 106, 287*n*
Hellmesberger, Joseph, 285, 288*n*
Hellmesberger String Quartet, 288*n*
Helm, Georg, 58
Henz, Matthäus, 269
Herder, Johann Gottfried von, 74, 264, 338
Herget, A., 145
Herlinger, Růžena, 440*n*
Hermann Lietz Country Boarding School (Haubinda), 275*n*
Herriot, Edouard, 292&*n*
Hertzka, Emil, xxiii, xxxvi, 41&*n*, 53, 91–92, 94–95, 96&*n*, 98, 106, 107&*n*, 108, 109&*n*, 110&*n*, 111–12, 113&*n*, 114&*n*, 115&*n*, 116, 118,

Hertzka, Emil, *continued*
 119&*n*, 122–23, 125&*n*, 126, 127&*n*, 128&*n*, 130–31, 132&*n*, 133–34, 139, 147, 158*n*, 208, 212, 226–27, 230, 231*n*, 232–33, 234&*n*, 235&*n*, 236, 238, 285–86, 287*n*, 301, 343–45, 347, 349–50, 353, 357, 360–63, 373, 381, 382&*n*, 429, 461, 462*n*; Plate 27
Herzmansky, Bernhard, xxxiii*n*, 71
Hesse, Max (publisher), 147, 291
Heuberger, Richard, 19
Heuss, Alfred Valentin, 192, 193*n*, 307
Heyer Museum, 97, 195*n*
Hildesheim, 290
Hindemith, Paul, xxxix, 191, 292, **318–23**, 361, 409, 434*n*
 Craft of Musical Composition, 318
 Ludus Tonalis, 318
 Mathis der Maler, 318
 string quartets, 320, 321*n*
Hindenburg, Paul von, 330&*n*, 333, 335, 337, 339*n*
Hirschfeld, Robert, xxiii, 87*n*, 230&*n*, 296
Hitler, Adolf, 218*n*, 275*n*, 413*n*
Hoboken, Anthony van, xiv*n*, xxiii, xxxvii, xl*n*, xlii&*n*, xliii, 105, 130, 141*n*, 142–43, 184, 187–89, 190&*n*, 191–92, 193&*n*, 195–96, 199–201, 203*n*, 204, 205&*n*, 206&*n*, 207*n*, 217, 221, 222*n*, 306&*n*, 307, 321*n*, 350, 376, 389, 391, 395, 398, 404–05, **418–40**, 441, 444–45, 446&*n*, 465–66, 484–85, 487*n*
 Joseph Haydn: Thematisch-bibliographisches Werkverzeichnis, 423, 424&*n*
Hoboken Dedication, *see* Photogram Archive
Hoehn, Alfred, 412, 413*n*
Hoffmann, Josef, 33*n*
Hofmannsthal, Hugo von, 27*n*, 71
Hofmeister, *see* Friedrich Hofmeister Musikverlag
Hohenzollern dynasty, 337, 338*n*; *see also* Wilhelm II, Kaiser
Hölderlin, [Johann Christian] Friedrich, 74, 357, 477
 Hyperion, 332, 358*n*
Holland, 146, 202, 434
Horwitz, Karl: String Quartet, 58
Hotel Bristol (Vienna), 7
Hotel Imperial (Vienna), 305, 308, 315
Huberman, Bronisław, xxiv, 189&*n*, 224, 312
Hugo, Victor, 42
Hupka, Felix, 354, 358

Hust, Christoph, 295
hyperinflation, xxx, 89–91, 272&n, 273, 287, 361, 379

Ibach, 347, 348n
Ibsen, Henrik: *Hedda Gabler*, 153
Iffert, August, 60, 61n
Igls, 316, 439
Illustrirtes Wiener Extrablatt, 230n
Immermann, Karl Leberecht, 6n
Imperial Association for German Musicians and Music Teachers, 389n
Imperial Culture Chamber (Germany), 413n
Imperial Music Chamber (Reichsmusikkammer; Germany), 214n, 412, 413n, 414
improvisation, 6n, 276–77, 279&n, 283, 285, 311
India, 465
Institute of Musical Art (New York), 311, 314n, 368, 397n, 467
International Musicological Society (Vienna chapter), 179–81
International Schubert Congress (Vienna, 1928), *see centenary under* Schubert, Franz
Istanbul, 223
Italian National Socialist Party, 346n
Italy, 116, 200n, 264, 271, 326, 343, 452
    Italian opera, 271, 326
Ivanow, O. de: String Quartet, 58

Jacobowski, Ludwig, 63, 64n
Jalowetz, Heinrich, 58
Janáček, Leoš, 203n, 434n
Jannequin, Clément, 193n
Japan, 163
Jean Paul, 337–38
Jews and Judaism, xxxvii, xli, 9n, 32, 38, 93, 106, 153, 159, 181&n, 182, 184, 212n, 224&n, 286, 294, 309, 312, 338n, 350, 353, 358&n, 359, 362, 377, 381, 385, 414; *see also* anti-Semitism *and* Jewishness *under* Schenker, Heinrich
Joachim, Joseph, 196, 366n, 367, 385, 393, 398, 399n
Jöde, Fritz, 292&n
Jonas, Oswald, xii, 315n, 368&n, 377, 388, 456n, 462&n, 463&n, 464&n, 465–66, 479, 481, 484n, 486, 487n; *see also* Oswald Jonas Memorial Collection (Riverside, California)

Judaism, *see* Jews and Judaism
Juilliard Music Foundation, 314n
Juilliard School of Music (New York), 314n, 397n
Julo (brother-in-law of Moriz Violin), 369, 371

Kabasta, Oswald, 462n
Kahn, Marianne, xxxn, 354
Kahnt, C. F. (publisher), 446
Kalbeck, Max, xxiv, 4, 8&n, 10, 17–19, 25, 30, 32, 87n, 102, 296; Plate 21
Kallmeyer, G., 272, 274
Kalmus, Alfred, xxiv, 104, 106, 108, 112–14, 115n, 248, 286, 287n, 461, 462n, 468, 471n, 478
Kalmus, Jacques, 287n, 462n
Kant, Immanuel: *Critique of Pure Reason*, 489
Karer Pass, 226–27
Karnes, Kevin C., 59, 180
Kärntnertor Theater (Vienna), 237
Karpath, Ludwig, 87n, 208–24; Plate 36
Kastropp, Gustav, 5n
Kauner, Hedwig, 145
Keilgasse, Vienna III, xliii, 104n, 363; Plate 11
Keller, Gottfried, 57n
Kern, Ludwig, 362, 363n
Kestenberg, Leo, xxiv, 213, 379–80, 404
Kestner, Prof., 383
Khuner, Paul, xxiv, 385n, 468, 484
Kiel, 145, 306–07, 375n, 401
    Conservatory, xxxi, 381, 403n, 441
    University, xxxi, 145, 375n
Kinsky, Georg, 97, 194, 195n, 199
Kirkpatrick, Ralph, 482, 483n
Kistner (publisher), 10, 14, 94n
Klagenfurt, 3, 45
Klammerth, Mr., 333n
Klasen, Willy, 3
Kleiber, Erich, 202, 203n, 430, 431n, 433
Kleines Journal, 326
Kleist, Heinrich von, 74
Klemperer, Otto, 202, 203n, 224n, 345, 433, 434n, 435
Klenau, Paul von, xxxix, 237–50; Plate 37
Klett-Cotta, 74; *see also* Cotta, J. G. (publisher)
Klimt, Gustav, 33n
Klingler, Fridolin, 366n
Klingler, Karl, 366n
Klingler Quartet, 366&n
Kobald, Karl, 215&n, 216, 219, 222, 223n
Koch, Friedrich Ernst, 339
Koch, Louis, 96&n, 97n, 192

Kolm, Betty, 152n
Kolodin, Irving, 456n
Königsberg, 436
    University, 365n
Kopfermann, Albert, xxiv, 236, 253
Kornfeld, Jeanette, see Schenker, Jeanette [Lie-Liechen]
Korngold, Julius, 87n, 160, 163
Köselitz, Johan Heinrich, see Gast, Peter
Koslovsky, John, 45, 327, 455n
Kral, Trude, xxxn, xliii, 383n, 458n
Kraus, Greta, xxxn, xliii, 383n, 458n, 462&n
Krefeld, 192
Krehl, Stephan, 349
Krenn, Franz, 2, 6n, 288n
Kretzschmar, Hermann, 115n, 160, 257
Kreuzer, Rodolphe, 200
Kroll Opera (Berlin), see Kroll Opera under Berlin
Kromer, Julius [Julo] Ritter von, 187, 198&n, 205, 206&n, 207
Kröner, Adolf, 74
Kröner, Paul, 74
Krupp A. G., 336–37, 339n
Kuhlau, Friedrich, 435
Kunstwart, Der, 261, 372, 381, 403, 405n, 469n, 471n
Kurth, Ernst, xxxix, 147, 273, 275n, 283, 289, 319, 322, 363, 369, 403n, 414–15, 417n
Kurz, H., 87, 229
Kurz, Selma, 365, 366n
Kux, Wilhelm, 3, 98, 99&n, 100

Lamberg, Ernst, 153, 166–69, 170&n, 171–72
Landesmann family, 353, 356
Landsberger, Hilda, see Rothberger, Hilda
Lange, Daniel de, 70n
Lange, Samuel de (Jr.), 441, 445, 446n
League of Nations, 266n, 369, 422
Lebert, Sigmund, 69, 70n
Lehmann, Lili, 19&n
Lehmann, Lotte, 296n
Leipzig, xxxvii, 3–4, 12n, 31, 59, 94n, 97, 114, 130, 131, 145–48, 149n, 191, 199, 202, 208–09, 234&n, 236, 274, 301–02, 306–07, 343, 355n, 363, 365n, 366n, 441, 446–47, 452, 471n
    Conservatory, xxxi, 191, 199, 446n
    Radio Orchestra, 203n
    University, 208–09, 365n, 373
leitmotive, 311

Lemberg, see L'viv (Lemberg)
Leonhardt, Carl, 273, 275n
Leschetizky, Theodor, 6n, 13
Lessing, Gotthold Ephraim, 264, 338
Ley, Stephan, 203, 204&n
Library of Congress (Washington), 97n
Liebscher, A., 261, 262n
Liebstöckl, Hans, 87n, 145
Lienau, Robert, 11&n
Liliencron, Detlev von, 4, 27&n, 28n, 65n
linear progressions, xxxix, 142, 310, 312, 313, 380, 389, 399, 407&n, 418, 437
Linz, 45, 203, 423
Liszt, Franz, 6n, 17n, 36, 37n, 194, 398, 460
Lobotka, Jella Pessel, 482
Loewe, Carl, 31
    "Kleiner Haushalt," 46
    "Nöck, Der," 46
London, 5, 93, 98&n, 99, 100, 101, 160, 192, 420, 424, 430, 444
long-range hearing (Fernhören), 242, 295
Lorenz, Alfred, xxiv, xxiv, 249&n, 322, 378, 380, 416, 437
Löwe, Ferdinand, xxiv, 71, 244
Loyda, Josef, 58
Lübeck, 295, 296n, 316
Ludendorff, Erich, 333, 337, 339n, 354, 355n
Ludwig, Ernst, 2
Lully, Jean-Baptiste, 420n
Luserke, Martin, 273, 275n
L'viv (Lemberg), 45
Lytle, Victor Vaughn, 479, 480n

Maas & Sons, Otto (publisher), 129, 133n
Madrid, 391
Magdeburg, 145
Magdeburgische Zeitung, 145, 326
Mahler, Gustav, 44, 53, 84, 209n, 230n, 286, 295–96, 298, 329, 344–45, 346n, 432
Mallarmé, Stéphane, 42
Mandruck (printing house), 131, 143
Mandyczewski, Eusebius, 98, 102, 144, 295, 296n, 307
Mann, [Paul] Thomas, 430
    Magic Mountain, The, 430
    Tristan, 431
Mannes, Clara, 314n, 397n, 466, 467&n, 472
Mannes, David, 314n, 397n, 466, 467&n, 472; see also David Mannes Music School (New York)

Mannes, Leopold, 314n
Mannes Music School, *see* David Mannes Music School (New York)
Mannheim, 5n, 7, 8n, 9, 11, 68, 70n
  Conservatory, 446n
Marpurg, Friedrich Wilhelm, 339&n
Marx, Adolf Bernhard, 322
Marx, Joseph, xxiv, 169, 170n, 171–73, 176–77, 214, 215&n, 216&n, 217&n, 218, 222&n, 223&n, 224, 386, 468; Plate 31
Marx, Karl, 164
Master Archive, *see* Photogram Archive
Matulke, Agnes, 346n
Mayer, Gustav, 430
Mayerhofer, Irene, xxxn, 3, 13n, 50&n
Meinert, Carl, 93n
Meiningen Court Orchestra, 305, 398
Mendelssohn, Arnold, 170
Mendelssohn, Felix, xxxviiin, 112, 281, 282n, 302, 337, 341n, 427
  songs
    "And'res Maienlied" (Op. 8, No. 8), 34
    "Pagenlied" (WoO 17, No. 2), 34
    "Schilflied" (Op. 71, No. 4), 34
    "Schlafloser Augen Leuchte" (WoO 4, No. 2), 34
  Songs without Words, 207
    "Venetianisches Gondollied" (Op. 30, No. 6), 207
  Variations sérieuses (Op. 54), 433
Mendelssohn Prize, 12n
Mendelssohn Stipend, 174
Mendl, (Chamber Counselor) Fritz, 153–54, 155&n, 156–57, 159–62, 166–67, 170
Merker, Der, 209n
Mery, Béla, 48&n
Messchaert, Johanna, 47
Messchaert, Johannes Martinus, xxxii, xxxiii&n, 26, **44–52**, 60–61, 62n, 64, 65n, 66, 67&n, 68, 196, 385, 393, 398; Plate 24
Meyer, Hans: *Form und Linie in der Musik*, 436
Meyerbeer Stipend, 174
middleground, 283, 350, 472
Mies, Paul, 145
Milstein, Nathan, 385
Ministry of Culture (Germany), 388
Ministry of Education (Austria), xxxvii, 173, 174n, 175&n, 176, 183, 191–92, 209&n, 210, 212, 213&n, 216n, 220, 223
Mitchell, William J., 483n

Mittler, Franz, 158n
modal mixture, 388, 409–11, 412n, 415, 417n
Monteverdi, Claudio, 420n
Morgan, John Pierpont (Jr.), 313, 314n
Mörike, Eduard, 247
Moscheles, Ignaz, 248
Motta, José Vianna da, 42
Mozart, Wolfgang Amadeus, xxxviiin, 51, 69, 91, 93n, 94–95, 130, 139, 189, 197, 206, 264, 277, 279, 297, 313, 362, 378, 397, 403n, 427, 432, 435, 460
  Don Giovanni, 136, 341, 419
  Piano Trio in E major (K. 542), 303
  piano works of, 61
    Adagio in B minor (K. 540), 61
    Rondo in A minor (K. 511), 61, 70n, 95n, 97
    Rondo in D major (K. 485), 95n
    piano sonatas, 91n, 108, 393
      Sonata in A major (K. 331), 265, 286, 288n
      Sonata in A minor (K. 310), 352, 354
  Requiem, 97
  String Quartet in C major ("Dissonance," K. 465), 350, 374–75
  symphonies, 132
    Symphony No. 40 in G minor (K. 550), 132n, 141–43, 202, 248, 363, 432n
    Symphony No. 41 in C major ("Jupiter," K. 551), 227
Mozarteum University of Salzburg, 175n
Muck, Carl, 214&n
Müller-Hartmann, Robert, 383
  Passacaglia for Piano (Op. 17a), 366n
Münchner Neueste Nachrichten, 145
Munich, xxxiv, xxxvi–xxxvii, 71, 94n, 130–31, 136, 142, 144–45, 161&n, 162, 168, 189, 237, 251, 262, 310, 323&n, 340–41, 351, 360, 363, 377, 381, 387, 419, 421, 430
  Academy of Music (State Music Hochschule), 298n, 431n
  Bach Society, 379n
  University, 365n
Music Forum, The, 465
Music Hochschule of the Academy of Arts (Berlin), *see* Academy of Arts *under* Berlin
Music Pedagogical Association (Vienna), 310
Music Teachers' Association of America, 488
Musical Quarterly, The, 347, 348n
Musical Times, The, 98n, 99&n, 100–01, 449n
Musick, De, 145

Musik, Die, 116, 145, 326, 343, 344, 346*n*, 390
Musik der Vergangenheit, 315*n*
Musikblätter des Anbruch, 115&*n*, 116&*n*, 117, 343, 353, 358, 362
Musikverein, *see under* Vienna
Musikwelt, Die, 145
Mussolini, Benito, 345, 430

Nagold, 269, 270*n*
  Teachers' Institute, 270*n*
National Library, *see* Austrian National Library (Vienna)
National Socialism, xli, 92*n*, 93, 215*n*, 218*n*, 274, 275*n*, 387–88, 413*n*, 490*n*
  Bierkeller Putsch, 275*n*
  propaganda, 224*n*
National-Zeitung (Basel), 311
Nazism, *see* National Socialism
Netherlands, 70*n*, 315*n*
Neue freie Presse, 17*n*, 19, 36, 42, 76, 85*n*, 184, 200, 215, 311
Neue Mozart-Ausgabe, 205*n*
Neue Musikzeitung, 145, 260*n*, 272*n*
Neue Preussische Kreuz-Zeitung, 326, 328, 331
Neue Zürcher Zeitung, 145
Neues Wiener Journal, 145, 217*n*
Neues Wiener Tagblatt, 19, 145, 209*n*
Neumann, Miss, 274, 275*n*
Neumeyer, David, 319
New Stuttgart Trio, 282*n*
New Vienna Conservatory, *see under* Vienna
New York, xliv, 93, 107&*n*, 199*n*, 311, 314*n*, 347, 368, 382*n*, 385*n*, 386, 396, 409*n*, 454, 456*n*, **465–90**
  Metropolitan Museum of Art, 314*n*
  Metropolitan Opera, 348*n*
  Public Library, xiii, 487*n*
Niecks, Frederick, 441
Nielsen, Carl (August): Symphony No. 2 ("The Four Temperaments," Op. 16), 42
Nietzsche, Friedrich, xli, 57*n*, 326–27, 334, 340–41, 417*n*, 457*n*
Nijmegen, 145
Norway, 68
Nováček, Ottokar, 12&*n*, 35
Novák, Vítězslav: *Gypsy Songs* (Op. 14), 34
Nuremberg, 430

obligatory register, 401
Ochs, Siegfried, xxv, 24&*n*, 248

Odefey, Alexander, 371*n*
Odescalchi, Princess Babette Clarissa, 203, 204*n*
Odescalchi, Prince Ladislaus, 203
Ohmann, Margarete, 326, 343, 346&*n*; Plate 38
Onégin, Sigrid, 347, 348*n*
Oppel, Reinhard, xxv, xxxi&*n*, 145, 191, 199, 202, 277, 286, 306–07, 375*n*, 378, 381, 394, 398, 421, 422*n*, 432, 488
  Messe für Vierstimmigen Chor (Op. 32), 306&*n*, 307, 421, 422*n*
Orchester, Das, 145
Ostdeutsche Rundschau, 230*n*
Oster, Ernst, xii, 487*n*
Oster Collection (New York Public Library), xiii, 2*n*, 118*n*, 240*n*, 251, 352*n*, 487*n*
Österreichische Credit-Anstalt, 315*n*
Österreichische Rundschau, 98
Oswald Jonas Memorial Collection (Riverside, California), xii, xiii, 2, 93*n*, 240*n*, 315*n*, 483*n*, 487*n*

Pairamall, Evelina, xxx*n*, 421, 422&*n*, 423*n*
Palestrina, Giovanni Pierluigi da, 340, 420
parallel fifths, xxxi, 128*n*, 267, 406
parallel octaves, xxxi, 128*n*, 267, 407
parallelism, 239, 401–02, 406–07
Paris, 94*n*, 101, 136&*n*, 143, 192, 313, 315*n*, 358*n*, 419–20, 426, 427&*n*, 428*n*
  Bibliothèque Nationale, 420*n*
  Conservatory, 192, 420*n*
Pauer, Ernst, 446*n*
Pauer, Max von, 441, 445, 446*n*
Paul, Jean, *see* Jean Paul
Pazeller, Elsa, 58
Penzoldt, Fritz, 347, 348*n*
Perger, Richard von, xxv, 24, 212
Pernter, Hans, 216&*n*, 217, 224
Pestalozzi, Johann Heinrich, 74
Peters, C. F. (publisher), xxxvii, 9, 14, 60, 96, 114, 122, 130, 146, 208, 241, 261, 262*n*, 301, 357–58, 402, 432
Pfitzner, Hans, 192
Pfohl, Ferdinand, xxv, 310, 351
Philadelphia, 488
Philharmonic Publishing House, *see* Wiener Philharmonischer Verlag
Photogram Archive, xiv, xxxvii, xlii–xliii, 94*n*, **187–207**, 246, 306, 418, 423*n*, 425, 426&*n*, 427&*n*, 428–29, 434&*n*, 446, 458*n*, 484–85

Pianoforte, Il, 145
Piazza, Henri, 94*n*, 136*n*
Pierpont Morgan Library (New York), 314*n*, 434*n*
Pietzner-Fayer, 185–86
Piller, 148
Piper, R. (publisher), 130, 202, 203*n*
Pollak, Egon, 364, 365*n*
Pollak, Robert, 303&*n*
Posa, Oskar, xxv, 50, 67*n*
    songs, 62
    "In einer grossen Stadt," 34
    "Irmelin Rose," 34
    Violin Sonata (Op. 7), 62
Prague, 43, 55*n*, 179, 358
Prieger, Erich, 95&*n*, 97
prolongation, 489
Prunières, Henri, 419, 420*n*
Prussia, 330, 333, 336–37, 338&*n*
    State Library (Berlin), 96, 97*n*, 145, 427*n*
Purcell, Henry, 420
Pürglitz Estate, 200

Radio Corporation (RAVAG), *see* RAVAG (Radio-Verkehrs-Aktiengesellschaft)
Radio Vienna (Radio-Wien), *see* Public Radio (Radio-Wien) *under* Vienna
Rameau, Jean-Philippe, 309, 314*n*
Rathenau, Walter, 336, 338*n*
Ratz, Erwin, xii, 487*n*
RAVAG (Radio-Verkehrs-Aktiengesellschaft), 187
Ravel, Maurice, 315*n*, 447
Reclam, Phillip (Jr.) (publisher), 119, 120*n*, 227*n*
Reger, Max, 28*n*, 59, 76&*n*, 84, 257, 277, 279, 280*n*, 285–86, 288*n*, 290, 329, 363, 395, 447
    Variations and Fugue on a Theme of Bach (Op. 81), 200*n*, 286, 288*n*
Reisnerstrasse, Vienna III, 103, 152, 168
Reitler, Josef, 223, 224*n*
Renner, Karl, 298, 299*n*
Revue musicale, 419, 420*n*
Reygersberg, 323*n*
Rhein- und Ruhr-Zeitung, 391
Rheinische Musik- und Theater-Zeitung, 169
Rhineland, xli, 169*n*, 388, 404
    Music Seminar (Duisburg), 387
Rickert, Prof., 248–49
Richter, Ernst Friedrich, 339, 381, 382*n*
Richter, Johann Paul Friedrich, *see* Jean Paul

Richtera, Leopold, 187, 190*n*, 196
Riegl, Alois, 179
Riemann, Hugo, 68, 70*n*, 78, 79*n*, 88, 160, 198, 319, 322, 335, 339, 369, 381, 382*n*, 392, 394*n*, 401–02, 447
Riemanns Musiklexikon, xxxii, 388, 392, 428, 429*n*, 441
Rieter-Biedermann, J. (publisher), 10
Rilke, Rainer Maria, 27*n*
Rintelen, Anton, 215*n*
Robert, Richard, 87*n*
Robitschek, Adolf (publisher), xxxiii&*n*
Rochlitzer, Ludwig, 192, 193*n*
Röder, C. G. (printing house), 131, 148, 149&*n*
Roentgen, Julius, *see* Röntgen, Julius
Rolland, Romain, 264, 292&*n*
Rome, 343, 346, 348*n*, 353
Röntgen, Engelbert, 71*n*, 72*n*
Röntgen, Julius, xxv, xxxiii&*n*, xxxiv, 44–45, 46*n*, 51, **59–72**; Plate 25
    Oud hollandsche boerenliedjes en contradansen, 67*n*
    Piano Quintet, 68, 70
Röntgen, Julius (Jr.), 72*n*
Röntgen Trio, 72*n*
Rosé, Alexander, 67*n*, 362, 363*n*
Rosé, Arnold, 9, 10*n*, 13, 18, 48, 50, 57, 67*n*; *see also* Rosé Quartet
Rosé Quartet, 9, 10*n*, 57
Rossini, Gioachino: *Barber of Seville, The*, 30
Rostock
    Philharmonic Orchestra, 71*n*
    University, 351*n*
Roth, Ernst, 106
Roth, Herman, xxv, xxx, 144, 161&*n*, 214&*n*, 257, 310, 357–58, 377, 434, 444&*n*; Plate 29
Rothberger, Alfred, xxxi, 160, 161*n*
Rothberger, Hilda, xxx–xxxi
Rothe, Barbara, 106, 124, 125*n*
Rothfarb, Lee, 37*n*, 257
Rothgeb, John, 251, 418
Rothschild, Alphons Mayer von, xxv, xxxvii–xxxviii, 13*n*, 33*n*, 80&*n*, 86, 87&*n*, 90, 162, 296*n*
Rothschild Artists' Foundation, xxxvii, 153*n*, 158&*n*, 164*n*, 181–82
Rothschild family, xxxviii, 315
Rottenberg, Ludwig, 64, 65*n*
Royal Conservatory of The Hague, 70*n*
Royal Swedish Academy, 65*n*

Rubinstein, Anton, 51
Rückert, Friedrich, 74
Rudolph von Habsburg-Lothrigen, Archduke of Austria, 425
Rudorff, Ernst, 208, 228, 229&n
Russia, 7, 271, 331n, 459&n

Saint Petersburg, 319
Sallenthin, Dr., 397
Salmhofer, Franz, 250
Salzburg, 313, 333n, 383, 423, 432
Salzer, Felix, xxv, xliii–xliv, 368&n, 376, 380, 383n, **454–64**, 465, 483n, 484n, 485, 487n; Plate 42
  Sinn und Wesen der abendländischen Mehrstimmigkeit (*The Meaning and Essence of Western Polyphony*), 454, 455n, 459n, 463
  "Sonata Form in Franz Schubert," 454
Salzer, Helene, 454
Samuel, Harold, 472, 473n
San Francisco, 396
Sanatorium Auersperg, 154
Sanatorium Schierke, 369
Santini Collection, 427, 428n
Sarajevo, 335
Saturn Verlag, 463, 464n, 484&n
Savart, Louis, 3
scale-step, 280, 283–84, 472, 473n
Scarlatti, Domenico, 22, 60, 320, 321n, 388, 483n
Schäfke, Rudolf, 415, 417n
Schalk, Franz, 288n
Scheidemann, Philipp, 209
Schelling, Friedrich Wilhelm Joseph, 74
Schenker, Georg, 375n
Schenker, Heinrich, Plates 1–4, 10–15
  accompanist, as, *see* performance activities *under* Schenker, Heinrich
  authorities and establishment, attitude to the, xxxvii, xxxviii&n, xl, **151–224**, 210n, 246, 428
  Brahms, relationship with, 8, 63, 72, 393, 398, 399n
  composer, as, xxxii–xxxiii, **2–43**, 75
  compositions, 2–3, 7, 9, 45, 51, 61n, 64
    Fantasy for piano (Op. 2), xxxii, 3, 7, 8n, 9, 11–15, 17–26, 32, 46&n
    Five Pieces for Piano (Op. 4), 3–4, 9, 13, 16&n, 17&n, 18–20, 26, 28, 46&n
    Hamlet, incidental music to, 2
    Ländler (Op. 10), 3, 22–24, 26

Schenker, Heinrich, *continued*
  compositions, *continued*
    Serenade for Horn and Piano, 2–3
    Six Songs (Op. 3), 3, 21, 27&n, 28n, 59, 63, 64&n, 65&n, 66
    String Quartet (fragmentary, unpublished), 13, 18
    Syrian Dances, xxxii–xxxiii, 26&n, 29n, **30–43**; Plate 9
    Three Songs (Op. 6), 3, 28
    [Three songs for mixed chorus] (Op. 7), 2–3, 22, 24, 29
    Two Pieces for Piano (Op. 1), 3, 6, 13n
    Two-voice Inventions (Op. 5), 3, 21, 59, 61, 63, 64n, 65
  compositions, performances of, 3, 7, 17&n, 29, **30–43**, 46, 63–64, 65n
  compositions, reviews of, 18–20, 29n, 42&n, 43&n
  contractual agreements, *see* financial and contractual matters *under* Schenker, Heinrich
  cultural outlook, xxx, xli, xliv, 60, 106, 107&n, 256–57, 263–64, 332n, 341; *see also* worldview *under* Schenker, Heinrich
  contemporaneous music and musical culture, view of, xxxv, xxxix–xl, xliv, 10n, 30–31, 45, 53, 54n, 57, 62n, 63–64, 76, 84, 118n, 152–53, 157–58, 188, 194, 196–97, 199, 226, 229n, 232n, 238, 245–46, 257, 260n, 264–65, 268, 271, 274, 283, 286, 288, 294–95, 311–14, **318–23**, 331, 342, 350, 353, 374, 425, 429, 450, 451&n; *see also* genius, views on *under* Schenker, Heinrich *and* Decline of the Art of Composition, The *under* theoretical, critical and pedagogical works *under* Schenker, Heinrich
  folk music, view of, xliv, 460
  jazz, view of, xliii, 392, 451&n
  opera, thoughts on, xxxiii, 45, 393, 394n
  Wagner, view of, xl, xliii, 82, 164, 231, 257, 264–65, 294, 302, 311, 316, 363, 364n, 449n, 450
  diaries, xi, xxx, 153, 179, 327, 350, 487n
  editorial works, 59
    Bach, Carl Philipp Emanuel, xxxiii–xxxv, 32n, 35–36, 62, 67, 69, 91, 133, 188, 384
    Bach, Johann Sebastian, xxxiii–xxxiv, 133, 227, 228n, 230, 353, 355n, 358

Schenker, Heinrich, *continued*
  editorial works, *continued*
    Beethoven, Ludwig van, xxxi, xxxiv–xxxvi, xxxix, xli, 75, 91, **93–105**, 109n, 110&n, 117, 121, 128, 133–34, 143, 158n, 199&n, 227, 232–33, 234&n, 235–36, 238, 254, 256, 258&n, 259–61, 262n, 264n, 267, 269, 274–75, 281, 282&n, 286–87, 288n, 290, 327n, 331&n, 338, 351, 352&n, 353–54, 357, 364, 381, 393, 397, 428, 442, 445; *see also* Beethoven, Ludwig van *and* elucidatory editions *under* editorial works *under* Schenker, Heinrich
    elucidatory editions (*Erläuterungsausgaben*), xxxi, xxxiv–xxxv, xxxix, xlii, 91, 93, 96, 109n, 110&n, 134, 199&n, 227, 228n, 232, 238, 254, 256, 258n, 259, 260, 262n, 264n, 267, 269, 270n, 274–75, 286–87, 288n, 290, 327n, 331&n, 338, 351, 352&n, 353–54, 355n, 393, 442, 445
    Handel, George Frideric, xxxiii
  education
    Bruckner, with, xxxii, 2, 284–85
    legal training, xxxii, xxxiv, 2, 152, 159&n, 208&n, 315n
    Vienna Conservatory, xxxii, 2
    Vienna, University of, xxxii, 2, 208
  financial and contractual matters, xxxvi, xlii–xliii, 2, 10, 12–13, 16, 18–19, 21, 24, 28, 32, 36–37, 39, 51, 60, 62, 64, 65n, 75, 76&n, 79, 83n, 85–92, 94, 96–98, 102, 103&n, 104&n, 105, 109, 110&n, 121&n, 123–25, 126&n, 127&n, 128, 131, 133–34, 137–39, 146, 149–50, **152–78**, 189, 191, 192n, 217, 231, 253, 262, 266–67, 269n, 283, 286, 304, 360, 379, 381, 383–84, 393, 419, 421, 422, 429, 436–37, 438n
  genius, views on, xxxii, xxxvi, xxxviii, xli, 62, 106, 107&n, 112, 114, 153n, 159, 243, 256, 257&n, 260, 263, 268, 283–84, 289, 292n, 312–13, 314n, 316, 327, 331, 332n, 334&n, 339, 342, 349, 351, 381, 385, 415, 429, 432, 464
  health, xlii, 126, 127n, 202, 204, 267, 310, 363n, 373, 375n, 378, 381, 383–84, 405, 432, 480
  Jewishness, xxxvii, xli, 32, 38, 106, 159, 181–82, 224&n, 294, 309, 312, 350, 358&n, 377, 385, 414

Schenker, Heinrich, *continued*
  legacy, views on his own, xxx, xxxviiin, xl, 154, 157, 294–95, 313, 353, 425–26, 438, 485
  legal disputes, xxxiv, xxxvi, **106–29**, 130, 138, 140, **152–78**, 367, 376, 381
  lessonbooks, xi, xliii, 203n, 420n
  manuscript studies, xxxix, **93–105**, **187–207**, **237–54**, 425, 427; *see also* Photogram Archive
  marriage to Jeanette, 93, 153
  music critic, as, xxxi, xxxiii, 10, 11n, 36, 44, 56, 111, 113n, 230, 233, 235, 292, 327
  performance activities, xxxii, 26, 34, **44–52**, 393
  performance practice, xxxix, 10, 46n, 59, **237–54**, 261, 265, 296–97, 305, 402, 421, 423n
  polemical style, xxxi, xxxvi, 30, 62n, 97, 106, 110&n, 111–12, 113&n, 124, 237, 281, 300, 305, 323, 332n, 466
  political views, xxxix, xliv, 106, 109, 111–13, 116, 164, 208–09, 256–57, 264, 266n, 271, 294, 313, 326–27, 331–33, 341, 348, 351&n, 388, 445; *see also* worldview *under* Schenker, Heinrich
  publishers, xxxiv–xxxvii, 3–5, 10, **73–150**; *see also* Breitkopf & Härtel (publisher) *and* Cotta, J. G. (publisher) *and* Drei Masken Verlag *and* Simrock, N. (publisher) *and* Universal Edition [UE] *and* Weinberger, Josef [Joseph] (publisher) *and* Wiener Philharmonischer Verlag
  teaching activities, xxxn, 5, 8n, 82, 117, 153, 157, 208, 217, 223, 262, 269n, 287, 294, 354, 362, 373, 389, 392, 408&n, 418–19, 420n, 421, 422&n, 433, 435, 437, **454–64**; *see also* pedagogy *under* Schenkerian theory
  theoretical, critical and pedagogical works
    Beethoven's Ninth Symphony, xxxviii–xxxix, xliii, 75, 91, 134, **226–36**, 244–45, 247, 248n, 251n, 252, 288n, 296n, 316, 397, 441, 448, 449n
    Contribution to the Study of Ornamentation, A, xxxiii, xxxiv&n, 59, 68, 70n, 71, 75, 181n, 384, 397, 445, 454
    Decline of the Art of Composition, The, 75&n, 78n, 81n, 82, 84n, 91, 210n, 228, 229n, 428

Schenker, Heinrich, *continued*
  theoretical, critical and pedagogical works, *continued*
    Five Analyses in Sketchform, xxxi, xliv, 28n, 128n, 131, 132n, 199n, 316n, 386–87, 400n, 403n, 407n, 454, 456n, 457&n, 471n, 473n
    "Johannes Brahms: Octaves and Fifths," xxxi, 128n
    Little Library (Kleine Bibliothek), 75, 91, 95&n, 96–97, 109, 110n, 134, 227n, 266&n, 267, 341, 351&n, 352&n; *see also* Pocket Library (Handbibliothek) *under* theoretical, critical and pedagogical works *under* Schenker, Heinrich *and* Tonwille, Der *under* theoretical, critical and pedagogical works *under* Schenker, Heinrich
    Masterwork in Music, The (Das Meisterwerk in der Musik), xxxvi–xxxvii, xl–xli, xliii–xliv, 113n, 118n, 126n, **130–50**, 189n, 200n, 206, 253, 287n, 288n, 291n, 310n, 314n, 315n, 318n, 321n, 327n, 358n, 364n, 367n, 378, 383n, 389, 391n, 403n, 405n, 409n, 417n, 424, 428, 432n, 447n, 449n, 451n, 465, 469n, 472, 473n
    New Musical Theories and Fantasies, xxxv, xxxviii, xliii, 74–92, 107n, 117, 121, 128, 160, 226–29, 328, 358, 371n, 397, 442–43, 449n
      Counterpoint, xxxv, xliii, 74–75, 76&n, 82n, 84n, 87n, 88–89, 90n, 92&n, 107&n, 117, 210n, 227, 229n, 232&n, 259, 262–63, 265, 267, 269–70, 332, 345, 351, 352&n, 354, 393, 428, 441, 443, 444n, 448, 477, 485
      Free Composition (Der freie Satz), xiii, xxxi, xlii–xliv, 28n, 75, 118n, 128n, 198, 199n, 206n, 217, 269, 285, 291–92, 358, 363n, 371n, 372&n, 373, 378, 381, 383–85, 390–91, 409n, 417, 428, 432, 438n, 441, 442&n, 450, 454, 460, 461n, 464, 466, 468, 478–79, 481–83, 485–86, 487&n, 488–89
      Theory of Harmony (Harmonielehre), xxxii, xxxiv&n, xxxv, xxxviii, 30, **74–92**, 95, 117, 182n, 216n, 217&n, 222n, 229n, 373, 389n, 412n, 417n, 461&n, 468, 469n, 472–73, 477, 485

Schenker, Heinrich, *continued*
  theoretical, critical and pedagogical works, *continued*
    Niloff's Table of Instrumentation, 37n, 231n, 234n, 396
    Pocket Library (Handbibliothek), 226, 227&n, 228; *see also* Little Library (Kleine Bibliothek) *under* theoretical, critical and pedagogical works *under* Schenker, Heinrich *and* Tonwille, Der *under* theoretical, critical and pedagogical works *under* Schenker, Heinrich
    "Tone System, The" (unpublished), xxxiv&n
    Tonwille, Der, xxxvi, xxxix, 75, 95n, 104, **106–29**, 130–32, 133&n, 139, 144, 227n, 231n, 244n, 246, 249, 266n, 269n, 273, 276–77, 281, 283, 285–86, 287&n, 288n, 290–91, 313, 327n, 342n, 343, 346n, 348–50, 351n, 352n, 353–54, 355n, 357, 358n, 359–64, 365&n, 366&n, 381, 382n, 393, 396, 429, 445, 472; *see also* Little Library (Kleine Bibliothek) *under* theoretical, critical and pedagogical works *under* Schenker, Heinrich *and* Pocket Library (Handbibliothek) *under* theoretical, critical and pedagogical works *under* Schenker, Heinrich
  typesetting of music examples, xxxvi–xxxvii, xli, xliv, 79, 80n, 82–83, 106, 108, 109n, 119, 129, 130–31, 136, 141–43, 144n, 147–48, 149&n, 198, 287n, 291n, 302n, 375, 400n, 408, 485
  worldview, xxx, xxxvi–xxxviii, 109–11, 113, 257, 266n, 271, 294, 313, 327, 331
Schenker, Jeanette [Lie-Liechen], xxvi, xxx&n, xxxi, xxxivn, xxxix, 29, 93, 107, 117n, 118n, 119&n, 127n, 128, 130–31, 153, 155n, 173n, 178n, 182, 194n, 198n, 212, 221, 240n, 251&n, 259n, 264n, 297, 304, 309, 314n, 315, 321, 326, 333, 342n, 351, 352&n, 353, 358–60, 362–63, 365, 367–68, 370, 375–76, 378&n, 381, 382&n, 385n, 386, 387, 403n, 471, 480–81, 483–84, 487n, 488–89; Plates 15–18
Schenker, Johann, 37n, 264n, 394n
Schenker, Julia, xxvi, xxxi, 194n, 233, 262
Schenker, Lie-Liechen, *see* Schenker, Jeanette [Lie-Liechen]

Schenker, Marcus, 37n
Schenker, Moriz [Mozio], xxvi, xxxi, 119n, 122n, 128n, 168, 354, 373, 375n, 376, 381
Schenker, Rebecka, 394n
Schenker, Sophie [Schifre], *see* Guttmann, Sophie [Schifre]
Schenker, Wilhelm, xxxi, 194n
Schenker Academy, *see* Heinrich Schenker Academy (Hamburg)
Schenker Documents Online, xiv
Schenker Institute (Hamburg), xli–xlii, xliv, 211n, 300, 311, 314n, 380, 382n, 383–84, 385n, 387, 416, 467n, 490&n
Schenker Institute (New Vienna Conservatory), 422n, 423n
Schenkerian theory
  Americanization, **465–90**
  dissemination, xli, xliii–xliv, **325–490**
  pedagogy, xxxi, xli, 191, 217, 223, 313, 442–43, **454–90**
Schenner, Wilhelm, 285, 288n
Scheu, Gustav, 127n
Scheuermann (bookshop), 387, 391&n, 395–96
Schicht, see structural levels
Schiedermair, Ludwig, 192, 193n, 395, 396n
Schiff, Anna, xxxi
Schiff, Jeanette, *see* Schenker, Jeanette [Lie-Liechen]
Schiff, Paul, xxxi
Schiff, Victor, xxxi
Schiller, Friedrich von, 74, 264
  Lied von der Glocke, 426n
  Wallenstein, 302n
Schillings, Max von, 237
Schindler, Anton Felix, 309, 421, 423n
Schirmer, G. (publisher), 478n
Schlesinger, Adolf Martin, 11&n, 101, 439
Schlesinger Music Library, 227n
Schmemann (bookshop), 391
Schmid, Ernst Fritz, 204, 205n
Schmid, Theodor Karl, 269, 270n
Schmid, Waldemar, 373, 375n, 403
Schmidt, Franz, xxvi, 173, 174&n, 214, 215&n, 222
Schmidt, Karl, 145
Schmidt, Leopold: *Joseph Haydn*, 144&n
Schmitz, Richard, 199n
Schnabel, Artur, 379n
Schneider, Hans, 417n
Schnerich, Alfred, 97
Schnitzler, Arthur, 71

Schoenberg, Arnold, xxxii–xxxiii, xxxix, 10n, **30–43**, **53–58**, 65n, 117, 191, 196, 203n, 224n, 230n, 232n, 238, 245n, 250, 257, 292, 301, 319, 322, 326, 344–45, 346n, 350, 361–62, 373–74, 401, 403n, 409, 415, 434n, 474
  Chamber Symphony No. 1 (Op. 9), 53, 57
  Eight Songs (Op. 6), 57n
  Four Songs (Op. 2), 57n
  Friede auf Erden, 440n
  Gurrelieder, 37n
  Music to Accompany a Film Scene, 439, 440n
  Pelleas und Melisande, 30, 37n, 39n
  Six Songs (Op. 3), 57n
  String Quartet No. 1 (Op. 7), 53, 57
  String Quartet No. 2 (Op. 10), 53
  Theory of Harmony, 30–31, 53, 117, 118n
  Three Pieces for Piano (Op. 11), 53
  twelve-tone method of, 30
  Two Songs (Op. 1), 57n
  Verklärte Nacht, 30
Schopenhauer, Arthur, 329, 337
Schott & Sons (publisher), 430
Schreier, Otto, 351&n
Schreker, Franz, 214n, 296n, 308&n, 345, 353, 362, 380, 382n
Schubert, Franz, xxxviiin, 44, 93n, 94, 95&n, 102, 132, 189, 282, 296n, 308, 320, 321n, 322, 341n, 362, 366, 369, 426, 427n, 454
  centenary, 188, 199, 200n
  Gretchen am Spinnrade (Op. 2, D. 118), 287n
  "Ihr Bild" ("I Stood in Dark Dreams," D. 957, No. 9), 271, 272n
  "Liebesbotschaft" (D. 957, No. 1), 46
  "Meeresstille" (D. 216), 46&n
  Moment Musical in F minor (D. 780, No. 3), 366
  "Nacht und Träume" (D. 827), 46&n
  Symphony in B minor ("Unfinished," D. 759), xxxv, xln, 307, 308n
Schubert Museum (Vienna), 189
Schumann, Elisabeth, 296n
Schumann, Robert, xxxviiin, 51, 60, 112, 282n, 341n, 362
  "beiden Grenadiere, Die" (Op. 49, No. 1), 46
  Fantasy (Op. 17), 11, 12n, 17–18
  Intermezzo (Op. 4, No. 5), 64
  Symphonic Etudes (Op. 13), 433
Schünemann, Georg, 214n, 380, 382n
Schuster & Loeffler (publisher), 301, 344–45, 346n

Schütt, Eduard, 13
  "Am Birnbaum," 34
  "Ewig mein bleibt, was ich liebe!," 34
  "Öffnet' ich die Herzensthür," 34
Schwäbische Merkur, 76n
Schwarzwald School (Vienna), 30
Scotland, 192, 445
Scotsman, The, 441, 452, 453n
Scott, Walter, 160
Scriabin, Alexander Nikolayevich, 388
Secessionist movement (Vienna), 33&n
Sedlmair, Sophie, 49n
Seidel's bookshop (Vienna), 105&n
Seitz, Karl, 423, 424n
Seligmann, Adalbert Franz, xxx, 85&n
Seminar for Private Music Teachers, 431n
Sezession, see Secessionist movement (Vienna)
Shaw, George Bernard: *Saint Joan*, 306
Siegel, Hedi, 454
Simrock, N. (publisher), 3–4, 10, 23&n, 24–25, 26&n, 27, 32, 75, 208
Singakademie (Vienna), see Singakademie under Vienna
Sittard, Alfred, 356&n
Smetana, Bedřich, 271, 312
Social Democratism, 257, 299n, 393, 423
Society for Creative Musicians, xxxiii, **53–58**
Society of the Friends of Music (Gesellschaft der Musikfreunde), see under Vienna
sonata form, xl, 78n, 257, 260 261n, 294, 305, 454
Sonderegger, Anton, 200n
Sonneck, Oscar, 347, 348n
Spengler, Oswald, 30, 342&n
  Decline of the West, The, 342n
Speyer, Edward, 98&n, 99–101
Spiegler, Hans, 304
Sporck, Ferdinand, 6n
Stamitz, Johann, 70n
Stark, Ludwig, 69, 70n
Starnberg (lake), 5
Stauber, Paul, 230&n
Steigentesch, August Ernst, 6n
Stein, Erwin, 58
Stein, Fritz, xxvi, 214&n, 369
Steiner, Franz, 68&n, 69, 72, 465
Steingräber, 355n
Steinhof, Prof., 427, 428n
Steinway, 356
Stendhal, 340
Stern, Alfred, 153n, 181&n, 182

Stern Conservatory (Berlin), 61n, 214n
Sternheim, Carl, 387
Stirling, Jane, xxvi, 143, 439
Stockhausen, Julius, 44, 60&n, 61n
Strasser, Otto, 200n
Straube, Karl, xxvi, 146–47, 208, 300, 308
Strauss, Richard, xxxv, 28n, 36, 37n, 44, 63, 76&n, 209n, 220, 257, 286, 297, 329, 344, 413n, 463n, 465
  Elektra, 264
  Sinfonia domestica, 53
Stravinsky, Igor, xl, 203n, 298n, 303, 311, 315n, 434n
  Concerto for Piano and Wind Instruments, 200n
Strecker, Dr., 430
structural levels, xxxv, 279n, 385
Strüve, Paul, 388
Stuttgart, xxxiv, 74, 144–45, 160, 227–28, 237, 260n, 269, 273, 345, 353, 445
  Conservatory, 441, 446n
  Music Hochschule, 275n
  Opera, 270n
Stuttgarter Zeitung, 377
Süddeutsche Zeitung Stuttgart, 282n
Supreme Court (Vienna), 166
Switzerland, 200n, 273, 306n, 316, 382, 446
Sylt, 203n, 382n, 430, 431&n
Symphonia, 145
synthesis, 64, 237, 280n, 283, 290, 294, 296, 311, 341, 385, 469n
Szalit, Paula, 5, 6n, 8&n
Szigeti, Joseph, 460&n

Tägliche Rundschau, 42
Tagore, Rabindranath, 465
Tautenhayn, Karl [Carl] Hermann, 199&n, 200n
Tautenhayn Quartet, 200n
Tchaikovsky, Pyotr Ilyich: Symphony No. 5 in E minor (Op. 64), 308
Temming, Max, 121n, 360, 361&n, 363n, 364–66, 382n
Tenants Harbor, Maine, 463, 479, 483
Tendler, Carl, 48&n
Terry, Charles Sanford, xxvii, 192, 446
Thausing, Moriz, 179
Theodor Kretschmann Music School, 224
Theresienstadt (Terezín) concentration camp, xi, xii, xxxi, 487n
Thomasberger, Konrad, 213&n

thoroughbass, xii, xl, 201, 206, 267, 315, 334, 341, 374, 381, 438, 482
Thuille, Ludwig, 237, 322, 381, 382n
Tirpitz, Alfred von, 337, 339n
Tomasz, Etta, 58
Tomay, Georg, xxxvii, 131, 147–49, 461&n
tonality/tonal system/tonal space, xlii, 63–64, 200n, 244, 318–19, 342, 377, 388, 409–11, 415
Tonkunst, Die, 368&n, 390, 465
Tonkünstler Orchestra Association, 299
Toscanini, Arturo, 147, 188, 460, 461
Tovey, Donald Francis, xliii, 441, 445, 449n, 452, 453n
Trieste, 45
Tübingen, 74
  University, 74, 260n
Turin, 145
Türkel, Siegfried, 153, 155–57, 159&n, 160–63, 165&n, 166, 170
Türtscher family, 397&n
Tyrol, the, 81n, 120n, 261, 291, 306

Überbrettl, 27n
Ulm, 269
Ungar, Fritz, xxvii, 368n, 463
United Kingdom, 441
United States of America, xli, xliii–xliv, 107, 144, 222&n, 264, 267, 314n, 316, 318, 342, 347, 360, 380, 388, 396, 397n, 434n, 451, 454, 457, **465–90**
Universal Edition [UE], xii, xiv, xxxi, xxxiii, xxxiv&n, xxxv–xxxvi, xxxviii–xxxix, 30, 37n, 38, 41&n, 43, 53, 59, 61n, 66n, 74&n, 75, 76n, 92n, 95, 97–102, 103&n, **106–29**, 130–34, 139, 158n, 199&n, 208, 217, 228n, 230, 231&n, 232–36, 249, 253–54, 258–60, 262&n, 267, 272, 286–87, 288n, 342, 344, 350, 352n, 353–54, 357, 366n, 367&n, 373, 382n, 384, 393–94, 429, 457n, 458n, 471n, 477, 478&n
University of California at Riverside, xii–xiii, 487n
Unterholzner, Ludwig, 145
Urlinie, xin, xxxv, 108, 109n, 132, 136, 142, 144n, 148, 149n, 188–89, 198, 199&n, 217, 256–57, 271, 273, 275n, 286, 287n, 290, 301, 316, 320–21, 341, 354, 358, 362, 369, 377, 381, 382n, 385, 389, 391, 394&n, 395–97, 399, 404, 407n, 413, 415, 417–18, 429, 434, 436–37, 447, 456&n, 457n, 468, 475

Ursatz, 310, 413, 468, 489

Velhagen & Klasing's Monatshefte, 203, 204n
Verdi, Giuseppe, 312, 314n
Vereinigung schaffender Tonkünstler, *see* Society for Creative Musicians
Versailles, Treaty of, 266n, 342
Victoria Hotel (Amsterdam), 52
Vienna, xxxii, xxxv, xli, 2–3, 24, 30, 34, 35n, 39n, 42n, 43n, 44–45, 54&n, 68, 70–72, 93, 98–99, 143, 145, 147&n, 148, 152–53, 155n, 158&n, 163&n, 169, 170, 173, 175n 179, 183–84, 189&n, 191, 203, 205&n, 208, 212–13, 217, 219, 223, 224, 238, 262, 265, 268, 292&n, 299, 308, 310, 313, 321, 328–29, 353, 356, 360, 363n, 368–69, 376, 380, 384, 385&n, 387, 390–91, 398, 420, 422–23, 424n, 426–27, 432, 434, 440n, 445, 454, 464, 481
  Academy, *see* Conservatory (Academy/Hochschule for Music and Performing Arts) *under* Vienna
  Bank Association (Wiener Bankverein), 153, 155&n, 156, 162
  Concert House, *see* Concert Society *under* Vienna
  Concert Society (Konzertverein), 68, 71, 209n, 237, 245n, 246n, 249, 296n, 329; *see also* Symphony Orchestra *under* Vienna
  Conservatory (Academy/Hochschule for Music and Performing Arts), xiv, xxxii, xxxvii, 2, 6n, 10n, 152&n, 153, 167, 169–77, 206, **209–24**, 226, 232, 288n, 296n, 298, 299, 300, 462&n, 478n
  Court Opera, *see* State (Court) Opera (Staatsoper, Hofoper) *under* Vienna
  Court Theatre (Hoftheater), 55n
  Folk Opera, *see* People's Opera (Volksoper) *under* Vienna
  Library in the City Hall (Wienbibliothek im Rathhaus), xiv
  Museum of the City of Vienna, 184–85
  Musikverein, 49n, 107
    small hall, 45
    large hall, 440n
  National Library, *see* Austrian National Library (Vienna)
  New Vienna Conservatory, 224n, 303n, 423
  People's Opera (Volksoper), 55n, 209n

Vienna, *continued*
  Philharmonic Orchestra, 10n, 147n, 175n, 306n
  Public Radio (Radio-Wien), 187, 190n, 196n, 200n
  Singakademie, 3–4, 29, 37
  Society of the Friends of Music (Gesellschaft der Musikfreunde), 37, 93, 97, 144, 296n, 302
  State (Court) Opera (Staatsoper, Hofoper), 10n, 19n, 71n, 245n, 366n
  Symphony Orchestra, 203n, 238, 375n, 440n, 462n
  University, xxxii, 2, 152, 179, 183, 193n, 200n, 208, 224, 296n, 423, 454, 465
"Vienna School" of art history, 179
Viennese Merchants' Guild, 57
Vilnius, 331&n, 332
Violin, Eduard, 357, 358&n, 360, 375n
Violin, Fanny, 356&n, 361, 363, 367&n, 370, 379, 383
Violin, Genoveva [Eva], xii, 370&n
Violin, Karl [Karli], 350, 357, 359n, 360–61, 368, 370, 372, 386n
Violin, Moriz [Floriz], xin, xxvii, xli, xliv, 4, 7, 13n, 32n, 34, 35n, 40, 42, 48n, 64, 72, 107, 121n, 144, 155, 182, 194, 208, 209&n, 210, 211&n, 212n, 223&n, 226, 297, 298&n, 299–300, 314n, **350–86**, 387–88, 389n, 403n, 408, 416–17, 466, 467n, 488, 490n; Plates 40–41
Violin, Valerie [Vally, Wally], 351&n, 356, 358, 361, 369, 370n, 372, 378, 386
Vogt Conservatory (Hamburg), 211n, 361n
voice-leading, xxxv, xliv, 130, 197, 249, 259, 265, 267, 276, 302n, 328, 330, 334, 350, 358n, 364, 372&n, 374, 376–78, 387–88, 399, 400n, 404, 413n
Volkmann, Ludwig, 146&n
Vossische Zeitung (Berlin), 145, 224n, 316
Vötterle, Karl, 202, 203n
Vrieslander, Klaus, 394
Vrieslander, Otto, xxvii, xxxi, xxxvii, xxxix, 87–89, 92, 105, 115&n, 117, 130–31, 134, 141–42, 144, 161&n, 162, 163n, 191, 199, 202, 203n, 205, 264n, 334&n, 338, 341, 343, 350–51, 363, 368, 377, 381–82, 384–85, 387, 389, 390, 391&n, 392, 394&n, 402, 403n, 405n, 422, 424, 426–27, 429, 431, 445, 466, 468, 469n, 470, 471n, 472–74, 475&n, 477, 488; Plate 29

Wagner, Richard, xl, xliii, 63, 82, 164, 214n, 230n, 231, 249n, 257, 265, 275n, 282n, 294, 302, 304, 311, 316, 321n, 340, 344, 351, 363, 364n, 436, 441, 449n, 450, 463n
  Parsifal, 329n
  Siegfried, 345–46
  Tristan und Isolde, 264, 275n
Waldeck, Arthur, 469n, 470
Waldheim & Eberle (printing house), 131, 136, 189, 375, 457&n, 458n
Walter, Bruno, 296n, 430
Waltershausen, Hermann Wolfgang, 430, 431n
Warburg, Gerald F., 380, 382n, 465
Wason, Robert, 74n, 318–19
Webenau, Wilma von, 58
Weber, Carl Maria von, 143
Webern, Anton von, 440n, 474
  Piano Quintet, 58
Wedge, George, xxvii, 311, 467
Weill, Arnold, xxxi
Weill, Kurt, 203n, 434n
Weill, Rosa, xxxi
Weimar, 430
  Court Theater, 55n
Weimar Republic, xxxviii, 214n, 256, 272n, 299n, 330n, 338, 348
Weinberger, Josef [Joseph] (publisher), xxvii, xxxiii, 30–32, 34, 38–39, 41, 43, 59–60, 62, 75, 106, 208; Plate 23
Weingarten, Paul, 10
Weingartner, Felix, 115n, 248–50, 297, 298n, 305
Weisbach [Weissbach], Hans, 202, 203n
Weisse, Adolf, 478n
Weisse, Hans, xiii, xxviii, xxix, xxxvii, xxxix, xli, xliii–xliv, 114, 131, 150, 179, 182n, 191, 213, 215&n, 222&n, 224, 301, 303–05, 307, 309–11, 316, 333&n, 350, 353, 355&n, 361&n, 362, 366, 368, 376–77, 378&n, 379–81, 382n, 383&n, 384, 385&n, 386&n, 390–91, 396, 405, 408, 409n, 421, 422&n, 429, 454, 455&n, 456&n, 461, 463, **465–90**; Plate 43
  Four Vocal Quartets with Piano Accompaniment (Op. 6), 366
  Octet in D major (1930), xliii, 309, 376, 379
  Six Bagatelles for Piano (1929), 376
  String Quartet (Op. 4), 304
  Variations and Fugue for Two Pianos, 476, 478
  Violin Sonata, 476
Weisse, Hertha, 386&n, 469–71, 478, 480, 483–84

Weisse, Monika, 483, 487
Weisse, Susannah [Susi], 477, 478n, 483
Weissgärber, Max, 200n
Wellesz, Egon, 221
Werfel, Franz, 312, 314n
Werker, Wilhelm, 292&n, 416, 417n
Westphal, Johann Jacob Heinrich, 201
Weyrich, Rudolf: Rondo for Piano, String Quartet, 58
Whittall, Arnold, 31, 53, 319
Wickersdorf, 144, 258n, 260, 261n, 269, 272–73, 275n
Wiener, Karl von, 209&n, 210, 211&n, 215n
Wiener Konzertverein, see Concert Society (Konzertverein) under Vienna
Wiener Morgenzeitung, 145
Wiener Neue Revue, 8, 10
Wiener Philharmonischer Verlag, xxxv, 243, 244n, 254
Wiener Singakademie, see Singakademie under Vienna
Wilhelm II, Kaiser, 326, 336–37, 338&n
Willfort, Manfred H., xliii, 383n, 457, 458n, 462&n
Willudden, 330
Wind Music Society (Bläser Vereinigung; Vienna), 57
Winter, Hugo, 106, 127n, 128
Wirth, [Karl] Joseph, 348&n
Wittgenstein, Leopoldine, 96, 97n
Wittgenstein, Ludwig, 97n, 454
Wittgenstein, Paul, 97n, 454
Wittgenstein family, 368, 376, 454
Wolf, Hans, 413, 414n
Wolf, Hugo, xxxv, 49n, 296, 450
 "Elfenlied," 34, 46
 "Gesang Weylas," 46

Wolf, Hugo, *continued*
 "Nachtzauber," 34
 "Nun lass' uns Frieden schliessen," 34
 "Ständchen," 34
 "Tambour, Der," 46
 "Zur Ruh, zur Ruh," 46
Wolf-Ferrari, Ermanno: Chamber Symphony in B♭ major (Op. 8), 57
Wolzogen, Ernst von, 27n
Workers' Symphony Concerts, 250
World War I, xxxix, xli, 91, 152n, 237–38, 256, 260, 263, 270n, 326–27, 330&n, 331&n, 332–33, 335–38, 339n, 344, 347, 351n, 359, 382n, 422, 441, 447, 468
World War II, 145n, 155n, 162, 188, 203n, 339n, 387–88
 British internment, 93
Wöss, Josef, 106
Wotquenne, Alfred, 201
Wunderer, Alexander, 175&n, 176–77
Wunsch, Hermann, 168, 169&n, 170
Württemberg State Theater (Stuttgart), 275n
Wyneken, Gustav, 261n, 282n, 290

Ysaÿe, Eugène, 398, 399n

Zaloziecki, Vladimir, 96
Zeit, Die, 8, 10
Zeitschrift für internationale Musikwissenschaft, 358
Zeitschrift für Musik, 145, 193n
Zemlinsky, Alexander von, 3, 54&n, 55n, 63
Zepler, Bogumil, 30
Zukunft, Die, 8, 10, 14–15, 271, 272n
Zürich, 70, 145
 Philharmonic Orchestra, 71n
Zwissler (publisher), 274, 286